ESSENTIALS OF CORRECTIONS

Fifth Edition

ESSENTIALS OF CORRECTIONS

G. LARRY MAYS AND L. THOMAS WINFREE, JR.

WILEY Blackwell

This fifth edition first published 2014
© 2014 John Wiley & Sons, Inc

Edition History: Wadsworth, Cengage Learning (4e, 2009; 3e, 2005)

Registered Office
John Wiley & Sons Ltd, The Atrium, Southern Gate, Chichester, West Sussex, PO19 8SQ, UK

Editorial Offices
350 Main Street, Malden, MA 02148-5020, USA
9600 Garsington Road, Oxford, OX4 2DQ, UK
The Atrium, Southern Gate, Chichester, West Sussex, PO19 8SQ, UK

For details of our global editorial offices, for customer services, and for information about how to apply for permission to reuse the copyright material in this book please see our website at www.wiley.com/wiley-blackwell.

The right of G. Larry Mays and L. Thomas Winfree, Jr. to be identified as the authors of this work has been asserted in accordance with the UK Copyright, Designs and Patents Act 1988.

Library of Congress Cataloging-in-Publication Data
Mays, G. Larry.
   Essentials of corrections / G. Larry Mays and L. Thomas Winfree, Jr. – Fifth edition.
      pages cm
   Includes bibliographical references and index.
   ISBN 978-1-118-53721-3 (pbk.)
   1. Corrections.   2. Corrections–United States.   I. Winfree, Latham T. (Latham Thomas), 1946-   II. Title.
   HV8665.M39 2014
   365–dc23

                          2013028445

A catalogue record for this book is available from the British Library.

Cover image: © Noam Armonn/Spaces Images/Corbis
Cover design by Simon Levy

Set in 10/12 pt Bembo Std by Toppan Best-set Premedia Limited
Printed and bound in Malaysia by Vivar Printing Sdn Bhd

1   2014

For Brenda;
Greg, Lisa, Mina, Robert, and Knox;
Gelaine, Gabe, Lucy, Oliver, Cooper, and Maggie.
Larry Mays

For Richard Vandiver, teacher, scholar, and mentor.
For Edwin E. Jeffery, husband, father, grandfather, great-grandfather, and good friend.
You both are missed.
Tom Winfree

CONTENTS

DETAILED CONTENTS

PREFACE

There are a variety of television shows and movies that deal with various aspects of law enforcement, some fictional and some real. However, the corrections component of the criminal justice system does not seem to garner the same amount of attention. This is interesting given that there are over 7 million adults in the United States under some form of correctional supervision, in addition to juveniles supervised and confined by the juvenile justice system. Furthermore, there are nearly 800,000 people employed in corrections at the local, state, and federal levels accounting for nearly $80 billion in annual payroll. By any measure, correctional agencies and operations in the United States are big business. Nevertheless, for many people much of the corrections component of the criminal justice system remains out of sight, and out of mind.

The two authors of this book have found the world of corrections to be both fascinating and frustrating. Collectively, we have spent more than 60 years working around, researching, and teaching about corrections. In some ways, the two of us feel like we know less now than when we began. Why is that? Several reasons seem apparent.

The field of corrections involves a complex array of people, places, institutions, and agencies. The successes of the dedicated people who work in this field seldom are publicized. The failures make local, state, national, and even international news. When we talk to our former students who work in corrections, they express an optimism that is borne of the conviction that they are doing something really worthwhile for society. By the same token, they are often disappointed that legislators, the general public, and the news media do not understand what they do, and thanks are seldom conveyed to them for a job well done. They also feel that the growing correctional populations and insufficient resources to manage those populations further handicap them. Like many employees of the criminal justice system, of which corrections is a big part, they point to the role that politics plays in the administration of punishment.

Additionally, the field of corrections is an ever-changing enterprise, and it is much different today than it was 20 or even ten years ago. Correctional agencies have been affected by changing laws at the state and federal levels, and the influence of prisoner litigation is an ever-present reality.

Finally, movements to improve the quality of correctional employees, their work environment, professionalization, and a heightened sense of ethics all play a major part in contemporary corrections. These three factors have made it challenging for us as we have worked on each successive edition of this book. Beginning with the first edition, our intent was to present a thorough but tightly focused textbook covering the essentials of corrections. The first edition had 11 chapters. When we did the second edition, we added an entire chapter on careers in corrections. The third edition brought two additional chapters: one on race and ethnicity and another on gender, and in this edition we have added a separate chapter on special needs inmates. Throughout the process, we have tried to maintain our focus on a book that covers the basics in the most thorough way possible.

THE GOALS OF THIS BOOK

The changing forces of corrections in the United States have now brought us to the fifth edition, one that presented its own challenges. As with past editions, we have pursued a number of goals in preparing this edition.

First, although we recognize that instructors must teach from the book, we want the book to be accessible intellectually to students from a variety of backgrounds and degrees of preparation. If students cannot grasp the material we have presented, then our efforts have been in vain. Comprehension is an essential step in mastery. So we view the students as our target audience.

Second, we have made every effort to present the material in a logical format. We want the material to flow from one chapter to the next and for the book to "tell a story." In this regard, we have attempted to minimize our separate voices in the writing process and to present the material as if it were written by one person. In each successive edition, this has become easier.

Third, we want to present the broad sweep of the corrections component to students who may or may not end up working in corrections. Although the aim was to make this an "essentials" book, we have been as thorough as possible without drowning students in a sea of interesting, but nonessential, information. We recognize that some colleges and universities may require this course whereas others offer it as an elective. Whichever the case, we want the students who read this book and complete the course to feel relatively secure in the breadth if not depth of their knowledge of corrections in the United States and the world beyond.

Fourth, we continue to include some materials that we consider classics in the field of corrections while focusing on the most recent material available. The newer material is taken from scholarly monographs, research articles, or federal government documents prepared by the Bureau of Justice Statistics or otherwise available through the National Criminal Justice Reference Service. However, as we (and most authors) are quick to acknowledge, as soon as a book is published the material included is already somewhat dated. Therefore, most of the data we have included ends with 2010. This date was chosen because it gave us the most complete figures for corrections operations, and it allowed us to compare "apples with apples" more readily.

As a result of these goals, we have pursued two strategies diligently in the creation of the fifth edition of our collaborative work: (1) We have updated and added material throughout the entire book at the suggestion of several reviewers and instructors who have used previous editions; and (2) we have eliminated some of the topics that no longer seem as essential. Nevertheless, we have retained our original promise to ourselves that we wanted a book that was understandable by students. Therefore, in the next section, we will outline the many changes that have occurred in the revision and production of this book.

THE FIFTH EDITION

Before considering the individual chapters, it is useful to outline some of the new features of this edition. In terms of reorganization, we have added an entirely new chapter on special needs inmates. Some of this information was included in different chapters in previous editions of the book, but this edition pulls all of this material together in one chapter and adds significant sections on immigration detainees and gay, lesbian, bisexual, and transgender inmates.

Most of the chapters have boxed materials dealing with current issues and controversies in corrections. Additionally, we have included boxes on international corrections in all chapters. We have had the feeling for some time that looking at how other countries address their correctional populations and problems helps students understand better what we do in the United States and why.

At the end of each chapter, we have provided three different devices that should help students develop a mastery of the material. First, we provide a list of key terms. These terms are emphasized and are defined for the students in the book's extensive glossary.

Second, we include a series of critical review questions. Rather than asking students simply to repeat information discussed in the text, our intent was for students to use these questions to test themselves on the degree to which they really grasp the material presented in the chapter. However, we believe that the questions can be used in quite a few different ways. For example, students can be assigned to answer the questions in small groups. The questions could also be used for essay exams.

Finally, we both believe very strongly in developing students' abilities to write, so in addition to the critical review questions, we have expanded the list of writing assignments in this edition. Each of these writing assignments is designed to have students create short (typically one to two page) essays that make them think critically and then express their answers in written form. We believe that both students and instructors will find these writing assignments useful and thought provoking.

ORGANIZATION OF THE TEXT

CHAPTER 1 *Introduction to Corrections* continues to provide an overview of the criminal justice system component that we call corrections. It gives students a brief look at the sweep of correctional agencies and institutions, and provides them with the basic terminology that they will need throughout the book.

CHAPTER 2 *A Brief History of Punishments and Corrections* deals with the issues of history and theory. These may not seem to be the most exciting topics to students, but we have long maintained that both are essential to understanding where we are today and how we got here. We have made every effort not to present material in this chapter as dry and boring statistics, but to make both history and theory come alive for students.

CHAPTER 3 *Sentencing and Criminal Sanctions* covers the topic of sentencing and criminal sanctions. We believe that students need to understand how offenders come into the domain of the

corrections system. Some of this material may have been covered in a previous class such as Introduction to Criminal Justice or Criminal Law. However, we are committed to making sure that students have a complete grasp of the material whether they have heard it before or not.

CHAPTER 4 *Probation and Community Corrections* contains material that has been substantially revised and updated. In previous editions, probation and parole were included in one chapter, and that chapter came much later in the text. Beginning with the fourth edition, we placed probation much earlier in the book (where it usually falls in the process) and combined it with material on community corrections (which was a separate chapter in the first three editions).

CHAPTER 5 *Jails and Detention Facilities* deals with jails and other types of short-term detention facilities. Often jails get little or no treatment in corrections books, but they represent the front door to all correctional processing that will follow. Not everyone in jail will be placed on probation or go to prison, but virtually everyone on probation or in prison has been in jail at some point.

CHAPTER 6 *Institutional Corrections* focuses on the institutional aspect of corrections, primarily jails and prisons. In some ways, institutional corrections gets an inordinate amount of attention. This element of the corrections work world certainly is the focus of much of the funding, research, and public thought when the word *corrections* is introduced.

CHAPTER 7 *Jail and Prison Inmates* covers information on the inmates housed in jails and prisons around the United States. This is one chapter where recent information is readily available from the US Bureau of Justice Statistics (BJS). Students can access the BJS website (**http://www.ojp.usdoj.gov/bjs/**) if they are interested in finding statistics for this class or other classes. They can also access current studies of a more general nature on corrections and related topics from the National Criminal Justice Reference Service (NCJRS) (**www.ncjrs.gov**). Instructors also might assign a little "scavenger hunt" by having students find facts and figures about certain correctional topics through either BJS or NCJRS.

CHAPTER 8 *Special Needs Inmates* deals with an increasingly problematic issue in corrections: inmates who have more than usual needs in terms of medical care, mental health care, treatment programming, and living arrangements. The groups incorporated into this chapter's discussions include adolescents and young adults; inmates with communicable diseases (especially HIV/AIDS and tuberculosis); those who are drug and alcohol dependent; inmates with mental health problems and mental illness; gay, lesbian, bisexual, and transgender inmates; and individuals being detained for immigration violations.

CHAPTER 9 *Parole and Prisoner Reentry* was added to the previous edition and, fortunately, several recent studies and data sources were available to help in the revision of this section. Although not prescriptive in its approach to prisoner reentry, the chapter does suggest that much more can be done to facilitate success in the lives of those who leave prison to live among us once again.

CHAPTER 10 *Careers in Corrections* first appeared in the third edition, although the title was a bit vague. Beginning with the fourth edition, we made this chapter's title much more explicit: *Careers in Corrections*. Furthermore, we have updated the information available from the Bureau of Labor Statistics that covers job outlook and potential salary structure for corrections positions nationwide. As always, students should be encouraged to check with their state corrections department to get the most up-to-date local information. Chapter 10 also has expanded discussions of professionalization and ethics for corrections employees.

CHAPTER 11 *The Administration of Corrections Programs* deals with professionalization and ethics, topics of continuing concern throughout criminal justice agencies. In this chapter, the discussions focus on the challenges faced by correctional administrators. We recognize that students will not step from college into an administrative position, but they will be working in an administrative environment and

working for managers and administrators. Our goal in this chapter was to sensitize students to the challenges faced by administrators (not only in corrections, but in practically every criminal justice organization).

CHAPTER 12 *Corrections Law and Inmate Litigation* discusses the crucial area of law and litigation. Whether they want to admit it or not, students who work in corrections will be involved in a career with high litigation potential. They may not be sued personally—although some might—but their agencies and organizations will be sued regularly. This chapter also updates some of the major cases (and changes) dealing with the death penalty in the United States.

CHAPTER 13 *Gender Issues in Corrections* was added to the third edition of the book, and we have continued to revise and update it for this edition. At any point in the criminal justice system, the inclusion of an in-depth discussion of women and their role as either clients or service providers is rare. We tried to raise the bar for discussions of gender in corrections by reversing this trend in Chapter 13. We review the worlds of incarcerated women and those in alternative programming, as well as suggest areas where women's needs are unique and distinct from those of male offenders. We close with an admittedly brief discussion of women as correctional employees. As we began work on the fifth edition we realized that this, unfortunately, is an area still somewhat overlooked by policy makers and corrections researchers.

CHAPTER 14 *Race, Ethnicity, and Corrections* delves into some critical and often provocative topics, including the definitions of race and ethnicity, sentencing disparities, disproportionate minority contacts with the criminal justice system, and the death penalty. In it, we introduce students to the various ways race and ethnicity affect offenders' lives, whether they are confined in prisons and jails or placed on probation and parole.

CHAPTER 15 *The Future of Corrections* is not, as in some textbooks, something of a throwaway. We have always wanted *Chapter 15, The Future of Corrections,* to present substantive material. Some of the discussions are clearly based on current research in terms of what works and what does not. Other discussions are speculative, and they deal with what might be called the science fiction of corrections. We have taken current technologies and some technologies under development, and have extrapolated these to imagine what the future of corrections might look like. We want this chapter to be significant, but also fun for both students and instructors.

COMPREHENSIVE ONLINE ANCILLARY RESOURCES

The revised and expanded ancillaries for this text are available on its companion website. To begin using this site please visit **www.wiley.com/go/mays5e**

Unlike the case of many textbook ancillaries, both the *Instructor's Section* and the *Student Section* have been prepared by the two authors of the text. We consider this to be a value-added feature, as the ancillaries for many introductory texts are written by third parties hired by the publisher.

These ancillaries have been substantially revised and expanded to go along with the new organization of the book. Additionally, the Instructor's Section includes new materials that we did not have space for in the text itself. We provide numerous suggestions for classroom exercises (such as discussions and group work), films, other books, and the types of guest speakers that might be appropriate at various points in the course.

Wiley has made available to students and instructors the following online resource materials:

- *A new student study guide:* This study guide is a new feature of the fifth edition. It is located in the Student Section. The guide will help students review materials from the chapters and help prepare them for classroom discussions,

assignments, and examinations. We want to acknowledge Dr Carolyn Dennis of Keiser University who prepared the study guide.

- *A list of web resources keyed to each chapter:* Both students and instructors will benefit from using these sites listed to update data in the chapters—and also to further explore topics that, of necessity, are covered somewhat briefly in the text. There is also a list of state-by-state corrections department websites provided.

- *Links to open-source videos.* These can be used along with the text to illustrate points covered in class and in the book's chapters.

- *Sample syllabi.* These will be especially helpful for instructors teaching this class for the first time, or who have not taught the course on a regular basis.

ACKNOWLEDGMENTS

A new edition of this book brought a new publisher and a new editor with whom to work. We want to thank Julia Teweles for her pursuit of us as authors and her confidence in us and this project. We would like to thank the many people who have served as reviewers throughout the life of this book. Their suggestions have proved to be very valuable and they are much appreciated. Also, there were a number of individuals who worked through the production process, including Julia Kirk, Project Editor. Eileen Winfree also was gracious enough to proofread and make suggestions on the entire manuscript as we got it ready for submission. Both of our wives qualify for sainthood as a result of the trials we have put them through over the years with our book projects.

G. Larry Mays
L. Thomas Winfree, Jr.

INTRODUCTION TO CORRECTIONS

LUCY ATKINS/CORBIS

Outline

Current Trends

Philosophies of Punishment

Outlooks on Corrections

The Role of Criminological Theories

Corrections Programs

Objectives

- To provide you with an understanding of the breadth and depth of corrections

- To acquaint you with the various philosophies and goals of punishment

- To reveal to you the role of criminological theory as a means to understand offenders

- To provide you with a contemporary view of corrections and a prospective look into its future

- To give you an overview of the various subjects explored in this textbook

Essentials of Corrections, Fifth Edition. G. Larry Mays and L. Thomas Winfree, Jr.
© 2014 John Wiley & Sons, Inc. Published 2014 by John Wiley & Sons, Inc.

INTRODUCTION

What comes to mind when you hear the word *corrections?* Do you think about prisons with massive stone walls and downtrodden inmates like those portrayed in dozens of movies? Perhaps you think about chain gangs, inmates in orange jumpsuits picking up trash along a highway, or prisoners in white uniforms hoeing in a line in a field. Do these images accurately reflect contemporary corrections?

The answer is *yes*, to a degree. But today *corrections* encompasses much more than the custodial supervision of convicted offenders inside or outside a secure facility. According to the US Department of Justice, at the end of 2010, an estimated 7.1 million adults in the United States (1 in 48 adults) were under some type of correctional supervision (Glaze 2011). Of this total, 4.06 million adults were on probation and another 840,676 were on parole. The rest, nearly 2.3 million adults, were confined in prisons and jails.

Probation. Parole. Prisons. Jails. These are critical components of corrections in the twenty-first century, but they are by no means the only components. According to the US Department of Justice, *corrections* "includes all government agencies, facilities, programs, procedures, personnel, and techniques concerned with the intake, custody, confinement, supervision, or treatment, or presentencing or pre-disposition investigation of alleged or adjudicated adult offenders, delinquents, or status offenders" (1981, 53). As used in this textbook, **corrections** refers to all government actions intended to manage adults who have been accused or convicted of criminal offenses and juveniles who have been charged with or found guilty of delinquency or a status offense.

In this chapter, we explore the philosophical and practical underpinnings of contemporary corrections. In order to gain a better understanding of our nation's formal response to criminals, we examine the philosophies that provide the foundation for "correcting" convicted offenders. Then we review the public and political attitudes that shape contemporary corrections policy, and the effects of those attitudes. Next we explore the explanations for crime that criminologists have developed over the past several centuries. Their theories will be especially useful when we start to consider the methods of treating convicted criminals. We conclude the chapter with a look at the nation's corrections programs. Before we begin our exploration of the essentials of corrections, however, we turn to an overview of current trends.

CURRENT TRENDS

Between the early 1980s and the end of the century, the United States experienced an enormous increase in the number of individuals under the supervision of adult correctional programs. In 1980, fewer than 2 million people were under any form of institutional or community supervision. As noted above, the nation's correctional systems reported more than 7 million detainees, inmates, and supervisees in 2010. As Figure 1.1 shows, between 1980 and 2007, the climb in the number of people age 18 and older under some form of supervision, especially in prisons and on probation, was steady and unrelenting. Beginning in 2009, after a 2 year plateau, the numbers started to move downward, led mainly by declines within the probation and jail populations.

Comparisons of prisoners by race and ethnicity yield controversial results (Guerino, Harrison, and Sabol 2011; Humes, Jones, and Ramirez 2011):

- In 2010, blacks accounted for 13.6 percent of the roughly 309.3 million people in the United States, or about 42 million individuals, but 40 percent of the inmates in state and federal facilities were black.

- About 50.5 million people, 16.3 percent of the total US population in 2010, were Hispanics, but they constituted 20 percent of the prison population that year.

- Non-Hispanic whites accounted for most of the remaining 196.8 million US residents in 2010, 63.7 percent of the total, but whites made up just 35 percent of the inmate population.

Another way to examine the racial and ethnic distribution of inmates is to look at *incarceration rates*,

FIGURE 1.1 Total population under the supervision of adult correctional systems and annual percent change, 1980–2010. *Source:* Glaze (2011, 1).

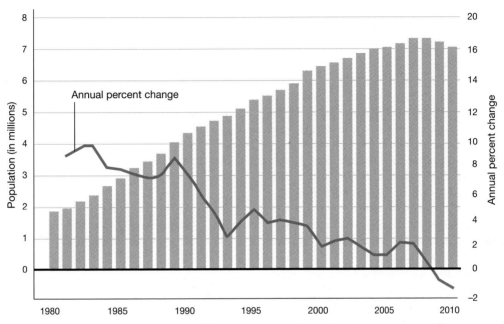

NOTE: Annual percentage change was based on within-year change in the probation and parole populations and year-to-year changes in the prison and jail populations. The annual percentage change in 1998 and 1999 was adjusted to account for expanded coverage of probation agencies during those years.

the number of people in a secure facility for every 100,000 (referred to in this text as per capita) people in a specific racial or ethnic group. Those rates confirm the race and ethnic disparities found within the nation's prison populations. For example, in 2010, the incarceration rate for every 100,000 black males in the United States ages 25 to 29 was 8,932 (down from 10,376 in 2002); among Hispanic males in the same age group, the rate was 3,892 (up from 2,394 in 2002); and among white males, the rate was 1,437 (up from 1,229 in 2002) (Glaze 2011; Harrison and Beck 2003).[1]

Since 2000, the rates for blacks and Hispanics have generally gone down, while those for non-Hispanics whites have increased, pushing the overall per capita incarceration rates for all racial and ethnic groups up from 476 in 2002 to 500 in 2010. Stated another way, and assuming current incarceration rates do not change, about one in three black males, one in six Hispanic males, and 1 in 17 white males are expected to go to prison during their lifetimes (Bonczar 2003).

We also find disproportionate rates for conditional release: three in ten probationers and four in ten parolees are black; and one in about eight probationers and nearly one in five parolees are Hispanic (Glaze and Bonczar 2011). Whites account for more than half of probationers but only four in ten parolees. Blacks and Hispanics as a group make up 43 percent of the nation's probationers and 57 percent of the parolees, well above their combined proportion in the general population. Since the late 1980s, the trend has been toward fewer black and Hispanic probationers and more black and Hispanic parolees, something we would expect given the explosion in incarceration rates for racial and ethnic minorities that began in the 1980s (Glaze and Bonczar 2011).

This unequal representation of blacks and Hispanics is often referred to as **disproportionate minority contact (DMC)**. Many corrections experts consider the overrepresentation of racial and ethnic minorities among those convicted and sentenced in the United States to be a national tragedy, a problem that begins with minority group member-police contacts. We review race and ethnicity at various points in the chapters that follow, and we examine disparities in sentencing and confinement in detail in Chapter 14.

Although women historically are underrepresented in the nation's correctional population, their proportion is growing. The number of female prisoners increased 21 percent (versus 13.4 percent for men) between 2000 and 2010: by the end of 2010, women accounted for 7 percent of all prisoners (Guerino, Harrison and Sabol 2011). In spite of these changes in women's incarceration, the 2010 incarceration rate for men was, at 943 per 100,000 males US residents, 14 times higher than for females (67 per 100,000 female US residents). In 2010, women made up 24 percent of those on probation (a 2 percent increase from 2000) and 12 percent of those on parole in both 2000 and 2010. As we relate later in this text, the growing involvement of women as clients of the nation's criminal justice system has created new and unique problems for correctional policy makers and practitioners alike.

What these statistics demonstrate is that corrections is a significant part of the criminal justice system in the United States. Moreover, the problem of expanding prison systems is not limited to the United States (see Box 1.1).

PHILOSOPHIES OF PUNISHMENT

In this book, we look at many different corrections programs, agencies, and institutions. Each one is guided by a punishment philosophy, a set of beliefs that defines both the potential and the limitations of corrections treatment. Throughout history, different philosophies have dominated the corrections field at different times. In this section, we explore the origins of these sometimes contradictory philosophies.

RETRIBUTION

One of the oldest correctional philosophies is retribution. In simplest terms, **retribution** is the belief that punishment must avenge for a harm done to another. Archaeologists have unearthed written codes dating back more than 3,500 years that clearly are based on retribution. For example, the Code of Hammurabi, which dates back to the eighteenth century BCE, provided, "If a man destroy the eye of another man, they shall destroy his eye. If he break a man's bone, they shall break his bone. If a man knock out a tooth of a man of his own rank, they shall knock out his tooth." Likewise, the Law of Moses stipulated that "thou shalt give life for life, eye for eye, tooth for tooth, hand for hand, foot for foot, burning for burning, wound for wound, stripe for stripe" (Exod. 21:23–25). From such harsh rules has come the *lex talionis*, the law of retaliation or revenge, a legal principle that requires a response in kind for crimes committed (*Encarta World Dictionary* 2009).[2]

The ancient concept of retaliation has aroused renewed interest since the 1970s. In the mid-1970s, the criminal justice system's ability to effect prosocial changes in criminals came under severe criticism (see the discussion of rehabilitation later). Simultaneously, a derivative of the *lex talionis* emerged. This new rationale for punishment, called *just deserts* or *retributive justice*, suggests that criminals earn society's wrath and deserve to be punished for the sake of punishment (Fogel 1975). Whether they learn to change (rehabilitation) or are frightened away from their criminal behaviors (deterrence) is irrelevant. They simply deserve punishment, much as those who violated laws in the days of the *lex talionis* deserved punishment. Only the forms of punishment are different, not the reasons for using them.

In the 1990s, critics of the corrections system suggested that the retributive justice philosophy had evolved into a philosophy of **penal harm**—the belief that punishment, particularly incarceration, should be uncomfortable. Since the 1980s, the prison population in the United States has increased at a far

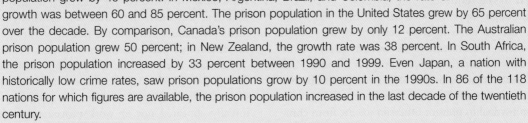

SPOTLIGHT ON INTERNATIONAL CORRECTIONS: THE INCARCERATION BOOM, A WORLDWIDE PHENOMENON   **BOX 1.1**

Observers note that prisons in the United States have undergone three decades of growth. This statement appears to be true internationally as well. For example, in 2000, Germany allocated the equivalent of $1.25 billion for new prison construction. This expansion plan was to increase prison capacity in the eastern German states by 50 percent and in the western states by 25 percent.

In general, the prison population in European nations grew 20 percent during the 1990s, but in more than half of these nations (not counting very small states) the prison population grew by 40 percent. In Mexico, Argentina, Brazil, and Colombia, the rate of growth was between 60 and 85 percent. The prison population in the United States grew by 65 percent over the decade. By comparison, Canada's prison population grew by only 12 percent. The Australian prison population grew 50 percent; in New Zealand, the growth rate was 38 percent. In South Africa, the prison population increased by 33 percent between 1990 and 1999. Even Japan, a nation with historically low crime rates, saw prison populations grow by 10 percent in the 1990s. In 86 of the 118 nations for which figures are available, the prison population increased in the last decade of the twentieth century.

Why are we seeing widespread growth in incarceration rates? The answers are complex and go beyond growth in crime rates. Roy Walmsley (2009) suggests five possibilities:

- the increasing belief in many countries that prison is the most effective response to crime;
- an increased fear of crime;
- a general loss of confidence in the criminal justice system;
- disillusionment with positive treatment alternatives (prison is a negative alternative); and
- a growing need for retribution

We should not lose sight of the fact that the United States, with just 5 percent of the world's population, has roughly 20 percent of the world's 9.9 million prison inmates. Nearly half of all sentenced prisoners are held in the United States. Moreover, although Western European nations have experienced dramatic prison population increases, the custody rate per 100,000 residents in most of these nations is less than 100. In the United States, the per capita rate for individuals held in state or federal prisons or in local jails is currently 732—the world's highest rate.

SOURCES: AUSTIN AND IRWIN (2001); CLEAR (1994); GLAZE (2011); WALMSLEY (2001, 2009).

greater rate than the prison system's ability to deal with it. The chief mechanisms of change were mandatory sentencing laws and restrictions on or even the abolition of discretionary parole.[3] "By promoting prison overcrowding and its related evils, the penal harm movement has clearly extended degradation, provocation, and deprivation well beyond the act of imprisonment to the daily *conditions* of confinement" (R. Wright 1996, 135).

DETERRENCE

The **deterrence** philosophy assumes that certain and severe punishment can "discourage future crime by the offender and by others" (US Department of Justice 1988, 90). This definition owes much to the writings of Cesare Beccaria, Jeremy Bentham, and other eighteenth-century philosophers.

Notice that there are two important dimensions here. The first is **specific deterrence**, the assumption that punishment dissuades the offender from repeating the same offense or committing a new one. The ultimate form of specific deterrence is the death penalty: we know with certainty that people who are executed for their crimes will not commit other crimes in the future.

Although specific deterrence may be very important in contemporary corrections, the second dimension—**general deterrence**—seems equally important. Specific deterrence would punish the individual offender so that he or she will not commit another offense; by contrast, general deterrence would punish the individual to prevent others in society from committing the same or similar crimes. This philosophy assumes that people can learn through the experience of others that punishments meted out to others serve as object lessons for the rest of us.

REHABILITATION

The most prominent correctional philosophy in this country for many years was **rehabilitation**, the belief that "providing psychological or educational assistance or job training to offenders" makes "them less likely to engage in future criminality" (US Department of Justice 1988, 90). Rehabilitation is based on the notion that people—whatever their age or their crime—can change. The key to change is treatment—individual and group counseling, drug and alcohol treatment, remedial education, and vocational education.

Between the 1950s and the 1970s, rehabilitation was the philosophy most frequently promoted by **penologists**, people who systematically study punishment. However, in the mid-1970s, an assessment of correctional programs brought the efficacy of rehabilitation into question (Lipton, Martinson, and Wilks 1975). Some critics wondered whether rehabilitation worked; others went even further, arguing that "nothing works"' (Martinson 1974). In a matter

of years, other studies found that rehabilitation is a viable basis for corrections (see, for example, Cullen and Gilbert 1982).[4]

If rehabilitation can work, why was such a gloomy picture painted in the 1970s? We have several possible answers. First, correctional treatment programs often were created with no evaluation component. Only after a few years of operation did someone (usually a funding agency) decide that it might be a good idea to find out whether a program was working. In the absence of formal evaluation criteria, assessments were based on anecdotal evidence or intuition, and often they were wrong. Many treatment programs were assumed not to work, often in the absence of hard evidence.

Second, many treatment program evaluations during the 1960s and 1970s made use of inadequate statistical techniques. Some of the programs that initially appeared not to work proved to work on reexamination.

Third, some treatment programs were almost designed to fail. They had no theoretical underpinnings, and their designers and implementers had only vague notions about what the programs should achieve. A number of the juvenile justice diversion programs system fit this category (Decker 1985). The stated purpose of these programs was to divert certain juvenile offenders *from* the formal process of adjudication, but no one specified where these youngsters should be diverted *to*.

In summarizing the research on rehabilitation, Joseph Rogers and Larry Mays (1987, 519–20) made several key points, ones that are no less relevant after nearly three decades:

- No treatment program works with every possible offender.
- Some programs may not work with any offenders.
- Some programs have a high degree of efficacy; that is, they work with a broad range of offenders.
- Unfortunately, some offenders cannot be rehabilitated.

Participants in correctional rehabilitation programs, much like clients of drug and alcohol treatment programs, get better when they want to get better and work towards that goal.

ISOLATION

Isolation is a very old correctional philosophy that has served two purposes throughout recorded history. The first is isolation as punishment: offenders were incarcerated in dungeons or towers to separate them from most human contact. The second is what we call the "rotten apple" response to criminal offenders: offenders were isolated to protect the rest of society from "spoiling." In this way, prisons and jails became dumping grounds for people society rejected because they were dangerous or simply unpleasant (see Welch 1996). What may also have been at work here is a defense mechanism of sorts. Inmates have low visibility: they are out of sight, out of mind. Criminals who are in jail are not a threat to law-abiding citizens, nor are they a reminder of the law's failure to protect those citizens.

INCAPACITATION

The contemporary version of isolation is **incapacitation**, "separating offenders from the community to reduce the opportunity for further crime while they are incarcerated" (US Department of Justice 1988, 90). At the core of this philosophy is the work of Marvin Wolfgang and his colleagues. Their Philadelphia birth cohort studies identified a group of high-risk and high-rate offenders (Wolfgang, Figlio, and Sellin 1972), who were later labeled "career criminals." An assortment of strategies—in particular, selective incapacitation—was developed to address the problems created by persistent offenders (Walker 2011).

At the heart of **selective incapacitation** lies the assumption that career criminals can be identified early on, as preteens or teens. Once these offenders are identified, the full force of the criminal justice system is brought to bear on them. Policymakers use selective incapacitation to ensure that career criminals are caught, convicted, and sentenced to a significant period of incarceration. The goal of policymakers is to reduce the crime rate substantially by removing persistent offenders from society for most if not all of their crime-prone years.

As some critics have pointed out, the career-criminal concept and the selective incapacitation approach are based on assumptions that are open to interpretation and challenge (Greenwood 1982; Walker 2011). The early identification of career criminals has been problematic. Also, selective incapacitation assumes that there is a finite number of high-rate criminals, and that if we catch those who are most persistent, no others are going to take their places. Both national and state governments have pursued this expensive strategy despite the lack of consensus on its value. Why? One answer may be that the image of the career criminal frightens the public, which creates an opportunity for savvy politicians. The upshot is that we are likely to continue to see references to career criminals and programs designed to deal with them for years to come.

REINTEGRATION

In the late 1970s through the early 1980s, most corrections professionals began to focus on reintegration. **Reintegration** recognizes the fact that a high percentage of the people in prison—probably more than 90 percent—eventually get out (Travis 2000). Once they get out, many of these offenders have a difficult time making a transition back into society. They must readjust to their families, to work, and to the label *ex-con*. Therefore, something must be done to help them make the transition from institutional life back into society.

The reintegration process is important for the inmate who has been released and for society. Most former inmates who fail to reenter society commit new crimes, usually within months of their release. By helping them make the transition to the free world, the corrections system can prevent crime and the offenders' eventual return to prison.

RESTITUTION

Restitution entails "having the offender repay the victim or the community in money or services" (US Department of Justice 1988, 90). Restitution was designed as an alternative to incarceration (Cromwell and Killinger 1994, 279–80), but in many jurisdictions today, judges incorporate restitution orders into probation conditions. Critics argue that restitution has become a probation add-on, a way of making probation more punitive, and part of the general trend toward requiring greater accountability from offenders.

RESTORATION

The most recent philosophy to gain followers in the field of corrections is **restoration** (see Box 1.2). Restorative justice, or the *balanced approach*, has been applied to juvenile and adult offenders (Armstrong, Maloney, and Romig 1990; Maloney, Romig, and Armstrong 1988). According to Gordon Bazemore (1992), the approach is based on three key elements:

- *Accountability* requires offenders to repay or restore victims' losses, much like restitution.
- *Community protection* weighs both public safety and the least costly, least restrictive correctional alternative.
- *Competency development* emphasizes remediation for offenders' social, educational, or other deficiencies when they enter the correctional system.

As Bazemore emphasizes, the key is balance: each of these elements should play an equal role in correcting deviant behavior (see Box 1.2).

What is the state of contemporary corrections? Do any of these philosophies underlie current correctional programs? Actually they all do in one form or another. Does one of them dominate? The answer is probably no. Much like the mental health field 30 or 40 years ago, contemporary corrections is caught

SPOTLIGHT ON INTERNATIONAL CORRECTIONS: RESTORATIVE JUSTICE IN BELGIAN PRISONS   BOX 1.2

Does restorative justice sound like a "New Age" correctional philosophy, cooked up by liberals at the end of the twentieth century? In fact, restorative justice's foundations can be seen in the practices of the ancient Greeks, Arabs, Romans, and Germanic peoples after the fall of Rome. The idea of restoring community harmony and balance after a crime has been committed is also found in numerous religious tracts associated with, among others, Buddhism, Hinduism, Taoism, and Confucianism.

Restorative justice is more than a philosophy; in many nations, it is a series of practices designed to change people's behavior. For example, in 1998, six Belgian prisons implemented restorative-justice programs that were intended to create a more positive prison culture. We will see in Chapter 7 that the culture inmates create in prisons tends to be negative and antiauthoritarian, not environments in which prosocial goals are likely to be met. In the Belgian prisons, restorative principles helped prisoners begin dealing with the aftermath of their crimes more personally and more openly while they were in prison. Inmates were encouraged to take responsibility for their actions. Through individual counseling and group work, staff members helped offenders recognize the physical, psychological, and emotional consequences of their offenses. Staff members also gave victims a brochure that described prison life for the offenders and the likely outcome of incarceration. Finally, the staff worked to end polarization between victim aid services and offender aid services, to build bridges between them and to explore the possibility of victim–offender communications while offenders were jailed. The pilot project was a success, and today each of Belgium's 30 prisons has a counselor who works to introduce restorative-justice concepts and practices inside the facility.

SOURCES: BRAITHWAITE (1999); NEWELL (2001); WINFREE (2002).

in a "model muddle" (Siegler and Osmond 1974). The problem: in trying to make themselves all things to all people, some corrections programs end up employing conflicting or competing elements. At the root of this muddle are political realities and public pressure—the topic we turn to next.

OUTLOOKS ON CORRECTIONS

Ask anyone in the criminal justice field today about the current public policy direction on crime, and you will likely get the same answer: punishment, punishment, and more punishment. Thomas Bernard (1992, 3–6) described a predictable cycle of responses to offenders, from lenient to harsh.[5] When people perceive that correctional treatment programs are too lenient, too soft on criminals, they call for harsher treatment. That is what is happening today. The public and policymakers generally feel that leniency contributes to criminality and that the only response to increased criminality is tougher punishment. So we find ourselves in the get-tough-on-crime part of the cycle.

Fueling that response is the belief that we are experiencing a crime wave. But the reality is that crime rates in most categories fell during the 1990s. According to the Federal Bureau of Investigation, the per capita violent crime rate peaked at slightly above 758 in 1991, dropping consistently throughout the rest of the decade and the first 5 years of the twenty-first century (Federal Bureau of Investigation 2011). In 2010, the per capita rates increased slightly for violent crime, but were still well below 404 per capita. For property crime rates, similar reductions were observed during this same period, dropping from a high of 5,140 in 1991 to 2,942 in 2010 (Federal Bureau of Investigation, 2011). The idea that a crime wave is sweeping the nation is largely a myth, and many would argue that the source of that myth is the media, which have helped spread and perpetuate the fiction of more than one crime wave.

When people believe that crime is on the rise, they turn to policymakers for solutions. That is what happened in the late 1970s and early 1980s. Politicians responded with get-tough-on-crime laws, key among them mandatory sentences for drug-related and other crimes. Those new laws, in turn, created a need for more jails and prisons. In the end, we have made more laws, made punishments more severe, and put more people behind bars. But at what cost do we pursue this policy? The economic costs of housing millions of offenders are staggering: they run to billions of dollars. And the social costs to offenders, to their families, and to society are incalculable.

Throughout much of our nation's history, prison incarceration rates changed slowly, over decades. For example, between 1870 and 1925, the per capita incarceration rate ranged from a low of 61 to a high of 79 (Cahalan 1986). In 1930, the rate moved above 100 and generally stayed between 110 and 115 until the late 1970s (Cahalan 1986). Then, the United States embarked on an "imprisonment binge" (Austin and Irwin 2001, 1). In the last two decades of the twentieth century, the incarceration rate rose from 138 to 461 per capita; between 1980 and 2010, the number of people in state and federal prisons went up over fourfold, from 329,821 to 1,509,475. By the end of the twentieth century, the United States was incarcerating people at the highest rate of any nation, a characterization that held through the first decade of the twenty-first century (see Box 1.1).

Table 1.1 shows the adult inmate population of the United States from 1980 to 2010. That population increased dramatically in both the absolute number of prisoners in federal and state prisons and local jails, and in per capita incarceration rates. In 1980, the nation's prison and jail systems held 501,886 inmates. By 1985, it had grown to nearly three-quarters of a million in population. Twenty-five years later, in 2010, the inmate population was at 2,258,203, more than four times the size of the 1980 correction system and three times that of the prison population reported in 1985. The incarceration rate increased 50 percent between 1980 and 1985, followed by another 133 percent increase between 1985 and 2010, and the peak rate to date was even higher in 2007! The federal prison system grew faster than either state or local systems: from 23,779 in 1980 to 198,339 inmates in 2010, an increase of more than sevenfold. By the end of the first decade in the twenty-first century, the US Bureau of Prisons operated the largest single prison

TABLE 1.1 **Adult inmate population, United States, 1980, 1985, 1990, 1995, 2000–2010.**

Year	Federal prisons	State prisons	Local jails	Total inmates	Per 100,00 rates (per capita)
1980	23,779	295,819	182,288	501,886	221
1985	35,781	451,812	256,615	744,208	313
1990	58,838	684,544	405,320	1,148,702	461
1995	89,538	989,004	507,044	1,585,586	601
2000	133,921	1,176,269	621,149	1,935,753	684
2001	143,337	1,180,155	631,240	1,961,247	685
2002	151,618	1,209,640	665,475	2,033,331	701
2003	161,673	1,222,135	691,301	2,081,580	712
2004	170,535	1,243,745	713,990	2,135,335	723
2005	179,220	1,259,905	747,529	2,193,798	737
2006	173,533	1,331,127	766,010	2,270,670	757
2007	179,204	1,353,646	780,581	2,313,431	765
2008	189,770	1,324,420	785,533	2,299,723	756
2009	196,318	1,319,426	767,620	2,283,364	743
2010	198,339	1,311,136	748,728	2,258,203	731

SOURCES: GUERINO, HARRISON, AND SABOL (2011); HARRISON AND BECK (2006, 2); MAGUIRE AND PASTORE (2001, 500); MINTON (2012); WEST, SABOL, AND GREENMAN (2010).

system in the United States, larger even than California (154,450 inmates) or Texas (152,403 inmates), its nearest rivals (Guerino, Harrison, and Sabol 2011, 19).

Our prisons and jails are critically crowded. Local, state, and national governments have all increased their inmate capacity, but it is clear that we cannot build ourselves out of the crowding crisis (Thompson and Mays 1991). It has been suggested that jail and prison capacity might drive prison population numbers (Klofas 1991). It is what some call the *Field of Dreams* theory: if you build a jail or prison, the inmates will come. It costs between $50,000 (for low-risk inmates) and $100,000 (for high-risk inmates) per bed space to build and an average of between $20,000 and $30,000 per year to house each inmate (Stephan 2004; Schmitt, Warner and Gupta 2010; South Carolina Department of Corrections 2012). Hence, policy makers and legislators—not to forget the public at large—need to consider carefully the answers to a series of critical questions. Specifically, have we reached the limit of what we can afford in number of people behind bars? Is $75 billion a year on corrections, with most going to

incarceration, too much? Finally, what about the social costs of incarcerating such a high percentage of the nation's minority youth? The point is that the get-tough-on-crime movement is not compatible with government downsizing and cutbacks, and the reality is that a clash between these two forces is looming.

THE ROLE OF CRIMINOLOGICAL THEORIES

When some students read or even hear the word *theory*, their minds snap shut and learning stops. To sneak theory into their work, writers and professors resort to trickery. They use terms like *framework*, *concept*, and *philosophy*. The authors of this textbook are not above this kind of trickery. Witness our description of the *philosophies* that underlie punishment. Deterrence, for one, is also a theory, as are most of the other philosophies we describe in this chapter.

Our current task—to help you understand why people commit crimes—is best achieved by describing both criminological theories and their practical aspects, particularly as they shape the nation's responses to crime. The details of these theories and the research that either supports or attacks their causal arguments are adequately described elsewhere (Akers and Sellers 2013; Winfree and Abadinsky 2010). Here we present a brief sampling of crime theories, with an emphasis on those with correctional implications. We start with the origins of criminological theories.

FROM FREE WILL TO DETERMINISM

Criminologists have spent more than 200 years applying philosophy and science to the study of crime.[6] Modern **criminology**, the scientific study of crime and criminals, is often dated from Cesare Beccaria's (1738–1794) late eighteenth-century attempts to apply what we now call *deterrence theory* to crime (see Chapter 2 for a discussion of this famous penal philosopher and early criminologist). Beccaria believed that people are rational beings endowed by their creator with free will and so are responsible for their own actions. Without certain and swift punishment that accords the unwanted act the required amount of severity, some people simply choose crime. The idea that criminals willfully choose to violate the law largely directed the study of crime for nearly a century.

In the 1870s, Cesare Lombroso (1836–1909) reported a criminological application for Charles Darwin's evolutionary theory. Criminals, according to what became known as the *Lombrosian* or *Italian school of criminology*, have few choices to make because their criminal tendencies are innate. Criminal behavior, then, is the result of **biological determinism**. Criminals are genetic misfits or biological throwbacks to earlier, primitive, and more violent beings.

Lombroso's ideas, first published as *The Criminal Man* in 1876, spawned a generation of deterministic anthropologists, psychologists, and economists. As determinists, these social scientists believed that forces beyond the individual's control were the source of criminal behavior. And as **positivists**, they looked for answers in measurable aspects of the human condition. Criminal anthropologists carried

on the work of early biological determinists as they grappled with the external measurable signs of internal crime inducing characteristics. Psychological determinists looked for forces in the human mind that could explain criminal conduct. Economic determinists, and later social determinists, believed that the distribution of wealth and the treatment of certain segments of society based on economic stratification created conditions ripe for criminality.

The implications of determinism for correctional practice are intriguing. If criminals are born, then society can do little to change them and prisons should function primarily as warehouses, storing this dangerous segment of society. However, if economic or social forces precondition certain people to become criminals, then changing those forces could alter an individual's pathway to crime. During the late nineteenth century, advocates of social change spoke out for *social engineering*, which in effect would rescue those placed by accident of birth in poor economic conditions. But Herbert Spencer (1820–1903) and some other sociologists railed against tinkering with society. Spencer, a social Darwinist, believed that government should not attempt to alter the lives of society's less fortunate in a substantial way. "The quality of society," he wrote, "is physically lowered by the artificial preservation of its feeblest members [and] the quality of a society is lowered morally and intellectually by the artificial preservation of those who are least able to take care of themselves" (1864, 313).

CRIME, CRIMINALS, AND DETERMINISTIC FORCES

Biological determinism did not disappear in the wake of conflicting evidence in the early twentieth century. In the late nineteenth century, it was widely believed that feeblemindedness was related to crime. The late-twentieth-century version of this idea alleges a link between intelligence and crime: the less intelligent the individual—measured by IQ score—the more likely he or she is to behave criminally. Other, more complex causal sequences link intelligence and crime by way of school performance and socioeconomic status. One contemporary

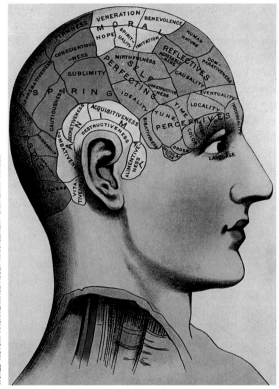

theory even suggests that certain racial groups are less intelligent than others—again, measured by IQ score—and so are more likely to live in poverty and be involved in crime (see, for example, Gordon 1987; Herrnstein and Murray 1994; and Wilson and Herrnstein 1985). Most criminologists reject the race-IQ-crime equation because it is not supported by research (Winfree and Abadinsky 2010, 131–34).

Attacks on the validity and utility of IQ testing, and the use of IQ scores to characterize the human potential, run squarely into a culture that values psychometric testing. As psychologist Curt Bartol warns, "IQ scores and the concept of intelligence should not be confused. The term *IQ* merely refers to a standardized score on a test. Intelligence, on the other hand, is a broad, all-encompassing ability that defies straightforward or simple definitions" (1991, 132). Nonetheless, support for IQ scores has deep roots in contemporary society, inside and outside race-based discussions (compare Chabris 1998; Fraser 1995; and Herrnstein and Murray 1994). Moreover,

some members of our society welcome race-based explanations no matter how weak the evidence.

Neopositivists would argue that school performance mediates between IQ scores and crime-proneness (Hindelang 1973). Youngsters with low IQ scores who later fail in school have higher delinquency rates and are more likely to commit crimes than are those with equally low IQ scores who manage to complete their schooling.

The correctional implications of IQ scores are built into the system. Nearly every convicted offender is subjected to some form of IQ testing. The scores are then used to determine subjects' mental functioning, likelihood of success in correctional treatment plans, and inmate classification (that is, low-functioning individuals may need special housing to avoid exploitation by other inmates). Although we are not sure what is being measured by IQ tests (Bartol 1991, 132), they continue to shape correctional practice and criminological discussions on the causes of individual criminality (Bartollas and Conrad 1992; Champion 2001).

Proponents of modern biological determinism insist that certain criminal behaviors have their origins in biochemical imbalances. For example, the crimes committed by drug addicts and alcoholics may be symptoms of other biochemical problems, among them a biological tendency toward addictive disorders (Gold, Washton, and Dackis 1985; Goleman 1990). Other biological determinists have attempted, with limited success, to link crime and hormone levels: for example, low levels of estrogen in women and high levels of testosterone in men. In one of the more interesting arguments about the role of biochemical imbalances, Lee Ellis (1991) asserts that criminals' blood exhibits low levels of a naturally occurring enzyme, monoamine oxidase (MAO). MAO helps regulate several key neurotransmitters, including those in the brain. Ellis observed that MAO is generally lower in three groups: males, youths and young adults (in their teens and twenties), and African Americans, three groups that are overrepresented in the criminal population.

Before we rush to order regular doses of MAO for members of these groups, it is important to note that the association between MAO and antisocial behavior is modest at best. Moreover, the idea that we can treat criminals with chemicals is not new: chemical therapies for criminals have been around for decades (Berman 1938; also see Hippchen 1982). Certain prison inmates could not be managed without the use of chemicals; and some parolees and probationers have chemical therapies included as a release condition. Many sex offenders are given hormone treatments in the belief that the hormones can control their sexual obsessions and so their conduct.

In addition to very real questions about the effectiveness of chemical therapies in controlling unwanted behavior, numerous moral and ethical dilemmas surround the forced or proactive treatment of offenders and people in at-risk groups. Can a democratic society subject its members to intrusive and disruptive biochemical treatments based on a probability that they might offend? Are we punishing people for what they *might* do? At what point does our collective need to feel safe outweigh individual liberties? And even if we can force treatment, should we?

Finally, **psychological determinists** believe that defects of the mind cause all misbehavior, including crime. Freudian psychoanalysts link human misbehavior to developmental issues originating with the following parts of the human **psyche**:[7] the **id** (the unconscious source of primitive and hedonistic urges), the **ego** (that part of the mind influenced by parental training and the like), and the **superego** (that part of the mind that is concerned with moral values). According to August Aichhorn (1925), the superego takes its form and content from children's efforts to emulate their parents or parental figures. Sometimes, the superego fails to develop properly, leaving only the ego to control the id's impulses. The problems usually stem from an abnormal relationship with parents or parental figures. Excessive control during a child's formative years can result in a superego that is too rigid and inflexible. Thinking bad and doing bad are often confused. The individual with an excessively controlling superego seeks punishment as a way of dealing with unconscious guilt. The person with a weak superego is unable to control aggressive, hostile, or antisocial urges. Given this set of psychological factors, crime is nearly inevitable.

Whether an individual has an overly strong superego or a very weak one, the prescribed treatment is the same. Through dream analysis and free association (talking about the first thing that comes to mind), the person with a poorly developed superego is made aware of the problem. With the guidance of a therapist, the individual eventually develops an appropriate superego and the inappropriate behavior stops.

BEHAVIOR MODIFICATION

An offshoot of behaviorism, **behavior modification** has perhaps the broadest practical implications of any psychological explanation of behavior. It begins with the premise that all behavior is the result of learned responses to various stimuli (Skinner 1974). From this perspective, deviant and criminal behaviors are inappropriate learned responses. Behavior is shaped by the presence or absence of various *reinforcers*, which stimulate behavior, and *punishers*, which retard or extinguish behavior. Because most crime involves a great deal of risk and very little reward, the role of behaviorism in causing crime mystifies some people. Psychologist Hans Eysenck explains: "An action followed by a small but immediate gratification will tend to be repeated, even though it is followed by a large but delayed painful consequence" (quoted in Taylor, Walton, and Young 1973, 47).

What is the practical role of behavior modification in corrections? Two forms have dominated the field over the past 30 years. The first, **reality therapy (RT)**, holds the offender accountable for his or her actions. In practice, RT is paternalistic and even authoritarian, which may explain its popularity with correctional workers. The therapist's moral standards must become the client's moral standards (Bersani 1989). The therapist develops a close relationship with the client and uses praise and concern as reinforcers, and the withdrawal of both as punishers. Through a lengthy interactive process, the client comes to see the error of his or her ways and, to gain favor with the therapist, ultimately behaves differently.

The second form of behavior modification program is built around a *token economy*. Good behavior earns the client rewards. Among the more important rewards for convicted criminals are such

things as early parole, temporary work or educational release into the community, and institutional privileges (including access to exercise or entertainment and better working conditions). Bad behavior yields punishments—for example, the loss of rewards, temporary isolation, or lower-paying and less-rewarding work.

Finally, psychology also provides insights into one of the most intriguing puzzles observed by correctional workers. Some "perfect" prison inmates—those who rarely complain about prison life or cause trouble for prison authorities—make poor candidates for release back into the community. Why? One answer may lie in **arousal theory**. That theory recognizes that some criminals have no conscience. **Psychopaths** (or *sociopaths*) commit crimes with no thought of conventional morality or of the consequences of their actions. According to Ellis (1990), because of a genetic defect, the brain functioning of psychopathic criminals quickly becomes habituated

to incoming stimuli. Low-arousal psychopaths find ordinary activities boring. When they take risks or commit crimes, they are looking to maximize their sensory stimulation. People with this disorder may literally be immune to efforts to alter their behavior. Low-arousal criminals receive little benefit from learning or punishment in most institutional environments because the existing stimulation barely keeps them awake (Bartol and Bartol 2011; Chesno and Kilmann 1975). By contrast, the world outside prison presents these people with too many stimuli, far more than they can manage without resorting to inappropriate behavior.

CRIME, CRIMINALS, AND SOCIAL FORCES

In the early twentieth century, sociologists emerged as major players in the ongoing quest to understand crime and criminals. These social scientists disavowed biological and psychological determinism, claiming they were too narrow and individualistic in orientation. Crime was a societal problem, not, as psychologists suggested, an individual problem.

In many sociological theories, crime is viewed as a consequence of social forces. Consider, for example, the contributions of the Chicago school of sociology to the study of crime. Looking at the relationship between greater Chicago and its inhabitants, social ecologists at the University of Chicago in the 1920s and 1930s believed it was the geographic area, not the people who inhabited it, that held the answer to understanding crime. They said crime emerged in certain communities because of disturbed, distressed, or incomplete social connections (Shaw and McKay 1942). These neighborhoods exhibited high mobility, as one ethnic group replaced another in conditions of extreme poverty, and as a result a lack of cohesiveness. City government largely ignored schools and parks in these areas to the point that they were deteriorating; and other public services were virtually nonexistent. Social ecologists claimed that this **social disorganization** found expression in criminal behavior.

Social disorganization explains the cause of criminal behavior; the **cultural transmission thesis** explains the persistence of criminal and other deviant values in successive generations. Together, these two components of social ecology helped shape an entire group of theories.

Edwin H. Sutherland, an early proponent of social ecology, summarized his ideas about the cultural transmission of criminality in his **differential association theory** (Sutherland and Cressey 1974). According to Sutherland, criminal values and behaviors are learned through social interactions. He called those values and behaviors *definitions*, and he suggested that those who become criminals are exposed to more definitions that support breaking the law than to definitions that support complying with the law. He believed that the sources of procriminal (and prosocial) definitions vary along four dimensions. Some sources—parents and childhood friends, for example—have an impact on early social development; they have high *priority*. Some sources are encountered with greater *frequency* than others. Often, exposure to certain sources lasts longer than exposure to others, so the former have greater

duration. Finally, the relationships with some sources have greater *intensity* than others because the individual respects those sources or has a stronger emotional tie to them.

Given the centrality of learning to the acquisition of criminal values and behaviors, could a person learn other, noncriminal ways? Donald Cressey, Sutherland's student and coauthor, believed that differential association could effect change.

Cressey (1955) advocated that offenders be exposed to prosocial definitions in a group context within correctional settings. Unfortunately, Sutherland left unexplored the means by which learning occurs. For example, we do not know why criminals learn certain definitions and not others—despite their exposure to great masses of information throughout their lives. This missing element makes it difficult to apply Sutherland's and Cressey's principles to a correctional setting.

Robert Burgess and Ronald Akers (1966) proposed that the missing element is **operant conditioning**: reward mechanisms encourage some definitions, whereas punishers extinguish others—concepts borrowed wholesale from behaviorism. In later refinements of his **social learning theory**, Akers (1985, 1992) articulated two central ideas. First, learning occurs through two mechanisms: **imitation**, which involves modeling behavior after that observed in others; and **differential reinforcement**, the operant-conditioning principle that people retain and repeat rewarded behavior and extinguish behavior that is punished. According to Akers, criminals learn motivating definitions—what he called **discriminative stimuli**—that either cast criminal behavior in a positive light or help neutralize the "undesirableness" of the behavior (1985, 50). In this way, thieves, for example, come to believe that burglary is an honorable vocation and that their victims, perhaps because they are rich or insured, do not deserve concern.

Victim–offender confrontation programs, which can be components of nontraditional settlements of violent and property crimes, have links to social learning theory. In addition to any other conditions for release into the community, offenders may be required to meet their victims, assuming the latter are willing. Therapists believe that offenders' discriminative stimuli are broken down by such meetings, especially when the offenders begin to see victims as human beings and understand their suffering. Offenders often find these confrontations very stressful, and few participants leave these meetings without being affected in some way.

Other correctional applications of social learning theory include **therapeutic communities**, residential programs in which offenders work together to change the attitudes and behaviors of all group members. In this case, reinforcers and punishers come from the offenders' peers, who are also engaged in the therapeutic process. Such communities offer those who want to change their attitudes and behaviors a supportive forum for expressing their best human emotions. These programs have been successful with both prison-confined and community-based felons (Wexler, Lipton, and Johnson 1988; Yablonsky 1989).

In line with the cultural transmission thesis, some researchers adopted a **subcultural hypothesis**: that crime largely emerges from delinquent or deviant subcultures. For example, delinquent youths may band together in gangs that reject both society and its values, reducing the impact of society's rejection of them (A. K. Cohen 1955). Alternatively, it might be that members of lower socioeconomic classes share similar concerns, including thrill-seeking behavior that may be illegal (Miller 1958). Still other subculturalists pointed to the existence of violent subcultures in society (Wolfgang 1958; Wolfgang and Ferracuti 1967). For these groups, violence becomes an accepted and expected way of dealing with all sorts of problems, especially questions of honor and manhood (Wolfgang and Ferracuti 1967).

Cultural transmission or social learning theorists, particularly Sutherland and Akers, base their explanations of crime and deviance on a single assumption: people learn to be deviant just as they learn to be conventional. Proponents of **social control theory** say that society provides the "social glue" that binds people together. Without this glue, people tend to engage in individual hedonistic activities, many of which violate the law. Social control theory is rooted in the work of Émile Durkheim (1897), a French sociologist who believed that many of society's ills, including crime, derive from times when the social fabric of society is weakened by war, economic changes, or other crises. He described the effect of this weakened state as **anomie** or a generalized sense of normlessness. During periods of major social and economic change, he insisted, society appears to reject laws and other norms, and crime, suicide, and other socially disturbing behaviors are more prevalent.

Durkheim viewed anomie as a societal condition, not something that could be observed in the individual. Two criminologists took different aspects of Durkheim's work and applied it to individual behavior. The first, Robert K. Merton (1957), believed that anomie is the result of the rift between culturally defined success (status and financial security, and the luxuries they provide) and limitations on the individual's ability to achieve that success (education, thrift, and hard work, for example). Merton developed several categories of adaptation to describe the individual's response to anomie. *Conformists* try legitimate means, including hard work and discipline, to achieve culturally valued goals. When they meet barriers, they stand face-to-face with the **anomic trap**: they can accept their fate, work hard, and achieve little; or they can turn to another adaptation. *Innovators*, unlike conformists, use illegitimate means to achieve success. Although Merton identified other adaptations, innovators pose the most direct problems for the criminal justice system.[8]

The implications of Merton's theory for corrections are straightforward but difficult to implement. Giving offenders the means to confront a life in which the deck may be stacked against them certainly has direct ties to Merton's anomie theory. That is, people facing the anomic trap must be offered legitimate alternatives that normally are not available to them. Increased educational opportunities or job training, both of which are found in correctional settings, provide good examples of legitimate alternatives.

Control theorist Travis Hirschi (1969) was a second criminologist influenced by Durkheim's work, in particular the discussion of the forces that hold society together. Hirschi believed that the **social bond** is the sum of the forces in a person's social and physical environment that connect that person to society and its moral constituents. The latter include social institutions—for example, family, school, and the law. Hirschi identified four types of ties between individuals and social institutions:

- *Attachment* is the affection for and sensitivity to members of social groups. Without attachments, the individual is free to deviate.
- *Commitment* refers to the individual's stake in conformity—how devoted he or she is to conventionality.
- *Involvement* is the extent to which the person engages in conventional activities.
- *Belief* explores the idea that the correctness of norms is variable, that norms (and laws) may not hold the same significance for all people in a society. The greater the belief in the society's norms, the lower the chance of delinquency.

Indeed, Hirschi believed that the probability of law-violating behavior is directly proportional to the extent to which any of these elements of the social bond are weakened.

As for correctional practice, convicted criminals may be among the most "debonded" individuals in society. If the social bond can be reestablished, and that is not a given, then rebonding would have to occur across all four dimensions. Consider our brief discussions of reintegration, restoration, and restitution. These philosophies and social bonding theory all imply that offenders must be made a part of the society from which they came, and that the links between offenders and the community must be reestablished (or, some would argue, established for the first time). The central warning of social bonding theory is that any treatment or rehabilitation program must address all aspects of an offender's relationship to the community. Moreover, conditions of probation or parole release must necessarily limit an offender's contacts with known criminals and prior criminal associates.[9] By minimizing negative distractions, the system encourages conventional bonding.

REVIEWING CRIMINOLOGICAL THEORIES

We have tried to accomplish three goals in this condensed discussion of crime theories. First, we have suggested a wide range of possible answers to several of the difficult questions people who work in the criminal justice system ask: Why do certain people commit crimes? Why do some stop? Why do others continue even after they are punished?

What do we do with the answers? This question leads to our second goal for this review of theories: understanding offenders' responses to the correctional system, their values, attitudes, outlooks, perspectives, and rationalizations. These theories also have the potential to inform correctional workers about what to expect from offenders placed in their charge. Certainly experience can give valuable insight, but theories yield far more systematic understanding of criminals' lives in general and of convicted offenders specifically. That is, theories can make the transition from civilian to correctional worker smoother for both keepers and kept.

Finally, an understanding of both philosophies of punishment and theories of crime helps penologists design better methods for treating offenders through prison-based therapeutic communities, conditional release, and other programs. (See Box 1.3 on the role of power in "causing" crime.) If society cannot change offenders' extra-institutional behavior—that is, if rehabilitation or deterrence is neither possible nor practical—then the goal of corrections at a minimum should be the proper, adequate, and humane treatment of those under correctional authorities' control. Before you dismiss these views as the ramblings of do-gooders, consider this: if you treat human beings as wild animals, abusing them at every turn, they tend to respond as wild animals. Now consider this: more than 90 percent of inmates are released into the community. Humane treatment is not just a moral issue; it is a practical matter too.

CORRECTIONS PROGRAMS

The United States has 51 correctional systems, a system in each state and a national system. If we add the District of Columbia and local systems in metropolitan areas like Los Angeles County and New York City, the number is even higher. Each of these criminal justice systems—and each system's corrections component—is different from the others, but we can identify three general categories of corrections programs: community-based programs, intermediate-sanctions, and institutional-placements.

POWER AND CRIME: A MISSING DIMENSION?   BOX 1.3

In the late 1960s and early 1970s, several important criminological theories emerged that attacked the dominant social structural, biological, and psychological theories for supporting the status quo. A growing and vocal group of criminologists said the study of crime should include the dimension of power: Who has it? Who doesn't? Who uses it? And to what ends?

Some of these critics, including Howard Becker and Edwin Schur, suggest that the state's power to label those accused of crimes is perhaps the greatest power and potentially the greatest evil. The label is proof of the state's authority to arrest, try, convict, and sentence lawbreakers. Ultimately, the truth of the label is irrelevant. Labeling theorists warn us that even people who are falsely accused can succumb to a label's power and become what the state calls them.

Other power-based theories of crime are rooted in Marxism. Marxists believe that the criminal justice system serves the interests of the wealthy (the capitalists), those who own the means of production and feed off the labor of the workers (the proletariat). Criminals, according to Richard Quinney and other neo-Marxists, are either victims of the system or freedom fighters, struggling against an unjust system. Later Marxists, including William Chambliss and Robert Seidman, redefined the relationships among capitalism, law, and crime: state authority emerged not simply as an instrument of oppression, but as an instrument for ensuring the long-term dominance of capitalism as a way of life.

Theories that speak to the state's power to arrest, try, convict, and sentence criminal offenders have important implications for policy, but implementing policy changes may be difficult, especially if the Marxists are correct. It is unlikely that a system with a vested interest in the status quo would adopt what Marxists are calling for: revolutionary changes in the balance of power.

But labeling theory raises different issues. For example, we know that a negative label has the power to change a person's life, to make that person become what he or she has been labeled. If we can avoid labeling young offenders, if we can keep them out of the system early on, we may reduce the likelihood of their committing future crimes. Schur describes what he calls **radical nonintervention**, that society and its agents of social control should overlook minor delinquent acts (for example, criminal trespass, petty vandalism, and shoplifting where restitution is made) to avoid labeling youngsters and possibly setting them on the path toward more serious criminality when they are older.

Labeling theorists also advocate for **deinstitutionalization**: they would like to see secure confinement abandoned as a punishment. Prisons for young offenders, goes this argument, are ill equipped to bring about change; instead, they are more likely to lead juvenile offenders deeper into the world of delinquency and crime. That effect is strengthened when young people leave the institution with the label *ex-con*. Deinstitutionalization programs for juvenile offenders have been tried on a limited scale with some success. Of course, both radical nonintervention and deinstitutionalization face an uphill battle for acceptance in a nation obsessed with punishment for its own sake.

SOURCES: BECKER (1963); CHAMBLISS AND SEIDMAN (1982); QUINNEY (1970); SCHUR (1973).

COMMUNITY-BASED PROGRAMS

Traditional programs of probation and parole are examples of community-based corrections efforts. These programs treat offenders in the community, under supervision and restrictions, rather than in an institution. Some penologists suggest that it is more effective to treat offenders in a natural environment, where the support systems established by their probation or parole officer can help them confront day-to-day problems and adjust to a life without crime. As discussed later in this book, this thinking is not always borne out, for various reasons.

Community-based programs can also include residential placement in a group home or halfway house (halfway in for probationers and halfway out for parolees). The assumption here is that the offender's original living arrangement is neither acceptable nor desirable. Group homes and halfway houses provide shelter, structure, and more constant surveillance than traditional probation or parole, and residents have a built-in support system and accountability group.

INTERMEDIATE-SANCTION PROGRAMS

Intermediate-sanction programs are among the fastest-growing programs in contemporary corrections. These programs fall somewhere between traditional probation and incarceration on the corrections continuum (Latessa and Allen 1999). Split sentences and intermittent confinement are two forms of intermediate sanctions: both require individuals convicted of crimes to serve brief periods of confinement in a local, state, or federal facility, followed by a period of community supervision. Intermediate sanctions, then, are both alternatives to incarceration and alternative forms of incarceration.

Not everyone agrees that court-ordered community service and restitution programs are intermediate sanctions. There is general agreement, however, that intensive probation supervision, house arrest, and electronic monitoring—all of which we discuss in later chapters—are examples of intermediate sanctions (Castle 1991; Gowdy 1993).

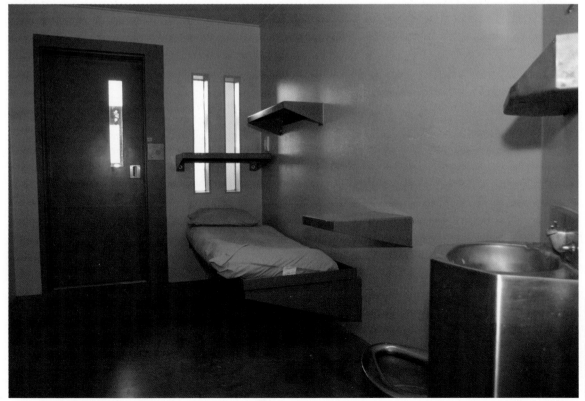

MIKE KARLSSON/ALAMY IMAGES

INSTITUTIONAL-PLACEMENT PROGRAMS

The area most closely associated with corrections is secure institutional confinement. Even here we find a variety of programs (US Department of Justice 1988, 58, 96). For example, offenders can be placed in jails, workhouses, or penal farms. And state and federal institutions range from low-security camps, farms, and ranches (often for juveniles or young offenders) to the most secure prisons.

Prisons in the United States typically fall into one of three security classifications: *minimum security* (inmates are relatively free to move around the facility), *medium security* (some freedom of movement within the institution), and *maximum security* (few or no opportunities for movement within the institution). To these traditional categories, some states have added *minimum restrictive security* or *close security*, two concepts discussed in Chapter 6. The decision to place a convicted criminal in an institution with a lower or higher security classification is a function of the severity of the offense and the likelihood of the offender's attempting to escape. Some facilities have been designed for more than one security level.

This brief overview is a reminder that corrections concerns a vast array of programs that operate in any number of settings, from the community to the most secure institution. We examine all of the various facets of corrections as we progress through this book.

SUMMARY

We expect corrections to achieve many goals in contemporary society. As a part of the American justice system, it touches the lives of millions of people every year. The key points to note from this chapter are the following:

- No universal agreement exists about what the word *corrections* means, and what exactly we are attempting to correct.

- In some ways, it is easiest to think of the corrections component of the criminal justice system as comprising a vast array of loosely connected agencies that fit within community responses, intermediate sanctions, and institutional placements.

- Generally speaking, there has been an explosive growth in the number of people under some form of correctional supervision during the past three decades.

- There are a variety of punishment philosophies, which include retribution, deterrence, rehabilitation, isolation, incapacitation, reintegration, restitution, and restoration.

- Criminological theories can help us understand the nature of human behavior and the appropriate responses to criminality. Most of these theories can be characterized as biological, psychological, or sociological. However, theories dealing with power and economics also have become prominent.

THINKING ABOUT CORRECTIONAL POLICIES AND PRACTICES: WRITING ASSIGNMENTS

1   Examine the trends in correctional populations since 1980 (Figure 1.1). The "slippage" of the past few years aside, what is the best way to characterize this graph? Now go online and find both a trend analysis for crime in the United States and victimization in the United

States (Note: They come from two different data sources), and characterize crime in the United States since the 1970s and 1980s. How do you reconcile the three different trends?

2 Think about the ways retribution may appear in modern correctional practices. Write a brief synopsis (2 to 3 paragraphs) taking a position about why retribution is or is not a legitimate correctional philosophy today. Explain your reasoning carefully.

3 In some ways, rehabilitation has fallen out of favor with the general public and even with some of those people who work in the corrections field. Prepare a 2 to 3 page summary about whether rehabilitation is a viable corrections goal. What programs today (institutional or extrainstitutional) still exemplify rehabilitation? Does it matter whether the offenders involved are juveniles or adults?

4 Search online for the term *restorative justice*. How many "hits" did you get? Develop a short paper explaining the key concepts that appear on many of the web sites that discuss restorative justice. Especially consider whether there is any consistency in the use and meaning of the term.

5 Go online and find the figures for your state's current prison population and the costs associated with housing these inmates. If this information is not available online, check your college or public library for a recent copy of the corrections department's annual report. As a last resort, you might contact a local representative of the state corrections department (from a nearby prison or probation and parole office) to see if he or she can provide you with this information. Are the figures easy to obtain? Is there a problem with using gross (aggregate) figures to calculate the per-inmate per-year cost? If you are able to obtain these figures, prepare a short paper (one page maximum) comparing these costs with your costs to attend college or university.

KEY TERMS

anomic trap	ego	reality therapy (RT)
anomie	general deterrence	rehabilitation
arousal theory	id	reintegration
behavior modification	imitation	restitution
biological determinism	incapacitation	restoration
corrections	isolation	retribution
criminology	*lex talionis*	selective incapacitation
cultural transmission thesis	operant conditioning	social bond
deinstitutionalization	penal harm	social control theory
deterrence	penologists	social disorganization
differential association theory	positivists	social learning theory
differential reinforcement	psyche	specific deterrence
discriminative stimuli	psychological determinists	subcultural hypothesis
disproportionate minority	psychopaths	superego
contact (DMC)	radical nonintervention	therapeutic communities

CRITICAL REVIEW QUESTIONS

1 What is being corrected in corrections, or is the term itself being misapplied?

2 How do you feel about a murder victim's next-of-kin asking to view the execution, pull the switch, or activate the syringes?

3 What is the difference between isolation and incapacitation? Is one more important than the other? Why or why not? If so, to whom?

4 Are there real limits to restitution? Do you think restitution is fair? Why or why not?

5 What three terms would you use to describe most nineteenth-century criminological theories? Justify the use of each term.

6 Are you offended by any of the forms of determinism described in the chapter? If yes, identify them and explain why you find them offensive.

7 Are we victims of our biology, or are we victims of our minds? Explain your answers.

8 How have twentieth-century sociologists helped us understand the social forces that produce criminals and criminal behavior? Distinguish between theories that explain the emergence of criminals and those that explain the crime rate.

9 Why is it important to understand the forces that shape our perceptions of crime, justice, and corrections?

10 Two of the boxes in this chapter address the international nature of corrections. What kinds of things have you learned about corrections from an international perspective that you did not know before? What kinds of things do you hope to learn?

NOTES

1 Although the gross number of people under supervision is instructive, especially if we are looking at growth or trends, the *per capita rate*—the rate per 100,000 people within a given racial or ethnic group—is more useful in making comparisons within groups or between years. The gross numbers tell us, for example, that the prison population increased between 1980 and 2010, but they do not tell us how much of that increase was linked to growth in the overall population. The per capita rate allows us to hold constant the increase in population. In our comparisons here, we have based the per capita rates on every 100,000 residents; the rates could also be calculated for a specific group (every 100,000 adults, for example, or every 100,000 people under age 18).

2 Literally, *lex talionis* translates from the Latin to mean the law of talion, the latter meaning exchange.

3 *Discretionary parole* is granted by a parole board, after a review of an inmate's criminal and institutional history and other relevant facts. Many of the

jurisdictions that have eliminated discretionary parole instead mandate the supervised release of inmates who have served a defined portion of their sentence.

4 While this phrase has long been attributed to Martinson, a careful reading of his 1974 work reveals that it was not so much that nothing worked as we cannot tell what does work, given the shortcomings in the evaluation literature.

5 Although Bernard focused on the juvenile justice system, his work applies to the adult justice system as well.

6 We are aware of a long tradition of crime "theories" going back to the mark of Cain, original sin, and other Judeo-Christian accounts of evil. There were also numerous attempts in the Middle Ages and the Age of Enlightenment to explain criminal conduct as possession by the devil or other evil spirits. There were even some interesting but inconclusive ideas about evil faces reflecting evil minds (the term for this is *physiognomy*). Equally interesting

and discredited were the phrenologists, who believed that bumps on the head indicate criminal proclivities. Our focus here is largely on the last 100 years of "scientific" criminology.

7 For psychologists, this term refers to the totality of the human mind, conscious and unconscious.

8 Merton identified two other adaptations. *Retreatists*, those who abandon both legitimate means to success and cultural goals of success for their own, usually more hedonistic, means and goals, could also be a source of trouble for the criminal justice system. In addition, *rebels*, who actively challenge all rules, including means and goals, are potentially thorns in the side of authority and, hence, problems for the justice system. We focus here on innovators to facilitate the discussion.

9 This condition could be linked to either social learning or social bonding. From a social learning perspective, criminal cronies are potential sources of procriminal definitions. From a social bonding perspective, ties to criminal cronies could weaken the bond to conventional society.

REFERENCES

Aichhorn, August. 1925. *Wayward youth*. New York: Viking Press.

Akers, Ronald L. 1985. *Deviant behavior: A social learning approach*, 3rd edn. Belmont, CA: Wadsworth.

Akers, Ronald L. 1992. *Drugs, alcohol and society: Social structure, process and policy*. Belmont, CA: Wadsworth.

Akers, Ronald L., and Christine S. Sellers. 2013. *Criminological theories: Introduction, evaluation, and application*, 6th edn. New York: Oxford University Press.

Armstrong, T., D. Maloney, and D. Roming. 1990. The balanced approach in juvenile probation: Principles, issues and application. *Perspectives* (Winter): 8–13.

Austin, James F., and John Irwin. 2001. *It's about time: America's imprisonment binge*. 3rd edn. Belmont, CA: Wadsworth.

Bartol, Curt R. 1991. *Criminal behavior: A psychological approach*, 3rd edn. Englewood Cliffs, NJ: Prentice Hall.

Bartol, Curt R., and Anne M. Bartol. 2011. *Criminal behavior: A psychological approach*, 9th edn. Upper Saddle River, NJ: Prentice Hall.

Bartollas, Clemens, and John P. Conrad. 1992. *Introduction to corrections*, 2nd edn. New York: HarperCollins

Bazemore, Gordon. 1992. On mission statements and reform in juvenile justice: The case of the "balanced approach." *Federal Probation* 56(3): 64–70.

Becker, Howard. 1963. *Outsiders: Studies in the sociology of deviance*. New York: Free Press.

Berman, Louis. 1938. *The glands regulating personality*. New York: Macmillan

Bernard, Thomas J. 1992. *The cycle of juvenile justice*. New York: Oxford University Press.

Bersani, Carl A. 1989. Reality therapy: Issues and a review of research. In *Correctional counseling and treatment*, 2nd edn., edited by P. C. Kratcoski. Prospect Heights, IL: Waveland Press.

Bonczar, Thomas P. 2003. Prevalence of imprisonment in the U.S. population, 1974–2001. *Bureau of Justice Statistics Bulletin*. Washington, DC: US Department of Justice.

Braithwaite, John. 1999. Restorative justice: Assessing optimistic and pessimistic accounts. In *Crime and justice: A review of research*, edited by Michael Tonry. Chicago: University of Chicago Press, 1–127.

Burgess, Robert, and Ronald L. Akers. 1966. Differential association-reinforcement theory of criminal behavior. *Social Problems* 14: 128–47.

Cahalan, Margaret W. 1986. *Historical corrections statistics in the United States, 1850–1984*. Washington, DC: US Government Printing Office.

Castle, Michael N. 1991. *Alternative sentencing: Selling it to the public*. Washington, DC: US Government Printing Office.

Chabris, Christopher. 1998. IQ since *The Bell Curve*. *Commentary* 106: 33–40.

Chambliss, William J., and Robert Seidman. 1982. *Law, order and power*. Reading, MA: Addison-Wesley.

Champion, Dean. 2001. *Corrections in the United States: A contemporary perspective*, 3rd edn. Upper Saddle River, NJ: Prentice Hall.

Chesno, Frank A., and Peter R. Kilmann. 1975. Effects of stimulation intensity on sociopathic avoidance learning. *Journal of Abnormal Psychology* 84: 144–50.

Clear, Todd R. 1994. *Harm in American penology: Offenders, victims, and their communities*. Albany: State University of New York Press.

Cohen, Albert K. 1955. *Delinquent boys: The culture of the gang*. New York: Free Press.

Cressey, Donald R. 1955. Changing criminals: The application of the theory of differential association. *American Journal of Sociology* 61: 116–20.

Cromwell, Paul F., and George G. Killinger. 1994. *Community-based corrections: Probation, parole, and intermediate sanctions*, 3rd edn. St. Paul, MN: West.

Cullen, Francis T., and Karen E. Gilbert. 1982. *Reaffirming rehabilitation*. Cincinnati, OH: Anderson.

Decker, Scott H. 1985. A systematic analysis of diversion: Net widening and beyond. *Journal of Criminal Justice* 13(3): 207–16.

Durkheim, Émile. 1897/1951. *Suicide*. Trans. J. A. Spaulding and G. Simpson. New York: Free Press.

Ellis, Lee. 1990. Conceptualizing criminal and related behavior from a biosocial perspective. In *Crime in biological, social, and moral contexts*, edited by L. Ellis and H. Hoffman. Westport, CT: Praeger.

Ellis, Lee. 1991. Monoamine oxidase and criminality: Identifying an apparent biological marker for antisocial behavior. *Journal of Research in Crime and Delinquency* 28: 227–51.

Encarta World English Dictionary. 2009. Retrieved on July 8, 2013 from: **http://www.bing.com/Dictionary/search ?q=define+lex+talionis&qpvt=lex+talionis&FORM=DTPDIA**

Federal Bureau of Investigation. 2011. *Uniform Crime Report, Crime in the United States, 2010*. Washington, DC: US Department of Justice. Retrieved on July 8, 2013 from: **http://www.fbi.gov/about-us/cjis/ucr/ crime-in-the-u.s/2010/crime-in-the-u.s.-2010/tables/10tbl01.xls**

Fogel, David. 1975. *". . .We are the living proof . . ." The justice model for corrections*. Cincinnati, OH: Anderson.

Fraser, Steven. 1995. *The bell curve wars: Race, intelligence, and the future of America*. New York: Basic Books.

Glaze, Lauren. 2011. *Correctional populations in the United States, 2010*. Washington, DC: U.S. Department of Justice.

Glaze, Lauren, and Thomas P. Bonczar. 2011. *Probation and parole in the United States 2010*. Washington, DC: US Department of Justice.

Gold, Mark S., Arnold M. Washton, and Charles A. Dackis. 1985. Cocaine abuse: Neurochemistry, phenomenology, and treatment. In *Cocaine use in America: Epidemiology and clinical perspectives*, edited by N. J. Kozel and E. H. Adams. Rockville, MD: National Institute of Drug Abuse, 130–59.

Goleman, Daniel. 1990. Scientists pinpoint brain irregularities in drug addicts. *New York Times*, June 26, B5.

Gordon, Robert A. 1987. SES versus IQ in the race-IQ delinquency model. *International Journal of Sociology and Social Policy* 7: 30–70.

Gowdy, Voncile B. 1993. *Intermediate sanctions*. Washington, DC: US Department of Justice.

Greenwood, Peter, with Allan Abramse. 1982. *Selective incapacitation*. Santa Monica, CA: RAND.

Guerino, Paul, Paige M. Harrison, and William J. Sabol. 2011. *Prisoners in 2010*. Washington, DC: US Department of Justice.

Harrison, Paige M., and Allen J. Beck. 2003. *Prisoners in 2002*. Bureau of Justice Statistics Bulletin. Washington, DC: US Department of Justice.

Harrison, Paige M., and Allen J. Beck. 2006. *Prisoners in 2005*. Washington, DC: US Department of Justice.

Herrnstein, Richard J., and Charles Murray. 1994. *The bell curve: Intelligence and class structure in American life*. New York: Free Press.

Hindelang, Michael J. 1973. Causes of delinquency: A partial replication and extension. *Social Problems* 20: 471–87.

Hippchen, Leonard. 1982. *Holistic approaches to offender rehabilitation*. Springfield, IL: Charles C. Thomas.

Hirschi, Travis. 1969. *Causes of delinquency*. Berkeley: University of California Press.

Humes, Karen R., Nicholas A. Jones, and Roberto R. Ramirez. 2011. *Overview of race and Hispanic origin: 2010. 2010 Census Briefs*. Washington, DC: US Department of Commerce.

Klofas, John M. 1991. Jail crowding. In *Setting the jail research agenda for the 1990s*, edited by G. Larry Mays. Washington, DC: National Institute of Corrections, 69–76.

Latessa, Edward J., and Harry E. Allen. 1999. *Corrections in the community*, 2nd edn. Cincinnati, OH: Anderson.

Lipton, Douglas, Robert Martinson, and Judith Wilks. 1975. *The effectiveness of correctional treatment*. New York: Praeger.

Lombroso, Cesare. 1876. *L'uomo delinquente [The criminal man]*. Milan: Hoepli.

Maguire, Kathleen, and Ann C. Pastore, eds. 2001. *Bureau of Justice Statistics sourcebook of criminal justice statistics 2000*. Washington, DC: US Department of Justice.

Maloney, D., Romig, D., and Armstrong, T. 1988. Juvenile probation: The balanced approach, *Juvenile and Family Court Journal*, 39(3): complete issue.

Martinson, Robert. 1974. What works? Questions and answers about prison reform. *Public Interest* 35: 22–54.

Merton, Robert K. 1957. *Social theory and social structure*. New York: Free Press.

Miller, Walter B. 1958. Lower-class culture as a generating milieu of gang delinquency. *Journal of Social Issues* 14: 5–19.

Minton, Todd D. 2012. *Jail inmates at midyear 2011—Statistical tables*. Washington, DC: US Department of Justice.

Newell, Tim. 2001. *Responding to the crisis—Belgium establishes restorative prisons*. London: ICPS.

Quinney, Richard. 1970. *The social reality of crime*. Boston: Little, Brown.

Rogers, Joseph W., and G. Larry Mays. 1987. *Juvenile delinquency and juvenile justice*. New York: Wiley.

Schmitt, John, Kris Warner, and Sarika Gupta. 2010. *The high budgetary cost of incarceration*. Washington, DC: Center for Economic and Policy Research.

Schur, Edwin. 1973. *Radical nonintervention: Rethinking the delinquency problem*. Englewood Cliffs, NJ: Prentice Hall.

Shaw, Clifford R., and Henry D. McKay. 1942. *Juvenile delinquency and urban areas: A study of rates of delinquency in relation to different characteristics of local communities in American cities*. Chicago: University of Chicago Press.

Siegler, M., and Humphry Osmond. 1974. *Models of madness, models of medicine*. New York: Macmillan.

Skinner, B. F. 1974. *About behaviorism*. New York: Knopf.

South Carolina Department of Corrections 2012. How much does it cost to build a prison? Frequently asked questions (FAQs). Retrieved July 8, 2013 from: **http://www.doc.sc.gov/faqs.jsp**

Spencer, Herbert. 1864/1961. *The study of sociology*. Ann Arbor: University of Michigan Press.

Stephan, James J. 2004. *State Prison Expenditures, 2001*. Washington, DC: US Department of Justice.

Sutherland, Edwin H., and Donald R. Cressey. 1974. *Criminology*, 9th edn. Philadelphia: Lippincott.

Taylor, Ian, Paul Walton, and Jock Young. 1973. *The new criminology*. New York: Harper & Row.

Thompson, Joel A., and G. Larry Mays, eds. 1991. *American jails: Public policy issues*. Chicago: Nelson-Hall.

Travis, Jeremy. 2000. *But they all come back: Rethinking prisoner reentry*. Washington, DC: US Department of Justice.

US Department of Justice. 1981. *Dictionary of criminal justice data terminology*. Washington, DC: US Government Printing Office.

US Department of Justice. 1988. *Report to the nation on crime and justice*, 2nd edn. Washington, DC: US Government Printing Office.

Walker, Samuel. 2011. *Sense and nonsense about crime and drugs*, 7th edn. Belmont, CA: Wadsworth.

Walmsley, Roy. 2001. World prison populations: Facts, trends and solutions. Background paper prepared for the United Nations Program Network Institutes Technical Assistance Workshop, Vienna, May 10.

Walmsley, Roy. 2009. *World prison population list*, 8th edn. London: King's College London, International Centre for Prison Studies.

Welch, Michael. 1996. *Corrections: A critical approach*. New York: McGraw-Hill.

West, Heather C., William J. Sabol, and Sarah J. Greenman. 2010. *Prisoners in 2009*. Washington, DC: US Department of Justice.

Wexler, Harry K., Douglas S. Lipton, and Bruce D. Johnson. 1988. *A criminal justice strategy for treating cocaine–heroin abusing offenders in custody*. Washington, DC: US Department of Justice.

Wilson, James Q., and Richard Herrnstein. 1985. *Crime and human nature*. New York: Simon & Schuster.

Winfree, L. Thomas, Jr. 2002. Peacemaking and community harmony: Lessons (and admonitions) from the Navajo peacemaking courts. In *Restorative justice: Theoretical foundations*, edited by Elmar G. M. Weitekamp and Hans-Juergen Kerner. Devon, UK: Willam, 285–307.

Winfree, L. Thomas, Jr., and Howard Abadinsky. 2010. *Understanding crime: Essentials of criminological theory*, 3rd edn. Belmont, CA: Wadsworth.

Wolfgang, Marvin E. 1958. *Patterns of criminal homicide*. Philadelphia: University of Pennsylvania Press.

Wolfgang, Marvin E., and Franco Ferracuti. 1967. *The subculture of violence*. London: Tavistock.

Wolfgang, Marvin E., Robert M. Figlio, and Thorsten Sellin. 1972. *Delinquency in a birth cohort*. Chicago: University of Chicago Press.

Wright, Richard. 1996. Afterword to *Life without parole: Living in prison today*, by Victor Hassine. Los Angeles: Roxbury, 129–39.

Yablonsky, Lewis. 1989. *The therapeutic community*. New York: Garden.

2 A BRIEF HISTORY OF PUNISHMENTS AND CORRECTIONS

BETTMANN ARCHIVE/CORBIS

Outline

Early History

The Age of Enlightenment, the State, and Criminal Sanctions

Prison Reform and Penitentiaries

The Pennsylvania System versus the Auburn System

Penitentiary Reform in the Nineteenth Century

From Rehabilitative Ideal to Justice Model

Objectives

- To orient you as to the role of corrections in human history

- To provide you with an understanding of how civilized nations refined their penal sanctions, leading to the creation of prisons and penitentiaries

- To acquaint you with the various nineteenth-century reform movements

- To reveal to you the importance of understanding the significance of the movement away from the rehabilitative ideal to the justice model for correctional practice

Essentials of Corrections, Fifth Edition. G. Larry Mays and L. Thomas Winfree, Jr.
© 2014 John Wiley & Sons, Inc. Published 2014 by John Wiley & Sons, Inc.

INTRODUCTION

The key to understanding contemporary correctional systems is an understanding of the historical and philosophical roots of punishment. How have societies through the ages dealt with offenders? The answer depends on the era, but generally punishments throughout recorded history tended to make the flesh suffer for the acts of the criminal, protect those in power, and exploit the labor of law-breakers.

- The ancient Greeks favored stoning and disemboweling offenders, but they also crucified, garroted, and drowned criminals when they felt it was appropriate.

- Centuries later, in ancient Rome, the state beheaded certain enemies of the Republic (and later of the Roman Empire) with ceremony. Most, but especially prisoners of war, were sentenced to life as galley slaves, where they often died chained to their oars in battle or from old age, illness, or injuries suffered at their masters' hands. Garden-variety criminals in ancient Rome were often stoned or buried alive.

- Following the ancient traditions, medieval English and French monarchs had their enemies disemboweled in a gory ritual. In the early Middle Ages, the most prevalent punishment was the forfeiture of property, especially land. By the late Middle Ages, English and French monarchs had begun to cut off the heads of traitors and, increasingly, common criminals.

- During the Renaissance, a time of discovery and enlightenment, the gallows had assumed a central role in capital punishments.

- At the end of the eighteenth century, Dr. Joseph-Ignace Guillotin, a French physician, proposed that France develop a more humane and uniform method of execution. A medical colleague, Dr. Antoine Louis, designed an efficient machine for shearing heads from bodies.

- In the late nineteenth and early twentieth century, courts in France—following the

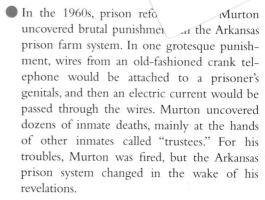

centuries-old exam... and other colonial ... nals to hard labor in d... goal was twofold: to p... build an infrastructure f...

- In the 1960s, prison refo... Murton uncovered brutal punishmei... in the Arkansas prison farm system. In one grotesque punishment, wires from an old-fashioned crank telephone would be attached to a prisoner's genitals, and then an electric current would be passed through the wires. Murton uncovered dozens of inmate deaths, mainly at the hands of other inmates called "trustees." For his troubles, Murton was fired, but the Arkansas prison system changed in the wake of his revelations.

What this brief but illustrative list points out is the wide range of criminal sanctions. It also suggests that punishments can be severe, even cruel. And it tells us that the inhumane treatment of criminals was not limited to ancient cultures.

EARLY HISTORY

A comprehensive history of punishments is beyond the scope of this chapter. But certain benchmark events, laws, and penal systems shaped communities' responses to crime and criminals. Most of these developments occurred during the past 3,000 to 4,000 years, paralleling the development of Western civilization.

CRIME AND PUNISHMENT IN PREHISTORIC CONTEXT

In prehistoric times, before the development of formal legal systems, the resolution of crime and punishment issues in clans and tribes relied heavily on rituals of reconciliation and, to a lesser extent, rituals of exclusion (Pfohl 1981; also see Gargarin 1986, 19–50, and Vinogradoff 1920, 299–389). Tribal rules in this prelegal stage passed orally from generation to generation and described inappropriate acts and appropriate sanctions. If someone violated a rule, the punishment usually was mild, and it would be carried out immediately by the entire community. For example, a person who showed up late for a meal might be teased by the group. In effect, the tribe would use humor to regain its authority, to remind the offender that he or she must comply with tribal rules. If the norm in question was more important and the sanction more severe, elders in the community might be called on to judge the transgressor. A thief who stole a bowl of fruit, for example, might be required to supply the victimized family with fruit over a prescribed period. Both parties—victim and perpetrator—had to agree on the justness of the settlement. Resolutions were less about deciding guilt or innocence and more about ending strife in a homogeneous community; the goal was reconciliation (Gargarin 1986, 21–23; Pfohl 1981, 83–84).[1] By definition, reconciliation is restoring balance; in the tribal context, it meant restoring the balance among victim, perpetrator, and the larger group. Restitution, then, was a common reconciliation ritual: the offender or the offender's kin had to repay the victim's loss.

Given the strong blood relationships in most tribes, the worst intragroup punishment was banishment or exclusion. In such situations, the norm violated would have to be a very important one, perhaps incest or the killing of one's parent. Banning the perpetrator from any future contacts with tribal members—including relatives—often meant more than the offender's symbolic death, as it was rare for any other group to accept such a person into its fold. Without food, shelter, and protection, a stone-age person's life expectancy declined dramatically. Anthropologists tell us that when faced with banishment, transgressors in tribal societies would often commit suicide rather than leave (Edgerton 1976).

Tribes typically reserved blood revenge for intergroup offenses. Tribal members were simply too valuable a resource to squander by killing them for rule violations. However, when that loss involved a serious injury or death, both parties usually agreed in advance to symbolic restitution (Pfohl 1981, 81–83). It might be possible that the transgressor would quite literally take the place of the injured or killed individual, becoming a member of the aggrieved family or serving as a slave.

IVY CLOSE IMAGES/ALAMY IMAGES

BABYLONIAN AND JUDAIC VIEWS ON PUNISHMENT

Historians often call Mesopotamia, the area between the Tigris and Euphrates rivers, "the cradle of civilization." Starting around 5000 BCE, in the city-states of the fertile southern plain between the two rivers, the first legal systems began to take form. Those early societies had dispute-resolution procedures but no formal rules. By the eighteenth century BCE, Babylonia had become the dominant state in the region. Historians credit the great Babylonian king Hammurabi (1792–1750 BCE) with codifying the country's many rules. Among the 282 clauses of the **Code of Hammurabi**, about 50 reveal Babylonian responses to crime and punishment. Fines and death penalties were common; so was the *lex talionis*, the principle of an eye for an eye and a tooth for a tooth (see Chapter 1). But according to Hammurabi's code, punishment was inflicted in the name of the city-state, not by the victim or the victim's relatives.

Roughly 800 kilometers to the west of Mesopotamia was Canaan. Here Judaism flourished as a religion, a culture, and a legal system. In this region of the world, the exchange of laws, like trade and commerce, was common. Consequently, the inclusion of the *lex talionis* in the **Law of Moses** is not surprising: "Your eye shall not pity; it shall be life for life, eye for eye, tooth for tooth, hand for hand, foot for foot!" (Deut. 19:21). Penalties for other misdeeds were equally harsh. For example, the punishment for practicing idolatry was death by the sword, and that could be the fate of an entire city if all of its residents had been led astray (Deut. 13:13–19), and death by public stoning was the fate of a son who was "stubborn and unruly" (Deut. 21:18–21). Still, although Mosaic penalties were severe, underlying the laws was a fundamental respect for human dignity: "If a man guilty of a capital offense is put to death and his corpse hung on a tree, it shall not remain on the tree overnight. You shall bury it the same day" (Deut. 21:22–23).

These "laws" represented, in many respects, the codification and ritualization of earlier normative practices. They also served another purpose. Specifically, rules of this nature, ones written down and passed in this form from one generation to the next, became the bedrock upon which city-states and later nations would be built. Often there was little distinction between the rules of the kings and the rules of the gods. The one set of rules served the interests of the other. The movement towards more secular views on law and punishments began to emerge in ancient Rome and Greece nearly 3,000 years ago.

GREEK AND ROMAN LAWS

Even after the establishment of the Greek city-states around 1000 BCE, parties continued to settle their disagreements by employing prelegal tribal norms or by consulting the oracles, a practice which reinforced the view that religion continued to have a hold over the affairs of men.[2] However, nearly all disputes in ancient Greece, including those arising from homicides, were private matters: their resolution was left to the injured party's family, the city-state typically playing no role. Draco, a seventh century BCE Athenian

politician and archon (chief magistrate), altered the traditional methods of dispute resolution.

It is no accident that Draco's reputation gave meaning to the word *draconian*: he was a harsh man. The Greek historian Plutarch, writing several hundred years later, observed: "It is said that [Draco] himself, when asked why he had fixed the punishment of death for most offences, answered that he considered these lesser crimes to deserve it, and he had no great punishment for more important ones" (Stewart and Long 1894). That may well have been an exaggeration, but we do know that in 621 BCE, Draco codified existing punishments for homicide and established procedures for applying them (Gargarin 1986, 88). Those accused of homicide could escape punishment by going into exile, an act Athenians viewed as an admission of guilt. Those who would not accept banishment were executed in especially brutal ways. The most fortunate criminals died by being thrown from a high place or by ingesting poison; those less fortunate died from starvation or exposure while staked in a public place. The harshness of his criminal sanctions aside—Draco's legacy of codified laws that were publicly displayed for all to see and interpreted only by the courts—cannot be denied.

In 594 BCE, after years of dissent and unrest, the Athenian elite elected the archon Solon (c. 639–c. 559 BCE), a respected poet and merchant. Solon ordered sweeping social and economic reforms that along with those made by Cleisthenes of Athens (c. 570–after c. 508 BCE) culminated in the creation of the Athenian democracy. Among Solon's first acts was the repeal of Draco's criminal penalties for all offenses except homicide, substituting new less "draconian" punishments for the rest. Like Draco, he also "published" his new laws in the *Prytaneum*, the religious and political hub of the city, so that all could know the laws and punishments for their violation. Among the new punishments were fines, public humiliation, and banishment. For example, the archon could order a "convicted" thief to give back the stolen property or its value and to pay a fine of an equal amount to the public coffers (Gargarin 1986, 9). Solon also distinguished between two kinds of lawsuits: private suits, brought only by injured parties, and public suits, which anyone could bring.

Aristotle called the public suit one of Solon's most democratic reforms (69).

The Romans were famous for borrowing everything from food and fashion to architecture from the Greeks. But they made an exception in their first major civil and criminal code, the **Twelve Tables** (Lewis and Reinhold 1990, 107). For almost 300 years following the founding of Rome (c. 750 BCE), the city's residents relied on customs for legal guidance and on the goodwill of Roman patricians to enforce them justly. But justice was rare, especially for Rome's lower classes. In the fifth century BCE, with Rome struggling to become a republic, a group of nobles codified the existing customs. The result was the Twelve Tables (Cary and Scullard 1975, 66–68). Legal scholars and historians regard the civil elements of the Twelve Tables and subsequent revisions dealing with property and contracts to be among ancient Rome's finest achievements (Gibbon 1932; Jolowicz 1954). Twenty-seven sections of Table VIII dealt with violations of criminal law and appropriate sanctions. Nine of the 27 sections required the imposition of the death penalty, for crimes as diverse as parricide, libel, arson, nocturnal meetings for any purpose, and treason. Those who bribed judges— as well as the judges themselves—were subject to capital punishment. In nearly all cases, the method of execution was as brutal as any practiced in ancient Greece. Some offenders were whipped until their flesh was laid bare and then crucified—a practice called *scourging*; others were bound hand and foot, placed in a sack with wild animals, and hurled into the sea.

Roman law evolved slowly, often over centuries. By the late third century BCE, two legal systems existed: *jus civile*, which dealt exclusively with relationships between Romans; and *jus gentium*, laws for foreigners. Romans, of course, retained more rights than noncitizens. After 100 BCE, Roman legislators enacted the *jus honorarium*, which allowed the decisions of magistrates to supplement and correct existing law. This method essentially formed the basis of **case law**. With the establishment of the Roman Empire in 27 BCE, the power to create laws shifted from the senate to the emperor.

By the sixth century all that remained of ancient Rome's glory was the Byzantine or Eastern Empire, headquartered in Constantinople. Justinian I (483–565) became emperor in 527, taking control of an empire embroiled in conflict (Norwich 1988, 181–90). His generals returned Africa and Italy to the empire but at great cost. Justinian found help in his quest to centralize control over the Empire in a recodification of the old Roman laws. He assigned the task to 12 scholars, who completed their work on the **Corpus Juris Civilis** in 535. Justinian's legal experts made few changes in the old laws. The punishments were those of old Rome; the penal sections were very brief. The importance of the **Justinian Code** was in its durability (Gibbon 1932): the Justinian Code remained in force until the fall of Constantinople and the Eastern Roman Empire in 1453. It would become the basis of modern Germanic law and of **canon law**, the law that governs churches, especially the Roman Catholic Church. The Justinian Code is also the progenitor of modern Romano-Germanic law and, indeed, the entire Civil Law legal system so popular in Europe and other parts of the world (Cannon 1997).

THE LAWS OF POST-ROMAN EUROPE

In 476, the Goths, one of the major groups of ancient Germans, deposed Romulus Augustulus, the last western Roman emperor. The fall of Rome signaled the beginning of the Middle Ages, which ended in the late fifteenth century with the reunification of Spain, the discovery of the Americas, and the European Renaissance. Most legal principles during medieval times combined elements of Roman Catholic canon law, tribal law, and the old Roman codes (Friedman 1977, 41).

The legal customs of the ancient Germanic tribes were called the **lex salica**. After the Ostrogoths and Visigoths invaded the Roman Empire, they came to recognize the value of formal laws; between the fifth and ninth centuries, the Germanic tribes codified the *lex salica* (Dopsch 1969, chap. 7). Germanic law dealt primarily with penal sanctions and procedures, although it also addressed property rights (Le Goff 1989, 27, 30–33). The Germanic tribes did not impose their legal system on those they ruled, allowing the Romans and others to use their own

ORONOZ ALBUM/SUPERSTOCK

laws. The Anglo-Saxons and other people of Europe merged the *lex salica* with their own cultural norms, the latter strongly rooted in blood ties and kinship.

Germanic tribal law allowed blood revenge, but the Goths quickly learned that blood revenge led to blood feuds. In the *lex salica*, then, they set out a schedule of monetary compensations for wrongdoing, called **botes**. For example, the **wergild** was the value placed on a murder victim: it varied by the victim's status in society. By paying this restitution to the victim's family, the murderer's family could avoid a blood feud. The descriptions of *botes* were detailed. Consider this passage about the compensation for mutilation:

> For tearing off someone else's hand, or a foot, an eye, the nose, 100 solidi,[3] but only 63 if the hand remains attached; for tearing off the thumb 50

solidi, but only 30 if it remains attached; for tearing off the index finger [the finger used to pull the bow string] 35 solidi; any other finger 30 solidi; two fingers together 35 solidi; three fingers together 50 solidi. (Le Goff 1989, 33)

Obviously, the *lex salica* was not the *lex talionis*: nearly every offense had a monetary value. Given the high value of a single gold solidus throughout Europe in the Middle Ages, when it could be worth 1,000 or more silver coins, these fines represented a considerable monetary loss to the offender.

With the establishment of feudalism in ninth-century Britain, a system of punishments, called **wites**, allowed the local lord or king to collect and keep the *botes*. This change was significant: for certain crimes, the victim was now the state. In murder cases, the amount of the wites varied with the status of the victim: slaves were worth one amount, freemen another, lesser nobility still more, and at the top was the king. Violations of the **king's peace**—crimes committed in the king's presence or against one of his officers—often resulted in fines ten times the normal amount or even in the offender's death (H. A. Johnson and Wolfe 1996, 38–39; Newman 1978, 106–7).[4]

Wites and laws in Saxon England were recorded in royal proclamations called *dooms* (Halsall 1998). Over the seventh and eighth centuries, the dooms became increasingly important in Britain, regulating life there (H. A. Johnson, Wolfe, and Jones 2008). After his conquest of Britain in 1066, William I ordered a survey of all English traditions, geography, and dooms. The result was the Domesday Book, the source of English common law.

CRIMES AND PUNISHMENTS IN THE MIDDLE AGES

The ancient Greeks and Romans rarely used imprisonment as punishment. Periodically, they would detain enemies of the state in abandoned rock quarries or in the cellars of fortresses and castles until the offenders could be punished. And in 640 BCE, Ancus Marcius (642–617 BCE) constructed Mamertime Prison, a vast underground prison complex

(Carter, Glaser, and Wilkins 1984, 4). After 476, Europe's rulers continued to use imprisonment primarily for pretrial detention—a practice Charlemagne (742–814) reinforced at the start of the ninth century, when he ordered that each county in his empire should keep a prison and maintain a gallows nearby. Hence, the ancient custom of using prisons to confine people, not punish them, continued through much of the early Middle Ages (Dunbabin 2002; Hinckeldey 1993; Newman 1978).

During the Middle Ages, corporal and capital punishments were largely reserved for those who threatened the king's peace and for religious offenders.[5] Medieval punishments, like those in ancient Greece and Rome, often served a religious function. For example, crucifixion, breaking on the wheel, and disembowelment combined torture and eventual death, to give the offenders the opportunity to confess before dying. Following feudal principles, medieval codes reserved many of the worst forms of capital punishment—for example, drawing and quartering, disembowelment, and beheading—for important political criminals, those who threatened the political status quo. Common criminals were executed quickly, by hanging or being impaled on a stake.

By the twelfth century, nobles were building larger and more-fortified castles—to defend the realm better against foreign and domestic enemies. Henry II of England (1133–1189) ordered each sheriff to build a prison within the county or shire, preferably in the royal castle (Dunbabin 2002). An alternative site for local prisons was near or in the gatehouse that protected the town walls. However, with a few notable exceptions—among them the Tower of London and the Conciergerie—royal buildings were seldom used for incarceration in the Middle Ages (Peters 1995); and when they were, the prisoners generally were awaiting the "pleasure of the monarch" or were being confined because they were politically too dangerous to run free and too well connected to be executed (see Box 2.1).[6] Living conditions in the royal prisons ranged from foul to reasonably comfortable, although commoners rarely saw conditions approaching the latter. In London's royal prison, inmates paid jailers fees for food, fuel, and bedding; these fees were regulated by public law (Peters 1995). The practice of charging fees continued in English jails into the fifteenth and sixteenth centuries and was brought to the American colonies.

EUROPEAN PUNISHMENTS AT THE END OF THE MIDDLE AGES

At the close of the fifteenth century, nearly all felonies—some 200 or more crimes—were punishable by death. As Graeme Newman (1978, 114–23) notes, common offenders, particularly those convicted of lesser crimes, often received corporal punishment—the stocks, the pillory, the whipping post, or pressing. Consider the following punishments, which were popular in England at the time and found their way into the English colonies as well (Newman 1978):

- The **stocks** were timbers with holes cut for feet and hands. The person in the stocks was seated on the ground or on a small stool. In the fourteenth century, stocks were found in every English jail; they served chiefly as a way to detain people before trial. In the seventeenth and eighteenth centuries, the stocks had become a punishment for crimes like public drunkenness.

- The **pillory** consisted of wood timbers set on a post, with restraining holes for head and hands cut into the timbers. Although the pillory was designed to shame the offender, sometimes the crowd would grow violent: "It was not uncommon for those sentenced to the pillory to be killed at the hands of angry spectators" (117).

- **Public whipping** may be the oldest and most widely used form of corporal punishment in the world. In the late Middle Ages, it was not uncommon for offenders to die during or after a whipping, particularly when the strokes were administered excessively harshly or the person's health was poor. Also, medical treatment was primitive in Tudor England and colonial America, increasing the likelihood of serious injury or death. Although whipping was seldom used in England after the seventeenth century, it continued to be employed as a

SPOTLIGHT ON INTERNATIONAL CORRECTIONS: FROM PALACES TO PRISONS   **BOX 2.1**

Today, the Tower of London is a much sought after tourist destination, an arsenal, a museum, and the repository of the queen's jewels. For most of its history, however, the Tower was a fortress and a royal residence. It was also the place where enemies of the crown awaited their fate—for most, execution on the Tower grounds or at nearby Tower Hill. The Tower was built by a Norman lord in the late eleventh century. Over the next several hundred years, many notable people met their fate there. Among them was Sir Thomas More (1478–1535), statesman, author, and martyr for the Roman Catholic Church. When England's Henry VIII (1491–1547) ordered More to disavow the Pope's authority in favor of the king's, More refused. In short order, More was imprisoned in the Tower and beheaded. A similar fate—albeit for different reasons—awaited Anne Boleyn, Henry's second queen consort. Elizabeth I, Henry's daughter by Boleyn, also imprisoned a number of high personages at the Tower, many of whom were later executed, including Sir Walter Raleigh, an explorer who helped colonize North America.

In Paris, on the Île de la Cité near Notre Dame, is the Palais de la Cité. It was built in the eleventh century by Robert II (c. 972–1031), also known as Robert the Pious, to consolidate his family's holdings in France. The Palais was enlarged over the centuries, and during the reign of Philip IV (1268–1314) parts of the complex took on a judicial function. In time, French rulers moved their residence from the Île de la Cité, and the structure functioned solely as a court of law and a prison.

The Conciergerie, the prison attached to the court at the Palais, was first used in the fourteenth century to detain suspects before trial; by the fifteenth century, it was one of the largest prisons in Paris. Its location was convenient: prisoners could be tortured to confess and then taken immediately to the court for sentencing; en route to the Place de Grève for execution, the condemned were allowed a brief detour to Notre Dame to make amends for their sins.

Many of the early inmates of the Conciergerie were political prisoners, people who in some way posed a threat to the king. Gabriel, Comte de Montgomery (c. 1530–1574), defied Charles IX (1550–1574) and was active in the Protestant Reformation; he was incarcerated and tortured in the tower that to this day bears his name. François Ravaillac (1578–1610), an alleged member of the conspiracy to assassinate Henry IV (1553–1610), was imprisoned in the Conciergerie and publicly tortured before being drawn and quartered by four horses. In 1676, Marie-Madeleine d'Aubray (c. 1630–1676) underwent water torture before she was decapitated in the Place de Grève. And in 1757, Robert François Damiens (1715–1757), who had attempted to assassinate Louis XV (1710–1774), underwent a particularly long and horrific torture before being quartered.

During the French Revolution (1789–1794) and the Reign of Terror (1793–1794), some of the most famous of the Conciergerie's inhabitants resided temporarily within its walls. The opening salvos of the revolution were fired at the Bastille, another famous fortress and prison in Paris. It, too, was used as a place of arbitrary and secret imprisonment at the whim of the crown. On July 14, 1789, a Parisian mob stormed the Bastille and set free its inmates. In the coming years, prisoners were taken from the Conciergerie and executed, among them Marie Antoinette (1755–1793) who was the Austrian-born wife of Louis XVI (1754–1792); and Maximilien Robespierre (1758–1794) who was one of the major leaders of the revolution and one of the architects of the Reign of Terror.

After the French Revolution, the Conciergerie was no longer royal property. It continued to function as a state prison until 1934. Today, the southeast corner of the Palais, the Quai des Orfevres, is a courthouse. Defendants here, however, need no longer fear the torture chambers of the Conciergerie.

SOURCES: CHANCE (2003); FISHER (1987).

method of discipline in American prisons into the twentieth century.

- **Pressing** was a particularly gruesome form of corporal punishment; it was used to convince suspected offenders to confess. The accused person was placed on a hard surface beneath a board. Weights were then added at regular intervals to the top of the board until the person either agreed to a plea or died.

Vagrants, idlers, debtors, and common prostitutes received different treatment in the late Tudor and early Stuart periods: the courts removed them from society and confined them for short terms in *houses of corrections* and *workhouses*. From there, these minor offenders would work on public and private projects. Workhouse inmates became an easily exploited source of labor. One of the most notorious English workhouses, St. Bridget's Well, or Bridewell, opened in 1557. Bridewell became a national model, and in 1576, Parliament ordered every county in England and Wales to establish Bridewell-style workhouses. The guiding principle was that by forcing people to work at difficult and unpleasant tasks, they would reform.

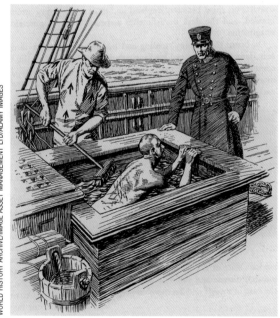

Beginning in the sixteenth century, **transportation**, a highly structured form of exile or banishment, was added to the death penalty as a method for removing offenders, even murderers, from society. Two factors influenced the use of transportation. First, the "new" houses of corrections and workhouses filled quickly. Second, colonialism required vast amounts of cheap labor. One way to encourage people to go to the colonies and discourage their return to England was to banish them in lieu of far more horrible fates. Parliament's passage of the Vagrancy Act in 1597 legalized the deportation of criminals deemed incorrigible. A royal order in 1617 allowed judges to issue a reprieve from any punishment—including the death penalty—if the offender was willing to work in an overseas colony. Parliament modified this law in 1718: all convicts sentenced to 3 or more years' imprisonment could choose transportation as indentured servants instead. Former indentured servants or penal colonists could never return to England. The British courts ordered an estimated 2,000 convicts a year transported to the American colonies from 1597 to 1776 (Sellin 1976, 73).

THE AGE OF ENLIGHTENMENT, THE STATE, AND CRIMINAL SANCTIONS

In the seventeenth century, Isaac Newton, Francis Bacon, John Locke, René Descartes, and Baruch Spinoza made enormous scientific and intellectual advances. Their work set the stage in the next century for the emergence of a group of philosophers and social critics who shared a belief in **natural law**—a system of rules and principles growing out of and conforming to human nature that can be discovered through reason without knowledge of or reference to society's artificial laws. Science, they believed, held the answers to all of society's challenges, social, political, economic, and moral, and the state was an instrument for human progress. This group of philosophers formed a rationalist, humanitarian, and scientific movement known as the **Age of Enlightenment**. And their thinking—especially the work of Montesquieu and Cesare Beccaria—had an important impact on law and punishment.

MONTESQUIEU

Charles-Louis de Secondat, Baron de La Brède et de Montesquieu (1689–1755) was an unlikely revolutionary, a highborn and well-educated nobleman who criticized the very caste system that produced him. A jurist and political philosopher, Montesquieu was a prolific author. In arguably his greatest work, *The Spirit of Laws* (1748), he compared republican, despotic, and monarchical governments. He advocated a balance of power among judicial, executive, and legislative branches. The separation of powers, Montesquieu believed, would ensure individual freedom.

Montesquieu also argued passionately about proportionality in punishment (Nugent 1977). Only despotic governments, he wrote, supported the severe punishment of criminals. Their goal: to induce terror in their citizens. He characterized monarchies and republics as more moderate forms of government. He believed these governments used punishment to prevent crime and to correct perpetrators: "Leniency reigns in moderate governments" (158).

CESARE BECCARIA

Any list of Enlightenment philosophers would be incomplete without Cesare Bonesana, Marchese de Beccaria (1738–1794), known to history as Cesare Beccaria. His crowning work, *On Crimes and Punishments* (1764), influenced generations of legal and penal reformers. Beccaria believed that punishment can deter crime, but only if it is certain, swift, and severe (see Chapter 1). Beccaria also espoused many ideas—for example, the segregation of inmates by age, gender, and offense—that were radical in his day. So radical were his suggestions that Beccaria initially published them under an alias. Proposing humane and just treatment for prisoners—convicted or otherwise—was as unpopular in the eighteenth century as it has been in recent times.

PRISON REFORM AND PENITENTIARIES

Two men, one an Englishman and one an American, translated the Age of Enlightenment's humanism and rationalism into philosophies of punishment that would profoundly influence their nations' responses to crime and punishment for generations. John Howard (1726–1790) was a squire (a member of the landed gentry) when, at the age of 47, he assumed the duties of sheriff of Bedfordshire. One of his responsibilities was to inspect the jails in his jurisdiction. He was appalled at the conditions he found. In travels to the European continent, Howard realized that squalor and exploitation were not necessary conditions of incarceration; he found that the prisons in England and Wales compared unfavorably with the Ghent House of Enforcement and other jails in Europe. In 1774, Howard began lobbying the House of Commons for change; 3 years later, his detailed and convincing account of the state of prisons in England and Wales was published (H. A. Johnson and Wolfe 1996, 129–30).

Howard's efforts to convince Parliament that conditions in jails must change succeeded: the **Penitentiary Act of 1779** created a new class of institution that largely incorporated Howard's concerns about humane treatment, productive labor, and sanitary living conditions.[7] As later reformers discovered, passing a law—and even building penitentiaries—was not the same as changing the way prisons were operated. Later generations of inspectors met with resistance from those charged with funding and implementing the necessary changes in the conditions of confinement. The criticisms of those opposed to higher spending for prison inmates in the late eighteenth century and early nineteenth century were not all that different from those voiced today: operating a humane prison costs too much money and prisoners deserve the lowest standard of living capable of sustaining life.

The American was Benjamin Rush (1745–1813), a highly regarded physician before he began his brief career as a penal reformer. Rush was a signer of the Declaration of Independence and counted among his friends such notables as Thomas Jefferson and John Adams. In 1786, Rush spoke out against a series of changes in Pennsylvania's penal law. He voiced two concerns: that punishment should not be public and that offenders' reformation could be achieved through punishment that encouraged penance (Hawke 1971; McKelvey 1936).

In 1787, the Friends' Society, or Quakers, of Pennsylvania formed the Philadelphia Society for Alleviating the Miseries of Public Prisons. Rush, a Presbyterian, attended the first meeting of the society, and he forever was associated with its goals. In 1789, the Society, with Rush as its primary spokesperson, attempted to improve the lot of inmates incarcerated at Philadelphia's Walnut Street Jail. The General Assembly agreed and designated the facility a penitentiary. A year later, a special cell block was erected where prisoners could be placed in solitary confinement, to meditate on their crimes and repent for them. In time, the former jail became a model of prison reform. Among its most impressive achievements: prisoners were paid for their work, men and women prisoners were separated, corporal punishment was forbidden, and religious instruction was required.

THE PENNSYLVANIA SYSTEM VERSUS THE AUBURN SYSTEM

Historians agree that throughout most of the first half of the nineteenth century, two prison systems vied for the attention of penal reformers in the nation and the world, the Pennsylvania system and the Auburn (New York) system.

EASTERN PENITENTIARY AND THE PENNSYLVANIA SYSTEM

Among the first truly new prisons, built from the ground up as state-run penitentiaries and guided by a penal philosophy other than prison-as-punishment, were two constructed in Pennsylvania. The first, Western State Penitentiary, opened in 1826 in Pittsburgh. The second, Eastern State Penitentiary, opened in 1829 at a site two miles outside Philadelphia, in an orchard that became known as Cherry Hill. These facilities were examples of what penologists call the **Pennsylvania system**, an imprisonment method in which offenders were kept in solitary confinement. The design of the new facilities reflected that method. The massive structures resembled gigantic stone wheels laid on their side; the cells lined corridors that extended like spokes from a central

FIGURE 2.1 The Layout of Philadelphia's Eastern Penitentiary.

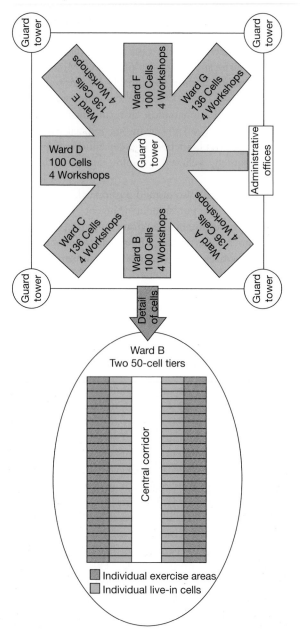

rotunda (see Figure 2.1). The cells at Eastern measured about 8 by 12 feet. Each had two locked doors: one leading into the corridor, the other to a small walled-in yard where the inmates engaged in solitary exercise and thought.

We have little evidence that the Pennsylvania system accomplished its goals. Likewise, only anecdotal evidence exists that it drove inmates insane or created a hardened class of criminals (Gibbons 1996, 352). Few states adopted the system's philosophy of solitary confinement by architectural design; even Pennsylvania abandoned the system in 1913. In a sense, the Pennsylvania system contained the seeds of its own demise in its basic philosophical element: solitary confinement. First, building and supervising individual cells for hundreds of prisoners were very costly undertakings. Second, separation and isolation did not allow for the profitable exploitation of inmate labor (McKelvey 1936). The Auburn system corrected both of these design shortcomings.

THE AUBURN SYSTEM

After the American Revolution, a series of events in New York State led to the creation of the **Auburn system**, which would compete with and eventually replace the Pennsylvania system. In 1796, the New York State legislature, following Pennsylvania's lead, abolished capital punishment for all offenses except first-degree murder and treason. As a result, the state experienced an immediate need for space to house convicted felons. The legislature authorized the construction of a prison in the Greenwich Village section of New York City. Newgate Prison, once a tin mine, opened in 1797. The prison housed adults and juveniles, men and women, many convicted of relatively minor offenses. By 1800, Newgate had nearly twice the number of inmates called for in its original design and had experienced two large-scale riots. Newgate Prison was ruled a failure by the state legislature and closed in the early 1820s, after a new prison had opened in upstate New York.

In 1816, the state legislature authorized construction of that new prison in the town of Auburn. The initial design of the Auburn Prison, as shown in

PHILIP SCALIA/ALAMY IMAGES

FIGURE 2.2 The Layout of New York State's Auburn Prison.

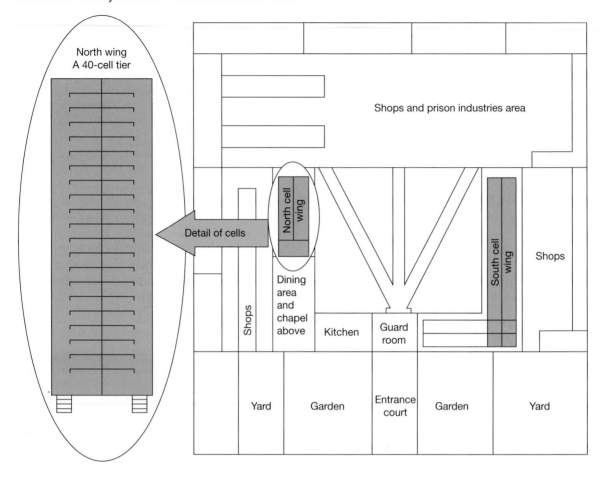

Figure 2.2, included two main cell wings: the prison's south cell wing had both two-person cells and congregate cells housing large groups of inmates; prisoners in the north cell wing were isolated in single-person cells. After a riot in 1821, William Brittin (d. 1821), the prison's first warden, rebuilt the north cell wing with solitary cells, each 7 feet long, 3 feet wide, and 7 feet high, set back to back and arranged in five tiers of 40 cells each.

The newly rebuilt north cell wing represented more than a change in prison architecture: when it was reoccupied in 1821, inmates followed a strict regimen of both physical and social isolation that was intended to subdue their "depraved hearts and stubborn spirits." These were the prison's worst inmates.

Less-dangerous prisoners lived in solitude three days a week and worked in groups the other four. The "least guilty and depraved" worked together in the prison workshops six days a week.

By 1825, the experimental three-class inmate system at Auburn Prison was abandoned, and even the north cell wing inmates were soon working together in light manufacturing workshops and eating in dining halls. When they were not working or eating, though, all inmates were confined to their cells to reflect on their crimes. Even reading—except the Bible—was strongly discouraged.

Regimentation was central to maintaining discipline at Auburn, but it was not the only tool used by the custodial staff. Guards strictly enforced a rigid

silent system: inmates marched, worked, and ate in complete silence. Prison officials instituted a number of other innovations too, many of which were used well into the twentieth century. One was the infamous *lockstep shuffle*: each inmate stood in line, his right foot slightly behind the left and his right arm outstretched with the hand on the right shoulder of the man in front of him. The column of men moved forward together in an undulating shuffle. The black-and-white striped uniform and cap also originated at Auburn, a dress code that survived into the 1950s in some state prisons.

Those inmates who violated the rules at Auburn usually came up against the whip. Elam Lynds (1784–1855), Brittin's successor and the man who has been "credited" by many with the punitive excesses of the Auburn system, said of flogging:

> I consider the chastisement by whip the most efficient and, at the same time, the most humane which exists; it never injures health, and obliges the prisoner to lead a life essentially healthy . . . I consider it impossible to govern a large prison without a whip. (quoted in Beaumont and Tocqueville 1832, 163)

Hard work, social isolation, strict regimentation, the silent system, and corporal punishment are the characteristics of a correctional philosophy that, along with its unique architectural design, we know as the Auburn system. Was it a success? If success means imitation, then the answer is yes. Auburn was the most emulated prison system of its day in the United States, spreading to 11 states and the District of Columbia in just a decade. In 1826, New York opened another maximum-security Auburn-style prison at Ossining (Sing Sing), employing prison labor almost exclusively. Another measure of success is longevity, and here, too, the Auburn system scores high marks. Some critics suggest that by the middle of the nineteenth century, the model had been largely compromised by overpopulation in existing prisons, but elements of the Auburn system were still in use into the twentieth century. Finally, the Auburn system receives mixed economic marks. Although they were less expensive to build and operate than Pennsylvania-style prisons, Auburn-type prisons rarely returned a profit. Prison contractors found the labor unreliable and the goods manufactured shoddy. Looking for cheap workers, contractors often got what they paid for.

The legacy of the Auburn system is hard to deny. First, modern prisons continue to rely on strict regimentation by security staff to maintain control in prison environments (Bartollas and Conrad 1992, 75; E. H. Johnson 1996, 48). Another legacy is the big-house layout: one- and two-person cells stacked in tiers and enclosed by high stone walls and guard towers (see Austin and Irwin 2001; and Irwin 1980). And yet another element is inmate classification by security-risk levels, a topic to which we return in later chapters. A final legacy, one felt almost from the day Auburn opened its doors, is the need to reform, a topic to which we turn next.

PENITENTIARY REFORM IN THE NINETEENTH CENTURY

Almost as soon as prisons in New York City, Cherry Hill, and Auburn opened to inmates, foreign visitors arrived and reported on what they saw. Some were complimentary; others were not. The result was the creation of an alternative correctional philosophy, one that emphasized prisoners' reformation and reintegration into society. It began, oddly enough, in the British penal colony at Van Diemen's Land, now known as Tasmania, off the coast of Australia.

ALTERNATIVES TO PRISON

In 1840, Captain Alexander Maconochie (1787–1860), a retired naval officer, arrived in Australia to become the superintendent of the penal colony at Van Diemen's Land. **Penal colonies** were isolated areas used for the confinement of convicted offenders; in most, geography or topography provided the means of confinement and control. Shocked by the conditions he found, Maconochie set about humanizing the facility. He proposed a plan to ready offenders for life in a free society, so that after their release they would not return to a life of crime (Barry 1958, 72). Unfortunately, Maconochie, like other penal reformers before and since, incurred the wrath of his superior, Sir John Franklin (1786–1847),

NORFOLK ISLAND.—THE CONVICT SYSTEM.

the lieutenant governor of Van Diemen's Land and a close friend. Franklin fired Maconochie before the treatment plan was fully implemented.

Maconochie's next stop was the superintendency of the penal colony at Norfolk Island, near Australia. The Colonial Office in London, which ran all of the Australian penal colonies, saw merit in Maconochie's ideas and approved a trial program. By the early 1840s, the office was under increasing pressure to rid itself of the penal colonies. Maconochie created a system of rewards—or **marks of commendation**—that were given to inmates for good behavior. An inmate with a fixed number of marks could earn the right to move freely about the colony or even a **ticket of leave**, early release from the colony. Misbehavior earned the offending party not the whip, but a loss of marks.

Conditions for the experiment at Norfolk Island were less than ideal. The inmate population was made up of new and doubly convicted offenders—inmates who had been convicted of new crimes since arriving on the island—and Maconochie, an independent and headstrong man, insisted that all inmates be treated the same. This did not sit well with the public, and Maconochie was recalled to England in 1844. The Norfolk Island experiment was abandoned a short time later, and the colony returned to a more punitive system of control.

Although Maconochie failed to change conditions on Norfolk Island, his innovations had a strong impact on the reorganization of the English penal system. As part of that reorganization, Parliament passed the **Penal Servitude Act of 1853**. The key component of the act was **parole**—the early release of prisoners to the supervision of local law enforcement. That same year, the Home Office commissioned Walter Crofton (1815–1897) to investigate living conditions in Irish prisons. In 1854, Crofton became director of the Irish prison system. Crofton, an admirer of Maconochie's effort at Norfolk Island, created what came to be called the **Irish ticket-of-leave system**. It consisted of four stages:

1 During the first three months, inmates were placed in solitary confinement and fed reduced rations. They did not work. Crofton believed that after three months of enforced idleness even the most shiftless inmate would be anxious to do something. The inmates' first real jobs were agricultural, requiring little skill and providing few rewards; however, inmates were given full rations at this point.

2 Working with other inmates in a prison on an island off the coast of Ireland, the industrious prisoner could earn marks for transfer to the third stage. This second stage consisted of four levels,

and it typically took inmates at least 12 months to progress through them; inmates could spend several years in this stage, depending on their original sentence and prison behavior.

3 Inmates in this stage worked in an open prison with few restrictions and only a handful of unarmed guards. The purpose was to show the inmates trust. Those inmates who in turn showed genuine signs of reformation could earn their promised ticket of leave.

4 Fourth-stage inmates were given a conditional release from prison. The inspector of released prisoners, a civilian employee, supervised Dublin's ticket-of-leave men; local police supervised parolees who lived outside Dublin.

Only inmates serving terms of three or more years were eligible for the Irish system.

Although there was considerable debate about the use of police as supervisors, and considerable political infighting among prison officials, the Home Office adopted Crofton's system for all of England in 1877. As we shall see in later chapters, the work of Maconochie, Crofton, and others greatly impacted the development of other alternatives to incarceration, including probation (Chapter 4) and parole (Chapter 9). Even in the nineteenth century, with its emphasis on heavy-handed penal sanctions, reformers began to seek alternatives to what was viewed as the prohibitively costly and socially damaging use of incarceration as punishment (cf., Beckett and Sasson 2004; Gibbons 1996; McKelvey 1936; Welch 2005).

FOREIGN OPPONENTS AND PROPONENTS

A number of foreign dignitaries visited prisons in the United States in the first half of the nineteenth century. Gustave de Beaumont (1802–1866) and Alexis de Tocqueville (1805–1859) were lawyers, magistrates, and widely traveled social critics. For nine months in the early 1830s, the pair toured the new nation's prisons, observing living conditions and talking with wardens and staff. On returning to France, Beaumont and Tocqueville prepared *On the Penitentiary System in the United States and Its Application to France* (1832), a generally favorable but candid look at US prisons. The French Revolution of 1848 interrupted plans to build a Pennsylvania-style prison system; and in 1853, France adopted a massive program of transportation to penal colonies. The most infamous French penal colony, part of which was Devil's Island, was located in French Guiana.

Another visitor was William Crawford (1788–1847), a London wine merchant and philanthropist commissioned by the British Home Office in the early 1830s to investigate the suitability of US prisons for Britain. Crawford traveled extensively, visiting penitentiaries in 14 states and the District of Columbia; he also stopped at a number of jails along the way. In a massive document, *Report on the Penitentiaries of the United States* (1834), he included detailed descriptions of all the facilities he visited.

By the late 1830s, the Home Office had approved plans for a model prison based on Pennsylvania's Eastern Penitentiary; that prison, later known as Pentonville, opened in 1842. Two years later, Reading Prison opened. (Recall the problems the British were having with their Australian penal colonies by the late 1830s and early 1840s.) The Pennsylvania approach alone quickly proved ineffective. By 1857, the Home Office was assigning every inmate to Pennsylvania-type solitary confinement for nine months, followed by placement in an Auburn-type regimen (Johnston 1969, xvi).

A fourth visitor to the US prisons was far less complimentary than Beaumont, Tocqueville, and Crawford. Charles Dickens (1812–1870) made several trips to the United States, the first in 1842. Not yet 30 years of age and already a celebrity, Dickens had by that time published five novels, including *Oliver Twist* (1837–1838) and *Nicholas Nickleby* (1839). He was no stranger to law, justice, and punishment, having served as a court stenographer and parliamentary reporter.

Dickens generally disliked American ways, but he reserved his most biting comments for the American penal system. Describing his visit to Eastern Penitentiary, he wrote,

> In the outskirts, stands a great prison, called the Eastern Penitentiary: conducted on a plan peculiar to the state of Pennsylvania. The system here is rigid, strict, and hopeless solitary confinement.

I believe it, in its effects, to be cruel and wrong . . . I believe that very few men are capable of estimating the immense amount of torture and agony that this dreadful punishment, prolonged for many years, inflicts upon the sufferer . . . I hold this slow and daily tampering with the mysteries of the brain, to be immeasurably worse than any torture of the body. (1842, 238)

Dickens, a master of detail, described a prison system that was very different from the system his contemporaries had seen.

THE CINCINNATI MEETING OF THE NATIONAL PRISON ASSOCIATION

In 1870, the National Prison Association (later the American Correctional Association), under the leadership of its first president, Rutherford B. Hayes (1822–1893), who later became US president, held its first National Congress on Penitentiary and Reformatory Discipline in Cincinnati. More than 130 delegates representing 24 states, Canada, and South America attended the congress. The graduated-release systems developed by Maconochie and Crofton were the centerpiece of discussion. The congress and the National Prison Association initiated the modern penal reform movement in America. Two names are synonymous with its implementation: Enoch Cobb Wines and Zebulon Reed Brockway.

ENOCH WINES: THE TRUE PENITENT Enoch Cobb Wines (1806–1879) was a scholar: he held three college degrees, including a doctorate of law. He was a secondary school teacher and a college educator, a Christian minister, and, during the last 17 years of his life, a penal reformer. His first book on crime and punishment, *The True Penitent Portrayed: A Doctrine of Repentance* (1864), was a reflection of Wines the scholar and Christian. He, like many of his reform-minded contemporaries, believed in the power of religious training and hard work to alter the course of human lives. Wines opposed the imposition of severe and regular punishment for its own sake. Instead, he advocated that those who wanted to reform criminals should first demonstrate their

concern for offenders by rewarding positive steps toward reformation and restricting the use of harsh punishment for those who failed. To this end, he supported both an approach built on the Irish ticket-of-leave system as a means of identifying progress, and the indeterminate sentence.

Wines died less than a decade after the Cincinnati conference, but through his writings, his influence on corrections in the United States continued well into the twentieth century. Still, Wines was largely an outsider—a theoretician and academician. It remained for others to implement his reform ideas, to translate theory into practice. Zebulon Brockway was one of the most prominent of those practitioners.

ZEBULON BROCKWAY: MASTER OF ELMIRA In the final quarter of the nineteenth century, Zebulon Reed Brockway (1827–1920) brought attention to the practical issues associated with corrections reform. Brockway's career began at age 21, when he became first a guard and, then quickly, a clerk at Connecticut's Wethersfield Prison. During the next 28 years, he served as superintendent of three different facilities, earning a national reputation as a penal reformer and innovator. For example, as superintendent of the Monroe County Penitentiary in upstate New York, he created programs intended to reform young offenders, a group that particularly interested him. Writing in his autobiography, *Fifty Years of Prison Service* (1912), Brockway described allowing inmates at the Michigan House of Correction a measure of self-governance. The passage of the indeterminate-sentence law by the Michigan legislature in 1867 was largely the result of his lobbying. But Brockway's most important contributions to corrections were made in a small town in upstate New York called Elmira.

Shortly after the Civil War, the New York legislature authorized construction of a "reformatory" to be built in Elmira, a 500-bed facility that would house first-time offenders between the ages of 16 and 30. When Elmira opened its doors to the first transfer inmates from Auburn in July 1876, Brockway was its superintendent. After a somewhat inauspicious transition period of about 4 years— marked by escapes and even staff murders—Brockway implemented his famous three-step program for inmates. Progression through the steps was based on a system of marks similar to those proposed by Maconochie and Crofton a generation earlier.

The first stage in the reformation process consisted of information gathering, an interview process Brockway often conducted personally. Today, this stage is called **intake**. New inmates began Brockway's program in the second of three "grades," where they were the objects of treatment by Elmira's staff. In what must have been one of the earliest prison-based internship programs, students and lecturers from nearby Elmira College provided inmates with a strong educational foundation. Other "medicine" in Brockway's treatment program included farm work, institutional maintenance, and even work in an iron foundry. When prison-based industries were temporarily outlawed in the 1880s, the young men of Elmira reformatory practiced daily their close-order drills with wooden rifles. Every month each inmate could earn three marks each for education, labor, and behavior. Those who earned full marks every month for six months moved to the first grade, the top level; full marks for a year could earn inmates a parole hearing and release, the final stage in Brockway's program. Marks were taken away for bad behavior and indolence, and inmates could be assigned to the third grade, the lowest level, for unsatisfactory behavior.

Brockway tightly controlled both the program and reports of its success and, far less often, its failures. He was a tireless self-promoter, and his early glowing reports led to widespread emulation of the reformatory model. Within a quarter-century, 12 states had adopted the reformatory model. By the early 1930s, nearly half the states had adopted reformatory plans for young offenders and even young adults based on the Elmira model.

FROM REHABILITATIVE IDEAL TO JUSTICE MODEL

The late 1800s were exciting times in the emerging fields of criminology and penology. Both disciplines had evolved from the work of Lombroso. During his

career, Lombroso identified four main types of criminals. Heredity, he suggested, was the main cause of criminal tendencies in all of them. As a consequence, there was essentially no way to alter criminal behavior. This was an important departure from the basic assumption underlying classical criminology—that laws and punishments act as a deterrent to criminal behavior. Moreover, Lombroso's theory was at odds with the reformation ideals of Wines, Rush, and Bentham, which had found expression in the work of Crofton and Brockway (see Box 2.2).

Lombroso's determinism directly influenced Continental European criminology, where rehabilitation for confirmed criminals was abandoned (H. A. Johnson and Wolfe 1996, 203). It had little direct influence on English or American penology. When US prison officials learned of Lombroso's ideas at the 1894 meeting of the National Prison Association, they rejected them "based on strong feeling that all men were responsible for their acts and, if sane, reformable by penological methods" (204). By the late 1800s, reformation held sway in penological

BENTHAM'S PANOPTICON: WHO'S WATCHING WHOM?

BOX 2.2

Jeremy Bentham (1748–1832) was a penal reformer and philosopher often mentioned in the same context as Beccaria, Howard, and Rush. A Scottish moralist, Bentham dabbled in penal reform. He believed that order and discipline could be achieved if inmates were under the constant supervision of a central inspector. Competing for a contract to build a central prison for England, Bentham proposed the panopticon, or inspection house. He envisioned a multitiered circular building with a glass inspection house at its hub. The windows of the inspection house would be louvered, consisting of movable slats that guards could open to keep watch over the prison's inmates. Bentham believed that the power of the inspection house model lay in its unpredictability: inmates would never know when they were being watched.

The panopticon was never built. Some critics argued that the factory Bentham proposed to operate at the prison would make the facility prone to corruption. Others believed that Bentham had failed to incorporate enough religious contemplation, despite the fact that the design called for a prison chaplain who would deliver sermons from the central hub to a captive congregation. The physical design did have its good points and was adopted in two English prisons, including Pentonville (1842), and in Western Penitentiary in Pennsylvania (1826) and Stateville Penitentiary in Illinois (1924).

SOURCES: BARNES AND TEETERS (1959); SCHAFER (1969, 106–8).

theory and practice. US penologists of this period believed that science held the key to understanding the disease—crime—and that medicine provided the model for its cure.

FROM MEDICAL MODEL TO REHABILITATION

After the pronouncements of the 1870 Cincinnati conference, prison administrators placed greater emphasis on reforming offenders. The most common approach was to develop an individualized treatment plan for each offender. Steeped in nineteenth-century positivism and progressivism, treatment equated crime with illness, and rehabilitation with cure.[8] A careful reading of Rush's writings reveals that diet and physical well-being were part of the good doctor's overall plan for a successful prison. Increasingly in the late nineteenth and early twentieth centuries, prison officials turned to the emerging social and behavioral sciences for answers to a vexing question: How can we change the criminal?

The **medical model** of corrections was the dominant approach to prisoner management in the early twentieth century. The specific treatment changed with new findings in social and behavioral sciences; in time, most prisons settled on group therapy and behavior modification as their treatments of choice. Prison administrators would add education and vocational training in the hopes of giving offenders skills that would be useful in free society.

A turning point in offender treatment came in 1929 with the adoption of a scientific treatment regimen by the US Bureau of Prisons. Within a decade, nearly every state had adopted the reality or the rhetoric of rehabilitation. **Rehabilitation**, the process of returning offenders to orderly or acceptable behaviors, became a primary goal of the nation's corrections systems. Between the 1870s and the 1950s, the locus of the rehabilitation process moved from the prison and reformatory to the community. **Reintegration**, a popular concept in the 1970s, provided a bridge between institution and community. Reintegration advocates understood the importance of minimizing the problems inmates encountered as they moved from a restrictive lifestyle to a free one. But a series of events in the mid-1970s cast doubt on rehabilitation's future in the US penal system.

"JUST DESERTS" AND THE JUSTICE MODEL OF PUNISHMENT

During the 20-year period following World War II, US prisons experienced a rash of inmate uprisings and riots. By the late 1960s, prison officials began to question the efficacy of prison-based rehabilitation (Clear and Cole 2003). Also, after a decade of legal and social liberalism in the 1960s, a wave of conservatism flooded the nation, cresting with Ronald Reagan's election to the presidency in 1980. One factor in the nation's move to the right was Robert Martinson's (1974) very negative report on corrections and adjudication programs, in which he questioned whether rehabilitation was possible within the current corrections system.

Other critics also questioned the system's ability to get the job done. For example, as the American Friends Service Committee noted in its report on punishment in the United States: "Retribution and revenge necessarily imply punishment, but it does not necessarily follow that punishment is eliminated under rehabilitative regimes" (1971, 20). In the early 1970s, the organization called for a moratorium on new prison construction.

Law professor and criminologist Norval Morris, concerned about the rights of all citizens, including prison inmates, responded to calls to abandon the prison system in *The Future of Imprisonment* (1974). Prisons, he speculated, would outlive him and all of his contemporaries. The challenge was to eliminate what Morris saw as a destructive conflict between the sentences meted out by judges and the treatment goals set by prison administrators. Indeed, Morris expressed little faith in the ability of the 1970s prison system to rehabilitate inmates. Prison, he wrote, is necessary to control the dangerous; moreover, it is the criminal's "just deserts" (xi). He called for new prisons solely for repetitively violent offenders. Treatment, he insisted, should be provided only for inmates who want to change: if criminals do not want to change, the government should not expend its resources to make them change, even if it could.

As the attacks on prison rehabilitation raged, David Fogel (1975) articulated a "new" model of justice. Like Morris, Fogel criticized the level of discretion exercised by officials charged with administering the medical model: "The justice perspective demands accountability from all processors, even the 'pure of heart.' *Properly understood, the justice perspective is not so much concerned with the administration of justice as it is with the justice of administration*" (192, italics in original).

Fogel espoused a punishment model in which offenders take responsibility for their own actions. The **justice model** rests on the assumption that individuals have free will: they choose to violate laws and so deserve to be punished. Within this model, rehabilitation and other forms of treatment should not be primary goals of corrections systems.

Just deserts and the justice model are mixtures of liberal thinking on crime and criminals (the concern for due process, monitoring the excesses of an all-powerful criminal justice system, and reining in an insulated correctional system) and conservative thinking (an emphasis on punishment for its own sake and retribution as embodied in the *lex talionis*). Also, the justice perspective seems to be a recasting of the classical views of humanity and crime: all rational human beings should be accountable for their own actions. Andrew von Hirsch characterizes this behavior as follows: "Someone who infringes on the rights of others does wrong and deserves blame for his conduct. It is because he deserves blame that the sanctioning authority is entitled to choose a response that expresses moral disapproval; namely, punishment" (1976, 49). But advocates of this model left a key question unanswered: What effect will a justice model of punishment have on corrections systems in the United States?

IMPLICATIONS FOR CONTEMPORARY CORRECTIONS

In a 1960s study that examined a group of men born in Philadelphia in 1945, criminologist Marvin Wolfgang and his colleagues found that about 6 percent of the participants accounted for about 50 percent of the group's criminal behavior (Wolfgang, Figlio, and Sellin 1972). In the 1980s, studies of repeat offenders confirmed that a relatively small percentage of career criminals accounted for most of the nation's crime (Blumstein et al. 1988; Greenwood 1982).

By the mid- to late-1980s, a simple solution began to take shape: *selective incapacitation*, the long-term incarceration of career criminals to limit their ability to commit new crimes. How do we identify career criminals? Here, again, the answer was simple: career criminals are repeat offenders, those who continue to appear in the justice and corrections systems. In short order, state and federal legislators began to limit the early release of offenders from prison and to pass **habitual-offender statutes** that would send others to prison for life.

How do we explain the widespread acceptance in this country of one of the most punitive and prison-oriented penal philosophies in history? Popular support for habitual-offender statutes, like the support for more prisons we described in Chapter 1, was rooted in the national obsession with the fear of crime (Austin and Irwin 2001, 5–7). The nation added getting tough-on-criminals to its political and social agendas. Politicians and citizens alike ignored the dire predictions of social scientists about the consequences of an imprisonment binge (Austin and Irwin; Clear 1994; Gottfredson and McConville 1987). Neither group seemed particularly interested in learning exactly who was in prison and for what crimes. The imprisonment rhetoric was far more important than its reality. Just over 30 years ago, the nation's prison population was under 350,000; today, it is greater than 2.25 million.

SUMMARY

The idea that those who break the rules of a community must pay is as old as civilization. In some ways, the community's responses have changed dramatically over the millennia; in other ways, we have not progressed very far in the search for appropriate penalties for lawbreakers. Some of the key points presented in this chapter include the following:

- The punishment philosophies that exist in the United States today have been influenced by practices that date back to the Code of Hammurabi and the Law of Moses.

- The Greeks and Romans laid the groundwork for what can be considered contemporary attitudes and practices toward punishment.

- The political and social philosophers from the Age of Enlightenment advocated that punishments should be swift, certain, and proportionate.

- The nation's focus on punitive measures for criminals regardless of type of crime or history of the offender has generated new laws and changes in sentencing policies that have resulted in unprecedented crowding in both jails and prisons.

- The Pennsylvania system and the Auburn system competed with one another during the early 1800s for the dominant form of prison operations. In the end, the Auburn system won.

- There were a variety of penal reformers in Europe and the United States. Influential Europeans were John Howard, Alexander Maconochie, Walter Crofton, Gustave de Beaumont, and Alexis de Tocqueville. In the United States, prison reformers included Benjamin Rush, Enoch Wines, and Zebulon Brockway.

- There has been a movement away from rehabilitation and the medical model of corrections. Today, much of the correctional focus is on "just deserts," incapacitation, and a renewed emphasis on retribution.

THINKING ABOUT CORRECTIONAL POLICIES AND PRACTICES: WRITING ASSIGNMENTS

1   "Law and punishment were far fairer before the advent of codified laws." Attack or defend this statement in a single-page answer.

2   In a single page, summarize the contributions of the Age of Enlightenment to modern theories of crime and punishment.

3 Develop a chart comparing and contrasting the Pennsylvania and Auburn prison systems. What are the strengths and weaknesses of each? Was the Pennsylvania system doomed from the start? Why or why not?

4 Write a brief (two pages maximum) essay on the differences between the medical model and the just deserts model.

5 Briefly review the history of punishment in Europe and the United States. What themes can you identify from the various sanctions invoked? Look to the future. What do you think lies ahead, given this brief history of punishments and corrections?

KEY TERMS

Age of Enlightenment
Auburn system
botes
canon law
case law
Code of Hammurabi
Corpus Juris Civilis
habitual-offender statutes
intake
Irish ticket-of-leave system
jus civile
jus gentium
jus honorarium

justice model
Justinian Code
King's Peace
Law of Moses
lex salica
marks of commendation
medical model
natural law
parole
penal colonies
Penal Servitude Act of 1853
Penitentiary Act of 1779
Pennsylvania system

pillory
pressing
public whipping
rehabilitation
reintegration
stocks
silent system
ticket of leave
transportation
Twelve Tables
wergild
wites

CRITICAL REVIEW QUESTIONS

1 The goal of early tribal punishments was to restore balance in the community. To that end, social groups relied primarily on reconciliation rituals, in particular restitution. To what extent was this goal similar to or different from the goals of restorative justice? (Be sure to address the issues of blood revenge and banishment in your answer.) Would these rituals work today?

2 The Code of Hammurabi and the Law of Moses have both been described as examples of *lex talionis*. How are they similar? How do they differ?

3 Did the ancient Greeks and Romans place a value on human life? In this sense, how were the laws in those societies different from the laws in earlier societies?

4 "Feudal law favored the rich and powerful." Is this statement accurate? Explain your answer.

5 Who are the de Tocquevilles and Dickenses of today? What forces shape our society's response to issues of crime and punishment?

6 Transportation was a way that many powerful European nations dealt with twin problems: Burgeoning offender populations (without the death penalty as a way to deal with most of them) and expanding geopolitical empires (that needed colonists). Could you see a way that transportation could reemerge in the twenty-first century (or in the near future)? Is this only a topic for science fiction?

7 In your opinion, who was the greater reformer, Enoch Wines or Zebulon Brockway? Explain your answer.

8   Correctional philosophy embraced the medical model and rehabilitation, if only briefly. What do you see as the great challenges to recapturing this orientation to corrections in the twenty-first century? How do you assess the need for such a return to the past?

9   Some suggest that the dramatic increase during the last two decades in both the number of prisons and the inmate population in the United States points to a "punishment binge." Do you agree with that assessment? If yes,

how do you feel about a corrections system that is becoming increasingly punitive? If not, how would you explain the country's preoccupation with building prisons and populating them?

10 Look at the history of corrections, which in many ways is the history of institutional corrects. What do the "lessons" of the way corrections developed tell us about contemporary and future approaches to "correcting" the behavior of criminals?

NOTES

1   This process of returning the community to peace through reconciliation captures the essence of restorative justice (see Chapter 1).

2   The oracles were both the people through whom the gods of ancient Greece and Rome spoke, and the places where mediums contacted the gods to ask for their help in making decisions.

3   A *solidus* was originally a Roman gold coin weighing roughly 4.5 grams. Introduced in the reign of Diocletian around 301, the coin was minted by various entities in Europe and the Middle East for at least 500 years (Porteous 1969; Spufford 1993).

4   Originally intended to protect the king from assassins and other malcontents, the king's peace provided the king's officers, in particular his tax collectors, some small measure of protection.

5   By the term *religious offenders*, we refer to the victims of the Holy Inquisition. Pope Gregory IX established the papal inquisition in 1233 as a means of combating heresy. Papal inquisitors often resorted to torture to secure confessions; they seldom put offenders to death, but imprisonment was common. The independent Spanish Inquisition, chartered by Ferdinand and Isabella of Spain in 1478 (and not abolished until 1834) was far harsher—and deadlier—than the Holy Inquisition of Rome.

6   Venetian jurists developed a precursor of modern-day alternatives to incarceration. Rather than subject convicted offenders to confinement, they sentenced debtors and other criminals to "self-binding detention": the offenders were not allowed to cross a bridge outside a specified area for 30 days (Dunbabin). If they paid their debts or otherwise behaved, the restriction was lifted; if they violated the terms of the self-binding confinement, they were jailed.

7   Howard's belief in the reformative power of hard yet productive work led to the coining of a new term: *penitentiary*. The word derives from the Latin *poenitentiae*, meaning "regret." Thus, the penitentiary was a place where those who violate society's laws are sent to think about their misdeeds and express their regret for them while performing hard labor to produce goods with real value.

8   *Progressivism* is the sum of the doctrines, principles, and practices of a group of late-nineteenth and early-twentieth-century philosophers, who believed that individual changes could be achieved through the continuous reconstruction of living experiences. The mechanisms of change were industrial training and agricultural and social education, all framed within the latest instructional techniques.

REFERENCES

American Friends Service Committee. 1971. *Struggle for justice*. New York: Hill & Wang.

Austin, James F., and John Irwin. 2001. *It's about time: America's imprisonment binge*, 3rd edn. Belmont, CA: Wadsworth.

Barnes, Harry Elmer, and N. K. Teeters. 1959. *New horizons in criminology*. Englewood Cliffs, NJ: Prentice Hall.

Barry, John Vincent. 1958. *Alexander Maconochie of Norfolk Island*. Melbourne: Oxford University Press.

Bartollas, Clemens, and John P. Conrad. 1992. *Introduction to corrections*, 2nd edn. New York: HarperCollins.

Beaumont, Gustave de, and Alexis de Tocqueville. 1832/1964. *On the penitentiary system in the United States and its application to France*. Carbondale: Southern Illinois University Press.

Beckett, Katherine, and Theodore Sasson. 2004. *The politics of injustice: Crime and punishment in America*. Thousand Oaks, CA: Sage.

Blumstein, Alfred, Jacqueline Cohen, Somnath Das, and Soumyo D. Moitra. 1988. Specialization and seriousness during adult criminal careers. *Journal of Quantitative Criminology* 4: 303–45.

Cannon, John. 1997. *The Oxford companion to British history*. New York: Oxford University Press.

Carter, Robert M., Daniel Glaser, and Leslie T. Wilkins. 1984. *Correctional institutions*. New York: Harper & Row.

Cary, M., and H. H. Scullard. 1975. *A history of Rome: Down to the reign of Constantine*, 3rd edn. New York: St. Martin's Press.

Chance, Clifford. 2003. *The Conciergerie: Palais de la Cite*. Paris: Éditions du Patrimone.

Clear, Todd R. 1994. *Harm in American penology: Offenders, victims, and their communities*. Albany: State University of New York Press.

Clear, Todd R., and George F Cole. 2003. *American corrections*. Belmont, CA: Wadsworth/Thomson Learning.

Dickens, Charles. 1837–1838. *Oliver Twist*. Philadelphia: Carey Lea and Blanchard.

Dopsch, Alfons. 1969. *The economic and social foundation of European civilizations*. New York: Fertig.

Dunbabin, Jean. 2002. *Captivity and imprisonment in medieval Europe, 1000–1300*. New York: Palgrave.

Edgerton, Robert. 1976. *Deviance: A cross-cultural perspective*. Menlo Park, CA: Cummings.

Fisher, Leonard Everett. 1987. *The Tower of London*. New York: Macmillan.

Fogel, David. 1975. *". . . We are the living proof . . ." The justice model for corrections*. Cincinnati, OH: Anderson.

Friedman, Lawrence M. 1977. *Law and society: An introduction*. Englewood Cliffs, NJ: Prentice Hall.

Gargarin, Michael. 1986. *Early Greek law*. Berkeley: University of California Press.

Gibbon, Edward. 1932. *The decline and fall of the Roman Empire*. New York: Modern Library.

Gibbons, Don C. 1996. Pennsylvania system. In *Encyclopedia of American prisons*, edited by Marilyn D. McShane and Frank P. Williams III. New York: Garland, 351–2.

Gottfredson, Stephen D., and Sean McConville. 1987. *America's correctional crisis: Prison population and public policy*. New York: Greenwood.

Greenwood, Peter, with Allan Abramse. 1982. *Selective incapacitation*. Santa Monica, CA: RAND.

Halsall, Paul. 1998. *Medieval sourcebook: The Anglo-Saxon dooms, 560–975*. New York: Fordham University. Retrieved July 8, 2013 from: **http://www.fordham.edu/halsall/source/560-975dooms.asp**

Hawke, D. F. 1971. *Benjamin Rush: Revolutionary gadfly*. Indianapolis: Bobbs-Merrill.

Hinckeldey, Christoph. 1993. *Criminal justice through the ages*. Rothenburg, Germany: Mittelalterliches Kriminalmuseum.

Irwin, John. 1980. *Prisons in turmoil*. Boston: Little, Brown.

Johnson, Elmer H. 1996. Auburn system. In *Encyclopedia of American prisons*, edited by Marilyn D. McShane and Frank P. Williams III. New York: Garland, 46–9.

Johnson, Herbert A., and Nancy Travis Wolfe. 1996. *History of criminal justice*, 2nd edn. Cincinnati, OH: Anderson.

Johnson, Herbert A., Nancy Travis Wolfe, and Mark Jones. 2008. *History of criminal justice*, 4th edn. Cincinnati, OH: Anderson.

Johnston, Norman. 1969. Introduction. *Report on the penitentiaries of the United States*, edited by William Crawford. Montclair, NJ: Patterson Smith.

Jolowicz, H. F. 1954. *Historical introduction to the study of Roman law*. Cambridge, UK: Cambridge University Press.

Le Goff, Jacques. 1989. *Medieval civilization, 400–1500*. Trans. Julia Barrow. New York: Blackwell.

Lewis, Naphtali, and Meyer Reinhold, eds. 1990. *Roman civilization: Selected readings: The Republic and the Augustan age*, vol. 1. New York: Columbia University Press.

Martinson, Robert. 1974. What works? Questions and answers about prison reform. *Public Interest* 35: 22–54.

McKelvey, Blake. 1936. *American prisons: A study in American social history prior to 1915*. Chicago: University of Chicago Press.

Morris, Norval. 1974. *The future of imprisonment*. Chicago: University of Chicago Press.

Newman, Graeme. 1978. *The punishment response*. New York: Pantheon.

Norwich, John Julius. 1988. *Byzantium: The early centuries*. New York: Viking.

Nugent, Thomas, trans. 1977. *Montesquieu, The spirit of laws*. Book 6. Berkeley: University of California Press.

Peters, Edward M. 1995. Prison before the prison: The ancient and medieval worlds. In *The Oxford history of the prison: The practice of punishment in Western society*, edited by Norval Morris and David J. Rothman. New York: Oxford University Press, 3–45.

Pfohl, Stephen J. 1981. Labeling criminals. In *Law and deviance*, edited by H. L. Ross. Beverly Hills, CA: Sage, 65–97.

Porteous, John. 1969. *Coins in history: A Survey of coinage from the reform of Diocletian to the Latin monetary union*. London: Weidenfeld and Nicolson.

Schafer, Stephen. 1969. *Theories in criminology*. New York: Random House.

Sellin, Thorsten J. 1976. *Slavery and the penal system*. New York: Elsevier.

Spufford, Peter. 1993. *Money and its use in medieval Europe*. New York: Cambridge University Press.

Stewart, Aubrey, and George Long. 1894. *Plutarch's lives*. London: Wm. Clowes & Sons, Ltd. Retrieved July 8, 2013 from: http://www.gutenberg.org/files/14033/14033-h/14033-h.htm#LIFE_OF_SOLON

Vinogradoff, Paul. 1920. *Outlines of historical jurisprudence: Introduction and tribal law*, vol. 1. Oxford, UK: Oxford University Press.

Von Hirsch, Andrew. 1976. *Doing justice*. New York: Hill & Wang.

Welch, Michael. 2005. *Ironies of imprisonment*. Thousand Oaks, CA: Sage.

Wines, Enoch Cobb. 1864. *The true penitent portrayed: A doctrine of repentance*. Philadelphia: Presbyterian Board of Publication.

Wolfgang, Marvin E., Robert M. Figlio, and Thorsten Sellin. 1972. *Delinquency in a birth cohort*. Chicago: University of Chicago Press.

SENTENCING AND CRIMINAL SANCTIONS

ALEX BEATON/ALAMY IMAGES

Outline

Objectives

- To help you understand how the criminal law affects corrections

- To provide you with an overview of the people, agencies, and organizations involved in sentencing

- To acquaint you with the various criminal sentencing options

- To help you distinguish between felony and misdemeanor sanctions

- To introduce you to the controversies surrounding the death penalty

- To show you the differences between indeterminate and determinate sentences

Essentials of Corrections, Fifth Edition. G. Larry Mays and L. Thomas Winfree, Jr.
© 2014 John Wiley & Sons, Inc. Published 2014 by John Wiley & Sons, Inc.

INTRODUCTION

Various social goals go into the sentencing process. These may correspond to the punishment philosophies discussed in the opening chapter: deterrence, incapacitation, isolation, rehabilitation, reintegration, restitution, restoration, and retribution. Sentencing also reflects other factors that judges, legislators, and the general public consider important (Banks 2009, Chapter 5; Singer and La Fond 2007, 20–29). For example, most people advocate **proportionality**, that punishment should be as severe as the crime was serious. Also, most criminal justice workers and members of the general public believe in **equity**, that similar offenders and similar offenses should be treated the same. Finally, many believe that a sentence should incorporate some recognition of the offender's criminal history; this is the notion of **social debt**.

The statement that a person is innocent until proven guilty means that the state must prove guilt and that the defendant need not prove innocence. This distinguishes the Anglo-American system of justice—called an **adversarial system**—from the inquisitorial system employed in the past by many European countries. In a traditional **inquisitorial system**, or **accusatorial system**, the defendant is presumed guilty unless he or she can prove innocence, a much more difficult task to accomplish. Today, however, all European states that are members of the Council of Europe have signed and ratified the European Convention on Human Rights, an agreement that binds them to protect certain key human rights pertaining to criminal procedure. Among those rights is the **presumption of innocence**. In terms of general regulations, then, there is no fundamental difference between European adversarial systems— the English system is most typical, the Italian system is less so—and the inquisitorial systems found in most of Europe, including, for example, Germany, France, and Austria (Reichel 2012).

The prosecution bears the burden of proof in criminal cases and must demonstrate a level of evidence sufficient to result in a conviction. In civil cases in the United States, juries are instructed to base their verdicts on the **preponderance of the evidence**. Although this term does not have a precise meaning, it is generally understood to mean that a verdict should be based on the amount of evidence necessary to decide the case in favor of one party or the other.

By contrast, in criminal cases, a verdict must be based on evidence sufficient to prove the defendant's **guilt beyond a reasonable doubt**. Again, this term does not have a precise definition, but usually we say that a reasonable doubt is "the state of mind of jurors in which, after the comparison and consideration of all the evidence, they cannot say that they feel an abiding conviction, a moral certainty, of the truth of a criminal charge against the defendant" (Rush 2003, 119).

Another concern in criminal law is the ***corpus delicti***, literally the "body of the crime." Despite what most people assume, *corpus delicti* does not necessarily refer to a dead body but, rather, refers to the elements that must be proved to establish that a crime has been committed. One of those elements is ***actus reus*** (in Latin, the wrongful act): an act is criminal only if it was committed overtly and resulted in harm. A wrongful act can take several forms, and the action does not have to be completed to be a crime.

For instance, in most states, if a man enters a convenience store, flashes a handgun, and demands money, he has committed the crime of armed robbery. What if the robber never makes it into the store? What if he is intercepted in the parking lot by a security guard or an off-duty police officer? Or what if an accomplice reports the crime to the police after it is planned but before it can be carried out? Attempts or conspiracies to commit a crime may be treated as less-serious forms of the crime, but they are crimes nonetheless.[1] Attempted crimes, conspiracies to commit crimes, and other efforts that fall short of completed acts are called **inchoate offenses** in criminal law (Dressler 2009).

SENTENCING: WHO DECIDES?

Most people aren't familiar with the sentencing process for those convicted of a crime. Even if a trial has been fairly public, sentencing often takes place after the adjudication is completed and after the public's fascination with the trial has faded. Once the press reports that an individual has been convicted, media attention typically focuses elsewhere.

Three elements of the sentencing process are a key to understanding that process: the decision makers, the decisions available to them, and the decision making process itself. In this section, we consider the first of these elements: the individuals who decide.

THE ROLE OF LAWMAKERS

Congress and each of the 50 state legislatures have the power to make **substantive law**, to define those behaviors that constitute crimes in the jurisdiction under their control. Legislatures also determine by statute, and courts add by case law, the law of criminal procedure. Unlike substantive law, which defines criminal behavior, **procedural law** governs the arrest, prosecution, and trial of criminal offenders.

All crimes are not equal: some are more serious than others. At the most basic level, we can divide all crimes into misdemeanors and felonies. All states do not define crimes in the same way, but misdemeanors are always the least serious and felonies are the most serious offenses.

According to the Department of Justice, **misdemeanors** are offenses "punishable by incarceration, usually in a local confinement facility, for a period of which the upper limit is prescribed by statute in a given jurisdiction, typically limited to a year or less" (1981, 132). In contrast, **felonies** may prescribe sentences of 1 year or more, including life in prison or the death penalty. Substantial fines also may be levied. Offenders incarcerated for felonies serve their sentences in state or federal prisons.

States can further differentiate degrees of seriousness within the misdemeanor and felony categories. For instance, some jurisdictions have a classification for infractions or violations. These offenses are often labeled **petty misdemeanors**, the least-serious crimes. The usual penalty for petty misdemeanors is a fine. Most states also distinguish among degrees (first, second, third) or classes (A or B, or I or II) of felonies (American Law Institute 1985; Dressler 2009). A first-degree felony or a Class A or I felony is more serious than the other degrees or classes are.

A second consideration in the classification of crime is the degree of personal involvement. Under English **common law**, the law that evolved from legal decisions based primarily on custom and precedent, a distinction was made between principals and accessories. **Principals** are those who actually commit a crime; **accessories** are individuals who contribute in some way to the crime's commission. In contemporary US criminal law, the federal government and most of the states have eliminated the distinctions between principals and accessories before the fact (before the crime is actually committed), although they still may treat accessories after the fact differently (see, for example, Schubert 2010, 195).

The third element of the criminal law of concern to lawmakers is *mens rea* (Latin: "guilty mind"), the intention to carry out a criminal act. **Criminal intent** can be specific (the perpetrator intends the harm caused the victim) or general (the perpetrator understood that harm was possible). Convictions for most crimes require that the offender's intent be proved. Intent is clear in an armed robbery: the state has very little to prove about intent if a person enters a convenience store, produces a handgun, and demands money. But when the charge is embezzlement, the state may have to establish that the offender took money with the intention of converting it to his or her own use.

Complicating the state's task of proving criminal intent are affirmative defenses. In an **affirmative defense**, the defendant admits to the facts of the crime but denies criminal intent, arguing that there were mitigating factors. For example, the **infancy defense** is the argument that the defendant was too young at the time the crime was committed to distinguish between right and wrong. According to the common law, children younger than age seven are incapable of forming criminal intent (Mays and Winfree 2012). Today, most statutes set the age between eight and ten.

One of the most controversial affirmative defenses is the **insanity defense**. In the insanity defense, the issue is the defendant's mental capacity at the time the offense was committed. Several different tests of the insanity defense have been applied over the years. The *M'Naughton* rule, which was first applied in England in 1843, addresses the defendant's understanding of the difference between right and wrong; the **irresistible-impulse test** refers to a mental defect that would prevent the defendant from using that understanding to control his or her behavior (Dressler 2009).

Although the entertainment and news media make much of the insanity defense, it is actually raised in only about 1 percent of the cases that go to trial, typically in cases involving homicide or attempted homicide (Walker 2006, 162). Moreover, the defense is successful in only 15 to 25 percent of the cases in which it is used. What the insanity defense has succeeded at is stirring up controversy. In response, 15 states have substantially altered or eliminated the insanity defense (FindLaw 2012; Dressler 2009).[2]

A third affirmative defense is **alibi**. Many students believe that an alibi is simply another word for excuse, but *alibi* comes from the Latin word *alius*, which means "elsewhere." Here, the defendant is not disputing the facts of the case but is saying, "I could not have committed this crime because I was somewhere else at the time it was committed."

A fourth affirmative defense is **entrapment**. This defense alleges that the police induced the criminal behavior, that the defendant would not have committed the crime in the absence of police intervention. Entrapment is a common defense, particularly where the charge is vice related (drug dealing, gambling, prostitution). The courts routinely rule that there is no entrapment if the police simply provide an opportunity for a person to do what he or she is already inclined to do (see, for example, *United States v. Russell* 1973). However, if police officers concocted the idea for the crime and then orchestrated events so the alleged offender could commit the act, they are guilty of entrapment.

There is one final note about affirmative defenses. In the US legal system, the state bears the burden of proving the elements of the offense: wrongful act and guilty mind. Only in the case of an affirmative defense does the burden of proof shift to the defendant.

In summary, lawmakers are responsible for defining criminal conduct, for defining substantive law, and defining the procedural rules that govern the criminal trial process. One component of that task is deciding the nature and the severity of sentences. Another is deciding whether sentences are indeterminate or determinate.

THE ROLE OF JURIES

As the "trier of facts," the jury is responsible for deciding who is telling the truth, what evidence means, and, eventually, whether the defendant is guilty. Saul Kassin reminds us that in the deliberation process, "Jurors are expected to base their opinions on an accurate appraisal of evidence to the exclusion of non-evidentiary sources of information" (2009, 175). Given the presumption of innocence, the jury decides whether that presumption has been sustained or whether the state has produced sufficient evidence to prove guilt beyond a reasonable doubt.

In most criminal cases, the jury's responsibilities have been discharged once it decides that the defendant is innocent or guilty. However, under certain circumstances—particularly in death penalty cases—the jury, rather than the judge, decides the sentence (see *Ring v. Arizona* 2002).

THE ROLE OF JUDGES

The jury is the trier of facts; the judge is the "trier of the law." The judge rules on trial procedures and evidence and decides what instructions will be given to the jury. In bench trials the judge serves as both trier of fact and trier of law.

In most criminal cases, once a verdict is reached, the judge requests a presentence investigation report and sets a date for sentencing. And in many states, the judge is responsible for imposing a sentence on the convicted offender. There is an important distinction here: lawmakers define crimes and, in the process, appropriate penalties; judges impose sentences, but lawmakers decide what sentences can be imposed.

SENTENCING: WHAT ARE THE CHOICES?

Among the sentences that legislatures regularly debate and prescribe are probation, fines and forfeitures,

misdemeanor sentences (including confinement in jail), felony sentences (including confinement in prison and intermediate sanctions), and the death penalty.

PROBATION

The Bureau of Justice Statistics defines **probation** as "a court-ordered period of correctional supervision in the community, generally as an alternative to incarceration" (Glaze and Bonczar 2011, 2). Probation is the most common criminal disposition in the United States for adult and juvenile offenders. At the end of 2010, just over 57 percent of the nation's offenders were on probation. This means that out of

more than 7 million people under correctional supervision in the United States more than 4 million people were on probation (Glaze 2011).

Several facts about probation are important to remember:

- Probation is a *sentence*. Although probation can be imposed on alleged violators, virtually everyone who is sentenced to probation has pleaded or been found guilty. The fact that probation is a sentence means that the court has continuing jurisdiction over probationers.

- Probation is a *judicial function*: it is imposed and supervised by a judge.

- The probation department, including the officers who work directly with offenders, can be a part of the court or an executive agency at the state level. In either case, probation officers must work closely with the sentencing judges. This is especially true in the preparation and presentation of presentence investigation reports.

- Probation is imposed *in lieu of incarceration*. It offers offenders a chance to remain in the community instead of serving a sentence behind bars.

- Probation is *conditional*. This means that the probationer's continued freedom depends on his or her meeting the terms of probation.

That so many offenders today are on probation is a by-product of the get-tough-on-crime trend. We are sending more people to jails and prisons for longer periods, and despite a building boom in prison facilities, we simply do not have bed space for all of the country's convicted offenders. The result? There are more people on probation and more of them serious offenders (see, for example, Glaze and Bonczar 2011).

With the changing makeup of the probationer population have come new, tougher probation conditions. For instance, several states have experimented with house arrest and electronic monitoring to track probationers' movements (see Ford and Schmidt 1985; Renzema and Skelton 1990). House arrest, with or without electronic monitoring, is designed to keep offenders off the street.[3]

The assumption here is that by confining offenders to their homes, they will be less tempted and will have fewer opportunities to commit new crimes. Although the effectiveness of house arrest is still being debated, some judges have turned to home confinement with increasing frequency. For many, house arrest has become more an add-on to probation than an alternative to incarceration (Clear 1988; also see Abadinsky 2012).

Another condition imposed on probationers is restitution, the court-ordered payment of money or services to the victim. In 2006, restitution was ordered for 18 percent of the felons convicted in state courts; most had committed property offenses (Rosenmerkel, Durose, and Farole 2009). Forcing probationers to make monetary payments to their victims creates several problems:

- It is easy for a judge to order that restitution be paid as part of a probated sentence, but the mechanics of collecting the money are another matter. In most jurisdictions, responsibility for collecting restitution falls largely to overburdened probation officers.

- A restitution order presumes some ability to pay. Often offenders, in particular juveniles, are unemployed or underemployed, and simply do not have the money to meet the restitution condition.

- Finally, some still question the purpose of restitution. Although advocates believe the practice increases offenders' accountability and victims' satisfaction, cause and effect are not always obvious. This has led critics to argue that restitution is simply another probation add-on.

Restitution can also take the form of court-ordered community service. Judges ordered 11 percent of the felons convicted in state courts in 2006 to perform community service in addition to any other sentence they received (Rosenmerkel, Durose, and Farole 2009). Supervision is a problem here also, and the effectiveness of the practice is questionable.

Clearly, probation and other noninstitutional sanctions provide an invaluable service to the courts and the community. We return to the topic of probation in Chapter 4.

FINES AND FORFEITURES

Fines and forfeitures of property or assets have long been penal sanctions. For instance, the Anglo-Saxons in Britain had a system of monetary payments called *botes* almost 1,500 years ago (see Chapter 2). These very old sanctions seem to have been rediscovered of late.

The most common application of fines is for traffic offenses. In most states, people charged with motor vehicle violations are subject to a fine and court costs. But the use of fines has been expanded in recent years. In 2006, 38 percent of the felons convicted in state courts were also ordered to pay a fine (Rosenmerkel, Durose, and Farole 2009).

Probably the most conspicuous use of fines in major criminal cases has come under the federal **Racketeer Influenced and Corrupt Organizations (RICO) Statute** (18 USC 1961–1968), a component of the Organized Crime Control Act of 1970. The law was designed to deal with organized crime, but since the 1980s, it has been applied to a variety of criminal activities. Those convicted of RICO violations, or their state-level equivalents, can find themselves facing hefty fines, ranging from hundreds of thousands to several million dollars. They may also be forced to forfeit the assets accumulated through their crimes.

Another type of monetary sanction is the **day fine**, or structured fine (Bureau of Justice Assistance 1996; Winterfield and Hillsman 1993). Day fines have been common for some time in Europe and South America, but they were not used in this country until the Richmond County (New York) Criminal Court implemented a pilot program in 1987.

In most US courts, fines are based on the nature of the crime. The legislature prescribes a range of fines for specific offenses, and the presiding judge imposes the appropriate amount on the convicted offender. The problem with this traditional approach is that it is not equitable: it places a disproportionate burden on lower-income offenders. The day-fine approach, because it ties the amount of the fine to the individual offender's ability to pay, sanctions all offenders proportionately.

When Laura Winterfield and Sally Hillsman (1993) evaluated the Staten Island Day-Fine Project in the early 1990s, they found that this sentencing option had been tried in a limited number of jurisdictions.[4] However, based on the Staten Island experience, Winterfield and Hillsman were able to draw several conclusions:

- Day fines could be implemented in most misdemeanor courts in the United States.
- On average, the amount of fines increased 25 percent under the day-fine program, and total fines increased 14 percent.
- Despite the increased amount of fines, collection rates were higher when day fines were imposed.

Day fines are **means-based penalties**, monetary sanctions that account for each offender's ability to pay. Moreover, day fines provide for "fairer punishments . . . without making the process of imposing fines too difficult or time-consuming for judges" (Winterfield and Hillsman 1993, 6).

One final note: Fines traditionally have been a revenue source used to support judicial or administrative operations. Since the 1980s, however, fines have been designated to support certain programs, especially those involving victims' assistance (US Department of Justice 1988, 96). In some ways, the use of fines in the criminal justice system today proves the adage that "everything old is new again." Although fines have been around for centuries, legislatures and the courts rediscovered them at the end of the twentieth century.

MISDEMEANOR SENTENCES

Remember that legislative bodies decide which offenses are misdemeanors and which are felonies. The distinction is important because how a crime is classified determines where incarcerated offenders are housed and for how long.

Misdemeanor sentences can take a variety of forms. Common misdemeanors are typically punishable by fines. Misdemeanors also can result in probation. But when most people think about misdemeanor sentences, they think about the county jail. County jails do play a significant role in the sanctioning of misdemeanants, as do county workhouses, penal farms, and other local detention facilities (see Chapter 5).

FELONY SENTENCES

For decades in this country, felony sentences meant prison. That is no longer true. Today, fines are increasingly being used, especially for crimes in which large sums of money change hands (drug trafficking, for example). Also, as a result of state prison crowding, courts often turn to probation for felony offenders (Glaze and Bonczar 2011). This means that probation is no longer the sentence of choice just for first-time and property offenders; it is becoming a common sentence for serious and repeat offenders—a fact that could lead to significant differences in the way probation services are structured and delivered (see Chapter 4).

Short of prison, convicted felons are subject to a variety of **intermediate sanctions**—punishments that are more severe than standard probation but less severe than imprisonment (Gowdy 1993). Day fines, house arrest, and electronic monitoring are some of the most common intermediate sanctions. Others, like intermittent confinement and shock incarceration, combine elements of probation with confinement.[5]

The use of intermediate sanctions has spread across the nation, to all levels of government. Former Delaware governor Michael Castle, for one, welcomed the change:

> People too often assume that public protection means prison, and that anything less than complete incarceration for all criminals will endanger public safety . . . Successful intermediate sanctions programs have been adopted in many communities, despite the burden of public resistance . . . Accomplishing change means putting an end to the old-fashioned and inaccurate concept that criminal justice means prisons and *only* prisons. (Gowdy 1993, 1)

Finally, convicted felons always face the possibility of imprisonment. The length of the potential sentence (1 year or more) and the place of incarceration (a prison instead of a county jail or other local correctional facility) distinguish felonies from misdemeanors. Convicted felons are more likely to be sentenced to prison if they are repeat **property offenders** or if they have committed one very serious **personal offense** (aggravated assault, rape, or robbery) (Glaze and Bonczar 2011; Rosenmerkel, Durose, and Farole 2009). In 2006, the likelihood of imprisonment for convicted felons ranged from 27 percent for people convicted of one felony to 96 percent for those convicted of three or more felonies (Rosenmerkel, Durose, and Farole 2009).

THE DEATH PENALTY

In some ways, a discussion of the death penalty does not belong in a book about corrections: the death penalty has nothing to do with correcting criminal behavior. But our topic here is sentencing, and the death penalty is a sentence that state legislatures mandate and the courts can impose under certain circumstances. It is important to note that the United States is the only Western nation that carries out capital punishment (see Box 3.1), making a discussion of the ultimate punishment even more important.

The death penalty has been in existence since this nation was founded. The United States adopted its laws and legal structure, including capital punishment, from England, where at one point virtually all felonies were punishable by death. Although the English have abandoned capital punishment, the United States remains one of a small group of nations to employ it.

In the decades following World War II, the number of people executed in the United States fell sharply (Figure 3.1). So steep was that fall that many pundits believed this country would follow the lead of other Western nations and would stop executing people either by law or in practice (Zimring and Hawkins 1986). In 1972, the US Supreme Court curbed the use of the death penalty, questioning the constitutionality of the sentence as then administered. Four years later, the Court upheld revised death penalty laws in several states. By the mid-1980s, the number of executions began to climb. The rise in the number of people executed in the United States paralleled the nation's imprisonment binge, so could be considered part of the penal harm movement described in Chapter 1.

The death penalty evokes strong reactions in those who oppose capital punishment under any circumstances and those who support it for all first-degree murders and, in some instances, for other crimes as well. Both of these groups constitute small but vocal minorities. Most Americans favor the death penalty for first-degree murder—or at least are not opposed to it—but are more ambivalent than the vocal advocates are.

People oppose or support the death penalty for various reasons. But at times, both groups argue their position on the same grounds. For example, both opponents and proponents of the death penalty may use the Bible to defend their views. Opponents might invoke the Ten Commandments: "Thou shalt

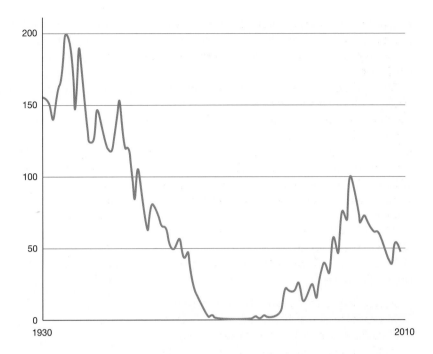

FIGURE 3.1 **People Executed in the United States, 1930–2010.**

Source: Snell (2011).

not kill." Proponents might counter with citations from Deuteronomy that describe the circumstances—for example, in cases of adultery, murder, or bestiality—that require citizens to stone the offending parties to death. Therefore, people of similar religious backgrounds may disagree about the death penalty.

Another area of dispute centers on the question of justice. Opponents argue that the death penalty in our society is not just because it is imposed disproportionately on those who are poor or who are minorities. Supporters would agree with Ernest Van den Haag (1975; Van den Haag and Conrad 1983) that the fact that some people receive the death penalty and others who are equally deserving do not does not make capital punishment any less just. Van den Haag reminds us that justice is giving people what they deserve, and that people who commit murder, especially premeditated murder, deserve to die.

Of course, debates about the morality or the fairness of the death penalty are largely philosophical. Other arguments are more practical. Consider, for instance, the economics of execution. Opponents argue that it is just as costly to execute a person,

especially after lengthy and expensive appeals, as it is to keep that individual in prison for life without the possibility of parole. Proponents argue just the opposite: executions are much less costly. Both groups agree on one point, however: the death penalty is final. Once a person has been executed, there is no opportunity to correct any mistakes that might have been made. The possibility of wrongful convictions and executing an innocent person troubles death penalty opponents; proponents say that appeals take care of virtually every correctable error and that few undeserving people are executed (see Mays 2012, 356–61). Advances in DNA testing have uncovered a number of unjust convictions in recent years. For example, in 2010, appeals courts in the United States overturned the convictions of 48 on death row (Snell 2011, 11). In many of those cases, DNA evidence was used or witnesses came forward to establish the innocence of people sentenced to death.

The final issue in the death penalty debate is legal and constitutional in nature. The framers of the Constitution presumed the existence of the death penalty. They provided in the Fifth Amendment that "no person shall be held to answer for a *capital*, or otherwise infamous crime, unless on a presentment

SPOTLIGHT ON INTERNATIONAL CORRECTIONS: THE DEATH PENALTY   BOX 3.1

Amnesty International reports that, as of 2010, a total of 96 nations and territories had abolished the death penalty for any crimes, and a small group reserved it only for exceptional crimes, such as those committed in wartime. Although the death penalty was technically a sanction in 30 other counties, those nations have not executed anyone in more than a decade. We can infer from their refusal to invoke the death penalty that the criminal justice systems in those 30 nations do not support capital punishment. Stated another way, on the issue of the death penalty, the United States is at odds with the punishment or sentencing practices of most of the world's nations and territories.

And what countries use the death penalty? There are 58 of them, including the United States. In 2010, at least 676 people were executed around the world. And most the world's executions took place in China, Iraq, Saudi Arabia, North Korea, Somalia, Yemen, and the United States.

SOURCE: AMNESTY INTERNATIONAL (2012).

or indictment of a grand jury . . . nor be deprived of *life*, liberty, or property, without due process of law" (emphasis added). A provision in the Eighth Amendment, the provision prohibiting cruel and unusual punishments, has been at the core of many appeals to the Supreme Court. In *Furman v. Georgia* (1972), the Court struck down the death penalty as it was being administered in more than 30 states. Numerous reasons were given, but the ruling focused on two factors: (1) juries had very broad discretion in deciding on the death penalty (not only for first-degree murder but, in some states, for rape, armed robbery, and a variety of other offenses); and (2) most states did not provide instructions concerning aggravating and mitigating circumstances.[6] What the Court was saying was that the death penalty was not cruel, but it was unusual because it was being imposed capriciously and arbitrarily. The Supreme Court did not say in *Furman v. Georgia* or in any subsequent case that the death penalty is unconstitutional in and of itself.

In 1976, in *Gregg v. Georgia*, the Court upheld the revised death penalty laws of Georgia and several other states. The revised laws departed from those that had existed before *Furman* in three major ways. First, the range of crimes punishable by death was severely narrowed—in most states to first-degree murder only. Second, death penalty states began to use **bifurcated hearings**: that is, they conduct a trial to determine the defendant's innocence or guilt; then, if the defendant is found guilty, they hold a sentencing hearing to determine whether the death penalty should be imposed. In both the original trial and in the sentencing hearing, the jury's verdict must be unanimous. If the jury's decision is not unanimous about a death sentence, the court imposes life imprisonment (in some states without the possibility of parole). Third, all states with the death penalty now provide for appeals, and in all but one, appeal—typically to the state supreme court—is automatic for defendants sentenced to die (Bonczar and Snell 2006, 3).

Today, 36 states and the federal government have the death penalty. Just 15 jurisdictions do not: Alaska, District of Columbia, Hawaii, Illinois (repealed in 2011), Iowa, Maine, Massachusetts, Michigan, Minnesota, New Mexico (repealed in 2010), North

TABLE 3.1 Executions and death row inmates by state, December 31, 2010.

Executions during 2010		Number of prisoners under sentence of death	
Texas	17	California	699
Ohio	8	Florida	392
Alabama	5	Texas	315
Mississippi	3	Pennsylvania	215
Oklahoma	3	Alabama	201
Virginia	3	North Carolina	158
Georgia	2	Ohio	157
Arizona	1	Arizona	133
Florida	1	Georgia	100
Louisiana	1	Tennessee	86
Utah	1	Louisiana	84
Washington	1	Nevada	81
		Oklahoma	71
		23 other jurisdictions	466
Total	46	Total	3,158

SOURCE: ADAPTED FROM SNELL (2011, 8).

Dakota, Rhode Island, Vermont, West Virginia, and Wisconsin. As shown in Table 3.1, the death penalty states executed 46 people in 2010. And at year's end, 3,158 others were on death row pending the results of a legal appeal or commutation of their sentence. From the time Gary Gilmore was executed in 1977, in the wake of the *Gregg* decision, through the end of 2010, five states have executed nearly two-thirds of the inmates sentenced to die in the United States: Texas (464 executions), Virginia (108), Oklahoma (94), Florida (69), and Missouri (67). Nine other states—Alabama, Arizona, Arkansas, Georgia, Indiana, Louisiana, North Carolina, Ohio, and South Carolina—executed between 20 and 49 people in the same period (Snell 2011, 15).

In 2010, the most common method of execution was lethal injection (36 states), followed by electrocution (nine states), lethal gas (three states), hanging (three states), and firing squad (two states). These numbers add up to more than 36 because some states employ more than one method. In fact,

TABLE 3.2 **Methods of execution by state, 2010.**

Lethal injection			Electrocution	Lethal gas	Hanging	Firing squad
Alabama	Kentucky	Oklahoma	Alabama	Arizona	Delaware	Oklahoma
Arkansas	Louisiana	Oregon	Arkansas	Missouri	New Hampshire	Utah
California	Maryland	Pennsylvania	Florida	Wyoming	Washington	
Colorado	Mississippi	South Carolina	Illinois			
Connecticut	Missouri	South Dakota	Kentucky			
Delaware	Montana	Tennessee	Oklahoma			
Florida	Nebraska	Texas	South Carolina			
Georgia	Nevada	Utah	Tennessee			
Idaho	New Hampshire	Virginia	Virginia			
Illinois	New York	Washington				
Indiana	North Carolina	Wyoming				
Kansas	Ohio					

SOURCE: ADAPTED FROM SNELL (2011, 6).

under certain circumstances, Arizona, Arkansas, Delaware, Kentucky, and Tennessee allow the condemned prisoner to choose the method. Table 3.2 lists methods of execution by state. Despite the variety of methods allowed by the various jurisdictions, 86 percent of the 1,060 inmates executed between 1977 and 2010 met their death by lethal injection; and another 13 percent died by electrocution (Snell 2011, 14). Lethal gas accounted for 11 deaths, hanging for three, and firing squads for three, including Gilmore's.

The available data on the death penalty suggest several important trends. First, the average stay on death row for those inmates executed in 2010 was 14 years and 10 months (this is 9 months longer than those executed in 2009) (Snell 2011, 1). The delay between sentencing and execution was largely a function of the lengthy appeal process. The cost to the government of that process and of housing death row inmates in special cell blocks or facilities is one of the arguments opponents of capital punishment rely on to counter those who contend that execution is cheaper than confinement. Second, the number of death row inmates has started to decline. During 2009, there were 15 fewer inmates on death row than there were at the end of 2009. Between 1977 and 2010, 7,879 federal and state inmates

entered prisons under death sentences, and 1,234 inmates were executed. During that period, 436 prisoners died of natural causes, and 3,359 were removed from death row because their convictions were overturned or their sentences commuted (Snell 2011, 18).

Third, historically a number of states allowed death sentences for youngsters below the age of 18, some as young as 14. In 1989, the US Supreme Court established 16 as the minimum age for imposing the death penalty (*Stanford v. Kentucky* 1989), and in 2005, the Court established 18 as the minimum age for death sentences (*Roper v. Simmons* 2005).

Finally, questions of race and ethnicity are prominent in the capital punishment debate. It is not correct to say that most of the inmates awaiting execution are members of racial or ethnic minority groups: in 2010, 55 percent of the prisoners on death row were white. But minorities—African Americans in particular—are overrepresented in the nation's death row population.[7] In 2010, for example, blacks made up 42 percent of the death row population; they made up about 12 percent of the general population that year (Snell 2011, 8). Between 1977 and 2010, about 57 percent of those executed were white (males and females), 34 percent were black, and about 7 percent were Hispanic (13).

SENTENCING: HOW ARE DECISIONS MADE?

It would seem to be fairly easy to figure out how much time an offender should get and then how much time that person should serve. But in practice, sentencing often is complicated by several factors. Some of those factors relate to judicial decision making; others relate to prosecutorial decision making in the form of plea bargaining.

JUDICIAL DECISION MAKING

Again, legislatures make laws that define criminal behaviors and punishments, and judges impose those punishments on convicted offenders in the form of sentences. In the sentencing role, judges traditionally have had a great deal of discretion. Although lawmakers defined sentences, they tended to define them in broad terms—a sentence of 2 to 5 years, for example. That began to change in the 1970s, as legislators began to set determinate and, later, mandatory sentences for certain crimes or certain offenders. Here, we examine an area where judges continue to have almost total discretion: the decision to impose concurrent or consecutive sentences.

The question of concurrent or consecutive sentences arises when a defendant is convicted of multiple offenses. **Concurrent sentences** are two or more sentences imposed and then served at the same time (Champion 2005, 54). The sentences do not have to be for the same term—all 10 years, for example. If they are different, the prisoner's release usually is calculated on the basis of the longest term. So, an offender sentenced to terms of 10 and 15 years to be served concurrently would not be released until the parole eligibility date for the 15-year sentence.

Consecutive sentences are two or more sentences imposed at the same time but served in sequence (Champion 2005, 56). The offender must serve all but the final sentence before he or she can be considered for release. For example, an offender sentenced to terms of 10 and 15 years to be served consecutively would have to serve the 10-year sentence before becoming eligible for release on the parole eligibility date for the 15-year sentence. Thus, consecutive sentences increase the maximum time an offender can be confined or under supervision.

How do judges decide between concurrent and consecutive sentences? Some suggest that concurrent sentences are one way in which judges protect defendants they believe have had too many charges brought against them—a plea-bargaining tactic we discuss later. Concurrent sentences have the effect of limiting time served to a single sentence, regardless of how many charges a defendant was facing. With consecutive sentences, judges have the power to maximize punishment. They are more likely to impose these sentences on repeat offenders or offenders who have committed crimes that are unusually cruel. It also has been suggested that some judges use consecutive sentences to retaliate against defendants who refuse to plea-bargain, insisting on their right to trial. This "jury trial penalty'" in effect says to the defendant, "You took up my time, now I'm going to take up some of yours" (Neubauer 2008).

PROSECUTORIAL DECISION MAKING: PLEA BARGAINING

Plea bargaining is the negotiation that goes on between the defense attorney and the prosecutor regarding sentences, counts, and charges. In effect, it is the attempt to exchange a guilty plea for some form of leniency. Plea bargaining has long been a component of the criminal justice system in the United States. Guilty pleas were entered in the first courts established in this country, and the bargaining process has been referred to in court proceedings as far back as the 1800s. Today, more than 90 percent of the felony cases in the United States each year are negotiated to disposition.

The average person believes that plea bargaining is all about the sentence and nothing else. Although the sentence is important, it is not the only focus of the negotiations. For example, a defendant may plea bargain, not to reduce the time served—with concurrent sentencing, the time served for one count or five counts could actually be the same—but to reduce the number of counts. In some states, the number of counts is one basis for the decision to charge a defendant as a *habitual offender*, a classification that can increase the term of incarceration and eliminate the possibility of parole.

The particular charge can be of concern too. The charge determines the length of the sentence and determines the form of the sentence. Consider homicide, for example. In most states, a conviction for first-degree murder carries a death sentence or a sentence of life in prison without parole. A person who pleads guilty to second-degree murder may spend many years in prison, but he or she cannot be sentenced to die.

Some argue that the nature of plea bargaining—the exchange of a guilty plea for leniency—can lead prosecutors to bring an excessive number of charges or more serious charges against defendants to gain a tactical advantage at the bargaining table. The two most prevalent types of overcharging are horizontal and vertical (see Davis 2007; Lippke 2011). **Horizontal overcharging** is the practice of charging a defendant with every possible criminal charge related to an offense and then using the lesser charges as bargaining chips. Ultimately, the defendant pleads guilty to the most serious offense, and the others are dismissed as part of the plea bargain.

Vertical overcharging is charging a suspect with more serious charges than can be proved in court, again to gain tactical advantage in negotiations with the defense. For example, the police may believe that an individual has committed second-degree murder, but the prosecutor charges the defendant with first-degree murder. The prosecutor can then offer to reduce the charge if the defendant agrees to plead guilty to that reduced charge. This tactic raises ethical questions about prosecutorial conduct (see Gershman 2009; Lippke 2011), but it also increases the likelihood of a defendant's entering into a plea agreement.

In the end, the impact of plea bargaining is a function of the prosecutor's attitude toward the defendant, the crime or crimes with which the defendant is charged, and the judge's response to the prosecutor's sentencing recommendations. Between negotiations regarding sentences, counts, and charges, and judges' authority to impose concurrent or consecutive sentences, it is difficult to predict the sentence in any particular case. What saves the process

from confusion? The answer is fairly simple: all the parties involved in the courtroom work group—judges, prosecutors, and defense attorneys—have a sense of what is a reasonable and fair sentence in a given case based on earlier cases (see, for example, Eisenstein and Jacob 1977; and Neubauer 2008). Samuel Walker (2011) and others call this the *going rate*. Given a particular set of facts, members of the courtroom work group will most likely agree on the appropriate sentence. This includes whether the defendant should receive probation and, if not, what a reasonable incarceration period should be.

SENTENCING STRATEGIES

In most jurisdictions, the courtroom work group is relatively free to craft a sentence based on the group's perceptions of the going rate. In the last few decades, however, some states have begun to limit the discretion of work group members, particularly judges. And like concurrent and consecutive sentences and plea negotiations, these sentencing strategies complicate the sentencing process.

DETERMINATE SENTENCES

For most of our recent history, state laws have used **indeterminate sentences**—ranges of time rather than specific periods—to define prison terms. So a statute might require a minimum of 2 years and a maximum of 5 years for a given offense (Champion 2005, 126). In most states, judges must impose the statutory range, although some states allow the judge to choose a specific term within the statutory range. The actual time served, however, is determined by a parole board.

In most of the states that use indeterminate sentences, inmates become eligible for parole after they have served some fraction—say a third or a half—of their minimum sentence. For example: an offender is sentenced to serve 1 to 5 years in a state that requires that one-half of the minimum sentence be served before parole can be granted. This offender would be eligible for parole (although not guaranteed to receive it) after serving just six months in prison. The discrepancies between sentences imposed and sentences served have led many groups to call for truth in sentencing (see, for example, Walker 2011).

In the 1970s, jurisdictions throughout the country began to define **determinate sentences**—specific periods of confinement—in their laws (Champion 2005, 78). Most of the states that have changed from indeterminate to determinate sentencing also have limited or eliminated parole. In its place, these states use some form of **good-time credits**: time deducted from a prison sentence for good behavior. The "discount rate" for good-time credits differs from state to state. In some states, it is as high as 50 percent—one day's credit for each day served—a rate that could halve the time inmates serve. When the federal government changed to determinate sentencing in 1987, Congress set the maximum good-time rate for federal prisoners at 54 days a year, or a 15 percent discount rate (see Mays 1989).

Traditionally, reform in the criminal justice system has the support of one or the other political camp: Right or Left. But determinate sentencing was supported by both conservatives and liberals (Walker 2011). Conservatives wanted truth in sentencing; that is, they wanted sentences that reflect the time an inmate would actually have to serve. They also felt that judges had too much discretion in sentencing. By contrast, liberals argued that parole boards had too much discretion, that they often base their decisions on factors unrelated to an offender's likely success on parole. Determinate sentencing, then, was designed to constrain the discretion of both judges and parole boards.

Within the criminal justice system, however, discretion never disappears; it simply passes to someone else. With determinate sentences, the chief beneficiaries have been prosecuting attorneys, a group that already enjoyed a great deal of discretion.

SENTENCING GUIDELINES

Sentencing guidelines prescribe the sentences judges must impose for certain crimes (based on the seriousness of the particular crime) and for certain offenders (based on the individual's criminal history). The objective is to limit the sentencing disparities that can occur from one offender to the next and from one judge to the next. Sentencing guidelines are based on determinate sentences; they take determinate sentences to the next level of specification. The prototype for sentencing guidelines comes from Minnesota, the first state in the country to develop guided sentences (Knapp 1984). Much has been written and said about Minnesota's sentencing process (see, for example, Knapp 1982, 1986; and Lagoy, Hussey, and Kramer 1978), but several issues are of importance to us here. First, the assumptions behind sentencing guidelines are that sentencing is a difficult process and that judges need all the help they can get. Underlying those assumptions is the belief that judges have too much discretion, which results in sentencing disparities. Sentencing guidelines, their proponents would argue, should promote more uniform sentences and limit the possibility of judges' abusing their sentencing powers (US Department of Justice 1988, 90–92).

Second, sentencing guidelines tend to focus on a limited number of factors. Minnesota's guidelines, for example, are based on a two-dimensional matrix (Knapp 1982, 1986; Mays 2012, 238). This means that the sentencing process considers only the present offense and the defendant's criminal history. Missing are factors such as race and ethnicity, economic status, drug or alcohol dependence, and employment history. Although judges might consider all of these relevant to their sentencing decisions, the Minnesota Sentencing Guidelines Commission believed they were not.

Third, sentencing guidelines do promote sentencing consistency, but they typically do not guarantee it. In most states, judges can depart from the guidelines by writing a justification for their decision to reduce or increase a prescribed sentence.

California is an example of a state that has taken sentencing guidelines a step further through the implementation of **presumptive sentences**—sentences calculated using a method defined in the statutes (Champion 2005, 199). Under this scheme, only the crime and the defendant's criminal history are variables in the determination of "normal" sentences. Here, too, judges can decrease or increase presumptive sentences by writing a statement that explains their reasons.

MANDATORY SENTENCES

One measure of increasing severity in sentencing is the development of **mandatory sentences**, penalties required by law for those convicted of certain offenses. Mandatory sentences can take several forms. One of the most common is *mandatory incarceration*. For example, Tennessee sets mandatory prison sentences for what it calls *Class X crimes*—first- and second-degree murder, aggravated rape, armed robbery, and other serious offenses. In addition, the law prohibits the dismissal or reduction of Class X charges without the trial judge's approval; the law also prohibits bail during an appeal and the use of suspended sentences or probation for Class X crimes (G. C. Thomas and Edelman 1988).

A second form of mandatory sentencing involves **mandatory minimums**, the least-severe penalties that can be imposed on offenders convicted of committing certain crimes. For instance, in 1974, Massachusetts adopted the Bartley-Fox handgun law, which mandates a minimum 1-year jail term for anyone carrying a gun without a license (see C).

Perhaps the most controversial form of mandatory sentencing stems from the so-called *three-strikes-and-you're-out legislation*. These laws mandate very long prison sentences—as long as life—for offenders found guilty of a third felony. Peter Benekos and Alida Merlo (1995) call these laws "politicized crime control policy" that moves beyond "getting tough" to "getting even tougher." As of 1995, 37 jurisdictions had proposed a three-strikes sanction. By 2004, 26 states and the federal government had adopted the sanction. The motivation behind the statutes seems to have been a small number of what Walker (2011) calls "celebrated" cases. One study of three-strikes sentencing notes,

> The intent of this campaign has primarily been to target dangerous offenders who habitually prey on innocent victims. The nature of this approach has involved an effort by both state and Federal legislators to enact policies that identify, and incapacitate for life, violent and/or nonviolent habitual offenders. (Turner et al. 1995, 16)

However, as Box 3.2 shows, both politicians and the public may be getting less than they bargained for, and paying more, with three-strikes sentencing.

BASEBALL MEETS CORRECTIONS   BOX 3.2

Nationwide, liberal and conservative politicians alike have rushed to demonstrate their outrage at heinous crimes, particularly crimes in which the perpetrator is a repeat offender. One response has been to introduce and pass three-strikes-and-you're-out legislation. Although these laws were intended to sanction habitual offenders more severely, they have had several unintended consequences as well.

One is cost. Peter Benekos and Alida Merlo suggest that harsher penalties remove the incentives for offenders to plea bargain, which increases the burden on criminal courts that are already shorthanded and constrained by space. To the costs of more judges, prosecutors, public defenders, and courtrooms, Benekos and Merlo add the costs of accommodating more prisoners: "There is little doubt that an immediate effect of the legislation will be to increase the already enormous prison population in the United States" (6).

These additional costs might be justified if the laws increased public safety, but not all of them do. Michael Turner and his colleagues note that many states include a number of nonviolent crimes in their habitual-offender statutes. This means that repeat property offenders, rather than violent personal offenders, are more likely to face third-strike sanctions. In the end, we may substantially increase the costs of operating our courts and our prisons to confine nonviolent offenders for life. Is it worth it?

SOURCES: BENEKOS AND MERLO (1995); TURNER ET AL. (1995).

AFTER THE VERDICT

Once a defendant has been found guilty, the judge typically delays sentencing until a presentence investigation can be completed. The investigation, which is carried out by the probation department, entails a thorough examination of the defendant's life history, including family, employment, personal, and legal status (see Chapter 4).

For every defendant who is placed on probation, a probation officer must develop, and a judge must approve, a probation plan that sets out the conditions the probationer must meet. If the convicted offender is sentenced to prison, a different set of actors comes into play. In most states, newly convicted felons who have been sentenced to prison are first sent to a correctional reception and diagnostic center. At this facility, staff members determine where each offender will be sent initially. In some states, judges have the authority to sentence individuals to specific facilities, but in most jurisdictions, this authority is reserved for the corrections department. Once the screening has been completed, new inmates are transported to the designated institution. There, they typically face more screening to determine whether assignment to the general population is appropriate and which housing unit seems best suited to their individual needs. One component of the screening is a risk assessment to determine the threat each inmate poses to the general population and the likelihood of a particular inmate's attempting to escape. Inmate housing usually does not change for the duration of the sentence unless the individual's circumstances change and a new assessment is made.

APPEALS

Prison inmates are stripped of many of their rights and practically all of their possessions, but they have an abundance of time. Some inmates spend their time scheming to escape, disturbing those around them, attempting to smuggle in contraband, and carrying on criminal enterprises within the prison walls. Others spend their time in more positive pursuits: enrolling in an educational program, learning a skill or trade, participating in bodybuilding, or using the prison's legal resources to challenge their convictions—we call them *jailhouse lawyers*.

Jailhouse lawyers are inmates who have developed an expertise at challenging their own convictions and those of other inmates (see, for example, J. Thomas 1988). Most are not attorneys, but they have studied the law and have learned how to write court documents. Through their expertise, these inmates have come to occupy a prominent role in prison society.

As a result of the potential power of jailhouse lawyers, some states have attempted to prohibit inmates from providing legal assistance to other inmates. Tennessee was one such state, and its policies prohibiting the activities of jailhouse lawyers were challenged before the US Supreme Court in *Johnson v. Avery* (1969). In that case, the Court held that inmates might be restricted but could not be prohibited from helping other inmates file appeals of their convictions or other legal documents (see Box 3.3). In 1977, the Court's decision in *Bounds v. Smith* expanded prisoners' access to the courts, making law books and other legal materials available to them in the institution and allowing them to consult with attorneys or paralegals who specialize in inmate appeals.

Inmates traditionally have used two legal mechanisms for appealing the conditions of their confinement or their convictions. For much of our history, the primary means of appeal has been the writ of habeas corpus (Mays 1981, 1984).

Under a **writ of habeas corpus** prisoners assert that they are being held unjustly and ask the court to require the state to justify the prisoners' conviction and incarceration. Thus, habeas corpus petitions challenge the very fact of incarceration, and a successful challenge means the conviction could be overturned and the prisoner retried or set free (Mays and Olszta 1989). Most inmates who are successful in their habeas corpus claims are retried rather than released. Although there has been a decline in civil rights cases in the past decade, since 1977, civil rights claims have played a more significant role than writs of habeas corpus in inmate appeals. Civil rights actions challenge not the fact of incarceration but the conditions under which an inmate is incarcerated.

JOHNSON V. AVERY, 393 U.S. 483 (1969)   BOX 3.3

The Tennessee Department of Corrections had a regulation that stated:

No inmate will advise, assist or otherwise contract to aid another, either with or without a fee, to prepare Writs or other legal matters. It is not intended that an innocent man be punished. When a man believes that he is unlawfully held or illegally convicted, he should prepare a brief or state his complaint in letter form and address it to his lawyer or a judge. A formal Writ is not necessary to receive a hearing. False charges or untrue complaints may be punished. Inmates are forbidden to set themselves up as practitioners for the purpose of promoting a business of writing Writs.

The petitioner was serving a life sentence in the Tennessee State Penitentiary when, in February 1965, he was transferred to the prison's maximum-security unit for violation of the policy. He appealed to the District Court of the Middle District of Tennessee for "law books and a typewriter." The district court held that the disciplinary confinement was unlawful and ordered him returned to his previous security classification.

The state of Tennessee appealed the district court's order, and the US Sixth Circuit Court of Appeals found in the state's favor. The court of appeals ruled that the state had an "interest . . . in preserving prison discipline and in limiting the practice of law to licensed attorneys" and that this interest "justified whatever burden the regulation might place on access to federal habeas corpus."

Justice Abe Fortas, writing for the US Supreme Court majority, noted, "In the absence of some provision by the State of Tennessee for a reasonable alternative to assist illiterate or poorly educated inmates in preparing petitions for post-conviction relief, the State may not validly enforce a regulation which absolutely bars inmates from furnishing such assistance to other prisoners." If Tennessee could not provide a *reasonable* alternative to jailhouse lawyering, the policy was unconstitutional.

One of the primary issues raised by inmates on appeal is access to the courts. Often, this is the most fundamental issue in the appeals process because it alleges that the inmate has been deprived of the legal references or assistance necessary to prepare whatever the substantive challenge may be. In many instances, *access to the courts* is really a catchall phrase for lack of counsel or ineffective representation by counsel. The appeal's substance indicates the appropriate remedy: If an inmate alleges that he or she is not receiving adequate legal assistance, the remedy would be to provide the necessary assistance. If the inmate alleges inadequate representation by counsel at trial, and the court finds that to be the case, the appropriate remedy would be a retrial.

Inmates also may challenge the trial procedures that resulted in their conviction. For instance, an inmate might claim that physical evidence or an admission of guilt was improperly admitted at trial. An inmate also could assert that he or she was denied the right to a jury trial or that the jury was improperly constituted. For example, in his appeal to the Supreme Court in *Batson v. Kentucky* (1986), the petitioner, a black man, alleged that blacks had been systematically excluded from his trial jury. The Court ruled that using race as a basis for excluding a juror is unconstitutional and remanded the case for further action. Another basis for appeal is the state's failure to try the case in a timely manner. The Supreme Court has defined in very broad terms what constitutes a speedy trial; today all of the states and the federal government have laws defining the time within which a suspect must be brought to trial, ranging from 60 to 360 days (Bureau of Justice Statistics 1988). If the time to trial exceeds the state's limits, many jurisdictions allow the trial court to dismiss all charges.

BOB DAEMRICH/ALAMY IMAGES

One of the most common bases of appeal is the judge's failure to instruct the jury properly—often by saying too much or too little. For instance, it can be an appealable error if the judge misstates a provision of the law. To prevent this, most judges simply read relevant portions of the law to the jury. An error of omission might be a judge's failure to instruct the jury on the general meaning of *probable cause* or on lesser included offenses for which the jury might find the defendant guilty. For example, in a first-degree murder trial, the judge normally gives instructions on first degree murder as well as second-degree murder, voluntary manslaughter, and involuntary manslaughter (Dressler 2009).

In appeals of criminal convictions, the appellate court must answer two basic questions: Was there an error? And was the error harmless? If the court finds an error but holds that it was harmless, the conviction usually is allowed to stand. If the error was not harmless, the appellate court may order the conviction

overturned and the defendant immediately released or held for retrial. In the case of a retrial, the trial court pays special attention to correcting the original error. In concluding this section, we should note several very important points:

- In general, the basis for an appeal is an error in law. That is, the judge must have made a mistake of some sort before or during the trial.

- Federal and state courts convict thousands of people each year, yet the percentage of cases appealed is fairly small.

- Of the convictions appealed, only a small percentage result in relief: Research from the late 1970s found that only about 3 percent of state appeals in federal courts succeed (US Department of Justice 1988, 88).

- Most successful appeals result in rehearings on specific issues or retrials of the case, not outright dismissals of the charges. Therefore, inmates are not leaving prisons in large numbers as a result of overturned convictions.

CONTEMPORARY TRENDS IN SENTENCING AND SOME THOUGHTS ON THE FUTURE

The punishment of criminal offenders in the United States has gone in two directions. First, there has been a movement to make sentences less severe for both adults and juveniles who commit minor offenses. We are diverting these offenders from the formal adjudication system and expanding the menu of sentences available to judges. These individuals are being sent to first-offender programs and driving while intoxicated (DWI) schools and are being ordered to perform community service in lieu of fines or incarceration.

At the same time, sanctions have become more severe for adults and juveniles who commit more serious crimes. The nation's perception of a crime wave, and the get-tough-on-crime laws legislatures are passing in response, mean that more offenders are being sentenced to prison for longer periods. The United States, say some critics, is in the midst of an imprisonment binge.

And what of the future? Certainly we expect the leniency shown first-time offenders to continue. We also expect penalties for habitual offenders to continue to be harsh. Some believe those penalties

should be even tougher. Some Americans, for example, are calling for the use of corporal punishment, the kind of punishment that is common in many Islamic and Asian countries (Newman 1983). Instead of sending people to prison—once thought to be a humane alternative to corporal or capital punishment—the state could subject them to caning (as is done in Singapore) and then release them. Although US jurisdictions probably will never cut off hands in the way some Islamic countries do, resurrecting public stocks may not be unrealistic.

Other suggestions make use of science and technology: genetic engineering to eliminate "criminal tendencies," electrodes implanted in an offender's brain to control behavior, and medications and surgical procedures to alter impulses. Already sexual predators are being treated with both surgical and chemical castration. And there are mood- and behavior-altering chemicals available that could be employed to "cure" criminal offenders.

Finally, the most exotic proposals involve vaporization or atomization, much like the transporter beam on the *Starship Enterprise*, or the use of cryogenics to deep-freeze offenders until some future date when their behavior can be modified by some yet-to-be invented method. It is also possible, given our current and future space travel technology that society will return to the transportation of prisoners to distant worlds where penal colonies will be established. Science fiction, you're thinking. But not really impossible.

SUMMARY

In this chapter, we have examined a broad range of issues dealing with the criminal law and particularly focusing on the sentencing process. Some of the major points covered in this chapter are the following:

- Legislative bodies define criminal behavior. They determine both the substantive law and procedural law. They distinguish felonies from misdemeanors and prescribe the appropriate punishments.

- Judges serve as the "triers of law" and juries serve as the "triers of fact" in cases that go to trial.

- Sentencing choices range from probation to fines, jail and prison sentences, and the death penalty.

- Prison sentences may be indeterminate or determinate and judges may impose them concurrently or consecutively.

- Offenders can appeal their convictions on writs of habeas corpus or through civil rights actions. The method of appeal chosen has implications for the most important form of relief.

THINKING ABOUT CORRECTIONAL POLICIES AND PRACTICES: WRITING ASSIGNMENTS

1   In a short essay (no more than one page) compare and contrast the elements of an adversarial system of justice with an inquisitional or accusatory system of justice.

2   There are several ways of categorizing or classifying crimes. List some of the different ways crimes are classified (especially based on seriousness) and provide a brief definition of each.

3   Divide the eight goals of sentencing into liberal and conservative categories. Write a few sentences for each one explaining your classification choice.

4   This is a difficult exercise, but it can be done. In no more than two pages, explain why you believe (or do not believe) that the death penalty serves a correctional purpose. This is not the same as taking a position for or against the death penalty. How do you feel about the possibility of an innocent person being executed?

5   Many inmates rely on the assistance of jailhouse lawyers to prepare their appeals for court. In a brief essay (two to three paragraphs), provide some of the reasons jailhouse lawyers write writs for other inmates.

KEY TERMS

accessories
accusatorial system
actus reus
adversarial system
affirmative defense
alibi
bifurcated hearings
common law
concurrent sentences
consecutive sentences
corpus delicti
criminal intent
day fine
determinate sentences
entrapment
equity
felonies
good-time credits

guilt beyond a reasonable doubt
horizontal overcharging
inchoate offenses
indeterminate sentences
infancy defense
inquisitorial system
insanity defense
intermediate sanctions
irresistible-impulse test
mandatory minimums
mandatory sentences
means-based penalties
mens rea
misdemeanors
M'Naughton rule
personal offense
petty misdemeanors

plea bargaining
preponderance of the evidence
presumption of innocence
presumptive sentences
principals
probation
procedural law
property offenders
proportionality
Racketeer Influenced and Corrupt Organizations (RICO) Statute
sentencing guidelines
social debt
substantive law
vertical overcharging
writ of habeas corpus

CRITICAL REVIEW QUESTIONS

1   What is meant by the concept of social debt, and how does it figure into the types and amounts of punishment that seem appropriate in a given case?

2   The chapter introduces the concepts of *actus reus* and *mens rea* in relation to the commission of crimes. What does each of these terms mean and why is each a necessary element in proving that a crime occurred?

3 The chapter discusses four of the most common affirmative defenses. What is an "affirmative defense," what are the four examples mentioned, and what distinguishes these defenses from any other defenses that might be raised?

4 Which of the eight goals of sentencing listed at the beginning of the chapter seem most influential today?

5 Define and describe the concept of probation. Based on the numbers provided in the chapter, how important is probation to the field of corrections in the United States? Explain.

6 Day fines are described as means-based penalties. What do we mean by this description? Why aren't day fines (or similar punishments) used more often in the United States? Do such penalties conflict with other notions of justice?

7 What are the different types of sentences that can be imposed on convicted offenders? Who decides which offenders get which sentences?

8 What do we mean by intermediate sanctions? Give examples of some of the punishments that would fit into this category.

9 Some say that sentencing is the most complex and time-consuming function performed by the courtroom work group. What are several factors that add to the complexity of the process?

10 What kinds of cases are likely to bring about calls for three-strikes-and-you're-out legislation? Have any of these types of cases been in the news lately? Describe one that has gone to trial and been decided. Do you agree or disagree with the outcome (verdict and sentence)? Explain your answer.

CASES CITED

Batson v. Kentucky, 476 U.S. 79 (1986)
Bounds v. Smith, 430 U.S. 817 (1977)
Furman v. Georgia, 408 U.S. 238 (1972)
Gregg v. Georgia, 428 U.S. 153 (1976)
Johnson v. Avery, 393 U.S. 483 (1969)

Ring v. Arizona, 536 U.S. 584 (2002)
Roper v. Simmons, 543 U.S. 551 (2005)
Stanford v. Kentucky, 492 U.S. 361 (1989)
United States v. Russell, 411 U.S. 423 (1973)

NOTES

1 In English common law, attempts and conspiracies to commit crimes were treated as misdemeanors; most jurisdictions now classify them as felonies (Dressler 2009).

2 The 11 states that have changed their laws are Alaska, Delaware, Georgia, Illinois, Indiana, Kentucky, Michigan, New Mexico, Pennsylvania, South Carolina, and South Dakota; the four states that have eliminated the insanity defense are Idaho, Kansas, Montana, and Utah.

3 Probationers under house arrest are allowed to work outside the home but usually must return directly home after work and remain there, except for emergencies, until they leave for work the next morning.

4 Maricopa County, Arizona; Richmond County, New York; four courts in Oregon; and one court each in Connecticut and Iowa.

5 *Intermittent confinement* involves alternating periods of incarceration and freedom. *Shock incarceration* is a short period of confinement, perhaps in a traditional prison or a military-style camp, followed by community supervision; it usually is reserved for first-time offenders.

6 *Aggravating circumstances* are factors relating to the commission of a crime that increase the seriousness of the offense; *mitigating circumstances* are factors surrounding the commission of a crime that could reduce the responsibility of the offender.

7   It is very difficult to determine the proportion of Hispanics on death row. Hispanics are an ethnic group, which means they could be classified in more than one racial category. We do know that Hispanics constituted more than 16 percent of the general population in the United States in 2010 and that they accounted for just over 12 percent of the death row inmates that year whose ethnicity was known (Snell 2011, 10). But the fact that many Hispanics are likely to self-identify as white could well mean that the 12 percent figure understates their prevalence among death row inmates. We discuss race and ethnicity in detail in Chapter 13.

REFERENCES

Abadinsky, Howard. 2012. *Probation and parole: Theory and practice*, 11th edn. Upper Saddle River, NJ: Prentice Hall/Pearson.

American Law Institute. 1985. *Model penal code*. Philadelphia, PA: American Law Institute.

Amnesty International. 2012. "Figures on the death penalty." Retrieved on July 9, 2013 from: from **http://www.amnesty.org/en/death-penalty/numbers**

Banks, Cyndi. 2009. *Criminal justice ethics: Theory and practice*, 2nd edn. Thousand Oaks, CA: Sage Publications.

Benekos, Peter J., and Alida V. Merlo. 1995. Three strikes and you're out! The political sentencing game. *Federal Probation* 59(1): 3–9.

Bonczar, Thomas P., and Tracy L. Snell. 2006. *Capital punishment, 2005*. Washington, DC: US Department of Justice.

Bureau of Justice Assistance. 1996. *How to use structured fines (day fines) as an intermediate sanction*. Washington, DC: US Government Printing Office.

Bureau of Justice Statistics. 1988. *Report to the nation on crime and justice*, 2nd edn. Washington, DC: US Government Printing Office.

Champion, Dean. 2005. *The American dictionary of criminal justice*, 3rd edn. Los Angeles, CA: Roxbury.

Clear, Todd R. 1988. A critical assessment of electronic monitoring in corrections. *Policy Studies Review* 7(3): 671–81.

Davis, Angela J. 2007. *Arbitrary justice: The power of the American prosecutor*. New York: Oxford University Press.

Dressler, Joshua. 2009. *Understanding criminal law*, 5th edn. Newark, NJ: LexisNexis.

Eisenstein, James, and Herbert Jacob. 1977. *Felony justice: An organizational analysis of criminal courts*. Boston: Little, Brown.

FindLaw. 2012. "Current Application of the Insanity Defense." Retrieved on July 9, 2013 from: **http://criminal.findlaw.com/criminal-procedure/current-application-of-the-insanity-defense.html**

Ford, Daniel, and Annesley K. Schmidt. 1985. *Electronically monitored home confinement*. Washington, DC: US Government Printing Office.

Gershman, Bennett L. 2009. "Why prosecutors misbehave." In *Courts and justice*, 4th edn., edited by G. Larry Mays and Peter R. Gregware. Long Grove, IL: Waveland Press, 321–31.

Glaze, Lauren E. 2011. *Correctional population in the United States, 2010*. Washington, DC: Bureau of Justice Statistics, US Department of Justice.

Glaze, Lauren E., and Thomas P. Bonczar. 2011. *Probation and parole in the United States, 2010*. Washington, DC: Bureau of Justice Statistics, US Department of Justice.

Gowdy, Voncile B. 1993. *Intermediate sanctions*. Washington, DC: US Department of Justice.

Kassin, Saul M. 2009. "The American Jury: Handicapped in the Pursuit of Justice." In *Courts and justice*, 4th edn., edited by G. Larry Mays and Peter R. Gregware. Long Grove, IL: Waveland Press, 154–83.

Knapp, Kay. 1982. The impact of the Minnesota sentencing guidelines on sentencing practices. *Hamline Law Review* 5: 237–56.

Knapp, Kay. 1984. What sentencing reform in Minnesota has and has not accomplished. *Judicature* 68: 181–9.

Knapp, Kay. 1986. Proactive policy analysis of Minnesota's prison populations. *Criminal Justice Policy Review* 1: 37–57.

Lagoy, Stephen P., Frederick A. Hussey, and John H. Kramer. 1978. A comparative assessment of determinate sentencing in the four pioneer states. *Crime & Delinquency* 24: 385–400.

Lippke, Richard L. 2011. *The ethics of plea bargaining*. New York: Oxford University Press.

Mays, G. Larry. 1981. Supreme Court disengagement from the exclusionary rule: The impact of *Stone v. Powell*. *Criminal Justice Review* 6(2): 43–6.

Mays, G. Larry. 1984. The Supreme Court and development of federal habeas corpus doctrine. In *Legal issues in criminal justice: The courts*, edited by Sloan Letman, Dan Edwards, and Daniel Bell. Cincinnati, OH: Anderson, 55–69.

Mays, G. Larry. 1989. The impact of federal sentencing guidelines on jail and prison overcrowding and early release. In *The U.S. sentencing guidelines: Implications for criminal justice*, edited by Dean J. Champion. New York: Praeger, 181–200.

Mays, G. Larry. 2012. *American courts and the judicial process*. New York: Oxford University Press.

Mays, G. Larry, and Michelle Olszta. 1989. Prison litigation: From the 1960s to the 1990s. *Criminal Justice Policy Review* 3(3): 279–98.

Mays, G. Larry, and L. Thomas Winfree, Jr. 2012. *Juvenile justice*, 3rd edn. New York: Wolters Kluwer Law & Business.

Neubauer, David W. 2008. *America's courts and the criminal justice system*, 9th edn. Belmont, CA: Wadsworth.

Newman, Graeme. 1983. *Just and painful: A case for the corporal punishment of criminals*. New York: Macmillan.

Reichel, Philip L. 2012. *Comparative criminal justice systems: A topical approach*, 6th edn. Upper Saddle Creek, NJ: Prentice Hall.

Renzema, Marc, and David T. Skelton. 1990. *Use of electronic monitoring in the United States: 1989 update*. Washington, DC: US Department of Justice.

Rosenmerkel, Sean, Matthew Durose, and Donald Farole, Jr. 2009. *Felony sentences in state courts, 2006—statistical tables*. Washington, DC: Bureau of Justice Statistics, US Department of Justice.

Rush, George E. 2003. *The dictionary of criminal justice*, 6th edn. New York: McGraw Hill.

Schubert, Frank August. 2010. *Criminal law*, 2nd edn. Austin, TX: Wolters Kluwer Law & Business.

Singer, Richard G., and John Q. La Fond. 2007. *Criminal law*, 4th edn. Austin, TX: Wolters Kluwer Law & Business.

Snell, Tracy L. 2011. *Capital punishment, 2010—statistical tables*. Washington, DC: Bureau of Justice Statistics, US Department of Justice.

Thomas, George C., III, and David Edelman. 1988. An evaluation of conservative crime control theology. *Notre Dame Law Review* 63(2): 123–60.

Thomas, Jim. 1988. *Prison litigation: The paradox of the jailhouse lawyer*. Totowa, NJ: Rowman and Littlefield.

Turner, Michael G., Jody L. Sundt, Brandon K. Applegate, and Francis T. Cullen. 1995. "Three strikes and you're out" legislation: A national assessment. *Federal Probation* 59(3): 16–35.

US Department of Justice. 1981. *Dictionary of criminal justice data terminology*. Washington, DC: US Government Printing Office.

US Department of Justice. 1988. *Report to the nation on crime and justice*, 2nd edn. Washington, DC: US Government Printing Office.

Van den Haag, Ernest. 1975. *Punishing criminals: Concerning a very old and painful question*. New York: Basic Books.

Van den Haag, Ernest., and John Conrad. 1983. *The death penalty: A debate*. New York: Plenum Press.

Walker, Samuel. 2006. *Sense and nonsense about crime and drugs: A policy guide*, 6th edn. Belmont, CA: Wadsworth.

Walker, Samuel. 2011. *Sense and nonsense about crime and drugs*, 7th edn. Belmont, CA: Wadsworth.

Winterfield, Laura A., and Sally T. Hillsman. 1993. *The Staten Island day-fine project*. Washington, DC: US Department of Justice.

Zimring, Franklin E., and Gordon Hawkins. 1986. *Capital punishment and the American agenda*. New York: Cambridge University Press.

PROBATION AND COMMUNITY CORRECTIONS

JIM WEST/ALAMY IMAGES

Outline

Objectives

- To provide you with an historical context for modern probation and community corrections

- To acquaint you with the mechanisms by which probation is provided, monitored, and revoked in contemporary US jurisdictions

- To introduce you to the evolving topic of community corrections

- To help you understand the issues and trends in probation and community corrections

Essentials of Corrections, Fifth Edition. G. Larry Mays and L. Thomas Winfree, Jr.
© 2014 John Wiley & Sons, Inc. Published 2014 by John Wiley & Sons, Inc.

INTRODUCTION

In this chapter, we examine the reasons federal, state, and local governments are willing to take the risks associated with nonsecure alternatives to prison and jail, and at the nature of probation and other community-based corrections programs. Community-based corrections and probation can be included in the same sentence handed down by the court. Thus, it is possible to consider probation to be one of the earliest forms of community corrections.

Before we examine those issues, however, we must consider several points. First, probation and community-based programs are key parts of the corrections mission in the United States. They stand as viable—and less costly—alternatives to incarceration. One factor that explains the utility of these programs is their variety: they range from interventions that remove offenders from the system even before the adjudication process begins to confinement short of incarceration in prison or jail.

Second, it is important to recognize that probation and community-based programs have both supporters and detractors. Program outcomes—particularly high-profile failures—are a source of contention between these two groups; other points of contention reflect philosophical differences about how society should treat convicted criminals (go back to the review of examination of "Philosophies of Punishment" in Chapter 1).

Finally, despite this ongoing debate, in time we expect probation *and* other community-based alternatives to incarceration will continue to dominate corrections. We base this statement on several sets of observations:

- As indicated in earlier chapters, most correctional institutions in the United States today are operating at or above their rated capacity. Local, state, and federal agencies can expand or replace them with larger facilities, but both actions are expensive and time consuming. If we have learned anything in the past decades, it is that we cannot build our way out of the jail- and prison-crowding crisis (see, for example, Thompson and Mays 1991; Welch 1994, 1996). Probation and community corrections continue to function as cost-effective alternatives to secure institutionalization (Sigler and Lamb 1995).

- The public, policymakers, and corrections administrators are not satisfied with the "lock them up or do nothing" choice that seemed to drive sentencing decisions in the past. Probation and community-based programs demand greater accountability from offenders than typically was required in standard probation programs. In addition, some would argue that in doing so they reduce the risk to public safety (DeMichele, Payne, and Matz 2011; Rackmill 1993).

- Probation and community corrections, because they offer more treatment options than in the past, have a greater likelihood of helping offenders become contributing members of society (Benekos 1990). This is especially true when the program emphasizes both the control *and* care of the client (Skeem and Machak 2008).

- Historically, probation and community corrections allowed those with a punishment and control orientation to maintain the fiction of treatment and therapy (Benekos and Merlo 1995). Today, both scholars and practitioners have begun to call for increased reliance on community corrections and a rejection of imprisonment as the first and best penal response (Listwan, Jonson, Cullen, and Latessa 2008; Lutze et al. 2012).

To summarize, this chapter has two primary functions. First, it introduces probation as a punishment and examines its history, process, current applications, and future. Second, it explores community-based alternatives to incarceration. Some of these alternatives serve as pretrial constraints on the liberty of the accused; others function as ancillaries to or in lieu of traditional probation. Our look at alternatives to secure facilities for accused and convicted offenders begins with the origins of probation.

THE HISTORY OF PROBATION

Probation is the conditional freedom granted an offender by a court. It is a test of whether the probationer can live in the community without committing new crimes or violate the conditions of release into the community. Even before probation had evolved into its current form, certain legal remedies allowed accused and convicted criminals alike to prove they deserved a second chance. Those remedies—the forerunners of modern probation—included judicial reprieve, bail, and release on one's own recognizance.

FORERUNNERS OF MODERN PROBATION

Judicial reprieve has a direct link to modern probation. A common practice in medieval English courts, **judicial reprieve** was the suspension of a penal sanction for a fixed time. A reprieve gave an offender time to petition the Crown for mercy, which was the only way a sentence—usually the death penalty—could be permanently set aside. Originally used only as a stay of execution, later courts used the judicial reprieve to delay any sentence indefinitely.

By the eighteenth century, English judges began suspending sentences in return for a specified period of good behavior. Once offenders proved they could live crime-free, they petitioned the Crown for a full or partial pardon. Judicial reprieve was also essential to the English transportation program: it allowed the courts to suspend the imposition of sentences for prisoners destined for a British colony. A century later, the US judicial system adopted the judicial reprieve. The importance of judicial reprieve for probation cannot be overstated. To give convicted offenders a second chance, judges needed a discretionary means to stop the imposition of a sentence. Judicial reprieve was ideal for this purpose.

For hundreds of years, bail and release on recognizance were the only means by which the accused could avoid confinement. **Bail** is money or property pledged to or held by the court to ensure that an arrested and charged individual will appear for trial. If someone other than the accused posts the bail, that person (or company) assumes responsibility for ensuring the accused appears in court at the scheduled time.

As practiced for centuries under English Common Law, **release on recognizance (ROR)** operated much like modern bail: the accused posted a bond or surety deposit with the court. Its formalization can be traced to the **Habeas Corpus Act of 1679**, an act of the English parliament, which stated: "A Magistrate shall discharge prisoners from their Imprisonment taking their Recognizance, with one or more Surety or Sureties, in any Sum according to the Magistrate's discretion, unless it shall appear that the Party is committed for such Matter or offences for which by law the Prisoner is not bailable" (British History Online 2012).

In 1830, ROR came to mean release from custody based solely on one's personal word to return for trial. It is highly likely that ROR was used in other US criminal cases prior to 1830; however, there are no official records of its application prior to this date (Grinnell 1941). That year, Boston Municipal Court Judge Peter Oxenbridge Thatcher allowed Jerusha Chase, a defendant he had found guilty of thievery, to leave the court's custody with the promise that she would return when her presence was required (Augustus 1852; Grinnell 1941). Apparently, Chase and several supporting friends persuaded Judge Thatcher that justice would better be served if Jerusha was not imprisoned but rather set free. The use of ROR as a sentencing alternative was appealed by a writ of certiorari to the Massachusetts's Supreme Court, but that writ was denied and the sentence stood (*Commonwealth v. Jerusha Chase* 1831; Grinnell 1941, 23). Seven years later, the Massachusetts legislature tied monetary sureties to recognizance. ROR is another important legal basis for what we call today probation. It remained, however, for a colorful Bostonian, John Augustus, to give the practice its name and a set of operational procedures.

JOHN AUGUSTUS: THE FATHER OF PROBATION

John Augustus was a wealthy shoemaker when he began an 18-year association with the Boston courts in a quasi-official capacity supervising individuals convicted by the court but released into his care for a period of time, something Augustus called probation. By his death in 1859, Augustus had "bailed on probation" 1,152 men and 794 women (Barnes and Teeters 1959, 554). Augustus believed that crime prevention was the intent of society's laws, and that sanctions should reform criminals, rather than simply punish. A member of the temperance movement, a religious and political effort to combat the evils of alcohol, Augustus was forever changed by a visit to a Boston courtroom. He described it this way: "I was in court one morning . . . in which the man was charged with being a common drunkard. He told me that if he could be saved from the House of Corrections, he never again would taste intoxicating liquors: I bailed him, by permission of the Court" (1852/1972, 4–5).

After carefully selecting his charges, Augustus helped them secure jobs and homes. He supervised them in the community, giving each one a set of conditions intended to yield prosocial changes. Augustus warned them that a return to the old ways would mean a return to court. At the end of a short supervision period, perhaps as little as two or three weeks, Augustus would give the court an impartial report on the offender's behavior. He coined the term probation, derived from a Latin word meaning to prove or test, as an apt description of his approach to bailing out and treating offenders. Augustus was the first to conduct presentence investigations, to set conditions of release, to make supervision mandatory, to report on probationers' progress, and to revoke the conditional release. Revocation was rare: Augustus claimed that only one of his first 1,100 probationers forfeited bail (Dressler 1962, 18).

THE GROWTH OF PROBATION SERVICES

After Augustus died, volunteers continued to provide probation for Boston's courts until the city hired a professional probation officer in 1878, the year the Commonwealth of Massachusetts adopted a probation statute. It was 1897, almost 20 years later, before a second state, Missouri, adopted a "bench parole

law" authorizing its courts to suspend sentences under certain conditions. The Missouri statute also provided that a "parole officer" supervise this misnamed form of probation (Glueck 1933, 231). Vermont (1898), Rhode Island (1899), New Jersey (1900), and New York (1901) quickly joined the probation services movement. Between 1903 and 1923, 20 more states and the District of Columbia added probation services. Two-thirds of the state legislatures legalized probation first for juveniles, sometimes taking as much as 20 years to enact similar provisions for adults (Johnson 1928, 12–13).

Federal authorities failed to embrace probation with the same enthusiasm as the states did. In the nineteenth century, federal judges suspended sentences in cases where imprisonment would have caused unusual hardship. In 1916, in *Killits (Ex parte United States)*, a first-time embezzler made full restitution and avoided prison. When the federal judge suspended a 5-year sentence, he referred to banker Killits's otherwise good reputation and high standing in the community. The Supreme Court ruled unanimously that the trial court did not have the constitutional authority to suspend the sentence. The National Probation Association and other probation proponents saw the decision as a mandate and lobbied Congress to pass enabling legislation. President Calvin Coolidge signed a probation bill into law in 1925, creating what we know today as the US Probation and Pretrial Services System.

THE ADMINISTRATION OF PROBATION

As previously noted, probation refers to the practice of conditionally releasing an offender into the community. The releasing authority is the trial court, part of the judiciary. However, either the judicial branch *or* the executive branch of state or local government provides probation services—distinctions in practice that owe as much to tradition as to policy (American Correctional Association [ACA] 2003). Table 4.1 shows that in most jurisdictions, responsibility for probation services lies with the executive branch of the state government. New York is the only jurisdiction that places control of probation with the local

TABLE 4.1 **Adult probation authorities in the United States, 2012.**

State Administration			Local Administration	
Judicial Branch	Executive Branch		Judicial Branch	Executive Branch
Colorado	Alabama	Nevada	Arizona	New York[a]
Connecticut	Alaska	New Hampshire	California	
Hawaii	Arkansas	New York[a]	District of Columbia	
Massachusetts	Delaware	North Mexico	Illinois	
Nebraska	Florida	North Carolina	Indiana	
New Jersey	Georgia	North Dakota	Kansas	
South Dakota	Idaho	Ohio	Pennsylvania[b]	
West Virginia	Iowa	Oklahoma	Texas	
	Kentucky	Oregon		
	Louisiana	Pennsylvania[b]		
	Maine	Rhode Island		
	Maryland	South Carolina		
	Michigan	Utah		
	Mississippi	Vermont		
	Missouri	Virginia		
	Montana	Wisconsin		
		Wyoming		

NOTES: [a]NEW YORK CITY DEPARTMENT OF PROBATION IS SEPARATE FROM THE NEW YORK STATE OFFICE OF PROBATION AND CORRECTIONAL ALTERNATIVES.
[b]IN TWO PENNSYLVANIA COUNTIES, PROBATION OFFICERS SERVE UNDER THE SUPERVISION OF THE LOCAL JUDICIARY; OTHERWISE, THEY ARE A STATE EXECUTIVE AGENCY.
SOURCES: AMERICAN CORRECTIONAL ASSOCIATION (2003); MODIFIED AND UPDATED BY THE AUTHORS.

executive (New York City Probation Department) and state executive (Office of Probation and Correctional Alternatives, under the New York State Division of Criminal Justice Services); Pennsylvania splits its probation services between the executive and judicial branches, but the latter is the case in only two counties.

ELIGIBILITY FOR PROBATION

The Supreme Court ruled in *United States v. Birnbaum* (1970) that probation is a privilege, not a right. The probation-granting authority is under no constitutional or statutory obligation to choose conditional release over incarceration. In fact, both federal and state statutes actually prohibit probation for certain types of offenses. For example, most states deny probation to offenders convicted of murder, kidnapping, or rape (Abadinsky 2011). In practice, half of all probationers are convicted of no crime more serious than a misdemeanor (Glaze and Bonczar 2011, 1).

PROBATION OFFICERS

The various jurisdictions in the United States take several different approaches to probation work. First, as reflected in Table 4.2, 17 states use probation-only officers. This model acknowledges that separate government entities grant probation and parole. That is, probation officers are sworn officers of the judicial branch, as are judges, attorneys, and even bailiffs. In many jurisdictions, judges or court administrators hire, train, evaluate, and fire probation officers. In

TABLE 4.2 Probation functions, including peace officer and firearms statuses, by jurisdiction, 2012.

Probation-Only Officers		Combined Probation/Parole Officers	
Arizona[a,e]	Massachusetts[c,f]	Alabama[a,d]	New Hampshire[c,d]
California[a,e]	Nebraska[c,f]	Alaska[a,e]	New Mexico[a,e]
Colorado[a,f]	New Jersey[c,f]	Arkansas[a,d]	North Carolina[b,e]
Connecticut[a,f]	New York[a,e]	Delaware[a,e]	North Dakota[a,d]
Georgia[a,d]	Ohio[b,e]	District of Columbia[a,f]	Oklahoma[a,e]
Hawaii[c,d]	South Dakota[c,f]	Florida[c,e]	Oregon[a,e]
Illinois[a,d]	Texas[c,e]	Idaho[a,e]	Pennsylvania[b,e]
Indiana[c,e]	West Virginia[c,e]	Iowa[a,e]	Rhode Island[c,f]
Kansas[c,f]		Kentucky[a,e]	South Carolina[a,d]
		Louisiana[a,d]	Tennessee[c,f]
		Maine[c,e]	Utah[a,d]
		Maryland[c,f]	Virginia[c,e]
		Michigan[c,e]	Vermont[c,f]
		Minnesota[c,f]	Washington[a,d]
		Mississippi[a,e]	Wisconsin[c,f]
		Missouri[c,e]	Wyoming[c,f]
		Montana[c,e]	US Probation and Pretrial Services[a,d]
		Nevada[a,d]	

NOTES: [a]ALL OFFICERS ARE CERTIFIED PEACE OFFICERS; [b]SOME OFFICERS ARE CERTIFIED PEACE OFFICERS; [c]NO OFFICERS ARE CERTIFIED PEACE OFFICER; [d]OFFICERS REQUIRED TO CARRY FIREARMS; [e]SOME SPECIALLY TRAINED OFFICERS CARRY FIREARMS OR FIREARMS ARE OPTIONAL OR CONDITIONAL, DEPENDING ON DUTIES; [f]NO OFFICERS MAY CARRY FIREARMS.
SOURCES: AMERICAN PROBATION AND PAROLE ASSOCIATION (2006, 2012); US COURTS (2007); MODIFIED AND UPDATED BY THE AUTHORS.

some jurisdictions, however, probation officers occupy state-level civil service positions. The second approach combines probation and parole functions. In 33 states, the District of Columbia, and the US Probation and Pretrial Services, officers either have mixed probation and parole caseloads or specialize in one or the other. Specialization recognizes the adjustment problems faced by individuals reentering society from prison as contrasted with probationers (Girard and Wormwith 2004).

A second set of issues addressed in Table 4.2 combines peace officer certification with the arming of probation officers, a practice that has been an issue among probation officers and authorities for decades (Brown 1990). No single prototype emerges from this table, although in 23 jurisdictions, including the US Probation and Pretrial Service, all officers are certified peace officers and must either carry weapons at all times or when performing special duties, such as arresting a probationer. Another pattern, found in 12 states, is where the probation officers are not certified peace officers and may not be armed while on duty. After these two the remaining combinations are a bit stranger. Probation officers are not certified as peace officers but must or may carry firearms or must carry them under certain circumstances in 11 jurisdictions. A rarer situation is when some agents are peace officers and are conditionally armed, which occurs in three jurisdictions. An equally rare combination, found in two states and the District of Columbia, is where certified peace officers are forbidden from carrying side arms. Unlike traditional law enforcement officers in the United States, then no single pattern concerning the peace officer and firearms statuses of probation officers has yet to emerge.

PRESENTENCE INVESTIGATION AND REPORT

A **presentence investigation (PSI)** is a detailed examination, prepared by a probation officer, caseworker, or other court officer, of a criminal defendant's life. The PSI reviews the offender's records (school, police, and, with a court order, medical records) and the thoughts of people who had regular contact with the offender (family members, friends, coworkers, teachers, coaches, religious leaders). The PSI also involves interviews with witnesses to the crime, the investigating police officers, and the victims or victims' next of kin. The product of this lengthy examination is a PSI report that contains a sentencing recommendation.

Few documents take on greater significance in a convicted-felon's life than the PSI report. It can spell the difference between probation and incarceration. In the past, PSI reports were lengthy; today, in most jurisdictions, the reports are short, standardized documents that probation officers present to the judge or the jury before sentencing. The fact that judges rarely reviewed the long-form PSI reports eased the move to more concise reports. The shorter forms lay out the key factors in a sentencing recommendation. Their courtroom experience—especially their understanding of the judge or judges they serve—may well shape the factors probation officers choose to include in PSI reports and even in their recommendations. Probation officers learn early in their careers what judges consider pertinent facts. In addition, the officers' bottom-line recommendations may reflect what they have observed at previous sentencing hearings or learned from other probation officers. Whatever the reason—the officers' investigative skills or their ability to write for the audience—the outcome is often the same: judges follow PSI recommendations between 70 and 90 percent of the time (Comptroller General of the United States 1976). While these estimates are over 30 years old, it is doubtful that the situation has changed. As we shall see, given modern risk-assessment methods, the current ratio is probably closer to the upper range (90 percent) than the lower (70 percent).

In the PSI, probation officers answer three questions. First, what circumstances promote a sentence other than prison? Second, what aggravating circumstances

suggest that prison, rather than a community-based sentence, is the best alternative for this offender? Third, does the defendant—now a convicted criminal—have special needs or problems that the free community can meet best? If the answer to the first or third questions suggests an alternative other than incarceration, then the court usually asks a follow-up question: Will the offender's continued presence in the community pose a public safety risk? As we will see later in this chapter, risk assessment is a critical part of offender classification and can depend a great deal on what is contained in the PSI.

Much of the PSI's content is legally hearsay: that is, someone other than the informant either saw or heard the defendant do or say something. Probation officers should crosscheck the validity and accuracy of both mitigating and aggravating information before including it. Although officers can extend tentative confidentiality to informants, the judge may require that informants testify to confirm the information's reliability (*Gardner v. Florida* 1977).

Two factors may intervene between a probation officer's recommendation and the trial court's sentence. First, we suspect that in a large number of cases, the prosecutor determines the sentence through the plea-bargaining process (see Chapter 3). What is the role of the PSI report if both prosecuting, defense attorneys, and the defendant agree on an appropriate sentence? In jurisdictions where PSI reports are prepared before trial, a report may well influence the plea agreement's terms. In addition, a report can validate the plea-bargain agreement, increasing the likelihood of the judge's approval.

Second, crowding may mean that jail or prison is not an option for some offenders. Simply put, if the choice is between incarcerating a violent offender with a long criminal record or a first-time nonviolent offender—no matter how serious the offense—the court is going to send the former to prison and to place the latter on probation.

RISK-MANAGEMENT CLASSIFICATIONS, CASELOAD, AND WORKLOAD ISSUES

Rather than simply dividing caseloads into felony or misdemeanor probationers, most probation departments make use of risk-management classifications. More than two-dozen classification instruments exist, most based on the National Institute of Corrections (NIC) Model Probation Client Classification and Case Management System or the Wisconsin's Correctional Assessment and Intervention System (CAIS) (Andrew, Bonta, and Wormwith 2006; Harris, Gingerich, and Whittaker 2004). The instruments generally recommend assignment to one of the following four supervision levels (Bartollas and Conrad 1992, 242; Jalbert et al. 2011):

- *Administrative* is for the lowest risk offenders, who are generally viewed as posing no serious public safety threat, along with virtually no history of crime. Probation officers' contacts with these probationers are minimal and are generally reactive-only, not proactive.

- *Minimum supervision* is for offenders who pose no significant public safety threat and have no history of serious crime (that is, their offenses mainly are misdemeanors or, in fewer instances, property felonies). These low-risk probationers generally contact their probation officer by mail or phone once a month or even less frequently.

- *Medium supervision* is for offenders who pose no significant threat to public safety but who do have histories of serious crime. These releasees must report in person at least once a month, and the officer may make occasional visits to their places of work or residence.

- *Intensive supervision* is for offenders who have histories of violent behavior. They must report to their probation officer several times a month and are subject to even more frequent workplace and home visits than are probationers under medium supervision.

Much depends on the correct classification of any given offender. Cases of misclassification, and incorrect supervision levels, abound in the popular press, as examples of "system failure." Box 4.1 contains a review of the issues and outcomes related to offender classification.

The number of clients, or **caseload**, assigned to a given supervision officer varies widely. **Workload** is a different correctional idea, and it refers to the amount of time needed to complete various tasks associated with supervising one's clients. As DeMichele (2007, 5) notes, caseload grows as the offender populations grow, while workload, tied to the hours in a day, week, month or year, remains stagnant. It is also important to note the distinctions between workload and caseload approaches and the implications for officers and their agencies. For example, the caseload approach focuses on the number of offenders assigned to an individual officer, while the workload approach addresses the amount of effort expended for the different tasks the officer must perform.[1] In the former, cases are assigned based on individual offender characteristics, while in the latter, assignment is linked to the expertise of a given officer. The caseload method assumes that each supervisee requires the same effort, while the workload method recognizes the importance of distributing tasks tied to the offenders' needs. Using a caseload approach, the number of cases supervised is typically determined in accordance with the supervision level assigned to the probationers (see Table 4.3). Using a workload method, the time spent on an individual case may vary according to supervision level, type of offense, and supervisee needs, a much more individualized approach that can lead to much less predictability as to an individual officer's output per month. In practice, officers using this approach have only so much time a month to spent on a given activity (e.g., case planning, conducting home visits, conducting office visits, communications with

TABLE 4.3 APPA recommended number of probation supervisees per officer.

Supervision Level (low to high)	Supervisees per officer	Available time per supervisee[a]
Administrative	No limit: 1,000	.12 hours
Minimum	200	.61 hours
Medium	50	2.44 hours
Intensive	20	6.04 hours

NOTES: [a]BASED ON AN ESTIMATED 122 HOURS PER MONTH IN A GIVEN OFFICER'S WORKLOAD (I.E., MINUS AVERAGE SICK AND VACATION LEAVE, HOLIDAYS, TRAINING TIME, AND NON-CASE TIMES).
SOURCE: DEMICHELE, BRIAN, AND MATZ (2011, 17); MODIFIED BY THE AUTHORS.

ZUMA PRESS INC/ALAMY IMAGES

others, reporting to the court, promoting supervisee accountability through strict monitoring of conditions, and enforcing conditions through arrest and formal sanctions). Community corrections professionals express more support for the caseload method than the workload approach (DeMichele and Payne 2007).

Reliable estimates of actual working ratios of supervisory officers to clients served are rare. Recent case-based workload assessments conducted by the American Probation and Parole Association (APPA) support a wide range of probationer-to-officer ratios, all based on the supervision level assigned to the probationer, as reflected in Table 4.3.

As noted above, the number of supervisees alone does not determine an officer's workload. Moreover, in some jurisdictions probation officers may have a **mixed caseload**—both misdemeanants and felons among the probationers they supervise. For these officers, the felony probationers are likely to be more time consuming. In jurisdictions in which officers work exclusively with misdemeanor probationers, caseloads of 500, 750, or even 1,000 are common. Misdemeanor probationers, the thinking goes, require less supervision; in effect, as administrative supervisees, they are paperwork probationers.

THE CONDITIONS OF PROBATION

The 1967 Task Force on Corrections identified the need for differential treatment of probationers. It asked that the conditions of release be tailored to

OFFENDER CLASSIFICATION AND PROBATION: A REVIEW
BOX 4.1

In the 1980s, probation authorities began experimenting with and then using offender classification and risk-screening instruments to help bring a higher level of predictability to probation (and parole) outcomes, and as a means of deciding who would benefit the most from community-based corrections programming. Andrews and colleagues observed that to be effective screening instruments must address the **risk principle** (i.e., determining the level of risk for recidivism posed by offenders), the **needs principle** (i.e., learning the offenders' criminogenic needs), and the **responsivity principle** (i.e., matching offenders' learning styles and cognitive abilities with program characteristics).

A wide array of instruments address some or all of these principles. For example, the Wisconsin Client Management Classification system (CMC) is a structured, interview-based assessment that puts offenders into one of five "strategy groups," each with different supervision levels and associated programming. The CMC's 45 questions address the subject's attitudes about their offense, their criminal history, family background, interpersonal relationships, current problems, and future prospects. The instrument also includes objective measures of the offender's criminal history and background, along with subjective assessments of the offender's behavior during the interview and impressions of the links between the client's needs and their criminogenic involvement, the latter made by classification officers. Used by 25 percent of all probation and parole authorities, the CMS is not strictly speaking a risk-assessment indicator but, rather, a supervision planning mechanism. This program is now known as the Correctional Assessment and Intervention System (CAIS) and is recognized as one of the best fourth-generation systems.

Andrews and colleagues have long been associated with offender classification/risk assessment, especially the Level of Service/Case Management System, known widely at the LSI-R or Level of Service Inventory-Revised. They identify that we are now in the fourth-generation of such clinical assessments, each generation improving the predictability of recidivism, what statisticians call predictive criterion validity. The "value of assessments resides in planning and delivering effective service. The (fourth generation) assessment instruments promote good planning and delivery" (Andrews et al. 2006, 23).

These systems may not resolve all problems; their presence may actually create new ones. As Ferguson observes about the implementation of "what works" in the corrections workplace, new challenges emerge, including the following: (1) the probation decision-makers' perceived loss of discretion; (2) the difficulties associated with obtaining quality information to assess the utility of such instruments; (3) the organizational maintenance of the needed resources and support levels; (4) the effective management of workloads, which may change by reducing duplication of effort (and perhaps jobs); and (5) the resistance of some entrenched personnel, from judges to probation officers, to any changes, but especially those that seem so technical and impersonal. Moreover, while instruments such as the LSI-R may be gender-biased, rendering them less useful for women (see also Chapter 14), Holtfreter and Cupp failed to find evidence supporting such a contention. In the end, these instruments remain just one more tool in deciding who goes to prison or jail and who stays in the community.

SOURCES: ANDREWS, BONTA, AND WORMWITH (2006); ANDREWS, ZINGER, HOGE, BONTA, GENDREAU, AND CULLEN (1990); DOWDEN AND ANDREWS (1999); FERGUSON (2002); GIRARD AND WORMWITH (2004); HARRIS, GINGERICH, AND WHITTAKER (2004); HOLTFRETER AND CUPP (2007).

meet each offender's and each offense's unique characteristics. That recommendation was not widely adopted: most jurisdictions continue to use an identical set of broad conditions for all releasees.

The following constitute the general conditions of probation in most jurisdictions:

- The probationer will report in person to the probation authority when released from custody and regularly for a stipulated period afterward; subsequently, the probationer will make written reports on a regular (often monthly) basis.
- The probationer will not violate state or federal statutes.
- If the police arrest or detain the probationer, he or she will make a report to the probation officer within a certain time (usually 48 to 72 hours).
- The probationer will not drink alcohol to excess (or at all, if this is a condition of release) and will not use, buy, possess, give, sell, or administer any controlled substances.
- The probationer will not own or have under his or her control any type of firearm.
- The probationer will not change his or her job or place of residence without the prior approval.
- The probationer will not leave the jurisdiction of the court without obtaining a travel permit.
- The probationer will not apply for a driver's license or a marriage license without prior approval.
- The probationer will not associate with people who have criminal records.
- The probationer will cooperate with the probation officer at all times, which includes providing correct and true information verbally and in writing.

A court can also order special conditions, for example, that the probationer must participate in a drug treatment or anger management program. Since the 1980s, many jurisdictions across the nation have tried a new tactic: intensive supervision. Used for both probationers and parolees (see Chapter 9 for the latter), the effect of intensive supervision is to increase officer oversight of individual system clients and effectively increase their workload, which, given fixed hours, means a lower ratio of officers to supervisees and an increase in the cost per supervisee. The logical question arising from such practices, then, is: Does the increased supervision (and cost) yield better results?

INTENSIVE SUPERVISION: DOES IT MAKE A DIFFERENCE?

Intensive supervision programs (ISPs) vary from state to state, but all monitor releasees closely. Curfews, multiple weekly contacts with case managers, strict enforcement of conditions, unscheduled drug testing, and community service requirements are common elements (Petersilia and Turner 1990). Because many ISP clients have lengthy drug histories, programs may enforce zero tolerance for drug use: one "dirty urine" and the releasee may be sent to jail or prison. Intensive supervision is time consuming, so the officers involved usually have far fewer cases than usual—just 20 to 25 a month, which increases other officers' caseloads.

A RAND Corporation assessment of ISPs for probationers around the nation raised as many questions as it answered (Petersilia and Turner 1990). The researchers convinced authorities to assign probationers randomly to either intensive supervision or regular probation. Researchers followed the test and control subjects for 1 year. The researchers were quick to acknowledge that the time available for the study was short: that is, the failure rate in 1 year was likely an understatement of what the failure rate would have been at 2 or 5 years. However, probation experts acclaim this as the largest experimental study of probationers or parolees ever undertaken.

An experimental evaluation of intensive probation for juvenile offenders conducted by RAND also found little support for the idea that a coordinated effort between probation officers, nonprobation service coordinators, child and family services social workers, alcohol and drug treatment specialists, mental health social workers, city recreation staff, mentors, police officers, community outreach workers, and restorative justice advocates would reduce recidivism (Lane et al. 2005). Researchers randomly assigned youths to the treatment (specialized intensive supervision) and control groups (normal processing), and after 2 years, there were no differences in recidivism or other official-record outcomes.

Collectively, these findings are problematic for ISP supporters. The adult study indicated that ISP releasees had a technical-violation rate twice that of the controls, and reoffended and returned to prison at a higher rate than those on regular probation. That the intensive programs had more and stricter rules may explain the former finding, and frequent monitoring apparently makes it easier for probation or parole officers to detect violations. The youth study revealed that a "softer" approach compared with a "harder" one does not make the juvenile probationers worse or more likely to fail.

According to RAND, ISPs cost more per releasee to administer and are not as effective as regular programs. "Our results suggest that ISP programs, as implemented in this study, are not effective for high-risk offenders if effectiveness is judged solely by offender recidivism rates" (Petersilia and Turner 1990, xii). The authors also maintained that the most compelling reason for the continued use of ISPs is the concept of *just deserts*, or letting the punishment fit the crime: "Routine probation clearly does not constitute just punishment for felons with serious prior records" (xiii).

A recent examination of ISP, one that employed a rigorous quasi-experimental design, found that intensive supervision reduced recidivism. As Jalbert, Rhodes and Flygare (2010) explained about their study, not only were the workloads lower for officers supervising ISP clients, but the underlying Evidence-Based Practices model required that agency resources be allocated according to the individual risks and needs of the probationer. They then compared various supervision-level outcomes with those generated by the evidence-based ISP program. Jalbert et al. (2010, 250, 251; see, too, Jalbert et al. 2011) found that ISP did indeed "have a salutary effect on probation outcome" and concluded that their study provided strong evidence that "case triage coupled with reduced caseloads for higher risk

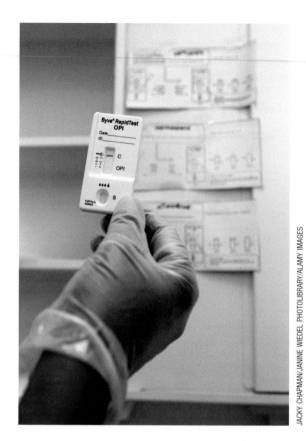

JACKY CHAPMAN/JANINE WIEDEL PHOTOLIBRARY/ALAMY IMAGES

offenders have beneficial effects on probation outcomes."

THE LENGTH OF SUPERVISION

In 1970, the American Bar Association (ABA) recommended that misdemeanant convictions receive a maximum of 2 years on probation, while felony convictions receive a maximum of 5 years on probation. These guidelines have not been widely accepted. Various jurisdictions impose probation for just 1 year or as many as 10 years (Abadinsky 2012). Actual probation sentences show some variability and depend in part on the crime for which the person was found guilty. For example, across the nation as a whole the mean probation sentence was 38 months, but persons convicted of murder and nonnegligent manslaughter received an average sentence of 71 months, with rape and robbery receiving mean sentences of 58 and 51 months respectively; the average sentences for the remaining index crimes hovered between 36 and 40 months (Rosenmerkel, Durose, and Farole 2009, 6).

The period served may not be the same as the period set at sentencing. In some states, statutes authorize judges to reduce the time remaining on a sentence or to end probation altogether if a probationer has exhibited good behavior. In most states, however, probationers must serve a statutory minimum before a court can intervene. Minimums range from 1 to 2 years, or from one-third to one-half of the probation sentence, whichever is less (Abadinsky 2012). In practice, the mean length of time served on probation, no matter the reason for leaving probation, has remained relatively constant at roughly 22 months for the past decade (Glaze and Bonczar 2011, 5).

MODELS OF SUPERVISION OFFICERS

These variable working conditions are further confounded by a dilemma observed decades ago by Klockars (1972). Some officers emphasize the law enforcement elements of their jobs (surveillance model officers), while others view themselves as serving a larger therapeutic function for their "clients" (treatment model officers). Still others, synthetic officers, attempt to balance the demands of each model, creating a third approach, the hybrid model.

The inclusion of ISP, risk-needs programs and specialty caseloads in the twenty-first century, supports the expansion of the hybrid model and the expanded use of synthetic officers (Skeem and Manchak 2008). However, as Skeem and Manchak further note, an entire generation of probation officers has come to the profession and worked in it without much exposure to either the treatment or hybrid models. As Lutze and associates observe about the new decarceration movement, success will result only by the restructuring of agencies to, in their words, "achieve positive outcomes for staff *and* offenders and by envisioning community corrections as a *human services profession* guided by an *ethic of care*" (2012, 54, emphasis added).

VIOLATIONS OF PROBATION

Probation has several different possible statutory outcomes. Between 1990 and early in the twenty-first century, approximately 60 percent of probationers successfully completed their sentences—early, late, or on schedule (Glaze and Bonczar 2006, 6; Gray, Fields, and Maxwell 2001, 539). Recently this figure has increased to 65 percent (Glaze and Bonczar 2011, 6). The remaining outcomes are less positive but not always ones that result in a prison or jail term. Death, discharge to another's custody on detainer or warrant, and transfer to an out-of-state probation authority account for about 1 percent apiece. About one in ten have what is described as an "unsatisfactory exit," which includes failing to meet all conditions of probation—normally only financial conditions—or early terminations; however, incarceration is not part of this outcome. Each year, roughly 3 to 4 percent abscond, while about the same percentage leave by some means, including deportation or transfer to ICE, release on bond, or a discharge by legislative mandate (e.g., a change in the law). The rest, about 16 percent, are incarcerated following a conviction for a new offense or a violation of one or more conditions of probation, the latter being called a **technical violation** (see Box 4.2). Accusations of either a new offense or a technical violation can trigger a revocation hearing.

THE PRELIMINARY HEARING

In the wake of two Supreme Court decisions, *Mempa v. Rhay* (1967) and *Gagnon v. Scarpelli* (1973), probation services nationwide adopted a standardized process for revocation. The probationer receives formal notice of the specific charges and a preliminary hearing date. The preliminary hearing determines probable cause that a violation has occurred. If the probationer fails to show up at the hearing, the court normally issues a failure-to-appear warrant. The warrant adds to the probationer's problems because it is a new charge and a technical violation in and of itself. If the probationer appears and enters a guilty plea, the court has the option of ordering imprisonment or issuing a reprimand, which is

TECHNICAL VIOLATIONS AND PROBATION REVOCATIONS: WHAT IS INVOLVED?   BOX 4.2

Technical violations are among the most controversial aspects of the revocation process. The probationer simply may have failed to notify the probation officer of a job change, missed a reporting date or a therapy session, or applied for a driver's license without prior consent. Critics, such as Czajkoski, R. Cohen, Cunniff and Shilton, argue that imprisonment is much too severe a penalty for these "crimes," suggesting the use of other, less-punitive sanctions, for example, house arrest, the loss of privileges, or fines. In most cases where the court orders probation revocation, the probationer has a new criminal charge, not just a technical violation. In the 1960s, Landis, Merger, and Wolff claimed that 80 percent of probation failures were for violations of probation orders. By the 1990s, Langan and Cunniff estimated this figure at about 60 percent, which is the best estimate for the current status of the ratio of technical violations to new felony convictions.

As Burke has noted, only state-level studies can reveal the actual rates and such studies summated for the nation as a whole do not exist. Nonetheless, a detailed study of Michigan probationers by Gray, Fields and Maxwell is instructive in this regard. They found that the most common type of violation was failure to report (34 percent), followed by a failed drug test (22 percent). New, nonassaultive crimes accounted for only 3 percent of the violations, and new, assaultive crime added another 3 percent. Most probationers who failed did so in the first 90 days of freedom. Although most probationers broke some rules, few committed serious crimes, findings consistent with a large body of research on probationers.

SOURCES: BORK (1995); COHEN (1995); BURKE (2007); CUNNIFF AND SHILTON (1991); CZAJKOSKI (1973); GRAY, FIELDS, AND MAXWELL (2001); LANDIS, MERGER, AND WOLFF (1969); SIMS AND JONES (1997); PETERSILIA AND TURNER (1990).

something like a stern warning. If the probationer waives the preliminary hearing or enters a plea of not guilty, the next step is a revocation hearing.

THE REVOCATION HEARING

In *Mempa*, the Supreme Court set specific guidelines for revocation hearings. Probationers should have the opportunity to testify and present witnesses. They also should be able to hear and cross-examine the state's witnesses and challenge any other evidence. Unless a compelling state interest exists, the accused also has the right to counsel.

Although these guidelines do not seem very different from those that define criminal trial procedures, revocation hearings and criminal trials are different in at least two important ways. First, as Abadinsky (2012) notes, proof at a revocation hearing need not meet the criminal law's rigid standard of proof beyond a reasonable doubt. Instead, the lower standard used in civil cases—a preponderance of evidence—applies. Second, evidence that would not normally find its way into a criminal case, including hearsay evidence, often is used in revocation hearings. Judges, in reaching their decisions, may consider any relevant information, including work records, therapy or treatment appointments kept and broken, and probationers' relationships with family and friends.

SENTENCING

If the hearing authority finds a probationer not guilty, he or she returns to probation. However, if the decision is that the defendant is guilty, the judge has several options. If the violations were relatively minor, the judge can sentence the offender to continued probation, perhaps with new conditions—assignment to a halfway house, intensive supervision, or electronic monitoring, for example. When the violations are grave or numerous or both, the court usually revokes probation and orders imprisonment.

In cases where the judge suspended sentencing pending the offender's successful completion of probation, the judge can impose whatever sentence the law allows for the original offense, up to and including the maximum. If the court did impose a sentence before releasing the offender on probation, the judge may choose to execute that sentence once he or she revokes probation.

PROBATION SERVICES TODAY

PROBATIONERS SERVICES

Probation accounts for four in seven of all adults under some form of correctional supervision in the United States. According to Table 4.4, state and federal probationers numbered 4.125 million at year's end 2010. Almost all of those probationers—99.8 percent—were under the supervision of state agencies. Texas and Georgia had 20 percent of all probationers. These two states are interesting because between 2009 and 2010, Texas was one of five states that helped account for half of all the nation-wide decreases in probationers (along with California, Florida, Maryland and Minnesota); Georgia was joined by three other states (Alabama, Arizona, and Pennsylvania) to account for 50 percent of the 2009–2010 growth. Changes in the probation populations in states that rely on it heavily can have an impact on national trends, a topic we revisit later in this chapter.

Another way to look at the numbers in Table 4.4 is to examine the rates per 100,000 adult residents in the country (per capita), the various regions, and the states. The per capita rate on December 31, 2005 for the nation was 1,721. This means that if you are in a restaurant with 59 other adults, one of you is probably on probation. However, Table 4.4 also suggests that it depends on where that restaurant is located. If you are dining in Indiana, Minnesota, or Rhode Island, where the per capita rate approaches or exceeds 3,000, odds are two probationers are sharing the restaurant; and in Idaho and Georgia, with a per capita rate of approximately 4,000 and 6,000, respectively, there are two and probably three probationers eating together. However, if you are in West Virginia or Utah, there may not even be one probationer dining with you. The per capita rate also varies by region of the country. The South had more people on probation at the end of 2010 (1,761,825) and more probationers per capita (2,008) than any other region. No other part of the nation had 1 million probationers. However, the rate for the Midwest (1,908) is close to that of the South. The per capita rates in the Northeast (1,351) and the West (1,337) are considerably lower, as were their absolute totals.

More appears to be at work here than geography. Local legal culture and state laws that encourage the use of alternatives to incarceration may be more relevant than straightforward geography. For example, the largest absolute increases between 2005 and 2010 occurred in California, Pennsylvania, Michigan, Illinois, and Minnesota. The largest absolute decreases during this time occurred in New York, Washington, the Federal System, District of Columbia, and Kansas. The 10 largest states by population—California, Texas, New York, Florida, Illinois, Pennsylvania, Ohio, Georgia, Michigan, and North Carolina—contributed the most to the nation's probation population, accounting for 2.43 million probationers or nearly 60 percent of the total.

PROFILES OF PROBATIONERS

The average probationer in 2010 was a white male, a characterization that had not changed in more than a decade (Glaze and Bonczar 2011, 33). Women, who constituted only 7 percent of those convicted of crimes, made up 24 percent of state probationers. The disproportion here may be a function of discrimination or a reflection of the fact that women tend to commit less serious offenses. Although blacks accounted for a smaller proportion of probationers than of those in jail or prison inmates, they were still present in the probation population at a percentage (30 percent) that was more than twice their proportion in the general population. Hispanics (13 percent) accounted for slightly fewer probationers than we would have expected if this status were a random occurrence. In addition, members of other minority groups made up only about 1 percent of the overall probationer population.

TABLE 4.4 Adults on probation, 2010.

Region and jurisdiction	Probation population, 1/1/2010	Entries: Reported	Entries: Imputed[a]	Exits: Reported	Exits: Imputed[a]	Probation population, 12/31/2010	Change, 2010: Number	Change, 2010: Percent	Number on probation per 100,000 U.S. adult residents, 12/31/2010
U.S. total	4,125,033	2,131,404	2,190,200	2,198,996	2,261,300	4,055,514	−69,519	−1.70%	1,721
Federal	22,587	11,287	11,287	11,171	11,171	22,703	116	0.50%	10
State	4,102,446	2,120,117	2,178,900	2,187,825	2,250,100	4,032,811	−69,635	−1.70%	1,711
Alabama	49,953	24,423	24,423	21,111	21,111	53,265	3,312	6.60%	1,474
Alaska[b]	6,739	1,209	1,209	989	989	6,959	220	3.30%	1,308
Arkansas	30,642	8,520	8,520	10,340	10,340	28,822	−1,820	−5.90%	1,307
California[c]	311,728	149,029	149,029	167,883	167,883	292,874	−18,854	−6.00%	1,047
Colorado[b,c,d]	78,432	53,111	53,500	55,262	55,600	76,289	−2,143	−2.70%	1,959
Connecticut[c]	55,553	26,040	26,040	28,686	28,686	52,907	−2,646	−4.80%	1,931
Delaware	16,831	12,992	12,992	13,510	13,510	16,313	−518	−3.10%	2,365
District of Columbia	8,055	6,989	6,989	5,977	5,977	9,067	1,012	12.60%	1,815
Florida[c,d]	267,448	209,566	210,600	219,180	220,400	256,220	−11,228	−4.20%	1,743
Georgia[c,e]	453,887	222,208	222,208	218,935	218,935	457,160	3,273	0.70%	6,208
Hawaii[c]	19,469	6,484	6,484	5,079	5,079	20,874	1,405	7.20%	2,066
Idaho[c,f]	56,975	43,365	43,365	47,447	47,447	52,893	−4,082	−7.20%	4,602
Illinois[c]	130,910	58,600	58,600	57,600	57,600	131,910	1,000	0.80%	1,344
Indiana[b,c]	131,635	92,378	92,378	95,266	95,266	128,747	−2,888	−2.20%	2,638
Iowa[b]	23,163	17,461	17,461	18,245	18,245	22,379	−784	−3.40%	963
Kansas	17,236	21,537	21,537	21,371	21,371	17,402	166	1.00%	812
Kentucky[c]	54,947	28,061	28,061	25,813	25,813	57,195	2,248	4.10%	1,714
Louisiana	42,259	17,050	17,050	15,396	15,396	43,913	1,654	3.90%	1,285
Maine	7,316	3,517	3,517	3,555	3,555	7,278	−38	−0.50%	693
Maryland[c]	95,017	48,438	48,438	55,274	55,274	88,181	−6,836	−7.20%	1,999
Massachusetts[b,c]	76,249	81,800	81,800	86,000	86,000	72,049	−4,200	−5.50%	1,378
Michigan[c,d]	185,416	110,422	124,500	113,944	128,500	182,333	−3,083	−1.70%	2,388
Minnesota	121,313	64,461	64,461	73,888	73,888	111,886	−9,427	−7.80%	2,760
Mississippi	24,276	10,170	10,170	7,653	7,653	26,793	2,517	10.40%	1,216
Missouri	57,805	23,755	23,755	24,131	24,131	57,429	−376	−0.70%	1,246
Montana[c]	10,091	4,021	4,021	4,019	4,019	10,093	2	0.00%	1,316
Nebraska	17,583	12,749	12,749	14,012	14,012	16,320	−1,263	−7.20%	1,194

Region/jurisdiction	Probation population, 1/1/2010	Reported entries	Reported exits	Entries, 2010	Probation population, 12/31/2010	Number change, 2010	Percent change, 2010	Number per 100,000
Nevada	12,300	6,467	6,933	6,933	11,834	−466	−3.80%	597
New Hampshire	4,600	3,082	3,335	3,335	4,347	−253	−5.50%	416
New Jersey	124,176	42,139	46,160	46,160	120,155	−4,021	−3.20%	1,788
New Mexico[d]	20,086	3,757	3,741	6,200	19,839	−247	−1.20%	1,301
New York	121,182	34,126	38,277	38,277	117,031	−4,151	−3.40%	769
North Carolina[c]	106,581	63,113	65,466	65,466	104,228	−2,353	−2.20%	1,442
North Dakota	4,206	2,756	2,672	2,672	4,290	84	2.00%	834
Ohio[b, c, d]	256,084	147,108	150,702	160,100	251,779	−4,305	−1.70%	2,841
Oklahoma[c]	27,067	9,635	11,045	11,045	25,657	−1,410	−5.20%	912
Oregon	39,607	15,103	14,864	14,864	39,846	239	0.60%	1,328
Pennsylvania[d]	171,329	91,858	83,890	83,890	179,297	7,968	4.70%	1,808
Rhode Island	25,924	—	5,100	5,800	25,164	−760	−2.90%	3,010
South Carolina	33,876	13,431	14,122	14,122	33,185	−691	−2.00%	939
South Dakota	6,602	3,202	3,264	3,264	6,540	−62	−0.90%	1,046
Tennessee	58,493	24,311	23,801	23,801	59,946	1,453	2.50%	1,232
Texas	426,208	165,551	173,081	173,081	418,678	−7,530	−1.80%	2,280
Utah	11,481	5,637	5,511	5,511	11,607	126	1.10%	590
Vermont[b, c]	6,833	3,891	4,420	4,420	6,304	−529	−7.70%	1,257
Virginia[c]	57,876	25,626	26,848	26,848	56,654	−1,222	−2.10%	923
Washington[b, c, d]	98,053	47,680	47,871	74,900	97,864	−189	−0.20%	1,882
West Virginia[c, d]	8,409	1,662	1,460	1,600	8,623	214	2.50%	597
Wisconsin	46,950	22,275	23,079	23,079	46,163	−787	−1.70%	1,052
Wyoming[c]	5,352	3,146	3,179	3,179	5,319	−33	−0.60%	1,270
Northeast	593,162	286,453	294,323	300,100	584,532	−8,630	−1.50%	1,351
Midwest	998,903	576,704	598,174	622,200	977,178	−21,725	−2.20%	1,908
South	1,761,825	891,746	909,012	910,300	1,743,900	−17,925	−1.00%	2,008
West	748,556	365,214	386,316	417,500	727,201	−21,355	−2.90%	1,337

NOTE: BECAUSE OF NONRESPONSE OR INCOMPLETE DATA, THE PROBATION POPULATION FOR SOME JURISDICTIONS ON DECEMBER 31, 2010, DOES NOT EQUAL THE POPULATION ON JANUARY 1, 2010, PLUS ENTRIES, MINUS EXITS. RATES WERE COMPUTED USING THE ESTIMATED U.S. ADULT RESIDENT POPULATION IN EACH JURISDICTION ON JANUARY 1, 2011.

— NOT KNOWN

[a]REFLECTS REPORTED DATA EXCEPT FOR JURISDICTIONS IN WHICH DATA WERE NOT AVAILABLE. DETAIL MAY NOT SUM TO TOTAL DUE TO ROUNDING.

[b]EXCLUDES PROBATIONERS IN ONE OF THE FOLLOWING CATEGORIES: INACTIVE, WARRANT, SUPERVISED OUT OF JURISDICTION, OR PROBATIONERS WHO HAD THEIR LOCATION TRACKED BY GPS.

[c]SOME OR ALL DETAILED DATA ARE ESTIMATED.

[d]DATA FOR ENTRIES AND EXITS WERE ESTIMATED FOR NONREPORTING AGENCIES.

[c]COUNTS INCLUDE PRIVATE AGENCY CASES AND MAY OVERSTATE THE NUMBER OF PERSONS UNDER SUPERVISION.

[f]COUNTS INCLUDE ESTIMATES FOR MISDEMEANORS BASED ON ENTRIES DURING THE YEAR.

SOURCE: GLAZE AND BONCZAR (2011, 30).

Half of all probationers in 2010 committed felonies; most (47 percent) of the rest committed a misdemeanor, with only about 2 percent on probation for some other kind of legal infraction (Glaze and Bonczar 2011, 33). A property crime was the most serious crime for 28 percent of the probationers, followed closely by drug law violations (26 percent). Violent offenses were the most serious crimes for one in five probationers. Public order offenses accounted for 18 percent of the probationers, but most of them (over 80 percent of the total) stood convicted of a DWI/DUI offense as their most serious crime. The most serious offense for the remaining 10 percent included many different kinds of crimes, none of which was more than 2 percent by itself.

Among the nation's 4 million-plus probationers in 2010, the supervision status of one in four was unknown and nearly 7 percent had absconded. In other words, we simply do not know the current supervisory status or location of one-third of all probationers.[2] Nearly 54 percent were on active status, while another 4 percent were inactive—waiting for termination. About 2 percent were under the control of another state's supervisory authority than the one that originally sentenced them or under some other supervisory status. The rest were small numbers and in a variety of statuses, including participation in a treatment program (less than 1 percent), financial conditions (1 percent), under an arrest warrant but free (4 percent), or some other status (2 percent).

TRENDS IN PROBATION

Besides jurisdictional variations in probation's use, the trends yield interesting insights into our nation's punishment system as well. Figure 4.1 provides a visual representation of 30-plus years of growth in the federal and state systems. The absolute number of adults on probation grew every year from 1983 to 2008. If we consider the annual percentage change

FIGURE 4.1 **Adults on probation at year end, 1980–2010.** *Source:* Glaze and Bonczar (2011, 2).

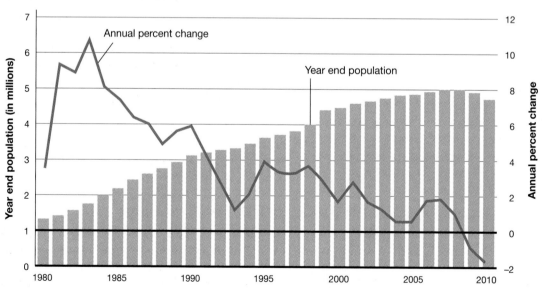

NOTE: Estimates may not be comparable to previously published BJS reports or other BJS statistical series. Counts reflect data reported by probation agencies within the reporting year, and annual change was based on the difference between the January 1 and December 31 population counts within the reporting year. Reporting methods for some probation agencies changed cover time and probation coverage was expanded in 1998 and 1999.

line in this figure, you will note that the trend here has been downward—with a few periodic rises—since the early 1980s. That is, while the probation population has grown every year over most of the past 30 years, its annual rate of growth has been a general downward spiral for most of this time. Between 1980 and 2010, the nation's probation population experienced a threefold increase; however, this observation does not mean that the population trend is or remains sharply upward. In 1983, the annual percent increase peaked at above 6 percent, dropping to around 4 percent by the late 1980s. It went up slightly at the beginning of the 1990s, only to drop below 2 percent in 1993, before spiking again in the mid-1990s to 4 percent, where it hovered until the late 1990s. Since the late 1990s, the trend has been one of less growth each year than the one before, with notable exceptions (2001, 2006–2008). Beginning in 2009 and continuing into 2010, the probation population actually declined for the first time in decades.

The per capita rate of state probationers increased markedly between 1980 and 2010, from 695 to 1,731, but the rate for federal probationers fell over the period, from 29 to 10. The latter finding is consistent with the implementation of the Sentencing Reform Act in the late 1980s and the rigid guidelines provided judges. There simply is very little room for judicial discretion, and, traditionally, probation—and other diversionary programs—was very much a product of that discretion. The overall per capita rate, however, fluctuated throughout the early 2000s, ranging from a high of 1,879 in 2004 to a low of 1,721 in 2010. The general trend here, like that for the annual percent change and absolute number of probationers, is downward by the end of the twenty-first century's first decade (Glaze and Bonczar 2011, 3).

Probation plays such a central role in US corrections that alternatives to it are often given only a secondary look. As we learn in Box 4.3, the fact that many nations around the world operate their penal systems without probation is almost beyond the belief of those who work in the US system. However, community alternatives to probation are becoming far more important to the US correctional scene, as we shall see in the next section.

THE ROLE OF COMMUNITY CORRECTIONS

In this section, we will introduce a term that may be new to many of you: **extrainstitutional punishment**. It means criminal sanctions administered outside a secure correctional facility. In Chapters 5, 6, and 7, we will discuss jails and prisons, the two basic types of secure institutions. Any corrections program that provides punishment or treatment outside a jail or prison is a form of extrainstitutional punishment. In this case, probation often serves as the mechanism by which the court releases an individual into the community and the means by which that same legal authority may remove community-corrections clients from it for failing to abide by their release conditions. Two terms—and their interrelationship with one another—are central to a complete understanding of community corrections: *intermediate sanctions* and *diversion*.

Intermediate sanctions are extrainstitutional punishments: they include all types of correctional programming between traditional probation and prison. These sanctions expand the scope of corrections programs in the United States; they also expand our capacity to punish convicted offenders. **Diversion** is the process of removing individuals from the formal system of prosecution and adjudication, and placing them in a less-formal treatment setting. For example, the trial court might agree to suspend proceedings against a substance abuser charged with drug dealing. The condition in this case probably would be zero tolerance for drug use. That is, if the treatment fails, the alleged offender will be tried and, if convicted, sentenced. However, if the treatment is successful, the court will drop all charges.

ORIGINS OF DIVERSION

Criminologists tie the modern concept of diversion to Edwin Lemert's (1951) work on **labeling**. Labeling is the process through which individuals adopt the characteristics of whatever it is they have been designated by those powerful enough to make the new status stick. Some sociologists would say that by branding a person a criminal, the criminal justice system contributes to that individual's negative

SPOTLIGHT ON INTERNATIONAL CORRECTIONS: PROBATION SERVICES IN EUROPE   BOX 4.3

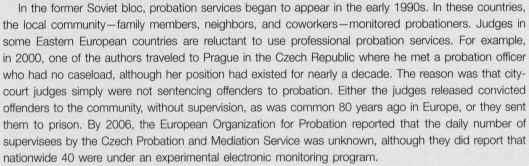

Today, we can find probation around the world. In common-law countries such as Great Britain, the supervised release of offenders was a logical extension of the bail system: a third party—a government department—would be responsible for probationers' conduct.

The transition was more difficult in civil-law nations, the legal tradition found in most European countries, where probation developed from the *sursis*, in effect a suspended sentence. The problem was that the *sursis* was unsupervised; conditioning it on supervision was thought to be an attack on basic privacy rights. At issue was the principle of strict legality found in most European penal codes. That is, the codes contain the criminal penalties; they are not something that judges can choose to impose. Only after World War I did the idea of supervised release take hold in Europe.

In the former Soviet bloc, probation services began to appear in the early 1990s. In these countries, the local community—family members, neighbors, and coworkers—monitored probationers. Judges in some Eastern European countries are reluctant to use professional probation services. For example, in 2000, one of the authors traveled to Prague in the Czech Republic where he met a probation officer who had no caseload, although her position had existed for nearly a decade. The reason was that city-court judges simply were not sentencing offenders to probation. Either the judges released convicted offenders to the community, without supervision, as was common 80 years ago in Europe, or they sent them to prison. By 2006, the European Organization for Probation reported that the daily number of supervisees by the Czech Probation and Mediation Service was unknown, although they did report that nationwide 40 were under an experimental electronic monitoring program.

The Netherlands, which has used probation as an alternative to prison for more than 180 years, recently privatized its system. In the early 1990s, the Dutch government decided to consolidate the 19 autonomous services—called the Dutch Federation of Probation Institutions—that provided various probation services. The goal was to reduce costs and improve services. The federation became the Dutch Probation Foundation, a private-sector entity. It operates under a single director general and consists of three national agencies. Dutch Probation Services, the largest, is responsible for all aspects of probation and works closely with the other two bodies. The Salvation Army Probation Department, the second agency, works with probationers who are homeless and with juveniles who present multiple behavioral and social problems. The third agency is CGZ Nederland, which works with substance-abusing offenders and those who are mentally ill. An integral part of the Dutch model is the use of volunteers. Each operational unit of Dutch Probation Services has a network of volunteers to help offenders reintegrate into society. This system has the advantage of extending the capacity of probation services without increasing their cost.

The public–private split in Europe comes down heavily on the side of the public sector, including former Soviet bloc nations as Bulgaria, Estonia, Hungary, Latvia, Lithuania, Moldova, Poland, Romania, Slovakia, and Slovenia. In 2001, Finland changed from a private sector system to one operated out of the Ministry of Justice. In German, only Baden-Württemberg operates a private sector probation service, the other states in Germany operating their own state-run programs. Austria's probation service—Neustart Austria—is a wholly private venture funded by the federal government.

SOURCES: EVANS (2002); EUROPEAN ORGANISATION FOR PROBATION (2012); VILLÉ, ZVEKIC, AND KLAUS (1997).

self-image, which in turn pushes that person to behave more like a criminal.

The connection between labeling theory and diversion programming is straightforward: if we can suspend proceedings before society labels the offender as a *delinquent* or *criminal*, we can prevent the negative effects of the label. Many proponents of diversion believe this is possible only if the diversion occurs *before* adjudication. Once a court finds an offender guilty of some crime, they insist, removing the individual from the system is simply a means of minimizing penetration (Whitehead and Lab 1999). At that point, some stigma has already attached to the offender, and all that placing him or her in a community corrections programming does is keep that individual out of jail or prison. Hence, the key to successful diversion, claim labeling theorists, is preadjudicatory removal from the system (Winfree and Abadinsky 2010).

TYPES OF DIVERSION PROGRAMS

Many types of diversion programs exist. Here we look at two categories that focus on self-awareness: educational or informational programs, and counseling or self-help programs (Enos and Southern 1996). Most diversion programs target first offenders. The goal of such programs is to keep first offenders from becoming persistent offenders. To do this, a program must start with an assessment of an offender's problems and then provide appropriate treatment. For example, educational programs focus on the educational needs of the participants. For juvenile offenders, tutoring or academic support for junior high school or high school courses is an expression of the educational dimension. Educational support for adults might entail a course in English as a second language or help with obtaining a GED certificate. Informational programs might teach about the consequences of criminal or delinquent behavior. For example, a program for first offenders charged with drunk driving might show a graphic film of an accident scene and follow that with a police officer or a judge addressing the legal consequences of driving under the influence. Although

these sessions usually stress course content, they often have a distinct "scared straight" orientation (Finckenauer 1982).

Counseling or self-help programs also can be informational. They tend to stress self-discovery and coping skills—anger management and problem solving, for example (Enos and Southern 1996; also see Lester and Braswell 1987). Some of these programs include the family, and family members help with the participants' treatment program. Whatever the emphasis of a specific program, the goals of educational and instructional diversion efforts generally are to help offenders identify and solve their personal problems.

SUCCESS AND FAILURE

Diversion programs suffer from a problem common to virtually all community corrections programs: lack of funding. Some look to the United Way or other community organizations for funding; others may ask businesses for donations. Typically, volunteers staff the programs. This means the staff is likely to be highly motivated, but it also means difficulties with long-term planning. Indeed, the two most persistent questions regarding diversion programs do not pertain to funding; they involve net widening and they are not very effective. **Net widening** is said to occur when a diversionary program designed to reduce the overall volume of contacts with and depth of penetration into the justice system does just the opposite. The implementation of diversion programs has made the social control net bigger and its mesh has been made finer. If diversion programs did not exist, say the critics, then many of their clients would not have been further processed by the justice system; rather, they would have been warned and released by the police or the prosecutor would have declined to prosecute or the courts would have put them on standard probation. In the case of community corrections, diversion programs increase the intrusion of state-agencies into the lives of program participants, perhaps increasing the likelihood of failure. Concerns of net widening have been a constant criticism of diversion programs (Austin and

Krisberg 1981). Although there have been mixed results, a body of research demonstrates that most diversion programs are net widening by their very nature (Decker 1985; see too McMahon 1990). The dilemma here is twofold: diversion programs increase the offender population in the programs themselves, and by diverting some people they free up space in traditional control facilities. Ultimately, diversion programs may have the effect of significantly increasing our capacity to punish.

The second criticism facing diversion programs centers on the evaluation of program effectiveness. Typically, diversion programs receive considerable praise for their client effectiveness. However, given that they deal with the least serious and, in some instances, most highly motivated offenders, it is not surprising that these programs show high success rates (see, for example, Latessa and Allen 1999, 134–35). Unfortunately, often these programs do not include an evaluation component and, as a result, anecdotal evidence provides the primary measures of success.

TYPES OF INTERMEDIATE SANCTIONS

Covering all forms of community corrections and sentencing alternatives is beyond the scope of this book. We give three examples: monetary repayments, community service, and house arrest. This is by no means an exhaustive review. However, it should give you a flavor of the alternative forms of extra-institutional sanctions available today. We also should note that many of these intermediate sanctions are not used as "stand-alone" punishments; rather, they are "add-ons" to other sanctions, including incarceration and traditional probation. The emphasis here is the use of intermediate sanctions as alternatives to incarceration.

FINES, FORFEITURES, AND RESTITUTION

As we have noted in Chapters 2 and 3, various cultures have used fines as criminal sanctions for a long time. Most people associate fines with traffic offenses; however, in the past two decades, the frequency of their use for major criminal acts, especially conspiracies, has increased. In Chapter 3, we discussed a modern variation of fines, the so-called *day fine*. Whatever the nature fines take, legal authorities will continue to use fines as extrainstitutional punishments as well as additional sanctions for some incarcerated offenders.

A second economic sanction is **asset forfeiture**. This too has been a weapon in the war against organized crime and Federal prosecutors frequently use it under the Racketeer Influenced and Corrupt Organizations (RICO) statutes (see Chapter 3). Finally, **restitution**—either alone or with probation—serves as an economic sanction. In some instances, restitution is a stand-alone extrainstitutional sanction, but courts use it even for individuals sentenced to jail or prison time.

SUCCESS AND FAILURE Economic sanctions are among the fastest-growing penalties in community corrections. What is the appeal of economic sanctions, and what do they accomplish? The appeal of this punishment seems reasonably clear. First, it can save money. They save bed spaces and per diem costs for every inmate not incarcerated. The potential savings could average as much as $30,000 per year per inmate, and the aggregate cost savings could be tremendous.

Furthermore, economic sanctions can generate revenue. Although we usually do not talk about fines and forfeitures as government funding sources, many jurisdictions view seized drug money and assets as revenue by state and local law enforcement agencies. Even if these moneys are not dedicated to additional law enforcement efforts, they go into the government's general funds and provide financial support that otherwise would not be available.

If fines and forfeitures are not alternatives to incarceration, but become probation and incarceration add-ons, then we have a different set of concerns. By targeting economic crimes, the intent of economic sanctions is to take the profit motive out of crime. If these tactics dissuade criminals from their illegal activities, then economic sanctions are successful, but participants in those activities, particularly organized-crime activities, may ultimately view fines and forfeitures as simply another cost of doing business. In these cases, economic sanctions are not deterrents but inconveniences.

COMMUNITY SERVICE

Community service is an area of community corrections that has seen enormous growth since the late 1970s. Like fines and restitution, community service has its roots in primitive legal codes and in notions such as reparations and restoration. In its modern form, community service is another alternative to incarceration. Community service programs seem especially appropriate for crimes such as spray painting graffiti or other forms of vandalism.

THE OBJECTIVES OF COMMUNITY SERVICE
The aim of community service is to secure benefits for the community and for the offender as well. The offender provides a service to the community, helping clean up graffiti, for example. At the same time, the offender seems to receive at least two major benefits. First, this sanction holds the offender accountable for the offense, which should help this person take responsibility for his or her future actions. Second, the offender benefits by avoiding incarceration and by not incurring a financial cost—a fine or restitution, for example—that may be difficult to pay.

TYPES OF PROGRAMS
In the cases that do not seem to warrant incarceration, a judge may order an offender to participate in projects that in theory should help the community. In some ways, like diversion programs, the only limits on community service projects are judicial imagination. For instance, the court may order offenders to work in community parks and recreation programs, or to clean up government offices. On occasion, offenders wash government vehicles. Normally, this work is part of standard probation or as a specific condition of probation. A probation officer or some other government official, such as a parks and recreation supervisor, may administer these efforts.

Other community service programs may require offenders to work in hospital emergency rooms (especially for drunk-driving cases) or facilities such as clinics, libraries, senior citizen centers, and schools. The objective is for the offender to develop a sense of accountability, to recognize that his or her criminal activity has harmed the community.

ISSUES IN COMMUNITY SERVICE
Community service would seem to be the least controversial community corrections programs imaginable, but this is not the case. Three issues plague community service endeavors. First, ensuring offenders' accountability presents many problems. Although offenders may appear for their assignments, this does not necessarily mean that the jobs are meaningful to them or that they learn any particular lesson by having fulfilled the court order. Second, there are questions about the supervision of offenders involved in community service projects. Simply because a judge has ordered an offender to perform a certain number of hours does not mean that the person will complete the duties assigned or even show up when ordered to. Someone will have to assume responsibility for holding the offender accountable, and often this task falls to overworked probation officers. The third and perhaps the most severe criticism of community service deals with punishment. Many members of the public do not believe that community service is real punishment. These projects may suffer from a lack of legitimacy as a result of this lack of credibility.

SUCCESS AND FAILURE
The degree to which community service projects address these three issues dictates the likelihood of their use. If the community-based sanctions cannot adequately address these issues, judges may not order community service. Nonetheless, Richard Maher and Henry Dufour (1987, 26) maintain that community service will continue to be part of the corrections continuum, if for no other reasons than prison crowding and the lack of tax dollars to support ever-increasing institutional populations. Maher and Dufour also contend that much of the existing enabling legislation keeps community service from being punitive. This undermines public confidence, and it lowers the threat of the sanction for offenders.

HOUSE ARREST WITH ELECTRONIC MONITORING

House arrest is a relatively old punishment concept that has been combined with a new enforcement mechanism: electronic monitoring (Lilly and Ball 1987).[3] Legal jurisdictions around the world have used house arrest with individuals not thought to be flight risks. More recently, authorities in the United States have used it with offenders who might be candidates for jail or prison. Historically, the presence of an armed guard at the offender's home enforced house arrest, or a police or probation officer made frequent checks to ensure that the offender indeed was at home. The advent of electronic monitoring changed the playing field for house arrest.

In April 1983, Albuquerque, New Mexico, District Court Judge Jack Love ordered the use of an electronic anklet for a probation violator. About the same time, other judges around the country had decided that the traditional ways of dealing with relatively minor offenders were ineffective. The typical choices were jail time or nothing. "Nothing'" actually consisted of a fine and probation, but not incarceration. Judge Love stumbled on the new electronic monitoring technology, which required fitting offenders with a tamper-resistant bracelet. The bracelet, coupled with a telephone transmitter-receiver device, allows manual or computer-assisted dialers to check on an offender's whereabouts (Ford and Schmidt 1985).

The normal procedure is to allow the offender to go to work or to have specified times when monitoring ceases, as long as the offender obtains prior approval. The monitoring officer might stipulate he or she will not engage in monitoring the subject, normally during the hours of 7:30 a.m. and 5:30 p.m. From 5:30 p.m. until 7:30 a.m., the officer expects the individual to be home; and when the dialer calls, the monitored person fits the device into the electronic receiver to send a verifying signal to the monitoring office.

If no electronic reply is given (or in case of equipment malfunction), the officer reports the subject as missing and dispatches one or more surveillance officers to the individual's home. **Surveillance officers** are typically sworn peace officers or other probation employees with limited arrest powers (i.e., they may only take probationers into custody or enter the homes of probationers without warrants). They patrol likely haunts of probation violators, check on probationers at night, and generally watch to see that releasees follow the rules. In this way, additional sets of eyes augment the probation officers' technology. Indeed, newer technology, tied to global positioning systems, allows authorities to know the exact location of clients 24 hours a day.

THE OBJECTIVES OF HOUSE ARREST WITH ELECTRONIC MONITORING What is house arrest with electronic monitoring intended to achieve? First, as an alternative to incarceration, house arrest should save jail and prison bed space. Additionally, every inmate-day we can free saves us money in the end. Therefore, house arrest may be one way to reduce rapidly escalating corrections costs. However, how can we offset or justify the additional cost of electronic monitoring? One answer to this has been that most jurisdictions that use electronic monitoring require program participants to pay a monthly monitoring fee.

Second, house arrest should save institutional space and should minimize the stigma and trauma faced by jail and prison inmates. One of the greatest dilemmas facing people who have served jail or prison sentences of any length is that reintegration into the community and their families is difficult. With house arrest, the problem of reintegration does not exist. Associated with the issue of community placement is the consideration that some treatment programs are available in the community but not in an institution. Therefore, offenders under house arrest may have access to more and better types of programming to meet their specific needs, and they may be required (and should be able) to pay all or part of the treatment costs because they are still employed.

SUCCESS AND FAILURE One of the major problems with any new correctional program is that they often appear on the scene and are proclaimed *the* solution to our problems. This has been the case with house arrest enforced by electronic monitoring. At this point, these programs have existed long enough for us to have a clear picture of what they can and cannot do. House arrest with electronic monitoring can be a very useful community corrections program, but it is not without problems.

As predicted, electronic monitoring appears to be a cost-effective alternative to incarceration. Because offenders must pay for the program, electronic monitoring often costs correctional systems little or nothing extra. However, the cost savings promised through additional free bed space is another matter.

In many jurisdictions, most candidates for electronic monitoring are not really on their way to jail or prison. As public opinion is often against using electronic monitoring with offenders who pose any significant risk, authorities typically use this method with low-risk offenders who are not likely to reoffend or to commit a serious violation under this form of supervision.

In those instances where house arrest and electronic monitoring divert offenders from incarceration, other offenders have likely filled up the "saved" bed spaces. Therefore, electronic monitoring may expand our capacity to punish. Another criticism of electronic monitoring is that it is not punitive enough. Many citizens and politicians feel that sending someone home to do time is not punishment, even if his or her freedom of movement is restricted.

Electronic monitoring (EM) opponents also note that this technique monitors a specific place, not specific behavior. Monitoring the offender's place might be important for a crime such as drunk driving, but for pedophiles or drug dealers, such monitoring may not be sufficient. James Quinn and John Holman (1991b) raised another concern: family conflict where offenders are under electronically monitored house arrest. Although their conclusions are less than definitive, Quinn and Holman conclude "that greater attention [needs to] be paid to offender household and related issues by professionals supervising offenders on [electronically monitored home confinement]" (190). Another issue is the fact that to date, through the first 20 years of their use, studies of EM were of such poor quality that there was no true picture of their ability to reduce recidivism or even control offenders living in the community (Renzema and Mayo-Wilson 2005). A study in Florida contradicts this conclusion. Researchers found that EM did not reduce the recidivism of violent offenders, but worked well among sex, property, and other offenders; furthermore, EM's effects were true across all levels of supervision for these types of offenders (Bales et al. 2010). After nearly a quarter of a century of use, the continued use of EM is based more on faith than large-scale evidence-based practices.

The most fundamental flaw facing EM may be that it has no theoretical underpinnings. Todd Clear (1988) examines all of the different justifications for punishment, from retribution to rehabilitation, and from deterrence to incapacitation, and finds electronic monitoring deficient on all points. He concludes that electronic monitoring is an add-on, a *net-widening* program in search of a purpose. Not everyone has been this critical, but definitive studies of EM's effectiveness are not yet available. If it cannot establish both economic and programmatic viability, electronic monitoring may not survive in its current form.

ISSUES IN COMMUNITY CORRECTIONS

Community corrections programs, like all components of corrections, face many issues. In this section, we explore several that seem to be most significant for the future of community-based programs.

GOVERNMENT AND PRIVATE SPONSORSHIP

Most jails and prisons are public facilities, funded by taxpayers and staffed by government employees. This is not the case with community-based programs. The private sector started and funded many alternatives to incarceration, especially diversion programs. Today, community corrections programs rely on a mix of local, state, and federal moneys as well as private funds.

Governments join with the private sector for a number of reasons. One is the scale of many community-based efforts. For example, consider a **halfway house** for substance abusers. This type of program might be too small for a government entity to operate efficiently but just the right size for a nonprofit community agency to make it succeed. In addition, the relatively small scale of local programs allows for the kind of innovative programming that governments want to encourage. Moreover, local programs are just that, *local*. They are in the community where the criminal justice system and its attendant treatment programs can best address the clients' needs. Finally, government funding of private sector programs becomes in effect a multiplier of the impact of the relatively small amount of funding any single organization can contribute.

There are two major drawbacks to a reliance on government funding, however. The first has to do with the uncertainties of government spending. Funding is one of the major struggles facing community corrections programs: program administrators are constantly trying to cobble together their own budgets for the coming year, and most programs are no more than a year away from financial extinction. It is very difficult to make long-term plans if you do not know whether your agency will survive the next budget cycle.

The second problem with multiple funding sources is that the programs are either accountable to everyone or accountable to no one. The former is bound to have an impact on what a program actually achieves, and the latter leaves the program's administrators to assess their own effectiveness— which is always a risky proposition.

The funding arrangements for community corrections may partly explain why these programs have expanded so widely in the past two decades. The programs' sponsorship and their unfortunate lack of accountability may also explain why there is so little in the way of research on their effectiveness. Even where researchers had an opportunity to examine the programs, the results are generally not very positive. In many community corrections programs, it is difficult to tell who is paying the bills and who is responsible for administration and program outcomes.

ADMINISTERING COMMUNITY-BASED PROGRAMS

One of the best things about extrainstitutional programs is that they attract energetic and creative employees. The staff members often are fresh out of college, their heads full of knowledge, and their hearts full of hope. To the extent that community corrections programs are effective, these young people deserve much of the credit. Their youth and enthusiasm help keep community-based programs from the malaise that seems to pervade firmly entrenched bureaucracies. In many correctional institutions, there is a sense among the staff that nothing is possible or that change is so difficult that it is not worth the effort. Long-time institutional employees often express levels of cynicism and hopelessness that are difficult to cure (Latessa and Allen 1999).

What happens to staff members over time, though, is one of the worst things about community corrections. The job is intense and demanding, and many simply burn out after a year or two. Turnover is a constant, and new hires face a steep learning curve. This means that most community agencies have very little in the way of institutional memory, which in turn means that no one learns from experience, and they keep making the same mistakes.

SUPPORTERS

Proponents of community corrections state their support in both negative and positive ways. For instance, from a negative perspective, they might say something like the following: "Institutional programs have proved largely ineffective in changing criminal behavior, so why not try something different?" They are not saying that community-based programs work and produce specific results; rather, they simply are saying that the community approach *could* work and that it would not do any worse than institutional programming.

Nevertheless, there are supporters of extrainstitutional punishment who find many positive aspects in community-based programs. One is cost-effectiveness: several of the programs currently being operated cost less per client per day to administer than institutional placements (Benekos 1990). Another is the relative absence of stigma: participants in community corrections can go about their everyday routine without the burden of the *ex-con* label. Proponents of extrainstitutional programming also believe that these treatment efforts are more effective for some offenders than institutionalization would be for several reasons

(McCarthy 1992). First, certain programs that are available in the community are not available in institutions. Second, community-based programs work with offenders in their "natural" environment, rather than in the artificial environment of a secure facility. As a result, offenders must learn to deal with family problems and the temptations presented by peers and crime opportunities. In an institution, they might talk about dealing with these issues, but in the community the reality of dealing with their problems confronts them head-on.

The final reason has to do with reintegration. Institutionalization makes it difficult for offenders, particularly for long-term prison inmates, to return to life on the outside (McShane and Krause 1993; Souryal 1997).[4] Not every offender is appropriate for extrainstitutional treatment, but those who are suffer fewer disruptions in their lives as a result of community-based treatment.

DETRACTORS

The critics of community corrections come from all points along the political spectrum—conservative, liberal, even moderate (see Walker 2011). Generally, though, their criticisms focus on cost, net widening, public safety, or effectiveness. Those who target program costs would admit that comparisons of the day-to-day costs of community-based versus institutional programs do make the extrainstitutional efforts look less expensive. They would argue, given that we continue to use institutional placements at the same or even a greater pace, these programs actually contribute to the upward budget spiral.

Cost and net widening are related. With each new community-based program, critics say, we bring more people into the corrections system. The outcome is more than a broader menu of treatment; it is more treatment, which means more cost. On the surface, it might appear that widening the net is a good thing, that it makes services available to more people. These services come with a shift of control to a correctional authority that otherwise might not be necessary. Clearly, there are two sides to this issue.

The third criticism leveled at community corrections is that the programs fail to protect public safety. Certain clients, critics insist, simply belong in jail or

prison, even at the cost of constructing additional bed space (DiIulio 2001; McShane and Krause 1993, 5). In the past, a number of the clients now participating in extrainstitutional programs would have been placed in correctional facilities. However, with institutional crowding a problem, alternatives to incarceration have become increasingly necessary. Opponents believe that we are sacrificing public safety for dollars and convenience.

Community corrections advocates must take the final criticism very seriously: do the programs work? If community-based programs do not reduce offenders' misbehavior, then it does not matter what else they do or what they cost (Latessa and Allen 1999, 401–8). Legal authorities must hold programs accountable, and their programmatic design—including services delivered and desired outcomes—must allow and even encourage objective evaluation.

THE SPECIAL CASE OF COMMUNITY STAKEHOLDERS

We already have referred to public perceptions of community corrections programs. Now we address the problems of selling the public on the acceptability of community-based programs in comparison to secure placements. For example, corrections programs depend on public tax dollars for support, and politicians depend on the public's support for reelection. Therefore, politicians are very sensitive to perceived changes in public opinion, particularly about crime and punishment issues. No politician wants to be seen as soft on crime. This means policy makers and community-corrections planners must consult state and local politicians when designing and implementing a community corrections program.

Members of the public also may get involved in the debate about community-based programming. Community members typically become incensed about program costs and the apparent lack of public safety. Program costs become an issue when the public views treatment as extravagant and that the programs coddle criminals.

Related to the program cost issue is concern for public safety. Most members of the public believe that when society punishes criminals, they really should be punished, and for most people, this means being locked up. Therefore, community-based programs start with the disadvantage that the public sees them as being inherently unsafe, and if members of the public feel that a program is unsafe, to them it *is* unsafe. Complaints about program safety typically develop when a program seeks public support. This is especially so when the program is based around a residential group home or halfway house. Community residents may form neighborhood associations to protest the facility's location. Fears about public safety make site selection one of the primary stumbling blocks to some community corrections programs, and one that requires a great deal of public relations work to effectively integrate these programs into the community.

THE FUTURE OF COMMUNITY CORRECTIONS

The future of certain parts of the corrections system is hard to forecast, but this is not true for community corrections. Currently, we rely on community corrections more than ever before, and at least three factors indicate that this trend is likely to continue. First, program costs on a client-for-client basis have proved to be lower for community corrections (Sigler and Lamb 1995). Although there is some concern about increasing overall corrections expenditures because of net widening, these programs typically are much less costly than incarceration. Furthermore, when judicial authorities leave offenders in the community, they can continue to work and support their families. Offenders also can be required, as part of their sentences, to help defray program costs. This is not an appropriate justification for a particular sanction, but in some instances, community-based corrections can generate revenue.

Second, we may be approaching the practical limit in the number of correctional institutions we can support in the United States. There will be some prison expansion, but much of the new building will replace worn-out facilities. As we have often noted, we cannot build our way out of a crowding crisis, and we cannot afford to build and operate increasingly secure institutions. Therefore, community-based alternatives will play a key role in corrections programming. These projects may be alternatives to incarceration or alternative forms of incarceration, but they will not be the fortress-like prisons we have relied on for almost two centuries in this country.

Finally, program effectiveness should be a factor in judicial selection of community corrections over institutionalization. However, are they effective? Two key reasons cause us to view many of these programs as ineffective. In some instances, efforts truly have been ineffective. We should identify and eliminate ineffective programs. However, other programs have not been evaluated at all, or the evaluations have been methodologically inadequate. In such cases, the projects are not at fault. Therefore, at the beginning of this new century, we need to be certain that every community corrections project has a rigorous evaluation component built into it. Because offenders continue to live at home, attend school, and often work outside the home, the correctional program does not have to prepare them to reenter society. If we can show that community corrections programs do no harm, that in fact they do some good, and that they reduce stigmatization and reintegration problems, these programs may be more than the wave of the future. As Lutze and associates (2012) have noted: The future is now.

SUMMARY

Probation and community corrections are similar correctional programs, but differ in important ways. From this chapter, you should especially note the following:

- Probation carries the major corrections burden for both adults and juveniles.

- The growth of probation services, which expanded tremendously during the 1980s and 1990s, has slowed in recent years.

It is unclear whether increasing the surveillance on probationers will result in lower recidivism. Likewise, supervision that is more intensive has a tendency to yield higher failure rates.

Intermediate sanctions, as a form of extrainstitutional punishments, share the goal of diverting offenders from deeper and more lasting movement through the labyrinth of contemporary criminal justice.

Many but not all forms of intermediate sanctions function as diversion from the system; some, especially fines and restitution, are viewed as add-on sanctions for both probationers and incarcerated offenders.

Modern technology and old-fashioned approaches to holding people accountable for their actions permeate the movement toward intermediate sanctions.

Modern criminal justice could not function in the United States without probation services, even though community-based corrections enhance the service delivery; eventually, the emphasis remains on traditional forms of supervision long associated with probation.

THINKING ABOUT CORRECTIONAL POLICIES AND PRACTICES: WRITING ASSIGNMENTS

1 Americans volunteer more time per 100,000 population than almost any other nation. Would probation services benefit from volunteerism? Prepare a one-page paper in response to this question.

2 Write an argument supporting the use of one of the three questions answered by the PSI to the exclusion of the other two. Address the use of hearsay evidence in your answer.

3 Prepare a brief, one-page essay on the total exclusion of technical violations in the consideration of probation revocation. Discuss both sides of the argument.

4 Complete an essay that starts with the following sentence: "Probation officers in the twenty-first century are exposed to forces that seem to pull them in multiple directions at once, the outcome of which could spell trouble for community corrections."

5 In the 1980s and early 1990s, many court officials viewed electronic monitoring as a limited tool. The technology was rudimentary and easily defeated by a persistent and creative offender. As we begin the second decade of the twenty-first century, the technology used to monitor a person whose liberty is tethered electronically is far more sophisticated than in Judge Love's day. Search the Internet for the most innovative technology available for monitoring offenders. Prepare a one-page brief of what is available and, if possible, the cost per unit.

KEY TERMS

asset forfeiture	intensive supervision programs	probation
bail	(ISPs)	release on recognizance (ROR)
caseload	intermediate sanctions	responsivity principle
community service	judicial reprieve	restitution
diversion	labeling	risk principle
extrainstitutional	mixed caseload	*sursis*
punishment	needs principle	surveillance officers
Habeas Corpus Act of 1679	net widening	technical violation
halfway house	presentence investigation (PSI)	workload

CRITICAL REVIEW QUESTIONS

1 What is the history of probation? Go back to Chapter 1 and look at the philosophies of punishment. Where does probation fit into this list?

2 Why is the work of probation officers so difficult? What is it about their caseload and workload that adds to the job's difficulty? (Later, you may wish to compare the clients of probation officers and parole officers, recognizing that in some jurisdictions, a given officer could have both kinds.)

3 "Probation is community corrections. Community corrections is probation." Attack or defend this claim.

4 The standard of proof in the revocation process is very different from the standard of proof at a criminal trial. Do you think that is fair?

5 Net widening is a focus of criticism raised in connection with diversion programs and other alternatives to incarceration. Briefly explain your understanding of net widening.

6 Labeling theorists believe that people act in accordance with society's expectations of them. Are there social forces or personal characteristics that might neutralize the labeling process? Explain your answer.

7 What kinds of cases seem most appropriate for fines and forfeitures? Would you be in favor of applying these sanctions to personal crimes like aggravated assault, rape, robbery, and homicide? Why or why not?

8 Is restitution an idea that looks better on paper than in practice? Do you believe that restitution is effective? What do you think would make it more effective? Explain your answers.

9 Is house arrest a punishment? Do you think it works better for certain types of offenders? Would you set a maximum duration for house arrest? Why?

10 How do the practices associated with probation and community corrections betray the public's right to safety and security? How do they provide for it?

CASES CITED

Commonwealth v. Jerusha Chase (Boston Municipal Court, 1831)

Ex parte United States 242 U.S. 27 (1916) (the *Killits* case)

Gagnon v. Scarpelli, 411 U.S. 778 (1973)

Gardner v. Florida, 430 U.S. 349 (1977)

Mempa v. Rhay, 389 U.S. 128 (1967)

U.S. v. Birnbaum, 421 F.2d 993 (2nd Cir., 1970)

NOTES

1 Discussion taken from DeMichele, Payne, and Matz. (2011, 6).

2 Discussion taken from Glaze and Bonzcar (2011, 36).

3 See Charles (1989), on uses with juveniles; Cooprider and Kerby (1990), on use at the pretrial stage; and Quinn and Holman (1991a), with an examination of this approach as a case management technique.

4 To understand the challenge facing long-term inmates when they leave an institution, rent the movie *The Shawshank Redemption* and pay careful attention to the character named Brooks. The portrayal of his life paints a graphic picture of what it is like to become institutionalized, to undergo prisonization (Clemmer 1940/1958).

REFERENCES

Abadinsky, Howard. 2011. *Drug use and abuse: A comprehensive introduction*. Belmont, CA: Wadsworth Cengage.

Abadinsky, Howard. 2012. *Probation and parole: Theory and practice*, 11th edn. Upper Saddle River, NJ: Prentice Hall/Pearson.

American Correctional Association (ACA). 2003. *Directory: Adult and juvenile correctional department, institutions, agencies, and probation and parole authorities*, 64th edn. Lanham, MD: American Correctional Association.

American Probation and Parole Association (APPA). 2006. *Adult and juvenile probation and paroles national firearm survey*, 2nd edn. Retrieved July 10, 2013 from: http://www.appa-net.org/eweb/Resources/Surveys/National_Firearms/docs/NFS_2006.pdf

American Probation and Parole Association (APPA). 2012. *Nation firearms survey* (updated). Retrieved on July 9, 2013 from: http://www.appa-net.org/eweb/dynamicpage.aspx?webcode=VB_SurveyFirearms

Andrews, D. A., James Bonta, and J. Stephen Wormwith. 2006. The recent past and near future of risk and/or need assessment. *Crime & Delinquency* 52(1): 7–27.

Andrews, D. A., I. Zinger, R. D. Hoge, J. Bonta, P. Gendreau, and F. T. Cullen. 1990. Does correctional treatment work? A clinically relevant and psychologically informed meta-analysis. *Criminology* 28(3): 369–404.

Augustus, John. 1852/1972. *A report of the labors of John Augustus*. Montclair, NJ: Patterson Smith.

Austin, James F., and Barry Krisberg. 1981. Wider, stronger and different nets: The dialectics of criminal justice reform. *Journal of Research in Crime and Delinquency* 18: 165–96.

Bales, William, Karen Mann, Thomas Blomberg, Gerry Gaes, Kelle Barrick, Karla Dhungana, and Brian McManus. 2010. *A qualitative and quantitative analysis of electronic monitoring*. Washington, DC: US Department of Justice.

Barnes, Harry Elmer, and N. K. Teeters. 1959. *New horizons in criminology*. Englewood Cliffs, NJ: Prentice Hall.

Bartollas, Clemens, and John P. Conrad. 1992. *Introduction to corrections*, 2nd edn. New York: HarperCollins.

Benekos, Peter J. 1990. Beyond reintegration: Community corrections in a retributive era. *Federal Probation* 54(1): 52–56.

Benekos, Peter J., and Alida V. Merlo. 1995. Three strikes and you're out! The political sentencing game. *Federal Probation* 59(1): 3–9.

Bork, M. V. 1995. Five-year review of United States probation data. *Federal Probation* 9: 27–33.

British History Online. 2012. Charles II, 1679: "An Act for the better secureing the Liberty of the Subject and for Prevention of Imprisonments beyond the Seas," Statutes of the Realm: volume 5: 1628–80 (1819), pp. 935–8. Retrieved on July 9, 2013 from: http://www.british-history.ac.uk/report.aspx?compid=47484

Brown, Paul W. 1990. Guns and probation officers: The unspoken reality. *Federal Probation* 54: 21–6.

Burke, Peggy. 2007. *When offenders break the rules: Smart responses to parole and probation violations*. Washington, DC: The Pew Center on the States.

Charles, Michael T. 1989. The development of a juvenile electronic monitoring program. *Federal Probation* 53(2): 3–12.

Clear, Todd R. 1988. A critical assessment of electronic monitoring in corrections. *Policy Studies Review* 7(3): 671–81.

Clemmer, Donald. 1940/1958. *The prison community*. New York: Holt, Rinehart & Winston.

Cohen, Robyn. 1995. *Probation and parole violators in state prison*, 1991. Washington, DC: US Government Printing Office.

Comptroller General of the United States. 1976. *Correctional institutions can do more to improve the employability of offenders*. Washington, DC: US Government Printing Office.

Cooprider, Keith W., and Judith Kerby. 1990. A practical application of electronic monitoring at the pretrial stage. *Federal Probation* 54(1): 28–35.

Cunniff, Mark A., and Mary K. Shilton. 1991. *Variations in felony probation: Persons under supervision in thirty-two urban and suburban counties*. Washington, DC: Criminal Justice Planners Association.

Czajkoski, Eugene H. 1973. Exposing the quasi-judicial role of the probation officer. *Federal Probation* 37(2): 9–13.

Decker, Scott H. 1985. A systematic analysis of diversion: Net widening and beyond. *Journal of Criminal Justice* 13(3): 207–16.

DeMichele, Matthew T. 2007. *Probation and parole's growing caseload and workload allocation: Strategies for managerial decision making*. Alexandria, VA: American Probation and Parole Association.

DeMichele, Matthew T., and Brian K. Payne. 2007. Probation and parole officers speak out—Caseload and workload allocation. *Federal Probation* 71(3): 3–35.

DeMichele, Matthew T., Brian K. Payne, and Adam K. Matz. 2011. *Community supervision workload considerations for public safety*. Washington, DC: Bureau of Justice Assistance.

DiIulio, John J., Jr. 2001. Prisons are a bargain, by any measure. In *Debating crime*, edited by David W. Neubauer. Belmont, CA: Wadsworth, 119–20.

Dowden, Craig, and D. A. Andrews. 1999. What works for female offenders: A meta-analytic review. *Crime & Delinquency* 45: 438–52.

Dressler, David. 1962. *The theory and practice of probation and parole*. New York: Columbia University Press.

Enos, Richard, and Stephen Southern. 1996. *Correctional case management*. Cincinnati, OH: Anderson.

European Organization for Probation (CEP). 2012. *Knowledgebase*. Retrieved on July 9, 2013 from: http://www.cep-probation.org/page/58/knowledgebase

Evans, Donald G. 2002. Spotlight on probation in the Netherlands. *Corrections Today* 64: 104–16.

Ferguson, Jennifer L. 2002. Putting the "what works" research into practice: An organizational perspective. *Criminal Justice and Behavior* 29: 472–92.

Finckenauer, James O. 1982. *Scared straight! and the panacea phenomenon*. Englewood Cliffs, NJ: Prentice-Hall.

Ford, Daniel, and Annesley K. Schmidt. 1985. *Electronically monitored home confinement*. Washington, DC: US Government Printing Office.

Girard, Lina, and J. Stephen Wormwith. 2004. The predictive validity of the level of service inventory-Ontario revision on general and violent recidivism among offender groups. *Criminal Justice and Behavior* 31: 150–81.

Glaze, Lauren E. 2011. *Probation and Parole in the United States, 2010*. Washington, DC: US Department of Justice.

Glaze, Lauren E., and Thomas P. Bonczar. 2006. *Probation and parole in the United States, 2005*. Washington, DC: US Department of Justice.

Glueck, Sheldon, ed. 1933. *Probation and criminal justice*. New York: Macmillan.

Gray, M. Kevin, Monique Fields, and Sheila Royo Maxwell. 2001. Examining probation violations: Who, what, and when. *Crime & Delinquency* 47: 537–57.

Grinnell, Frank W. 1941. The Common Law history of probation: An example of the "equitable" growth of criminal law. *Journal of Criminal Law and Criminology* 32: 14–34.

Harris, Patricia, Raymond Gingerich, and Tiffany A. Whittaker. 2004. The "effectiveness" of differential supervision. *Crime & Delinquency* 50: 235–71.

Holtfreter, Kristy, and Rhonda Cupp. 2007. Gender and risk assessment: The empirical status of the LSI-R for women. *Journal of Contemporary Criminal Justice* 23(4): 363–82.

Jalbert, Sarah Kuck, William Rhodes, Christopher Flygare, and Michael Kane. 2010. Testing probation outcomes in evidence-based settings: Reduced caseload size and intensive supervision effectiveness. *Journal of Offender Rehabilitation* 49(4): 233–53.

Jalbert, Sarah Kuck, William Rhodes, Michael Kane, Elyse Clawson, Bradford Bogue et al. 2011. *A multi-site evaluation of reduced probation caseload size in an evidence-based practice setting*. Washington, DC: US Department of Justice.

Johnson, F. R. 1928. *Probation for juveniles and adults*. New York: Century.

Klockars, Carl. 1972. A theory of probation supervision. *Journal of Criminal Law, Criminology, and Police Science* 64, 549–57.

Landis, J. R., J. D. Merger, and C. E. Wolff. 1969. Success and failure of adult probationers in California. *Crime & Delinquency* 6: 34–40.

Lane, Jodi, Susan Turner, Terry Fain, and Amber Sehgal. 2005. Evaluating an experimental intensive supervision program: Supervision and official outcomes. *Crime & Delinquency* 51: 26–52.

Latessa, Edward J., and Harry E. Allen. 1999. *Corrections in the community*, 2nd edn. Cincinnati, OH: Anderson.

Lemert, Edwin. 1951. *Social pathology*. New York: McGraw-Hill.

Lester, David, and Michael Braswell. 1987. *Correctional counseling*. Cincinnati, OH: Anderson.

Lilly, J. Robert, and Richard A. Ball. 1987. A brief history of house arrest and electronic monitoring. *Northern Kentucky Law Review* 13(3): 343–74.

Listwan, Shelley Johnson, Cheryl Lero Jonson, Francis T. Cullen, and Edward J. Latessa. 2008. Cracks in the penal harm movement: Evidence from the field. *Criminology & Public Policy* 7: 423–65.

Lutze, Faith E., W. Wesley Johnson, Clear, Latessa, and R. N. Slate. 2012. The future of community corrections in now: Stop dreaming and take action. *Journal of Contemporary Criminal Justice* 28(1): 42–59.

Maher, Richard J., and Henry E. Dufour. 1987. Experimenting with community service: A punitive alternative to imprisonment. *Federal Probation* 51(3): 22–7.

McCarthy, Bernard J. 1992. Community residential centers: An intermediate sanction for the 1990s. In *Corrections: Dilemmas and directions*, edited by Peter J. Benekos and Alida V. Merlo. Cincinnati, OH: Anderson, Academy of Criminal Justice Sciences, 173–92.

McMahon, Maeve. 1990. Net widening: Vagaries of a concept. *British Journal of Criminology* 30: 121–49.

McShane, Marilyn D., and Wesley Krause. 1993. *Community corrections*. New York: Macmillan.

Petersilia, Joan, and Susan Turner. 1990. *Intensive supervision for high-risk probationers: Findings from three California experiments*. Santa Monica, CA: RAND.

Quinn, James F., and John E. Holman. 1991a. The efficacy of electronically monitored home confinement as a case management device. *Journal of Contemporary Criminal Justice* 7(2): 128–34.

Quinn, James F., and John E. Holman. 1991b. Intrafamilial conflict among felons under community supervision: An examination of the cohabitants of electronically monitored offenders. *Journal of Offender Rehabilitation* 16 (3/4): 177–92.

Rackmill, Stephen J. 1993. Community correction and the Fourth Amendment. *Federal Probation* 57(3): 40–5.

Renzema, Marc, and Evan Mayo-Wilson. 2005. Can electronic monitoring reduce crime for moderate to high-risk offenders? *Journal of Experimental Criminology* 1: 215–37.

Rosenmerkel, Sean, Matthew Durose, and Donald Farole. 2009. *Felony sentencing in state courts, 2006-statistical tables*. Washington, DC: US Department of Justice.

Sigler, Robert, and David Lamb. 1995. Community-based alternatives to prison: How the public and court personnel view them. *Federal Probation* 59(2): 3–9.

Sims, B., and M. Jones. 1997. Predicting success or failure on probation: Factors associated with felony probation outcomes. *Crime & Delinquency* 43: 314–27.

Skeem, Jennifer L., and Sarah Manchak. 2008. Back to the future: From Klockars' model of effective supervision to evidence-based practice in probation. *Journal of Offender Rehabilitation* 47(3): 220–47.

Souryal, Sam S. 1997. Romancing the stone or stoning the romance? In *Crime and justice in America*, edited by Paul F. Cromwell and Roger G. Dunham. Upper Saddle River, NJ: Prentice Hall, 342–53.

Thompson, Joel A., and G. Larry Mays, eds. 1991. *American jails: Public policy issues*. Chicago: Nelson-Hall.

US Courts. 2007. *Beginnings of probation and services*. Retrieved August 7, from: http://www.uscourts.gov/FederalCourts/ProbationPretrialServices/History.aspx

Villé, Renaud, Ugljesa Zvekic, and Jon F. Klaus. 1997. *Promoting probation internationally*. Rome: United Nations Interregional Crime and Justice Research Institute.

Walker, Samuel. 2011. *Sense and nonsense about crime and drugs*, 7th edn. Belmont, CA: Wadsworth.

Welch, Michael. 1994. Jail crowding. In *Critical issues in crime and justice*, edited by Albert R. Roberts. Thousand Oaks, CA: Sage, 251–76.

Welsh, Wayne N. 1996. Jail overcrowding and court-ordered reform: Critical issues. In *Visions for change: Crime and justice in the twenty-first century*, edited by Roslyn Muraskin and Albert R. Roberts. Upper Saddle River, NJ: Prentice Hall, 199–214.

Whitehead, John T., and Steven P. Lab. 1999. *Juvenile justice: An introduction*, 3rd edn. Cincinnati, OH: Anderson.

Winfree, L. Thomas, and Abadinsky, Howard. 2010. *Understanding crime. Essentials of criminological theory*. Belmont, CA: Wadsworth Cengage.

5 JAILS AND DETENTION FACILITIES

Outline

Objectives

- To provide you with a short history of jails
- To help you understand the differences between jails and other types of detention facilities
- To acquaint you with the problems female inmates face in jails
- To explain the differences in jail architectural designs
- To provide you with information on the types of people who work in jails and the functions they perform
- To introduce you to the major issues with which jails must cope
- To acquaint you with the "new generation" jail concept

INTRODUCTION

Jails were part of this country's earliest history, dating back to Virginia's Jamestown Colony in the 1600s. By the time of the Revolutionary War, many villages and towns had what was often called a *common jail*. Even in colonial times, jails were built, financed, and operated locally. The buildings were simply but sturdily built, and they were small. Few had the room to separate inmates—hence the name *common jail*. Males and females, adults and children, hardened criminals and undesirables, all typically were housed in a single room or a small number of cells.

As with so many other elements of the US criminal justice system, English settlers brought the institution of the jail with them. In a 1984 report, the Advisory Commission on Intergovernmental Relations (ACIR) noted that with the concept

Essentials of Corrections, Fifth Edition. G. Larry Mays and L. Thomas Winfree, Jr.
© 2014 John Wiley & Sons, Inc. Published 2014 by John Wiley & Sons, Inc.

of jails, the settlers also brought with them "county responsibility, sheriff administration, and fee-type compensation" (3).

Jails today fulfill several functions, but early English jails existed primarily to hold prisoners until they could be tried or executed. Like their English counterparts, early colonial jails primarily held people awaiting trial or punishment: incarceration was not itself a punishment. By the mid-1800s, though, the colonists had broken with this English tradition as well. Jails in this country were now housing three types of inmates: those awaiting trial, those convicted but awaiting sentencing, and those sentenced to serve jail time (ACIR 1984, 3–4).

This was the role jails continued to play in the United States throughout the nineteenth century and much of the twentieth century. They grew in number, and they increased in size, but jails still performed the same functions. Moreover, the quality of the nation's jails also remained largely unchanged.

CONTEMPORARY JAIL AND DETENTION FACILITIES

Conditions in this country's jails through the eighteenth century were primitive; some would say that conditions in contemporary jails are not much better. In the early 1970s, the National Advisory Commission on Criminal Justice Standards and Goals suggested, "The jail has evolved more by default than by plan. Perpetuated without change from the days of Alfred the Great, it has been a disgrace to every generation" (1973, 273). Since those words were written, the conditions in many jails have improved. Before we look at changes during the past three decades, though, we examine what makes a jail a jail and also jail demographics in the United States.

WHAT IS A JAIL?

Any number of facilities—from work camps to penitentiaries—can be used to house prisoners. What makes jails different from the rest? In its definition, the Bureau of Justice Statistics (2012) notes that "Jails are locally-operated short term facilities that hold both inmates awaiting trial or sentencing or both, and those sentenced to terms of less than 1 year, typically misdemeanants." A jail, then, is a facility, typically under the control of a city or county government, that houses a diverse population of pretrial detainees, convicted misdemeanants serving short sentences, and convicted felons awaiting transportation to prison. Box 5.1 shows something of the range of responsibilities of contemporary jails.

Jails occupy a unique place in the criminal justice system: they are the gateway to that system. But they are not prisons, and prisons are not jails. Felons may be housed in jails temporarily, but they do not serve time in jail.

Drawing on the characteristics defined by a number of observers, we can identify three that distinguish contemporary jails from prisons. First, jails house *various populations*. Unlike prisons, which tend to house convicted felons of a single gender, jails hold all kinds of people, male and female, young and old, misdemeanants and felons. Often between half and two-thirds of the average daily population (ADP) of jails are pretrial detainees who do not have the money to make bail. Probation and parole violators can also be detained in jail while they await judicial or administrative hearings, and convicted felons en route to state or federal prisons may spend several weeks in jail until bed space becomes available in a secure facility. Jails also house misdemeanants serving sentences of up to 1 year.

Among convicted jail inmates, an estimated 70 percent have used drugs regularly, and about the same percentage use alcohol. One in three jail inmates was drinking alcohol during the commission of the crime that resulted in his or her arrest, and slightly less than 30 percent were using other drugs when they committed their offense. One-quarter committed a drug offense (James 2004) and 8 percent of that group—more than 30,000 inmates—are convicted driving while intoxicated (DWI) offenders (James 2004, 3).

Some of the people in jails have not been charged with or convicted of crimes: they are people with mental illness or communicable diseases, and they are being held until a place can be found for them in a treatment program (Ditton 1999; also see Mays and Judiscak 1996). One jail inmate in seven was

FUNCTIONS SERVED BY JAILS

BOX 5.1

Among the functions served by jails are the following:

- Receive individuals pending arraignment and hold them awaiting trial, conviction, or sentencing.
- Re-admit probation, parole, and bail bond violators and absconders.
- Temporarily detain juveniles pending transfer to juvenile authorities.
- Hold people who are mentally ill pending their movement to appropriate health care facilities.
- Hold individuals for the military, for protective custody, for contempt, and for the courts as witnesses.
- Release convicted inmates to the community when they have completed their sentences.
- Transfer inmates to federal, state, or other authorities.
- House inmates for federal, state, or other authorities because of crowding in their facilities.
- Operate community-based electronic monitoring or other supervision programs

SOURCE: MINTON (2011, 3).

homeless in the year before incarceration (James 2004, 9). At midyear 2005, nearly two-thirds (64 percent) of jail inmates had mental health problems (James and Glaze 2006). One-third of all jail inmates have a physical impairment and a staggering 37 percent have a medical problem upon admission to jail, but less than half had seen a health care professional about the problem (Maruschak 2006, 1). The rate of confirmed human immunodeficiency virus/acquired immunodeficiency syndrome (HIV/AIDS) infection among jail inmates is ten times higher than it is in the general population (Maruschak 2004). Sociologist John Irwin (1985) has characterized the modern jail as an institution used to incarcerate the "rabble." He included in the rabble members of the permanent urban underclass as well as the disorderly or unruly segments of society.[1]

A second characteristic that sets jails apart is *location*. Jails traditionally are located in central business districts, often in the same building as, or immediately adjacent to, the county courthouse. Prisons, by contrast, frequently are situated in relatively remote locations.

Third, jails are unique because of the *way they are administered*. Most US prisons are operated by state corrections departments or the US Bureau of Prisons. Roughly 70 percent of US jails are operated by elected sheriffs (Kerle and Ford 1982). These officials typically come from a law enforcement background, and relatively few are even marginally interested in jail operations. For most sheriffs, jail management is a responsibility that is incidental to the office. This means that jails are both financially and operationally subordinate to law enforcement. To some degree, the problem with having law enforcement officials administer jails is that jails are not really law enforcement entities. By the same token, although jails are confinement facilities, they are not fully a part of the criminal justice system's corrections component.

Jails are not prisons. They also are not temporary **detention facilities** like the drunk tanks and lockups in police stations, facilities that hold people for no more than a day or two, until they can be formally charged, processed, and transported to a jail for booking.

HOW MANY JAILS?

Another factor distinguishes jails from prisons: jails are much more numerous. In 2005, there were 1,719 state and 102 federal prisons in the United States (Stephan 2008). By contrast, the 2006 national census of jails identified 3,283 federal, state, and local jails (Stephan and Walsh 2011). The number of jails decreased slightly from the previous census in 1999, and the trend since 1970 has been downward.[2] Small jails have generally disappeared. They have been combined with larger jails in a county jail system or merged with jails in other cities or adjacent counties in a regional facility.

HOW MANY INMATES?

In 2010, 809,360 people were under some form of jail supervision, 748,728 of them actual inmates (Minton 2011, 12). The "average" jail housed roughly 260 inmates. This is deceiving, however, because it is difficult to talk about the average jail in the United States: jails are unique facilities within the criminal justice system, and each jail is itself a unique facility.

Sabol and Minton (2008) found that nearly 60 percent of US jails have a rated capacity of 99 or fewer inmates, yet these jails house only about 8 percent of the nation's jail inmates. Previous national censuses of jails indicated that about half of the small jails are located in the South (also see Mays and Thompson 1988). But nationwide, the clear trend is toward fewer small jails and more medium to large jails.

Most local incarceration facilities have seen their populations decrease steadily since 1999. From 2000 to 2007 jail populations increased nationwide from 621,148 to 780,581. However, by 2009 inmate numbers had declined to 767,434 and in 2010 they were 748,728 (Sabol and Minton 2008; see also Minton 2011).

Each of the population numbers given here was for a specific day of the year in question. Although these one-day numbers do say something about occupancy in relation to capacity, and by implication the degree of crowding in jails, they do not reflect the actual number of inmates who pass through jails in a given year. The best estimates tell us that about 13 million people are admitted and released from the nation's jails each year, with slightly more admitted than released (Sabol and Minton 2008, 2). But this number, which is based on total bookings, overstates the actual number of *individuals* brought into and released from jails. Although most detainees are only booked once in a year, others may go in and out many times during a given year. Allowing for repeat detainees, we estimate that somewhere between 6 million and 10 million people are held in the nation's jails each year.

JAILS AND WOMEN

We discuss the gender distribution of the inmate population more fully in Chapter 13. However, three facts about women in jail help explain how contemporary jails are structured and operated.

First, the adult population in US jails traditionally has been overwhelmingly male (Table 5.1). In 2010, for example, there were 656,360 men in this nation's jails, 87.6 percent of the inmate population. However, both the numbers of men and women have decreased from 2007 to 2010, and the percentage of female inmates has declined from 12.8 percent of the population to 12.3 percent (Minton 2011, 7).

Second, female inmates are nearly twice as likely as male inmates to test positively for HIV, on average 2.3 percent versus 1.2 percent (Maruschak 2004, 8). The percentage of positive tests varies by race and ethnicity. The highest occurrence (3.0 percent) is found among black (non-Hispanic) women, who are also the largest single group of female inmates; white males have the lowest occurrence (0.6 percent)

TABLE 5.1 **Inmates in US jails, by gender, 2007–2010.**

Gender	Number of inmates			
	2007	2008	2009	2010
Male	679,654	685,862	673,728	656,360
Female	100,520	99,670	93,706	92,368

SOURCE: ADAPTED FROM MINTON (2011, 7).

(Harlow 1998, 3; Maruschak 2004, 8). Given the tendency of the corrections system generally, and the jail system in particular, to relegate women's needs to second place after men's, these figures do not bode well for female inmates who test positive for HIV.

Finally, although most women inmates are held in mixed-population jails, some are incarcerated in women-only facilities. Single-gender jails are rare. In 1999, with 3,365 public jails nationwide, there were only 13 jails exclusively for women, down from 18 in 1992 (Stephan 2001; Stohr and Mays 1993).

JAIL FUNCTIONS

Jails can differ greatly from county to county, even within the same state. The research of two individuals—Patrick Jackson and John Klofas—has

contributed greatly to our understanding of the differences among jails.

Jackson (1988) examined the operations of three California jails: the Los Angeles County Central Jail, the San Francisco Jail, and the Yolo County Jail. These jails differed not only in the size of the population served, but also in how they were used by local authorities and how that affected the makeup of the inmate population. For example, the Los Angeles County jail was used primarily to house suspects who had been arraigned, so the inmates there tended to be charged with more serious crimes. By contrast, authorities in San Francisco used the jail there to detain people charged with public-order offenses (such as drunkenness and vagrancy); most of the inmates spent relatively short periods in confinement. The Yolo County Jail was typical of many small jails in the United States. It served a rural population, and it booked and held inmates at a

SCOTT HOUSETO/ALAMY IMAGES

fairly low rate. The typical inmate in this facility had been charged with drunk driving or a public order offense. Despite the differences in the functions of these jails, Jackson found that most of the inmates in all three facilities fell easily into Irwin's "rabble" characterization.

Klofas also has added to our understanding of jails through his jail-use typology (1987, 1988, 1991a). He described four types of jails based on booking rates and holding rates:

- **Holding jails** book inmates at a low rate but detain them for some time. This type of jail would be consistent with Jackson's (1988, 1991) assessment of the Los Angeles County Central Jail.

- **Processing jails** book people at a high rate but hold them for a relatively short time—like the San Francisco facility Jackson studied.

- **Low-use jails** both book and hold inmates at very low rates. Low-use jails, such as the Yolo County facility, are most often found in rural counties or small towns.

- **High-use jails** both book and hold inmates at high rates. An example would be any major urban facility, like Chicago's Cook County Jail.

THE DESIGN OF JAILS

The physical layout of a jail defines the nature of the supervision there. With advances in technology, with new tools for overseeing inmate activities, the configuration of jails has evolved through at least three phases.

The most traditional jail design, shown in Figure 5.1, is a **linear design**, with cells opening onto long straight hallways (W. R. Nelson 1988). In facilities with a linear design, custody personnel work outside the cells and make periodic rounds. To see what a particular inmate is doing, an officer has to look into the individual's cell. This pattern of inmate management is called **intermittent supervision**. Officer supervision here is less regular than in other forms.

Second-generation jails make use of closed-circuit television cameras or other devices to increase the surveillance of inmate activities in common areas. The basic layout of these facilities still is linear, and officers still have to walk down a hallway and look into cells to check on individual inmates, but monitoring devices allow **remote supervision** of prisoners and staff members at jail entrances (sally ports), in booking areas, in drunk tanks, and in corridors. This form of inmate supervision is most common in jails

FIGURE 5.1 Linear-Design Jail.

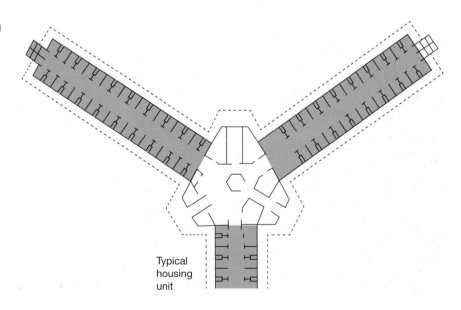

Typical housing unit

FIGURE 5.2 **Podular-Design Jail: A New Generation.**

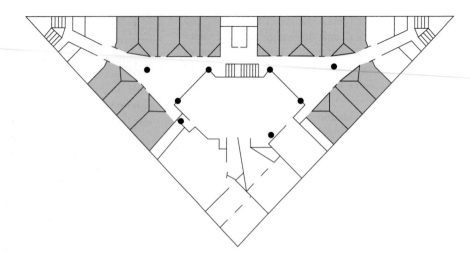

and prisons with low staff-to-inmate ratios because it allows a small number of corrections officers (COs) to supervise a large number of inmates.

Third-generation design commonly is found in **new-generation jails**. This design holds the promise of not just bigger jails but also better ones. The **podular design** departs from linear design by housing inmates in pods (Zupan and Menke 1991). The pods are triangular structures, their perimeter lined with 16 to 46 small sleeping rooms, and their center left open as a dayroom or program area (Figure 5.2).[3] One goal of the design is to make inmates feel safer: at certain times they can retreat to their own sleeping quarters and shut, and perhaps lock, the door (Zupan and Stohr-Gillmore 1988).

The podular design also has given rise to a new form of inmate management (R. M. Davis 1987). Remember that inmate management in linear-design jails is either intermittent or remote. COs periodically make rounds past or through inmates' cells to see whether any prohibited activity is taking place. After an officer wanders by, inmates are free to return to whatever they were doing for another 30 to 45 minutes. In new-generation jails, inmates are under the **direct supervision** of corrections officers 24 hours a day. Direct supervision eliminates many of the traditional barriers between inmates and staff, allowing staff members greater interaction with and control over prisoners. Of course, direct contact with inmates requires new interpersonal skills for COs

who have worked only in traditional facilities. It also requires a more open, participative management style by administrators.

Although new-generation jails do not solve all the problems of contemporary jails, they do offer hope on a number of fronts (Conroy, Smith, and Zupan 1991; Wallenstein 1987). First, evidence indicates that direct supervision means jails can be built to standard commercial construction specifications, which means less money spent making the facilities secure and installing protective devices (W. R. Nelson 1988). Second, research indicates that inmates not only may feel safer but actually may be safer in new-generation jails (Sechrest 1989a; Zupan and Menke 1991; Zupan and Stohr-Gillmore 1988). Third, after the initial apprehension of moving from a traditional jail to a direct-supervision jail, job satisfaction among staff members increases and remains relatively high (Stohr, Self, and Lovrich 1992). The key would seem to be more training in communications and human relations skills for staff members, which may require hiring more and better qualified employees and, in all likelihood, paying them more (McCampbell 1990).

JAIL ADMINISTRATION

Jails fit into one of a small number of administrative patterns. Again, sheriffs' departments operate about

DEAN HANSON/CORBIS

70 percent of US jails (Kerle and Ford 1982). In some counties, jail administration is a county department, and the head of that department is appointed by the county government. Under this arrangement, the jail administrator reports to the county manager, the county judge, or the board of supervisors. A third arrangement places control of the jail under the chief of police. This is most common in counties that have combined police and sheriff's departments or in large cities that operate their own jails. Fourth, in a number of very large urban areas—Dade County (Florida), Los Angeles County, and New York City, for example—the jails are part of a local corrections department (Haque 1989). In these areas, each facility may be designated for a special use: possibly one jail for females, another for pretrial detainees, and another for inmates actually serving time.

The administrative arrangement often indicates the significance of the jail's operating budget. Administration-by-sheriff can mean money and attention goes to law enforcement instead of jails.

Additionally, the type of jail administration can indicate the pay, status, and personnel deployment patterns. We now turn our attention to personnel.

JAIL EMPLOYEES

The layout and administration of a jail are critical to its performance. But the greatest influence on the jail's day-to-day operations is the ability of the people who work there. In a survey of problems facing Texas jails, Kellar (2001) found that human resource issues were first in importance. Among those concerns are officer retention, pay, understaffing and employee assignments and quality.

THE NUMBER OF EMPLOYEES

Most jails are understaffed (Kerle 2002; Mays and Thompson 1991). In 2006, there were an estimated

234,000 jail employees nationwide, an average of 1 employee for every 3.3 inmates (up from 1 to 2.9 inmates in 1999). The majority of those employees were serving as detention/corrections officers. Understaffing is particularly acute in small and rural jails, and during the night shift in many jails (see Ruddell and Mays 2011). In some counties, it is not uncommon to have the jail's night shift staffers working two jobs—CO and dispatcher, for example (Kerle and Ford 1982). In linear-design jails, this may mean that inmates are unsupervised for long periods, a situation ripe for inmate assaults on one another and for suicides.

EMPLOYEE ASSIGNMENTS AND QUALITY

It is virtually impossible to separate work assignments and employee quality: both are related to the facility's dominant administrative system.

In the traditional approach to staffing, custodial personnel are simply sheriff's deputies assigned to work in the jail. These employees tend to come from five groups (F. R. Ford 1993; Rowan 1993; Struckhoff 1989):

- New hires awaiting the start of a training-academy class.
- Newly trained deputies awaiting assignment to road patrol.
- Deputies who have requested a jail assignment (not uncommon among older deputies who have become tired of the rigors of patrol).
- Deputies on limited duty because of accidents or injuries.
- Deputies who are being disciplined.

The result is that many jail employees are in their positions for some reason other than personal choice, and not all of them are happy about their placement. This can lead to problems with inmates, other employees, and supervisors.

Under the second administrative system, sheriffs or jail administrators develop two separate career tracks: one for patrol deputies and one for detention facility personnel. These are distinct and not interchangeable career options. Therefore, personnel cannot simply transfer from one function to the other. This ensures continuity in the operations of jails, and staff members who are better trained. But the fact that detention officers often are paid less than patrol officers, a reflection of the comparative value sheriff's departments tend to place on corrections officers, can lower the quality of the people who choose the corrections track (Rowan 1993).

Two ways of improving the quality of jail employees are through better training and better compensation. In many states, training is minimal. Programs teach the technical aspects of facility operations (for example, using physical restraints, writing reports, and disciplining inmates) and human relations (interpersonal communications skills, dispute resolution). According to the American Jail Association and other groups, what is needed is not law enforcement training, although it involves elements of law enforcement training, and it is not corrections or prison training either. In the end, jail training is distinctive. It should focus on issues like working with people who are mentally ill or suicidal, diffusing conflict, and anger management for inmates and staff.

The nature of jail training is one reason some sheriff's departments have decided to separate the law enforcement and custody career paths. Law enforcement officers carry weapons and generally receive training during a period of 10 to 20 weeks (400 to 800 hours). By contrast, custody officers are not armed and may receive only two to four weeks (80 to 160 hours) of training. These differences may explain why jail personnel are paid less and why they have or are perceived to have second-class status.

MAJOR JAIL ISSUES

By design, jails deal with social problems, which may be one of the reasons they exhibit so many problems themselves. Here we address a number of the problems that affect jail operations, particularly those that seem most resistant to change.

LOCAL POLITICS

A major problem facing contemporary jails is that they are a product of their local political environment

(ACIR 1984; National Advisory Commission 1973; Thompson 1986). Most are administered by a sheriff's department; at the same time, they are subject to the policy directives and funding controls of a city council, a county commission, or a county board of supervisors (Ricci 1986). Sometimes, jails are caught in the middle of a standoff between a sheriff from one political party and a coalition of county commissioners from another. The result is often a policy stalemate.

The political problems of jails become all too apparent in the budget process. Jails must compete in budget negotiations with schools, roads, health care, solid-waste disposal, and parks and recreation. All of these programs are far more popular with voters than are jails.

LOCAL FUNDING

A second problem jails face is local financing. Jails are the victims of low funding priorities, and they suffer because counties have relatively inflexible revenue bases (National Advisory Commission 1973). Most of the counties in the United States rely heavily, if not exclusively, on property taxes, and students of local government have long recognized that property taxes, of all revenue sources, are the least responsive to local economic growth.

When we combine political conservatism ("Lock 'em up, and throw away the key") with fiscal conservatism ("Public money shouldn't be wasted on bad people and the jails that house them"), we find jails suffering a conflicting experience (Mays and Thompson 1991, 11–12; Ruddell and Mays 2011). Thus, jails must house an increasing number of inmates in aging facilities that are too small and are poorly maintained.

Two states—Ohio and California—devised innovative ways to help jurisdictions cope with the shortcomings in the local financing of jails. In the 1980s, in an effort to deal with a persistent lack of funds for prison construction, Ohio moved from reliance on general-obligation revenue bonds to the use of lease-purchase agreements (DeWitt 1986d). This approach—which was extended to cover jail construction in 1986—offers several advantages over traditional financing methods. For instance, a lease

does not obligate the government to ongoing debt. Additionally, lease agreements can be negotiated over a relatively short time. And, perhaps most importantly, lease agreements, unlike bond issues, seldom require voters' approval.

California also takes a different approach to funding jail construction and improvement (Lammers and Morris 1990). As a result of voter initiatives like Proposition 13 (a 1978 initiative that established property tax limitations) California created the County Jail Capital Expenditure Fund, a general-obligation bond pool of money accessible to counties throughout the state. From 1980 to 1988, the fund made more than $1.45 billion available to counties that were struggling to deal with "litigation, deterioration, and crowding" in their jails (2).

LOCATION ISSUES

Some of the problems jails face can be solved only through expansion, construction, or relocation. Expansion often is the least costly alternative when the issue is simply one of needing more space. But expansion may not be feasible in a jail's present location, or it may not be possible to expand a building that is more than 50 years old.

For some counties, the issue is not the size of the jail but its suitability (Hall 1987). Here, it may be necessary to build a new facility. The preferred site usually is at or near a jail's present location: often the courthouse and jail-related services (lawyers' offices, bail-bonding businesses) are located near the jail and have a vested interest in keeping the jail where it is. If new land must be purchased, the county faces a funding dilemma (Orrick 1989). Acquiring additional property for the building and parking, even under the government's right of eminent domain, can be a lengthy and expensive process.

Most counties faced with a major jail expansion or relocation project are forced to look for property away from the traditional central business district. Remote locations are more feasible today because of video arraignments, which allow judges and lawyers to be in one place while the prisoners are in another. One disadvantage of nontraditional sites is accessing utilities. Another is the opposition of neighboring landowners, who have nothing against a jail as long as it's not in their backyard (Mays and Czerniak 1992–1993; Welsh et al. 1991). In the face of organized opposition, politicians have been known to back down from a jail relocation decision.

MAKESHIFT STRUCTURES

For some counties, the problem of jail crowding is chronic, but for others, it is acute. The problem is worse during the weekend, when jail populations often swell (US Department of Justice 1983). Three factors are at work here: First, law enforcement activity over the weekend can put additional prisoners—especially those charged with crimes like DWI—into jails. Second, in some jurisdictions judges may not be available over the weekend to conduct bail hearings as often as they do during weekday business hours. This leaves some prisoners languishing in jail over the weekend simply because they cannot make an initial appearance before a judicial officer until the start of business Monday morning. Third, judges are increasingly imposing weekend sentences on certain offenders, particularly those convicted of DWI (May 1978).

In some counties, especially large urban counties, crowding is a chronic problem that requires a long-term solution. These counties may be faced with the choice of adding new facilities or expanding their current ones (Cunniff 2002).

One of the promising approaches to dealing with jail crowding is the use of **jail annexes** or **satellite jails**, structures that house the overflow from main jails. These alternative structures may be built as an annex or make use of an existing structure, a former school or warehouse, for example. At one time, New York City converted two former British troop ships into jail barges that were moored in the East River (Haque 1989; Welch 1991). Some jail annexes are high-tech, built with the latest technology; others are decidedly low-tech.

Converting an existing structure into a satellite jail offers savings in time and money: the building already exists in some form and so only needs modification. Even building a jail annex can be less costly than building a central jail: most of these structures do not have to conform to the higher security standards required in central jails. This is because they

often are used to house work-release inmates and other prisoners who need less security than the jail's general population.

Opposition to makeshift facilities comes primarily from two groups. Michael Welch (1991) argues that the use of alternative structures expands our capacity to punish. That is, when counties can add jail space quickly and relatively inexpensively, they never have to address the underlying issues: Whom are we jailing? Why? They can just keep incarcerating more and more people. The second group argues that what administrators call "temporary solutions" tend to be fairly enduring because crowding is a chronic problem. They insist that the use of alternative structures keeps decision makers from focusing on the root of the problem: the patterns of jail use.

PRIVATIZATION

One of the most hotly debated issues in corrections is **privatization**, the movement toward having

L. THOMAS WINFREE, JR.

corrections facilities or specific functions within those facilities constructed or operated by private contractors (see, for example, Logan 1990; Mays and Gray 1996; and Robbins 1988). Although we explore this issue in greater depth in Chapters 11 and 14, we examine its application to jails here (see, especially, Collins 1987a, 1987b).

Privatization provides several advantages for counties looking for ways to deal with many of their jail problems (McCullough and Maguigan 1990; J. Ward 1990). For instance, the private sector may be able to help a county finance the renovation or construction of a jail when the taxpayers have refused to approve a capital bond issue, or the private sector may offer the county a turnkey option in a lease-purchase agreement. In either situation, a private contractor handles the construction and then turns the operation over to a public-sector agency (Bowen and Kelly 1987). Experience in many counties has demonstrated that private-sector organizations are able to buy land and build jails more quickly and at less cost than governments (Hackett et al. 1987).

Counties also may be able to save money by contracting with private vendors for specific services. A **public–private partnership** is an arrangement in which a government makes a legal agreement to purchase specific services from a private-sector supplier (Cox and Osterhoff 1991). Among the most common services are food services, medical care, counseling, education, and job training.

The private approach to total facility management has been criticized on several counts. For example, some authorities believe that the private sector has little or no business operating detention facilities (see, for example, Feeley 1991; Gilbert 1996; Robbins 1988). These authorities insist that the jail and prison operations are inherently a government function. However, there is precedent for public-private partnerships: the private sector has been involved in the corrections system in various ways throughout its development.

Other critics base their opposition to privatization on the way governments are charged for services, usually a per diem charge per inmate. They argue that this kind of pricing arrangement creates an incentive for private contractors who own or operate facilities to spend less on inmates and to keep the beds as full as possible to maximize their profits.

One argument for privatization is that private contractors can provide certain goods and services at much-reduced cost. For example, when a county needs to buy sheets and towels for a jail, it must advertise for bids, which can take time and does not guarantee the lowest possible price. By contrast, private jail operators are free to purchase whatever they need from suppliers with whom they have negotiated quantity discounts or long-term contracts. This holds true particularly for purchases of cleaning and janitorial supplies and food. In most counties, private-sector companies may well be able to operate a jail at lower cost than the government (Hackett et al. 1987).

Another advantage of privatization is the potential reduction of legal liability. Many private contractors specify that any jail they build and operate will conform to American Correctional Association (ACA) standards. This means that new facilities are eligible for accreditation, which is a defense when inmates sue over the conditions of confinement. Of course, local policymakers must be aware that contracting for jail operations does not exempt them from legal liability. It generally means the county's liability is reduced or shared with the private operator (see Chaires and Lentz 1996).

Privatization to date has not had a significant impact on the number of jails in the United States and the number of private facilities is decreasing. At midyear 1999, there were 47 private jails in this country, 1 percent of the nation's jails. By 2006 this number had declined to 37. Seven states—Texas (8); California (5); Pennsylvania (4); Florida (3), Missouri (3), New Mexico (3), and Tennessee—had 29 of the nation's private jails (Stephan and Walsh 2011, 10).

JAIL STANDARDS

The development of jail standards has been going on for over three decades. The ACA issued its first edition of *Standards for Adult Local Detention Facilities* in 1977; the third edition was published in 1991 (ACA 1991). The ACA's standards cover a number of areas, among them training and staff development, building and safety codes, security and control, safety and emergency procedures, inmate rights, food service, sanitation and hygiene, health care, and work and industries programs. Additionally, some states have expanded the minimum standards, adding requirements concerned with the construction and operations of facilities.

It is difficult to locate data on the number of jurisdictions that have jail standards in place. Nevertheless, the American Correctional Association (2012) reports that 32 states have some form of jail standards. However, in most states these standards are voluntary and they do not include mandatory audits or inspections.

Jails in those states with mandatory standards, regular inspections, and enforcement mechanisms have more effective programs and operating procedures (Thompson and Mays 1988a). More to the point, jails in those states are more likely to provide inmates with medical care in the facility itself, and to screen inmates for physical and emotional problems, and for alcohol abuse. These jails also keep inmates confined to their cells for fewer hours a day. Most important, these facilities have substantially fewer inmate deaths—by natural causes or suicide— than do their nonstandard, noninspected counterparts (Thompson and Mays 1988a, 1988b).

Given the growing number of lawsuits brought by inmates regarding jail conditions, we are likely to see more states adopt standards on an increasing number of those conditions, and more vigorous inspections and enforcement. As many jail administrators have learned, having jail standards does not keep a jail from being sued, but having standards and adhering to them can greatly reduce both the mishandling of inmates and the rates at which lawsuits are brought and won.

REMOVING JUVENILES FROM ADULT JAILS

Since the 1970s, and some would say even earlier, there has been ongoing debate about the incarceration of juvenile offenders in adult jails (see Schwartz 1989, 1991). One of the major provisions in the Juvenile Justice and Delinquency Prevention Act of 1974 was the removal of juvenile detainees from

TABLE 5.2 **Juvenile inmates in US jails, 2007–2010.**

Juvenile inmates	Number of inmates			
	2007	2008	2009	2010
Held as adults	5,649	6,410	5,846	5,647
Held as juveniles	1,184	1,294	1,373	1,912
Total juvenile inmates	6,833	7,704	7,219	7,559

SOURCE: ADAPTED FROM MINTON (2011, 7).

adult jails. That has yet to happen. In fact, recent research shows that the number of juveniles in adult jails still is relatively high.

As Table 5.2 shows, 7,559 juveniles were being detained in US jails in 2010 (Minton 2011, 7). Most people assume that these are the worst of the worst juvenile offenders, a shaky assumption at best. In many small rural counties, there is no juvenile detention center, and so the options often are adult jail or nothing.

Most jail administrators are reluctant to house juveniles in their facilities under any circumstances. The issue is liability. Juvenile detainees must be housed out of sight and sound of adult offenders (Dale 1988). The result is that these youngsters often end up in the most remote sections of jails, in locations where the risk of assault and suicide is the greatest.[4]

For most counties, the solution has been relatively simple: build a separate juvenile detention center to house these youngsters. If a county does not have a sufficient population of young offenders or the economic resources to support its own juvenile detention facility, it might join with an adjacent city or county to create a regional facility, a solution that is occurring with adult jails (Stephan and Walsh 2011).

Another issue with juvenile offenders is the dramatic increase in their overall number in US jails. In 1990 they numbered 2,301 ballooning to 7,615 in 2000. This has since remained fairly constant (Minton 2011, 7). One explanation is that a number of jurisdictions have targeted their get-tough-on-crime policies at young offenders. As a result, large numbers of youngsters are being tried as adults, and they are being housed in adult jails until their cases have been tried.

THE PHYSICAL PLANT

Jails suffer a great deal of wear and tear, not only from the number of inmates passing through each year, but also from routine vandalism. One approach to dealing with this problem is to construct all or nearly all jail space as maximum-security space. This means building jails out of reinforced concrete and steel, materials that are nearly indestructible.

A second approach to maintaining a jail's physical plant is through direct inmate supervision. In new-generation jails, COs are located in the housing pods along with the inmates. This not only reduces assaults on inmates, but also reduces vandalism and the destruction of property. Because supervision is direct and constant in podular-design jails, there is less wear and tear on the facilities, which means commercial-grade materials can be used in their construction.

INMATE PROGRAMMING

Not all of the problems facing contemporary jails are the result of crowding, staff, or the physical plant. Many stem from the inmates themselves. Irwin (1985) characterized them as rabble (also see Welch 1989). Certainly many of them live at society's margins even when they are not incarcerated. They tend to be drawn disproportionately from racial and ethnic minorities, and, in general, from the lowest socioeconomic strata. They often have **special needs**, physical, psychological, or medical problems that require treatment or special services (James and Glaze 2006; Karberg and James 2005; Maruschak 2006), and many of them are unemployed. In other words, these people have problems outside jail, and when they come to jail, they bring those problems with them. We will deal with the problems of special needs inmates further in Chapter 8.

Any number of programs are available to address the physical, emotional, and socioeconomic problems of jail inmates. But three factors limit their implementation in jails. The first is time. Much of the jail inmate population is transient, there for a matter of

days or weeks. Even those who are serving time measure their sentences in months, rather than years.[5] This is not an excuse for a lack of programming, but it means that jail administrators have to find ways to make constructive use of whatever time they have with inmates. The two other factors that limit the programming jails are able to offer are a lack of physical space and money.

MEDICAL TREATMENT AND PROGRAMS Infectious diseases—among them, drug-resistant tuberculosis, various forms of hepatitis, and sexually transmitted diseases—pose threats to jail inmates and staff (Maruschak 2006). Most jails are ill equipped to deal with any one of these problems, let alone several at one time. One of the most dramatic health-care issues facing contemporary jails involves inmates with HIV or those who have developed AIDS (Maruschak 2004). Jail inmates seem particularly susceptible to AIDS because many of them have histories of intravenous drug use and may engage in needle sharing and other risky activities.

When the 1999 census of jails was conducted, 1.7 percent of the nation's jail inmates were reported to be HIV-positive; that percentage was slightly lower (1.3 percent) but virtually unchanged in 2002. Interestingly, the number of HIV-positive inmates decreased from 6,711 in 1993 to 4,871 in 2002 (Maruschak 2004, 8). The distribution of HIV-positive inmates was not uniform across the United States. In fact, the largest jails reported the highest infection rates. Statistics from the 1996 survey of local jails shows that HIV/AIDS cases vary by gender, race and ethnicity, age, marital status, and education (Harlow 1998). In general, the highest rates were reported for black (non-Hispanic) women, Hispanics, inmates over 35 years of age, and widowed or divorced inmates (Maruschak 2004).

There were 42 AIDS-related jail deaths in the United States in 2002 (down from 58 in 2000). From 2000 to 2002, 155 jail inmates in the United States died from AIDS-related illnesses. These illnesses continue to be a leading cause of inmate deaths.

Although there have been no documented cases of job-related HIV infection of corrections officers (Hammett and Moini 1990; Maruschak 2001;

Takas and Hammett 1989), inmates who are HIV-positive pose an assortment of problems for jails. First, uninformed and untrained staff members may be anxious about working with inmates who are carrying the AIDS virus. The fear of contamination—however unrealistic—is always present. Second, other inmates may panic if they learn that someone with HIV is housed in the jail's general population. Third, there can be legal repercussions for administrators who segregate HIV-positive inmates from the general population, especially if that segregation takes on a punitive dimension. Finally, jails assume medical responsibility for all of those inmates they house (Lawrence and Zwisohn 1991; Welch 1989). Therefore, as part of each jail's programming, there must be ongoing AIDS awareness education for both staff members and inmates.

COUNSELING PROGRAMS Estimates are that from half to two-thirds of the inmates in jails are drug or alcohol abusers (Mays, Fields, and Thompson 1991; D. J. Wilson 2000). Many of these inmates are suffering from withdrawal, and—given that one in three was homeless before being jailed—some are conspicuously malnourished. They need medical treatment as well as counseling to stabilize their physical and emotional conditions. Drug- and alcohol-dependent inmates may also bring serious psychological problems into the jail environment, and these inmates may be prime candidates for suicide in jail (Kennedy and Homant 1988; Winfree 1988; Winfree and Wooldredge 1991; Wooldredge and Winfree 1992).

In a 1998 survey, one in ten jail inmates reported an emotional or mental condition, and a similar number reported an overnight stay in a mental hospital. Based on these two criteria, one in five jail inmates is reported to have had recent mental health problems (James and Glaze 2006). Inmates who are mentally ill are more likely than other inmates to report one or more of the following problems: drug or alcohol use at the time of the offense, drug use in the month before the offense, a history of alcohol dependence, and fighting while drinking. After arriving in jail, these inmates tend to get into fights and break rules more often than other inmates. It makes sense, then, for jails to screen incoming inmates for

signs of substance abuse and mental illness, provide them with immediate care and treatment, and promote some type of long-term solution to whatever problem is at the root of their chemical dependence.

What can jails do for substance abusers? First, they need to provide detoxification facilities and treatment programs such as Alcoholics Anonymous and Narcotics Anonymous. Staff members can conduct these programs, or they may be available through community groups and organizations. Of course, access to detoxification facilities and drug treatment programs is directly related to the size of the facility: the larger the jail, the more likely it is to run medical facilities and substance abuse programs. The critical size appears to be 250 or more inmates: seven out of ten facilities this size or larger report having substance abuse programs (D. J. Wilson 2000, 7). At the other extreme, only about one in three of the jails holding fewer than 50 inmates offer substance abuse treatment, and only about one in four have detoxification facilities. In the 2006 national jail census, researchers found that overall about 10 percent of the jails in the United States offered drug or alcohol treatment (Stephan and Walsh 2011).

Mental health problems may extend beyond substance-abusing inmates. Researchers have characterized the jail as contemporary society's mental health clinic (Jerrell and Komisaruk 1991; Kalinich, Embert, and Senese 1988, 1991; Senese, Kalinich, and Embert 1989). As a result of the movement to deinstitutionalize many of those formerly committed to state psychiatric hospitals, people who need mental health care are left to live on the streets of most large cities (Judiscak 1995). Supposedly, care was to be provided for these people through community mental health programs. However, because most of these programs are underfunded and understaffed, a host of potential clients do not receive the services they need. After these people wander the streets long enough, their often bizarre appearance and behavior bring them into contact with local law enforcement officers, who put them in jail to appease citizens' complaints or as a "mercy booking" (Jerrell and Komisaruk 1991). In the end, it seems we have deinstitutionalized a population in need but criminalized its mental health treatment (Haddad 1993; Hecht and Smithhart 1987).

Ironically, many jail inmates receive no better mental health treatment in jail than they did when they roamed the streets. According to a 1998 survey, about 40 percent of mentally ill jail inmates received some form of mental health services (Ditton 1999). Most of those who were mentally ill (34 percent) were given medication. Fewer than 10 percent were admitted overnight to a mental hospital or treatment program, but more than half received counseling or therapy. The key, as Todd Clear and George Cole (2003) observe, is the diversion of those who are mentally ill away from jails by the judicious screening, interviewing, and evaluating of pretrial detainees.

REHABILITATIVE SERVICES Another group of programs for jail inmates can be classified under the general heading **rehabilitative services**. These programs can include religious activities provided by local churches or jail chaplains, recreation, sessions on coping skills and anger management, and instruction in parenting techniques (for both male and female inmates). These efforts do two things: they teach skills and abilities that are relevant in the outside world, and they make constructive use of inmates' time in jail. Unfortunately, research involving a group of women-only jails found that although inmates are eager to take part in these programs, few jails provide enough programs to actually meet inmates' needs (Gray, Mays, and Stohr 1995).

EDUCATION AND VOCATIONAL TRAINING Many jail inmates are unemployed at the time of their arrest. This is often because they lack education and marketable job skills (Harlow 2003). For some, long criminal histories have rendered them virtually unemployable (Tewksbury and Vito 1994; Western and Petit 2000). Lack of sufficient employment means that many jail inmates cannot post even a modest bail and the vast majority of them cannot afford an attorney. Frequently, inmates go to court on relatively minor charges without an attorney and simply plead guilty to the charges. For them, the "process is the punishment" (Feeley 1979).

OTHER LOCAL DETENTION FACILITIES

Several options other than county or regional jails are available to local authorities for short-term incarceration. Although at some point we may witness more alternatives to incarceration, the public mood today points to an increase in the amount and forms of incarceration.

MINIMUM SECURITY FACILITIES

One category of alternatives to traditional jails is minimum security facilities. Virtually all jails are built to maximum-security specifications. This is an inefficient system because maximum-security space is the most expensive to construct, because bed space in jails is at a premium, and because most jail inmates do not require maximum-security confinement. As a result of this, a number of local jurisdictions are constructing sections of new jails or completely separate facilities—satellite jails—to house lower-risk inmates.

This approach seems particularly appropriate for certain inmates. For example, individuals charged with shoplifting and other minor property crimes seldom warrant anything more than minimum-security custody. The same is probably true for most of those charged with DWI, especially those sentenced to serve weekend terms. What these inmates need is a place to report to and a set of walls, perhaps enclosed by a fence, to contain them for their 48-hour-or-so stays.

POLICE LOCKUPS

One of the most pervasive detention facilities in the United States is the **police lockup**. (See Box 5.2 for a look at lockups and jails in other countries.) There are so many, in fact, that we do not have an exact count, although estimates run as high as 15,000 facilities around the country (Abadinsky and Winfree 1992). Several features distinguish lockups from other types of detention facilities:

● Most lockups are located in a police building. In some cities, old service stations or other renovated structures have been pressed into service as lockups (see, for example, Welch 1991).

- Lockups temporarily detain suspects until they can be interrogated or fully processed by the police and then transferred to the county jail.

- Research tells us that lockups are dangerous places (Winfree 1988). Because they are temporary holding structures, inmate activities are not monitored as closely as they would be in a central jail. This often results in higher levels of inmate-on-inmate assaults and higher numbers of inmate deaths than are found in jails or prisons.

COUNTY WORKHOUSES AND PENAL FARMS

In many US counties, separate facilities are maintained for misdemeanants serving terms longer than 90 days. Instead of holding inmates serving 6- to 12-month sentences in the main jail, the county may

operate a workhouse or a penal farm. These low-security facilities tend to be located away from the courthouse and the central business district, where jails traditionally are situated. Inmates serving time in these longer-term facilities have a variety of work responsibilities. For instance, they might perform maintenance in parks and on roads, or do farming. They also might be responsible for maintaining government vehicles. Also, workhouses and penal farms may offer programming opportunities that are not available in central jails. Workhouses and penal farms may be more common in rural settings, but even urban counties may operate facilities for longer-term inmates outside the central jail setting.

STATE-RUN JAILS

Throughout this chapter, we have been saying that jails are locally operated and funded facilities, and that these features distinguish them from prisons.

DAVID ALAN HARVEY/MAGNUM PHOTOS

Local jails are run by large cities, counties, and regions; the states may assist those local governments, and some operate their own jail systems.

State assistance of local jails can take several forms: the development of jail standards, jail inspections and certification, and funding for construction and operations, for example. The Commonwealth of Virginia, for example, has established regional detention centers (Liebowitz 1991). These 12 regional jails are used by 24 counties and 11 cities.

SPOTLIGHT ON INTERNATIONAL CORRECTIONS: POLICE LOCKUPS, REMAND FACILITIES, AND PRISONS

BOX 5.2

Jails—short-term incarceration facilities administered and operated locally—are relatively rare outside the United States. What happens in other countries to people awaiting arraignment or to postconviction misdemeanants? In most European nations, those accused of crimes are taken as quickly as possible before a magistrate, who advises them of the charges and their right to pretrial release. Most are simply released at that point on a money or property bond or on their word that they will return for trial. With the exception of those accused of capital crimes, detention is usually the last resort.

In some nations—France is one example—the police, with judicial approval, can temporarily detain a person accused of what the French describe as "flagrant" felonies or misdemeanors for as long as 24 hours; the prosecutor can extend the detention for cause for another 24 hours. Similar procedures were common in the former Soviet Union, but they lacked judicial oversight. In postcommunist Poland, pretrial detention—called *preliminary detention*—is an option only if there is probable cause that the suspect committed the offense and one or more of the following conditions exists: (1) the accused is a flight risk or has no permanent residence; (2) there is reason to believe that the accused may attempt to obstruct justice, for example by suborning perjury; (3) the penalty for the charge is at least an 8-year sentence, or the individual has been convicted and the sentence is more than 3 years; or (4) there is reason to believe the accused will commit another crime. Japan has a unique approach to pretrial detention. In theory, accused persons can be detained for as long as 23 days without bail unless they confess. Not surprisingly, most suspects confess; only rarely are people detained for the full 23 days.

Where are pretrial detainees housed if there are no jails? They usually are housed temporarily—from a few hours to a few days—in a police lockup, a short-term holding facility like the police lockups in the United States. If a decision is made to continue to detain them, they often go to a state-run prison. The Prague City Jail in the Czech Republic is actually a jail and a prison: the facility houses both accused and convicted misdemeanants and felons, men and women, children and adults.

In some legal systems, those accused of crimes but not yet convicted are called *remand prisoners*; the rest are simply *convicts* or *prisoners*. The term *remand* is from the Latin *remandere*, "to send back." In those systems, a legal authority can send an accused back to jail (or prison) pending further investigation of the charges. Often the only way to distinguish between remand prisoners and other prisoners is their clothing: the former wear their own, while the latter wear state-issued clothing.

Our point: in most developed nations, pretrial detention is a far rarer occurrence than it is in the United States, where heavy reliance on monetary bail ensures that certain people—largely the poor—are detained before trial.

SOURCES: REICHEL (2002, 14–15, 261, 310); PERSONAL OBSERVATIONS OF L. THOMAS WINFREE, JR. (JULY 2000).

Six states have taken assistance a step further. Alaska, Connecticut, Delaware, Hawaii, Rhode Island, and Vermont all operate their own jails (Stephan 2008). In these states, either state size or population led to the development of state-run jails. For example, Delaware is a small state, with just three counties. Instead of each county struggling to operate its own jail, Delaware combined the operation of state prisons and county jails in a state-run facility.

In the future, we may begin to see state-run jails in larger and more populous states. Consider the case of Texas. The 237 jails in Texas have been dealing with persistent crowding for almost three decades. Since the early 1980s, when the prisons operated by the Texas Department of Criminal Justice were placed under court order to reduce crowding, sentenced felons have been backing up in county jails (Stephan and Walsh 2011; Taft 1979). The result of local jail crowding has been a boom in jail expansion.

Eventually the state stepped in to offer counties relief from a dilemma of the state's making. In 1992, the Texas legislature created a new category of offenders, "state jail felons" (Harris-George, Jarrett, and Shigley 1994). To house these inmates and provide relief for overcrowded prisons, the state has built several regional facilities. Each region contains either a Mode 1 or Mode 2 state jail. The Mode 1 jails eventually will house 17,000 inmates and will be operated by the Institutional Division of the Department of Criminal Justice. The Mode 2 jails will provide another 7,000 beds and will be operated by the Community Supervision Department, the county probation agency (Harris-George, Jarrett, and Shigley 1994). This movement, coupled with the construction of additional prison space, has dramatically reduced inmate population crowding in some areas.

Although not every state can follow the lead of Virginia and Texas, states should play a greater role in dealing with the dilemmas facing jails (Thompson and Mays 1991). The creation of state-assisted and state-run jails is one possible solution to some of the persistent problems faced by contemporary jails.

TRENDS IN CONTEMPORARY JAILS

Given the demand for local space for detention and the increasingly complex functions jails carry out, jails will undoubtedly continue to play a major role in local criminal justice. At least two trends are likely to persist: consideration of alternatives to incarceration and innovations in architectural styles (new-generation jails).

ALTERNATIVES TO INCARCERATION

Some observers have said that we cannot build ourselves out of the crowding crisis in today's jails and prisons (see, for example, Klofas 1991b; Welsh et al. 1991). Many jurisdictions have built a new jail only to see it filled in a matter of months. However, in the short-run the addition of bed space—about 2.5 percent or 22,000 beds annually since 2000—has reduced some of the crowding problems faced by jails (Minton 2011, 2).

In the future, whatever the public's mood, local governments may be forced by space and budget constraints to consider alternatives *to* incarceration rather than alternative forms *of* incarceration. Some counties have reached the conclusion that not everyone convicted of a crime needs to serve time in jail. Policymakers in these counties have decided that jail space is a precious commodity and that it must be used wisely (see Jackson 1988; Klofas 1991a).

A variety of alternatives to incarceration exist, and we discuss them at length throughout this book. Here we look at them briefly and in the context of jail space. Underlying each of these alternatives to incarceration is the assumption that every jail bed saved or emptied is one less jail bed that has to be built.

We have talked about house arrest and electronic monitoring as alternatives to incarceration (see D. Ford and Schmidt 1985; and Renzema and Skelton 1990). The key to evaluating these programs can be stated as a simple question: Would the person placed on house arrest or electronic monitoring actually go to jail if these programs were not available? Advocates say yes. They believe that electronic monitoring is one solution to jail crowding (see, for example, Hipschman 1987). But opponents say no. They argue, and the evidence seems to confirm, that house arrest and electric monitoring are add-ons to probation and parole, that they do not save bed space in jails. Clear (1988), for example, in an examination of the use of electronic monitoring, finds it is not a true alternative to incarceration. In examining the approach in light of traditional goals, he characterizes electronic monitoring as a program in search of a correctional philosophy.

The problem might lie in the decision to use them only with certain offenders rather than in the programs themselves. Because of public opinion—or politicians' perceptions of public opinion—house arrest and electronic-monitoring programs tend to be used with low-risk offenders, people who are unlikely to cause a major disaster or a public outcry if the programs fail. Most of these offenders would not be jailed even if house arrest and electronic monitoring were not available, which means that many of these programs are not alternatives to incarceration.

Some would argue that house arrest and electronic monitoring are limited by their nature to use with low-risk offenders. One of the chief criticisms of these programs is that they monitor an individual's location, not his or her behavior. This can be important in preventing drunk drivers from hurting themselves or others, but it may not be effective for individuals convicted of selling drugs or child pornography.

NEW-GENERATION JAILS AND BEYOND

Traditionally, the architecture of local jails has been a particularly troubling problem. Most local jurisdictions build new jails very infrequently—typically, once every 20 to 30 years; so, most architects have very little training and experience in the design of detention facilities. Together these factors mean that the design of a new jail may well repeat past structural mistakes (blind spots, for example), or that a new jail may be very attractive but not especially functional.

Since the late-1970s, the architecture of jails has changed dramatically (Goldman 2002). If we look at that change, we see that jail design and construction in the future will likely be dictated by five elements: lower operating costs, lower construction costs, speed of construction, flexibility of space, and expandability. All of these elements are related in some way to the inescapable conclusion about jails in the twenty-first century: we cannot continue to build and operate jails in this nation in the same way we have for the past two centuries.

The design of jails inevitably is related to their operating costs. As private-sector contractors have learned, a properly designed facility may allow for the elimination of staff posts throughout the jail. A **post** is any position that must be staffed 24 hours a day. The elimination of a post is an important cost-saving measure. In fact, the numbers are astounding: to staff one post, a jail must employ about five people. That means that using a design that eliminates two or three posts can save the personnel costs of 10 to 15 employees—with salaries and fringe benefits, between $400,000 and $600,000 a year.

Lowering construction costs is a fairly simple issue: construction costs are high because most housing units in jails are built to maximum-security standards, which, in the past, has necessitated the use of materials of the highest security grade possible. But two recent innovations seem to indicate that jails can be built with less-costly materials. Direct inmate supervision—the constant surveillance found in new-generation jails—allows jails to dispense with some of the high-security materials they have relied on in the past and still be sure that inmates are not escaping or vandalizing the facility or getting hurt. So, new-generation jails are being built with certain commercial-grade materials—solid-core wooden doors instead of steel doors, for example—without compromising security (see Kerle 1998; W. R. Nelson 1988).

The second cost-saving innovation is precast concrete materials, which have greatly reduced construction costs in general and appear to do the same for the costs of building new jails. One of the pioneers in the use of prefabricated concrete cell modules was Pinellas County, Florida (DeWitt

1986a, 1986b). The Pinellas County Jail was built with three connected octagonal units. One of the units houses the jail's support functions and control center; the other two were designed to hold 192 inmates in eight 24-inmate pods. The concrete elements were cast off-site and then joined during construction. The final cost to Pinellas County: $14,500 per inmate, or $29,000 for each two-person cell (DeWitt 1986b, 1986c). This compares with traditional estimates of about $50,000 per bed space in most new jails. Construction cost is also related to construction speed. Prefabricated materials save both money and time. In the construction of public facilities, speed is a factor in site selection and the bidding process.

Site selection continues to be a problem for new jail construction (see Mays and Czerniak 1992–1993). Many jurisdictions have gone through painful and protracted site selection processes only to have the community rally behind cries of "Not in my backyard!" And once a site is chosen and a design is finalized, the bidding process for goods and services can be cumbersome and extended.

At this point, the private sector may enter the picture again. Private-sector companies have become involved in jail construction and operations business by promising to save governments time through the private procurement of land for construction and streamlined procedures for purchasing goods and services. If the private sector is able to deliver on its promise to save time, it is going to save local governments money as well.

An ongoing dilemma facing most contemporary jails is not so much a lack of space as the inflexibility of available space (National Advisory Commission 1973, 275). Most jails are constructed to be operated one way over the life of the building. Unfortunately, jails' needs change. When they do, administrators have a difficult time converting, say, bed space to recreation space, or space for male inmates to space for female inmates. This is an area where designers and architects can help by creating flexible spaces that can easily be converted to other uses. The problem, of course, is that the design elements that make spaces flexible—picture movable walls—by definition are not secure; and in the design of jails, security inevitably wins over flexibility. Even new-generation jails do not offer functional flexibility. Administrations can relabel a space, but they cannot reconfigure it.

Finally, modern jails must be expandable. Expansion is almost impossible in existing jails. These jails have been built in city centers as part of, or adjacent to, the county courthouse. They are often located on very small and very expensive parcels of land with little parking. Expansion choices under these conditions are limited. Adding stories to an existing structure is an expensive proposition and, depending on the building's engineering, may not be possible. And even if adjacent land in the central business district is available for building an addition, the cost of that land may be prohibitive. In the absence of on-site options, central jails are choosing to expand through satellite facilities, and some are choosing to leave downtown altogether, even if it means separating the jail and the courthouse. This option, though less convenient, usually reduces the cost of the site, makes plenty of free parking available for employees and visitors, and, perhaps most important, allows for future expansion.

For those jails that do not have the land to move outward, expansion often takes the form of housing pods attached to the jail's central core. These pods usually are not up to the security standards of the main structure, so they tend to be used for work-release and other low-security inmates. The primary security issue in this context—and a strong argument for separate housing for low-risk prisoners—is keeping those prisoners well apart from the general population, to minimize the likelihood of their introducing contraband into the more secure jail environment.

SUMMARY

There are more jails and detention facilities in this nation than any other kind of correctional facility. Jails and detention facilities process perhaps as many as 13 million people a year, keeping them for as little as a few hours to as long as a year or more. In reviewing the nature and functions of local jails, keep the following points in mind:

- Jails are distinct from prisons in a variety of ways, although they may serve similar functions.

- Jails house males and females, adults and juveniles, pretrial detainees and convicted offenders, and a wide range of inmates with special needs.

- For the most part in the United States jails are locally funded and locally operated, often by law enforcement agencies. Some states assist with the funding or operation of local jails, and six states have state-run jail systems.

- The number of jail inmates has increased dramatically since 1980. Although men still outnumber women in jail, the percentage of women has been increasing more rapidly than has the percentage of men.

- Jail architecture has evolved during the past 30 years or so, and many new jails employ a podular design and direct-supervision of inmates.

- Although crowding has been a persistent problem, expansion efforts nationwide now have many jails operating at less than 100 percent of capacity.

THINKING ABOUT CORRECTIONAL POLICIES AND PRACTICES: WRITING ASSIGNMENTS

1 Write a brief paragraph on each of the three main characteristics that distinguish jails from prisons. Add others to this list if you can think of some.

2 In a one- to two-page essay, discuss the status of jails in the criminal justice system. Especially note the factors that influence their status. Can you suggest ways to improve this status?

3 This is a position paper. Take a stand one way or the other on the proposition: Jails can greatly benefit from expanded inmate programming. In your paper, clearly state the reasons for the position you've taken.

4 Rank the issues confronting jails from the one that is most likely to be resolved locally to the one that is least likely to achieve such resolution and explain how you arrived at these conclusions.

5 "New generation jails make life too easy for inmates, increasing the likelihood that they will reoffend." Attack or defend this statement in a brief essay.

KEY TERMS

detention facilities	linear design	processing jails
direct supervision	low-use jails	public–private partnership
high-use jails	new-generation jails	rehabilitative services
holding jails	podular design	remote supervision
intermittent supervision	police lockup	satellite jails
jail	post	special needs
jail annexes	privatization	

CRITICAL REVIEW QUESTIONS

1   Briefly describe the range of functions served by local jails.

2   John Irwin characterizes inmates as rabble. What kinds of people make up the inmate population of jails? What impact do inmates have on the functions of and conditions in local jails?

3   It is common in describing the number of inmates in corrections facilities to talk about the average daily population of inmates. Why is it difficult to determine the ADP of local jails?

4   What has happened to the number of jails in the United States since the 1970s? Discuss the reasons for this change.

5   Describe the basic designs used in the construction of US jails. What effect has technology had on the design of local jails? What does each design imply about the interactions of staff members and inmates?

6   Who is primarily responsible for administering jails in the United States? Why? Are there other administrative structures that work as well or better? Explain your answer.

7   Think about the possible justifications for privatizing local jails. What might motivate a county commission to privatize the local jail?

8   Most inmates in jails are there for just a short time. How does that influence the programs that are available to them and their ability to take advantage of these programs? Recognizing the constraints of time, which three types of programs make the most sense to you? Explain your answers.

9   Infectious diseases pose unique problems to confined populations like those found in jails. How might the nation's jails better meet those challenges?

NOTES

1   Irwin spent 5 years in prison in the 1950s for armed robbery. When he was released, he went to college and eventually earned a doctorate in sociology. He went on to teach at the university level and to write about and work with prisoners.

2   Previous censuses were conducted in 1970, 1972, 1978, 1983, 1988, 1993, and 1999, and in each report the number of jails decreased. In 1970, the census reported 4,037 jails; in 1972, 3,921; in 1978, 3,493; in 1983, 3,338; in 1988, 3,316; in 1993, 3,304; and in 1999, 3,376.

3   In some facilities, the pods are slightly larger and so hold more inmates.

4   In general, juvenile detainees are at the highest risk of suicide (Winfree 1987, 1988; Winfree and Wooldredge 1991).

5   Although one jail administrator once commented that he had inmates "serving life on the installment plan" (Saxton 1991).

REFERENCES

Abadinsky, Howard, and L. Thomas Winfree, Jr. 1992. *Crime and justice: An introduction.* Chicago: Nelson-Hall.

Advisory Commission on Intergovernmental Relations (ACIR). 1984. *Jails: Intergovernmental dimensions of a local problem.* Washington, DC: ACIR.

American Correctional Association (ACA). 1991. *Standards for adult local detention facilities*, 3rd edn. Laurel, MD: ACA.

American Correctional Association (ACA). 2012. *Core jail standards*. Retrieved on July 10, 2013 from: http://www.aca.org/standards/pdfs/CoreJailStandards.ppt

Bowen, Bruce, and Dierdre Kelly. 1987. Lease-purchase financing for jails. *American Jails* 1(1): 57.

Bureau of Justice Statistics. 2012. What is the difference between jails and prisons? Retrieved on July 10, 2013 from: http://bjs.ojp.usdoj.gov/index.cfm?ty=qa&iid=322

Chaires, Robert, and Susan Lentz. 1996. Some legal considerations in prison privatization. In *Privatization and the provision of correctional services: Context and consequences*, edited by G. Larry Mays and Tara Gray. Cincinnati, OH: Anderson, Academy of Criminal Justice Sciences, 31–60.

Clear, Todd R. 1988. A critical assessment of electronic monitoring in corrections. *Policy Studies Review* 7(3): 671–81.

Clear, Todd R., and George F. Cole (2003). *American corrections*, 6th edn. Belmont, CA: Wadsworth.

Collins, William C. 1987a. Privatization: Some legal considerations from a neutral perspective, part I. *American Jails* 1(1): 40–45.

Collins, William C. 1987b. Privatization: Some legal considerations from a neutral perspective, part II. *American Jails* 1(2): 28–34.

Conroy, Robert, Wantland J. Smith, and Linda L. Zupan. 1991. Officer stress in the direct supervision jail. *American Jails* 5(5): 34–6.

Cox, Norman R., Jr., and William E. Osterhoff. 1991. Managing the crisis in local corrections: A public–private partnership approach. In *American jails: Public policy issues*, edited by Joel A. Thompson and G. Larry Mays. Chicago: Nelson-Hall, 227–39.

Cunniff, Mark A. 2002. *Jail crowding: Understanding jail population dynamics*. Washington, DC: US Government Printing Office.

Dale, Michael J. 1988. Detaining juveniles in adult jails and lockups: An analysis of rights and liabilities. *American Jails* 2(1): 46, 47, 50.

Davis, Russell M. 1987. Direct supervision as an organizational management system. *American Jails* 1(1): 50–3.

DeWitt, Charles. 1986a. *California tests new construction concepts*. Washington, DC: US Government Printing Office.

DeWitt, Charles. 1986b. *Florida sets example with use of concrete modules*. Washington, DC: US Government Printing Office.

DeWitt, Charles. 1986c. *New construction methods for correctional facilities*. Washington, DC: US Government Printing Office.

DeWitt, Charles. 1986d. *Ohio's new approach to prison and jail financing*. Washington, DC: US Government Printing Office.

Ditton, Paula M. 1999. *Mental health and treatment of inmates and probationers*. Washington, DC: US Government Printing Office.

Feeley, Malcolm. 1979. *The process is the punishment: Handling cases in a lower criminal court*. New York: Russell Sage Foundation.

Feeley, Malcolm. 1991. The privatization of prisons in historical perspective. *Criminal Justice Research Bulletin* 6(2): 1–10.

Ford, Daniel, and Annesley K. Schmidt. 1985. *Electronically monitored home confinement*. Washington, DC: US Government Printing Office.

Ford, Francis R. 1993. Politics and jails, part II. *American Jails* 7(1): 11–6.

Gilbert, Michael J. 1996. Private confinement and the role of government in a civil society. In *Privatization and the provision of correctional services: Context and consequences*, edited by G. Larry Mays and Tara Gray. Cincinnati, OH: Anderson, Academy of Criminal Justice Sciences, 13–20.

Goldman, Mark. 2002. *Jail design review handbook*. Washington, DC: National Institute of Corrections.

Gray, Tara, G. Larry Mays, and Mary K. Stohr. 1995. Inmate needs and programming in exclusively women's jails. *Prison Journal* 75: 186–202.

Hackett, Judith C., Harry P. Hatry, Robert B. Levinson, Joan Allen, Keon Chi, and Edward D. Feigenbaum. 1987. *Contracting for the operation of prisons and jails*. Washington, DC: US Government Printing Office.

Haddad, Jane. 1993. Managing the special needs of mentally ill inmates. *American Jails* 7(1): 62–5.

Hall, David B. 1987. Jail facility renovation and expansion. *American Jails* 1(1): 38–9.

Hammett, Theodore, and Saira Moini. 1990. *Update on AIDS in prisons and jails*. Washington, DC: US Department of Justice.

Haque, Ekram U. 1989. New York City Department of Correction: The successes and challenges of a giant system. *American Jails* 2(4): 51, 55.

Harlow, Caroline Wolf. 1998. *Profile of jail inmates 1996*. Washington, DC: US Department of Justice.

Harlow, Caroline Wolf. 2003. *Education and correctional populations*. Washington, DC: US Department of Justice.

Harris-George, Becky, Herbert H. Jarrett, and Richard T. Shigley. 1994. State jails: Texas' answer to overcrowding! *American Jails* 8(5): 17–20.

Hecht, Frank R., and Ramon Smithhart. 1987. Management of the acute and chronically mentally ill inmate: A new experience. *American Jails* 1(3): 10–2.

Hipschman, D. C. 1987. Electronic monitoring now makes house arrest a viable way to alleviate overcrowding. *American Jails* 1(1): 63–4.

Irwin, John. 1985. *The jail: Managing the underclass in American society*. Berkeley: University of California Press.

Jackson, Patrick G. 1988. The uses of jail confinement in three counties. *Policy Studies Review* 7(3): 592–605.

Jackson, Patrick G. 1991. Competing ideologies of jail confinement. In *American jails: Public policy issues*, edited by Joel A. Thompson and G. Larry Mays. Chicago: Nelson-Hall, 22–39.

James, Doris J. 2004. *Profile of jail inmates, 2002*. Washington, DC: US Department of Justice.

James, Doris J., and Lauren E. Glaze. 2006. *Mental health problems of prison and jail inmates, 2006*. Washington, DC: US Department of Justice.

Jerrell, Jeanette M., and Richard Komisaruk. 1991. Public policy issues in the delivery of mental health services in a jail setting. In *American jails: Public policy issues*, edited by Joel A. Thompson and G. Larry Mays. Chicago: Nelson-Hall, 100–15.

Judiscak, Daniel. 1995. Why are the mentally ill in jail? *American Jails* 9(5): 9–15.

Kalinich, David, Paul Embert, and Jeffrey D. Senese. 1991. Mental health services for jail inmates: Imprecise standards, traditional philosophies, and the need for change. In *American jails: Public policy issues*, edited by Joel A. Thompson, and G. Larry Mays. Chicago: Nelson-Hall, 79–99.

Karberg, Jennifer, and Doris J. James. 2005. *Substance dependence, abuse, and treatment of jail inmates, 2002*. Washington, DC: US Department of Justice.

Kennedy, D. B., and R. J. Homant. 1988. Predicting custodial suicides: Problems with the use of profiles. *Justice Quarterly* 5(3): 441–56.

Kellar, Mark. 2001. *Texas county jails, 2001: A status report*. Retrieved on July 10, 2013 from: http://www.tcjs.state.tx.us/docs/Final%20DraftTJSbu.pdf

Kerle, Kenneth E. 2002. Women in the American world of jails: Inmates and staff. *Margins* 2(Spring): 41–61.

Kerle, Kenneth E., and Francis R. Ford. 1982. *The state of our nation's jails*. Washington, DC: National Sheriffs' Association.

Klofas, John M. 1987. Patterns of jail use. *Journal of Criminal Justice* 15: 403–11.

Klofas, John M. 1988. Measuring jail use: A comparative analysis of local corrections. Paper presented at the annual meeting of the American Society of Criminology, Chicago.

Klofas, John M. 1991a. Disaggregating jail use: Variety and change in local corrections over a ten-year period. In *American jails: Public policy issues*, edited by Joel A. Thompson and G. Larry Mays. Chicago: Nelson-Hall, 40–58.

Klofas, John M. 1991b. Jail crowding. In *Setting the jail research agenda for the 1990s*, edited by G. Larry Mays. Washington, DC: National Institute of Corrections, 69–76.

Lammers, Norma Phillips, and Mark O. Morris. 1990. *Jail construction in California*. Washington, DC: US Department of Justice.

Lawrence, James E., and Van Zwisohn. 1991. AIDS in jail. In *American jails: Public policy issues*, edited by Joel A. Thompson and G. Larry Mays. Chicago: Nelson-Hall, 116–28.

Liebowitz, Morton J. 1991. Regionalization in Virginia jails. *American Jails* 5(5): 42–5.

Logan, Charles H. 1990. *Private prisons: Cons and pros*. New York: Oxford University Press.

Maruschak, Laura M. 2001. *HIV in prisons and jails, 1999*. Washington, DC: US Department of Justice.

Maruschak, Laura M. 2004. *HIV in prisons and jails, 2002*. Washington, DC: US Department of Justice.

Maruschak, Laura M. 2006. *Medical problems of jail inmates*. Washington, DC: US Department of Justice.

May, Edgar. 1978. Weekend jail: Doing time on the installment plan. *Corrections*, March, 28–38.

Mays, G. Larry, and Robert Czerniak. 1992–1993. The political problems of planning for a new jail: Dona Ana County, New Mexico's experience. *Texas Journal of Political Studies* 15(1): 31–45.

Mays, G. Larry, and Tara Gray, eds. 1996. *Privatization and the provision of correctional services*. Cincinnati, OH: Anderson, Academy of Criminal Justice Sciences.

Mays, G. Larry, and Daniel L. Judiscak. 1996. Special needs inmates in New Mexico jails. *American Jails* 10(2): 32–41.

Mays, G. Larry, and Joel A. Thompson. 1988. Mayberry revisited: The characteristics and operations of America's small jails. *Justice Quarterly* 5(3): 421–40.

Mays, G. Larry, and Joel A. Thompson. 1991. The political and organizational context of American jails. In *American jails: Public policy issues*, edited by Joel A. Thompson and G. Larry Mays. Chicago: Nelson-Hall, 3–21.

Mays, G. Larry, Charles B. Fields, and Joel A. Thompson. 1991. Preincarceration patterns of drug and alcohol use by jail inmates. *Criminal Justice Policy Review* 5(1): 40–52.

McCampbell, Susan W. 1990. Direct supervision: Looking for the right people. *American Jails* 4(4): 68–9.

McCullough, H. Laws, and Timothy S. Maguigan. 1990. APRICOR: Proving privatization works. *American Jails* 4(4): 46–9.

Minton, Todd D. 2011. *Jail inmates at midyear 2010— statistical tables*. Washington, DC: Bureau of Justice Statistics, US Department of Justice.

National Advisory Commission on Criminal Justice Standards and Goals. 1973. *Corrections*. Washington, DC: US Department of Justice.

Nelson, W. Raymond. 1988. *Cost savings in new generation jails: The direct supervision approach*. Washington, DC: US Department of Justice.

Orrick, David. 1989. New construction as a solution to jail overcrowding: Some policy and funding implications. *American Journal of Criminal Justice* 14(1): 71–86.

Reichel, Philip L. 2002. *Comparative criminal justice systems: A topical approach*. Upper Saddle River, NJ: Prentice Hall.

Renzema, Marc, and David T. Skelton. 1990. *Use of electronic monitoring in the United States: 1989 update*. Washington, DC: US Department of Justice.

Ricci, Kenneth. 1986. What can county commissioners do about their jails? *Prison Journal* 61: 14–8.

Robbins, Ira P. 1988. *Legal dimensions of private incarceration*. Washington, DC: American Bar Association.

Rowan, Joseph R. 1993. Politics in jail operations— Some good, some bad. *American Jails* 6(6): 58–60.

Ruddell, Rick, and G. Larry Mays. 2011. Trouble in the heartland: Challenges confronting rural jails. *International Journal of Rural Criminology* 1(1): 105–31.

Sabol, William J., and Todd D. Minton. 2008. *Jail inmates at midyear 2007*. Washington, DC: Bureau of Justice Statistics, US Department of Justice.

Saxton, Samuel F. 1991. Reintegration: A strategy for success. In *Setting the jail research agenda for the 1990s*, edited by G. Larry Mays. Washington, DC: National Institute of Corrections, 58–63.

Schwartz, Ira M. 1989. *(In)justice for juveniles: Rethinking the best interest of the child*. Lexington, MA: Lexington Books.

Schwartz, Ira M. 1991. Removing juveniles from adult jails: The unfinished agenda. In *American jails: Public policy issues*, edited by Joel A. Thompson and G. Larry Mays. Chicago: Nelson-Hall, 216–26.

Sechrest, Dale K. 1989a. Population density and assaults in jails for men and women. *American Journal of Criminal Justice* 14(1): 87–103.

Senese, Jeffrey D., David B. Kalinich, and Paul S. Embert. 1989. Jails in the United States: The phenomenon of mental illness in local correctional facilities. *American Journal of Criminal Justice* 14(1): 104–21.

Stephan, James J. 2001. *Census of jails, 1999*. Washington, DC: US Department of Justice.

Stephan, James J. 2008. *Census of state and federal correctional facilities, 2005*. Washington, DC: Bureau of Justice Statistics, US Department of Justice.

Stephan, James, and Georgette Walsh. 2011. *Census of jail facilities, 2006*. Washington, DC: Bureau of Justice Statistics, US Department of Justice.

Stohr, Mary K., and G. Larry Mays. 1993. *Women's jails: An investigation of offenders, staff, administration and programming*. Washington, DC: National Institute of Corrections.

Stohr, Mary K., Ruth L. Self, and Nicholas P. Lovrich. 1992. Staff turnover in new generation jails: An investigation of its causes and prevention. *Journal of Criminal Justice* 20(5): 455–78.

Struckhoff, David. 1989. Deputies or correctional officers in jails: Is there a controversy? *American Jails* 2(4): 32–4.

Taft, Philip B., Jr. 1979. Backed up in jail. *Corrections*, June, 26–33.

Takas, Marianne, and Theodore M. Hammett. 1989. *AIDS bulletin: Legal issues affecting offenders and staff*. Washington, DC: US Department of Justice.

Tewksbury, Richard A., and Gennaro F. Vito. 1994. Improving the educational skills of jail inmates. *Federal Probation* 58(2): 55–9.

Thompson, Joel A. 1986. The American jail: Problems, politics, prospects. *American Journal of Criminal Justice* 10: 205–21.

Thompson, Joel A., and G. Larry Mays. 1988a. The impact of state standards and enforcement procedures on local jail performance. *Policy Studies Review* 8(1): 55–71.

Thompson, Joel A., and G. Larry Mays. 1988b. State–local relations and the American jail crisis: An assessment of state jail mandates. *Policy Studies Review* 7(3): 567–80.

Thompson, Joel A., and G. Larry Mays. 1991. Paying the piper but changing the tune: Policy changes and initiatives for the American jail. In *American jails: Public policy issues*, edited by Joel A. Thompson and G. Larry Mays. Chicago: Nelson-Hall, 240–6.

US Department of Justice. 1983. *Report to the nation on crime and justice*. Washington, DC: US Government Printing Office.

Wallenstein, Arthur M. 1987. New generation/direct supervision correctional operations in Bucks County, Pennsylvania. *American Jails* 1(1): 34–6.

Ward, Julia. 1990. Bay County Jail and Jail Annex: A case for private enterprise in corrections. *American Jails* 4(4): 38–42.

Welch, Michael. 1989. Social junk, social dynamite and the rabble: Persons with AIDS in jail. *American Journal of Criminal Justice* 14(1): 135–47.

Welch, Michael. 1991. The expansion of jail capacity: Makeshift jails and public policy. In *American jails: Public policy issues*, edited by Joel A. Thompson and G. Larry Mays. Chicago: Nelson-Hall, 148–62.

Welsh, Wayne N., Matthew C. Leone, Patrick T. Kinkade, and Henry N. Pontell. 1991. The politics of jail overcrowding: Public attitudes and official policies. In *American jails: Public policy issues*, edited by Joel A. Thompson and G. Larry Mays. Chicago: Nelson-Hall, 131–47.

Western, Bruce, and Becky Petit. 2000. Incarceration and racial inequality in men's employment. *Industrial and Labor Relations Review* 54(1): 3–16.

Wilson, Doris James. 2000. *Drug use, testing, and treatment in jails*. Washington, DC: US Department of Justice.

Winfree, L. Thomas, Jr. 1987. Toward understanding state-level jail mortality: Correlates of death by suicide and by natural causes. *Justice Quarterly* 4: 51–71.

Winfree, L. Thomas, Jr. 1988. Rethinking American jail death rates: A comparison of national mortality and jail mortality, 1978, 1983. *Policy Studies Review* 7(3): 641–59.

Winfree, L. Thomas, Jr., and John Wooldredge. 1991. Exploring suicides and deaths by natural causes in America's largest jails: A panel study of institutional change, 1978 and 1983. In *American jails: Public policy issues*, edited by Joel A. Thompson and G. Larry Mays. Chicago: Nelson-Hall, 63–78.

Wooldredge, John D., and L. Thomas Winfree, Jr. 1992. An aggregate-level study of inmate suicides and deaths due to natural causes in U.S. jails. *Journal of Research in Crime and Delinquency* 29(4): 466–79.

Zupan, Linda L., and Ben Menke. 1991. The new generation jail: An overview. In *American jails: Public policy issues*, edited by Joel A. Thompson and G. Larry Mays. Chicago: Nelson-Hall, 180–94.

Zupan, Linda L., and Mary K. Stohr-Gillmore. 1988. Doing time in the new generation jail: Inmate perceptions of gains and losses. *Policy Studies Review* 7(3): 626–40.

INSTITUTIONAL CORRECTIONS

ZUMA PRESS INC/ALAMY IMAGES

PHILIP SCLIA/ALAMY IMAGES

Outline

Objectives

- To acquaint you with the unique problems of prison management and operations

- To give you insights into the rich and varied history and evolution of institutional corrections at both the state and federal levels

- To give you a working understanding of the types and functions of prisons, penitentiaries, and other correctional institutions for long-term confinement

- To orient you to the important topic of prison labor, past and present

- To establish the idea of the "new prison" as a recurring theme in corrections

Essentials of Corrections, Fifth Edition. G. Larry Mays and L. Thomas Winfree, Jr.
© 2014 John Wiley & Sons, Inc. Published 2014 by John Wiley & Sons, Inc.

INTRODUCTION

This chapter focuses on institutional corrections. It examines the nation's prisons and prison systems. Jails and detention facilities are also correctional institutions, but they face different albeit related challenges. In some ways, then, the world inside of jails and detention facilities is a microcosm of the prison world; hence, some of the topics found in this chapter bear more than a passing resemblance to those discussed in Chapter 5. Technically, however, a prison is a correctional facility operated by a state or the federal government for the confinement of convicted felons who are serving sentences in excess of 1 year.[1] Nearly all are operated at the state or federal level. Most states have at least two such facilities, one for men and a separate one for women, although it is also possible that the incarceration of some or all female felons is privatized or contracted to an out-of-state correctional facility.

Traditionally, correctional experts have viewed prisons as a prime example of the **total institution**. Social anthropologist Erving Goffman defined total institutions as physical and social environments in which others control nearly every aspect of residents' daily lives (see Box 6.1). He further observed the following about such social worlds: "Their encompassing or total character is symbolized by the barrier to social intercourse with the outside and to departure that is often built right into the physical plant, such as locked doors, high walls, barbed wire, cliffs, water, forests, or moors" (1961, 4). Inmates make few choices for themselves. Prison authorities tell them when and where to eat, work, exercise, and sleep. In the extreme, inmates cannot move about the facility without permission. The greater the control exercised over the inmates, the more total the institution. Few institutions in twenty-first century US society exhibit higher levels of control over participants' lives than do prisons, and this includes the prisoners and those charged with managing them inside the prison walls.

Are the characteristics of total institutions necessarily bad? Is it wrong that certain religious orders isolate their members and require unquestioning obedience from them? Would you want individual members of the armed forces making their own decisions about decorum, dress, and discipline?

RITES OF PASSAGE AND THE DEHUMANIZATION OF INMATES   BOX 6.1

In his classic work *Asylums*, Erving Goffman described various total institutions, including prisons. Prisons, he observed, protect society from those who pose a threat; moreover, the inmate welfare is secondary to institutional security. According to Goffman, when inmates enter a total institution, they undergo **rites of passage**, rituals that reinforce the idea that the inmates are no longer free, that they are "the property" of the institution. A key element in these rites of passage, practiced to a greater or lesser extent in all total institutions, is **dehumanization**—the process of stripping inmates of their personhood. In prisons, it begins when officials take away new inmates' personal belongings, lining them up for medical and psychological screening, and issuing uniforms.

The objective of dehumanization is not just the inmates' acceptance of their nonperson status. For Goffman, the dehumanization process is complete when the keepers no longer think of the kept as human beings. Such a mindset creates the controlled environments that define total institutions, and it tends to limit the extent to which the keepers can participate in any meaningful way in affecting prosocial changes in the kept.

SOURCE: GOFFMAN (1961).

The obvious answer to all of these questions is, in a word, no. Similar questions could be asked about prison inmates. For example, are prisons today truly total institutions, especially as the concept was first described by Goffman? If prison personnel did not place the appropriate restrictions on inmates' freedom, they would be failing at perhaps their most important assigned task, protecting society. What are the appropriate types and levels of restrictions? Ultimately, some deprivations of liberty, or the placement of limits on the ability of prison inmates to move about a correctional facility and beyond, is essential for the operation of *most* prisons. The larger issue is that while we acknowledge the need for control in prisons, society may question the methods used by some—but not all—of them to achieve security and control over inmates.

In this chapter, we describe prisons that have no walls or fences, yet the inmates remain under the control of prison authorities. We also describe other examples of institutional corrections that despite their locations and security measures have, at times, lost control of their inmates. Controlling prisoners may be less a function of barbed wire and dehumanization than it is about effective management.

PRISONER MANAGEMENT

Most prisons are in practice total institutions as those tasked with their operation must assume responsibility for virtually all phases of the inmates' lives. This is not an easy task, for inmates commonly resist what they view as efforts at external control. Indeed, it is the combination of the operational goals of a given prison, the security levels provided within the prison, and the classification levels assigned to its inmates that determines the methods and severity of control employed by prison administrators. We begin our look at prisoner management with a review of two organizational goals fulfilled to a greater or lesser extent by all prisons, moving next to a review of prison security levels, and finally examine the systems of inmate classification that facilitate the attainment of these goals within the system of available security levels.

INSTITUTIONAL GOALS

Prisons have two widely acknowledged—and some would argue conflicting—goals: custody and treatment. **Custody** is the legal or physical control of a person. Prison authorities are responsible for inmates' legal *and* physical control. This means they have an obligation to provide for inmates' basic needs; however, that obligation is secondary to protecting the public. **Treatment** is a term borrowed from medicine by early penal reformers and refers to a type of therapy associated with a particular diagnosis. Many inmates have broad-ranging medical and psychiatric or psychological needs, ones they possessed upon entry into the facility and others they developed in response to life in a total institution. When screening detects emotional or psychological problems, the treatment may involve individual or group counseling; when a prisoner's history suggests socioeconomic factors, the treatment may involve education or vocational training.

Which goal is paramount? The answer depends on whom you ask. However, as the common adage goes, you cannot treat them if you cannot keep them. As Susan Craig (2004, 968) observes, "The goal of controlling inmates subsumes all other goals. Even rehabilitative programming, which may involve time away from the prison routine or better quarters than can be had in the general population, is a privilege that may be granted or taken away." Much of the conflict between such institutional goals reflects the differences between those responsible for the custody and the treatment of inmates (Sykes 1958). That conflict can—and often does—spill over into the respective work worlds of those who are responsible for the services intended to achieve one goal or the other.

Custody is the primary responsibility of correctional officers (COs).[2] One simple objective guides these men and women: to ensure the safety and security of the institution and its staff, and then its inmates. Authority, regimentation, and architecture are the COs' chief tools (Farmer 1977; Lombardo 1984). The mix of these elements defines the prison's security level, a topic we examine in detail later in this chapter. Historically, COs rarely have more than a high school education; perhaps as a result, their career advancement is limited within the prison system (see Chapter 10 for more on this career path). The position of COs in the prison management hierarchy mandates that they be suspicious of any unusual exchanges—verbal or physical—occurring between inmates and, in some situations, between inmates and staff members. They must be on the lookout for illegal drug and home-brew liquor stashes, weapons, and other contraband, as well as overt or covert behavior that could signal an inmate uprising. Although riots pose a constant threat, they rarely occur. Among the people who provide treatment for inmates are counselors, caseworkers, case managers, psychologists and psychiatrists, social workers, activities coordinators, chaplains, educators, nurses, and physicians. Almost all of these service providers hold baccalaureate degrees and many hold work-related graduate degrees. With the exception of some caseworkers, case managers, and activities coordinators, few of these employees have prior work experience in prisons. Although they tend to earn less than do their peers in noncorrectional settings, treatment providers usually receive higher compensation than all but the highest-ranking COs.

In addition to education and income, working conditions distinguish custodial staff from treatment staff. Correctional officers work in cellblocks and yards with large numbers of prisoners. Treatment personnel typically work in other physical locations, often in private or semiprivate offices or in classrooms, where they interact with individual inmates or with small groups. In most US prisons, COs wear military-style uniforms; treatment staff rarely wear uniforms.

Perhaps the greatest divergence between custodial staff and treatment staff is philosophical. COs tend to control by intimidation. In addition, they can develop a generalized distrust for most inmates because it is their job to be suspicious. By contrast, treatment providers cannot force inmates to learn or to deal with their psychological problems. The success of treatment programs rests on establishing trust relationships between providers and inmates. Where COs tend to resort to coercion, treatment providers employ persuasion; where the former rely on suspicion and wariness, the latter resort to nurture, trust, and hope. On all of these crucial points, custody

and treatment personnel are generally unable to find common ground (Street, Vinter, and Perrow 1966; Zald 1968).

It would be wrong to assume that the correctional personnel charged with maintaining security cannot perform human services functions, essentially helping to bring about prosocial changes in prison inmates, or that treatment staff cannot work to maintain security, although the countervailing forces associated with each goal can create a difficult balancing act for both sets of staff (Inderbitzin 2007). As Hepburn and Albonetti (1981) observed more than 30 years ago, the conflict is not between the jobs performed by the various staff; rather, it is a product of the organizational goals that drive security and treatment decisions about specific inmates housed in a given prison. Prisons house inmates across a range of security risk levels. If a facility has all (or mostly) low-risk inmates, then the conflict between treatment and security is likely to be lower; while, in a maximum security facility that houses high-risk inmates, the conflict is likely to be far greater.

The primacy of control in the policies and practices of prison administration seems undisputed (DiIulio 1987; Reisig 1998). It is a widely believed, but little tested, idea that a highly controlled prison is a safe prison (Craig 2004). Pitting one organizational model against another seems counterproductive, leading to a general undermining of social cohesion, order, and rehabilitation (Craig 2004). A more productive approach, suggest some critics of contemporary prison management, would be a less restrictive model (King 2009–2010; Pollock et al. 2012). This more permissive approach should lead to better social cohesion, "a necessary precondition not only to an orderly prison but to one that fulfills its rehabilitative goals as well" (Craig 2004, 1127–28).

Giving hope to the hopeless may be as important as controlling them. As Dinitz (1981, 9) observed, in the wake of prison riots at Attica and Santa Fe, two of this nation's most violent prison uprisings: "The hopeful prison engenders in inmates the hope that their lives will improve." Without such hope and even in the presence of the most controlling of environments, prisons might actually be more difficult to control, not less. And, as importantly for society, the products of such prisons are unlikely to succeed for long outside the prison walls. Given the wide support in the public and among policy makers for a merger of rehabilitation and retribution as goals of contemporary corrections (Kifer, Hemmens, and Stohr 2003, 48), this suggestion may be more than just a random entry on the twenty-first century "wish list" for corrections.

What do we know about COs' views on the goals of corrections? Most researchers report that COs see incapacitation (security and control) as the prison's primary goal and rehabilitation as a distant third or fourth, after either retribution or deterrence (Cullen et al. 1989; Kifer, Hemmens, and Stohr 2003; Paboo-jian and Teske 1997). The attitudes of COs are important to goal achievement in any institution. As Misty Kifer and associates (2003, 67) observe about the COs as the prison's "street level bureaucrats": "They hold the power to either carry out or destroy the institutional mission."

SECURITY LEVELS

Prison officials must lock up some inmates for nearly 24 hours a day, especially those who pose a risk of escape or serious harm to others. Other inmates could live free in the community, and no one would be in any greater danger than before their release. The risk that attaches to inmates defines a prison's physical appearance and security provisions and its all-important *security level*.

MAXIMUM SECURITY **Maximum security** is the highest security level found in most prison systems. Correctional authorities reserve it for inmates who represent the greatest threat to society, the institution, and other inmates. High stone or concrete walls typically enclose older maximum-security prisons. In newer facilities, chain-link fences, topped with razor wire, provide external security. Modern prison architects strategically place tall gun towers in corners or in the center of the facility. From this vantage point, armed COs have an unobstructed view of the wall or fence and buildings, and of the outside perimeter.

The buildings within a maximum-security prison typically are stone, reinforced concrete, or cinder-block structures. Most of these prisons are linear, and access to and from the cells is controlled by means of a **sally port**, an entryway secured by two steel or barred doors with glass or screen inserts. In addition, fences and gates separate maximum-security cellblocks from one another and from other parts of the prison. In most maximum-security prisons, COs patrol the central security zones, basically hubs through which all inmates must pass as they move about the facility.

Inmates have virtually no privacy in maximum-security prisons. Unarmed COs move about the corridors. In addition, depending on a facility's current capacity, inmates may share a cell with two or three others. COs conduct frequent scheduled and unannounced **inmate counts**, during which a staff member must physically view each inmate. Some prisons use a system not unlike supermarket bar codes to track inmates as they move about the facility. COs may make unannounced **shakedowns**, searches of cell areas and inmates for weapons, drugs, and other contraband. Most intrusive are **body cavity searches**, examinations of inmates' mouths, anuses, and vaginas. COs resort to this kind of search after an inmate has moved from a lower security area of a facility to a more secure one, or when a shakedown has failed to uncover suspected contraband.

COs monitor all visitations electronically or by direct supervision, except those with attorneys. COs may prohibit physical contact between inmates and visitors. Prisoners and their visitors may be required to communicate through a screened barrier or by telephone or intercom, both of which are subject to monitoring. Prison security staff monitor external telephone calls as well. The intent of these security measures is to prevent inmates from formulating escape plans, smuggling in contraband, and committing crimes inside or outside the prison.

MEDIUM SECURITY **Medium security** is less restrictive and regimented than maximum security. In fact, some medium-security facilities are not even called *prisons*. They are *correctional facilities* or *institutions*. Unless it is a converted maximum-security facility, most medium-security prisons do not have high masonry walls. Instead they may be enclosed by a double chain-link fence topped by razor wire. The

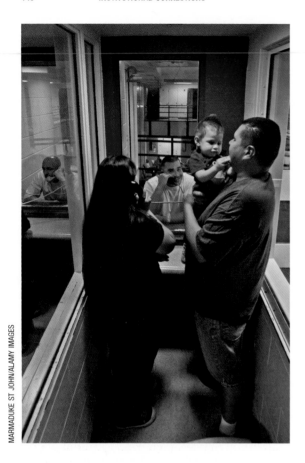

MARMADUKE ST JOHN/ALAMY IMAGES

is likely to be secure, these facilities rely on less-sophisticated and less expensive gates and doors to control movement throughout the institution. Inmate counts and searches, unless warranted by breaches in security, occur with less regularity in medium-security facilities than in maximum-security prisons.

The relaxation of security and regulations in medium-security facilities demonstrates these inmates pose a much lower risk of escape or violence than do inmates in maximum-security prisons. Classification personnel transfer inmates between medium- and maximum-security prisons in response to good or bad behavior. Medium-security facilities may actually adjoin maximum-security facilities, allowing for quick and inexpensive transfers.

MINIMUM SECURITY Minimum security is the least restrictive form of prison custody. Often minimum-security facilities look like college campuses, ranches or farms, or work camps. Minimum-security facilities for women often look like cottages, based on decades-old thinking that a homelike environment better serves the needs of women. Inmates in a minimum-security facility pose no security risk. They often are nonviolent offenders (for example, white-collar or professional criminals) or first-time offenders, are under short sentences (unless they are older inmates), or are about to be released from custody.

You might assume from descriptions of minimum-security facilities that these inmates have it easy compared with others. Certainly minimum security is much less oppressive and restrictive than either medium or maximum security. However, inmates still are not free to come and go as they please. They must follow institutional rules and regimentation. They are still the objects of physical and psychological abuse from COs and other inmates. In fact, many inmates prefer higher-security facilities, where routine monitoring and limited interactions with other prisoners mean less victimization by fellow inmates.

INMATE CLASSIFICATION

By the middle of the nineteenth century, prison reformers lobbied for the classification of inmates

area between the fences may have sensors or other devices that warn of escape attempts. Most such prisons also have strategically located gun towers, and COs provide roving security around the perimeter on foot or in vehicles.

In medium-security prisons, living units may be arranged like dormitories, with 50 or more inmates sleeping in a huge open area. In podular-design facilities, inmates may have small individual cells for sleeping and common areas for the rest of the time. In either case, inmates share readily accessible shower areas. Medium-security prisons also have fewer rules than do maximum-security facilities. Inmates may be required to wear institutional clothing only when working at their assigned tasks or on other prison business; otherwise, they may wear their "civilian clothes." Inmate movements around the prison are also less restricted. Although the central control area into broad categories. In response, prison administrators began to separate men from women, adults from children, those with communicable diseases from those who were reasonably healthy, and property offenders from murderers, robbers, and thieves. Zebulon Reed Brockway's unstructured discussions with incoming inmates to the Elmira Reformatory eventually gave way to intake interviews—specialized personnel questioned new inmates about their criminal and social histories—supplemented by psychological testing. Psychological and personality testing, first widely used on draftees during World War I, became the basis of early prison classification systems during the first three decades of the twentieth century. Individual treatment models, fueled by positivism, translated into the adoption of many screening, testing, and diagnostic techniques intended to help prison officials segregate inmates into manageable groups. By the 1930s, prison classification schemes focused on psychiatric diagnoses, which often had little to do with the actual services available.

Classification systems developed after World War II assessed the threat offenders posed to the general public. Relying largely on inmates' criminal records, personality inventories, and interviews—tempered by the individual assessor's personal experiences in the penal system—a prison employee called a classification officer, case manager, or case worker would recommend a security level for each prisoner. This system worked for over 20 years. Then prisoner classification systems changed in two ways during the 1970s. First, a series of appellate cases made clear that classification systems could blunt inmate charges of harsh conditions during confinement. *Holt v. Sarver* (1969) was an Arkansas case that took several years to work its way through the appellate courts. The decision in *Holt* was the first to identify the link between living conditions and housing assignments, a basic element of all classification schemes. *Morris v. Travisono* (1970) was the first case to result in a court ordering a state (Rhode Island) to design a classification system because such a system "is essential to the operation of an orderly and safe prison" (965). Finally, in *Pugh v. Locke* (1976), an Alabama case, an appeals court judge tied inmate treatment to classification systems. Classification is not a right, wrote

the judge, but it is a primary force in bringing any prison system to a treatment level that is constitutionally acceptable (also see Craddock 1996).

As a result of these court decisions, classification systems had to meet three goals (Craddock 1996, 90):

- Classification staff must assign inmates to the *least-restrictive security level* possible to provide for the safety of the community at large, the staff, and other inmates.

- The system must incorporate the *assessment of inmates' needs* on a regular and recurring basis, while not excusing inmates from responsibility for their own behavior.

- Staff members should encourage prosocial change by extending *positive incentives* to those inmates who exhibit control over their own behavior.

A second change was the abandonment of a large number of inmate treatment programs. We described the medical model in Chapter 2, an approach that relies on science for the tools to change human behavior. In the late 1960s and early 1970s, the medical model came under attack on two fronts. Liberals viewed it as a form of mind control and the misapplication of science to social ills. Conservatives believed it pampered rather than punished criminals. In response, prison systems scaled back or phased out their treatment programs. By the late 1970s and early 1980s, just as the courts were formalizing classification processes and, in effect, making them mandatory, specialized prison-based treatment programs became less popular, as pundits questioned their usefulness (Bonta and Andrews 2007; see too Martinson 1974). By default, then, classification had less to do with the treatment of inmates and more to do with their custody.

Today, prisoner classification systems typically combine two or more methods from the following models (Craddock 1996, 91–92):

- In **consensus-based classification systems**, prison personnel, based on their experiences with problem inmates, identify the factors that determine risk.

- **Equity-based classification systems** attempt to treat all inmates the same. They weigh only those factors that relate to the current offense—violence, for example, or the nature of the crime.

- **Prediction-based classification systems** base inmate classifications on a range of legal, psychological, social, and even medical information about the offender. The goal is both to predict and to control inmate behavior by making classification decisions based on scientifically verifiable information.

In practice, the combination of models has led to at least five approaches to inmate classification (Craddock 1996, 92), all far more objective than those employed even 20 years ago. Roughly one-quarter of the states base their classification systems on selected elements of psychometric tests that they have developed or taken from standardized tests such as the Minnesota Multiphasic Personality Inventory (MMPI) and the Quay Adult Internal Management System (Buchanan and Whitlow 1987). A further quarter of the states have adopted the **Custody Determination Model** developed by the National Institute of Corrections (NIC). This model bases custody and security assignments on such factors as the offender's expression of violence before and since incarceration, the offender's history of alcohol and drug abuse, and the severity of the current offense. In addition, a third quarter of the states and the federal government use a system developed by the **US Bureau of Prisons (BOP)**. This system focuses on a number of factors, including the severity of the current offense, the time the inmate may serve on the current sentence, and the inmate's history of incarceration, escapes, and violence (Bureau of Prisons 2006).

The remaining states are split between two models. Approximately one in ten of the states uses the **Correctional Classification Profile**, a system created by the Correctional Services Group (Buchanan and Whitlow 1987). This profile assesses an inmate's needs based on the risk posed to both the institution and the public at large. It examines eight dimensions: medical and health needs, mental health needs, security and public risk needs, custody and institutional risk needs, educational needs, vocational training needs, work skills, and the distance between the prison and the location of the inmate's family. Finally, another 10 percent of the states use a combination of the NIC and BOP models.

Classification officers, who like their predecessors also may be called case managers or case workers, implement these systems in today's prisons. They are generally considered to be noncustodial support staff, positioned as they are between the custodial and treatment staff. As you will learn in Chapter 10, this position may also have higher educational requirements than a CO and pay better, as the former have duties and responsibilities that are different from correctional officers in most prisons. Classification officers conduct initial intake assessments, review test results and inmate records, and make recommendations for institutional placement. They may also perform rule-enforcement functions, such as reviewing rule infractions and recommending sanctions for those found to be guilty. They may also work with inmates to find an appropriate work or living reassignments, assist with educational goal attainment, and facilitate engagement in rehabilitation programs, such as anger management courses or drug abuse counseling. Prior to release, the classification officer may work with the inmate to develop an individualized reentry plan. Any recommendation made by the classification officer would typically go to a committee for approval, although the actual placements often owe more to the availability of space in a given living area, treatment program, job, or the like than to a classification officer's recommendations. Moreover, as suggested in Box 6.2, the work of the classification officer, once based largely on highly arbitrary and subjective criteria, has taken on a new look in the twenty-first century.

PRISON TYPES AND FUNCTIONS

Several design elements distinguish contemporary prisons from one another. A prison meant to house low-threat nonviolent inmates is not going to look the same as one that is designed to protect society from the most dangerous offenders, nor is it going to cost as much to build. If all prisons had to meet the same security standards, taxpayers would have to

CALIFORNIA'S CLASSIFICATION SYSTEM

BOX 6.2

In the 1990s, California redesigned its inmate classification system. The new design, like the old one, is a point system: the more points, the higher the inmate's security level. However, the means by which classification officers assign points in the new system is less subjective or arbitrary than in the previous one: they assign points by means of an inventory at the time each inmate enters the system. Among the factors considered are these:

- Gang activities (gang members are more troublesome) or disruptive group behavior.

- Age (younger offenders are more troublesome); history with the criminal justice system (inmates with longer histories are more troublesome).

- Mental health (those with a history of emotional problems tend to be more troublesome).

Classification officers assign certain factors in an inmate's record a mandatory minimum score: for example, 52 points for inmates sentenced to death or to life without parole, 28 points for inmates serving multiple life sentences, and 19 points for inmates with a history of escapes. The system eliminates *stability factors*, including being married, being employed, having more education, and prior military service. Finally, this system employs a user-friendly form.

During a period of 24 months, Richard Berk and his associates randomly assigned 19,318 incoming male inmates to an experimental group (new classification system) and a control group (old classification system). Later, they followed up on reports of inmate misconduct—what the California Department of Corrections and Rehabilitation (CDCR) called 115s—as a measure of the instrument's effectiveness. What did the researchers find? First, staff members accepted and supported the new form: they found it easy to use and useful. Second, the mandatory minimums made the new system more transparent than the old method of overriding a classification that seemed too low for a dangerous inmate. Third, the researchers reported that those indicators discarded in the new system but reported only for the control group were unrelated to that group's prison misconduct. Fourth, the new system resulted in fewer Level I classifications (lowest security risk) and a net increase in Level III classifications. Fifth, the new classification system sorted inmates "substantially better by level of risk when serious misconduct was the sole concern, not all misconduct. That is, the revised classification score works better than the [old] classification score in predicting serious misconduct" (241). Finally, inmate scores changed slightly faster; hence, CDCR was able to move inmates to lower-security facilities faster than was possible in the old system.

After deploying the Inmate Classification Score System (ICSS) for more than a decade, CDCR commissioned an "expert panel" study of the state's two-stage system. The study generated five different inmate datasets, one reflecting classification score reviews and the remaining four examining the outcomes for a range of Close Custody Designation questions pertaining to sentence types (i.e., 15–50 year, life, and multiple life sentences). Close Custody Designations could override the preliminary classification scores, resulting in a mandatory minimum classification. Farabee and associates concluded that there are no natural "breaks" in preliminary classification scores that predict who is more likely to be a behavioral risk to the prison; however, "the likelihood of behavioral infractions increases with preliminary score" (2). The researchers also found that mandatory minimum scores "trap" inmates who may

(Continued)

(Continued)

pose low threats to the institution and other inmates. Age and preliminary classification scores were better, than the actual placement classification score determined by the mandatory minimums, at predicting who would be "trapped". Finally, moving a person to the next higher housing classification level does not suppress institutional misconduct. In summary, the researchers suggested that preliminary classification scores, based on the revised system, should not be overridden by CDCR Mandatory Minimum factors. Moreover inmates with preliminary scores at the threshold of between two housing levels can safely be placed in the lower level. Finally, Close Custody Designations should not be used as a proxy for the risk posed by an inmate for either escape or other behavioral misconduct. Few modern classification systems have been subjected to this level of review and assessment.

SOURCES: BERK ET AL. (2003); FARABEE ET AL. (2011).

pay for a number of unnecessarily expensive facilities. The good news is that not all prisons are created in the same way, and the costs of building and maintaining them reflect those differences. In structures used for the long-term confinement of prisoners, form follows function.

PRISON DESIGN

Facility design is the general plan for a prison physical complex. Prison designers must incorporate a wide range of activities, from supplying food for inmates and doing their laundry, to office space for administrative staff. The variety of functions involved in housing hundreds of people presents designers with many of their greatest challenges. Cost is also a factor in the layout of prisons. Some designs are cheaper to build but are more expensive to maintain than those with higher front-end costs. Of course, security—external and internal—is a crucial design

issue. Does the facility require walls or fences? Does it need individual cells or cells for two or more inmates? Must it include large open areas for work or recreation, or smaller areas where supervision is easier?

Figure 6.1 shows the five basic designs used in building prisons in this country during the past 200 years. Philadelphia's Eastern Penitentiary, which when viewed from above looks like a cross-section of a spoked wheel, was a radial-design prison. New York's Auburn Prison is a modification of this design: from above, the wheel appears cut in half. The spokes in the radial-design contain cells and functional areas—the prison laundry, the kitchen, and dining area, gymnasiums, and work areas, for example. One spoke contains the administrative offices and the prison's main entrance. The spokes spread out from a hub, in effect the "Times Square" of the facility: anyone moving from spoke to spoke must pass through this area.

FIGURE 6.1 **Overhead Views of Prison Designs.**

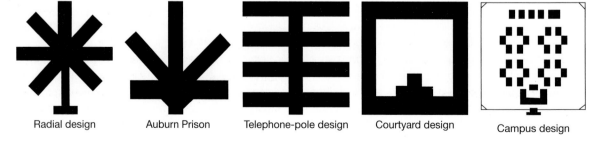

Radial design Auburn Prison Telephone-pole design Courtyard design Campus design

The **radial-design prison** and the Auburn design, which is often described as half a radial prison, have strengths and weaknesses. For securing the prison and facilitating physical searches of inmates, they have few peers. Both are built around a central Times Square sally port area, through which everyone must pass to enter the prison's work, residential and administrative wings. In the case of an inmate disturbance or riot, whoever controls Times Square controls the facility. However, the radial-design prison has never been popular in the United States. Only a few facilities are still active, among them the main facility at the US Penitentiary at Leavenworth (Kansas) and New Jersey's Rahway and Trenton state prisons and a few prisons built after 1970 that employed the design (Nagel 1973).

The **telephone-pole design prison** has a central corridor (the pole) for easy movement around the facility. Wings set at right angles to the central corridor (the cross-members of the pole) house the cells and functional and administrative areas. In these prisons and in radial-design prisons, floors typically are stacked one above the other, an arrangement that allows for the housing of inmates with different classifications in the same facility, while limiting their contact with one another. On the negative side inmates can easily barricade the central corridor during riots and disturbances. Taking back control of the central corridor from entrenched inmates is a difficult task. The telephone pole design is most common in maximum-security prisons, like Marion (Illinois), Somers (Connecticut), and Jackson (Georgia).

The **courtyard-design prison** relies on the institution's walls for security. Although prison experts view the courtyard design to be one of the more modern prison plans, the design is not unlike that of the fortresses and castles with central courtyards that have served as prisons for centuries in Europe. Examples include the Conciergerie in Paris and the Tower of London (see Chapter 2). In the modern courtyard-design prison, all institutional units, including housing, education, health care, industry, and dining, face a central and often expansive courtyard. All doors, except those providing entrance to administrative areas, open to the courtyard, and nearly all movement throughout the facility squeezes through the central courtyard, a natural chokepoint. The courtyard itself may contain recreational areas or park-like areas.

Prison architects often joined the courtyards to create a "daisy chain" of structures, each an almost self-contained unit. This flexibility makes the design especially useful for jurisdictions that anticipate a need for additional space. The courtyard design is also very useful when a facility must house inmates of different classification levels: inmates of the same classification share the same courtyard unit. One shortcoming, however, is that all prisoners in a given courtyard unit must share the same common area, no matter how high the units are stacked. The courtyard design is common to megaprisons and large-scale prison complexes located in the same geographic area.

Prison designers may favor form over function. Policymakers might be responding to a public that does not want a forbidding structure in its town. Alternatively, the facility may serve only low-risk adult inmates, young offenders, or women prisoners.[3] Jurisdictions that do not want a traditional-looking prison often choose a **campus-design prison**. Such facilities more closely resemble a small college than a prison: clusters of living units, which look like private homes but have large dormitory wings, and functional buildings that look like classroom buildings and libraries. Campus-design prisons downplay patrols and perimeter security. Casual visitors may have trouble spotting COs or distinguishing the inmates from the staff. In some medium-security campus design prisons, several chain-link fences, topped by concertina razor wire, and several secure gates provide perimeter security, but facilities that house low-risk inmates may have no fence at all.

BUILDING DESIGN AND INMATE SUPERVISION

The outside of a prison rarely yields insights into the physical layout of the living units. The living units are where inmates typically spend most of their time. Nevertheless, a walk through a living unit quickly reveals the layout and, in turn, the approach to managing the facility. The **linear design** is among the oldest designs currently in use. In this design, one- or two-person cells line a hallway. COs control movement in and out of the cell area from one end of the hallway, usually by means of a sally port. A secure hallway connects the doors, which face each other. They operate electronically or manually, but both doors cannot open at the same time—a security measure that both staff and inmates often find a nuisance.

The traditional linear design allows secure movement through the area by COs or by inmates in transit to and from their cells. In prisons based on the Pennsylvania model, the cells face one another across the hallway, and cells typically have an exterior window. In prisons based on the Auburn model, the cells are set back to back in a block. The hallway, instead of separating the cells, is a walkway around the cells (see Figure 2.2). When they look out of their cells in this layout, inmates look onto other buildings or prison walls.

What does the linear design tell us about a prison's approach to supervision and inmate management? Security is paramount, but supervision in such a facility is *intermittent*. Unless a CO is standing in front of a cell or has a direct line of sight into a cell, it is almost impossible to maintain visual contact with the cell's occupants. This means that COs and other workers have only sporadic contact with inmates while the inmates are in their cells—from 16 hours a day in most cases to as many as 23 hours a day.

A **modified linear design** typically does not place the cells in a straight line. Instead, sally ports control access from a central security area to clusters of cells, which may share a common area (also called a *day area*). Each cell, which is generally open except during sleeping hours, holds one, two, or more inmates. In some facilities, the cells in a cluster are stacked in two or more stories; the upper levels open to the common area on the first floor. In variations on this design, the living unit functions much like a dormitory, with dozens of beds or bunk beds arranged in the area. Despite the openness of this design, the fixtures and doors of these living units are hardened against inmate vandalism, and movement around the day area is tightly controlled.

Surveillance in the modified-linear-design living area is also indirect: COs rely heavily on electronic monitoring, two-way mirrors that look into each cell from a secure gallery area behind the individual cells, and viewing windows. COs rarely enter the common area.

Podular design represents a break with two traditions: linear living areas and intermittent supervision. Pods generally are triangle-shaped structures lined with individual cells that share a central day area. Like modified-linear-design units, cells in the pods can be stacked, opening onto a single common area. Nevertheless, the similarities end there. Podular-design units are less secure: cell doors often are standard solid core doors that the inmate can choose to lock, and a single steel door rather than a sally port usually controls entry to the pods.

One criterion of modern podular design is *direct supervision*: COs spend most of their workdays in the common area among the inmates. Although this would seem to make the COs more vulnerable to inmate assaults, it actually gives them greater control. "Management by walking about," a common practice in business and education, is both more personal and more reliable than either intermittent or remote surveillance. Direct supervision also provides a more humane work environment for COs and living environment for inmates (Zupan 1991).

PRISON LABOR

Work as punishment has a long history. The use of readily and cheaply available inmate labor has always made economic sense to labor contractors, including prison wardens. Before development of the modern penitentiary, many prisons were mines, farms, or public-works projects requiring large pools

MIKAEL KARLSSON/ALAMY IMAGES

of laborers. As the idea of the penitentiary gained a foothold in England and the United States, so did the concept of prison industries. Penal reformers believed that in addition to their economic value, prison industries were a cure for the idleness that plagued inmates in early houses of detention.

FROM THE AUBURN PRISON FACTORY TO THE GREAT DEPRESSION

In the 100 years after Auburn Prison and its imitators opened their doors in the early 1800s, three forms of prison industries evolved:

● Under the **contract system**, prison wardens sold inmate labor to private vendors, who provided the necessary machinery, tools, raw materials, and even supervisory staff. Usually, the factory was near or in the prison, where the vendor would rent space from the warden. When this form of prison labor came under attack, prison administrators took over the production of finished goods, which they then sold (Schaller 1982).

- The **lease system** was a modification of the contract system that came into use after the Civil War. Under this system, private vendors paid a fixed fee, generally to the warden, for prison labor. Often, the work occurred off-site on farms or in mines. The lease system, which closely resembled the indentured servitude outlawed by the Thirteenth Amendment, largely affected African American and poor white males in the South (Sellin 1976, 145).

- In the late 1800s, the **state-use system** evolved in response to charges of unfair competition from prison labor. This system created a *sheltered market*, in which prison labor does not compete directly with private industry; instead, prison systems use inmate labor to produce goods consumed by the prison system itself or by state government (Schaller 1982). In some states, the work is limited to the production of license plates or the construction of new prison facilities; in others, most notably Texas, prison labor produces everything consumed by inmates, from food to clothes.

The early purveyors of prison labor learned a hard truth: free labor is worth every penny you pay for it. For example, Auburn Prison, which was literally a factory within prison walls, took more than 10 years to show a modest profit (Durham 1989).

Profitability did not account for all the problems associated with the use of prison labor. In the 1890s, prison industries and cheap prison labor came under attack on three fronts (McKelvey 1936, 93–118). First, a group of manufacturers, the National Anti-Contract Association, campaigned against the use of prison labor, arguing that competitors who were using prison labor were able to undersell them on labor costs alone. Second, the emerging labor union movement targeted prison labor for competing

unfairly with workers in the free market. Finally, a series of scandals involving the exploitation of prison workers erupted in the late 1800s. In fact, charges were brought against the Elmira reformatory and Zebulon Brockway. Legislatures in eastern states, including Massachusetts, New York, and Pennsylvania, were among the first to use prison labor and then to create laws curbing its use (McKelvey 1936, 126–44). In 1887, Congress enacted legislation that outlawed the contracting of federal prisoners (201).

Despite a strong antiprison labor movement with broad public support, the widespread use of prison labor continued until the Great Depression. In January 1929, 10 months before the stock market crash that caused the Depression, President Herbert Hoover signed the **Hawes-Cooper Act** into law. The act made all inmate-manufactured goods transported through a state subject to that state's laws. By the early 1930s, dozens of states had laws restricting the manufacture, transportation, and sale of prison-made goods. This made it illegal for manufacturers to move prison-made goods across those states for sale in an unrestricted state. Moreover, the costs of rerouting the goods more than offset the savings realized from the use of prison labor. These factors dealt prison industry a near-fatal blow.

By the mid-1930s, millions were out of work. Congress responded to the crisis by passing the 1935 **Ashurst-Sumners Act**, which made it a crime for the interstate transportation of prison-made goods into a state whose laws restricted their sale. The law also encouraged those states that still allowed the sale of prison-manufactured goods to enact restrictive legislation. By 1940, every state restricted the sale of inmate-manufactured goods. Although prison inmates continued to produce goods for state use, federal control of interstate commerce ended prison industries for the next 40 years.

CONTEMPORARY PRISON INDUSTRIES

The 1970s, notes Duffee (1989, 350), provided a climate of change for prison industries in the United States. At the start of the 1980s:

- labor unions no longer exerted the political influence they had from the 1930s to 1950s;

- state and federal legislators were encouraging prison managers to become more efficient and to cut costs;

- prisoners' rights activists had successfully attacked post-incarceration barriers to employment for convicted felons, increasing the value of prison-based vocational training; and

- rehabilitation was out, and work, along with the security it brought the institution, was in.

- The Free Ventures Project, a seven-state experiment in private enterprise, gave inmates real jobs and real skills with post-incarceration marketability.

In 1979, Congress enacted Public Law 96–157, which created the **Private Sector/Prison Industries Enhancement Certification (PS/PIEC)** program. The law removed most of the restrictions placed on inmate-manufactured goods by the Hawes-Cooper and Ashurst-Sumners acts. Just three restrictions remained in place. First, the pay inmates working in private-sector prison industries receive must be the same rate paid for similar work in the local area. Second, before beginning a prison construction project, state officials must consult local labor unions. Third, inmate employment cannot displace workers in the private sector, cannot involve work for which there is a surplus of labor in the locality, and cannot impair existing contracts for services.

Legislatures in nearly half the states repealed state-use-only statutes between 1970 and 1985. In their place were new laws that allowed the limited sale of prisoner-manufactured goods to the private sector (ACA 1986; Flanagan and Maguire 1993). The net effect of the federal and state legislation was a resurgence of interest in prison industries. **Joint-venture programs**—sometimes, as in California, still called Free Venture Programs—could serve as models for other collaborative efforts between prison administrators and the private sector. However, only about 0.3 percent of all prisoners in the United States participated in certified joint-venture programs.[4] About 200 certified private employers used more than 5,000 prison inmates by 2004.

Do these programs work? That is, do they achieve their intended goals? By several benchmarks, the impact of such work on inmate reentry appears to be significant. A 2006 National Institute of Justice (NIJ) study revealed that participants in traditional prison industries found work sooner and survived longer after release than did inmates who did something other than work while incarcerated, and prison industries enhanced programs faired even better than did their cohort in traditional prison work (Smith, Bechtel, Patrick Smith, Wilson-Gentry 2006). As Moses and Smith (2007) stated, not only was recidivism lower, but inmate labor also benefited taxpayers and inmates. For example, as of 2006, nearly one-quarter of PIECP wages went for room and board; not quite 40 percent went to the inmates and 10 percent of their wages were "banked" for post-release use; another significant fraction went to the Internal Revenue Service. Even the federal victims fund received a significant portion. By these combined measures, claimed Moses and Smith, prison "real work" programs work.

Is the use of prison labor a good idea? The answer depends on whom you ask. Busy inmates are certainly less unhappy than ones who have nothing to do in prison other than wait for the time to pass. It is important to recall that the proportion of the total inmate population engaged in meaningful and financially rewarding employment is very small. The potential for work-related abuses is fairly high (Sloan, n.d.). There is also reason to be concerned about the rights of prison laborers, as they enjoy few legal protections and are susceptible to the same market forces as workers in the free society. For example, prison inmates have been negatively impacted by the economic downturn that began in late 2007, as thousands of inmates lost their jobs (Kirklin 2011).

FEDERAL PRISON SYSTEM

Congress authorized the construction of three federal penitentiaries in 1891. Until that time, state prisons and local jails housed federal prisoners. It took more than a decade to build and open the first of the new prisons. While construction was under way, federal prisoners went to the former military prison in Leavenworth, Kansas. The first new federal penitentiary opened in 1902 in Atlanta, Georgia; 4

years later, two other inmate-constructed federal penitentiaries opened at Leavenworth and McNeil Island (Washington). In the 1920s, the federal prison system added a women's prison, a youth facility, and a detention center, operated by the Justice Department and supervised by the superintendent of prisons and prisoners (US BOP 1994). The Volstead Act—which enforced the Eighteenth Amendment's prohibition on the sale, manufacture, and transportation of all alcoholic beverages—was passed in 1919, and a series of new federal laws making heroin, cocaine, marijuana, and other substances illegal was passed in the 1920s. These law-enforcement initiatives, and new federal laws protecting banks and criminalizing the interstate theft of automobiles, brought thousands of new felons into the federal prison system.

On May 14, 1930, President Hoover signed legislation creating the US Bureau of Prisons (US BOP 2006a). The bureau's charge was to centralize and make the administration of the federal prison system consistent, to professionalize the prison service, and to provide more humane care for federal prisoners. Over the next few years, the BOP opened several new federal correctional facilities, including the US Penitentiary at Lewisburg (Pennsylvania) and prisons at El Reno (Oklahoma), La Tuna (Texas), and Milan (Michigan). In 1933, the Medical Center for Federal Prisoners opened in Springfield, Missouri.

The number of inmates housed by the BOP between 1940 and 1980 grew slowly, from 20,000 to nearly 25,000 (US BOP 1997). Changes in federal antidrug policies, parole policies, and sentencing mandates led to a huge increase in the number of federal prisoners in the 1980s. For example, in 1986 the federal prison population stood at more than 40,000 sentenced and yet-to-be-sentenced inmates, an increase of close to 16,000 inmates in just 5 years. In less than a decade, the number of inmates had more than doubled. In 2012 the federal prison population was over 218,000 (Government Accountability Office 2012).

FEDERAL FACILITIES PROFILE

The federal government classifies its facilities by security level: high, medium, low, minimum, and administrative. Bureau personnel assign these designations by weighting, in order of importance, the impact of seven features: external patrols, gun towers, external security barriers, external detection devices, type of housing, internal security features, and staff-to-inmate ratios. A detailed look at the different types of federal facilities is provided below. About 45 percent of the federal prisoners are housed in minimum security facilities; medium security federal facilities house a slightly lower percentage, roughly 42 percent; the rest are residents of the BOP's maximum security correctional facilities, including about 400 at the Florence supermax penitentiary. We begin with the high security US Penitentiaries and other special facilities that are also operated at high security.

HIGH SECURITY

The high-security prisons in the federal system are **US Penitentiaries (USPs)**. They have a highly secure perimeter, usually consisting of walls or several strongly reinforced fences. Inmates live in multiple- and single-occupant cells. COs maintain close control over inmates' movements, and the staff-to-inmate ratio of 1:2 is the highest for any federal prison facility. Internally and externally, high-security facilities resemble the maximum-security prisons found in most state systems.

The BOP's 20 USPs house high-risk male inmates.[5] Two, USP-Atlanta (Georgia) and USP-Leavenworth (Kansas) are more than 100 years old. USP-Lewisburg (Pennsylvania) came into the system in 1932, followed by USP-Terre Haute (Indiana) in 1940. The BOP built no new federal penitentiaries for nearly 20 years, until USP-Lompoc (California) opened in 1959, followed by USP-Marion (Illinois) in 1963. It was another 30 years before the opening of USP-Allenwood (Pennsylvania) in 1993. By 2007, 13 more federal penitentiaries had opened, including USP-Atwater (California); USP-Beaumont (Texas); USP-Big Sand (Kentucky); USP-Canaan (Pennsylvania); USP-Coleman (Florida); USP-Florence-High (Colorado);[6] USP-Florence-ADX (Colorado); USP-Hazelton (West Virginia); USP-Lee (Virginia); USP-McCreary (Kentucky); USP-Pollock (Louisiana); USP-Tucson (Arizona), and USP-Victorville (California). Between 1993 and 2007, the BOP more than tripled the number of high-security facilities it operates, each of which was built to house between 500 and 1,500 inmates. Federal executions are carried out at the Special Confinement Unit at USP-Terre Haute.

MEDIUM SECURITY

More than half of all facilities operated by the BOP are **federal correctional institutions (FCIs)**, run as medium-security facilities or, less often, as medium- and administrative-security facilities.[7] At this security level, the perimeters are double-fenced, usually strengthened with electronic security devices. Inmates live in one-, two-, or three-person cells. Internal controls are not as tight as they are in high-security facilities, but they are strict, and the staff-to-inmate ratio averages 1:3. This security ranking is comparable to the medium-security level in state prison systems.

LOW SECURITY

All low-security federal facilities are FCIs. In these facilities, perimeters are double-fenced; 20 to 30 or more residents live in dormitories or cubicles; and the staff-to-inmate ratio averages 1:4. One of these facilities is a female-only facility. Three others are mixed-gender facilities. All four operate at low or low administrative-security levels. The BOP does not run any facilities for women at higher security levels. The only option for higher-risk females sentenced for federal felony violations is to place them in an administrative-security facility.

MINIMUM SECURITY

The BOP operates a few **Federal Prison Camps (FPCs)**, all minimum-security facilities. Many are located adjacent to a larger institution—a federal penitentiary, correctional institution, medical center, or detention center—that draws on the FPC population for workers; others are located on military bases. The camps have limited or no perimeter fencing, house inmates in dormitories, and have a relatively high staff-to-inmate ratio (1:10). **Campers** are the lowest risk of all federal prisoners. Most are white-collar criminals or other nonviolent offenders. FPC–Alderson (West Virginia), the oldest continually functioning federal women's facility, and FPC–Bryan

(Texas) both house only women; the rest house only men.

The BOP also operates **Satellite Prison Camps (SPCs)**. Like FPCs, the BOP operates SPCs as minimum-security camps, adjacent to a main facility, and, again like FPCs, their primary function is to house an accessible workforce for the more secure facility. However, the capacity of satellite camps is smaller than that of the FPCs. Each satellite camp houses between 100 and 500 inmates, and each FPC houses between 500 and 800 inmates. Most of the satellite camps house men; a handful of these camps incarcerate women only. Together, federal minimum- and low-security levels are roughly equivalent to the minimum-security classification used in state prisons.

ADMINISTRATIVE FACILITIES Administrative Facilities are special-use prisons that provide a range of security conditions for a range of inmates. Like jails, these facilities house inmates at all risk levels. The BOP operates a variety of facilities with administrative-security classifications. All the BOP's **Metropolitan Correctional Centers/Metropolitan Detention Centers (MCCs/MDCs)** are administrative-security prisons. These institutions are relatively new: the BOP opened the first MCC/MDC facilities in the mid-1970s. In many ways, these facilities resemble large jails. They house between 700 and 2,500 male and female inmates of virtually every possible legal designation: accused, convicted, and in-transit federal felons and misdemeanants. Only one **federal medical center (FMC)** treats women exclusively. The rest treat only men or women at an adjacent camp. A sixth medical facility, the Medical Center for Federal Prisoners (MCFP), also treats only men. The **federal detention centers (FDCs)**, one of which houses male inmates exclusively, primarily hold short-term federal detainees.

Three special-use facilities are unique. The first is the **Federal Transfer Center (FTC)**, located in Oklahoma City, and home to the BOP's airline. This facility is responsible for coordinating the movement of inmates between other facilities.[8] The second special-use facility, the **Secure Female Facility (SFF)** located at USP Hazelton (WV), exclusively houses female offenders. Third, the BOP designation of **Administrative-Maximum (ADMAX)** refers to its

super-max penitentiary, also called USP-Florence-ADX. This facility and its role in the federal prison system are revealed in Box 6.3.

Finally, the BOP operates an administrative unit called the **Federal Correctional Complex (FCC)**. There are 14 FCCs around the nation. They are a cluster of institutions with different missions and security levels, all located in close proximity to one another. Perhaps the most famous of these is the Federal Correctional Complex at Florence, Colorado, home of USP-Florence-ADX, FCI-Florence, and USP-Florence High; the complex houses approximately 1,500 inmates.

According to the 2005 Census of State and Federal Correctional Facilities (CSFCF), the BOP's 29,755 staff, including more than 14,000 COs, was supervising 145,780 inmates in 102 correctional facilities.[9] Nearly 75 percent of these facilities were moderately large, housing between 1,000 and 2,499 inmates; only two housed 2,500 or more inmates. The remainder, about one in four had an average daily capacity of less than 1,000 inmates. The BOP-operated system is crowded, operating at 137 percent of its rated capacity. In terms of security levels, about four in ten operate as either minimum or medium security facilities. A total of 20 federal facilities are designated as maximum security institutions, including the supermax penitentiary at Florence, Colorado.[10]

PROGRAMS PROFILE

The federal government operates many programs at its more than 100 secure facilities. Four emphases are clear: work, education, vocational and occupational training, and drug treatment.

WORK Work is important for at least three reasons. First, it keeps the inmates busy for extended periods. All able-bodied federal inmates have a job. Second, good work habits, combined with vocational training, can lead to a successful post-release job placement. Third, inmates provide a ready labor pool in the prison for institutional jobs.

Federal facilities operate two main work programs. The BOP formed the first, **Federal Prison Industries, Inc.**, in 1934 (US BOP 2009). Today

BEYOND MAXIMUM SECURITY: SUPERMAX PRISONS

BOX 6.3

The **supermax prison** exceeds even maximum-security prisons in control and custody. The supermax is reserved for the "baddest of the bad," those inmates who pose such a threat to other prisoners and staff that they must be locked down 23 hours a day in single-person cells. Prisoners are fed in their cells and have few opportunities to mix with one another. There are two staff members for each inmate in this facility. These special features mean that such prisons cost two to three times more than a standard maximum-security facility to build, maintain, and operate. More than 30 states and the federal government have one or more of these units. While the nation's state prison systems operate few supermax prisons, many maximum-security prisons and even jails have a supermax cell, hallway, or wing—called the **administrative segregation unit**—where inmates who break rules can be isolated, usually for short periods.

The BOP currently operates one supermax federal prison, USP-Florence-ADX. Administratively, this 575-bed stand-alone facility is part of the USP-Florence. USP-Florence-ADX has six levels of security. Based on the inmates' security classification, they may or may not have access to the facility's visitors center, administration section, classrooms and program areas, chapel, gymnasium, or commissary. Even access to the health services center may be restricted: if a high-risk inmate needs medical care, the services may go to the prisoner, rather than vice versa.

What effects do extended periods of isolation, the absence of normal stimuli, and a controlling environment have on the individual inmate's psyche? Do those effects increase with the term of incarceration? Do the conditions in these facilities have a negative impact on certain inmates in particular, those with mental illness, for example? Do the methods used in these facilities constitute cruel and unusual punishment? Jenesia Pizarro and Vanja Stenius suggest that such prisons have the potential to increase all the pains of imprisonment and thereby further damage inmates' mental health while failing to make appreciable inroads into their need for treatment. Maureen O'Keefe and associates disagree, suggesting that the effects of standard administrative segregation on the physical and mental health of inmates may be overstated. However, at least six inmates at USP-Florence-ADX have committed suicide and many others have attempted suicide or engaged in self-mutilation. Given a 2012 federal class-action suit against the BOP concerning the operation of USP-Florence-ADX, the needed legal guidance may be coming from the federal courts.

SOURCES: COHEN (2012); MAUER (1985); MEARS (2006); O'KEEFE, KLEBE, STUCKER, ET AL. (2010); PIZARRO AND STENIUS (2004); RIVELAND (1999); US BOP (1994, 2006A, 2006B).

UNICOR, the Federal Prison Industries' trade name, has the following five goals (US BOP 2003, 15):

- employ and provide job skills training to as many inmates as possible to help them prepare for a productive—and crime-free—return to the community after their release;

- contribute to the safety and security of federal prisons by keeping inmates constructively occupied;

- produce market-priced, quality goods for sale to the federal government;

- operate in a self-sustaining manner; and

- minimize any negative impact on private business and labor.

UNICOR provides work assignments for 8 percent of the BOP system's work eligible inmates (US BOP 2011). The program operates 88 factories at 66 BOP facilities. Inmates manufacture and refinish furniture;

produce textiles, clothing, and paintbrushes; refurbish vehicle components; assemble electrical cable and radio mounts for military applications; craft signs and other metal products; and recycle. In the fiscal year 2011, the typical inmate worked between 35 and 44 hours a week. The best-paying jobs are typically in UNICOR: inmates in the program earn from $.23 to $1.15 an hour (US BOP 2006a, 6). UNICOR's sales were $745 million in 2011.

The second work program is general maintenance of the BOP facility, also called facility support services. About 75 percent of federal inmates work at institutional jobs, in health services, food services, educational and recreational services, the law library, the business office, and maintenance. Inmates working in their facility earn considerably less money—from $.12 cents an hour for farming, forestry, and ranching, to $.40 an hour for non-UNICOR goods production (US BOP 2006a, 6).

EDUCATION

All BOP institutions offer literacy classes, English as a Second Language (ESL), adult continuing education, parenting classes, library services, wellness education, and instruction in leisure-time activities. Inmates without a high school diploma or General Educational Development (GED) certificate must participate in literacy programs for at least 240 hours or until they receive a GED. Inmates without GEDs are ineligible for higher paying jobs in UNICOR. Non-English-speaking inmates are required to participate in ESL until they show English proficiency. In 2005, the GED program enrolled nearly 24,000 inmates and more than 6,000 received their GEDs.

VOCATIONAL AND OCCUPATIONAL TRAINING

The BOP supports hundreds of occupational training programs, apprenticeship programs, and advanced occupational education programs, as they are available in 98 percent of all federal secure facilities (Stephan 2008, Appendix table 18). On any given day, about 10,000 inmates participate in these programs. In a given year, inmates complete more than 10,000 occupational training courses. Inmates also have access to courses offered by a broad range of technical schools, community colleges, and 4-year colleges and universities. The US Department of Labor, Bureau of Apprenticeship Training registers all apprenticeship programs at BOP facilities. Although some programs serve thousands of inmates, other programs are small and unique; for example, each year about 100 inmates complete a 10-week course in Commercial Truck Driving Basics, preparing them to take the test to obtain a commercial driver's license.

DRUG TREATMENT

All federal facilities offer psychological and psychiatric counseling, compared with just two-thirds of state prisons and less than half of private facilities (Stephan 2008, Appendix table 18). One focus of counseling is substance abuse—a logical response given the large number of drug-involved inmates in the federal system. Given that for over one-half of all federal prisoners, a drug offense is their most serious crime, BOP must provide drug treatment to every eligible inmate.

The BOP operates three primary drug treatment programs along a drug-treatment continuum (US BOP 1994; 2006a). The first step is **drug education**, an information-oriented program available to almost all inmates in federal facilities. Every year, more than 15 percent of federal inmates participate in this program. The next step involves the **nonresidential drug abuse treatment**, an outpatient program consisting of individual and group counseling, self-help groups, and seminars. Less than 10 percent of federal inmates participate in this program. About one-half of all federal facilities have a **residential drug abuse treatment program**; this program reaches about 10 percent of the federal inmates, constituting roughly one-third of federal inmates with serious drug-related problems. The program is voluntary, and inmates who sign up begin 9 months of unit-based education and intensive individual and group counseling.

STATE PRISON SYSTEMS

Table 6.1 includes the number and incarceration rates in federal and state institutions between 1925 and 2011, broken down by gender. Early statistics are notoriously unreliable. However, between 1925 and

TABLE 6.1 Inmates in federal and state prison, by gender, 1925–1980: five-year intervals and 1981–2011 (yearly).

Year	Males		Females		Total	
	Number[a]	Per capita rate[b]	Number[a]	Per capita rate[b]	Number[a]	Per capita rate[c]
1925	88,231	149	3,438	6	91,669	79
1930	124,785	200	4,668	8	129,453	104
1935	139,278	217	4,902	8	144,180	113
1940	167,345	252	6,361	10	173,706	131
1945	127,609	193	6,040	9	133,649	98
1950	160,309	211	5,814	8	166,123	109
1955	178,655	217	7,125	8	185,780	112
1960	205,265	230	7,688	8	212,953	117
1965	203,327	213	7,568	8	210,895	108
1970	190,794	191	5,635	5	196,429	96
1975	231,918	220	8,675	8	240,593	111
1977[d]	274,244	255	11,212	10	285,456	129
1980	303,643	275	12,331	11	315,974	139
1981	339,375	304	14,298	12	353,673	154
1982	379,075	337	16,441	14	395,516	171
1983	401,870	354	17,476	15	419,346	179
1984	424,193	370	19,205	16	443,396	188
1985	459,223	397	21,345	17	480,568	202
1986	497,540	426	24,544	20	522,084	217
1987	533,990	453	26,822	22	580,812	231
1988	573,587	482	30,145	24	603,732	247
1989	643,643	535	37,264	29	680,907	276
1990	699,416	575	40,564	32	739,980	297
1991	745,808	606	43,802	34	789,980	313
1992	799,776	642	46,501	36	846,277	332
1993	878,037	698	54,037	41	932,074	359
1994	956,566	753	60,125	45	1,016,691	389
1995	1,021,059	789	63,963	47	1,085,022	411
1996	1,068,123	819	69,599	51	1,137,722	427
1997	1,120,787	853	73,794	54	1,194,581	444
1998	1,167,802	885	77,600	57	1,245,402	461
1999	1,221,611	913	82,463	59	1,304,074	463
2000	1,246,234	915	85,044	59	1,331,278	469
2001	1,343,164	896	92,979	58	1,345,217	470
2002	1,313,053	906	97,491	60	1,380,370	476
2003	1,368,866	915	101,179	62	1,470,045	482
2004	1,391,781	920	104,848	64	1,496,629	486
2005	1,418,406	929	107,518	65	1,525,810	491
2006	1,456,366	943	112,308	68	1,568,674	501
2007	1,482,524	955	114,311	69	1,596,835	506
2008	1,493,670	952	114,612	68	1,608,282	504
2009	1,502,002	949	113,482	67	1,615,487	502
2010	1,500,936	948	112,867	66	1,613,803	500
2011	1,487,393	932	111,387	65	1,598,780	492

NOTES: [a]THIS FIGURE IS FOR ALL PERSONS UNDER THE CONTROL OF THE NATION'S STATE AND FEDERAL CORRECTIONAL AUTHORITIES, INCLUDING BOTH SENTENCED AND UNSENTENCED PRISONERS.
[b]PRISONERS PER 100,000 RESIDENTS OF GENDER NOTED.
[c]PRISONERS PER 100,000 RESIDENTS.
[d]IN 1977, THERE WAS A TECHNICAL CHANGE IN THE WAY THE RATES WERE CALCULATED. FROM THAT YEAR FORWARD, JURISDICTION COUNTS VERSUS CUSTODY COUNTS WERE USED. JURISDICTION COUNTS INCLUDE ALL INMATES FOR WHOM A COURT HAS LEGAL, BUT NOT NECESSARILY PHYSICAL, CUSTODY.
SOURCES: CARSON AND SABOL (2012, 23, 31); HARRISON AND BECK (2002, 6; 2003, 5; 2004, 4; 2005, 4; 2006, 4); LANGAN ET AL. (1988); MAGUIRE AND PASTORE (2002, 494); WEST AND SABOL (2008, 18–20; 2010, 28, 30–31).

1970, the overall rates typically rose slowly, leveled off, and then dropped: the rate in 1970 (96 per 100,000) was close to the rates recorded in 1925 and in 1945. In 1975, the rate was 111 per 100,000. It rose steadily throughout the next four decades. In fact, by 1986 it had nearly doubled, doubling again over the next 10 years. By 2007, the rate was 506, an increase of more than 400 percent in a period of 40 years. Never before in the 80-plus years of recorded national prisoner statistics had there been an increase of as much as 100 percent in a similar time span. We would be remiss, however, if we did not note a recent trend. Beginning in 2008, there has been a downward movement in the overall incarceration rate for prisons, largely accounted by for deceases in state-level incarceration rates (Carson and Sabol 2012). It is important to note that 70 percent of the decrease in state prison populations between 2010 and 2011 was due to California's Prison Safety Realignment Program, which was court-precipitated (Carson and Sabol 2012, 1).

The patterns observed for male and female inmates are also instructive. In 1975, the rate for male inmates was 220 per 100,000 US male residents, and prisons held 231,918 male inmates. In 2007, the male rate was 955, with nearly 1.5 million male inmates. The rate for women in 1975 was 8, and there were only 8,675 female inmates in the nation's prisons. By 2007, the nation's prisons held more than 114,000 female inmates, and the per capita rate stood at 69. There are more women in prison today than there were prisoners of both genders in 1925, and the per capita incarceration rate for women has been creeping toward the total rate reported in 1925. But again, the rates for both genders peaked in 2007 and began inching downward over the subsequent 3 years. It remains too soon to suggest that the upward spiral in prison incarceration rates has been broken, but it is an interesting trend nonetheless.

STATE FACILITIES PROFILE

The 50 states operate 1,719 correctional facilities, 70 percent (1,190) of which are confinement facilities.[11]

Only about 4 percent of state facilities hold 2,500 or more inmates. About 24 percent of state facilities hold between 1,000 and 2,499 inmates. A further 17 percent house between 500 and 999 inmates each. More than one-half of the nation's correctional facilities house fewer than 500 inmates. A few states—including Florida, Georgia, California, Michigan, New York, and Texas—have many very big public correctional facilities that house 1,000 or more inmates. As Box 6.4 shows, the nation's 415 private facilities present different profiles and programming from those in the public sector.

In terms of classification levels, about 54 percent of state facilities operate at the minimum or low security level, largely due to the fact that most community corrections facilities are operated at that level. Another 25 percent of all such institutions operate as medium-security institutions. The remaining 21 percent are maximum-security prisons, including those that operate at super-maximum and close- and high-supervision levels. As a rule, those states that operate correctional systems with very large facilities (those that house 1,000 or more inmates) also have the most maximum security prisons.

PROGRAMS PROFILE

WORK Jobs are important to state prison systems, but less uniformly so than in the federal system. Work programs are available in 87 percent of the nation's 1,719 state-level correctional facilities. As with federal prisons, the term "facilities support services" best describes nearly all job programs in both types of facilities, meaning the inmates take care of the prison and its grounds, as 72 percent report this form of work program. Agricultural and farming programs are found in 17 percent of state facilities. Public works assignments—including highway and street cleaning—exist in 46 percent of the publicly operated correctional facilities. Prison industries, so common at the federal level, are found in 25 percent of state-level facilities. Indeed, the manufactured goods produced in prison industries tend to be products consumed by the prison or state, including

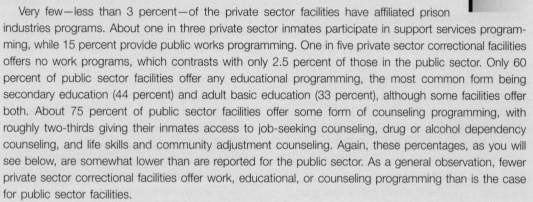

PRIVATE CORRECTIONS: THE REST OF THE STORY

BOX 6.4

Between 2000 and 2005 the number of private facilities contracted to the state or federal governments increased by nearly 60 percent, one-quarter of the growth occurring in the federal sector: one in five private sector inmates were federal felons. In terms of size, two-thirds of the private facilities housed fewer than 100 inmates, largely because three-quarters of them were community-based correctional facilities. This conclusion is reinforced by the observation that nearly 90 percent of all private correctional facilities operate at the minimum security level, while only 2 percent are maximum security facilities.

Very few—less than 3 percent—of the private sector facilities have affiliated prison industries programs. About one in three private sector inmates participate in support services programming, while 15 percent provide public works programming. One in five private sector correctional facilities offers no work programs, which contrasts with only 2.5 percent of those in the public sector. Only 60 percent of public sector facilities offer any educational programming, the most common form being secondary education (44 percent) and adult basic education (33 percent), although some facilities offer both. About 75 percent of public sector facilities offer some form of counseling programming, with roughly two-thirds giving their inmates access to job-seeking counseling, drug or alcohol dependency counseling, and life skills and community adjustment counseling. Again, these percentages, as you will see below, are somewhat lower than are reported for the public sector. As a general observation, fewer private sector correctional facilities offer work, educational, or counseling programming than is the case for public sector facilities.

SOURCE: STEPHAN (2008).

furniture, refurbished vehicles, license plates, and signs of all descriptions and materials.

State prison inmates average $.56 an hour, about $.10 an hour more than federal inmates do. Most inmates work between 20 and 44 hours a week. Texas and a few other states pay their inmates nothing. In the state system, as in the federal system, farming, forestry, and ranching pay the least, on average $.31 an hour. The highest-paid state prisoners work in maintenance, repair, or construction (all $.94 an hour) and goods production ($.84 an hour).

EDUCATION AND VOCATIONAL TRAINING Educational and vocational training programs are widespread in state corrections (Harlow 2003; Stephan 2008). About 66 percent of state-operated facilities provide at least adult basic education (ABE), usually leading to a GED. About 50 percent operate vocational,

technical, prerelease, or job-readiness training. Roughly 32 percent of state prisons have special education programs, including programs for people with learning disabilities. College programs also operate in 32 percent of public facilities, but fewer than 8 percent operate study release programs.

TREATMENT PROGRAMS One of the most pressing needs among state prisoners is drug treatment (Mumola and Karberg 2006; Stephan 2008). Drug, mental health, and sex-offender programs receive varying degrees of attention—and resources—in state corrections systems. Nine out of ten state-operated facilities offer inmates counseling services. The most common of these, found in 72 percent of public facilities, focus on drug and alcohol dependence, substance abuse, and drug awareness programs. Psychological or psychiatric counseling is less common, found in about 55 percent of public facilities, roughly the same percentage having training in life skills, community adjustment, and employment skills. Counseling programs for people with HIV/ AIDS are less common: only about 50 percent of all public confinement and community-based facilities offer them.

THE PRISON OF THE FUTURE

What will the prison of the future look like? This is more than a rhetorical question. In the late eighteenth century, the English philosopher and social theorist Jeremy Bentham proposed the panopticon, an idea introduced in Chapter 1. This radical prison design, with its inspection tower in the center of a circular prison, was initially adopted and then abandoned as the design for the English National Penitentiary at Millbank. The idea was to provide a physical environment where a few officers could supervise the work of hundreds of inmates, as well as provide for their moral training. No true panopticon was ever constructed, although dozens of prisons around the world have included architectural and security elements of Bentham's idea of the prison of the future.

Over a century later, Frank C. Richmond, the Director of Psychiatric Field Service for the State Board of Control of Wisconsin, speculated about the prison of the future. He was responding to a challenge from Sanford Bates, the first director of the Federal Bureau of Prisons, who observed the following 5 years earlier: "How can we devise a system that will be at once a present protection and still comprehend a program of sound humanitarian rehabilitation" (Richmond 1935, 735). Richmond made five suggestions that he thought should be incorporated into such a prison. First, prison architecture and construction should lend themselves to programs of constructive rehabilitation, giving prominence to medical, education, and mental hygiene facilities. Second, prison staff at all levels should have training in the science of human behavior, with a priority given to hiring college-educated personnel. Third, while work is essential, prisoners and their labor must not be exploited and "private interest in prison

labor is to be abolished" (737). Fourth, while men (and we assume women) may be punished en masse, corrective and protective treatment plans must be individualized for each inmates. However, Richmond echoes the concerns of Bates before him (and many subsequent generations of penologists): "The great problem, then, is to harmonize the police and custodial function of the prison with the educational and correctional function" (739). The final suggestion is to stop using the word prison to describe the new "ideal institution," substituting names more suited for their corrective and treatment functions such as institutes and centers named for correctional leaders. While some of Richmond's suggestions sound quaint and idealistic in the twenty-first century, most still resonate with those who study institutional corrections. Importantly, Richmond recognized that form (i.e., a facility's physical features) and function (i.e., what the facility's staff did for and to their charges) were interrelated; moreover, what we call something (e.g., a prison) and someone (e.g., a prisoner) matters.

Is a utopian prison possible? Joycelyn M. Pollock and her associates' (2012) review of five actions that would move the United States' corrections in the direction of a more functional prison system reflected the ideas of Dr. Richmond. First, the nation's prisons should commit to the principles of restorative justice and rehabilitation. Second, staff recruitment should seek out and retain personnel who are committed to these principles. Third, the prison's climate must be changed so that inmates can focus on change rather than survival. Fourth, prisons should adopt evidence-based rehabilitative programming, models based on success. Finally, Pollock and her associates emphasize that those committed to change must understand and find a way to overcome the forces that have a vested interest in the "prison industrial complex" (60). Due in part to these forces and the United States' troubling history of corrections, they conclude "that prisons will never be utopian, but they can be more just, more humane, and more effective as a place to change lives. Evidence suggests this is what the public wants" (Pollock et al. 2012, 60). In spite of this measured cynicism about contemporary and future prisons, consider the Norwegian prison highlighted in Box 6.5.

SPOTLIGHT ON INTERNATIONAL CORRECTIONS: THE WORLD'S NICEST PRISON   BOX 6.5

Since 1982, Norway has operated Bastøy prison, what has been called the world's nicest prison. It is a minimum security facility located on a one-square mile island. At night, nearly all of the 69 staff members take the 15-minute ferry ride to the mainland, leaving only five employees to supervise 115 inmates. Inmates are housed in wooden cottages or in a former mansion that closely resembles a college dorm; the prison's farm employs most inmates. However, they have much free time to wander the island's beaches or ride horses. What are the crimes of the inmates? They are serving time for murder, rape, and heroin trafficking, among other serious crimes.

In a nutshell, many observers see this prison as a resort, a place people would pay to visit. Indeed, CNN reporter John Sutter called it "the holiday version of Alcatraz." However, it is at its core still a prison. Liberty is restricted to the island. Escape attempts occur, but infrequently. The next stop for those who escape and are caught is a maximum security prison and an extended sentence. There are few rules, including the absence of a formal dress code for inmates or correctional officers; however, everyone works. Indeed, Bastøy has a strong programmatic commitment to the provision of rehabilitative services that work, especially those that target inmate reintegration.

Does the Norwegian approach to punishment and rehabilitation work? First, we need to recognize that Norwegian courts employ far shorter prison sentences than do similar courts in the United States. For example, a rapist-murderer might be sentenced to 10 years. Second, recidivism in Norway's prison system is very low, hovering at 20 percent. However, Bastøy's reported recidivism rate is even lower at 18 percent. It may not be a utopian prison, but it is unlike any prison found in the United States.

SOURCE: SUTTER (2012).

SUMMARY

Correctional institutions play an essential role in the protection of society from some of its more dangerous law-breaking members. Whether the state or federal governments operate them, such facilities must balance multiple goals, including custody and treatment, although the former tends to trump the latter. Some other key points presented in this chapter include the following:

● A prison is a total institution specifically designed for punishment, but the punishments rendered must be humane and follow guidelines based on the US Constitution and defined by federal and state laws and court decisions.

● Security arrangements—especially those found in maximum-security or supermax prisons—can and do create bleak living conditions for those subjected to them; there is a dynamic give-and-take, then, between inmates' rights and the need to protect society, the institution, and inmates themselves.

● Today, prisons have also become an economic force as communities compete for new prisons: prisons mean jobs that are nonpolluting, renewable, and, except for private prisons, protected by civil service regulations.

● Jail or prison terms are what the public demands when criminals are convicted.

THINKING ABOUT CORRECTIONAL POLICIES AND PRACTICES: WRITING ASSIGNMENTS

1 You are a mid-level unit manager at a state prison. Your boss has asked you to prepare a one- to two-page policy brief on why custody goals should be "softened" to engage COs more in the rehabilitative process. What do you say?

2 Nearly every state's department of corrections (DOC)—or state-level agency that manages long-term correctional institutions—maintains an accessible website for public accountability and personnel recruitment purposes. Visit your state's DOC website. Go to the webpage for one or more of the facilities found in your state and see if you can determine the design. Then look at the facilities' security level and stated goals for inmates. Prepare a one- to two-page paper summarizing each element: design, security level, and institutional goals for inmates. *Note:* If you cannot find such a website for your own state, look for one for a nearby state.

3 Labor unions and others have long argued against the use of prison labor, insisting that it can cost workers on the outside their jobs. What do you think? Would your answer be different if you knew that a prison laborer could replace you or a friend? What would you say if prison officials paid inmates the prevailing wage? Do you think that would appease the unions' concerns? Can you think of any other ways to accommodate the unions' concerns? Prepare a one- to two-page paper that briefly addresses these questions.

4 In this chapter, we present a lot of information about prison security levels. In the previous chapter, you learned about jail security levels. In a one- to two-page paper, compare and contrast life in prisons and jails in terms of security levels. How are they similar? How do they differ? Where would you rather spend a year and why?

5 Apart from putting prison inmates on a desert island or a futuristic modular prison in space, what do you think the prison of the future should look like? What should be emphasized? Explain how you reached this conclusion.

KEY TERMS

administrative facilities
Administrative Maximum United States Penitentiary (ADMAX)
administrative segregation unit
Ashurst-Sumners Act
body cavity searches
campers
campus-design prison
classification officer
consensus-based classification systems
contract system
Correctional Classification Profile
courtyard-design prison

custody
Custody Determination Model
dehumanization
drug education
equity-based classification systems
Federal Correctional Complex (FCC)
Federal Correctional Institutions (FCIs)
Federal Detention Centers (FDCs)
Federal Medical Center (FMC)
Federal Prison Camps (FPCs)

Federal Prison Industries, Inc.
Federal Transfer Center (FTC)
Hawes-Cooper Act
inmate counts
joint-venture programs
lease system
linear design
maximum security
medium security
Metropolitan Correctional Centers/Metropolitan Detention Centers (MCCs/MDCs)
minimum security
modified linear design

nonresidential drug abuse
    treatment
podular design
prediction-based classification
    systems
Private Sector/Prison
    Industries Enhancement
    Certification (PS/PIEC)

radial-design prison
residential drug abuse
    treatment program
rites of passage
sally port
Satellite Prison Camps (SPCs)
Secure Female Facility (SFF)
shakedowns

state-use system
supermax prison
telephone-pole design prison
total institution
treatment
UNICOR
US Bureau of Prisons (BOP)
US Penitentiaries (USPs)

CRITICAL REVIEW QUESTIONS

1   When you were reading Goffman's contribu-
    tions to our understanding of total institutions,
    did you see any parallels between prisons and
    colleges or universities?

2   Briefly summarize the main conflicts between
    custody and treatment as institutional goals for
    prisons, paying close attention to the role of
    staff. In what other kinds of total institutions
    might attempts to attain these goals be less
    difficult?

3   Why is classification essential to the smooth
    functioning of prisons?

4   Describe prison growth throughout the twen-
    tieth and early twenty-first centuries. What do
    you make of the overall trends and the trends
    for female offenders? [*Note:* We return to this
    topic in Chapter 13.]

5   The federal prison system has grown tremen-
    dously since changes in sentencing laws in the
    1980s. What characteristic of federal prisons is
    most instructive about these changes?

6   What do you think of making prison inmates
    pay their own way by taking out a share of
    their wages to pay for room and board? Why
    are such programs useful? Why might they be
    counterproductive?

7   What do you think are the most impressive
    aspects of the federal prison system? How likely
    are these characteristics to find their way into
    state systems?

8   Which prison-based programs do you think
    hold the most promise for helping inmates turn
    around their lives? Which are a waste of time
    and money?

9   What are prisons not doing for (or to) inmates
    that they should consider? Be sure to provide
    your reasons for each answer.

10 Is it reasonable to ask what the prison of the
    future might look like? Explain your answer.

CASES CITED

Holt v. Sarver, 300 F.Supp. 825 (ED Ark. 1969). 309 F.
    Supp. 362 (E. Ark. 1970), aff'd. 442 F.2d F.2d 304
    (8th Cir. 1971)

Morris v. Travisono, 310 F.Supp. 857 (DRI 1970)
Pugh v. Locke, 406 F.Supp. 318 (MD Ala. 1976)

NOTES

1. Prisons have many names, including *penitentiaries* or *correctional facilities*; for the sake of convenience we generally use the term *prison* to refer to all state and federal correctional facilities, unless a special reason exists for using another name.

2. Correctional officers were once called prison guards. In some facilities they are still known by that name or are called corrections officers, prison officers, prison warders, or detention officers.

3. Although women inmates are classified no differently from men, and are likely to include low-, medium-, and high-risk individuals, policymakers seem to think that walled facilities are not appropriate for women. See Chapter 13 for more on our "genderized" correctional system.

4. The Office of Justice Programs (OJP), which administers the PS/PIEC program, reported 39 jurisdictions certified to operate private-sector prison industries; however, nine did not have active partnerships as of 2004 (Office of Justice Programs 2004).

5. The BOP operated USP-Alcatraz as a maximum security facility from 1933 to 1963.

6. The "High" designation is used solely to distinguish this prison from the BOP's super-max prison, USP-Florence-ADX, which is described later in this chapter.

7. USPs that are designated to hold medium-security inmates are also operated at this level.

8. The BOP operates its own airline, using aircraft seized under federal racketeering laws.

9. The US Census Bureau and, more recently, the Bureau of Justice Statistics have conducted the CSFCF every 5 or 6 years since 1971. The census includes all public and private correctional facilities operating in the United States. According to Stephan (2008, 1), whose report on the 2005 census is the most recent one available, the following types of facilities are specifically included: prisons and prison farms, prison hospitals, centers for medical treatment and psychiatric confinement; boot camps; centers for reception; diagnosis; classification; alcohol and drug treatment; community correctional facilities; facilities for parole violators and other persons returned to custody; institutions for youthful offenders; and institutions for geriatric inmates. Specifically excluded were city, county, and regional jails and private facilities that did not house primarily state or federal inmates, as well as facilities for the military, US Immigration and Customs Enforcement (see Chapter 8), US Marshals Service, and correctional hospital wards not operated by correctional authorities.

10. The 2005 CSFCF describes 17 maximum security penitentiaries; however, three more were subsequently brought online.

11. This material is also taken in part from Stephan (2008). However, the report does not separate confinement facilities, what we have chosen to call prisons, from community-corrections facilities. Unless specifically indicated, the state facilities profile information includes both kinds of facilities. This is not a problem for the previous discussion of BOP confinement facilities, as the federal government does not operate community-corrections facilities itself, but instead subcontracts these operations to the private sector.

REFERENCES

American Correctional Association (ACA). 1986. *A study of prison industry: History, components, and goals.* Washington, DC: US Government Printing Office.

Berk, Richard, Heather Ladd, Heidi Graziano, and Jong-Ho Baek. 2003. A randomized experiment testing inmate classification systems. *Criminology & Public Policy* 2: 215–42.

Bonta, J., and D. A. Andrews. 2007. *Risk-need-responsivity model for offender assessment and rehabilitation.* Ottawa, Ontario, Canada: Public Safety Canada.

Buchanan, R. A., and K. L. Whitlow. 1987. National evaluation of objective prison classification systems: The current state of the art. *Crime & Delinquency* 32: 272–90.

Bureau of Prisons. 2006. *Program statement: Inmate security designation and custody designation.* Washington, DC: US Department of Justice.

Carson, E. Ann, and William J. Sabol. 2012. *Prisoners in 2011.* Washington, DC: US Department of Justice.

Cohen, Andrew. 2012. An American gulag: Descending into madness at supermax. *The Atlantic.* Retrieved on July 11, 2013 from: **http://www.theatlantic.com/national/archive/2012/06/an-american-gulag-descending-into-madness-at-supermax/258323/**

Craddock, Amy. 1996. Classification systems. In *Encyclopedia of American prisons,* edited by Marilyn D. McShane and Frank P. Williams III. New York: Garland, 87–96.

Craig, Susan Clark. 2004. Rehabilitation versus control: An organizational theory of prison management. *Prison Journal* 84: 928–1149.

Cullen, Francis T., Faith E. Lutze, Bruce G. Link, and Nancy T. Wolfe. 1989. The correctional orientation of guards: Do officers support rehabilitation? *Federal Probation* 58: 33–42.

DiIulio, John J., Jr. 1987. *Governing prisons: A comparative study of correctional management.* New York: Free Press.

Dinitz, Simon. 1981. Are safe and humane prisons possible? *Australian and New Zealand Journal of Criminology* 14: 3–19.

Duffee, David E. 1989. *Corrections: Practice and policy.* New York: Random House.

Durham, Alexis M. 1989. Origins of interest in the privatization of punishment: The nineteenth and twentieth century American experience. *Criminology* 27: 107–39.

Farabee, David, Ryken Grattet, Richard McCleary, Steven Raphael, and Susan Turner. 2011. *Expert panel study of the inmate classification score system.* Sacramento, CA: State of California, Department of Corrections and Rehabilitation, Office of Research, Research and Evaluation Branch.

Farmer, Richard E. 1977. Cynicism: A factor in corrections work. *Journal of Criminal Justice* 5: 237–46.

Flanagan, Timothy J., and Kathleen Maguire. 1993. A full employment policy for prison in the United States: Some arguments, estimates, and implications. *Journal of Criminal Justice* 21: 117–30.

Goffman, Erving. 1961. *Asylums.* Garden City, NY: Anchor.

Government Accountability Office. 2012. *Bureau of prisons: Growing inmate crowding negatively affects inmates, staff, and infrastructure.* Washington, DC: Government Accountability Office.

Harlow, Caroline Wolf. 2003. *Education and correctional populations.* Washington, DC: US Department of Justice.

Harrison, Paige M., and Allen J. Beck. 2002. *Prisoners in 2001.* Washington, DC: US Department of Justice.

Harrison, Paige M., and Allen J. Beck. 2003. Prisoners in 2002. *Bureau of Justice Statistics Bulletin.* Washington, DC: US Department of Justice.

Harrison, Paige M., and Allen J. Beck. 2004. *Prisoners in 2003.* Washington, DC: US Department of Justice.

Harrison, Paige M., and Allen J. Beck. 2005. *Prisoners in 2004.* Washington, DC: US Department of Justice.

Harrison, Paige M., and Allen J. Beck. 2006. *Prisoners in 2005.* Washington, DC: US Department of Justice.

Hepburn, John, and Celeste Albonetti. 1981. Role conflict in correctional institutions: An empirical examination of the treatment-custody dilemma among correctional staff. *Criminology* 17: 445–60.

Inderbitzin, Michelle. 2007. A look from inside: Balancing custody and treatment in juvenile maximum-security facility. *International Journal of Offender Therapy and Comparative Criminology* 51: 348–62.

Kifer, Misty, Craig Hemmens, and Mary K. Stohr. 2003. The goals of corrections: Perspectives from the line. *Criminal Justice Review* 28: 47–69.

King, Sue. 2009–2010. Reconciling custodial and human service work: The complex role of the prison officer. *Current Issues in Criminal Justice* 21: 257–72.

Kirklin, Jackson Taylor. 2011. Title VII protections for inmates: A model approach for safeguarding civil rights in America's prisons. *Columbia Law Review* 111: 1048–89.

Langan, Patrick A., John V. Fundis, Lawrence A. Greenfield, and Victoria W. Schneider. 1988. *Historical statistics on prisoners in state and federal institutions, year end 1925–1986.* Washington, DC: US Department of Justice.

Lombardo, Lucien X. 1984. Group dynamics and the prison guard subculture: Is the subculture an impediment to helping inmates? *International Journal of Offender Therapy and Comparative Criminology* 29: 70–90.

Maguire, Kathleen, and Ann C. Pastore, eds. 2002. *Bureau of Justice Statistics Sourcebook of Criminal Justice Statistics 2001.* Washington, DC: US Department of Justice.

Martinson, Robert. 1974. What works? Questions and answers about prison reform. *Public Interest* 35: 22–54.

Mauer, Marc. 1985. *The lessons of Marion: The failure of a maximum security prison: A history and analysis, with voices of prisoners*. Philadelphia: American Friends Service Committee.

McKelvey, Blake. 1936. *American prisons: A study in American social history prior to 1915*. Chicago: University of Chicago Press.

Mears, Daniel. 2006. *Evaluating the effectiveness of supermax prisons*. Washington, DC: Urban Institute.

Mears, Daniel., and Cindy J. Smith. 2007. Factories behind fences: Do prison "real work" programs work? *NIJ Journal*. 257: 32–36.

Mumola, Christopher, and Jennifer C. Karberg. 2006. *Drug use and dependence, state and federal prisoners, 2004*. Washington, DC: US Department of Justice.

Nagel, William G. 1973. *The new red barn: A critical look at the modern American prison*. New York: Walker.

Office of Justice Programs. 2004. *Prison industry enhancement certification program*. Program brief. Washington, DC: US Department of Justice.

O'Keefe, Maureen L., Kelli J. Klebe, Alysha Stucker, Kristin Sturm, and William Leggett. 2010. *One year longitudinal study of the psychological effects of administrative segregation*. Colorado Springs, CO: Colorado Department of Corrections.

Paboojian, A., and R. H. C. Teske. 1997. Pre-service correctional officers: What do they think about treatment? *Journal of Criminal Justice* 25: 425–33.

Pizarro, Jenesia, and Vanja M. K. Stenius. 2004. Supermax prisons: Their rise, current practices and effect on inmates. *Prison Journal* 84: 248–64.

Pollock Joycelyn M., Nancy L. Hogan, Eric G. Lambert, Jeffrey Ian Ross, and Jody L. Sundt. 2012. A utopian prison: Contradiction in terms? *Journal of Contemporary Criminal Justice* 28: 60–76.

Reisig, M. D. 1998. Rates of disorder in higher-custody state prisons: A comparative analysis of managerial practices. *Crime & Delinquency* 44: 229–45.

Richmond, Frank C. 1935. Prison of the future-and a fifth suggestion. *Journal of Criminal Law and Criminology* 25: 733.

Riveland, Chase. 1999. *Supermax prisons: Overview and general considerations*. Washington, DC: US Department of Justice.

Schaller, Jack. 1982. Work and imprisonment: The overview of the changing role of prison labor in American prisons. *Prison Journal* 62: 3–11.

Sellin, Thorsten J. 1976. *Slavery and the penal system*. New York: Elsevier.

Sloan, Bob. n.d. The prison industries enhancement certification program: Why everyone should be concerned. *Prison Legal News*. Retrieved on July 11, 2013 from: http://www.prisonlegalnews.org/

displayArticle.aspx?articleid=22190&AspxAutoDetectCookieSupport=1

Smith, Cindy J., Jennifer Bechtel, Angie Patrick, Richard Smith, and Laura Wilson-Gentry. 2006. *Correctional industries preparing inmates for re-entry: Recidivism and Post-release employment*. Washington, DC: US Department of Justice.

Stephan, James J. 2008. *Census of state and federal correctional facilities, 2005*. Washington, DC: Bureau of Justice Statistics, US Department of Justice.

Street, David, R. D. Vinter, and Charles Perrow. 1966. *Organization for treatment*. New York: Free Press.

Sutter, John. 2012. CNN—Welcome to the world's nicest prison. Retrieved on July 11, 2013 from: http://www.cnn.com/2012/05/24/world/europe/norway-prison-bastoy-nicest/index.html

Sykes, Gresham M. 1958. *The society of captives: A study of a maximum security prison*. Princeton, NJ: Princeton University Press.

US Bureau of Prisons (BOP). 1994. *The state of the bureau: 1993*. Washington, DC: US Government Printing Office.

US Bureau of Prisons (BOP). 1997. *Quick facts*. Washington, DC: US Government Printing Office.

US Bureau of Prisons (BOP). 2003. *Federal Prison Industries (UNICOR): Annual report 2002*. Washington, DC: US Department of Justice.

US Bureau of Prisons (BOP). 2006a. *State of the Bureau 2005*. Washington, DC: US Department of Justice.

US Bureau of Prisons (BOP). 2006b. *About the Federal Bureau of Prisons*. Washington, DC: US Department of Justice.

US Bureau of Prisons (BOP). 2009. *Factories with fences: 75 years of changing lives*. Washington, DC: US UNICOR.

US Bureau of Prisons (BOP). 2011. *Fiscal year 2011 annual management report to the Congress of the United States*. Washington, DC: UNICOR.

West, Heather C., and William J. Sabol. 2008. *Prisoners in 2007*. Washington, DC: US Department of Justice.

West, Heather C., and William J. Sabol. 2010. *Prisoners in 2009*. Washington, DC: US Department of Justice.

Zald, M. N. 1968. The correctional institution for juvenile offenders: An analysis of organizational "character." In *Prison within society: A reader in penology*, edited by Lawrence Hazelrigg. New York: Doubleday-Anchor, 229–46.

Zupan, Linda L. 1991. *Jails: Reform and the new generation philosophy*. Cincinnati, OH: Anderson.

JAIL AND PRISON INMATES

7

ROBIN NIELSON/CORBIS

Outline

Objectives

- To give you a sense of who are the nation's jail and prison inmates

- To acquaint you with the culture and everyday life of those imprisoned by local, state, and federal authorities

- To give you a framework for understanding the violence found in many correctional institutions, from the exploitation of individual inmates to prison riots

- To provide you with a baseline understanding of the breadth and depth of issues confronting those who work on a daily basis with prison and jail inmates

Essentials of Corrections, Fifth Edition. G. Larry Mays and L. Thomas Winfree, Jr.
© 2014 John Wiley & Sons, Inc. Published 2014 by John Wiley & Sons, Inc.

INTRODUCTION

Who is serving time in the nation's jails and prisons? Does one racial or ethnic group dominate the "inmate class"? What do inmates do for sex? How dangerous is institutional life for inmates *and* staff? These questions are typical of what students ask when a corrections class turns to the subject of inmates. You may have other questions. In fact, we hope you do.

Twenty years ago, college students were unlikely to have much personal experience with either jails or prisons. Today, conditions are different. If you are female, you are more likely than your mother was to have such an experience. If you are Hispanic, your probability of incarceration has increased since your parents' day. If you are an African American male, one in four of your peers may end up in prison and even more are likely to see the inside of a jail.

Confused? Concerned? Enraged? Are you curious about what is going on in the nation's jails and prisons? That story begins with the characteristics of jail inmates.

CHARACTERISTICS OF JAIL INMATES

Jails incarcerate men and women, adults and juveniles. Law and custom dictate that we must segregate by sight and sound the men from women, and the adults from juveniles. In addition, most jails house many different types of inmates (see Chapter 5). Gaining an accurate and current picture of inmates in jails is a difficult task, because of their large number (more than 3,200) and fluid populations (more than 13 million inmates per year). Once every 5 years or so, the Bureau of Justice Statistics (BJS) conducts a census of jails, including public and private, state and federal facilities, with the most recent one in 2006 (Stephan and Walsh 2011). Periodically, the BJS also provides a profile of jail inmates based on surveys or sampling of jails. In addition, the federal Bureau of Prisons (BOP), through various sources, provides limited information about its "jail" inmates. We use all such sources in our look at local and federal jail inmates.

FIGURE 7.1 Conviction Status of Adult Jail Inmates, 2005. *Source:* Minton (2011, 8).

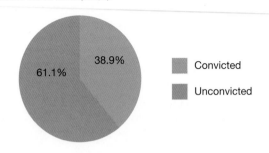

LOCAL JAIL INMATES

Just over 38 percent of all local jail inmates are unconvicted of any crime (Figure 7.1). Investigators interviewing witnesses to crimes or "persons of interest" may temporarily confine them in a jail or lockup. Moreover, jail authorities may also incarcerate mentally ill persons until social services can find a place for them. Jails serve as a place of confinement for people convicted of misdemeanors; jails also hold convicted felons while they await transfer to prison or while their cases are under review by a local court. This wide range of inmates—in combination with gender and age differences—means that jails are unique institutions in the nation's correctional system.

At midyear 2010, the nation's local jails held an estimated 748,728 inmates (Minton 2011). Another 60,632 individuals were under jail supervision but lived outside the facility, for example, participating in weekend-in-jail programs, electronic monitoring, home detention, day reporting, community service, treatment programs, and other types of out-of-jail supervision. This type of supervision has declined from the peak of 72,852 in 2008 and the number is lower than that reported over a decade earlier in 2000 (65,884).

The 2010 overall jail incarceration rate of 242 inmates for every 100,000 US residents was up from 2000 when it stood at 220, but it was down from 259 in 2007 (Minton 2011). Slightly more than 44 percent of jail inmates were non-Hispanic whites;

non-Hispanic blacks made up less than 40 percent of the adult jail population. The Hispanic proportion (about 15 percent) was nearly identical to this particular ethnic group's contribution to the national population. The percentage of white inmates increased from 41.9 percent in 2000 to 44.3 percent in 2010. For blacks in the same period the percentages decreased from 41.3 percent to 37.8 percent. For Hispanics and those of other races (or those who were reported as multi-racial) the percentage remained relatively unchanged.

FEDERAL JAIL INMATES

In 2006, the BOP operated 12 jails—metropolitan correctional centers, metropolitan detention centers, and federal detention centers—that held about 13,000, about three-fourths of them not convicted of any crime (Stephan and Walsh 2011, 3). As is the case in most jails, the vast majority were men. Nearly two-thirds of the inmates were white; just under a third were black. Asians, Pacific Islanders, American Indians, and Alaskan Natives accounted for a very small fraction of the inmate population. These detention facilities, like most BOP facilities, operated in excess of capacity. Local jails housed roughly 30,000 federal prisoners for such diverse agencies as the BOP, the Bureau of Immigrations and Customs Enforcement (ICE), the US Marshals Service, and the Bureau of Indian Affairs (Minton 2011).

CHARACTERISTICS OF PRISON INMATES

What do we know about the people populating the nation's prisons? Our answer to this question is constrained by the immense size of our prison systems and the cost of conducting regular surveys of each facility. As a result, as with jails, our information about prison inmates is sporadic and, in some cases, a bit out-of-date. Nonetheless, there are some bright spots. Annually, the BOP provides a statistical report summarizing its inmate population. At the state level, we must rely on more sporadic reporting. That is,

periodically, the BJS conducts a census of all prison facilities—the most recent in 2005 (Stephan 2008). However, the information in those reports typically is sparse. For some information, we must turn to other sources, among them a 1997 survey of prison inmates (Bureau of Justice Statistics 2000).

STATE PRISONERS

Given 50 different reporting systems and 1,826 public and private institutions for adult offenders, it is difficult to obtain a complete picture of the nation's nonfederal inmates. We do have some informative fragments, however. For example, looking at Figure 7.2, we see that in 2010, non-Hispanic blacks accounted for nearly 38 percent of all state prison inmates, whereas non-Hispanic whites made up just over 32 percent of the state prison population. Hispanics accounted for just over one in five state prisoners, a smaller percentage than for federal inmates. In addition, like federal inmates, state inmates were disproportionately male (over 93 percent) (see Figure 7.3)

FIGURE 7.2 **Race, Ethnicity, and Gender of State Prisoners, 2010.** *Source:* Guerino, Harrison, and Sabol (2011, 26).

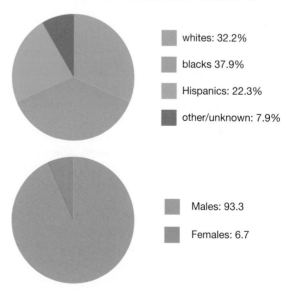

whites: 32.2%

blacks 37.9%

Hispanics: 22.3%

other/unknown: 7.9%

Males: 93.3

Females: 6.7

FIGURE 7.3 Race, Ethnicity, and Gender of Federal Prisoners, 2005. *Source:* US Bureau of Prisons (2010).

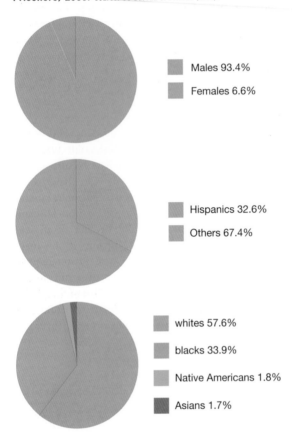

Males 93.4%

Females 6.6%

Hispanics 32.6%

Others 67.4%

whites 57.6%

blacks 33.9%

Native Americans 1.8%

Asians 1.7%

TABLE 7.1 State prisoners by most-serious offenses, 2008–2009.

	2008	2009
Crimes against persons	715,900	726,100
Murder	175,200	179,000
Manslaughter	16,500	16,900
Rape	67,500	67,800
Other sexual assault	98,300	99,600
Robbery	183,100	185,700
Assault	137,100	138,100
Other violent	38,400	39,000
Property crimes	263,400	261,900
Burglary	129,800	131,000
Larceny	21,300	49,900
Motor vehicle theft	50,400	19,800
Fraud	34,100	33,200
Other property	27,800	28,000
Drug	255,700	242,900
Public order	116,100	121,000
Other	14,300	13,900

SOURCE: GUERINO, HARRISON, AND SABOL (2011, 28).

Private-sector prisons—there were 415 of them in 2005—housed 128,195 inmates at the end of 2010. Here, too, the vast majority of inmates (94 percent) were men (Stephan 2008).

The average state prisoner is a 32-year-old black male (Bureau of Justice Statistics 2000). Among state prison inmates, 57 percent have never been married; another 26 percent are divorced, separated, or widowed. The rest say they are married. About 5 percent are citizens of another country, a rate far below that observed for federal inmates. Within this overwhelmingly male prison population, inmates have, on average, 12 years of schooling. Fewer than 15 percent of state prison inmates have more than a high school education, a rate about half that of

federal prisoners. Of the state inmates serving time in 1997, more than 56 percent report alcohol or drug use in the month before they committed their current offense, and nearly 33 percent were using drugs at the time of their arrest for the current offense (Maguire and Pastore 1999, 508).

Table 7.1 shows the number of state inmates serving time in 2008 and 2009 based on their most serious offense. In most categories there was an increase from 2008 to 2009. There were between two and three times as many inmates serving time for crimes against persons as there were serving time for property crimes. One interesting comparison involves property crimes and drug-related offenses. In both 2008 and 2009 there were nearly as many inmates serving time for drug offenses as there were for all property crimes combined. The nation's "war on drugs," waged since the 1980s, clearly has had an impact on state prison populations.

One factor that has driven prison populations in the past decade is the movement toward "truth-in-sentencing." Most states adopted truth-in-sentencing guidelines as the result of federal pressure. In 1994, Congress authorized incentive grants to states that conformed to the 85-percent standard. To qualify for these grants, states were required to ensure that persons convicted of certain violent crimes—for example, murder, rape, robbery, and aggravated assault—serve not less than 85 percent of their sentences. In exchange, the national government would provide the state with additional funds for new state jails and prisons. The National Institute of Justice reports that in 2005 41 states and the District of Columbia had passed some form of truth-in-sentencing legislation, and 28 states and the District of Columbia had met the legislative criteria for federal grant funding (Rosich and Kane 2012).

James Austin and John Irwin predict that the remaining states will not jump on the truth-in-sentencing bandwagon. Of 28 jurisdictions that had adopted sentencing standards by 1998, only six adopted the standards as a result of federal incentives. Austin and Irwin observed that because of increased incarceration levels, crowding, and new construction, a kind of **imprisonment binge** would continue into the foreseeable future.

> It now appears that the remaining states are less likely to adopt such draconian laws, as they recognize the substantial prison and operating costs associated with such sentencing policies. Nonetheless, the damage has been done. . . . The long-term consequences of longer prison terms coupled with higher parole violation rates will require further continuation of the imprisonment binge. (Austin and Irwin 2001, 241)

We return to this important topic in Chapter 15.

FEDERAL PRISONERS

Figure 7.3 shows the race and ethnicity, and gender of federal prisoners in 2009. Fewer than 40 percent of those prisoners were non-Hispanic blacks; about 57 percent were white, while slightly less than 2 percent were either Native American or Asian. In terms of ethnicity, about 32 percent were Hispanic. The vast majority—over 93 percent—of federal prisoners was male. The average federal prisoner was 37 years old. Nearly seven in ten federal prisoners were US citizens, 26.7 percent were noncitizens, and the remaining portion was of unknown status. A large contingent (17.8 percent) was citizens of Mexico. The federal prison population has grown dramatically in recent years. In 1980, the system held fewer than 20,000 inmates. By 2005, 166,173 people were being housed in federal prisons, and in 2010 there were 190,642 federal inmates. Table 7.2 shows the number of federal prisoners in 2000, 2009, and 2010 by the offenders' most serious crime. **Drug offenses** clearly played a primary role in the overall growth of the prison population during the period from 2000 to 2010. The absolute number of offenders in the other categories grew somewhat, but nowhere near the size of the drug-offender population. In 1980, there were about as many drug offenders as there were property offenders; by 2005, although the number of property offenders had about doubled, the number of drug offenders had increased more

TABLE 7.2 Federal prisoners by most-serious offenses, 2000, 2009, 2010.

	2000	2009	2010
Crimes against persons	13,740	15,010	14,830
Homicide	1,363	2,863	2,769
Robbery	9,712	8,389	8,242
Other violent	2,665	3,758	3,818
Property crimes	10,135	11,088	11,264
Burglary	462	425	392
Fraud	7,506	7,841	8,063
Other property	2,167	2,822	2,809
Drug offenses	74,276	96,735	97,472
Public order offenses	32,325	63,714	65,873
Immigration	13,676	21,739	21,377
Weapons	10,822	27,941	28,821
Other	7,827	14,035	15,675
Other	1,263	1,339	1,203

SOURCE: GUERINO, HARRISON, AND SABOL (2011, 30).

than 15 times, and between 2000 and 2010 the number of drug offenders increased again by nearly one-fourth. Stated another way, in 2010, over one-half of federal prisoners were drug offenders, another roughly 8 percent were personal offenders, 6 percent were property offenders, and about 34 percent were public-order offenders. Notice that the number of federal offenders convicted of violent crimes was relatively stable; but the proportion of offenders in this category, like that of property offenders, declined.

Three factors underlie these trends. First, in the 1970s, President Richard Nixon declared a War on Drugs, a war Ronald Reagan vowed to carry on when he became president in 1981. A crucial front in that war was the international drug trade, and both administrations targeted foreign nationals who were smuggling illegal drugs (see, for example, Currie 1993; Harlow 1994; Inciardi 1992; Pollock 2004; Walker 2006). The result was an exponential growth in the number of federal prisoners and, over time, a fundamental change in their nationality. In 1991, 18 percent of federal prisoners were not US citizens; by 2009, nearly 27 percent of federal prisoners were foreign nationals (Bureau of Justice Statistics 1994; US BOP 2009).

Second, the nation's courts began getting tough on drug offenders in the 1980s. Congress enacted the *Sentencing Reform Act of 1984*, the so-called truth-in-sentencing law, which mandated specific sentencing guidelines for federal judges (see Chapter 3). Under the act, which went into effect in late 1987, federal offenders must serve a minimum of 85 percent of their actual sentence (Sabol and McGready 1999). The law did not significantly increase the duration of sentences in the federal courts, but it did increase the average time served by 75 percent. In 1986, federal prisoners were serving, on average, 58 percent of maximum sentences; by 1997, they were serving 87 percent of those sentences, higher than the 85 percent standard. We can attribute approximately 65 percent of the dramatic increase in the federal prison population to the increase in time served. The Sentencing Reform Act has affected violent criminals and drug offenders in particular. Between 1986 and 1997, the average sentence for violent offenders increased from 65 months to 76 months; and the average sentence for drug offenders

increased from 30 months to 66 months. For their part, public-order offenders saw their average sentence increase from 9 months in 1986 to 31 months in 1997.

Finally, those who have violated the nation's immigration laws constitute a unique offender group, one typically buried within several offense categories (for example, they are present in both the drug laws and public order offense categories). In 2005, the federal government detained 19,572 people because of actions taken by the Bureau of Immigration and Customs Enforcement (ICE) (Harrison and Beck 2006). ICE detained almost 6,000 people in its own facilities or in facilities under exclusive contract to the bureau. BOP facilities and other federal correctional institutions held 900 of these detainees. Under intergovernmental agreements, a form of contract between two or more units of government, state prisons, local jails, and other nonfederal facilities held 12,500 ICE inmates. Interestingly, just under half had violated US immigration laws alone, meaning they were classified public-order offenders; the rest were being held pending trial on criminal charges or had been convicted on a criminal charge in addition to an alleged or proved immigration law violation. In nearly all cases, the federal government deports those offenders held on felony convictions who also violated immigration laws but only after they serve their sentence. Eventually, most people convicted only of immigration law violations also are deported.

JAIL AND PRISON CULTURE

In the 1940s, Donald Clemmer gave penologists a new way of thinking about prison inmates. Clemmer was once a correctional officer at Menard (Illinois) penitentiary. He used his experiences and other observations in his classic study, *The Prison Community*, first published in 1940. The community he describes is a powerful inmate subculture, complete with rules and regulations, values, and prejudices. **Prisonization**—the mechanism by which one becomes a member of that subculture—is the process through which prison inmates "take on in greater or less degree the folkways, mores, customs, and general culture of the penitentiary" (Clemmer 1940/1958, 299).

The prison community, Clemmer believed, is not a highly integrated body of men or women. Some prisoners are more deeply committed and involved than are others. According to Clemmer, prisonization is highest among inmates with the following seven characteristics (302):

- a long sentence;
- an unstable personality originating in pre-prison life;
- no positive relationships outside the prison walls;
- a readiness and capacity for integration into the inmate subculture;
- complete acceptance of an inmate code as a reflection of the inmate subculture's norms and values;
- living in the same cell or in close proximity with others of like persuasion; and
- participation in gambling and homosexual behavior.

Clemmer described a world unseen except by those who lived or worked in it. His work shaped prison studies for generations of penologists.

CHARACTERISTICS OF THE INMATE SUBCULTURE

A *subculture* is a social group that exhibits unique characteristics, including norms, rules, and regulations, that distinguish it from—and often place it in conflict with—the larger society. According to Clemmer, the **prison subculture** is negativistic, its animosity directed equally at the prison staff and at the free society. Whatever prison authorities or society values, the prison subculture devalues.

Inmates new to prison life are **fish**, a term that indicates their low and easily exploited status in the subculture. When they arrive, more experienced inmates may take them aside and explain the facts of prison life. If the fish are weak or fail to understand the code, other inmates will exploit them. If they are strong or learn to use the system to their own benefit, they may rise to positions of leadership in the subculture. Most inmates in the prison community simply try to stay out of trouble and just do their time.

THE INMATE CODE

The attitudinal and behavioral norms of prison subculture make up the **inmate code**. Lloyd Ohlin (1956: 28) explained the rules this way: "The code represents an organization of criminal values in clear-cut opposition to the values of conventional society, and to prison officials as that society's agents." Gresham Sykes and Sheldon Messinger (1960) identified the code's five basic tenets.

- *Never interfere with the interests of other inmates.* Above all else, this means do not betray another inmate, particularly to the authorities; however, it also means keeping out of other inmates' business and generally being loyal to your own class—the cons.
- *Don't lose your head.* In other words, play it cool and do not get involved in matters that have nothing to do with you.
- *Don't exploit other inmates.* Specifically, keep your word, pay your debts, and do not steal from other inmates. If this tenet does not ring true given the behavior of many inmates, see the fourth tenet.
- *Don't be weak.* If you whine, cop out, look for special privileges from guards or other authority figures, or are easily taken advantage of by others, then you deserve to be exploited or worse.
- *Punish violators quickly and severely.* Proof beyond a reasonable doubt is not necessary; suspicion can be enough to set the inmates' wheels of justice in motion.

The code has little variety in penalties. Most code violations result in corporal punishment or death. There is no appeals process. If an inmate believes that a violation of some provision of the inmate code has occurred, then that person is generally free to act as he or she sees fit. This normative expectation explains the significance most inmates attach to physical strength. Many prisoners form extensive alliances in the interest of self-preservation.

INMATE ROLES AND ADAPTIVE BEHAVIORS

What kind of student are you? How would your friends or your professors describe you? Do you have a life outside school? The answers to these questions help define who you are on and off campus. Similar questions about inmates define who they are in their unique social setting. Joseph Fishman (1934) provided an early glimpse into the life of prison inmates. In *Sex in Prison*, Fishman wove a rich tapestry of images about a system of social arrangements he called the *prison subculture*. In particular, he found the language of the inmates unique, and they used it to describe their relationships with one another, including, as we describe later, sexual ones.

Beginning in the 1940s and continuing for several decades, prison researchers explored the ways that inmates adapted to the prison code, especially through the mechanism of role types. For example, Clarence Schrag (1944) suggested that inmates play at least four different roles:

- **Right guys** are those rare inmates who follow all of the precepts of the code, are the most prisonized of all prison or jail residents. They tend to be antisocial, which only increases their status. Right guys are what inmates think of as model prisoners.

- **Con-politicians** are inmates with money and influence, the latter with both guards and other inmates. Moreover, through skill and manipulation, they can obtain virtually any good or service wanted by inmates with enough money to pay. These inmates are pseudo-social: they pretend to be prosocial while engaging in antisocial conduct.

- **Outlaws** are inmates who rely on force and physical violence to obtain what they want from other inmates. Given the exploitation found in jails and prisons, some inmates need outlaws for protection, but most inmates avoid them.

- **Square Johns** are inmates who follow the prison's official rules, take part in institutional programming, and generally ignore all but the snitching provision of the inmate code. Square Johns are low on the prison subculture hierarchy. Despite being convicts, these individuals are prosocial; they are the least prisonized of Schrag's role types.

In the 30 years following Schrag's definitions, other prison researchers described role-types similar to those observed by Schrag, although the specific names changed depending on the region of the country and the era in which the researcher studied the prison (Garabedian 1963; Leger 1978; Rabow and Elias 1969; Sykes and Messinger 1960; Thomas and Foster 1975; Zingraff 1975). Their common point was clear: inmate responses to imprisonment varied but generally tended to reflect an appreciation for the inmate code's values, in either its adoption or its rejection.

Irwin, an ex-convict and well-respected academician, provides some of the most profound insight into inmate adaptations to institutional life. According to Irwin (1970), in addition to the specific roles prisoners adopt, they also engage in one or more strategies or adaptive behaviors, to survive. The first is **doing time**, which means that the inmates view the prison experience as a "temporary break in their careers, one which they take in stride" (69). The goals are to keep busy, pass time, make life as easy as possible, and keep out of trouble. Professional criminals, including thieves and other property offenders, commonly "do time." A second strategy is **jailing**. Prisoners who are jailing do not think of the world outside as home. Many of them grew up as wards of the state in institutional settings, and jail or prison is where they feel most comfortable. These inmates look for positions of power and authority. The third strategy is **gleaning**, getting as much out of prison as possible (Irwin 1970, 76). Gleaning may start small, for example, an inmate learns to read. Knowledge becomes its own reward, and soon these inmates are branching out into vocational training, personal growth and enrichment, and advanced educational programs. Even taking part in physical activities like weightlifting and body shaping is a form of gleaning. The goal here is simply self-improvement (78).

As Irwin explained it, "Not all inmates can be classified neatly by these adaptive styles. Some vacillate from one to another, and others appear to be following two or three simultaneously" (1970, 68). At some time or another, however, nearly all inmates use one or more of these strategies.

SEX AND INSTITUTIONAL LIFE

The issue of homosexual inmates, ones who either were homosexual prior to incarceration or "came out" during their imprisonment, is addressed in the next chapter. At this point, we are more concerned with general sexual contacts in prisons and jails. For instance, in the 1930s, Fishman studied the role of sex in creating the prison subculture. Subsequent researchers have provided additional insights. Gender and race add important elements to our understanding of prison sex. Some prison-based studies have revealed that males were more likely to express homophobic attitudes, but blacks were more tolerant of homosexuals than were white inmates, a finding that reflects the greater tolerance of blacks in general toward homosexuality (Hensley 2000). Generally, **punks**, or the more passive participants, enjoy lower status in the prison than do **wolves**, the aggressors who rarely view themselves as homosexuals (Bowker 1981; Richmond 1978; also see Sykes and Messinger 1960).

Sex in men's jails and prisons can be a consensual act, an economic exchange identical to prostitution in the free world, or a forced act of violence between an aggressor and a victim, a form of rape. Daniel Lockwood (1980) observed that even consensual acts between male inmates could involve coercion if one inmate gives another three choices: "fight, flee, or fuck." Inmates tend to see forcing sex on others as a show of strength and masculinity. Some inmates turn tricks for survival; that is, they exchange sex for protection. Inmates can also achieve status from their work as male prostitutes. A new prostitute at a southeastern boys' training school observed the following to one of this text's authors: "Now the other guys pay attention to me. I've got all the smokes and lighters I want." (Cigarettes and lighters are usually important parts of the inmate economy.)

In contrast, Rose Giallambardo (1966), Esther Heffernan (1972), and Alice Propper (1981) independently reported that for the most part, homosexual activities among women inmates are voluntary. In those liaisons, *studs*, *butches*, or *pimps* take the masculine role, and *femmes*, *broads*, or *foxes* take the feminine roles. Prostitution also occurs in women's prisons, with *chippies* or *tricks* selling themselves to studs. Giallambardo observed that switching roles—that is, changing from a stud to a femme—is common. Propper noted that these liaisons and extended families give female inmates "security, companionship, affection, attention, status, prestige, and acceptance" (155).

How do staff members feel about prison homosexuality? The answers to this question are fragmentary, but instructive, and may depend on one's role in the prison hierarchy. Few studies look at upper-level managers (Hensley and Tewksbury 2005). An exception to this generalization, a study of 226 wardens throughout the nation, revealed that, irrespective of the type of institution in which they serve, wardens believed that inmate sexual activities, consensual and coercive, were rare. Interestingly, female and nonwhite wardens reported that a higher percentage of inmates had consensual sex than did their male and white counterparts (Hensley and Tewksbury). Nonetheless, most of this study's wardens believed that significant numbers of their inmates were sexually inactive, a conclusion that is at odds with inmate-based studies.

Part of the problem may lie in the social and physical distance between the wardens and their inmates, although official and even unofficial reports of inmate-on-inmate sexual assaults—let alone inmate assaults on staff—eventually reach the warden's desk. The fact that all forms of prison sex are rule-breaking behavior in almost every US prison suggests that administrators may know that it is happening but choose not to acknowledge it, a dangerous response given the threats posed by infectious diseases and violent victimizations (Hensley and Tewksbury 2005; Lockwood 1980; Sylvester, Reed, and Nelson 1977).

Correctional line-staff provide additional insights. Their attitudes toward homosexuality, like those of the public, vary greatly. There seems to be a contradiction between what officers say and do about inmates' sexual habits, in that most indicate they would or should report prison sexual misconduct, but few actually do report it (compare Eigenberg 1994, 2000; Lockwood 1980; Wooden and Parker 1982). Unlike prison administrators who appear to underestimate prison inmates' sexual activity, officers may overestimate it, including the incidence of rape, especially when compared with the inmate self-reports (Nacci and Kane 1983).

Perhaps correctional officers—the prison and jail beat cops—simply chose not to "see" rapes and other sexual assaults for a number of reasons (Eigenberg 2000). Estimates by COs may actually be based on what they have heard from their coworkers and even inmates, rather than what was actually observed, hence the over-estimates. The COs, then, may hear about the same rapes several times from different sources. Beyond indifference to the fate of inmates or being coerced to look the other way, both of which could get them in trouble if the results are serious injury or death, correctional officers may view such acts as consensual, may be too embarrassed to confront the inmates about it, or may have difficulty determining the consensual nature of the act. Moreover, some officers view aggressors as true homosexuals and those in passive roles as unwilling victims (Eigenberg 2000). They also support the inmate-endorsed idea that homosexuality is a functional and situational alternative to other sexual outlets. Finally, some officers view the inmate-victims of forced sexual encounters as getting what they deserve (Eigenberg 1989, 1994). Thus, the range of perspectives toward prison homosexual contacts represented by prison line-staff is considerable (Eigenberg 2000).

What is the real picture of sexual violence among inmates? We answer this question later in this chapter, when we return to the issue of institutional violence. We turn next to a related question: What is the origin of the prison culture?

THE ORIGINS OF INMATES' SOCIAL ORGANIZATION

Clemmer believed that prison subculture reflects inmate reactions to incarceration. Nevertheless, as he acknowledged, "Men who come to prison are not greatly different from those already there . . . Most persons admitted to prison already possess 'criminality' in various degrees" (1951, 313, 319). Lloyd McCorkle and Richard Korn (1954) also concluded that the deprivations of prison life shape the inmate subculture. Prisoners are isolated from most beneficial social contact with the outside world; they can rarely form relationships with people who are not criminals. According to the **deprivation hypothesis**, a major function of the inmate subculture's normative system is to prevent the internalization of social rejection and its conversion into self-rejection. An inmate subculture "permits the inmate to reject his rejecter rather than himself" (18).

Sykes (1958, 65–78) coined the term **pains of imprisonment** to describe the inmate's emotional reaction to the loss of liberty, goods and services, heterosexual relationships, autonomy, freedom of movement, and security. The inmates' collective response to these pains took on the characterization of **solidary opposition**. Sykes and Messinger (1960) proposed that inmates attempt to neutralize imprisonment's emotional consequences by forming their own community. As the inmates move in "the direction of solidarity, as demanded by the inmate code, the pains of imprisonment become less severe" (11).

Clemmer's observation that inmates enter prison with values and experiences left the door open for a competing perspective, the **cultural importation hypothesis**. Irwin and Donald Cressey (1962) contended that the inmate culture has beliefs, attitudes, and lifestyles with obvious parallels in the outside world, particularly the world of the inner cities, where crime is commonplace. Research on the prison community generally supports the idea that prisoners bring the inmate code and subculture with them. For example, Charles Wellford (1967) suggested that the deprivation hypothesis overlooks the obvious relationship between inmates' preprison activities and their commitment to the inmate code. He insisted that preprison involvement in the "criminalistic subculture" is the key to understanding prisonization (203).

Is the negativism of the prison community a response to the rigors of prison life? Alternatively, does it derive from city streets? Charles Thomas (1970) believes that prisonization is a function of both sets of experiences. The deprivation hypothesis does not adequately explain all of the elements of the inmate subculture. Consider the prison economy, which depends for its existence on barter and smuggling, practices that reflect extra-institutional values and experience. In addition, the cultural importation hypothesis neglects other aspects of the subculture—for example, homosexual activity as a replacement for heterosexual contact (also see Hensley 2000). According to Thomas, a comprehensive model must include not only deprivation and importation factors, but also factors such as the frequency and quality of inmates' contacts with people and groups outside the prison. Also important is the extent to which self-perceived stigmatization negatively affects inmates' life after release. As Thomas argues, a comprehensive model must incorporate the degree to which prison interrupts extra-prison support networks—such as nurturing relationships with friends and family in the outside world. The inclusive model describes a social environment in which imported aspects of prisonization interact with imprisonment pains. This model also encompasses "a broader variety of influences that provide a more sophisticated understanding of why a particular type of subcultural system emerges within so many prisons and why inmates vary in their degree of integration into that system" (Thomas and Petersen 1977, 55; also see Wooldredge 2003). The utility of the concept of prisonization is not limited to prisons in the United States, as Box 7.1 makes clear.

PRISON CULTURE IN THE TWENTY-FIRST CENTURY

Much of the groundbreaking research on the inmate subculture dates back to the 1940s and 1950s. Does an inmate code operate in contemporary prisons? Is there a solidary inmate social system today? Prison communities today appear organized by the principles of a negativistic code similar to that described by Clemmer, Sykes, and others. Whether that code supports solidary opposition is a separate question (Bottoms 1999; Irwin and Austin 1993; Irwin, Schiraldi, and Ziedenberg 1999; R. C. McCorkle, Meithe, and Drass 1995).

More than 30 years ago, Irwin (1980) suggested that the inmate subculture's hallmark unity has fragmented into competing groups based largely on race and ethnicity. His work confirmed Leo Carroll's (1974) findings about race relations in a Rhode Island maximum-security prison. Carroll observed that even after the racial integration of prisons in the years following World War II, inmates separated themselves by race in their living arrangements, in the prison theater, and even in the gym (160, 162,169). James Jacobs (1977) also described how African American street gangs gained a foothold and expanded their power base in Stateville (Illinois) Penitentiary, and eventually took over the prison community. Although white and Hispanic gangs extended their reach into Stateville, their numbers were smaller, and they had far less influence than the black gangs did. In prisons across the nation, loyalty to the "inmate class" became loyalty to one's race, ethnic group, clique, or gang. As Irwin and Austin note, "Prison populations have become much more racially heterogeneous and divided, and the old prison leaders have lost control over other prisoners" (Irwin and Austin 1993, 74).

Joycelyn Pollock (2004) uses three sets of forces to summarize the nature of prison life:

- The black market, where anything from drugs to sex can be purchased or bartered.
- Racial tension, which accounts for much prison violence and often is associated with prison gangs that have ties to similar groups outside the prison.
- Prison violence, committed by both inmates and staff.

Pollock observes that for many—if not most—inmates, the goal is just to survive:

For some [prison] is home for decades. Whereas many "rip and roar" and engage heavily in the inmate subculture, others try to find some semblance of safety by choosing job assignments that take them away from the mainstream and avoid the mess hall and yard and any other place where they may get in trouble . . . They, in effect, [have] created a world within a world, moving

Prisonization has proved to be one of the most enduring and flexible concepts in corrections. This characterization includes cross-cultural studies of the phenomenon. The inmate social system, the inmate code, and inmate slang have proved to be useful in prison studies in Scandinavia, Korea, Scotland, Mexico, Israel, New Zealand, Germany, England, and Spain. The research shows that the more rigid the prison structure, the stronger the inmates' social system, and the less conventional their attitudes. Almost without exception, prisonization is associated with antisocial behavior and strong resistance to authority.

True comparative studies of prisonization's effects, however, are rare. Forty years ago, Hugh Cline, in a study of prisonization in 15 different Scandinavian prisons, was unable to find support for the deprivation hypothesis. Instead, he found a positive relationship between inmates' criminal experience and the antisocial climate of the prison subculture. Over 30 years ago, Ronald Akers and his associates surveyed prison inmates in the United States, Mexico, England, Germany, and Spain. Despite low prisonization in Mexico, the authors concluded, "A recognizable nonconformist inmate culture is found everywhere" (547). Winfree and his colleagues surveyed medium-security inmates in two prisons, one in New Mexico, and another in New Zealand during the mid-1990s. Prisonization levels in both facilities were similar, and so were the levels of respect accorded to different offender types by inmates in both prisons. For example, the lowest-ranked offenders in both prisons were child molesters, and among the highest ranked were burglars who specialized in commercial establishments (ranked first in New Zealand and third in New Mexico). Inmates around the world may not think the same on all issues, but on some, there appears to be considerable agreement.

SOURCES: AKERS, HAYNER AND GRUNNINGER (1977); WINFREE, NEWBOLD, AND TUBB (2002).

through the chaotic and trouble-plagued social world of the prison, but not a part of it. (116)

The inmate code may be alive and well, but the object of inmate loyalty has changed. Inmate relationships have become far less predictable. Right guys and older, more experienced inmates no longer play a major role in settling inmate disputes. One consequence of these shifting loyalties is an increase in prison violence.

VIOLENCE IN CORRECTIONAL INSTITUTIONS

Prison-based violence represents one of the greatest pressures against effective prison management,

threatening both inmates and staff (Cullen, Latessa, Burton, and Lombardo 1993; Griffin and Hepburn 2006; Wolff et al. 2007). Violence in the nation's correctional institutions takes many forms. Inmate-initiated victimizations and prison riots are of particular interest to prisoners, staff, and the public.

INMATE VIOLENCE

When you crowd hundreds of thousands of people, half of whom have already demonstrated their willingness to resort to violence and many of the rest with antisocial tendencies, into small and inhospitable spaces, you should not be surprised when they engage in violent behavior directed toward each other, their keepers, and the physical plant itself. Three primary types of inmate-initiated violence are of particular interest: physical violence, psychological victimization, and economic exploitation.

PHYSICAL VIOLENCE In 2008 the Bureau of Justice Statistics (BJS) reported that local jails experienced 960 deaths and in 2009 the number was 948 (Noonan and Carson 2011). Jailhouse suicide, a topic we treat in depth later in this chapter, was the leading cause of jail deaths (29 percent) between 2000 and 2009. Heart disease accounted for another 22 percent of the jail inmate deaths during this period. Intoxication deaths added slightly more than 7 percent, and no other specified cause was responsible for more than 5 percent of the deaths during this time period. The number of murders in jails is small (about 23 in 2009); injuries from fights or assaults are more common. For example, in 1996, the last year for which such data are available, one in seven male inmates and one in ten female inmates reported being involved in a fight since entering jail (Harlow 1998). Fights were even more numerous among inmates younger than 25: an estimated one in five reported being in a fight or being punched. Yet, half of inmates believed jail was as safe or safer than the city streets.

A clearer picture of inmate sexual violence is starting to emerge. In 2003, George Bush signed into law the Prison Rape Elimination Act (PL 108–79), mandating that the BJS develop a new national data collection system on the incidence and prevalence of sexual violence in correctional facilities (Beck and Harrison 2006).

In 2005, local jails reported 1,700 allegations of sexual violence, of which investigations substantiated 336. The rate of allegations per 1,000 inmates was less than two per 1,000 jail inmates. The rate of substantiated sexual assaults per 1,000 jail inmates in 2004 was 0.45. Victims or another inmate reported three-fourths of the cases in which an investigation later substantiated the charges; staff reported less than 30 percent.

Jail inmates also assault staff. A partial picture of this conduct emerged in the 1999 BJS census of jails (Stephan 2001), where nearly 9,300 inmate assaults on staff occurred in local jails. This translated to a rate of 18 per 1,000 inmates. Four staff members died as a result of the assault.

Prisons present an even bleaker picture of deaths and assaults. In 2009, the nation's private, state, and federal prisons reported 3,408 inmate deaths (Noonan and Carson 2011). Most prison deaths—more than 88 percent—resulted from illnesses, including cancer (911 deaths), heart disease (870), liver disease, 258), AIDS-related (94), and other illnesses (881). Only 55 inmates—again fewer than 2 percent—died of injuries caused by another inmate. This figure represents a significant change from 25 years ago. In 1980, the prison homicide rate was 54 per 100,000 inmates. By 1990, the per capita rate (per 100,000) had dropped to eight, declining by a further 50 percent to four per capita in 2009.

Although prisons are less lethal places than in the past, prisoners and staff remain at risk. State and federal prison authorities reported more than 34,000 assaults on inmates in 2000 (Stephan and Karberg 2003, 10). Based on the average daily population of the reporting facilities, this works out to a victimization rate of 28 violations per 1,000 inmates. However, other inmates are not the only objects of physical violence in prison: inmates also assault correctional officers and other staff. In 2000, prison authorities reported nearly 18,000 incidents involving inmates and staff, resulting in a rate of 15 staff assaulted for every 1,000 inmates.

The Prison Rape Elimination Act of 2003 also mandated that BJS provide insights into sexual violence in prisons (Beck 2012). As a result of this mandate, BJS sponsored a second national survey of 167 state and federal prisons, 286 local jails, and ten "special confinement facilities" to assess the ongoing issue of sexual violence in confinement. The survey of 76,459 inmates found that 2,861 reported experiencing sexual victimization within the previous 12 months. This resulted in an estimated number of 88,500 sexual victimizations nationwide (or about 4.4 percent of prison inmates and 3.1 percent of jail inmates). Among the prison inmates, 2.1 percent reported being victimized by another inmate, 2.8 percent reported being victimized by a staff member, and 0.5 percent said they had been victimized by both. For jail inmates, 1.5 percent said they had been victimized by another inmate, 2 percent said their victimizer was a staff member, and 0.4 percent reported being victimized by both groups (Beck 2012; Beck et al. 2010).

Such reports, based on official institutional records and survey responses, may be the tip of the iceberg. A survey of inmates serving time in 14 prisons in a mid-Atlantic state found far higher prevalence rate estimates, ranging from 129 to 346 for inmate-on-inmate assaults and 83 to 321 for staff-on-inmate assaults (Wolff et al. 2007). Another study of prison inmates in seven midwestern prisons revealed that 16 percent had been pressured to participate in sexual contact and 7 percent of the inmates had been raped in their current facility (Struckman-Johnson and Struckman-Johnson 2000). National estimates suggest that as much as 20 percent of the inmate population of any prison is victimized by both property and personal crime, a victimization rate that is higher than that reported by the public (Wooldredge 1998, 2003). In particular, the victimizations suffered by older inmates, which in prison means inmates 50 and older, may be even higher. John Kerbs and Jennifer M. Jolley (2007), who interviewed 65 elderly inmates, concluded that such inmates "appear to represent attractive targets because of their age-related declines in health and because of their diminished social status amid younger predators who act on and exploit ageist attitudes, beliefs, and behavior that ultimately deprive elders of their safety and security" (212).

In 1990, there were 10,731 assaults on staff in prisons, a rate of 17.1 per 1,000 inmates (Stephan and Karberg 2003). By 1995, the number of assaults had increased to 14,165, but increases in the prison population lowered the rate to 14.8 per 1,000 inmates. By 2000, the number of assaults on staff in both state and federal facilities grew to 17,952, but again the rate per 1,000 inmates fell, to 14.6. The risk of staff assault is not the same at all facilities: maximum-security facilities reported 24.5 assaults per 1,000 inmates; minimum-security prisons, only 4.9 assaults per 1,000 inmates. In 2000, five prison employees died because of their injuries, down from 14 in 1995. The number of major prison disturbances—those involving five or more inmates—increased from 317 in 1995 to 806 in 2000.

PSYCHOLOGICAL VICTIMIZATION Psychological victimization is the threat of physical harm. Hans Toch (1976) noted that the prison's climate of violence

has no equivalent elsewhere. According to Toch, "Inmates are terrorized by other inmates, and spend years in fear of harm. Some inmates request segregation, others lock themselves in, and some are hermits by choice" (47–48). Some prison researchers suggest that crowding may be one cause of psychological victimization. We know that laboratory rats confined in a crowded cage will turn on one another and eat their way to a more manageable number. People are not rats, and crowding alone probably does not induce victimization (Gaes and McGuire 1985). Still, Toch insists that the ability of individual inmates to cope with prison or jail is "challenged by every consequence of crowding" (1976, 56).

Beyond the separation of victim and victimizer, there are few effective fixes for this form of violence. Moreover, there are no effective preventive measures either. Once inmates learn about winning through intimidation, preventing the victimization of a given inmate is very difficult.

ECONOMIC EXPLOITATION Economic exploitation is another form of violence against inmates by inmates. Most jails and prisons support two inmate economies. The facility's store, commissary, or canteen is the center of the **legitimate inmate economy**. Inmates have cash deposited in their accounts by friends or relatives or earn credits through their labor. Normally, the legitimate economy is credit-based: inmates without credit at the canteen cannot make any purchases, even of soap, towels, toothpaste, or other basic hygiene essentials. A few corrections systems allow inmates to carry small amounts of cash for purchases at the canteen (Santos 1996).

The second economy is the **sub rosa inmate economy**, an underground marketplace that exists outside the legitimate inmate economy. The volume of goods and services that flows through a large prison's *sub rosa* economy in a given year may reach millions of dollars. The *sub rosa* economy consists of two parts (Lankenau 2001). The first is a gray market, where inmates exchange or barter scarce items for illegal or quasi-illegal commodities, like drugs, sex, or the payment of illegal gambling debts. The second element is a black market, where the items themselves are illegal and considered contraband. As one might expect, the value of items on the black market

EGMONT STRIGL/IMAGE BROKER/ALAMY IMAGES

tends to be higher, reflecting the associated risks and rarity of the items (Lankenau).

There is interplay between the legitimate and *sub rosa* economies. A pack of cigarettes may cost, for the sake of argument, $1.50 for an inmate with money in his or her canteen account. That same pack of cigarettes can cost several times its retail value when purchased from an inmate merchant. Of course, the canteen probably does not extend credit, whereas the inmate merchant might—at a high interest rate. Hence, many inmates owe a considerable amount of money to their not-so-friendly inmate merchant, money that is payable on demand in cash, equivalent merchandise, or in services defined by the inmate holding the debt. As Box 7.2 suggests, prison authorities sometimes inadvertently manipulate the legitimate economy, placing pressures on both the gray and black market.

Many administrators view the *sub rosa* economy as unavoidable. The drugs and other contraband it controls reduce the tensions and frustrations associated with institutional life (Kalinich 1996; Pollock 2004). Imagine the public-relations nightmare if the corrections administration went into the business of providing what is now considered contraband.

The underground inmate economy is complex. It provides goods and services that are in great demand, but almost all of them illegal. Like any high-volume illegal business, it generates large amounts of cash, in itself an incentive for theft, robbery, extortion, and blackmail. Now consider the goods sold through the *sub rosa* economy. Inmates pay high prices for those goods, which is a form of victimization. The theft of that illegal object or substance is also a risk in a prison environment. Such victims have no recourse. How can they complain about another inmate's stealing something that they should not have had in the first place? Crime-involved victims are not unique to prison or jail settings, as even in the free society drug dealers have drugs, guns and cash stolen from

THE CHANGING VALUE OF TOBACCO IN THE CORRECTIONAL ECONOMY   BOX 7.2

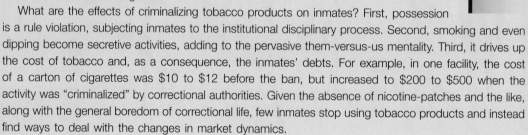

Attempts to control tobacco in correctional settings earnestly began in the 1980s. More recently, prisons have become smoke-free, reflecting changing values and public concerns. Related to these trends in health policies and practices, efforts at controlling tobacco in prisons and jails have taken several forms: (1) outright bans on any form of tobacco anywhere at the facility and (2) restrictions on where inmates can use it. The net effect is to drive this commodity from both the legitimate prison economy and the gray *sub rosa* economy into the black market, where it coexists with cell phones, moonshine, and illicit drugs.

What are the effects of criminalizing tobacco products on inmates? First, possession is a rule violation, subjecting inmates to the institutional disciplinary process. Second, smoking and even dipping become secretive activities, adding to the pervasive them-versus-us mentality. Third, it drives up the cost of tobacco and, as a consequence, the inmates' debts. For example, in one facility, the cost of a carton of cigarettes was $10 to $12 before the ban, but increased to $200 to $500 when the activity was "criminalized" by correctional authorities. Given the absence of nicotine-patches and the like, along with the general boredom of correctional life, few inmates stop using tobacco products and instead find ways to deal with the changes in market dynamics.

SOURCE: LANKENAU (2001).

them or thieves have their ill-gotten gain taken from them, by stealth and force. Such victims, wherever they reside, get little sympathy from the criminal justice system, and indeed could find themselves charged with a crime at worst or rule violation at best, should they be so foolish as to report the offense.

RIOTS AND OTHER DISTURBANCES

A **prison riot** is "a collective attempt by inmates to take over part or all of the prison. Riots may be expressive (usually spontaneous) or instrumental (planned with some goal in mind)" (Hawkins and Alpert 1989, 254). In 1993, a total of 21 corrections systems reported 186 incidents; however, only seven were designated a riot (Lillis 1994).

A HISTORY OF CONTEMPORARY PRISON RIOTS Historically, prison riots were common, as you learned in Chapter 2. In early American prisons, inmates sometimes rioted within months of the facility opening. Several more recent prison disturbances have become part of modern prison lore. One was the 1946

takeover of Alcatraz, labeled the *Battle of Alcatraz* by the warden at the time. Alcatraz—called "The Rock" by inmates and guards alike—was a federal penitentiary on an island in San Francisco Bay. It was home to the nation's most dangerous prisoners. The takeover was actually a failed escape attempt. Authorities responded with the combined firepower of federal prison guards, Marines, and Army soldiers, and the Coast Guard and harbor police patrolled the waters around The Rock throughout the three-day uprising (Johnston 1949). Residents of San Francisco watched as antitank rockets, aided by small arms and machine gun fire, blasted away at inmates trapped in a single cellblock, along with their guard hostages. The prison's construction was largely responsible for the fact that only three inmates and two guards died, and that just one inmate and 14 officers were injured. After the riot, Alcatraz remained open another 17 years; in 1963, the remaining prisoners were transferred to US Penitentiary (USP)—Atlanta.

The assault that ended the 1971 Attica Prison uprising was the bloodiest encounter between two groups of Americans in the twentieth century (New York Special Commission on Attica 1972). Attica Prison is in the farming community of Attica, 30 miles east of Buffalo. Guard retaliation against two inmates precipitated the riot. It ended after four days with a police firestorm that left ten hostages and 29 inmates dead, and another three hostages, 85 inmates, and one state police trooper wounded. The rioting inmates had killed one guard and three inmates. The investigations of the riot reached the same conclusion: the inmates failed to realize that to those in charge, the lives of the inmates' hostages were only slightly more important than were the lives of the inmates themselves (Badillo and Haynes 1972; Oswald 1972; Wicker 1975).

Another deadly riot occurred in 1980 at the Penitentiary of New Mexico. In 36 hours, the prison became a killing ground, as convicts rampaged through the facility. Most of the 33 dead in the Santa Fe prison riot were snitches or inmates against whom other prisoners had grudges (Bingaman 1980; Colvin 1982; Mahan 1982). Inmates assaulted and sodomized 11 guards. An army of prison guards, state police officers, and National Guardsmen restored order in the facility. The irony of the Santa Fe riot was that several dead snitches had warned officials about the inmates' frustration with crowded conditions: the facility was at 150 percent of its rated capacity. Before the riot, a group of inmates initiated a suit against New Mexico, citing administrative incompetence, corruption, and nepotism. After the riot, and the failure of officials to act, New Mexico entered into a 20-year-long consent decree empowering the federal district court to oversee the operation of all of the state's medium- and maximum-security prisons.

EXPLAINING PRISON RIOTS What triggers a prison riot? Social scientists have identified four types of riots, each triggered by a different set of circumstances. For example, during the 1940s and 1950s, dozens of prisons in the nation were the scene of **frustration riots** between a unified inmate subculture and prison authorities. As Irwin observed about this period in penal history: "After prisoners were convinced that treatment programs did not work (by the appearance of persons who had participated fully in those treatment programs streaming back into prison for new crimes or violation of parole), hope shaded to cynicism and turned to bitterness" (1980, 63). Inmates were also responding collectively to prisons' brutal and crowded living conditions in the decade after World War II. Between 1950 and 1953, the nation experienced more than 50 prison riots (McCleery 1968, 130).

With the integration of US prisons in the 1960s, race joined frustration as a cause of prison riots, but the prison community had changed. Rising black consciousness outside the prison took on radical dimensions inside as well. The Nation of Islam (the Black Muslims), a major separatist organization, confronted prison officials with demands based on religious freedom. The traditional inmate social system broke down, and the pace of prison riots increased. In 1969 and 1970, 98 riots took place (Reid 1981, 204). A political racial conflict was a crucial factor in many if not most of what were essentially prison-based **race riots** (Garson 1972; Jacobs 1979).

The social forces of the late 1960s and early 1970s increasingly politicized prison inmates. The inmates' manifesto—the demands they submitted to prison officials during the 1970 strike at Folsom (California) Prison—combined both their racial and their political concerns. The **political riot** came of age at Attica in 1971. Richard Hawkins and Geoffrey Alpert (1989) made the following observations about the Attica riot:

> The existence of a political ideology and stable inmate factions such as the Black Muslims created a united front among inmates. Inmates, organizing after the riot started, defined the uprising as a political act, which bridged diverse inmate interests. The prisoners at Attica used the Folsom manifesto as their model for structuring demands. (257)

Politicizing the prison social system did not survive long in the turbulent 1970s with the emergent fragmentation of the inmate subculture. Not surprisingly, the object of violence was less the institution or officials than it was fellow inmates (Colvin 1982). The emergent **rage riots** were often spontaneous, an expression of real or perceived inmate frustration with mistreatment. Inmate conflicts or the authorities' efforts to break up inmate conflicts sometimes triggered the riots. Other rage riots were instrumental in nature—to destroy parts of the facility or to get even with certain inmates or groups of inmates. The archetype of the instrumental rage riot occurred at the Santa Fe penitentiary in 1980.

Future prison riots may involve complex motivations. Some may be over living conditions, as the Attica riot was. Others may involve inmate frustrations, fears, or rage, as the Santa Fe and earlier riots did. Still others may involve multiple sets of factors, as did the uprising at Folsom. Many prisons are very heterogeneous; the solidary inmate subculture is largely passé. In those facilities, small groups of inmates may riot for very special and personal reasons (Hawkins and Alpert 1989, 262–65). For example, two riots occurred in 1989 among federal prison inmates at FDC–Oakdale (Louisiana) and USP–Atlanta. The rioters were Cubans facing deportation to their homeland. They rioted over their legal status. Both of these riots ended in negotiated settlements; a similar one involving Cuban detainees 4 years later at Federal Correctional Institution (FCI) –Talladega (Alabama) required an assault by federal authorities. The retaking of FCI–Talladega occurred without serious injuries to either hostages or detainees (Useem et al. 1995).

INMATE ISSUES

We conclude our examination of jail and prison inmates with a brief look at two issues: prison gangs and jailhouse suicide. We make no claim that these are the only inmate issues; nothing could be further from the truth. However, these concerns have plagued jails and prisons almost since their inception. Moreover, they show no sign of disappearing. These issues, and the racial problems we described earlier, threaten the fragile status quo of US correctional facilities.

PRISON GANGS

Prison gangs are not part of the traditional inmate subculture. They are cliques and informal groups

BOB SCHULTZ/AP/PRESS ASSOCIATION IMAGES

organized principally or even exclusively on racial or ethnic lines. The major gangs in US prisons today include the "Mexican Mafia," "La Nuestra Familia," the "Aryan Brotherhood," the "Black Guerrilla Family," and the "Texas Syndicate" (see Box 7.3). As a rule, prison gangs require either murder or blood-drawing initiations. All have ties, however tenuous, to gangs outside prison, so inmates have a supportive social system in and out of the correctional setting. For example, the Aryan Brotherhood, a white supremacist group, maintains ties with motorcycle gangs on the outside, many of which are involved in the illicit drug trade. Inside, these groups compete for the lucrative prison drug business.

Prison gangs are not just a problem for correctional facilities in California, Texas, and New York. More than a decade ago, a survey by the American Correctional Association (ACA) found prison gangs—what the ACA calls **security threat groups**— in 40 state prison systems and the District of Columbia, and in the US Bureau of Prisons (ACA 1994). Indeed, the state systems most affected by gangs were Illinois, with 48.1 percent of the prison population

EUROPEAN PRESS AGENCY/ALAMY IMAGES

(14,900) gang members, and New Jersey, with 24.4 percent of the population (6,000) gang members. The study also found 1,153 different security threat groups with 46,190 members. Overall, roughly 6 percent of the nation's prison population belonged to a prison-based gang.

THE THREAT TO PRISON SAFETY AND SECURITY Prison gangs have replaced the solidary inmate social system, and that has created problems for prison authorities. In addition to the racial conflict they engender, gangs feud and form alliances, which create security and control problems. For example, the EME and NF have had an ongoing blood feud since 1968. In its struggle with the EME, the NF allied itself with two very different groups, the white supremacist AB and the BGF. Defining these relationships in a fluid environment is difficult, however. For instance, members of rival cliques from street gangs may unite

to provide protection for members. They also may exert control over the *sub rosa* inmate economy. Likewise, members of affiliated gangs outside the prison may find themselves with divided loyalties behind the walls.

Second, conventional wisdom suggests gangs are the source of much prison violence. The prison environment—with its associated deprivations—itself promotes violence, including violence directed at staff (Jiang and Fisher-Giorlando 2002). Gang members typically have a higher frequency of assaults on both staff and other inmates than nongang members (Huebner 2003), even when factors such as age, ethnicity, violent history and prior incarceration are taken into consideration (Griffin and Hepburn 2006). Indeed, as mentioned several times in this chapter, inmate assaults on staff are highest in those institutions with a maximum-security classification, facilities where the restrictions on inmates' lives are the greatest.

PRISON GANGS IN A NUTSHELL

BOX 7.3

The first recorded prison gang was Walla Walla (Washington) State Penitentiary's Gypsy Jokers Motorcycle Club. For most of the past 30 years, however, five groups have been major players in most of the nation's larger prisons:

- *Mexican Mafia (EME).* Prison officials report members of this gang in at least nine state prison systems and in the federal prison system. The EME models its leadership on the structure and behavior of the Italian Mafia, with much of its original leadership coming from urban regions of Southern California. The group's primary activity—in and out of prison—is selling drugs; however, its members allegedly engage in other criminal activities, including prostitution and illegal gambling.

- *La Nuestra Familia (NF).* This gang, composed mainly of rural Northern California Hispanics, has a board of directors. The longstanding feud between the EME and the NF often forces the California Department of Corrections and Rehabilitation to send members to different institutions. In addition to protecting NF members, this gang engages in the same kinds of prison-based criminal enterprises as do the other groups.

- *Black Guerrilla Family (BGF).* Prison activist George Jackson founded this unusual prison gang in the late 1960s. The BGF, despite its Maoist orientation, participates in the capitalistic inmate economy. The group is highly dependent on a charismatic leader and central committee. Prison authorities also consider it a highly dangerous gang because its members routinely assault prison staff. Prison gang experts believe the BGF has strong ties to gangs outside prisons, particularly in Chicago.

- *Texas Syndicate (TS).* Texas residents of Hispanic descent formed this group at California's Folsom State Prison. In the mid-1970s, the Texans found themselves caught between members of the EME and NF; creating the TS was a means of self-defense. The TS is a paramilitary group whose members are legendary for their patience in taking revenge for an insult or a violation of the inmate code.

- *Aryan Brotherhood (AB).* The AB's members come from biker gangs and other neo-Nazi groups outside prison. Like ethnic gangs, the AB protects its members and engages in a wide range of criminal activities; however, the prison-based drug trade is their primary focus. AB members are widely recognized as indiscriminately and unpredictably violent.

SOURCE: PELZ (1996).

What is the relationship between gangs and violence? A few studies suggest that gang members may be responsible for more than their share of prison violence, especially drug and fighting infractions (Ohio Department of Rehabilitation and Correction 1998; Shelden 1991). Gerald Gaes and his associates (2002) made perhaps the first systematic assessment of the contribution of gang affiliation to prison violence and other forms of inmate misconduct. In their study of the entire BOP male population, the researchers found that gang members had increased rule infractions and crimes within prisons, even after controlling for security classification, previous violent behavior, and other background factors. They also report that inmates who were closer to the core of a gang's leadership were more likely to resort to violence, a finding that is consistent with research on street gangs (Klein 1995; Spergel 1995).

Third, riots and other prison disturbances often create a power vacuum that new gangs are all too ready to fill. For example, following the riot at the New Mexico Penitentiary in 1980, two gangs emerged. One, the Sindicato Nuevo Mexico, is the largest organized prison gang in New Mexico and an offshoot of the EME. In Texas, similar evolutionary processes took place after a court decision ended that state's infamous building tender system. **Building tenders** were inmates tacitly acknowledged by prison administrators to have informal social control of a given inmate area (Crouch and Marquart 1989; Stojkovic 1996). Before *Ruiz v. Estelle* (1980), building tenders maintained economic and social control over their respective buildings in the Texas prison system. Ultimately, gangs emerged to fill the power vacuum created by the elimination of the building tenders (Fong 1990). In Ohio, researchers found similar cases of gangs emerging as riot organizers and negotiators Ohio (Huff and Meyer 1997).

RESPONDING TO PRISON GANGS What can prison authorities do about prison gangs? In the 1990s, Connecticut's Department of Corrections initiated a three-phase program for members of security-risk groups at designated institutions. In the first phase, prison staff members reclassify inmates to a higher security level, meaning that often they end up in a **close-custody unit**, a form of administrative segregation. The goals of this phase are cultural sensitivity and harmonious living: members of various security-risk groups all live together. Once they sign a letter of intent to renounce their gang affiliation, inmates enter Phase II. In this phase, the facility's classification staff groups the inmates into squads of 12, many of whom are members of different gangs. Each squad engages in all daily activities as a group. The emphasis here, again, is on cultural sensitivity and getting along, but understanding the alternatives to gang membership is also important. After 60 days or so, inmates enter Phase III. The final phase adds programming on anger and violence management to the earlier elements. After approximately 90 days, once they have formally renounced their gang membership, inmates return to the general population.

Other states, particularly those with large gang problems, approach prison-based gangs in a less systematic fashion. The California prison system uses a prison classification system to break up gangs by sending members to different facilities. Nevertheless, gangs remain a major power in California prisons (ACA 1994). By contrast, throughout most of the 1980s, Texas would house gang members in separate facilities, a practice that essentially created small gang fiefdoms (Fong 1990). Another strategy is to create small, semiautonomous, self-contained institutions of approximately 50 to 100 inmates (Levinson and Gerard 1973). The same team of specialists supervises all inmates with similar classifications and release dates. This **unit management** approach helps break up existing ties based on race, ethnicity, or gangs. The intended result is the emergence of a new form of prosocial group cohesion.

A fourth strategy is to create *gang-free facilities (GFFs)*. A GFF is a minimum-security prison, and the inmates assigned to it must have no gang affiliations, memberships, or associations, as determined by classification staff. Generally, staff and inmates view gang-free prisons as safer and less-violent institutions. In one study, gang-free prisons had a higher concentration of whites, sex offenders, and inmates wanting to enter programming; moreover, guards observed that in prisons with gangs, inmates tend to resolve their own disputes; by contrast, in GFFs, resolving inmate disputes becomes the work of the correctional officer (Rivera, Cowles, and Dorman 2003). The question remains: Do they work? For one perspective on GFFs, see Box 7.4. Whatever strategy a prison tries, breaking up the power of gangs is as difficult in prison as it is on the streets. Prisons gangs remain a complex problem that to date has defied resolution.

JAILHOUSE SUICIDE

Jailhouse suicide refers to suicides occurring in jails *and* prisons. In jails, suicide (often by hanging) is the second leading cause of death, after illness (Noonan and Carson 2011). Although there are nearly twice as many people in prison as in jails, in 2009 the number dying by suicide was about two-thirds that reported for jails. Suicide is also the second ranked

DO GANG-FREE FACILITIES WORK?

BOX 7.4

In the late 1990s, 2 years after conversion of a minimum-security prison to a gang-free prison, researchers interviewed three groups of inmates. One group comprised inmates who had been confined at the facility before and after conversion, a second comprised inmates transferred into the gang-free facility from other minimum-security prisons during conversion, and a third group was composed of newly admitted offenders sent from the state's reception and classification unit. All three cohorts were volunteers. The researchers were interested in learning how the inmates viewed the new prison environment, but especially along the following prison environmental dimensions: level of activity, social stimulation, social support from staff, level of privacy, level of freedom to move about and engage in rewarding activities, emotional feedback derived from the social community, and personal safety. The researchers used a focus group approach, which entailed bringing three cohorts together in groups of 9 to 12 inmates and asking them a series of questions during 90-minute sessions.

Did the inmates accept the facility's change to a GFF? Two elements of personal control—choice and predictability—influenced inmates' acceptance, but there were group differences as well. For example, members of the group that had been at the facility before and after conversion did not like the new regime's restrictiveness, and thought that their individual autonomy and options had been negatively affected. The transfer group had similar feelings of dissatisfaction. Both groups expressed concern that the administration was inconsistent in the application of rules and policies, a condition probably due in some measure to the transition. The newly arrived inmates saw things more positively. They uniformly used as their base of comparison jails and other correctional facilities. Interestingly, all three cohorts discounted the negativity prison administrators associated with gangs, and they saw the current facility problems as owing much to the absence of gangs and the consolidation of power in correctional officers' hands. Gang rules, the inmates claimed, were always clear; the rules of this institution in change were not and therefore worrisome. Inmates were unsure whether the level of safety in the facility was because of the absence of gangs or because the facility had always been a safe one. Clearly, the viability of the GFF concept has yet to be fully tested.

SOURCES: RIVERA, COWLES, AND DORMAN (2003).

cause of death for prison inmates, after illnesses. Prison suicides are troublesome, but other health-related problems—like HIV/AIDS, infectious diseases, drug abuse, and general mental health problems—tend to command more attention from prison officials. It is important, therefore, to review suicides in jails and prisons separately.

Jail suicide rates have declined from 129 per 100,000 in 1983, when they accounted for the majority (56 percent) of all jail deaths to 41 in 2009, when they were second to illness (Noonan and Carson 2011, 5). The fact that nearly half of jail suicides occur within the first week of custody—one

in seven on the same day they are processed into jail—suggests a close tie between the detention event and suicides. In 2009, the highest jail suicide rates were for males, who were much more likely to commit suicide than females (43 versus 27), and whites, whose jail suicide rate (80) was more than three times that of Hispanics (25) and five times greater than black inmates (16). Younger jail inmates, those younger than 18, and older inmates, those over 55, were much more likely to commit suicide in jail than those who were 18 to 54.

In prisons, most suicides (over 52 percent) occurred after 23 months of confinement. Prison suicides, despite what might be seen as a natural propensity toward depression and despair associated with long-term incarceration, occur less frequently than in local jails. The absolute number of suicides in 2009 was 201, about two-thirds the number that committed suicide in jail (Noonan and Carson 2011). Since 1980, when it stood at 34, the rate per 100,000 inmates fell by more than 50 percent to 15 in 2009. Between 2001 and 2009, males were more likely than females to commit suicide in prison (16 versus 11). The per capita (per 100,000) suicide rate for whites was 25, which was higher than for either Hispanics (18) or blacks (8). Interestingly, Asians (51) had the highest suicide rate.

Can local and state authorities reduce "jailhouse" suicides? One response was to create descriptive profiles of who is likely to commit suicide while confined (Kennedy and Homant 1988). One problem with this approach is that staff do not always take seriously the expression of suicide ideas and attempts (Haycock 1989), a practice that can backfire on correctional officials (Danto 1973). Suicide-prevention profiles rely heavily on demographics, physical and mental condition, and criminal history and current disposition. Do such profiles work? In a study of jail suicides in New York State, researchers found a 150 percent reduction in suicides after implementation of a comprehensive suicide-prevention program that included the use of a high-risk profile (Cox and Morschauser 1997). However, the integration of suicide profiles into prison and jail admission screening and, perhaps most importantly for prisons, ongoing prisoner management is far from complete (Winter 2003). In particular, we are just beginning to understand the impact of such factors as crowding, prison deprivations, and bullying on prison suicides (Blaauw, Winkel, and Kerkhof 2001; Huey and McNulty 2005). After more than 20 years of systematic study and much progress in reducing the suicide rates in jails and prisons, we are only beginning to grasp the significance of this correctional issue.

SUMMARY

In this chapter, we explored the residents of the nation's prisons and jails. What we have learned is that these populations are heavily minority in composition. Today's inmate shares much in common with his or her predecessor of 25, 50, or even 100 years ago because many of the challenges—deprivations—they face have not changed; however, in other important ways, prisoners are changing to meet a new prison world. Key points of interest to consider in this chapter are as follows:

- Prisoners today face many of the same pains of imprisonment and deprivations that confronted those confined in jails and prisons 50, 75, and even 200 years ago.

- What is different about jails and prisons today is that the populations are far less cohesive than they were just 30 years ago.

- Although the demise of inmate solidarity can be good from an administrative perspective—for example, there is less organized inmate resistance to prison rules and regulations—it can also have less-positive effects.

- Inmates have become far less predictable: the instances of their responding to real or imagined insults with violence have increased dramatically.

- The strict enforcement of restrictive and sometimes meaningless rules that define what inmates can and cannot do to embellish their living spaces has led to a prison environment that is more drab and monotonous than ever.

- Never a pleasant living environment, current conditions in the nation's jails and prisons may be worse than they were in the 1950s, largely because of what has been described as an imprisonment binge.

THINKING ABOUT CORRECTIONAL POLICIES AND PRACTICES: WRITING ASSIGNMENTS

1 In a one-page essay explain one of these two propositions: (1) jail and prison inmates are the same because . . . ; or (2) jail and prison inmates are different because. . . .

2 The populations of local and federal jails are quite different. Given discussions about sentencing policies and federal priorities over the past decade or more, prepare a paper that explores why these differences exist. Keep this paper and review it after reading Chapters 13 and 14. Has your answer changed?

3 Look at the forces driving the imprisonment binge. Prepare a one-to-two-page critical assessment of those forces and suggest ways that policy makers could reverse this trend and slow the binge.

4 You are the warden of a medium-security prison. After a surge in race-based violence, you decide to segregate your facility by race because inmates—by living arrangements, dining-hall practices, and recreational activities—have already achieved considerable segregation. Prepare a one-to-two-page paper with your best arguments, preparing to deal with charges of racism.

5 We concluded this chapter with two inmate-centered issues. Which issue do you think would place the greatest burden on public budgets to resolve? Which issue do you think poses the greatest threat to inmates' quality of life and therefore deserves attention first? Even if you select the same issue, give your rationale for each in a one-to-two-page paper.

KEY TERMS

building tenders
close-custody unit
con-politicians
cultural importation
    hypothesis
deprivation hypothesis
doing time
drug offenses
economic exploitation
fish
frustration riots
gleaning

imprisonment binge
inmate code
jailing
legitimate inmate economy
outlaws
pains of imprisonment
political riot
prison gangs
prisonization
prison riot
prison subculture
psychological victimization

punks
race riots
rage riots
right guys
security threat groups
solidary opposition
Square John
sub rosa inmate economy
unit management
wolves

CRITICAL REVIEW QUESTIONS

1 What do the race/ethnicity, gender, and conviction status statistics tell us about the jail population in the United States? Are the prison statistics for these characteristics the same or different? Why would that be?

2 Do the available statistics indicate that state prisoners and federal prisoners are similar, or are they different? If there are any differences, what would account for the disparity?

3 Which single statistic about federal prisoners do you find most interesting? Explain your choice.

4 Which single statistic about state prisoners do you find most interesting? Explain your choice.

5 What do we mean by "truth-in-sentencing?" What factors would drive states to adopt truth-in-sentencing laws, and what might the consequences (intended or unintended) be of such laws?

6 What do you think is the worst aspect of the inmate code? What would bother you least if you were a member of the inmate subculture?

7 Based on your reading of this chapter (and other information you can find) explain whether the inmate subculture code today is the same as it was when pioneering research on prisons was done in the 1950s and 1960s.

8 Do you think the inmate subculture is primarily a product of incarceration or of inmates' experiences outside?

9 What kind of violence do you think inmates fear most and why?

10 Review the role of importation and deprivation in creating the inmate social system. What do these ideas tell you about prison gangs?

CASE CITED

Ruiz v. Estelle, 503 F.Supp. 1265 (S.D. Tex. 1980)

REFERENCES

Akers, Ronald, H. Hayner, and W. Grunninger. 1977. Prisonization in five countries: Types of prison and inmate characteristics. *Criminology* 14: 527–54.

American Correctional Association (ACA). 1994. *Gangs in correctional facilities: A national assessment*. Laurel, MD.

Austin, James F., and John Irwin. 2001. *It's about time: America's imprisonment binge*, 3rd edn. Belmont, CA: Wadsworth.

Badillo, Herman, and Milton Haynes. 1972. *A bill of no rights: Attica and the American prison system*. New York: Outerbridge & Lazard.

Beck, Allen J. 2012. *Prison Rape Elimination Act of 2003—PREA Data Collection Activities, 2012*. Washington, DC: Bureau of Justice Statistics, US Department of Justice.

Beck, Allen J., and Paige M. Harrison. 2006. *Sexual violence in correctional facilities, 2005*. Washington, DC: Bureau of Justice Statistics.

Beck, Allen J., Paige M. Harrison, Marcus Berzofsky, Rachel Caspar, and Christopher Krebs. 2010. *Sexual victimization in prisons and jails reported by inmates, 2008–09*. Washington, DC: Bureau of Justice Statistics, US Department of Justice.

Bingaman, Jeff. 1980. *Report of the attorney general on the February 2 and 3, 1980, riot of the Penitentiary of New Mexico*, 2 vols. Santa Fe, NM: Office of the Attorney General.

Blaauw, Eric, Frans Willem Winkel, and J. F. M. Kerkof. 2001. Bullying and suicidal behavior in jails. *Criminal Justice and Behavior* 28: 279–99.

Bottoms, Anthony E. 1999. Interpersonal violence and social order in prisons. In *Prisons*, edited by Michael Tonry and Joan Petersilia. Chicago: University of Chicago Press, 205–81.

Bowker, Lee M. 1981. Gender differences in prisoner subcultures. In *Women and crime in America*, edited by Lee M. Bowker. New York: Macmillan, 409–19.

Bureau of Justice Statistics. 1994. *Comparing state and federal prison inmates*, 1991. Washington, DC: US Department of Justice.

Bureau of Justice Statistics. 2000. *Correctional populations in the United States*, 1997. Washington, DC: US Government Printing Office.

Carroll, Leo. 1974. *Hacks, blacks and cons*. Lexington, MA: Lexington Books.

Clemmer, Donald. 1940/1958. *The prison community*. New York: Holt, Rinehart & Winston.

Clemmer, Donald. 1951. Observations on imprisonment as a source of criminality. *Journal of Criminal Law and Criminology* 41: 311–19.

Colvin, Mark. 1982. The 1980 New Mexico prison riot. *Social Problems* 29: 449–63.

Cox, J., and P. C. Morschauser. 1997. A solution to the problem of jail suicide. *Journal of Crisis Intervention and Suicide Prevention* 18: 178–84.

Crouch, Ben M., and James W. Marquart. 1989. *An appeal to justice: Litigated reform of Texas prisons.* Austin: University of Texas Press.

Cullen, Francis T., Edward J. Latessa, Velmer S. Burton Jr., and Lucien X. Lombardo. 1993. The correctional orientation of prison wardens: Is the rehabilitative ideal supported? *Criminology* 31(1): 69–92.

Currie, Elliott. 1993. *Reckoning: Drugs, the cities, and the American future.* New York: Hill and Wang.

Danto, B. L. 1973. The suicidal inmate. In *Jailhouse blues: Studies of suicidal behavior in jail and prison,* edited by B. L. Danto. Orchard Lake, MI: Epic.

Eigenberg, Helen M. 1989. Male rape: An empirical examination of correctional officers' attitudes toward male rape in prison. *Prison Journal* 58: 39–56.

Eigenberg, Helen M. 1994. Rape in male prisons: Examining the relationship between correctional officers' attitudes toward male rape and their willingness to respond to acts of rape. In *Prison violence in America,* 2nd edn., edited by Michael C. Braswell, Reid H. Montgomery, and Lucien X. Lombardo. Cincinnati, OH: Anderson, 145–65.

Eigenberg, Helen M. 2000. Correctional officers and their perceptions of homosexuality, rape, and prostitution in male prisons. *Prison Journal* 80: 415–33.

Fishman, Joseph F. 1934. *Sex in prison.* New York: National Liberty Press.

Fong, Robert S. 1990. The organizational structure of prison gangs. *Federal Probation* 54(4): 36–43.

Gaes, Gerald, and William J. McGuire. 1985. Prison violence: The contributions of crowding versus other determinants of prison assault rates. *Journal of Research in Crime and Delinquency,* 22(1): 41–65.

Gaes, Gerald, Susan Wallace, Evan Gilman, Jody Klein-Saffran, and Sharon Suppa. 2002. The influence of prison gang affiliation on violence and other prison misconduct. *Prison Journal* 82: 359–95.

Garabedian, Peter G. 1963. Social roles and processes of socialization in the prison community. *Social Problems* 11: 139–52.

Garson, G. David. 1972. Force versus restraint in prison riots. *Crime & Delinquency* 18: 411–21.

Giallambardo, Rose. 1966. *Society of women: A study of women's prison.* New York: Wiley.

Griffin, Marie L., and John R. Hepburn. 2006. The effect of gang affiliation on violent misconduct among inmates during the early years of confinement. *Criminal Justice and Behavior* 33: 419–48.

Guerino, Paul, Paige M. Harrison, and William J. Sabol. 2011. *Prisoners in 2010.* Washington, DC: Bureau of Justice Statistics, US Department of Justice.

Harlow, Caroline Wolf. 1994. *Comparing federal and state prison inmates.* Washington, DC: US Department of Justice.

Harlow, Caroline Wolf. 1998. *Profile of jail inmates 1996.* Washington, DC: US Department of Justice.

Harrison, Paige M., and Allen J. Beck. 2006. *Prisoners in 2005.* Washington, DC: US Department of Justice.

Hawkins, Richard, and Geoffrey P. Alpert. 1989. *American prison systems: Punishment and justice.* Englewood Cliffs, NJ: Prentice Hall.

Haycock, J. 1989. Manipulation and suicide attempts in jails and prisons. *Psychiatric Quarterly* 60(1): 85–98.

Heffernan, Esther. 1972. *Making it in prison: The square, the cool and the life.* New York: Wiley.

Hensley, Christopher, Cindy Struckman-Johnson, and Helen M. Eigenberg. 2000. Introduction: The history of prison sex research. *Prison Journal* 80: 360–67.

Hensley, Christopher, and Richard Tewksbury. 2005. Wardens' perceptions of prison sex. *Prison Journal* 85: 186–97.

Huebner, Beth M. 2003. Administrative determinants of inmate violence: A multi-level analysis. *Journal of Criminal Justice* 30(2): 107–17.

Huey, Meredith P., and Thomas L. McNulty. 2005. Institutional conditions and prison suicide: Conditional effects of deprivation and overcrowding. *Prison Journal* 85: 490–514.

Huff, C. Ronald, and M. Meyer. 1997. Managing prison gangs and other security threat groups. *Corrections Management Quarterly* 1(2): 10–18.

Inciardi, James. 1992. *The War on Drugs II.* Mountain View, CA: Mayfield.

Irwin, John. 1970. *The felon.* Englewood Cliffs, NJ: Prentice Hall.

Irwin, John. 1980. *Prisons in turmoil.* Boston: Little, Brown.

Irwin, John., and James Austin. 1993. *It's about time: America's imprisonment binge.* Belmont, CA: Wadsworth.

Irwin, John., and Donald Cressey. 1962. Thieves, convicts and the inmate culture. *Social Problems* 10: 142–55.

Irwin, John., V. Schiraldi, and J. Ziedenberg. 1999. *American's one million nonviolent prisoners*. Washington, DC: Justice Policy Institute.

Jacobs, James B. 1977. *Stateville: The penitentiary in mass society*. Chicago: University of Chicago Press.

Jacobs, James B. 1979. Race relations and the prison subculture. In *Crime and justice*, vol. 1, edited by Norval Morris and Michael Tonry. Chicago: University of Chicago Press, 1–28.

Jiang, Shanhe, and Marianne Fisher-Giorlando. 2002. Inmate misconduct: A test of the deprivation, importation and situational models. *Prison Journal* 82: 335–58.

Johnston, James. 1949. *Alcatraz: Island prison and the men who live there*. New York: Scribner's.

Kalinich, David. 1996. Contraband. In *Encyclopedia of American prisons*, edited by Marilyn D. McShane and Frank P. Williams III. New York: Garland, 111–15.

Kennedy, D. B., and R. J. Homant. 1988. Predicting custodial suicides: Problems with the use of profiles. *Justice Quarterly* 5(3): 441–56.

Kerbs, John J., and Jennifer M. Jolley. 2007. Inmate-on-inmate victimization among older male prisoners. *Crime & Delinquency* 53: 187–218.

Klein, Malcolm W. 1995. *The American street gang*. New York: Oxford University Press.

Lankenau, Stephen E. 2001. Smoke 'em if you got 'em: Cigarette black markets in US prisons and jails. *Prison Journal* 81: 142–61.

Leger, Robert G. 1978. Socialization patterns and social roles: A replication. *Journal of Criminal Law and Criminology* 69: 627–34.

Levinson, Robert B., and Roy E. Gerard. 1973. Functional units: A different correctional approach. *Federal Probation* 37: 8–16.

Lillis, J. 1994. Prison escapes and violence remain down. *Corrections Compendium* 19: 6–21.

Lockwood, Daniel. 1980. *Prison sexual victimization*. New York: Elsevier.

Maguire, Kathleen, and Ann C. Pastore, eds. 1999. *Bureau of Justice Statistics sourcebook of criminal justice statistics 1998*. Washington, DC: US Department of Justice.

Mahan, Sue. 1982. An "orgy of brutality" at Attica and the "killing ground" at Santa Fe: A comparison of prison riots. In *Coping with imprisonment*, edited by N. Parisi. Beverly Hills, CA: Sage, 65–78.

McCleery, Richard H. 1968. Correctional administration and political change. In *Prison within society: A reader in penology*, edited by Lawrence Hazelrigg. New York: Doubleday-Anchor, 113–49.

McCorkle, Lloyd, and Richard Korn. 1954. Resocialization within walls. *The annals of the American Academy of Political and Social Sciences* 293: 5–19.

McCorkle, R. C., T. D. Miethe, and K. A. Drass. 1995. Roots of prison violence: A test of the deprivation, management, and "not-so-total" institution models. *Crime & Delinquency* 41: 317–31.

Minton, Todd D. 2011. *Jail inmates at midyear 2010—statistical tables*. Washington, DC: Bureau of Justice Statistics, US Department of Justice.

Nacci, P., and T. Kane. 1983. The incidence of sex and sexual aggression in federal prisons. *Federal Probation* 7: 31–36.

New York Special Commission on Attica. 1972. *Attica*. New York: Bantam.

Noonan, Margaret E., and E. Ann Carson. 2011. *Prison and jail deaths in custody, 2000–2009—statistical tables*. Washington, DC: Bureau of Justice Statistics, US Department of Justice.

Ohio Department of Rehabilitation and Correction, Bureau of Research. 1998. *Descriptive analysis of protective control inmates*. Columbus.

Ohlin, Lloyd. 1956. *Sociology and the field of corrections*. New York: Russell Sage.

Oswald, Russell G. 1972. *Attica: My story*. Garden City, NY: Doubleday.

Pelz, Mary E. 1996. Gangs. In *Encyclopedia of American prisons*, edited by Marilyn D. McShane and Frank P. Williams III. New York: Garland, 213–18.

Pollock, Joycelyn. 2004. *Prisons and prison life: Costs and consequences*. Los Angeles: Roxbury.

Propper, Alice M. 1981. *Prison homosexuality: Myth and reality*. Lexington, MA: Lexington Books.

Rabow, Jerome, and Albert Elias. 1969. Organization boundaries, inmate roles, and rehabilitation. *Journal of Research in Crime and Delinquency* 6: 8–16.

Reid, Sue Titus. 1981. *The correctional system*. New York: Holt, Rinehart & Winston.

Richmond, K. 1978. Fear of homosexuality and modes of rationalization in male prisons. *Australian and New Zealand Journal of Sociology* 14(1): 51–57.

Rivera, Beverly D., Ernest L. Cowles, and Laura G. Dorman. 2003. An exploratory study of institutional change: Personal control and environmental satisfaction in a gang-free prison. *Prison Journal* 83: 149–70.

Rosich, Katherine J., and Kamala Mallik Kane. 2012. Truth in Sentencing and State Sentencing Practices. *NIJ Journal* 252. Retrieved on July 11, 2013 from: http://www.nij.gov/journals/252/sentencing.html

Sabol, William J., and John McGready. 1999. *Time served in prison by federal offenders, 1986–1997.* Washington, DC: US Department of Justice.

Santos, Michael G. 1996. Commissaries. In *Encyclopedia of American prisons*, edited by Marilyn D. McShane and Frank P. Williams III. New York: Garland, 100–102.

Schrag, Clarence. 1944. Social role types in a prison community. Master's thesis, University of Washington, Seattle.

Shelden, Randall. 1991. A comparison of gang and nongang members in a prison setting. *Prison Journal* 71(2): 50–60.

Spergel, Irving A. 1995. *The youthful gang problem.* New York: Oxford University Press.

Stephan, James J. 2001. *Census of jails, 1999.* Washington, DC: US Department of Justice.

Stephan, James J. 2008. *Census of state and federal correctional facilities, 2005.* Washington, DC: Bureau of Justice Statistics, US Department of Justice.

Stephan, James J., and Jennifer C. Karberg. 2003. *Census of state and federal correctional facilities, 2000.* Washington, DC: US Department of Justice.

Stephan, James J., and Georgette Walsh. 2011. *Census of Jail Facilities, 2006.* Washington, DC: Bureau of Justice Statistics, US Department of Justice.

Stojkovic, Stan. 1996. Building tenders. In *Encyclopedia of American prisons*, edited by Marilyn D. McShane and Frank P. Williams III. New York: Garland, 66–69.

Struckman-Johnson, Cindy, and David Struckman-Johnson. 2000. Sexual coercion rates in seven Midwestern prison facilities for men. *Prison Journal* 80: 279–390.

Sykes, Gresham M. 1958. *The society of captives: A study of a maximum security prison.* Princeton, NJ: Princeton University Press.

Sykes, Gresham M., and Sheldon L. Messinger. 1960. Inmate social system. In *Theoretical studies in social organization of the prison*, edited by Richard A. Cloward et al. New York: Social Science Research Council, 5–19.

Sylvester, S.F., J. Reed, and D. Nelson. 1977. *Prison homicides.* New York: Spectrum.

Thomas, Charles W. 1970. Toward a more inclusive model of the inmate contraculture. *Criminology* 8: 251–62.

Thomas, Charles W., and David M. Petersen. 1977. *Prison organization and inmate subcultures.* Indianapolis: Bobbs-Merrill.

Thomas, Charles W., and Samuel Foster. 1975. On the measurement of social roles adaptations in the prison community. *Criminal Justice Review* 1: 11–21.

Toch, Hans. 1976. A psychological view of prison violence. In *Prison violence*, edited by Albert K. Cohen, George Cole, and Robert G. Bailey. Lexington, MA: Heath, 43–58.

US Bureau of Prisons (BOP). 2009. *State of the Bureau 2009.* Washington, DC: US Department of Justice.

US Bureau of Prisons. 2010. State of the Bureau 2010. Retrieved on August 5, 2013 from: http://www.bop.gov/news/PDFs/sob10.pdf

Useem, Bert, Camille Graham Camp, George M. Camp, and Renie Dugan. 1995. *Resolution of prison riots.* Washington, DC: US Department of Justice.

Walker, Samuel. 2006. *Sense and nonsense about crime and drugs: A policy guide*, 6th edn. Belmont, CA: Wadsworth.

Wellford, Charles. 1967. Factors associated with adoption of the inmate code. *Journal of Criminal Law, Criminology and Police Science* 58: 197–203.

Wicker, Tom. 1975. *A time to die.* New York: Quadrangle.

Winfree, L. Thomas, Jr., Greg Newbold, and S. Houston Tubb III. 2002. Prisoner perspectives on inmate culture in New Mexico and New Zealand: A descriptive study. *Prison Journal* 82: 213–33.

Winter, Melinda M. 2003. County jail suicides in a midwestern state: Moving beyond the use of profiles. *Prison Journal* 83: 130–48.

Wolff, Nancy, Cynthia L. Blitz, Jing Shi, Jane Siegel, and Ronet Bachman. 2007. Physical violence inside prisons: Rates of victimization. *Criminal Justice and Behavior* 34: 588–99.

Wooden, W., and J. Parker. 1982. *Men behind bars: Sexual exploitation in prison.* New York: Plenum.

Wooldredge, John D. 1998. Inmate lifestyles and opportunities for victimization. *Journal of Research in Crime and Delinquency* 35: 480–502.

Wooldredge, John D. 2003. Keeping pace with evolving prison populations for effective management. *Criminology & Public Policy* 2: 253–58.

Zingraff, Matthew T. 1975. Prisonization as an inhibitor of effective personalization. *Criminology* 13: 366–88.

SPECIAL NEEDS INMATES

8

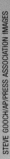

STEVE GOOCH/AP/PRESS ASSOCIATION IMAGES

Outline

Objectives

- To catalog the members of special needs inmate groups

- To reveal the issues associated with special needs inmates

- To explore the costs associated with providing correctional services to such inmates

- To examine the pressures that special needs inmates create for institutional corrections

- To give a sense of why special needs inmates are vulnerable to both inside and outside pressures

Essentials of Corrections, Fifth Edition. G. Larry Mays and L. Thomas Winfree, Jr.
© 2014 John Wiley & Sons, Inc. Published 2014 by John Wiley & Sons, Inc.

INTRODUCTION

Nearly all prisons house inmates who by reason of a special set of circumstances, physical, cultural or social conditions, and unique legal statuses are at an increased risk of victimization. This victimization could come from other inmates, staff or even the society outside prison or jail. The kinds of victimization could be economic, social, psychological, political, legal, and physical. Just who are these inmates? In a 2009 report, the United Nations Office on Drugs and Crime (UNODC) notes the following about special needs inmates:

> There are certain groups that are in a particularly vulnerable position in prisons and who therefore need additional care and protection. Some people may experience increased suffering due to inadequate facilities and lack of specialist care available to address their special needs in prison. The prison environment itself will exacerbate their existing problems. These include prisoners with mental health care needs, prisoners with disabilities and older prisoners. Some are at risk of abuse from other prisoners and prison staff, due to prejudicial attitudes and discriminatory perceptions entrenched in society itself, which are more pronounced in the closed environment of prisons. Such groups may suffer from humiliation, physical and psychological abuse and violence, due to their ethnicity, nationality, gender and sexual orientation . . . Most of these prisoners are, in fact, vulnerable due to more than one reason. They suffer both due to their existing special needs, which are intensified in prisons, and due to the additional risks they confront, stemming from their particular status (p. 2).[1]

Briefly, **special needs** inmates constitute a class of inmates for whom imprisonment creates a greater likelihood that their civil and human rights will be violated. To this UNODC list, we have added incarcerated children, adolescents, and young adults and foreign national inmates, two additional groups who by reason of their unique statuses are more vulnerable to physical, social and legal abuses. We begin with the youngest prison and jail inmates.

INCARCERATED CHILDREN, ADOLESCENTS, AND YOUNG ADULTS

While the vast majority of correctional clients nationwide are adults, state and local correctional systems also have the responsibility for supervising children and adolescents (individuals under 18 years of age) as well as young adults (18–24 years of age). In this section we will examine the scope of the correctional population that includes people in these two age groups and explore some of the challenges they present to correctional agencies.

THE YOUNG AND THE RESTLESS

One of the trends that could spell disaster for future correctional populations is the tendency to incarcerate younger, more violent offenders, an offshoot of the nation's get-tough movement. These chronic offenders are state-raised—they have lived in and out of state-controlled institutions their entire lives—and streetwise. They are unlikely to be sent to special young-offender units or facilities. Instead, they are mainstreamed with offenders who have similar criminal records.

As the new generation of state-raised youths enters prison, they may face an increasingly divided inmate population, one divided along lines of race and ethnicity, and by age as well. Violent young offenders will enter the corrections pipeline, but fewer than in the past will leave the nation's prisons, increasing the proportion of those who are older.

This trend has at least two implications for corrections: We will be filling prisons with people who know no life other than juvenile and adult correctional facilities, and we will be creating an extremely disaffiliated class of people. Cut off from noncriminal society for long periods and given little hope of altering their lives, long-term inmates are a prison administrator's worst nightmare. Rehabilitation aside, they must be managed in correctional settings for decades. They also constitute a threat to older, more-vulnerable inmates, the likely "targets of opportunity" for violent young offenders (Vito and Wilson 1985). Prison classification systems can reduce the contact between these two groups of inmates.

However, these strategies have their limits. Consequently, mixing very young and very old populations has the potential to create yet another problem for jails and prisons that has roots in the free community: the mistreatment of the elderly (Douglas 1995).

In the following sections we will examine the incarceration of juvenile and young adult offenders in a variety of correction settings. Of particular interest will be juvenile detention centers, adult jails, juvenile correctional facilities, and adult prisons.

JUVENILES IN LOCAL DETENTION FACILITIES

Although this may not include a complete accounting, in 2008 the Office of Juvenile Justice and Delinquency Prevention found that nationwide there were about 734 local jurisdictions operating juvenile detention facilities. These facilities house youngsters from 10 years of age to the upper age of jurisdiction for the local juvenile courts (17 in most states). **Juvenile detention centers** may be free-standing structures or they may be part of larger city or county jail complexes. Detention centers (sometimes called juvenile halls) operate very much like adult jails, and they provide short-term incarceration prior to, or immediately following, juvenile court adjudication (Hockenberry, Sickmund, and Sladky 2011; Sickmund 2010).

In 2008 when the OJJDP took its one-day census, the 734 detention centers reporting indicated that they housed over 32,400 juveniles or about 44 youngsters on average per facility. There has been a general decline in the number of youths incarcerated since 2000, and between 2006 and 2008 there was a 12 percent decrease in the number of juveniles in custody.

As a result of fewer juvenile arrests, most detention facilities were operating at or below their rated capacity. In fact, in 2008 45 states detained fewer youngsters than they did in 2006. The result of this population decrease has been that fewer youngsters are suffering some of the pains of imprisonment. For instance, juvenile detention centers traditionally have been characterized as dangerous places for the youngsters they hold. However, in 2008 detention centers reported only one of the six suicide deaths that occurred in juvenile facilities nationwide. There

were two other deaths that resulted from accidents (Hockenberry, Sickmund, and Sladky 2011, 9). Nevertheless, juvenile detention centers are places where youngsters are threatened, beaten, and sexually assaulted by other inmates and occasionally by staff members.

JUVENILES IN ADULT JAILS

An ongoing dilemma for local corrections has been the housing of youngsters in adult jails. One of the original mandates of the Juvenile Justice and Delinquency Prevention Act of 1974 was the removal of juveniles from adult jails (see Schwartz 1989, 1991). Federal funding to the states was tied to efforts to move detained juveniles from adult jails and place them in separate juvenile detention centers. A deadline was set for this goal, but Congress changed the cutoff dates several times in the process of reauthorizing the Office of Juvenile Justice and Delinquency Prevention (OJJDP). Nevertheless, the numbers of accused delinquents continued to decline from a nearly 4,000 average daily population in the 1970s to a low of 1,009 in 2005. In 2010 the number stood at 1,912 (Minton 2011, 7). The complicating factor is that this number doesn't tell the complete story, since in 1993 the Bureau of Justice Statistics started counting not only adolescents held as juveniles but also those held as adults. Table 8.1 shows the numbers of both populations between 2000 and 2010.

Holding youthful offenders in adult jails poses at least two sets of problems. First, from an operational standpoint jails must provide **sight-and-sound separation** between adolescent and adult offenders. Many of the youngsters housed in adult jails are held in small, rural counties that have small jails. The space in these facilities is not always flexible and this presents a problem when adults must be separated from juveniles, and males must be separated from females. If the jail has only 10 or even 20 cells this becomes a housing nightmare.

Second, housing youthful offenders in adult jails potentially exposes them to adult offenders and to staff members whose job is to deal with adult offenders. Ideally, there should be custody and other staff members whose sole function is to deal with the

TABLE 8.1 **Inmates under the age of 18 held in local jails, 2000, 2005–2010.**

	2000	2005	2006	2007	2008	2009	2010
Held as adults	6,126	5,750	4,835	5.649	6,410	5,846	5,647
Held as juveniles	1,489	1,009	1,268	1,184	1,294	1,373	1,912

SOURCE: MINTON (2011, 7).

youngest inmates. As a practical matter, this may not be possible.

JUVENILES IN SECURE JUVENILE FACILITIES

Juveniles committed to long-term sentences (usually more than 1 year) typically are housed in juvenile correctional facilities. These facilities can be open or low-security operations (such as ranch or wilderness camp programs or residential treatment centers) or they can be secure operations such as state training or industrial schools (see Hockenberry, Sickmund, and Sladky 2011). Most state training schools can hold offenders until they become 21 years old, at which time they are released or turned over to the state corrections department for incarceration. Nationwide there are approximately 85 ranch, wilderness, or marine camp programs and 210 state training schools. In 2010, OJJDP reported that 48,427 adolescents were held in state custody as a result of juvenile court commitments. Not all of these youngsters were held in secure facilities, but about 28,000 of them were (Hockenberry, Sickmund, and Sladky 2011; Sickmund et al. 2011). Many of the state training schools that serve as secure commitment facilities resemble adult prisons, and some of the youngsters housed in these institutions eventually "graduate" to adult prison time.

ADOLESCENTS AND YOUNG ADULTS IN ADULT PRISONS

In addition to those youngsters adjudicated as juvenile delinquents, a small number of adolescent offenders (between 1 and 2 percent of all accused delinquents) are transferred to criminal courts where they are tried as adults. Technically these youngsters are no longer juveniles but adults and they can be sentenced to serve time in adult prisons.

The most recent figures available on this population come from the Bureau of Justice Statistics which reported that in 2009 there were 2,779 prison inmates under the age of 18 and in 2010 there were 2,295 (Guerino, Harrison, and Sabol 2011). In addition, there were 829 inmates who were 18 or 19 years old, and 1,538 who were aged 20 to 24 (Glaze 2011).

These adolescent and young-adult inmates present a number of problems for correctional authorities. First, a small number of them are first-time serious offenders who have no experience of incarceration. These inmates are often referred to as "fish" and they represent prime targets for assault, sexual abuse, and exploitation by experienced prisoners (see Chapter 7). Prisons are faced with two choices in such situations: they can place these inmates in the general prison population and hope they can survive and learn to adapt, or they can place them in protective custody and forever brand them as weaklings. Neither choice is particularly optimal.

Second, as confirmed by correctional authorities, these youthful inmates can be disruptive as they try to establish their reputations within the inmate hierarchy. They can become very predatory as they try to "out-tough the toughs" and, in particular, they try to prey on the most vulnerable of the inmates.

Third, as we have already indicated, some youthful offenders fit into the category of state-raised youths. They have "done time" as juveniles and now they are "doing" adult institutional time. Such youngsters know how to do time and they become firmly entrenched in the negativistic inmate culture. The more they fit into the inmate world, the more difficult it is for them in the outside world when, or if, they are released.

INMATES WITH MEDICAL NEEDS

Both jails and prisons face a wide array of inmate medical needs. Many inmates come into the correctional environment with poor or no records of medical care. Therefore, once they are incarcerated their medical needs become the responsibility of the local, state, or federal agencies that house them.

HIV/AIDS

HIV-positive refers to the documented presence of the Human Immunodeficiency Virus in a human being, suggesting that the person in question could develop **AIDS** (Acquired Immunodeficiency Disorder

Syndrome), which weakens the immune system and allows opportunistic infections and cancers to develop. HIV and AIDS are highly problematic for correctional systems, in both the control and spread of the virus and the syndrome in the inmate population. All 50 states, the District of Columbia, and the US Bureau of Prisons have the authority to test inmates for HIV. Most (43) jurisdictions test if an inmate shows HIV-related symptoms or at the inmate's request. Twenty jurisdictions test high-risk inmates, and 23 test inmates involved in an incident— an alleged rape, exposure to another individual's blood, or an assault by an inmate suspected of being HIV-positive.

The number of HIV-AIDS inmates in the nation's prison systems increased from 17,551 in 1991 to 25,807 in 1999, dropping slightly over the following few years (Maruschak 2004, 2006). Until the middle of the first decade of the twenty-first century, the

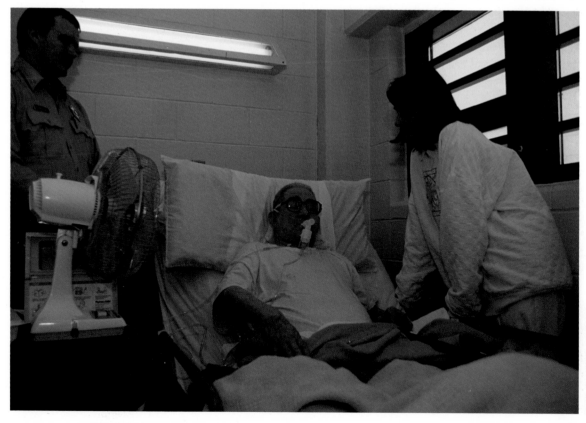

number of reported HIV-AIDS cases among state and federal prison inmates was consistently in the 21,000-plus range, and the number of HIV/AIDS cases as a percentage of the total custody population remained relatively flat, hovering just under 2 percent. Towards the end of that decade, however, the number of cases and the percent of the population reported to be HIV positive or have confirmed AIDS dropped precipitously, in terms of both the absolute number (18,515) and percent of prison population (1.5 percent). It is also worth noting that New York (with 3,080 cases), Florida (2,920), Texas (2,394), and California (1,098) house the largest numbers of HIV-AIDS inmates, continuing to account for one-half of the total (Maruschak 2012).

As reflected in Figure 8.1, the 2001 rate of AIDS-related deaths in US state prisons was over twice that found in the general population. By 2004, the AIDS death rate in state prisons was one and one-half times the rate found in the general population. The rate dropped even further through the rest of the decade,

until in 2010 it was below that found in the US general population. Expressed another way, the raw number of AIDS-related deaths in state prisons had dropped from a peak of 1,010 in 1995 to 72 in 2010. In 2001, the three main singular causes of death were, in declining order, heart disease, cancer and AIDS-related disorders; at the end of the decade, AIDS-related disorders were a distant fifth, replaced by liver disease and suicide (Noonan and Carson 2011). AIDS-related deaths in federal prison are relatively rare events, having occurred only seven times in 2010.

As a result of the relatively short-term periods of confinement, our insights into AIDS/HIV in jails are far less detailed. In 2002, two-thirds of all inmates reported ever being tested for HIV (Maruschak 2004, 9). Of those tested, 1.3 percent were HIV-positive, a decrease over the 1999 Jail Census, when it was 2 percent. The nation's jails reported that 42 people died of AIDS-related issues while in jail; however, many jails—especially those with limited

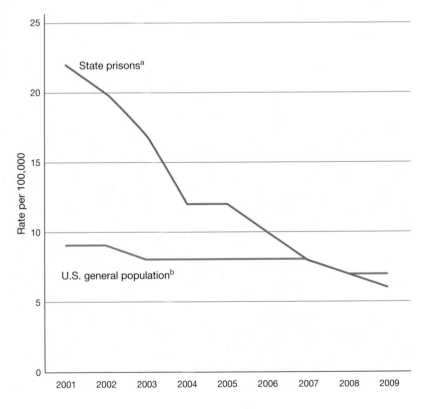

FIGURE 8.1 **Rate of AIDS-related deaths in state prisons and in the US general population among persons aged 15–54, 2001– 2009.** *Source:* Maruschak (2012, 3).

or nonexistent medical facilities—transport severely ill or dying inmates to area hospitals, where they eventually die. As a result, these figures probably do not accurately reflect the jail death rate for AIDS. The jail death statistics do, however, give some interesting insights, ones paralleling what has been reported for prisons. Specifically, at the start of the twenty-first century, deaths related to HIV-AIDS stood as the number two cause of death among jail inmates, after heart disease; 9 years later, HIV-AIDS was the fourth leading cause of jail deaths, after heart disease, cancer and alcohol/drug intoxication (Noonan and Carson 2011, 5). Indeed, a jail inmate was as likely to be a homicide victim or die of an accident as to die of HIV-AIDS, as all three had a mortality ratio of 3:100,000 jail inmates (Noonan and Carson 2011, 6).

What works to intervene or prevent HIV in the highly vulnerable inmate population? The general consensus among health experts is that prison and jail populations present unique challenges for HIV prevention programming (Bryan et al. 2006; Swartz, Lurigio, and Wiener 2004). Given the high incidence of drug-using inmates, risky sexual behavior, and generally poor health habits, these groups are less than ideal candidates for health care education. Peer educators appear to have some success, especially in the area of condom use and beliefs about personal susceptibility to the disease (Bryan et al.). What is equally clear, however, is that prison and jail administrators must tailor individual programs to meet the needs of low-, moderate-, and high-risk inmates if they hope to be successful, an unlikely response from the nation's cash-strapped correctional systems (Swartz et al.). Judged by the downward movement in both HIV-AIDS confirmed cases and deaths among jail inmates, current policies are having the desired effect.

TUBERCULOSIS

Tuberculosis is a highly contagious disease of the lungs, intestines, and joints. It is spread primarily by inhalation. Tuberculosis is potentially a greater threat to inmates in US jails and prisons than is either HIV/AIDS or any sexually transmitted disease. There are four important reasons for this (Hammett and Harrold 1994):

- *Transmittal mechanism*: TB can become airborne. Older prisons and jails generally have inadequate ventilation systems, and they often recycle the same air throughout the facility. This practice helps spread the TB bacterium (*Mycobacterium tuberculosis*) throughout the facility.

- *Symptomology*: people infected with TB may remain symptom-free for long periods (as is the case with those who are HIV-positive).

- *Drug-resistance*: during the past two decades, epidemiologists (scientists who study the incidence and characteristics of disease) have recorded the appearance of a **multiple drug-resistant tuberculosis (MDR-TB)**, one that does not respond to traditional treatment.

- *Disease progression*: those who are infected with both HIV and MDR-TB have twice the risk of developing active TB, as do those who test positive for TB alone.

Tuberculosis in jails and prisons poses a health risk not only to inmates but also to the staff and even to the general population. To date, neither the nation's jail and prison systems nor its health systems have responded to this threat as effectively as they have to AIDS/HIV and hepatitis. Air circulation and cleaning systems are becoming more sophisticated in newly constructed facilities, but in older jails and prisons, fitting the systems retrospectively is expensive and not a high priority.

HEPATITIS

Another highly contagious disease that threatens the nation's prisoners is hepatitis. There are several forms of this disease: the most serious are hepatitis B and hepatitis C. Both are viral diseases that attack the liver. In most cases, the hepatitis B virus (HBV) is a limited infection. Most victims recover in a matter of months; people with weakened immune systems, however, can become lifelong carriers and may develop cirrhosis (scarring) of the liver, cancer, or liver failure and eventually die. HBV responds well to immunization if diagnosed within two weeks of exposure. The hepatitis C virus (HCV) is far more dangerous: about 80 percent of its victims develop a chronic infection. Both forms of the disease are spread through infected blood, most commonly through sharing needles or sexual contact.

In 2000, nearly 70 percent of all state correctional institutions reported that they had a policy to treat inmates for HCV (Beck and Maruschak 2004). The most common approach was to test those inmates who presented symptoms of the disease, followed by those who requested testing. In the 12 months before the survey was conducted, more than 57,000 inmates were tested in the nation's prison system: 31 percent were positive for HCV. More than 6,000 inmates in state prisons received treatment for HCV over these same 12 months. Currently, estimates of the prevalence of HCV infection in prison inmates place it far higher than that of the general US population. Among prison inmates, between 16 and 41 percent have ever been infected with HCV, and 12 to 35 percent are chronically infected; these latter figures are 10 to 20 times the estimates for the general US population (Center for Disease Control and Prevention 2012).

The 2000 census also revealed that about 70 percent of the nation's prisons provide HBV vaccinations. About one in three prisons with an existing policy in 2002 actually administered the three-dose series. And one in eight prisons had policies to vaccinate all inmates as a preventive measure. About 14,000 state prison inmates completed the series between July 1, 1999, and June 30, 2000.

FEMALE MEDICAL NEEDS

Incarcerated women present gender-specific problems for corrections authorities. Appellate courts have recognized the existence of women's prisons as evidence that women and men have different needs, and that those needs must be accommodated.

MEDICAL SERVICES Few jails or prisons have gynecologists or obstetricians on call, let alone on the facility's staff. The majority of jails do not have even a general practitioner on staff. A female inmate who needs to see a medical specialist or requires a mammogram or some other screening procedure may have to wait months for a referral. In addition to gender-specific medical needs, women also have higher rates of drug abuse when they enter the corrections system. They test positive for HIV at proportions higher than men, and are disproportionately more likely than men to have drug- and mental-health related issues.

PRIVACY This concern is just as real for men who are supervised by women as it is for women who are supervised by men (Zupan 1992). The only difference is in prevalence: the percentage of female COs, especially in jails, is low. The courts have upheld objections to opposite-sex supervision in areas of "protected privacy" (toilets and showers, for example). Many jails simply do not have enough female COs to guarantee both the supervision of inmates and their privacy.

EXPLOITATION AND DEGRADATION BY COs The potential for sexual exploitation of heterosexual female inmates by COs certainly exists. Women are more vulnerable than men in this regard, a fact revealed by their social systems in jails and prisons. Women inmates are looking for protective, nurturing, affective relationships, which typically makes them more susceptible to exploitation. Also, many COs continue to treat female inmates as "errant children" (Pollock-Byrne 1990, 122), which contributes to the already high frustration levels many inmates experience (Fox 1984).

MOTHERHOOD Many jails refuse to allow minor children to visit their mothers; and prisons may severely restrict the number and duration of family visits. A woman who gives birth to a child in prison may lose her child to state authorities or have her parental rights restricted. In nearly every case, the child is taken away from the mother shortly after birth. A few states operate cottages within the prison compound for short- or long-term care of inmate babies, or allow mothers who have recently given birth to reside temporarily in a community-based center (Chapman 1980).

TRAINING, COUNSELING, AND REHABILITATION Since their inception, training and rehabilitation programs at women's prisons have reinforced gender stereotypes.

The only widely available programs are those geared to "traditional" women's work: cosmetology, food preparation and service, sewing, housekeeping, and the like. A few real-world job-training programs do exist in women's prisons, although they tend to offer little variety. Few jails offer their female inmates any job training or vocational education. And other institution-based programs, including drug rehabilitation and general counseling, even in women-only jails, which should be among the best institutions of this type for women, exhibit significant shortcomings.

From 2000 to 2010 the number of women in prison in the United States grew from 93,324 to 112,822. Even though their incarceration rate has grown faster than that of men, their percentage of the total prison population only increased from 6.7 percent to 6.9 percent (Guerino, Harrison, and Sabol 2011). The increase in absolute numbers suggests that worse times for women prisoners and prison administrators may be ahead. Because women inmates are fewer in number, their needs receive less attention and money. If the past is a guide to the future, even if women's numbers should double during the next 20 years, the resources allocated to women inmates' unique needs will not keep pace. Women in jails and prisons are a bereft group, largely forgotten by the public, by policy makers, and even by researchers (Fletcher and Moon 1993, 6–7).

INMATES WITH MENTAL ILLNESS AND MENTAL HEALTH PROBLEMS

Jail and prison inmates with mental illness or other types of mental functioning deficiencies pose a variety of problems for correctional authorities. And, as we will see in the following sections inmates with mental illness are at the center of a host of social problems.

SCOPE OF THE PROBLEM

In approaching this special needs population, two terms will be used in a general sense (as opposed to a strictly technical or clinical sense). First, the term **mental health problem** is a broad designation for a variety of mental functioning issues that includes genetic issues and both drug- and alcohol-induced psychoses. For example, depression, inability to sleep (insomnia), sleeping too much (hypersomnia), and persistent anger or irritability could be considered symptoms of mental health problems (James and Glaze 2006, 2). These types of problems may be treated through individual or group counseling and therapy (Beck and Maruschak 2001).

Second, the term **mental illness** is normally associated with more focused and severe medical conditions such as schizophrenia, bipolar disorder, delusions, or hallucinations (Beck and Maruschak 2001; James and Glaze 2006). Conditions such as these typically require intensive treatment, hospitalization, and psychotropic drug treatment.

Based on these two terms, reports from the Bureau of Justice Statistics show that in 1998 there were 283,000 prison and jail inmates in the United States who were mentally ill. This figure represented 16 percent of the state prison inmates, 7 percent of the federal prison inmates and 16 percent of local jail inmates (Ditton 1999, 1). Furthermore, in 2005 56 percent of the prison and jail inmates in the United States reported having a mental health problem. This included 705,600 state prison inmates along with 78,800 in federal prisons, and 479,900 in local jails (James and Glaze 2006). In comparison to the general population of the United States, prison and jail inmates are more than five times more likely to report some type of mental health disorder (56 percent versus 11 percent). Therefore, whether we use clinical diagnoses or self-report mechanisms, mental health issues are significant concerns in correctional facilities of all types and at all levels in the United States.

It is important to note at this point that mental health problems are not equally distributed in correctional populations in the United States. A few brief demographic elements will illustrate this point. To begin with female inmates report substantially higher levels of mental health problems than do males: 73 percent versus 55 percent in state prisons and 75 percent versus 63 percent in local jails (James and Glaze 2006, 1).

Furthermore, race or ethnicity also must be considered. In state prison inmate populations, 62 percent of white inmates, 55 percent of black inmates, and 46 percent of Hispanic inmates reported having mental health problems. For jail inmates the numbers were 71 percent for whites, 63 percent for blacks, and 51 percent for Hispanics (James and Glaze 2006, 4).

Finally, age is also an issue when dealing with mental health problems in corrections. Inmates aged less than 24 tend to report the highest rates of mental health problems. By contrast, those over the age of 55 reported the fewest problems. This may be a reflection of the populations we are most likely to incarcerate, or may be an indication of issues related to institutional adjustment: the youngest inmates struggle to adjust to prison and jail life and the oldest have already acclimated themselves to institutionalization.

ASSOCIATED ISSUES

Research by the Bureau of Justice Statistics also demonstrates that inmates with mental health problems also exhibit other social maladies. First, many of these inmates have drug and alcohol dependency problems along with (or resulting in) their mental health issues. They are slightly more likely than other inmates to have been under the influence of drugs or alcohol at the time they committed the most recent offense for which they were arrested.

Second, inmates with mental health problems were more than twice as likely as other inmates to have been homeless in the year prior to their most recent arrest (20 percent versus 9 percent). Related to the issue of homelessness, 38 percent of prison inmates and 47 percent of jail inmates who were mentally ill were unemployed at the time of their arrest (Ditton 1999, 5). They also reported having longer criminal histories than inmates who were not mentally ill.

Third, inmates who experienced mental health problems frequently came from families with a history of drug or alcohol abuse, and over one-half had a family member who had been incarcerated (including almost 24 percent who had an incarcerated parent and over 40 percent who had an incarcerated sibling). Related to the issue of family chaos or instability, twice as many state prisoners with mental health issues as those who did not (18 percent

versus 9 percent) had lived in foster homes or institutions as children. In the jail inmate population the difference was more than twice as much, 14 percent versus 6 percent (James and Glaze 2006, 4).

Finally, mentally ill inmates reported a significant amount of physical or sexual abuse prior to incarceration. Male state prison inmates with mental illness were more than twice as likely as other male inmates to report that they had been physically abused growing up (27 percent versus 11 percent). They were almost four times more likely to report sexual abuse (15 percent versus 4 percent). For female state prison inmates the numbers are even more dramatic and astounding: about 68 percent report physical abuse and nearly 59 percent report sexual abuse during their lifetime. The numbers for female inmates in local jails are lower for physical abuse (60 percent) but higher for sexual abuse (almost 64 percent).

Taken together these problems paint a picture of individuals who live disorderly and troubled lives. They have relatively few social supports in terms of families and friends and most have ongoing interactions with the criminal justice system. Therefore, any hope they have for treatment frequently must come from correctional institutions.

TREATMENT PROGRAMS AND RESOURCES

In a 2000 survey, 1,394 (95 percent) of the nation's 1,558 public and private prisons reported that they offered inmates some type of mental health services (Beck and Maruschak 2001). The most secure institutions are most likely to offer mental health services, and the services frequently provided were therapy or counseling (84 percent), administration of psychotropic drugs (83 percent), and screening at intake or admission (78 percent). Out of the nearly 1.4 million inmates in state and federal prisons in 2000, 150,900 participated in mental health counseling or therapy programs, 114,400 received psychotropic drugs, and another 18,900 were under 24-hour care (Beck and Maruschak 2001; Guerino, Harrison, and Sabol 2011).

By 2005, almost 97 percent of the public correctional facilities in the United States provided counseling and other specialized programs to treat inmates suffering from mental health problems and related issues. Typically, the types of programs offered were counseling (78 percent of the facilities), drug and alcohol awareness counseling (74 percent), and psychological counseling (58 percent) (Stephan 2008, 6). Once again, these numbers indicate something of the scope of this problem for correctional agencies, and the amount of resources that they must expend to deal with mental health and related issues.

INSTITUTIONAL ADJUSTMENT

One of the primary reasons for focusing on mental health issues in prisons and jails is that inmates with these types of problems can be dangerous to themselves, to other inmates, and to staff members. They also disrupt the smooth operation of any prison or jail. For example, when examining the records of repeat offenders, 53 percent of the mentally ill state prison inmates had at least one sentence for some type of violent offense. This contrasts with 45 percent of the nonmentally ill inmates. Along with their violent criminal histories, mentally ill inmates are more likely to cause disciplinary problems within prisons or jails. In fact, in 1998 36 percent of mentally ill state prisoners reported being involved in a fight compared to 25 percent of other prisoners. As a result, these inmates—who already have longer sentences than the nonmentally ill—may be faced with institutional disciplinary procedures such as administrative segregation and the loss of good time credits. Simply speaking, prisons and jails cause problems for mentally ill inmates, and mentally ill inmates cause problems for prisons and jails. A case is made in Box 8.1 that the same could be said of older inmates, as many of them are vulnerable to exploitation simply due to their age, and their age creates medical management problems for the institution's administrators.

GAY, LESBIAN, BISEXUAL, AND TRANSGENDERED INMATES

As revealed in Chapter 7, prison sexuality can involve either inmate-inmate or inmate-staff relationships.

There is much consensual sexual contact in both types of relationships, although neither is viewed with particular favor by prison and jail administrators.[2] That is, by policy, most residential correctional facilities do not condone and may officially forbid sexual contacts, even of a consensual nature, between inmates. However, unless the sexual contact is of a nonconsensual nature and it comes to the official notice of prison administrators, correctional officers and others who come in daily contact with inmates tend to ignore inmate-inmate sexual relationships. Even when it is reported, unless the act involved coercion or violence, the likely outcome is a minor administrative sanction against both parties, such as the loss of library privileges or removal of one's personal entertainment device. Sexual contacts between inmates and staff are not only frowned upon, but also officially forbidden. Inmate-staff sexual relationships can result in a disciplinary action being taken against the inmate and, in all likelihood, either the suspension or termination of the prison employee.

Within the larger context of sex and institutional corrections, a further inmate group has its own unique challenges. Moreover, the administrators of the jails and prisons in which these particular special needs inmates are housed may face a range of issues related to absent or incomplete policies and problematic staff practices whenever such inmates enter their facility. We refer here to inmates who arrive at intake or "come out" while in prison or jail as gay, lesbian, bisexual, or transgendered persons, collectively designated as **GLBT inmates**. The distinctions presented in Box 8.2 are instrumental to this discussion.

There simply is no reliable estimate of the number of GLBT inmates in the nation's prisons and jails, although researchers have provided some fragmentary insights. For example, a recent national study guardedly estimates that nine million Americans identify as members of the GLBT community (Gates 2012). This figure means that about 3.5 percent of the adult population is gay, lesbian, or bisexual, with about 0.3 percent indicating that they are transgender. Sexton, Jenness, and Sumner (2010) provide the basis for an estimate of transgendered persons in California's prisons. They attempted to interview

GERIATRIC INMATES: THE OLD AND THE INFIRM   BOX 8.1

T he cost of incarcerating an elderly prison population is another age-related problem. Prison gerontologists report that imprisonment, especially extended periods of repeated incarceration, accelerates the aging process. The lack of proactive medical care, poor life habits, inadequate nutrition, and the like translate into years lost. A prisoner who is 50 years old may have the physiology and medical history of a 70-year old.[3]

The mental problems associated with growing old, particularly psychiatric disorders such as hypochondria and depression, are believed to be higher in elderly prisoners than among elderly people living in the community. Providing for the medical, dental, and mental health needs of older offenders may be second only to providing care for AIDS/HIV sufferers in terms of per inmate costs.

Short of new legislation that targets the release of elderly, infirm, and low-threat inmates, we suspect that executive clemency may be the only means for releasing these high-cost prisoners. Also, as penalties become harsher, they are less likely to be employed with or applied in full force to these populations. Irrespective of whether increasing numbers of older inmates enter the system, prisons are "growing" their own elderly populations, as inmates age through their sentences.

SOURCES: ADAMS AND VEDDER 1961; ALSCHULER 1980; GOETTING 1980; GOLDEN, 1984; LYNCH 1988; MCCOY 1984; MEITHE 1987; WALKER 2011.

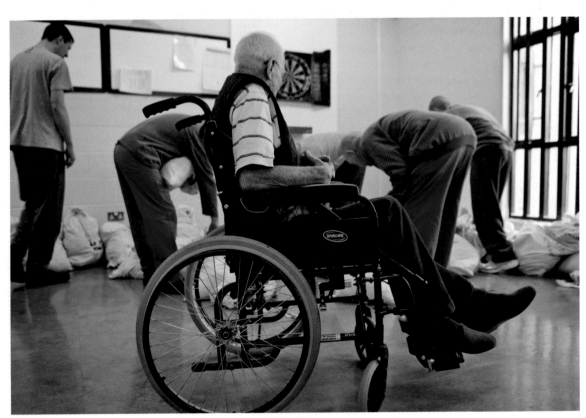

ANDREW AITCHISON/ALAMY IMAGES

GENDER AND SEXUAL ORIENTATIONS: KEY DISTINCTIONS BOX 8.2

Gender identity or gender orientation is a person's self-conception as either male or female that is independent of biological sex. **Sexual orientation** refers to the preferred sexual partner of the individual. In general usage, the following typical designations are instructive:[4]

- Gay: a person with a male gender identity and male anatomy who is sexually attracted to other males.

- Lesbian: a person with a female gender identity and a female anatomy who is sexually attracted to other females.

- Bisexual: person with either a female gender and female anatomy or a male gender and male anatomy who is sexually attracted to both men and women.

- Transgender: a person whose internal gender identity is at odds with his or her physical anatomy. This can be diagnosed as a medical disorder called **Gender Identity Disorder (GID)**, which is defined in the *Diagnostic and Statistical Manual for Mental Disorders (DSM-IV)* as the presence of persistent and strong cross-gender identification for which medical treatment and surgical procedures may be recommended. These individuals may be either "trans-man", a person moving physically from female to male characteristics, or "trans-woman", a person physically moving from male to female characteristics. In terms of sexual orientation, transgendered people can be gay, lesbian, bisexual, or straight relative to their own internal gender identity.

SOURCES: AMERICAN PSYCHIATRIC ASSOCIATION (2007); LEACH (2011).

every transgendered person held in that state's prisons for men. Their final sample of 315 individuals represented an estimated 95 percent of all transgendered persons in those institutions. Extrapolating from this number, we can estimate that 0.2 percent of the population in California prisons for men in 2008 were transgendered individuals, a number that, given the absence of similar estimates for transgendered persons in prisons for women, comports well with national estimates.[5]

What is clearly established under law in the United States is that no one may be discriminated against based on his or her sex, race, color, creed, religion, and nation origin. With regards to gender identity or sexual orientation the case law and codes are less clear.[6] As a matter of policy, prison or jail inmates may not suffer the loss of dignity, human or civil rights, or services simply because they are gay, lesbian, bisexual, or transgendered. However, the establishment of such rights has been, like the

recognition of inmate rights generally, a case-by-case uphill legal battle. Consider, by way of example, the following section of the Federal Bureau of Prisons' *Inmate Information Handbook* (2012, 46) under the section entitled "Your Healthcare Rights and Responsibilities": "You have the right of access to health care services regardless of race, color, creed, sexual preference, or national origin. Health services include medical, mental health, dental and all support services." There is no other mention of sexual preference in the handbook. As will become clear next, case law and policies are still evolving with regards to defining the complete parameters of the rights of the GLBT community.

POLICIES AND PRACTICES

The nation's prisons and jails have been slow to respond to issues created by the presence of GLBT inmates (Edney 2004; Tarzwell 2006; Tewksbury and

Potter 2005). Consider, for example, the following protocols developed for processing transgendered individuals, many of whom are often charged with prostitution and other sex-crimes:

- *Booking name* The arrestee's "adopted name" of self-reference should be included, as well as the birth name, either as a primary or AKA name. If no official identification documents are available, the adopted name should be used, rather than "Jane Doe" or "John Doe."
- *Forms of address* Staff should use the pronoun appropriate for that person's gender self-identity. Should this be unclear, then the staff should ask respectfully the inmate's preference.
- *Strip searches* Unless the instant offense involved a weapon or controlled substance, the inmate should be strip-searched only in the event an officer has reason to believe there is an imminent danger or need for such a procedure. Such searches should be conducted by two officers of the gender requested by the transgender inmate. If no preference is expressed by the inmate, then the search should be conducted by officers of the same gender as the inmate's gender presentation. Failing all else, the search should be conducted by one male and one female officer. (Scheel and Eustace 2002)

Once in-processed, additional challenges emerge for correctional staff, especially those entrusted with classifying and assigning inmates to institutional living arrangements. Three interrelated concerns merit special attention: treatment of transgendered persons who have undergone partial or complete surgical procedures to modify their sexual characteristics, the use of preventive detention, and conjugal visits.

GLBT INMATES AND HOUSING ASSIGNMENTS Traditionally, GLBT individuals, when incarcerated, face a daunting choice. They can request a housing assignment in a protective custody or segregation unit inside the facility on the basis of their sexual orientation or gender identity, which effectively "outs"

them to the administration and inmates (there are few secrets inside prisons and jails), or they take their chances living in the general population. **Protective custody (PC)** is a specialized form of imprisonment intended to segregate, isolate, and insulate an inmate from a particular harm or threat, which is usually noted specifically in the institutional protective custody order. Prisoners may request a transfer to protective custody or it may be ordered by prison administrators, upon the recommendation of correctional officers, classification staff, or other prison/jail staff members. **PC units** within a prison or jail are generally segregated from the facility's general population by secure doors or other physical barriers. They may consist simply of special cells or cell blocks within the larger correctional institution or entire wings of the prison or jail, depending on demonstrated administrative needs.

Housing decisions involving transgendered inmates are either straightforward or complicated (Tarzwell 2006). In most jurisdictions a completely transgendered person, one who finished the process of moving physically from one biological sex to the other through the process of **sexual reassignment surgery (SRS)**, is classified as the re-assigned sex and housed in the appropriate prison facility or unit of a local jail. However, if the individual has not completed the SRS, then he or she will, in all likelihood, be assigned to a correctional facility intended for persons of his or her birth sex. Trans-males and trans-females are, almost without exception, placed directly into protective custody; rarely are they offered the opportunity to move into the general population (*Farmer v. Brennan* 1994; Leach 2011).

Even when a request for protective custody is made, prison officials may not honor it. However, failure to place an inmate who has requested such a housing assignment could create liability issues for the prison or jail. For example, in *Johnson v. Johnson* (2004) the Court ruled on a gay inmate's Fourteenth Amendment claim; the plaintiff, who had been repeatedly raped and sold as a sexual slave for 18 months, asserted that the officials' failure to protect him was motivated by his sexual orientation. The Court affirmed this position, saying: "Neither the Supreme Court nor this court has recognized sexual orientation as a suspect classification [or protected group]; nevertheless, a state violates the Equal Protection Clause if it disadvantages homosexuals for reasons lacking rational relationships to legitimate governmental aims" (*Johnson v. Johnson* 2004, 532). This latter statement is crucial, since it has long been the government's contention, one upheld by successive court decisions, that GLBT inmates may be held in segregated custody exclusively due to sexual preferences, orientation or identity (*Smith v. Walker* 2007). For transsexual prisoners, the US Supreme Court has established the legal standard for liability—deliberate indifference to a known substantial risk of serious harm—in *Farmer v. Brennan* (1994). Simply being gay, lesbian, or bisexual is not a sufficient cause in itself to warrant special protective measures; such measures need to be taken in the case of a transgendered inmate where there is a substantial risk of serious harm. Ultimately, the prison or jail officials may have an overarching and legitimate "penological interest" to segregate homosexual inmates for safety and security reasons (*Veney v. Wyche* 2002).

CONJUGAL VISITS

Inmates do not enjoy a right to conjugal visits (*Lyons v. Gilligan* 1974), although such programs exist in at least six states: California, Connecticut, Mississippi, New Mexico, New York, and Washington (Rogers 2008; Wolfe n.d.). At present, California and New York allow conjugal visits for inmates who are in civil unions or married to someone of the same sex, providing the partner is willing to follow the institutional rules and regulations that govern such visitations (e.g., prior medical examination, background examination, full-body search prior to and after visitation). The Federal Bureau of Prisons does not allow conjugal visitations, and it is not generally viewed as part of the policy of the nation's jails to allow them. It may well be that in the states that allow conjugal visits for heterosexual married and domestic partners, legal challenges could cause them all to allow for such visitations by same-sex partners or they will need to disallow such visits altogether.

ASSOCIATED ISSUES

Over the past 20 years or more, GLBT inmates have asserted their basic human and civil rights, using litigation the same way as other inmates seeking religious rights and reductions in cruel and unusual punishments have. Moreover, inmates and staff interpersonal responses to GLBT inmates create additional barriers to inmate adjustment to the "prison community." GLBT inmates, but especially transgendered inmates, may also have special medical needs that threaten to overwhelm already understaffed prison and jail medical systems. We turn next to a review of each of these associated issues.

GLBT SEXUAL VICTIMIZATIONS

In Chapter 7, we described the nature of sexual activity in prisons and the level of violence, much of which involves sexual assault and related abuse. Both such concerns are not expressly related to an inmate's sexual orientation or gender identity, whether they are the victims or perpetrators. However, GLBT inmates report much higher levels of physical and sexual abuse than do other inmates (Beck and Johnson 2012; Edney 2004). For example, in a 2008 study of released prison inmates, 3.5 percent of heterosexual males reported being sexually victimized by another inmate, while bisexual and homosexual males reported a number that was ten times higher; for females, the inmate-on-inmate sexual victimizations were for heterosexuals 13 percent, bisexuals 13 percent, and lesbians 18 percent, higher than for heterosexual males, but lower than for bisexual and gay males (Beck and Johnson 2012, 5). Transgender male inmates are even more likely to report sexual victimizations while in prison than are gays or bisexual men, with lifetime prevalence peaking at nearly 90 percent (Sexton, Jenness, and Sumner 2009). For correctional staff contacts, the differences are instructive: for males, 5.2 percent of heterosexuals, 17.5 percent of bisexuals, and 11.8 percent of gays indicated staff-on-inmate sexual victimizations; for females, 3.7 percent of heterosexuals, 7.5 percent of bisexuals, and 8 percent of lesbians indicated staff-on-inmate sexual victimizations (Beck and Johnson 2012, 16).

OTHER FORMS OF VICTIMIZATION

GLBT inmates often face more subtle forms of victimization while incarcerated, including the loss of human dignity and respect. They are often publicly ridiculed by inmates and staff alike (Farber 2009; Kunzel 2008). One view often reported as held by correctional officers in particular is that the overt behavior of gay inmates in part brought on or precipitated jailhouse rapes (Eigenberg 1989, 1994, 2000a, 2000b). At least one recent study suggests that the attitudes of staff may be softening. In particular, Cooke and Lane (2012), sampling correctional officers in 13 Florida jails, observed following:

> Overall, officers in this sample had relatively low levels of victim blaming and perceived inmates who report rape as credible, though they tended to perceive some inmates as more blameworthy and less credible, a finding consistent with prior research in both general public and correctional settings.

Housing can also create problems for both the correctional facility and GLBT inmates. For example, gay and transgendered male inmates may be placed in single-occupancy cells, even if they do not ask for or wish such a housing arrangement. This matter was settled in *Veney v. Wyche* (2002). In this case, a Virginia male homosexual inmate was denied a transfer from a single-occupancy cell to a double-occupancy cell. The federal appeals court, upholding the dismissal of the inmate's complaint, noted that, the veracity of the plaintiff's claim aside, his rights had not been violated as no "fundamental rights" were involved and that homosexual males are not a "suspect (or protected) class." Moreover, prison safety and security concerns legitimately drove the officials' decision to assign the inmate to a single-occupancy cell since, according to the Court in *Veney v. Wyche* (2002): (1) housing homosexuals and homosexuals together could increase sexual activity, leading to reductions in prison security; (2) homosexual activities between cellmates could lead to heightened levels of certain communicable diseases, including HIV; (3) housing heterosexuals and homosexuals together could cause friction (but only in the case of males, since it was noted by the court that female heterosexuals are far more tolerant of homosexuality than are heterosexual males); and (4) homosexuals are at greater risk of being sexually attacked in prison than heterosexuals.

SPECIALIZED MEDICAL ISSUES Persons undergoing or who have undergone SRS have, according to case law, "serious medical needs," particularly in terms of the continuation of hormone treatments (*Wolfe v. Horn* 2001; *Kolisek v. Maloney* 2002). For example, a transgendered inmate housed in a facility of the Federal Bureau of Prisons must have had a medical diagnosis of GID and begun hormone replacement treatment prior to assignment to the BOP; otherwise, inmates who later complain of this medical condition are not eligible for transgender-related medical procedures. Those so diagnosed and treated prior to incarceration will only be maintained at the level when they entered the facility (Federal Bureau of Prisons 2005, 43). At present, no legal authority must assist incarcerated individuals in completing SRS (*Los Angeles Times* 2011).[7] However, appellate court decisions in 2011 and 2012, one in Wisconsin and the other in Massachusetts, have paved the way for state-funded SRS, citing Eighth Amendment issues (*Field v. Smith* 2011; *Kolisek v. Spencer* 2012).

In May 2012, the US Department of Justice (2012) announced new rules that respond directly to the vulnerabilities of GLBT prisoners. Key provisions of the policy, which extend beyond BOP facilities and include those administered by the US Department of Homeland Security (DHS), are following: (1) security staff must be trained in how to conduct respectful search of transgender inmates, (2) transgender inmates cannot be assigned to a male or female facility based solely on their anatomy, and (3) transgender inmates must be given the opportunity to shower separately from other inmates. Overall, the new rules are intended to prevent, detect and respond to prison rape, as mandated by the Prison Rape Elimination Act of 2003. It remains to be seen the extent to which this DOJ policy will have an impact on not only the treatment of GLBT inmates in federal facilities, but also extend into state and locally operated prisons and jails.[8]

UNAUTHORIZED IMMIGRANTS AND THE US CORRECTIONAL SYSTEM

Few public policy topics ignite people on all sides of the political spectrum as does the question of foreign nationals and crime in the United States,

JIM WEST/ALAMY IMAGES

especially if the foreign nationals in question are undocumented aliens. Often those who identify themselves as adopting an anti-immigrant stance view the question of citizenship as us-versus-them. As Box 8.3 reveals, the answer to the question "Who is a citizen?" is a complex one.

POLICIES AND PRACTICES

The immigration question is not simply a matter of us-against-them. As was made clear in Box 8.3, just as there are many different forms of us, there is also more than one form of them; however, the ones of most concern to the federal government are **ICE detainees**. Specifically, immigration detainees are defined as persons held for immigration violations in federal, state, and locally operated prisons and jails, as well as in privately operated facilities under exclusive contract and ICE-operated facilities. Persons serving time in a local jail or in state or federal prison for either a criminal or immigration offense may be turned over to ICE after completing their sentence.

Estimates of undocumented immigrants in the United States vary from 7 to 20 million (Knickerbocker 2006). The Center for Immigration Studies[9] maintains that there are 10.8 million *illegal immigrants* (Camarota and Zeigler 2009); the Pugh Hispanic Center[10] claims that there are 11.9 million *unauthorized immigrants* (see Passel and Cohn 2009). DHS's Office of Immigration Studies contends that the number of unauthorized immigrants living in the US in 2010 was 10.8 million, down from a peak of 11.7 million in 2007 (Hoefer, Rytina, and Baker 2011, 1). A reasonable estimate, then, is that there are between 11 and 12 million individuals whose residence in the United States is illegal, unauthorized, or undocumented.[11] Of this number, three-quarters are Hispanic, and six in ten are Mexican nationals (Passel and Cohn 2009, i).

Since the 1990s, the federal government has followed several different policies. The National Strategic Plan, begun in 1994, focused on the areas of highest illegal activities, in an attempt to curb illegal immigration and drug trafficking and included such high profile programs as Operations Hold the Line

CITIZENS, UNDOCUMENTED ALIENS, AND OTHERS: CRITICAL DISTINCTIONS   BOX 8.3

US Citizenship and Immigration Services (CIS) recognizes the six legal statuses. Three of these statuses are generally not problematic for Immigration and Customs Enforcement (ICE), the DHS agency empowered to enforce the Immigration and Nationality Act (INA, Title 8 U.S.C. 1101). First, the "lawfully present" are immigrants or noncitizens that have been inspected and admitted into the United States and have not overstayed the period for which they were admitted, or have current permission from the CIS to stay or live in the United States. Second, "qualified aliens" are lawfully present immigrants defined as one of the following: (1) individuals lawfully admitted for permanent residence (LPRs); (2) individuals who are admitted to the United States as refugees; (3) individuals who have been granted asylum; (4) Cuban/Haitian entrants who were paroled into the United States or given other special status; (5) abused spouses or children, parents of abused children, or children of abused spouses; (6) individuals who have been granted parole into the United States for at least a period of 1 year (or indefinitely) under the INA, including "public interest" parolees; (7) individuals granted withholding of deportation or removal under the INA; (8) individuals who were admitted to the United States as conditional entrants prior to April 1, 1980; and (9) Amerasians who were born to US citizen armed services members in Southeast Asia during the Vietnam War. Third, "nonqualified aliens" are noncitizens who are lawfully present in the United States and who are not included in the definition of qualified aliens and include, but are not limited to: (1) citizens of Marshall Islands, Micronesia or Palau; (2) immigrants paroled into the United States for less than 1 year; (3) immigrants granted temporary protected status; or (4) nonimmigrants who are allowed entry into the United States for a specific purpose usually for a limited time are also nonqualified, including business visitors; students; and tourists.

The sole problem immigration category for ICE is the "undocumented alien." Undocumented aliens are noncitizens without a lawful immigration status as previously defined, and who either (1) entered the United States illegally or (2) were lawfully admitted but whose status expired or was revoked by actions of the CIS.

The final two categories include individuals who are either citizens or nationals, neither of which is of interest to ICE. There are six ways a person can be classified as a "U.S. citizens." First, a person is a citizen if they were born in the United States or its territories (Guam, Puerto Rico, and the US Virgin Islands; also residents of the Northern Mariana Islands who elected to become US citizens). Second, citizenship is extended to American Indians born outside the United States without regard to immigration status or date of entry if they were born in Canada and are 50 percent American Indian blood (but need not belong to a federally recognized tribe); or they are members of a federally recognized Indian tribe or Alaskan Native village or corporation. Third, individuals can become naturalized US citizens. Fourth, individuals born abroad to at least one US citizen parent, depending on conditions at the time of their birth, are citizens. Fifth, individuals who turn 18 years of age on or after February 27, 2001 automatically become US citizens if the following conditions are met while the individual is under age 18: (1) the individual is granted lawful permanent resident (LPR) status; (2) at least one of the individual's parents is a US citizen by birth or naturalization; and (3) the individual resides in the United States in the legal and physical custody of the citizen parent; or was adopted according to the requirements of INA 101 and resides in the United States in the legal and physical custody of the citizen parent. Finally, an individual who turned 18 before February 27, 2001 would have automatically become a citizen if, while the individual was still under 18, he or she became a lawful permanent resident and either of his or her parents naturalized. Such individuals also may be citizens when only one parent naturalized, if the other parent was dead or a US citizen by birth, or if the individual's parents were separated and the naturalized parent had custody.

The final category consists of "U.S. nationals," who are persons who owe permanent allegiance to the United States and may enter and work in the United States without restriction. The following are the only persons classified as US nationals: (1) persons born in American Samoa or Swain's Island after December 24, 1952; and (2) residents of the Northern Mariana Islands who did not elect to become US citizens.

SOURCE: WASHINGTON STATE DEPARTMENT OF HEALTH AND SOCIAL SERVICES (2012).

and Gatekeeper, both of which were viewed as relatively successful in their limited goals. In 2005, in the wake of the 9/11 attacks, two programs were initiated. One, called the National Border Patrol Strategy, was created by Customs and Border Patrol (CBP) and the second was DHS's Secure Border Initiative: the former emphasized prevention through deterrence, while the latter called for an increase in the number of agents, improved detention and removal capacity, and greater reliance on technology. By the mid-2000s, these programs had morphed into a three-point approach to prevent illegal entry into the United States, including the greater use of expedited removal, increase the use of detention prior to removal proceedings, and increase the percentage of apprehended persons with a federal immigration crime (Rosenblum 2012).

There are basically two issues with respect to immigration detainees. First, ICE's Office of Enforcement and Removal Operations (ERO) deals directly with immigrant detainees. According to the ICE (2013), the ERO identifies and apprehends removable aliens, detains these individuals when necessary, and removes illegal aliens from the United States. The ERO prioritizes the apprehension, arrest, and removal of convicted criminals, those who pose a threat to national security, fugitives, and recent border entrants. Individuals seeking asylum also work with ERO. Second, once detainees who are accused of an immigration crime have been convicted, then they are transferred from ERO custody through the US Marshals Service to the Federal Bureau of Prisons, where they serve their sentence or, in some

cases, are exchanged with their nation of origin for a US citizen-inmate.

We have reasonably good information about the number of individuals who are, in a given year, ICE detainees and immigration-law violators in federal custody. Apprehensions refer to instances where foreign nationals are caught inside the United States illegally, while the US Department of Justice uses the term arrest to indicate that an individual has been booked by US Marshals for violating federal immigration law.[12] For example, immigration detentions peaked in 2000 at 1.8 million, declining to slightly more than 500,000 in 2010, their lowest level since 1972 (see Table 8.2). By contrast, arrests increased from 25,500 in 2000 to a record high of nearly 85,000 in 2009, before declining slightly in 2010 to 82,438. The pattern in the first decade of the twenty-first century, then, was for arrests to increase over threefold, while detentions experienced a similar decline. These figures are important since the volume of detentions and arrests determines the number of potential detainees and foreign nationals imprisoned for immigration law violations and other crimes. Most detentions (87 percent) and arrests (92 percent) occurred along the US–Mexico border. According to the information contained in Figure 8.2, even on the southwestern border, some sectors are busier than others, as about half of the apprehensions and about one-fourth of the arrests occurred in the Tucson Sector.[13]

The first group consists of apprehensions where the offender is not further processed for federal felony prosecution. ICE detainees can be subsequently

TABLE 8.2 **Deportable aliens located[a]: fiscal years 1925 to 2010.**

Year	Number	Year	Number
1925	22,199	1968	212,057
1926	12,735	1969	283,557
1927	16,393	1970	345,353
1928	23,566	1971	420,126
1929	32,711	1972	505,949
1930	20,880	1973	655,968
1931	22,276	1974	788,145
1932	22,735	1975	766,600
1933	20,949	1976[b]	1,097,739
1934	10,319	1977	1,042,215
1935	11,016	1978	1,057,977
1936	11,728	1979	1,076,418
1937	13,054	1980	910,361
1938	12,851	1981	975,780
1939	12,037	1982	970,246
1940	10,492	1983	1,251,357
1941	11,294	1984	1,246,981
1942	11,784	1985	1,348,749
1943	11,175	1986	1,767,400
1944	31,174	1987	1,190,488
1945	69,164	1988	1,008,145
1946	99,591	1989	954,243
1947	193,657	1990	1,169,939
1948	192,779	1991	1,197,875
1949	288,253	1992	1,258,481
1950	468,339	1993	1,327,261
1951	509,040	1994	1,094,719
1952	543,535	1995	1,394,554
1953	885,587	1996	1,649,986
1954	1,089,583	1997	1,536,520
1955	254,096	1998	1,679,439
1956	87,696	1999	1,714,035
1957	59,918	2000	1,814,729
1958	53,474	2001	1,387,486
1959	45,336	2002	1,062,270
1960	70,684	2003	1,046,422
1961	88,823	2004	1,264,232
1962	92,758	2005	1,291,142

Year	Number	Year	Number
1963	88,712	2006	1,206,457
1964	86,597	2007	960,756
1965	110,371	2008	791,568
1966	138,520	2009	613,003
1967	161,608	2010	516,992

NOTES: ªDEPORTABLE ALIENS LOCATED REFER TO BORDER PATROL APPREHENSIONS AND ICE ADMINISTRATIVE ARRESTS. PRIOR TO 1952, DATA REFER TO BORDER PATROL APPREHENSIONS; ᵇINCLUDES THE 15 MONTHS FROM JULY 1, 1975 TO SEPTEMBER 30, 1976 BECAUSE THE END OF DATE OF FISCAL YEARS WAS CHANGED FROM JUNE 30 TO SEPTEMBER 30. SOURCE: US DEPARTMENT OF HOMELAND SECURITY (2011A).

FIGURE 8.2 Apprehensions by Border Patrol sector and criminal immigration suspects arrested in US district courts on the Southwest border, 2010. *Source:* Motivans (2012, 8).

NOTES: A **deportable person** is an alien in and admitted to the United States subject to any grounds of removal specified in the Immigration and Nationality Act. This includes any alien illegally in the United States, regardless of whether the alien entered the country by fraud or misrepresentation or entered legally but subsequently lost legal status. Tucson District Court has 21,275 arrests.

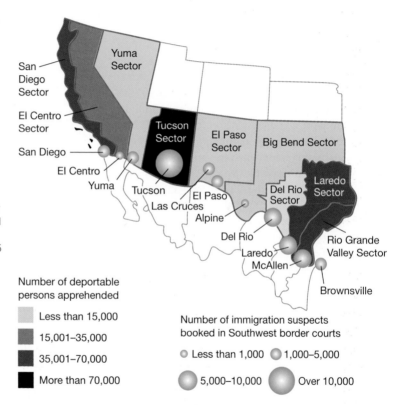

charged with a federal misdemeanor—entry without inspection—and their cases quickly resolved by the actions of a federal magistrate. This path is followed by most first time illegal entrants, particularly those eligible for expedited removal.[14] The median period of detention—most detainees remain in custody and not given bail—is a matter of days. Given the large volume of detainees versus arrestees, it is not surprising that ICE's 350-plus public and private sector detention facilities, with a maximum holding capacity of slightly more than 33,000 individuals, processed a total of 363,000 immigrants in 2010 (ACLU 2012; US Department of Homeland Security 2011b).

Arrestees account for a second cluster of unconvicted detainees. Nine out of ten alleged immigration violators prosecuted in US district courts are charged with illegal reentry or other aggravated immigration offenses. The median time for a felony prosecution from filing, which generally takes place within two weeks of arrest, to disposition was about nine months in 2010. Given a perceived flight risk, nearly all defendants tried for an immigration felony in US district court were detained, in this case under the authority of the US Marshals Service, usually in a BOP-operated federal detention facility. Nearly all defendants plead guilty in court; eight out of ten convicted defendants received a prison sentence. The median felony sentence was 15 months in 2010, down from 24 months in 2002; the median misdemeanor sentence was 4 months in 2010, compared to 3 months in 2002.

The second group of detainees consists of those individuals convicted of a federal felony and admitted to the Federal Bureau of Prisons. In 2010, this was 29 percent of all BOP admissions, up from 19 percent in 2000, a clear result from changing federal immigration-law enforcement policy. Roughly eight out of ten immigration offenders in federal prison were Mexican nationals. Nearly all (97 percent) were male. In 2010, among the 22,230 non-US citizens in federal prison, nearly half (47 percent) stood convicted of drug-related offenses, followed closely by an immigration offenses (43 percent); other offenses accounted for the remainder.

ASSOCIATED ISSUES

The detention of unauthorized immigrants, including deportable aliens, is associated with a number of additional issues. The economic and social costs of immigrant detention are of concern, especially given the hidden nature of both sets of costs. That is, the detention facilities themselves tend to be located in rural or small-town America; moreover, most unauthorized immigrants lack legal representation and few individuals speak on their behalf. A second issue is the privatization of immigrant detention, meaning there is a constituency of companies across the nation that have a vested interest in seeing the current policy of detention continue. Finally, a small group of unauthorized immigrants quite literally have become the embodiment of Philip Noland, the

protagonist in Edward Everett Hale's (1863) short story, "The Man without a Country."

THE COSTS OF DETAINING UNAUTHORIZED IMMIGRANTS

Calculating the costs of detaining unauthorized immigrants, particularly those detained by ICE's ERO, is straightforward. The ACLU (2012) provides the following estimates: Per diem costs range from $122 to $166 for each detainee or from $44,500 to $60,590 each year. On any given night, DHS spends an average of $5.5 million on detention. In the fiscal year 2012, the Obama administration requested a record-breaking $2 billion for immigrant detention.

The social costs of detention are more difficult to calculate. As noted in the UNODC (2009) report on immigrant detention worldwide (see Box 8.4), detainees often lack contact with families and friends, do not enjoy a right to legal representation (particularly those accused solely of unlawful entry without inspection), and lack basic shelter, food, and health care, all of which are true of detention facilities in the United States. Many ERO detention facilities are little more than tent cities, intended as temporary housing. Often women and children are housed under such conditions, leading to possible intergenerational psychological and social problems that have yet to be studied. In short, in no other situation in US corrections—short of the internment of Japanese-Americans during World War II—have families been incarcerated in this manner.

DETAINING UNAUTHORIZED IMMIGRANTS AND DEPORTABLE ALIENS FOR PROFIT

Corporate America has long viewed prisons as a profit zone (Chang and Thompkins 2002). Since 2005 and the evolution of the ICE policy that emphasizes detention and quick removal, ERO resources have become strained—ICE has only eight facilities of its own—to the point where private corporations and other government entities have been seconded into the detainment business (Wilder 2007). The privatization of detention for unauthorized and deportable aliens—there are seven contract detention facilities utilized by ICE—is problematic since the oversight of human rights violations at such facilities is difficult without

SPOTLIGHT ON INTERNATIONAL CORRECTIONS: IMMIGRATION DETAINEES AROUND THE WORLD

BOX 8.4

According to international law, persons detained solely on the basis of their irregular immigration status, what ICE calls immigration detainees, should not be held with prisoners who have committed criminal offenses. According to the UNODC, an irregular immigration status on its own should not be used as the basis for detention, "unless there are well-founded reasons for safety and security that justify such detention" (p. 78). In short, detention should be the action of last resort, either as a pretrial measure or as a penal sanction for an unauthorized immigrant, and should physical detention be necessary, such individuals should be kept apart from "common" criminals.

The UNODC also observes that worldwide foreign nationals who fall into the category of immigrant detainees are often at a disadvantage when they interact with the detaining nation's criminal justice system. This observation is in part due to increasingly punitive measures leveled against foreign national offenders in many Member nations, race- and cultural-based discrimination, limited awareness of legal rights and legal access within the detaining nation, the absence of social networks, and economic marginalization. Rather than detain and incarcerate, the UNODC recommends that Member nations develop alternative "non-custodial measures and sanctions and sentencing measures to avoid discrimination in their consideration of alternatives to prison" (p. 80). However, the majority of nations worldwide have no policies designed to avoid discrimination and related harmful consequences that immigration detainees often suffer. For example, in many Asian and Gulf States persons who are trafficked or migrant workers in abusive situations often find themselves incarcerated. In Europe, foreign suspects are far more likely to be convicted and sentenced to prison, than a "domestic" suspect.

The problems of immigrant detainees continue during incarceration, as worldwide they face linguistic challenges, cultural and religious conflicts and discrimination, an absence of social support networks, ineligibility for institution-based treatment, education, training and related programming, and post-incarceration liabilities, such as deportation or continued indefinite imprisonment, even for long-term unlawful residents (see Associated Issues below). Incarceration creates unique challenges for nearly all inmates. For those individuals whose only "crime" is being an unauthorized immigrant, either seeking a better life or possibly fleeing human traffickers and getting caught in the net of immigration officials, the stigma of being a detainee can be difficult to understand or overcome, even upon release. Becoming an immigrant detainee can also mean being incarcerated alongside violent criminals in marginal living conditions. Often they are assaulted, coerced, or intimidated by other inmates, who see immigrant detainees as vulnerable and without advocates inside or outside the prison, adding another layer of victimization to the detainee's criminal justice experience.

SOURCES: UNODC (2009); WACQUANT (2006).

direct government involvement. Moreover, local jails and state prisons, where detained immigrants have even less access to health and welfare resources, are increasingly used by ICE's ERO to house detainees at considerable cost (and profit). ICE has contractual agreements with state and local governments for more than 350 facilities that collectively house over 50 percent of the detainee population (US Department of Homeland Security 2009, 5). For example, in 2008 and 2009, 13 California jails received over $100 million to house ICE immigration detainees (Gorman 2009). What is important to recognize is that the vast majority of immigration detainees are under civil detention orders, not criminal detention orders issued prior to or as a result of a court appearance in a US district court (Gorman 2009). For all intents and purposes, the current ICE policy on immigration has created an environment that produces offenders for profit (Feltz 2007).

LIFE IN PRISON WITHOUT TRIAL
Most people believe that Hale's story of a man who is stripped of his citizenship and must wander the world onboard a naval vessel is entirely a work of fiction. In fact, a number of figures throughout history have been stripped of their citizenship for various reasons, and as a result, possessing no national documentation, are stateless people. US immigration law allows for the indefinite imprisonment of persons found deportable from or inadmissible to the United States. Such people would receive practically no constitutional rights, including bail prior to any hearing and no Fourth or Sixth Amendment rights during the hearing; moreover, the Ex Post Facto clause would not shield the accused of new liability for past deeds (Capitaine 2001, 769–70). If the accused is found to be illegally in the United States or a deportable person, the latter generally a situation in which a legal resident has been convicted of a felony, the judge would have no option but to order deportation. At this point, the waters become muddy. If the accused is the citizen of a nation which no longer exists or that will not allow that person to repatriate,

then such individuals are held indefinitely at the pleasure of the Attorney General, resulting in detainment in one of the 350-plus ICE facilities around the nation. In 2001, some 3,600 individuals fell into this state of legal limbo, unwanted by the United States and unable to repatriate to their nations of legal residence (Capitaine 2001, 772). By 2005, the most recent statistics available, there were about 1,200 individuals detained indefinitely but under deportation orders (Detention Watch Network 2006). However, the Supreme Court ruled in *Zadvydas v. Davis* (2001) and *Clark v. Martinez* (2005) that indefinite, potentially permanent civil detention is unconstitutional since the Due Process clause applies to all persons within the United States, irrespective of their legal status.

Since 2001, several bills (HR 4437 and HR 1932) have been proposed by Congress to legitimize indefinite detentions for illegal immigrants. The most recent such bill, the "Keep Our Communities Safe Act of 2011" (HR 1932) did not make it out of committee. Tan's (2011) analysis of this bill is particularly critical, as he notes the following about such legal maneuvers:

> In a time of fiscal crisis, it is incumbent on policy-makers to take a hard look at what the government's growing expenditures on immigration detention have actually bought. Prolonged and indefinite immigration detention is costly, wasteful, and contrary to our constitutional values. Rather than expand our detention system based on the myth of the ubiquitous "criminal alien," Congress and the Obama administration should be limiting detention mandates and making more effective use of the government's limited law enforcement resources. (Tan 2011, 9)

Nevertheless, under the section 412 of the *USA Patriot Act* suspected terrorists may be detained indefinitely.[15] In Box 8.5 we look briefly at terrorists and their fate around the world, suggesting that in the minds of many, these are the world's most special inmates.

THE MOST SPECIAL INMATES: TERRORISTS AND THEIR IMPRISONMENT   BOX 8.5

Once individuals suspected of committing terrorist acts are detained, the wheels of justice begin to grind, in some cases very slowly. After a determination of guilt has been made, determining the appropriate sanctions for persons is difficult involving the determination of a balance between the community's need to be safe and secure and the best interests of the convicted persons, all within the letter and spirit of penal law and constitutional protections. Progressing from arrest to punishment, then, involves many detention decisions that create unique social, legal, economic, and political problems for the government overseeing the process. Thus, nations around the world wrestle with how to treat such individuals and keep to international and national standards of human and civil rights. Indeed, it could be argued that terrorists are the most special inmates incarcerated by any nation. Several examples are instructive in this regard.

The British have a long history of attempting to contain terrorists, responding to a series of bombings and assassinations during the 1970s. Currently, the British house terrorist suspects at Her Majesty's Prison Belmarsh, a category A (highest security classification) prison, located outside London. Within Belmarsh, there is a second prison, one dedicated to housing Great Britain's most dangerous terrorist suspects and convicted offenders. In the early twenty-first century it was known as Britain's version of Guantanamo Bay, as 11 individuals were held at Belmarsh and several related facilities indefinitely without charges or trials under their version of the USA Patriot Act. The law lords, who at the time were Great Britain's highest court, ruled against such imprisonment as breaching human rights (Human Rights Watch).

Since the 9/11 attacks the United States has aggressively sought the capture, detainment, trial, and punishment of terrorists, most of whom have some links to the international terrorist group al-Qaida (Shane). Guantanamo Bay, Cuba, enjoys a high profile in this regard, especially as there are currently over 170 inmates held there, many detained without trial for upwards of a decade or more. However, the BOP reports that it houses 362 people convicted of terrorism-related cases, nearly 90 percent of whom are held in connection with acts of international terrorism.

Finally, it is interesting to note given arguments about indefinite detentions of terrorists as essential for national security that 600 former Gitmo prisoners have been released since 2001, including 200 who have served their sentences and been freed from prison. The Director of National Intelligence reports that only 16 percent have subsequently engaged in terrorist acts (Grandoni).

SOURCES: GRANDONI (2012); HUMAN RIGHTS WATCH (2004); SHANE (2011).

SUMMARY

This chapter addressed a highly charged topic: special needs inmates. Without doubt, many readers will query what all the fuss is about, or they will suggest that such inmates deserve what they get. The point of this chapter is to articulate the position that a humane society owes all of its citizens, including those who by their actions have had their freedom curtailed, basic services, no matter how the extent to which their actions or personal characteristics may offend some members of the public. Key points of interest to consider are the following:

- Children, adolescents, and young adults are held in prisons and jails, in spite of federal legislation to the contrary. Moreover, the children of unauthorized immigrants are detained, often for long periods of time, largely because their fate is determined by civil and not criminal court actions, meaning their detention is not a punishment, at least in legal theory.

- Prisons and jails are ill-equipped to provide adequate medical treatment for inmates who either enter these institutions with an illness or develop a medical issue while incarcerated. Indeed, for some highly contagious diseases, including hepatitis and multiple drug-resistant tuberculosis, the design of prisons and jails creates a breeding ground for pandemics.

- Women's needs are rarely met inside most prisons and jails, even those designed specifically for them.

- Inmates suffering from mental diseases or disorders often find themselves ignored by the nation's jails and prisons, abused by other inmates, and returned to society in worse condition than when they were first incarcerated.

- The medical, legal, and physical needs of GLBT inmates have long been ignored; moreover, they suffer high victimization levels at the hands of other inmates and correctional staff.

- The detention of unauthorized immigrants borders on a national disgrace, especially when considering the fate of families and children who are detained, the use of indefinite detention, and related legal issues. Tens of thousands of men, women and children are detained in living conditions that would be unacceptable for convicted criminals.

- Few of these groups of special needs inmates enjoy the same legal protections as the majority of prison or jail inmates, and most face high levels of physical and emotional abuse.

KEY TERMS

AIDS
Citizenship and Immigration
    Service (CIS)
conjugal visits
deportable person
gender identity
Gender Identity Disorder
    (GID)
gender orientation

GLBT inmates
hepatitis C virus
HIV-positive
ICE detainees
Immigration and Customs
    Enforcement (ICE)
juvenile detention centers
mental health problem
mental illness

multiple drug-resistant
    tuberculosis (MDR-TB)
PC-units
protective custody (PC)
sexual orientation
sexual reassignment surgery
    (SRS)
sight-and-sound separation
special needs

THINKING ABOUT CORRECTIONAL POLICIES AND PRACTICES: WRITING ASSIGNMENTS

1 This chapter has discussed a number of types of special needs inmates. Write a one-page essay in which you prioritize these categories from those with the most critical needs to those with the least critical needs. Provide a brief justification for your ranking.

2 Conduct an Internet search for the term "special needs inmates." How many sources do you find for this term? What are some of the sources that might be useful in preparing a term paper?

3 Many critics of the US correctional system look at the incarceration of mentally ill inmates, including those who were diagnosed prior to imprisonment and those who developed symptoms during incarceration, as a grievous failing of our entire justice system. Create a chart with two columns. In the left column, indicate the rationale, both practical and moral, for releasing such inmates into the care of a free-society facility for their treatment. In the right column, indicate the same kinds of reasons that support the continued incarceration of the mentally ill.

4 Women in prison face gender-specific problems. If you were the assistant director of your state department of corrections and had been given the task of developing a policy statement prioritizing the needs of female inmates in state prisons, where would you start? Are there reliable sources for this assignment? Explain.

5 A jail near you experiences an outbreak of MDR-TB. Of the entire jail population 40 percent and 20 percent of the staff test positive for tuberculosis. How would your local community respond to this situation? What should the jail authorities have done to prevent this outbreak?

CRITICAL REVIEW QUESTIONS

1 Create a summary list of special needs inmates. Which ones would create similar problems for the justice system if they had not been sentenced to prison, but instead were released on probation? Would the problems, in your estimation be larger or smaller? Explain your answer.

2 Review the problem of incarcerating young people. At what age do you think young persons should be held fully accountable for their crimes and subject to a prison term? Explain how you reached this conclusion.

3 Inmates with medical needs have long been ignored by jails and, to a lesser extent, by prisons. Review the issues associated with such needs and conduct an Internet search for case law that describes the state's responsibility to provide basic medical services. What is the trend in correctional law with respect to medical needs?

4 Women represent a unique prison and jail population. List each of the special needs associated with incarcerating women. Rank them from the most pressing downward, and explain how you reach this ranking.

5 Which infectious disease, HIV/AIDS or TB, seems to pose the greatest problem for the nation's prisons and jails? Look for Bureau of Justice Statistics publications to support your answer.

6 Why is it essential for a jail or prison to develop, implement or review housing policies for GLBT inmates? List all of the reasons, including your rationale for their inclusion.

7 Case law on state-paid SRS for incarcerated felons is one of the most controversial medical concerns facing the nation's prisons and state coffers. What are the issues? What is the current status of this controversial topic?

8 Who is a citizen? This is a hot issue in US politics and criminal justice practice. Provide an overview of the issues and the nation's response to it. What do you think lies ahead for the corrections field in this regard? Explain your thinking.

9 Since September 11, 2001, several federal agencies have turned their attention to the War on Terrorism, including the Bureau of Immigration and Customs Enforcement. How has the War on Terror affected the treatment of undocumented aliens in this country?

10 After reviewing the content of this chapter, do you think terrorists are the most special inmates? Explain your thinking in answering this question. What about terrorists as a worldwide correctional issue?

CASES CITED

Clark v. Martinez, 125 S.Ct. 716 (2005).

Farmer v. Brennan, 511 US 825 (1994).

Field v. Smith 653 F.3d 550 (7th Cir., 2011).

Johnson v. Johnson, F.3d. 503, 512 (5th Cir., 2004).

Kolisek v. Maloney, 221 F.Supp.2d 156 (D.Mass., 2002).

Kolisek v. Spencer, No. 00-12455 (District Court, District of Massachusetts September 4, 2012).

Lyons v. Gilligan, 382 F.Supp. (Dist. Court, ND Ohio, 1974).

Smith v. Walker, U.S. Distr. LEXIS 94773 (C.D. Ill. December 28, 2007).

Lyralisa Stevens versus California, No. 11-10372 (9th Cir., California, 2012).

Veney v. Wyche, No. 01-6603, 293 F.3d 726 (4th Cir., 2002).

Wolfe v. Horn, 130 F.Supp.2d 648 (E.D.Pa., 2001).

Zadvydas v. Davis, 533 U.S. 678 (2001).

NOTES

1 Persons under sentence of death are included in the UNODC report; however, we have included discussions of the death penalty at other places in this textbook and will not review them here. You may wish to ask your instructor to elaborate on the issues related to long-term residence on death row.

2 Human Rights Watch (2001) observes that much alleged consensual sex in prisons is in fact sexual slavery, where the rape victims are intimidated into pretending that the sexual activity is consensual. Such victims become, in essence, the literal property of their rapists. There are no extant studies that tell us how much of the so-called consensual sex in prisons actually is a form of slavery. For their part, most prison wardens support the position that both violent and consensual prison sexual activities in their respective prisons occur at far lower levels than is reported in popular and scientific outlets (Hensley and Tewksbury 2004).

3 Some prison systems classify prisoners as elderly at age 40; others use age 60 as the benchmark category for elderly inmates; still others use a different definition altogether. One study that made use of the 40-and-above category claims that about 16 percent of the nation's prisoners were elderly in 1991; in reality, only 1 percent were aged 60 or older (J. Lynch et al. 1994).

4 Besides the "traditional" designations of GLBT, some scholars recognize a fifth category, *questioning*, which refers to individuals experimenting with their sexual and gender identities. Finally, a rarely encountered category is the *inter-sex individual*, a person who has the sexual characteristics of both sexes. These characteristics can be internal, external or both, but the male or female organs are almost never complete.

5 In 2008, California prisons for men housed a total of 162,050 inmates (Sabol, West, and Cooper 2009, 20).

6 State laws vary widely with respect to discrimination based on gender identity or gender expression. Hate crimes based on sexual orientation or gender identity are punishable by federal law and also covered by many state statutes. Inmates have been convicted

of violations of federal law for alleged hate crimes against GLBT inmates.

7 The most recent case, *Lyralisa Stevens v. California*, is currently under a writ of certiorari for appeal to a higher court.

8 Included in the new set of rules is the following provision: "A State whose Governor does not certify full compliance with the standards is subject to the loss of five percent of any Department of Justice grant funds that it would otherwise receive for prison purposes, unless the Governor submits an assurance that such five percent will be used only for the purpose of enabling the State to achieve and certify full compliance with the standards in future years" (42 U.S.C. 15607(c)). The final rule specifies that the Governor's certification applies to all facilities in the State under the operational control of the State's executive branch, including facilities operated by private entities on behalf of the State's executive branch (US Department of Justice 2012, 2).

9 The Center for Immigration Studies (CIS) is a nonpartisan, nonprofit making research organization that advocates immigration reduction in the United States. It maintains a website at **www.cis.org/**

10 The Pew Hispanic Center is a nonpartisan research organization that seeks to improve understanding of the US Hispanic population and to chronicle Latinos' growing impact on the nation. The Center does not take positions on policy issues. It maintains a website at **www.pewhispanic.org/**

11 "Unauthorized immigrants" are all foreign-born noncitizens residing in the country who are not "legal immigrants." These definitions reflect standard and customary usage DHS and academic researchers. Careful readers will note that that different entities use slight variations on these terms, including the US State Department, which refers to unauthorized immigrants as "undocumented aliens." Language is everything.

12 Unless otherwise noted, the following material is taken from Motivans (2012).

13 Sector refers to any one of 21 geographic areas into which the United States is divided for the Department of Homeland Security's Border Patrol activities. The nine sectors (El Centro (CA), San Diego (CA), Yuma (AZ), Tucson (AZ), El Paso (TX), Big Bend (TX), Del Rio (TX), Laredo (TX), and Rio Grande Valley (TX)) that cover the Mexican–US border are the busiest in the nation, accounting for over 90 percent of the immigration arrests.

14 Under the Illegal Immigration Reform and Immigrant Responsibility Act of 1996, the DHS is authorized to remove certain inadmissible aliens from the United States in an expedited fashion. This Act covers aliens who are inadmissible because they have no entry documents or because they have used counterfeit, altered, or otherwise fraudulent or improper documents. The aliens may arrive in, attempt to enter, or may have entered the United States without having been admitted or paroled by an immigration officer at a port-of-entry. Under this Act, the DHS has the authority to order their removal, and the aliens are not referred to an immigration judge except under certain circumstances. Specifically, they may make a claim to lawful status in the United States or demonstrate a credible fear of persecution if returned to their home country.

15 Section 412 has the following limitation on definite detention: "An alien detained solely under paragraph (1) who has not been removed under section 241(a) (1)(A), and whose removal is unlikely in the reasonably foreseeable future, may be detained for additional periods of up to six months only if the release of the alien will threaten the national security of the United States or the safety of the community or any person."

The US government has overcome this limitation for hundreds of terrorist suspects.

REFERENCES

Adams, Mark E., and Clyde B. Vedder. 1961. Age and crime: Medical and sociologic characteristics of prisoners over 50. *Geriatrics* 18: 177–81.

Alschuler, A. W. 1980. Sentencing reform and parole release guidelines. *University of Denver Law Review* 51: 237–45.

American Civil Liberties Union. 2012. *Immigrant rights: Immigration detention.* Retrieved July 16, 2013 from: **http://www.aclu.org/immigrants-rights/detention**

American Psychiatric Association. 2007. *Diagnostic and statistical manual of mental disorders*, 4th edn. Washington, DC: American Psychiatric Association.

Retrieved July 16, 2013 from: www.psychiatryonline.com

Beck, Allen J., and Candace Johnson. 2012. *Sexual victimization reported by former state prisoners, 2008.* Washington, DC: US Department of Justice.

Beck, Allen J., and Laura M. Maruschak. 2001. *Mental health treatment in state prisons, 2000.* Washington, DC: Bureau of Justice Statistics, US Department of Justice.

Beck, Allen J., and Laura M. Maruschak. 2004. *Hepatitis testing and treatment in state prisons.* Washington, DC: US Department of Justice.

Bryan, Angela, Reuben N. Robbins, Monica S. Ruiz, and Dennis O'Neill. 2006. Effectiveness of an HIV prevention program in prison among African Americans and Caucasians. *Health Education & Behavior* 33: 154–77.

Camarota, Steven A., and Karen Zeigler. 2009. *A shifting tide: Recent trends in the illegal immigrant population.* Washington, DC: Center for Immigration Studies.

Capitaine, Victoria Cook. 2001. Life in prison without trial: The indefinite detention of immigrants in the United States. *Texas Law Review* 79: 769–89.

Center for Disease Control and Prevention. 2012. *Correctional facilities and viral hepatitis.* Retrieved July 16, 2013 from: http://www.cdc.gov/hepatitis/Settings/corrections.htm

Chang, Tracey F. H., and Douglas E. Thompkins. 2002. Corporations go to prison: The expansion of corporate power into the correctional industry. *Labor Studies Journal* 27(1): 45–69.

Chapman, Jane Roberts. 1980. *Economic realities and the female offender.* Lexington, MA: Heath.

Cook, Carrie L., and Jodi Lane. 2012. Examining differences in attitudes about sexual victimization among a sample of jail officers: The importance of officer gender and perceived inmate characteristics. *Criminal Justice Review* 37(2): 191–213.

Detention Watch Network. 2006. Indefinite detention fact sheet. Retrieved July 16, 2013 from: http://www.detentionwatchnetwork.org/node/302

Ditton, Paula M. 1999. *Mental health and treatment of inmates and probationers.* Washington, DC: Bureau of Justice Statistics, US Department of Justice.

Douglas, Richard L. 1995. *Domestic mistreatment of the elderly: Towards prevention.* Washington, DC: American Association of Retired Persons.

Edney, Richard. 2004. To keep me safe from harm? Transgender prisoners and the experience of imprisonment. *Deakin Law Review* 9: 327–38.

Eigenberg, Helen M. 1989. Male rape: An empirical examination of correctional officers' attitudes toward rape in prison. *The Prison Journal* 68: 39–56.

Eigenberg, Helen M. 1994. Rape in male prisons: Examining the relationship between correctional officers' attitudes toward male rape & their willingness to respond to acts of rape. In *Prison violence*, 2nd edn., edited by M. Braswell, R. Montgomery, and L. Lombardo. New York: Anderson, 145–65.

Eigenberg, Helen M. 2000a. Correctional officers and their perceptions of homosexuality, rape, and prostitution in male prisons. *The Prison Journal* 80: 415–33.

Eigenberg, Helen M. 2000b. Correctional officers' definitions of rape in male prisons. *Journal of Criminal Justice* 28: 435–49.

Farber, Bernard J. (ed.) 2009. Homosexual and bisexual prisoners. *AELE Monthly Law Journal* 6: 301–10.

Federal Bureau of Prisons. 2005. *Program statement: Subject: Patient care*, P6031.01. Washington, DC: US Department of Justice.

Federal Bureau of Prisons. 2012. *Inmate information handbook.* Retrieved July 23, 2013 from: http://www.bop.gov/locations/institutions/big/BIG_aohandbook.pdf

Feltz, Renee. 2008. A new immigration policy: Producing felons for profit. *NACLA Report on the Americas. Report: Detention.* November/December. New York: North American Congress on Latin America.

Fletcher, Beverly R., and Dreama G. Moon. 1993. In *Women prisoners: A forgotten population*, edited by B. R. Fletcher, L. D. Shaver, and D. G. Moon. Westport, CT: Praeger, 5–13.

Fox, James. 1984. Women's prison policy, prisoner activism, and the impact of the contemporary feminist movement: A case study. *Prison Journal* 64: 15–36.

Gates, Gary J. 2012. LGBT identity: A demographer's perspective. *Loyola Law Review* 45: 693–714.

Glaze, Lauren E. 2011. *Correctional population in the United States, 2010.* Washington, DC: Bureau of Justice Statistics, US Department of Justice.

Golden, Delores. 1984. Elderly offenders in jail. In *Elderly criminals*, edited by Evelyn S. Newman, Donald J. Newman, Mindy L. Gewirtz, and associates. Cambridge, MA: Oelgeschlager, Gunn and Hain.

Gorman, Anna. 2009. Cities and Counties Rely on US Immigrant Detention Fees. *The Los Angeles Times.*

March 17. Retrieved July 16, 2013 from: http://articles.latimes.com/2009/mar/17/local/me-immigjail17

Grandoni, Dino. 2012. Only 16 percent of released Gitmo prisoners become terrorists again, *The Atlantic Wire*. March 5. Retrieved July 16, 2013 from: http://www.theatlanticwire.com/global/2012/03/only-16-percent-released-gitmo-prisoners-become-terrorists-again/49522/

Guerino, Paul, Paige M. Harrison, and William J. Sabol. 2011. *Prisoners in 2010*. Washington, DC, Bureau of Justice Statistics, US Department of Justice.

Hale, Edward Everett. 1863. The man without a country. *The Atlantic Monthly* 12 (73): 665–80.

Hammett, Theodore, and Lynne Harrold. 1994. *Tuberculosis in correctional facilities*. Washington, DC: US Department of Justice.

Hensley, Christopher, and Richard Tewksbury. 2004. Wardens' perceptions of prison sex. *The Prison Journal* 85(2): 186–97.

Hockenberry, Sarah, Melissa Sickmund, and Anthony Sladky. 2011. *Juvenile residential facility census, 2008: Selected findings*. Washington, DC: Office of Juvenile Justice and Delinquency Prevention, US Department of Justice.

Hoefer, Michael, Nancy Rytina and Ryan C. Baker. 2011. *Estimates of the unauthorized immigrant population residing in the United States: January 2010*. Washington, DC: US Department of Homeland Security.

Human Rights Watch. 2001. No escape: Male rape in U.S. prisons. V. rape scenarios. Retrieved on 23 July 2013 at http://www.hrw.org/reports/2001/prison/report5.html

Human Rights Watch. 2004. U.K.: Law lords rule indefinite detention breaches human rights. New York: Human Rights Watch. December 16. Retrieved July 16, 2013 from: http://www.hrw.org/en/news/2004/12/15/uk-law-lords-rule-indefinite-detention-breaches-human-rights

Immigration and Customs Enforcement. 2013. About ICE: Enforcement and removal operations. Retrieved on 23 July 2013 at http://www.ice.gov/about/offices/enforcement-removal-operations/

James, Doris J., and Lauren E. Glaze. 2006. *Mental health problems of prison and jail inmates*. Washington, DC: Bureau of Justice Statistics, US Department of Justice.

Knickerbocker, Brad. 2006. Illegal immigrants in the US: How many are there? *Christian Science Monitor*, May 16.

Kunzel, Regina G. 2008. *Criminal intimacy: Prison and the uneven history of modern American sexuality*. Chicago: University of Chicago Press.

Los Angeles Times. 2011. Inmate loses bid for tax-payer paid sex-change operation. September 22. Retrieved July 16, 2013 from: http://articles.latimes.com/2011/sep/22/local/la-me-transgender-20110922

Leach, Donald L. 2011. *Managing lesbian, gay, bisexual, transgender and intersex inmates: Is your jail ready?* Aurora, CO: National Institution of Corrections Information Center. Retrieved July 16, 2013 from: http://nicic.gov/Library/period315

Lynch, P. J. 1988. Criminality in the elderly and psychiatric disorder: A review of the literature. *Medical Science and the Law* 28: 65–74.

Lynch, James P., Steven K. Smith, Helen A. Graziadei, and Tanutda Pittyathilchun. 1994. *Profile of inmates for the US and England and Wales, 1991*. Washington, DC: US Department of Justice.

Maruschak, Laura M. 2004. *HIV in prisons and jails, 2002*. Washington, DC: US Department of Justice.

Maruschak, Laura M. 2006. *Medical problems of jail inmates*. Washington, DC: US Department of Justice.

Maruschak, Laura. 2012. *Medical problems of prisoners*. Washington, DC: Bureau of Justice.

McCoy, Candace. 1984. Determinate sentencing, plea bargaining bans, and hydraulic discretion in California. *Justice System Journal* 9: 256–75.

Meithe, T. D. 1987. Charging and plea bargaining practices under determinate sentencing: An investigation of the hydraulic displacement of discretion. *Journal of Criminal Law* 78: 155–76.

Minton, Todd D. 2011. *Jail inmates at midyear 2010—statistical tables*. Washington, DC: Bureau of Justice Statistics, US Department of Justice.

Motivans, Mark. 2012. *Immigration offenders in the federal justice system, 2010*. Washington, DC: US Department of Justice.

Noonan, Margaret E., and E. Ann Carson. 2011. *Prison and jail deaths in custody, 2000–2009: Statistical Tables*. Washington, DC: US Department of Justice.

Passel, Jeffrey S., and D'Vera Cohn. 2009. *A portrait of unauthorized immigrants in the United States*. Washington, DC: Pew Hispanic Center/Pew Research Center.

Pollock-Byrne, Joycelyn M. 1990. *Women, prison and crime*. Pacific Grove, CA: Brooks/Cole.

Rogers, Patrick. 2008. Conjugal visits: Preserving family bonds behind bar. Retrieved July 16, 2013 from: http://www.legalzoom.com/marriage-divorce-family-law/marriage-domestic-partnership/conjugal-visits-preserving-family-bonds

Rosenblum, Mark R. 2012. *Border security and immigration enforcement between ports of entry.* Washington, DC: Congressional Research Services.

Sabol, William J., Heather C. West, and Matthew Cooper. 2009. *Prisoners in 2008.* Washington, DC: US Department of Justice.

Scheel, Murray D., and Claire Eustace. 2002. *Model protocols on the treatment of transgender persons by San Francisco County Jail.* Retrieved July 16, 2013 from: http://www.transgenderlaw.org/resources/sfprisonguidelines.doc

Schwartz, Ira M. 1989. *(In)justice for juveniles: Rethinking the best interest of the child.* Lexington, MA: Lexington Books.

Schwartz, Ira M. 1991. Removing juveniles from adult jails: The unfinished agenda. In *American jails: Public policy issues*, edited by Joel A. Thompson and G. Larry Mays. Chicago: Nelson-Hall, 216–26.

Sexton, Lori, Valerie Jenness, and Jennifer Sumner. 2009. *Where the margins meet: A Demographic assessment of transgender inmates in men's prisons.* Irvine, CA: University of California.

Sexton, Lori, Valerie Jenness, and Jennifer Macy Sumner. 2010. Where the margins meet: A demographic assessment of transgender inmates in men's prisons. *Justice Quarterly* 27(6): 835–66.

Shane, Scott. 2011. Beyond Guantánamo, a web of prisons for terrorism inmates. *The New York Times.* December 10.

Sickmund, Melissa. 2010. *Juveniles in residential placement, 1997–2008.* Washington, DC: Office of Juvenile Justice and Delinquency Prevention, US Department of Justice.

Sickmund, Melissa, T. J. Sladky, Wei Kang, and Charles Puzzanchera. 2011. *Easy access to the census of juveniles in residential placement.* Retrieved July 16, 2013 from: http://www.ojjdp.gov/ojstatbb/ezacjrp/

Stephan, James J. 2008. *Census of state and federal correctional facilities, 2005.* Washington, DC: Bureau of Justice Statistics, US Department of Justice.

Swartz, James A., Arthur J. Lurigio, and Dana Aron Weiner. 2004. Correlates of HIV-risk behaviors among prison inmates: Implications for tailored AIDS prevention programming. *Prison Journal* 84: 486–504.

Tan, Michael. 2011. *Locked up without end: Indefinite detention of immigrants will not make America safer.* Washington, DC: Immigration Policy Center, American Immigration Council.

Tarzwell, Sydney. 2006. The gender lines are marked with razor wire: Addressing state prison policies and practices for the management of transgender prisoners. *Columbia Human Rights Law Review* 38: 167–220.

Tewksbury, Richard, and Potter, R. H. 2005. Transgender prisoners—A forgotten group. In Stan Stojkovic (Ed.), *Managing special populations in jails and prisons* (pp. 15.1–15.14). New York: Civic Research Institute.

UN Office on Drugs and Crime. 2009. *Handbook on inmates with special needs.* New York: United Nations.

US Department of Homeland Security. 2009. *Immigration and custom enforcement detention bedspace management.* Washington, DC: US Department of Homeland Security.

US Department of Homeland Security. 2011a. *2010 yearbook of immigrant statistics.* Washington, DC: US Department of Homeland Security.

US Department of Homeland Security. 2011b. *Annual Report: Immigration Enforcement Actions: 2010.* Washington, DC: US Department of Homeland Security. Retrieved July 16, 2013 from: http://www.dhs.gov/xlibrary/assets/statistics/publications/enforcement-ar-2010.pdf

US Department of Justice. 2012. *National standards to prevent, detect, and respond to prison rape: Executive summary.* Washington, DC: US Department of Justice. Retrieved July 16, 2013 from: http://www.ojp.usdoj.gov/programs/pdfs/prea_executive_summary.pdf

Vito, Gennaro F., and Deborah G. Wilson. 1985. Forgotten people: Elderly inmates. *Federal Probation*, March, 18–24.

Wacquant, Loïc. 2006. Penalization, depoliticization, racialization: On the over-incarceration of immigrants in the European Union. Chapter in Sarah Armstrong and Lesley McAra (eds.), *Contexts of control: New perspectives on punishment and society.* Oxford: Clarendon Press.

Washington State Department of Health and Social Services. 2012. Citizenship and alien statuses: Definitions. Olympia, WA: Washington State Department of Health and Social Services. Retrieved July 16, 2013 from: http://www.dshs.wa.gov/manuals/eaz/sections/CitizenshipAndAlienStatus/citizengenelig.shtml

Wilder, Forrest. 2007. Detention archipelago: Jailing immigrants for profit. *NACLA Report on the*

Americas. Report: Detention. May/June. New York: North American Congress on Latin America.

Wolfe, Zachary. n.d. *Gay and lesbian prisoners: Recent developments and a call for more research.* West Brattleboro, VT: Prison Legal News. Retrieved July 16, 2013 from: **https://www.prisonlegalnews.org/**

displayArticle.aspx?articleid=20578&AspxAutoDetectCookieSup port=1

Zupan, Linda L. 1992. Men guarding women: An analysis of the employment of male correctional officers in prisons for women. *Journal of Criminal Justice* 20: 297–309.

PAROLE AND PRISONER REENTRY

MIKAEL KARLSSON/ALAMY IMAGES

Outline

Origins of Parole

The Administration of Parole

Violations of Parole

Prisoner Reentry

Parole and Prisoner Reentry Today

Objectives

- To provide you with an historical context for modern parole and prisoner reentry

- To acquaint you with the mechanisms by which parole is provided, monitored, and revoked in contemporary US jurisdictions

- To introduce you to the evolving topic of prisoner reentry as distinct from and related to parole

- To give you insights into the issues and trends in parole and prisoner reentry

Essentials of Corrections, Fifth Edition. G. Larry Mays and L. Thomas Winfree, Jr.
© 2014 John Wiley & Sons, Inc. Published 2014 by John Wiley & Sons, Inc.

INTRODUCTION

For many of us, one of the greatest injustices of the US system of criminal justice is that convicted felons are free to commit new crimes before they fully "pay" for the old ones. It does not seem fair that so many criminals are roaming the streets when the state or federal government should lock them up in jail or prison. Members of the public do not feel safe in their homes or in their communities, taking extra precautions when they go out at night, traveling well-lit streets, and avoiding certain neighborhoods. Back in their houses, they check the bars on windows and doors, and use alarm systems. Because criminals are free, goes this line of thinking, the rest of us are prisoners.

Is this what you think too? Even if you do not agree with those who would like to see all criminals locked up until they no longer pose a threat to society, you have to admit that such arguments lead to other important questions, ones we will examine in this chapter. Consider Todd Clear and James Austin's (2009:312) **iron law of prison populations**, which states that prison populations are first and foremost determined by the number of people sent to prison and second by the amount of time the prisoners reside in them. As a corollary of this law, they observe the following: There is no way to change the prison population without changing either the number of people who go to prison or how long they stay there. Parole or other forms of early prisoner release is clearly one way to manipulate the iron law of prison populations at the *back end*, just as changing the rules for reincarcerating parolees upon technical violations would reduce the number of people (re) entering prison, or the *front end* of the process.

Then there is Jeremy Travis's **iron law of imprisonment**. As Travis (2005) observed in *But They All Come Back: Facing the Challenges of Prisoner Reentry*, except for the very few prison inmates who die in prison, all the rest eventually "come home." That is, nearly all will return to the free society. By age 23, one in three US adults has an arrest record, for something other than a minor traffic violation (Barnes et al. 2012). Well in excess of a half-million inmates leave the nation's prisons each year, joining another 300,000 individuals who continue in their tenuous

and conditional status as parolees. The Bureau of Justice Statistics gives us another set of insights into prisoner reentry, one that bolsters Travis's iron law of imprisonment: 95 percent of all state prisoners will leave prison at some point; eight in ten of these releases are to parole supervision (Bureau of Justice Statistics 2007; Glaze and Bonczar 2011). These are not trivial observations. The issue then becomes not *if* they return, but *when*. Related questions include the following: *What* are the conditions of release? *What* are their fates, once released? *What* is society doing to assist them in their reentry?

In this chapter, we look at the important idea of prisoner reentry into the community and the primary mechanism by which inmates accomplish this reentry: parole. Parole is one of the oldest and most widely practiced means of reentering the free society, but in the past 20 years, state and federal authorities have instituted other means of reentry. We turn first to an examination of parole, starting with its origins.

ORIGINS OF PAROLE

Parole is a conditional release from prison. The term comes from the *parole d'honneur*, a French phrase meaning "word of honor." In medieval times, a defeated knight could give his word of honor to withdraw from combat and leave the battlefield, escaping injury or death. By the eighteenth century, the medieval custom had become law. Section VII of the Lieber Code, the laws of war prepared for the Union army during the Civil War, governed the use of parole at first by the North and then by both sides: captured soldiers received an offer of freedom in exchange for their word of honor not to reenter the hostilities. Participation was voluntary and many people were paroled more than once (Catton 1960). Later in the nineteenth century, the Declaration of Brussels and the Hague Convention made parole practices part of international law (Friedman 1972). These practices established the idea that an imprisoned person could be freed in exchange for a promise to behave in accordance with a set of agreed-on conditions. It took many years, however, for the practice to enter the penal system.

PAROLE: FROM AN ENGLISH PRACTICE TO US LAW

Alexander Maconochie used a system of marks and conditional release for inmates sentenced under indeterminate sentences on Norfolk Island in the 1840s. The English Parliament enacted the Penal Servitude Act in 1853, allowing prisoner release on a ticket-of-leave under police supervision. That same year, Walter Crofton became director of the Irish prison system. He was aware of Maconochie's work on Norfolk Island. A year later, Crofton created the **Irish ticket-of-leave system** as a way of releasing ex-convicts into the community through the four stages described in Chapter 2. The **inspector of released prisoners**, the first parole officer, aided the police in this effort.

The Irish ticket-of-leave system provided a model for conditional prisoner release, but it was neither the only one nor the first. Indeed, even before Maconochie's experiment, Massachusetts started the first US parole system in 1837. In spite of Massachusetts's exemplary efforts, attempts to create similar systems in other states came up against the beliefs that placing an ex-offender under police supervision was un-American (Abadinsky 2012). Parole came into widespread use in the United States only after its adoption by New York State.

When Bostonian G. S. Howe wrote a letter to the New York Prison Association in 1846 suggesting that prisoners "might be so trained as to be left upon their parole during the last period of their imprisonment with safety" few took notice (Klein 1920, 417). In 1874, Crofton wrote to the New York Prison Association about the adoption of his leave and supervision method. A part of the necessary legal mechanism for the implementation of Howe's and Crofton's suggestions was already in place in New York. That is, the New York State legislature had already passed **good-time laws** in 1817. These laws allowed prison officials to shorten an inmate's prison term in exchange for good behavior. The establishment in 1876 of the indeterminate sentence put all the pieces in play. In that year, New York State created both a system of "indeterminate" sentences setting a minimum and maximum prison term, and legislation permitting parole release of those who

had served the minimum; parolees were required to report monthly to citizen volunteers known as **Guardians** (New York State Division of Parole 2007).

One of the earliest institutions to use the New York state reentry program was Zebulon Reed Brockway's Elmira reformatory (see Chapter 2). However, post-release supervision was part of Elmira's approach in name only, as it included virtually nothing that would aid ex-offender reentry (Abadinsky 2012). Indeed, most of the first early-release programs were essentially release-and-return programs: few inmates had the resources they needed once they left prison to turn around their lives. In time, though, prisoner aid societies began to transfer attention and resources from people in prison to those conditionally released from prison. In the tradition of John Augustus's work with probationers, volunteers supervised paroled offenders in the community, for example, New York State's Guardians. In 1845, Massachusetts hired the first state employee whose job it was to help parolees adjust to free world life. The duties of Massachusetts's first parole officer included assisting released prisoners in finding jobs and providing them with tools, clothing, and transportation at state expense. It would be many years before other states followed the Massachusetts's example and hired professional parole supervisors.

PAROLE AND THE GREAT DEPRESSION

During the Great Depression of the 1930s, parole's use grew as never before. In the mid-1920s, the nation was releasing about 20,000 parolees a year, as it had been for 20 or more years. Between 1930 and 1940, the number of people released on parole increased to more than 40,000 (Cahalan 1986, 50), a trend that was fed by three sets of interrelated forces. First, by the end of the first decade of the twentieth century, only three states—Florida, Mississippi, and Virginia—did not have a prisoner release statute (Cahalan 1986, 170). At the federal level, parole began in 1910 (see Box 9.1). Consequently, the mechanism for early prison release was in place in nearly every state and the federal government before World War I.

Second, both the per capita (per 100,000) incarceration rate and actual prison populations in the

United States grew dramatically between the world wars. In 1923, the prison population was at 74 inmates per 100,000 people, a rate comparable to that reported in 1890 (Cahalan 1986, 30). By 1940, a year before the United States entered World War II, the rate had risen to 125, an increase of nearly 69 percent. In 1931, the National Commission on Law Observance and Law Enforcement delivered a bleak report on the nation's overcrowded prisons. Parole was one answer to the crushing economic burden of building and maintaining prisons during the Great Depression.

Third, federal laws passed during the Great Depression (see Chapter 6) restricted the sale of products created using prison labor, increasing the economic burden on the states. The number of inmates in prison was rising and the profits accrued from using them as a source of cheap labor were falling. Interestingly, then, it was also the economic conditions associated with the Great Depression as much as the pressures exerted by prison reformers that led to parole's extended use in the 1930s, as the states struggled with ways to make their budgetary restrictions support an increasingly expensive prison system (Abadinsky 2012).

PAROLE IN THE TWENTY-FIRST CENTURY

According to Graeme Newman (1958, 4), parole did not originate from a single program or experiment; it grew out of many different practices, including the transportation of prisoners to America and Australia, the English/Irish ticket-of-leave system, and experimental early release programs in Massachusetts and New York. Today, parole continues to evolve. One important change has to do with the nature of early release. Instead of earning parole, most state and federal prisoners leave correctional institutions today under a mandatory early-release system, methods we will address later in this chapter. Most parole programs do not even pretend to meet inmates' rehabilitative and reintegrative needs. Their objective is to give overburdened prison systems a way to control their inmate population. That is, as a prison closes in on its legal capacity, prison administrators begin to release prisoners who are close to their release dates

and who have presented few disciplinary problems while incarcerated (Winfree, Sellers et al. 1990; Winfree, Wooldredge et al. 1990). However, relying solely on backdoor methods to reduce the nation's burgeoning prison populations in the twenty-first century may not be enough, especially in light of the iron law of prison populations.

Next we turn to a consideration of the administration of parole, examining how the various jurisdictions have responded to these pressures. Before that, however, you may wish to review Box 9.1, which describes the federal parole system's history—a cautionary tale for all such release mechanisms.

THE ADMINISTRATION OF PAROLE

Unless an inmate dies in prison or jail, he or she reenters society in one of five ways.

- **Commutation of sentence** is an extraordinary action by the executive branch of government. Legally, commutation literally means exchanging one punishment for another less severe one. Practically, it means the release of an inmate from prison in consideration for time served. The chief executive can commute sentences for illness, impending death, or other compassionate reasons. In some states, an inmate's early release is possible if the inmate is very ill or debilitated by disease or terminally ill. Such releases, which go by many names that reflect their extraordinary nature, are rare, and self-serving for the institution: They save huge medical costs and, in most cases, pass them along to cities and counties where the releasees reside until their deaths or recoveries. Such releases are generally permanent.

- A **pardon** is another form of executive clemency or mercy and is a rare event. Under the US and various state constitutions, the chief executive—the president or governor—may grant a pardon or forgiveness for some or all past criminal deeds. In some instances, pardons restore rights taken away from convicted felons; in others, pardons cause the convicted

THE EVOLUTION AND DEMISE OF THE FEDERAL PAROLE SYSTEM   BOX 9.1

The practice of paroling federal prisoners dates to 1910, when each of the three federal penitentiaries established parole boards to grant conditional release into the community. These boards consisted of each institution's warden and physician, joined by the Washington-based Superintendent of Prisons. Twenty years later, with the creation of the Bureau of Prisons, a single Washington-based Board of Parole was established. By 1950, this board consisted of eight full-time presidential appointees, who reported directly to the US Attorney General.

Throughout the early 1970s a series of organizational changes reflected the BOP's growth since World War II. The board was restructured into five regions, with a board member assigned to each one. The remaining three members, including the board's chair, remained in Washington at national headquarters. The board was also re-titled the US Parole Commission in 1976 and consolidated within the Department of Justice as an independent agency. The Commission was expanded to nine members, broken out into the chair, five regional commissioners, and a three-member National Appeal Board.[1]

The 1980s saw many changes in the US Parole Commission. When Congress passed the *Comprehensive Crime Control Act of 1984*, it created the US Sentencing Commission to establish sentencing guidelines for the federal courts under a regime of determinate sentences. The Parole Commission's chair is a nonvoting, ex-officio member of the Sentencing Commission. On November 1, 1987, the sentencing guidelines went into effect. The Parole Commission retained jurisdiction over federal defendants who committed crimes prior to that date; however, those whose crimes occurred on or after that date were not eligible for parole. All federal felons sentenced after this date are given a release date determined at sentencing, based on the sentencing guidelines, and are subject to a term of supervised release, managed by officers of the US Probation and Pretrial Services, which summarizes this mission as follows:

> [Supervised release is] a term of supervision served after a person is released from [federal] prison. The court imposes supervised release during sentencing in addition to the sentence of imprisonment. Unlike parole, supervised release does not replace a portion of the sentence of imprisonment but is in addition to the time spent in prison. US probation officers supervise persons on supervised release.

What was the ultimate fate of the US Parole Commission? In fact, that has yet to be determined. It was scheduled to be phased out first in 1992, but was given a reprieve until 1997, owing to concerns about federal prisoners who were eligible for parole. In 1996, another extension pushed the termination date out to 2002. However, Congress authorized additional responsibilities for the Commission in the *National Capital Revitalization and Self-Government Improvement Act of 1997*. Since August 5, 2000, it has had jurisdiction over parole and mandatory release supervision and revocation decisions for persons serving District of Columbia code felony sentences; moreover, the Parole Commission was reduced to five commissioners. It was scheduled for final dissolution in 2005; however, at this writing, the Commission, consisting of the chair and three commissioners, is still in operation under the terms of the 1997 legislation.

SOURCES: HOFFMAN (2003); US COURTS (2013); US SENTENCING COMMISSION (2013).

felon's immediate release from confinement. In some jurisdictions, including the federal government, a pardon board reviews all requests for executive clemency and makes recommendations to the chief executive. However, it is ultimately within the power of the chief executive to pardon quite literally any convicted felon under his or her legal authority.

- **Expiration release** is an unconditional release from prison when the offender's sentence—minus any good-time credits—ends. This is not a form of parole: inmates released at the end of their term are not under supervision and do not have to meet any other conditions for release.

- Correctional authorities initiate **discretionary release** when they believe an inmate is ready for life on the outside. This system is found in states that have retained some elements of indeterminate sentencing. Another government entity, usually a parole board, must concur and authorize the parole. Typically, inmates released under this system must adhere to certain restrictions including limitations on their movement in the community, types of persons with whom they can associate, and even where they live or whether they can buy or drive a car. This system is an outgrowth of the medical model and indeterminate sentencing.

- Many inmates today leave custody under **mandatory release**. Once an inmate has served a statutorily defined minimum length of time, his or her release is nearly automatic. The prison authority simply informs the paroling or releasing authority that the offender has served this statutorily defined limit, and supervised release begins. In some cases, the releasing authority can deny release if the individual is deemed to pose a present risk to the community. In such systems, a fixed set of guidelines governs the actual release. In some states and the federal government this method is referred to as **supervised release**, as it extends supervision upon exiting the state's prison system to as much as one-third of the original

sentence. In many jurisdictions using this type of release mechanism, probation officers provide post-release supervision.

Table 9.1 contains a summary of how the federal government, the District of Columbia, and nearly all states have responded to the need to release prisoners. Maine is not reported since it has not used parole for offenders convicted since 1973. Minnesota and Virginia also claim that they do not have parole; however, the former releases inmates under the mandatory system, and the latter reports both discretionary and mandatory releases. Interestingly, the second most common pattern revealed in this table is a mixed model, which largely depends on state law or parole board practices. The discretionary model dominates the state systems. Several states maintain that they do not parole inmates; however, all report parole intakes and releases, following either the discretionary or mandatory/supervised release models.

ELIGIBILITY FOR PAROLE

In many jurisdictions, the key to understanding parole is an inmate's **parole eligibility date**, the earliest point at which the inmate can leave prison. Calculating this date varies by jurisdiction and release model. First, the inmate must be eligible for parole. For example, in some jurisdictions, those convicted of first-degree murder or aggravated homicide must serve a "natural life" sentence. They will never leave prison unless the president or state governor pardons them or they receive a commutation of their sentence. Many inmates "complete" their natural life sentences and end up in the prison cemetery.

The second criterion depends on whether the jurisdiction employs mandatory release or discretionary release. In mandatory-release jurisdictions, time served is the deciding factor: if the inmate has served the minimum term required by law, he or she is eligible for a parole hearing. Good-time credits and other ways of reducing the time an inmate must serve before he or she is eligible for release help compress this important period. The inmate may be told the date of his or her parole hearing soon after entering prison or shortly before the hearing, depending on institutional policy.

TABLE 9.1 **Models of parole and post-supervision release.**

Discretionary only		Mandatory only	Combination of methods	
Alabama	New Hampshire	Alaska	California[a]	New Jersey[b]
Arkansas	New Mexico	Arizona[h]	Colorado[b]	New York[g]
Georgia	North Dakota	Delaware	Connecticut[c]	Ohio[i]
Hawaii	Oklahoma	D. of Columbia[h]	Florida[d]	Oregon[j]
Idaho	Pennsylvania	Illinois	Louisiana[b]	South Carolina[g]
Iowa	Rhode Island	Indiana	Maryland[b]	Texas[g]
Kansas	South Dakota	Minnesota[f]	Michigan[e]	Washington[b]
Kentucky	Tennessee	Mississippi	Nevada[b]	
Massachusetts	Utah	North Carolina		
Missouri	Vermont	Virginia		
Montana	West Virginia	Wisconsin[h]		
Nebraska	Wyoming	Federal System[h]		

NOTES: [a]CALIFORNIA HISTORICALLY USED THE MANDATORY METHOD, BUT SINCE 2011 HAS MOVED TO A NEW SYSTEM (SEE BOX 9.2); [b]ALLOWS DISCRETIONARY PAROLE, BUT HOLDS INMATES UNTIL MANDATORY THRESHOLD IS MET; [c]INMATES ARE ELIGIBLE AT 50 PERCENT (DISCRETIONARY) OR 85 PERCENT (SUPERVISED RELEASE) OF SENTENCE, DEPENDING ON THE CRIME(S) OF WHICH THEY ARE CONVICTED; [d]EMPLOYS THREE TYPES OF SUPERVISION, DEPENDING OFFENSE TYPE AND DATE OF CONVICTION; [e]FOR NON-LIFE SENTENCES, PAROLE BOARD GAINS JURISDICTION AFTER MINIMUM SENTENCE, LESS GOOD TIME OR DISCIPLINARY CREDITS; MAXIMUM SET BY STATUTE AND MINIMUM BY JUDGE; [f]NO PAROLE BOARD; MOSTLY EMPLOYS SUPERVISED RELEASE, WHICH LASTS ONE-THIRD OF THE SENTENCE; SOME MANDATORY RELEASES; [g]EMPLOYS DISCRETIONARY OR MANDATORY/SUPERVISED RELEASE, BASED ON PAROLE BOARD DECISION, BUT MAINLY DISCRETIONARY; [h]MAINLY EMPLOYS SUPERVISED RELEASE; [i]HEARINGS TO DETERMINE NEED FOR POST-RELEASE CONTROL AND HOW LONG; MAINLY EMPLOYS MANDATORY RELEASE, BUT DEPENDS ON WHEN THE CRIME WAS COMMITTED AND THE TYPE OF OFFENSE, ESPECIALLY FIRST DEGREE FELONIES AND SEX OFFENSES; [j]PAROLE BOARD HAS JURISDICTION OVER 10% OF PRISONERS; RESTS ARE SUBJECT TO MANDATORY RELEASE.
SOURCES: BUREAU OF JUSTICE STATISTICS (2007); GLAZE AND BONCZAR (2011); UPDATED BY THE AUTHORS AT THE RELEVANT WEBSITES FOR THE FEDERAL GOVERNMENT, EACH STATE, AND THE DISTRICT OF COLUMBIA.

Mandatory-release regimes, generally found in states using determinate sentencing, give eligible inmates an estimated release date. Without any institutional-based problems, these inmates will leave prison after serving a specified portion of their sentence, minus any good-time credits, under terms of supervision that are generally indistinguishable from those given to parolees. In truth-in-sentencing states, this practice is often called the "85-percent-rule," meaning convicted felons will serve 85 percent of their sentence (Sabol et al. 2002).[2] Even in such regimes, a post-release review board or commission may examine pending releases; these entities can delay release, short of sentence expiration, due to concerns about post-release failure.

In most discretionary-release systems inmates become automatically eligible for a parole hearing after serving a minimum amount of time expressed in months. This method is common in states using indeterminate sentencing. In still other discretionary-release jurisdictions, inmates are automatically eligible

for a parole board hearing after serving a specified portion—often expressed as a percentage—of the minimum or maximum sentence, depending on the nature of their most instant offense. For example, persons convicted of a type of homicide for which they are eligible for parole will serve a portion of the maximum sentence. To reiterate, the determination of a positive release decision in discretionary systems rests with the parole board. In both cases, prison behavior can be considered when rendering a parole decision.

Until recently, whether parole itself is a right was unclear, in spite of the fact that nearly all states' websites devoted to parole or early release eligibility declare it to be a privilege and not a right. In a 2011 Supreme Court decision, this issue was addressed in straightforward and unanimous fashion. Parole can be a right extended at the state level, but there is no Constitutional right to parole. In this case, Damon Cooke was convicted of the attempted murder in 1991; the sentence was up to life in prison, under

California's indeterminate sentencing laws. At his most recent parole hearing, the board ruled that Cooke was still "an unreasonable risk" to the community and denied him parole. He lost an appeal at the state level; however, the Ninth US Circuit Court ruled in his favor, arguing that the parole authority did not have enough evidence to deny Cooke parole; in essence, he had a right to parole. The US Supreme Court disagreed; the Court wrote, in a *per curiam* decision: "Whatever liberty interest exists is, of course, a *state* interest created by California law. There is no right under the Federal Constitution to be conditionally released before the expiration of a valid sentence, and the States are under no duty to offer parole to their prisoners" (*Swarthout v. Cooke*; emphasis in the original).

GRANTING PAROLE: THE PAROLE BOARD

Parole boards operate under two basic models. **Independent parole boards** are free of any other state agency's control and generally report directly to the governor. Such boards make all release and revocation decisions for parolees in their jurisdiction. In a handful of states (see Table 9.2), independent parole boards may also be responsible for parolee supervision. A review of state paroling authority websites reveals that only about 20 states use the independent parole board model, including some in the Old South (e.g., Alabama, Arkansas, Florida, Georgia, Kentucky, and Tennessee), and several in the West (e.g., Arizona, Idaho, Montana, Nevada, New Mexico, Utah, and Wyoming).

Consolidated parole boards are autonomous panels within the governmental department responsible for administering correctional institutions or community corrections. These boards make all release and revocation decisions; parolee supervision is usually the responsibility of another unit within the department of corrections. Some states use the same authority—the department, board, or commission of probation and parole—to supervise both probationers and parolees (see Table 4.2). Consolidated parole boards dominate the state and the federal systems, including jurisdictions with very large prison populations such as California, New York, Ohio, Texas,

Pennsylvania, and the federal system. Given the widespread claim that consolidated parole boards provide greater continuity of services and are able to process large numbers of post-release supervisees, these patterns are not entirely surprising.

The actual composition of parole boards, whichever model the state employs, varies widely. Even the number of board members varies from three part-time members (Alabama) to 12 (California) or 19 (New York) members, while even for large boards, as few as three may form a quorum and make release decisions. People who serve on independent boards typically do not know much about corrections, prisons, or parole before they become members. In sharp contrast to that characterization, a few states, such as Arkansas, and most Canadian Provinces mandate that one member must be a social scientist or criminal justice faculty member at a 4-year university. Members are usually appointed directly by the governor or nominated by a statewide commission and then appointed by the governor; generally, they serve part-time and are paid a nominal salary or per diem expenses. Critics of this model often point to its lack of insight into the process and the needs of offenders.

By contrast, the composition of the consolidated parole board, sometimes referred to as the **institutional model**, typically employs full-time corrections professionals. Although members of consolidated boards begin with an understanding of institutional needs and inmates' needs, they are subject to pressure from their own agency and other state and local criminal justice agencies, and the potential for abuse of their discretion may be greater than it is for independent parole board members.

Parole boards also go by many names. There is no one dominant pattern. Moreover, its title is not tied to whether the paroling authority is an independent entity or a consolidated agency. Sixteen state agencies are boards of pardons, probation, or paroles, handling two or more functions.[3] Twenty-six other states have a state parole board.[4] A third pattern is the parole commission, found in five states.[5] Prison releases in the District of Columbia fall under the jurisdiction of the US Parole Commission. A few agencies have unique names, such as Arizona's Board of Executive Clemency, Hawaii's Paroling Authority,

California's Board of Parole Hearings, Illinois's and Kansas's Prisoner Review Board, the Minnesota's Supervised Community Release, and Washington's Intermediate Sentence Review Board. Clearly, the agencies that, to a great or lesser extent, decide who leaves prison, when, and under what conditions function under many organizational models and have nearly as many names.

PAROLE AND POST-RELEASE DECISION MAKING: POLICIES AND PROCEDURES

After the appropriate authority makes the decision to consider an inmate for early release the parole board assesses all relevant information. In states that set indeterminate sentences, the board establishes minimum and maximum sentences. Given the emphasis on treatment and suitability for release in these states, the board may consider evidence of the inmate's progress toward rehabilitation. The members usually examine an inmate's current and past crimes along with the following:

- any indication of repentance for his or her prior criminal acts;
- any indication of prior adjustment in the community;
- the inmate's physical, emotional, and mental health;
- the adequacy of the parole plan, including questions about a job, a residence, and social support systems in the community; and
- a summary report of the inmate's institutional conduct, including disciplinary reports, participation in programs, and the like. The presentence investigation (PSI) report may find its way into the parole board's deliberations and the members may hear from the prosecuting attorney and the offender's victims

The problems of discretion, arbitrariness, and prediction would seem to be missing from parole decisions in states that use mandatory-release procedures. That is, the issues associated with bad decisions based on good information (or good decisions based on bad information) disappear, as do concerns for the parole board's abuse of discretion—essentially, it has none. Once an offender is statutorily eligible for parole, three criteria alone determine its award:

- The inmate generally must have followed the correctional institution's rules and regulations.
- The inmate must not pose a significant public safety risk.
- The inmate must not have committed a crime so serious that his or her release would lead citizens to question the validity of the criminal justice system or to disrespect the law.

Even under this system, however, parole boards enjoy considerable discretion. Consider the third item in the list. How do the members decide whether a specific criminal's release is going to anger the public? In some cases, the public's reaction is relatively easy to predict—the release of a convicted child molester, for example, is likely to be met with protest—but there is no way to be sure how the community is going to respond in every case. Decisions here, then, are largely subjective.

It is also important to recognize that in most systems, the parole boards are more than an administrative entity. They also have quasi-judicial powers, including the power to:

- issue subpoenas;
- compel the attendance of witnesses;
- compel the production of books, papers and other documents pertinent to the subject of its inquiry; and
- administer oaths and take the testimony of persons under oath.

These powers extend to the revocation of parole as well, a topic addressed later in this chapter.

PAROLE DECISIONS: RISKS AND REMEDIES

A parole decision that angers the public is largely a political mistake; a parole decision that compromises the safety of the public could well be a life-threatening mistake. For example, the Maine parole board was disbanded and parole ceased owing to a lack of public confidence in both the board and the practice (Sharon 2011). To minimize a parole decision's adverse risk to public safety of a parole decision, about half the states—whether they use the discretionary-release model or the mandatory-release model—employ a statistical method (Ruanda, Rhine, and Wetter 1994). For example, Colorado's Actuarial Risk Assessment Scale requires the inmate's case manager to respond to a series of questions. Three items center on the inmate's institutional adjustments. The inmate's prior criminal record is the focus of three other items. Only one item specifically addresses the current offense; another asks about current and prior criminal activities. The final three items deal exclusively with the offender's personal life: employment, marital status, and age. Based on the total score, the inmate is classified a high, medium-high, medium, or low parole risk. As with similar instruments used in other states, Colorado's scale is regularly validated by comparing inmates' records to predicted and actual parole outcomes (Patzman and English 1994).

Risk-screening instruments for parolees are similar to those used for probationers (see Box 4.1). They help intake personnel make suitable institutional assignments and determine inmate suitability for release prior to their termination date. The final recommendation can come from prediction tables, case managers, or both. Ultimately, in cases of discretionary parole, the parole board decides. Hearings are typically quite short, usually no more than ten minutes. Unless a statute specifically requires it, a parole board does not have to hold formal hearings or even inform prisoners of why they were denied parole. When the authority grants parole, inmates rarely want to know why.

In jurisdictions where parole boards still have a lot of discretion, members try to reduce the number of what statisticians call **false positives**, parolees who looked to be good risks but later committed a crime. Rather than subject the public to danger and themselves to embarrassment, members of parole boards tend to deny parole to what statisticians would call **false negatives**, inmates who would have made a success of their parole. Where mandatory release is the law, unless there are compelling reasons not to grant parole, early release is almost automatic.

The realities of creating correctional responses to political pressures concerning widely publicized false positives and subsequent policy changes, such as three-strikes legislation and truth-in-sentencing laws, led to the mass incarcerations reported in the late 1990s and early 2000s (Clear 1994; Clear and Austin 2009; Cullen 1995). As suggested in Box 9.2, California provides an important test case for this challenge.

PAROLE OFFICERS

Chapter 4 related how the various jurisdictions in the United States take several different approaches to probation and parole work. The emphasis here is on release from prison. In jurisdictions where they are used, parole officers receive their authority from the executive branch. Most **parole officers** or **parole agents**, therefore, are state-level civil service employees. Others are combination **probation/parole officers (PPOs)**, and may be either local employees or state employees (see Table 4.2 for an overview of which states employ each type). Several states and the federal government no longer offer parole. As some inmates in these jurisdictions received parole dates before the law changed, probation officers provide for their post-release supervision. Other jurisdictions have so few parolees that the local probation officers supervise their release.

Table 9.2 summarizes field supervision service providers. The state-level department of corrections is the most common pattern of employment for post-release agents/officers, found in 36 states. Those agents or officers who supervise prison releases in five states work directly for the parole board. In two states supervisory staff are employed by the state-level department of community corrections. The courts oversee parole in the Federal System, the District of Columbia and Iowa. Finally, six states have other patterns of employment, but in most of them, the agents/officers work for a department of public safety.

The number of clients assigned to a given parole officer—like the caseload of probation officers—varies widely. Reliable estimates of the actual ratios for parole officers to clients served, as was the case

CALIFORNIA'S PUBLIC SAFETY REALIGNMENT

BOX 9.2

In May of 2011, the US Supreme Court upheld a three-judge panel's decision that the State of California was obligated to reduce its prison population to 137.5 percent of its rated capacity. Justice Anthony M. Kennedy, writing for the majority in a five to four decision that was decided along ideological lines,[6] described a failed prison system, one that did not deliver even minimal care to prisoners with serious medical and mental health problems. As a result that system produced "needless suffering and death." California was given 2 years to bring its system into compliance with this standard.

On October 1, 2011, the California instituted a new Public Safety Realignment, based on two laws that were intended to reduce the number of inmates. At the front end, California planned to place new nonviolent, nonsexual offenders under county jurisdiction, allowing the counties to release these inmates under a county-led post-release community supervision program (PRCS), funded in part by the state, and not employing the state's parole system. Normal attrition, then, would be relied upon to reduce the currently overcapacity prison system's population. California's prisons held 165,062 people at the end of 2010, which was before the landmark decision, and 149,569 a year later. The prison population was moving in the right direction, but the Supreme Court decision translated into no more than 110,000 prisoners at current rated capacity.

Faced with the twin realities of the iron law of prison populations and the iron law of imprisonment, California resorted to traditional parole, in this case unconditional release, for some 52 percent of prison releasees in the final quarter of 2011; these parolees had no post-release stipulations. Indeed, from 2010 to 2011 unconditional releases increased by nearly 700 percent. About this situation, the Bureau of Justice Statistics notes the following: "Since California incarcerates more individuals than any other state except Texas (10.8 percent of the US state prison population), changes in California's prison population have national implications."

This emerging situation begs several important questions. First, rather than react to court-mandated changes in correctional policies, why don't states act preemptively to avoid situations where policy is driven by legal necessity and not evidence-based exemplars? Is California a bell-weather for other states—and the federal system—which are also over capacity? Finally, why is this discussion important? Answers to some, but not all of these questions, lie in the rest of this chapter.

SOURCES: *BROWN V. PLATA* (2011); CARSON AND SABOL (2012, 4, 5).

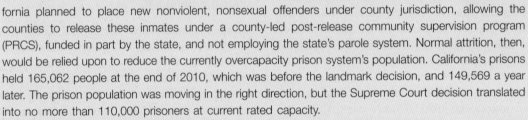

for probation officer–probationer ratios, are rare. In many jurisdictions, parole officers or probation officers who supervise parolees typically oversee a smaller number of releasees than do probation officers working entirely with probationers. This difference owes much to the fact that parolees are often viewed as posing a higher risk to the community than do probationers (DeMichele and Payne 2007; Girard and Wormwith 2004; see too Petersilia 1998). However, over the past several decades any putative differences between lower risk probationers and

higher risk parolees may have disappeared, as probationers' characteristics increasingly mirror the prison population, given that more than one half of all probationers are convicted felons (Taxman, Shepardson, and Byrne 2004, 3). It is not surprising, therefore, that the American Probation and Parole Association's report entitled *Probation and Parole's Growing Caseloads and Workload Allocation: Strategies for Managerial Decision Making* (DeMichele 2007) describes caseloads and workloads built around the risks, needs, and responsivity to various treatments of

TABLE 9.2 Field supervision service providers.

Type	Jurisdiction	
Parole Board	Alabama	Pennsylvania
	Georgia	Tennessee
	New Jersey	
Department of Corrections	Alaska	Montana
	Arizona	Nebraska
	California	New Hampshire
	Colorado	New Mexico
	Connecticut	New York
	Delaware	North Dakota
	Florida	Ohio
	Idaho	Oklahoma
	Illinois	Oregon
	Indiana	Rhode Island
	Kansas	South Dakota
	Kentucky	Utah
	Louisiana	Vermont
	Maine	Virginia
	Michigan	Washington
	Minnesota	West Virginia
	Mississippi	Wisconsin
	Missouri	Wyoming
Department of Community Corrections	Arkansas	South Carolina[a]
Courts	District of Columbia[b]	Federal System[c]
	Iowa	
Others	Hawaii[d]	Nevada[e]
	Maryland[d]	North Carolina[d]
	Massachusetts[e]	Texas[f]

NOTES: [a]DEPARTMENT OF PROBATION, PAROLE, AND PARDON SERVICES; [b]COURTS SERVICES AND OFFENDER SUPERVISION AGENCY; [c]US PRETRIAL AND PROBATION SERVICES; [d]DEPARTMENT OF PUBLIC SAFETY; [e]DEPARTMENT OF PUBLIC SAFETY AND SECURITY; [f]DEPARTMENT OF CRIMINAL JUSTICE.
SOURCES: CREATED BY THE AUTHORS FROM INFORMATION AVAILABLE AT THE RELEVANT AGENCY WEBSITES.

the person being supervised and does not simply divide them into two groups, probationers and parolees (National Institute of Corrections 2011; see too Andrews and Bonta 2007; Andrews and Dowden 2007). In essence, the descriptions of caseloads and workloads of probation officers (Chapter 4) also apply to parole officers and post-release supervisors.

CONDITIONS OF PAROLE

The official **parole agreement** generally lists a state's standard conditions of parole; these conditions are often indistinguishable from the conditions the state sets for probationers. If an inmate has special needs, his or her special conditions of parole also become part of the parole agreement. Consider, by way of example, the following set of conditions, which are part of a standard parole agreement in West Virginia:[7]

- Must report [to their parole officer] within 24 hours [of release].
- Stay within a certain area.
- Obtain permission before changing residence or employment.
- Obtain and maintain employment.
- Maintain acceptable, nonthreatening behavior.
- Must not possess firearms or weapons.
- Report any arrest within 24 hours.
- Complete monthly written report.
- Report as instructed.
- Must not use drugs or alcohol or enter drinking establishments.
- Must not break any state or local laws.
- Abide by other written requirements.
- Pay $40 supervision fee monthly.
- Sex Offenders of children cannot live with anyone under 18.
- Sex Offenders must register with WV State Police within 3 days.
- Allow contacts at home or employment without obstruction.
- Submit to search of person, residence or motor vehicle at any time by Parole Officers.

MIKE KARLSSON/ALAMY IMAGES

Some prison inmates, however, pose unique reintegration problems, largely due to public concerns about their presence in the community and statutory requirements that may restrict their release to terms of mandatory parole, even when the state provides discretionary parole to other offenders (DeMichele, Payne, and Katz 2011). Consider, for example, the case of sex offenders, who constitute roughly 2 percent of the parolee population (Glaze 2003, 4). The West Virginia conditions of parole contain several special conditions for sex offenders. In other states, additional conditions are common. Their parole can hinge on agreeing to at least two special conditions: that they cannot frequent places where children gather (for example, playgrounds, schoolyards, and skating rinks) and that they must participate in a specific outpatient therapy program. When paroled, their release conditions usually include intensive supervision. This means more

home visits than would normally be the case and, in some jurisdictions, mandatory polygraph tests, services that also increase the workloads of parole officers (English et al. 2003; English, Pullen, and Jones 1996; Sample and Bray 2003).

Despite the widespread belief that paroled sex offenders pose a serious threat to the community (see, for example, Pallone 2003), a significant body of research suggests that sex offenders have a very low recidivism rate, certainly lower than burglars, for example, who are seldom assigned special conditions of release (Sample and Bray 2003). These findings suggest that paroling authorities may be over-allocating scarce resources to a relatively low-risk offender or, at a minimum, diverting resources from other parolees at the same or higher risk of reoffending. We return to the topic of sex offenders in Chapter 14. As Richard Wright (2003, 99–100) has observed about sex offender supervision, it is often difficult to separate the science from the politics.

LENGTH OF SUPERVISION

State and federal laws govern the duration of parole. Typically, parolee supervision lasts for a minimum period, from as little as six months to as much as 7 or more years, depending on the jurisdiction and the original charge (that is, serious violent crimes may merit very long paroles). In jurisdictions employing mandatory release, a parolee may leave prison after serving two-thirds of his or her sentence and be required to continue on parole for the remaining one-third. Good or even exemplary behavior on parole generally does not shorten its length, short of a pardon or other act of executive clemency (Abadinsky 2012). By contrast, bad behavior can mean a return to prison or an extended period of supervision. Most states empower the parole authority to discharge parolees before the end of the mandated supervision period once the minimum has been satisfied. Again, there is considerable variation among the states in terms of how much time on parole is enough.

VIOLATIONS OF PAROLE

Parole has two possible outcomes: success and failure, continued residence in the free society or return to prison. In 2010, 52 percent of the parolees completed the term of supervision and earned unconditional release, a figure that has increased from 45 percent, where it had stood from the mid-1990s to 2009 (Glaze and Bonczar 2006, 9; 2011, 9). Failure is a complex term, covering several different statuses. For example, among the 48 percent of parolees that were unsuccessful, some returned to prison (33 percent), transferred to another jurisdiction for supervision (1 percent), died (1 percent), absconded (9 percent), or otherwise exited from parole (1 percent). These success rates are consistently lower than those reported for probationers, which was 65 percent in 2010 (Glaze and Bonczar 2011, 6).

Parolees (and probationers) who fail commit new offenses and technical violations. Once the parole officer learns of an alleged offense, he or she confers with a supervisor about the next step. If the alleged offense is serious, the parole officer asks the court of jurisdiction to issue an arrest warrant for the parolee. Once in custody, the parolee is likely to remain there until the issue is resolved: few states allow parolees to post bail. If the offense is not serious, the parole officer, after assessing the parolee's threat to the community and flight risk, may ask the court to issue a **citation**, a legal document roughly equivalent to a traffic ticket. The citation orders the parolee to appear at a violation hearing. In most states, a parole officer who observes a violation in person can immediately take the parolee into custody, an act called a **summary arrest**. In 2010, among the 33 percent of parolees who returned to incarceration, seven in ten were simply revoked, while slightly more than one-fourth received a new conviction and sentence. In Box 9.3, we address another important question: Who fails on parole?

THE PRELIMINARY HEARING

In *Morrissey v. Brewer* (1972), the Supreme Court ruled that parolees, like probationers, have limited due process rights. The Court did not mandate that a preliminary hearing take place before the parole board: its only stipulation was that the hearing had to be before a neutral party. Often a **hearing officer**, typically a supervisory-level or senior member of the parole agency staff, conducts the preliminary hearing. Here, too, the preliminary hearing is to determine probable cause. The parolee's case officer presents the government's case. Should the officer fail to make the case for a violation, the parolee returns to supervision. Should the hearing officer find that probable cause exists for one or more violations, he or she may remand the parolee to jail until the revocation hearing.

It is interesting to observe that the rate at which parolees return to prison as a result of a revocation decreased from 12 percent in 2000 to 9 percent in 2009, while those who committed a new offense and returned to prison remained at 4 percent during this

WHO FAILS ON PAROLE?   BOX 9.3

A 3-year study of recidivism for the National Institute of Justice (NIJ) followed a group of 272,111 former state inmates conditionally released in 1994. During the study period, 25 percent were arrested on a new charge (almost all for committing a felony or a serious misdemeanor), convicted, and sentenced to prison. Another 26 percent were sent back to prison solely for a technical violation of their conditions of release. After 3 years, then, nearly 52 percent of the releasees were back in prison, either serving a new sentence or serving their original one. As a group, the inmates had accumulated 4.1 million arrests prior to release; in the next 3 years, they added 744,000 arrests.

Who failed and who succeeded? Car thieves, those in prison for receiving or selling stolen property, larcenists, burglars, robbers, and those possessing, using, or selling illegal weapons failed at the highest rates, all above 70 percent. Among those with the lowest failure rates were murderers, sex offenders, rapists, and drunk drivers, all roughly at 50 percent or lower. Property offenders had the highest arrest rates within 3 years of release (74 percent) followed by drug offenders (68 percent), and public-order offenders and violent offenders (62 percent each). Finally, researchers found that the younger the offender, the higher the recidivism rate.

The researchers found that those releasees who served the most time—61 months or more—had a significantly lower rearrest rate than those who served less time. Violent offenders—inmates who generally receive the longest sentences—actually had lower recidivism rates than did nonviolent offenders, especially rapists and other sexual predators. It may be that these people, having spent more time in prison, stay out of trouble because they do not want to go back. Alternatively, it may be that the stringent conditions of their release, combined with regular and frequent supervision, limit their opportunities to commit new crimes.

For the same reasons, fewer conditions and less monitoring—and the lure of easy money on city streets—may combine to make it easier for property offenders and drug offenders to reoffend. The NIJ statistics are not an explanation for recidivism, but they punctuate the difficulties of predicting parolees' behavior.

SOURCE: LANGAN AND LEVIN (2002).

time (Glaze and Bonczar 2011, 10). Perhaps, as Burke (2007; see too Orrick and Morris 2012) recommended, decisions to revoke parole on the basis of technical violations should be undertaken with care and based on a concern for public safety and not simply the violation of a given rule.

THE REVOCATION HEARING

The makeup of the hearing board varies from state to state. Often the jurisdiction's parole board decides whether an alleged violator should return to incarceration or to parole. Whoever serves, the tribunal's neutrality is crucial: its members must have no stake in the outcome. Although the revocation hearing is more exhaustive and comprehensive than the preliminary hearing, many legal niceties are missing. Again, if the preponderance of evidence supports the alleged violation, the board has several options, including continuing parole with restricted freedom or incarcerating the parolee. When the hearing board, functioning as a quasi-judicial body, finds in the parolee's favor, supervision continues.

Jurisdictions vary greatly in their responses to two other key concerns. First, the parole violator may not have to serve the rest of his or her original sentence before a second parole. Unless the violation involves a new offense, eligibility may be statutory and likely occurs in a relatively short time. Second, paroling authorities also differ in their views on time served under parole supervision. In some states, this time does not count toward the original sentence; in others, parolees receive credit for their time in the community.

PRISONER REENTRY

Classic parole has largely been a failure. Its rates of success (and failure) have been unchanged for more than a decade (Glaze and Bonczar 2006), which some pundits might say is a sign of success. Many offenders find themselves caught in the justice turn-stile, entering, exiting and reentering prison in a cycle that seems to have no end (Theis, Winfree, and Griffiths 1982). However, two facts about prisoners—their huge numbers in prison and that they will nearly all return to society—suggest that the status quo is not good enough. This sentiment has precipitated a dialogue in the corrections community during the past several decades about what can be done to create a more successful inmate reentry system. The fact that discretionary parole was being replaced by release systems over which the prisons and parole authorities had little control suggested to many correctional policy makers that the nation needed a new perspective on reentry.

For many correctional experts, practitioners, and critics of the current system, prisoner reentry is that new perspective. As Joan Petersilia (2001, 360) so aptly observed: "Virtually no systematic, comprehensive attention has been paid by policy makers to deal with people after they are released, an issue that has been termed prisoner reentry." She based this statement on four sets of observations:

- *Determinate sentences means automatic release:* Statutorily, under current determinate sentencing guidelines, there is little the state or federal government can do to delay a person's release from incarceration. Most releasees go back into the community—and living conditions—from which they came before conviction, sentencing, and imprisonment. Now the conventional wisdom is that some control over a person's release date, as a way to respond to an inmate's unique issues and problems, many brought about by incarceration, is a good idea.

- *More parolees have unmet needs:* Spending longer periods behind bars means that releasees' contacts and support systems outside prison are more fragile or nonexistent. Importantly, given more prisoners in less space and with less money, treatment programs have been pared back, resulting in untreated physical and mental illnesses among the inmate population. Inmate skill and education training, never high, have been further degraded because of the imprisonment binge, "at a time when inmates need *more* help, not less" (Petersilia 2001, 363; also see Petersilia 2003). A number of current prison issues—including the expanded use of super-max prisons, increases in gang- and race-based violence, and higher than previously noted levels of mental illness among newly arrived inmates—means that the treatment and rehabilitative needs of contemporary prisoners are peaking, along with their numbers in prison.

- *Parolee supervision replaces services:* A key function of parole officers, in whatever form they are manifested, was to provide services to the releasees as they entered the community. Caseloads have skyrocketed, as one would expect given the increases in the number of parolees in both the state and federal systems. Petersilia (2001, 364) also points out that 20 percent of the prisoner releasees are under no supervision because they "max out" their sentences. These are exactly the people who need supervision and services most and will get none.

- *Most parolees return to prison:* Two-thirds of all parolees will return to prison within 3 years (Langan and Levin 2002). This statistic comes as no real surprise when you consider the general absence of social support networks, marketable work skills, and acceptable social skills, along with low educational attainment.

Ultimately, the current system—or what it has evolved into during the past 25 years—has serious flaws. What is needed is a recasting of parole and prisoner reentry into a system designed for success, not failure. The current movement toward a "no parole" system—one without discretion—does not appear to hold the answer. In Petersilia's (2001, 372) words: "When parole boards have no ability to select who will be released, they are forced to supervise a more serious parolee population and not one of their own choosing . . . Parole officers say that parole has lost its power to encourage inmates toward rehabilitation and sanction parole failures." A system based on a prisoner reentry perspective, by contrast, may hold much promise.

DEFINING PRISONER REENTRY

Prisoner reentry is not about semantics. This is not just a new way to express the old ideas. The concept of **prisoner reentry** is an old one. John Irwin (1970), in *The Felon,* used the term to describe release from prison and adjustment into the free society more than 40 years ago. During the 1990s, the term took on a more formalized meaning with respect to release from prison. However, as Travis (2005, xxi) observes about the unprecedented return of ex-convicts: "Reentry is the process of leaving prison and return to society. Reentry is not a form of supervision, like parole. Reentry is not a goal, like rehabilitation or reintegration. Reentry is not an option. An emphasis on reentry reflects the iron law of imprisonment: they all come back." It is also influenced strongly by the iron law of prison populations: The nation needs to restructure how it can reduce the burden on its prisons, while simultaneously providing for successful reentry and both public safety and security.

Reentry centers the prisoner release and reintegration debate on a new set of parameters. First, reentry can help redefine the role of prisons in society. The question becomes this: "How can prisoners best be prepared for their inevitable return?" Bridging between corrections-based institutional programming and community programming should be an essential element of any prisoner reentry program, no matter the conditions of release.

Second, prison managers must redefine their responsibilities beyond just holding inmates and releasing them at a specified time. "Prison administrators have a broader social obligation to prepare these prisoners for the inevitable return home" (Travis 2005, xxii). Unsupervised, maxed-out inmates have the same interest in successful reentry as any supervised inmate; the state's interest in reconnecting them to "positive and productive ties" is no different than for their highly supervised peers (Travis 2005, xxii).

Third, reentry is central to the thoughtful reconsideration of the nation's sentencing policies, whether it is "three-strikes" practices, sex offender civil commitments, or drug-law violations. Determinate sentences offer no substitute mechanisms for reintegrating offenders back into the community; indeed, they ignore the iron law of imprisonment. As Travis states it: "A sentencing policy that shows [violent, mentally ill and drug-addicted prisoners] the door makes little sense" (2005, xxiii).

Fourth, reentry shows us that successful reintegration and its impact on the offender and his or her family is at least as important a goal as lowered recidivism. Although the ties are not automatic, improving the former may have a positive impact on the latter.

Last, reentry allows policy makers, practitioners, and the public to see that prisoner release and reintegration have a dynamic connection to all other social policies, including but not limited to employment, public health, families and children, housing, community strengthening, and civic participation.

ELEMENTS OF SUCCESSFUL REENTRY

What are the elements of a successful reentry system? Travis (2005, 323–52) lists the following five action principles as essential for effective reentry:

1 *Prepare for reentry:* full employment of inmates in real work, preferably with learned skills and aptitudes that will translate into jobs upon release; the key is to work from entry to exit—and beyond into the community—with realistic, attainable training and treatment goals. Fully empowered inmates have their needs met in terms of work

opportunities, health care, family ties, community roles, and last but perhaps most importantly, their own personal expectations for reintegration. Time, money, and other resources invested here, claim proponents, will yield dividends upon release and reintegration.

2 *Build bridges between prisons and communities:* building bridges is a powerful metaphor, and one that is central to prisoner reentry. Bridges need to be built between criminal justice agencies, some operating as if they are the only element in the justice process. As we have seen throughout this text and this chapter in particular, those responsible for prisoner reentry at different junctures may have little contact with one another. The goal is to change this situation. Bridges are also needed between prisons and private organizations, especially when they have services to offer for reentering inmates. Travis suggests that it should not just be up to the prison staff to build these bridges, but that individual inmates should assume increased responsibility for working on the linkages as well. Finally, bridges need to be built between the corrections agency and the community. Not only will prisoners benefit, but so will the facility itself. "Prison administrators need to engage the world outside the prison walls" (Travis 2005, 332).

3 *Seize the moment of release:* the moment of release is not the end of the process. Prison staff should help bridge the gulf, more real than just symbolic, between the prison world and the outside world. Families should be involved. Transitional housing should be provided. Soon-to-be released inmates should be given an orientation. They should be "welcomed home," a small but important message to someone leaving prison. The symbolic and the tangible come together in this element of successful reentry.

4 *Strengthen the concentric circles of support:* the metaphor of concentric circles, with the returning inmate at the center, helps us understand the overlapping support and protection mechanisms needed for successful reintegration. The family is the first circle; its significance cannot be overstated. Next is the peer group. This circle is a

tricky one, as some peers are the source of negative influences. Sometimes the plan needs to include new, socially supportive, prosocial peer groups. The third circle, encompassing the previous two, is made up of community institutions. What is important to recognize about this circle is that working with it benefits the ex-prisoner, and the community gains a new perspective on prisons and prisoners. The social services circle provides jobs, public assistance, drug treatment, transitional housing, and the like, often for both reentering offenders and their families. Criminal justice agencies—especially parole and police services—make up the final circle. If they understand the role and scope of the other circles, this final element can play a central role in successful reintegration and quite possibly lowered recidivism.

5 *Promote successful reintegration:* Avoiding the confrontational nature of traditional release programs and emphasizing short-term, attainable goals is part of promoting reintegration as a real possibility rather than an ideal. Important transitional milestones must be acknowledged and praised. Everyone within the circles of support should engage in a new culture of reintegration that acknowledges just how far ex-offenders travel from their old lives in prison to their new lives in the community.

Travis's elements resonate with others. For example, Richard Seiter and Karen Kadela (2003) examined what works, what does not work, and what is promising in prisoner reentry. Their conclusion: programs that emphasize vocational training and work release are effective in reducing recidivism and preparing ex-offenders for jobs with marketable skills, all central to Travis's action elements for effective reentry. Seiter and Kadela also noted that prison-based drug treatment programs ease the transition from prison to the community. They did not find as much support for existing educational programs, which they classified as promising at best. In concert with Travis, they found that prerelease centers and programs could reduce recidivism (see too Williams 2007). None of these findings are unexpected: Travis's and Petersilia's (1998, 2001, 2003) ideas, among

close inspection of Table 9.3 reveals, these statistics represent only part of the overall picture of contemporary parole in the United States.

Most parolees fall under state authority, although the proportion of federal parolees, nearly 12 percent, is far higher than the 1 percent of federal probationers in the country. An important point about federal parole may help clarify the relatively large number of federal releasees. In the late 1980s, the *Sentencing Reform Act of 1984* went into effect. The intent of the act was to phase out parole by 1992. Anyone sentenced by a federal court on or after November 1, 1987, left prison on supervised release, not parole (see Box 9.1 for more on this Act). Indeed, as previously mentioned a dozen states or more moved from parole to some form of supervised release during this same time frame or, in the cases of Maine and Minnesota, even before the federal reforms took place.

Among federal entries, then, there were two types of supervision for individuals leaving prison: traditional parole, which accounts for less than 3 percent of all releasees, and supervised release, which accounts for nearly all of the rest. The reverse is true of state releases, where only about 6.5 percent were supervised releases and the rest were either discretionary parolees released by a parole board (28 percent) or mandatory parolees (44.5 percent) released from prison owing to determinate sentencing, good-time provisions, or emergency releases. Another small fraction, about 9 percent of the state releasees and less than 0.1 percent of federal releasees, had their paroles reinstated after a violation. Although the terms are different, these release formats—and the lives of the releasees—are, as we learned, very similar.

More than 14 percent of state parolees—about one in seven parolees—live in California, which also has a comparatively high per capita rate (per 100,000). In addition, the combined parolee populations of California, New York, Pennsylvania, and Texas account for almost 50 percent of the nation's state parolees. However, these are some of the nation's most populous states. Again, look at the per capita rates in Table 9.3 for a moment. The highest rate is for the District of Columbia. Even some states with populations smaller than the "big four" have per capita rates well above the national average, including Oregon, Arkansas, and Louisiana.

others, are based on decades of scientific study about what works, what does not work, and what shows promise in corrections. What is new is the redirection of the debate toward defining movement from the prison community to the free community, recognizing that it has as a beginning entry into the system and may not end even when the ex-offender reenters the community. Indeed, as the "Spotlight on International Corrections" in Box 9.4 makes clear, the concern for successful offender reentry is not limited to the United States.

PAROLE AND PRISONER REENTRY TODAY

On December 31, 2010, there were 840,676 parolees in the United States, a rate of 357 parolees for every 100,000 adult residents (Table 9.3).[8] However, as a

SPOTLIGHT ON INTERNATIONAL CORRECTIONS: PARDON AS A REINTEGRATION TOOL IN CANADA

BOX 9.4

One way to change for the better the lives of offenders in dramatic fashion is to expunge their criminal conviction records. Jobs are harder to get with a felony conviction record; ex-felons find many careers closed to them. Lying is one way around these difficulties. When it involves a criminal record, misrepresentation is grounds for immediate termination—if discovered. Moreover, it could lead to further criminal charges. The barriers that a criminal record puts between the ex-offender and a normal life impede reintegration itself.

Canada, among other nations and some US states, has an answer to this problem: the pardon. Essentially this practice amounts to setting aside one's criminal convictions through a process of partial expungement. Nearly all persons with criminal records who make an application to the Canadian National Parole Board (NPB) for a pardon—99 percent—routinely receive them. The costs are minimal, the paperwork not onerous.

Does it work? Alternatively, does this practice allow dangerous criminals to hide in plain sight in Canada? Rick Ruddell and L. Thomas Winfree provide some insights into these questions. Examining more than 30 years of NPB data, they found that most of the recipients—nearly 97 percent—were successful. In just over 3 percent of the cases, the pardon was revoked because of further crime or filing a fraudulent pardon application.

Several factors may explain this program's success. First, the ex-offenders must apply, complete the paperwork, and pay the fees. That is, they must be suitably motivated, which experts on human behavioral change tell us is essential if change is to occur. Second, successful applicants must not have had an indictable offense, or felony, in the past 5 years. In other words, they have already demonstrated an ability to lead a crime-free—or arrest-free—life for an extended period. Finally, there are protections. Although the previous records are sealed, they remain available and may be used at any subsequent sentencing, so in this sense, the records are not completely expunged from the criminal justice system.

SOURCE: RUDDELL AND WINFREE (2006).

Then there are the states with very small per capita parole numbers, ones below 100 per 100,000 adult residents in that state or roughly one-third the national per capita rate. There are two groups of such states, the first including Massachusetts, Nebraska, North Dakota, Oklahoma, and Rhode Island. There is no single reason for these low rates. Some of these states have small prison populations, even taking into consideration state populations; others have relatively high numbers of prisoners, but do not parole as many of them. The one common element is that all five in this group utilize discretionary parole exclusively. Before we reach the conclusion that it is all about discretionary parole, consider a final group of five states—Delaware, Florida, Maine, North Carolina, and Virginia—that also have per capita parole

rates under 100. Maine is a special case, having abolished parole in the 1973. Unlike the first group, however, the remaining four states do not use the same parole model (see Table 9.1) and similar to that group are a mixture of states with large and small prison populations. The far lower per capita rates in all ten of these states and the very high rates in many other states, then, appear to be related to state-specific parole laws, policies and practices.

PROFILES OF PAROLEES

Whites were in a plurality among parolees (42 percent) in 2010, although blacks were close behind (39 percent), followed by Hispanics (18 percent) and American Indian/Alaska Native (1 percent), and

TABLE 9.3 Adults on parole, 2010.

Region and jurisdiction	Parole population, 1/1/2010	Entries	Exits	Parole population, 12/31/2010	Change, 2010 Number	Change, 2010 Percent	Number on parole per 100,000 U.S. adult residents, 12/31/2010
U.S. total	837,818	565,264	562,478	840,676	2,858	0.3	357
Federal	100,598	47,873	42,919	105,552	4,954	4.9	45
State	737,220	517,391	519,559	735,124	-2,096	-0.3	312
Alabama	8,429	3,024	2,447	9,006	577	6.8	249
Alaska	1,923	593	427	2,089	166	8.6	393
Arizona	8,186	12,880	13,073	7,993	-193	-2.4	161
Arkansas	21,077	9,395	9,366	21,106	29	0.1	957
California[b]	106,371	166,340	167,782	105,133	-1,238	-1.2	376
Colorado	11,655	8,978	9,619	11,014	-641	-5.5	283
Connecticut	2,873	3,413	3,392	2,894	21	0.7	106
Delaware	519	516	475	560	41	7.9	81
District of Columbia	5,992	2,222	2,043	6,171	179	3.0	1,235
Florida	4,323	6,528	6,758	4,093	-230	-5.3	28
Georgia	23,709	13,622	12,240	25,091	1,382	5.8	341
Hawaii	1,831	814	795	1,850	19	1.0	183
Idaho	3,447	1,863	1,353	3,957	510	14.8	344
Illinois	33,162	26,578	33,731	26,009	-7,153	-21,6	265
Indiana[b]	10,989	10,607	10,724	10,872	-117	-1.1	223
Iowa[b]	3,259	2,312	2,374	3,197	-62	-1.9	138
Kansas[b]	5,010	4,793	4,740	5,063	53	1.1	236
Kentucky	12,601	9,154	7,127	14,628	2,027	16.1	438
Louisiana	23,607	15,755	13,160	26,202	2,595	11.0	767
Maine	32	1	1	32	0	0.0	3
Maryland[a]	13,195	6,378	6,378	13,195	0	0.0	299
Massachusetts	3,253	4,507	4,500	3,260	7	0.2	62
Michigan	24,374	12,137	12,025	24,486	112	0.5	321
Minnesota	5,435	5,706	5,334	5,807	372	6.8	143
Mississippi	5,426	3,423	2,415	6,434	1,008	18.6	292
Missouri	18,857	11,570	11,006	19,421	564	3.0	421

Montana	1,007	580	601	986	−21	−2.1	129
Nebraska	823	1,147	1,029	941	118	14.3	69
Nevada	4,186	4,625	3,847	4,964	778	18.6	250
New Hampshire	1,883	1,284	1,194	1,973	90	4.8	139
New Jersey	15,356	8,183	7,976	15,563	207	1.3	232
New Mexico	3,157	510	521	3,146	−11	−0.3	206
New York	49,950	23,461	24,869	48,542	−1,408	−2.8	319
North Carolina[a]	3,544	3,833	3,756	3,621	77	2.2	50
North Dakota	363	818	754	427	64	17.6	83
Ohio	14,575	6,655	9,154	12,076	−2,499	−17.1	136
Oklahoma[a]	2,970	596	939	2,627	−343	−11.5	93
Oregon	22,117	8,799	8,425	22,491	374	1.7	750
Pennsylvania	96,014	53,156	53,300	95,870	−144	−0.1	967
Rhode Island[b]	537	488	469	556	19	3.5	67
South Carolina	6,419	3,053	3,060	6,412	−7	−0.1	182
South Dakota	2,748	1,706	1,611	2,843	95	3.5	455
Tennessee	11,556	4,595	3,854	12,157	601	5.2	250
Texas[a]	104,943	33,050	33,230	104,763	−180	−0.2	570
Utah	3,185	1,780	2,024	2,941	−244	−7.7	150
Vermont[a]	1,087	513	568	1,032	−55	−5.1	206
Virginia[a]	2,565	1,060	1,001	2,624	59	2.3	43
Washington	6,563	5,733	5,340	6,956	393	6.0	134
West Virginia	1,889	1,302	1,395	1,796	−93	−4.9	124
Wisconsin	19,499	6,995	6,930	19,572	73	0.4	446
Wyoming[a]	749	360	427	682	−67	−8.9	163
Northeast	170,985	95,006	96,269	169,722	−1,263	−0.7	392
Midwest	139,094	91,024	99,412	130,714	−8,380	−6.0	255
South	252,764	117,506	109,644	260,486	7,722	3.1	300
West	174,177	211,855	214,234	174,202	−175	−0.1	320

NOTE: BECAUSE OF NONRESPONSE OR INCOMPLETE DATA, THE PAROLE POPULATION FOR SOME JURISDICTIONS ON DECEMBER 31, 2010, DOES NOT EQUAL THE POPULATION ON JANUARY 1, 2011, PLUS ENTRIES, MINUS EXITS. ALL AGENCIES REPORTED PAROLE ENTRIES AND EXITS FOR 2010. RATES WERE COMPUTED USING THE ESTIMATED U.S. ADULT RESIDENT POPULATION IN EACH JURISDICTION ON JANUARY 1, 2011.

[a]SOME OR ALL DATA WERE ESTIMATED.

[b]POPULATION EXCLUDES PAROLEES ABSCONDER OR SUPERVISED OUT OF STATE CATEGORIES.

SOURCE: GLAZE AND BONCZAR (2011, 40).

Asian/Native Hawaiian, other Pacific Islander (1 percent).[9] Males far outnumbered females on parole (88 percent versus 12 percent). Given sustained increases in number of women in prison observed during the past 20 years, it is not surprising that the proportion of parolees who were female increased from 10 percent in 1995 to 12 percent in 2010, a nearly 20 percent jump. However, men dominated the parolee population in 2000, as they did the prison population. Except for the increase in female parolees, these figures were virtually unchanged from those observed in 2000.

Nearly all parolees in 2010 (95 percent) were felons, a much higher percentage than for probationers who committed felonies. When considering their most serious offense, more parolees were drug offenders (35 percent) than were property offenders (24 percent) or violent criminals (27 percent). Public order or other crimes were the most serious offense for 12 percent of all parolees. Weapons offenses added another 3 percent. More than 80 percent of parolees were on active supervision while 7 percent were inactive, meaning that they no longer regularly reported to their parole supervisors. The percentage

of parolees who were absconders (6 percent) was lower than that reported for probationers. Out-of-state supervision for parolees, by contrast, was higher than that for probationers (4 percent versus 2 percent).

TRENDS IN PAROLE AND PRISONER REENTRY

Figure 9.1 provides a visual representation of 30 years of growth in the federal and state parole systems. It contains both the annual percentage change and the yearend population on parole. With respect to the former, parole grew at an average rate of roughly 7 percent a year. But this characterization hides what actually was happening to the institution of parole, that is, parole populations experienced annual percentage increases ranging from 6 percent to 16 percent from 1982 through 1992, when the percentage growth stabilized either side of 2 percent. Throughout the first decade of the twenty-first century, then, the growth rate moved up very slowly, then headed down and finally ended the decade in the negative (2009), rising slightly in 2010.

FIGURE 9.1 **Adults on parole at year end, 1980–2010.** *Source:* Glaze and Bonczar (2011, 2).

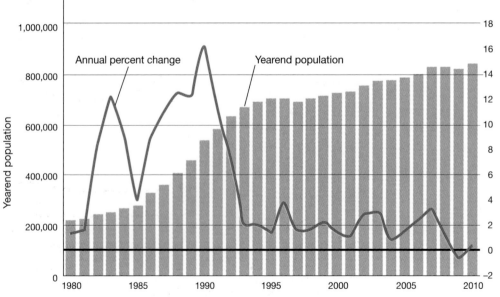

The actual number of parolees also experienced dramatic growth between 1980 and 2010. By 2010, the number of parolees in the country had more than tripled, from 222,036 to 784,408 (Glaze and Bonczar 2011). Between 1990 and 2005, the average annual growth rate for parole was similar to that of probation. However, the parole rate also increased more than 150 percent between 1980 and 2010. The change in the federal parolee rate, given the elimination of discretionary parole between 1987 and 1992, was in the wrong direction. In 1980, the federal per capita parole rate stood at 12. By 2010, the rate had increased to 45; it was more than three and one-half times the earlier federal parole rate and more than four times the federal probation rate.

This counterintuitive trend may reflect the flood of inmates into federal prisons following the Sentencing Reform Act of 1984 (see Box 9.1). To deal with the front-end pressure on facilities and staff, the US Bureau of Prisons began using supervised release programs on the back end of a sentence. Indeed, this is precisely what happened between 1991—when the federal parole population stood at 21,000-plus

(within 2,000 parolees of where it had been for nearly 5 years)—and 1992, when it ballooned to nearly 40,000. Over the past 20 years it has more than doubled again. Given the relatively high overcapacity rate reported for federal prisons in 2011, which stood at 138 percent of the rated capacity on December 31, 2011, the federal system of prisoner release is having difficulty keeping pace with demands on it (Carson and Sabol 2012, 31).

The methods of release tell us the rest of the story. Specifically, we are interested in how these policy shifts have impacted the methods of release from prison. In 1980, before three-strikes and truth-in-sentencing laws, mandatory sentencing, and restrictions on parole practices, 58 percent of releasees left prison on discretionary parole, while less than 20 percent of the releasees left under mandatory parole and most of the rest completed their sentences and were not subject to post-release supervision (Glaze and Bonczar 2006, 8). In the twenty-first century, mandatory parole has become the most prevalent form of release, used in about 40 percent of all prison releases. Figure 9.2 gives details of prison

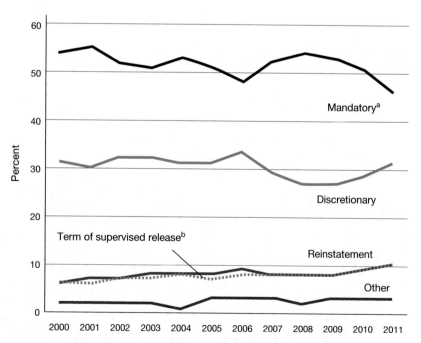

FIGURE 9.2 Entries to parole, by type of entry, 2000–2011.
Source: Maruschak and Parks (2012).

[a]Includes data reported as term of supervised release by states and the District of Columbia from 2008 to 2011.
[b]Federal data only. Includes estimates for 2000 to 2007.

releases since 2000. What is interesting about these statistics is that after 20 years of decline, the use of mandatory release has declined slightly (2000–2011), offset by an equal increase in discretionary releases (2000–2011). Whether these trends continue depends on how state legislatures—and the US Congress— respond to the pressures of mass incarceration and come to grips with the influences of both the iron law of imprisonment and the iron law of prison populations.

As Travis (2005) observed—and reports on prison populations and parole reinforce—nearly all parolees will eventually return to the community.[10] And, according to the provisions of Clear and Austin's (2009) iron law of prison populations, there are only two ways to gain control of the nation's over-extended prison system. States can either slow down the entries or speed up the exits. Those states with large prison systems must have supportive parole or supervised release systems. Their only alternative would be to free prisoners with no supervision. This is a situation that few people believe would be good for the nation. Moreover, one important lesson of the reentry research is that if we expect releasees to make that adjustment we must ease them back into society with an entire repertoire of social, work, and relational skills, a format that can only be provided the ex-prisoners through a system that resembles parole or supervised release.

SUMMARY

Parole and prisoner reentry—like Chapter 4's probation and community corrections—are similar to each other, but differ in important ways as well, especially given the specific way most jurisdictions use parole and the rather generic use of the term *prisoner reentry*. From this chapter, you should especially note the following:

- Parole allows the executive branch to exercise a similar measure of control and to provide a similar measure of security for what many view as a more dangerous population (people not eligible for probation or other community-based corrections programs).

- Parole or supervised release gives the offender an opportunity to show that he or she can live lawfully and productively in the free community.

- Parole allows both jail and prison systems to relieve the pressure of crowding.

- The War on Drugs and other legislative initiatives, along with state and federal movements to restrict or eliminate parole (through determinate sentencing), have swelled the number of inmates in jails and prisons, and with that increase has come an increase in the use of parole.

- The number of people entering the justice funnel is unlikely to decrease in the near future. This means that parole and other means of prisoner reentry are likely to remain important alternatives to incarceration.

- The future of prisoner release may depend on the extent to which policymakers take to heart the action principles underlying prisoner reentry as a new way of viewing the reintegration of ex-offenders into the community.

- Contrary to the position widely endorsed in the 1980s and 1990s, parole is not dead. States have abandoned it, only to reconstitute it, often in response to pressures created by the iron law of prison populations at the end of the millennium. Even Maine, which made the most complete break of all with parole, was experiencing political and social pressures to restore the system.[11] Parole, in its many manifestations, has proven itself an integral and responsive part of the nation's correctional system.

THINKING ABOUT CORRECTIONAL POLICIES AND PRACTICES: WRITING ASSIGNMENTS

1 Criminal justice has very few "laws," at least the kinds that allow us greater insights into the operation of the system's component parts. This chapter references two of them. What are they? (*Hint*: One of them is found in Note 1.) How can knowledge of these laws help the nation deal with the problem of prisoner reentry?

2 The use of parole varies widely across the nation, from state to state, from region to region. Speculate as to reasons why these differences occur. Is this a matter of cultural and social variability or are other explanations at work?

3 Visit your state's prisoner release authority home page. Look for a discussion of supervisory agents and policies governing their use. Sometimes, this information is found under a FAQ heading or career opportunities. Next, visit the homepage of a prisoner release agency that has a different policy on firearms for parole officers. For example, if your state requires that they carry firearms, find one that does not or makes it optional. Can you determine from these web pages why each agency has adopted its respective policies? Prepare a summary of what you found and which one makes the best argument.

4 In an era of mandatory release's growth and the decline of discretionary release, provide at least two reasons why the states and the federal government may want to return to the use of parole boards and discretionary prison release. Why is this likely or unlikely to happen? Describe your thoughts on these questions in an essay.

5 Prepare a brief, one-page essay on the total exclusion of technical violations in the consideration of parole revocation. Discuss both sides of the argument. (*Hint*: You may want to cite one of the laws mentioned in the first question in this list.)

KEY TERMS

citation	independent parole boards	parole agents
commutation of sentence	inspector of released prisoners	parole agreement
consolidated parole boards	institutional model	parole eligibility date
discretionary release	Irish ticket-of-leave system	parole officers
expiration release	iron law of imprisonment	prisoner reentry
false negatives	iron law of prison	probation/parole officers
false positives	populations	(PPOs)
good-time laws	mandatory release	summary arrest
guardians	pardon	supervised release
hearing officer	parole	

CRITICAL REVIEW QUESTIONS

1 What does the history of parole suggest about the practice? Explain that history and its linkages to current methods of prisoner reentry.

2 Which type of parole board—independent or consolidated—seems better equipped to render the most equitable parole decisions? Explain your answer.

3 The demise of discretionary release from prison was predicted in the 1980s and early 1990s. What is the basis of this prediction? What is its current status? Include in your answer an appreciation for the professional parole commission as an alternative to the parole board.

4 Table 9.1 contains a great deal of information. How would you summarize it? What do you believe is the most difficult aspect of a parole officer's job? Explain your answer.

5 The federal government has created one of the nation's largest prison systems since sentencing reforms in the late 1980s. Apply the iron law of prison populations to this micro-example of "mass federal incarceration" and describe how the number of federal inmates could be reduced.

6 Would you rather be a probation officer or a parole officer? Explain your answer.

7 Summarize the trends in parole between 1980 and 2010. Which single fact about these trends do you find most interesting and why?

8 Early parole proponents had to weave a path through US values and economic necessities. If you look at parole and other prisoner release mechanisms in the twenty-first century what do you see as the forces marshaling against early release of prisoners? Provide a summary of what you see as the main contemporary arguments against early release.

9 What legal changes to the criminal justice system would you support to reduce the number of offenders entering the parole systems? (Remember that changes we make in the criminal justice system are likely to have an effect on other systems, among them health care and social services.)

CASES CITED

Brown v. Plata, No. 09–1233. Argued November 30, 2010—Decided May 23, 2011.
Morrissey v. Brewer, 408 U.S. 471 (1972.

Swarthout v. Cooke, 562 U.S. _____ (2011) [USSC 10-333]

NOTES

1 In 1950, the Board was assigned the task of providing parole decisions for the Youth Corrections Division, a task that absorbed by the Commission in 1976.

2 It is important to observe that the 85-percent rule does not extend to all crimes, even in states that use it. For example, some states use it only for crime corresponding to the Federal Bureau of Investigations Part I Violent Crimes, while other states use it for all crime, including misdemeanors (Sabol et al. 2002).

3 Alabama, Connecticut, Georgia, Idaho, Louisiana, Missouri, Montana, Oklahoma, Oregon, Pennsylvania, South Carolina, South Dakota, Tennessee, Texas, and Utah.

4 Alaska, Arkansas, California, Colorado, Delaware, Indiana, Iowa, Kentucky, Massachusetts, Michigan, Mississippi, Missouri, Nebraska, New Hampshire, New Jersey, New Mexico, New York, North Dakota, Ohio, Oregon, Rhode Island, Tennessee, Vermont, Virginia, West Virginia, and Wyoming.

5 Florida, Maryland, Nevada, North Carolina, and Wisconsin.

6 Even the dissenters were split. Justice Scalia filed a dissent, joined by Justice Thomas; Justice Alito filed a separate dissent, joined by Chief Justice Roberts.

7 Obtained from the following website: **http://www.wvdoc. com/wvdoc/ParoleServicesResources/StandardConditionsof Parole/tabid/143/Default.aspx** (last accessed July 16, 2013)

8 It is important to note that although we use the term *parolee* in this discussion, these statistics include persons released from prison or jail because of mandatory release programs or other forms of conditional release. However, even the Bureau of Justice Statistics calls these people *parolees.*

9 The following discussion is taken largely from Glaze and Bonczar (2011), Appendix Table 15.

10 We would be remiss if we did not acknowledge the observations of our former colleague Joseph Rogers, who wrote in 1989 (p. 21): "First, 99 percent of those entering prison eventually return to society to become our neighbors in the communities where we live and work." Roger was off a bit on the figure (99 percent versus 95 percent), but then he was basing his calculations on 1980s sentencing practices.

11 In 2011, 70 Maine legislators signed a bill intended to review the possibility of bring back parole for some offenders; victims-rights advocacy groups and politicians who contend the bill would conflict with the governor's exclusive rights to extend clemency opposed the bill (Sharon 2011). At this time, parole is denied to nearly all of Maine's prison inmates.

REFERENCES

Abadinsky, H. 2012. *Probation and parole*, 11th edn. Upper Saddle River, NJ: Prentice Hall.

Andrews, D.A., and J. Bonta. 2007. *Risk-need-responsivity model for offender assessment and rehabilitation, 2007-06*. Ottawa, Canada: Public Safety Canada.

Andrews, D.A., and C. Dowden. 2007. The risk-need-responsivity model of assessment and human service in prevention and corrections: Crime-prevention jurisprudence. *Canadian Journal of Criminology and Criminal Justice* 49(4):439–64.

Barnes, R., M.G. Turner, R. Paternoster, and S.D. Bushway. 2012. Cumulative prevalence of arrest from ages 8 to 23 in a national sample. *Pediatrics* January: 21–7.

Bureau of Justice Statistics. 2007. *Reentry trends in the US: Releases from state prisons*. Retrieved June 25, 2007 from: http://www.ojp.usdoj.gov/bjs/reentry/reentry.htm

Burke, P. 2007. *When offenders break the rules: Smart responses to parole and probation violations*. Washington, DC: The Pew Center on the States.

Cahalan, Margaret W. 1986. *Historical corrections statistics in the United States, 1850–1984*. Washington, DC: US Government Printing Office.

Carson, E.A., and W. J. Sabol. 2012. *Prisoners in 2011*. Washington, DC: US Department of Justice.

Catton, Bruce. 1960. *The American heritage picture history of the Civil War*. New York: Outlook.

Clear, Todd R. 1994. *Harm in American penology: Offenders, victims, and their communities*. Albany: State University of New York Press.

Clear, Todd R., and J. Austin. 2009. Reducing mass incarceration: Implications of the iron law of prison populations. *Harvard Law and Policy Review* 3: 307–24.

Cullen, F.T. 1995. Assessing the penal harm movement. *Journal of Research in Crime and Delinquency* 32(3): 338–58.

DeMichele, Matthew T. 2007. *Probation and parole's growing caseload and workload allocation: Strategies for managerial decision making*. Alexandria, VA: American Probation and Parole Association.

DeMichele, M.T., and B.K. Payne. 2007. Probation and parole officers speak out—Caseload and workload allocations. *Federal Probation* 71(3): 30–5.

DeMichele, Matthew T., B.K. Payne, and A.K. Katz. 2011. *Community supervision workload considerations for public safety*. Washington, DC: Bureau of Justice Assistance.

English, Kim, Linda Jones, Diane Pasini-Hill, Diane Patrick, and Sidney Cooley-Hill. 2003. *The value of polygraph testing in sex offender management*. Washington, DC: US Department of Justice.

English, Kim, Suzanne Pullen, and Linda Jones. 1996. *Managing adult sex offenders: A containment approach*. Lexington, KY: American Probation and Parole Association.

Friedman, Leon. 1972. *The law of war: A documentary history*, vol. 1. New York: Random House.

Girard, Lina, and J. Stephen Wormwith. 2004. The predictive validity of the level of service inventory-Ontario revision on general and violent recidivism among offender groups. *Criminal Justice and Behavior* 31: 150–81.

Glaze, Lauren E. 2003. *Probation and parole in the United States, 2002*. Washington, DC: US Department of Justice.

Glaze, Lauren E., and Thomas P. Bonczar. 2006. *Probation and parole in the United States, 2005*. Washington, DC: US Department of Justice.

Glaze, Lauren E., and Thomas P. Bonczar. 2011. *Probation and parole in the United States, 2010*. Washington, DC: US Department of Justice.

Hoffman, P.B. 2003. *The history of the federal parole system*. Washington, DC: US Parole Commission.

Irwin, John. 1970. *The felon.* Englewood Cliffs, NJ: Prentice Hall.

Klein, Philip. 1920. *Prison methods in New York State.* New York: Columbia University Press.

Langan, Patrick A., and David J. Levin. 2002. *Recidivism of prisoners released in 1994.* Washington, DC: Bureau of Justice Statistics.

Maruschak, L.M., and E. Parks. 2012. *Probation and Parole in the United States, 2011.* Washington, DC: U.S.US Department of Justice.

National Institute of Corrections. 2011. *Parole essentials: Practical guides for parole leaders, 4. Special challenges facing parole.* Washington, DC: National Institute of Justice.

New York State Division of Parole. 2007. *History of parole in New York State.* Retrieved June 25, 2007 from: http://parole.state.ny.us/INTROhistory.asp

Newman, Charles L. 1958. *Sourcebook on probation, parole and pardons.* Springfield, IL: Charles C. Thomas.

Orrick, E.A., and R.G. Morris. 2012. Do parole technical violators pose a safety threat? An analysis of prison misconduct. *Crime & Delinquency.* Retrieved July 16, 2013 from: http://cad.sagepub.com/content/early/2012/11/28/0011128712465585.abstract

Pallone, Nathaniel J. 2003. Without plea bargaining, Megan Kanka would be alive today. *Criminology & Public Policy* 3: 83–96.

Patzman, John, and Kim English. 1994. *Parole guidelines handbook.* Denver: Division of Criminal Justice.

Petersilia, J. 1998. Probation in the United States, Part 2. *Perspectives.* Summer. Retrieved July 16, 2013 from: http://www.appa-net.org/eweb/Resources/PPCSW_12/docs/su98pers42.pdf

Petersilia, J. 2001. Prisoner reentry: Public safety and reintegration challenges. *Prison Journal* 91: 360–5.

Petersilia, J. 2003. *When prisoners come home.* New York: Oxford University Press.

Rogers, J. W. 1989. The greatest correctional myth: Winning the war on crime through incarceration. *Federal Probation* LIII(3): 21–8.

Ruanda, J., E. Rhine, and R. Wetter. 1994. *The practice of parole boards.* Lexington, KY: Council of State Governments.

Ruddell, Rick, and L. Thomas Winfree, Jr. 2006. Setting aside criminal convictions in Canada: A successful approach to offender reintegration. *Prison Journal* 86: 452–69.

Sabol, W.J., K. Rosich, K. M. Kane, D. Kirk, and G. Dubin. 2002. *Influences of truth-in-sentencing reforms on changes in states' sentencing practices and prison populations, executive summary.* Washington, DC: US Department of Justice.

Sample, Lisa L., and Timothy M. Bray. 2003. Are sex offenders dangerous? *Criminology & Public Policy* 3: 59–82.

Seiter, Richard P., and Karen R. Kadela. 2003. Prisoner reentry: What works, what does not, and what is promising. *Crime & Delinquency* 49: 360–88.

Sharon, S. 2011. Maine lawmaker proposes restoring state's parole system. *Maine Public Broadcasting Network News,* 5 May 2011. Retrieved July 16, 2013 from: http://www.mpbn.net/News/MPBNNews/tabid/1159/ctl/ViewItem/mid/3762/ItemId/16372/Default.aspx

Taxman, F., E. Shepardson, and J. Byrne. 2004. *Tools of the trade: A guide for incorporating science into practice.* Washington, DC: National Institute of Corrections.

Theis, Harold E., L. Thomas Winfree, Jr., and Curt T. Griffiths. 1982. Correlates of the parole-reparole process: An examination of "revolving door" corrections. *Corrective and Social Psychiatry and Journal of Behavior Technology Methods and Therapy* 28: 121–30.

Travis, Jeremy. 2005. *But they all come back: Facing the challenges of prisoner reentry.* Washington, DC: Urban Institute.

US Courts. 2013. *Term of supervised release.* Retrieved July 16, 2013 from: http://www.uscourts.gov/FederalCourts/ProbationPretrialServices/CommonlyUsedTerms.aspx

US Sentencing Commission. 2013. *About the commission.* Retrieved July 16, 2013 from: http://www.justice.gov/uspc/about-comm.html

Williams, T. H. 2007. What works? Evidence-based practices in parole and probation. *Journal of Community Corrections* 16(4): 5–7.

Winfree, L. Thomas, Jr., Christine S. Sellers, Veronica Smith Ballard, and Roy R. Roberg. 1990. Responding to a legislated change in correctional practices: A quasi-experimental study of revocation hearings and parole board actions. *Journal of Criminal Justice* 18(3): 195–215.

Winfree, L. Thomas, Jr., John Wooldredge, Christine S. Sellers, and Veronica S. Ballard. 1990. Parole survival and legislated change: A before/after study of parole revocation decision making. *Justice Quarterly* 7(1): 151–173.

Wright, Richard. 2003. Sex offender registration and notification: Public attention, political emphasis, and fear. *Criminology & Public Policy* 3: 97–104.

CAREERS IN CORRECTIONS 10

Outline

Institutional Corrections: Correctional
Officers and Counselors

Community-Based Corrections:
Probation and Parole Officers

Community-Based Corrections:
Counselors and Other Workers

Workplace Challenges

The Trend Toward Professionalization

Finding a Job

Internships and Cooperative Education

Job Prospects

Correctional Employee Ethics

Objectives

- To help you understand the various jobs available in corrections

- To introduce you to some of the major challenges facing correctional employees

- To explain to you the movement toward correctional professionalization

- To help you in the job application process, including finding internships

- To introduce you to the ethical dilemmas faced by corrections employees

Essentials of Corrections, Fifth Edition. G. Larry Mays and L. Thomas Winfree, Jr.
© 2014 John Wiley & Sons, Inc. Published 2014 by John Wiley & Sons, Inc.

INTRODUCTION

"What can I do with a degree in criminal justice . . . or sociology, psychology, social work, or whatever?" Our students always ask this question. University and college instructors typically spend a great deal of time advising students who want to work in the criminal justice system. In this chapter, we explore the work experiences of different corrections professionals, and offer insights into finding and applying for corrections positions.

One of the first things students are pleased to discover is that corrections is a large and expanding segment of the US labor market. For example, in 2008, of the nearly 2.5 million people employed in criminal justice systems, 794,825—roughly a third—worked in corrections: 36,770 (5 percent) at the federal level, 485,759 (61 percent) at the state level, and 272,296 (34 percent) at the local level. The total number of corrections employees at all levels in the United States grew by more than 470,423 people between 1982 and 2008. In the same period, state and local expenditures for corrections (including payrolls) increased from $9.03 billion to $79.6 billion, far outpacing inflation (Hughes 2006; Kycklehahn 2012). Positions are increasingly available in the public and private sectors for people interested in working with accused and convicted offenders. Some students are reluctant to explore a career in corrections because they do not want to work in a jail or a prison—that should not discourage them. Yes, there are many jobs available in institutional settings, but there also are a good number of jobs in noninstitutional settings. In this chapter, we describe what is available both inside and outside secure facilities, for people with associate degrees all the way to doctoral degrees. We explore many specific career options here, along with the advantages and disadvantages of particular jobs, approximate pay scales, workloads, promotion opportunities, hiring restrictions, and public- versus private-sector employment. We conclude this chapter with a discussion of employee ethics.

Money is always a topic of conversation with students. Usually, instructors start their replies, when asked how much one can expect to make in corrections, with something like the following: "In public service, you can't expect to make a lot of money." Consider that the average yearly salary for all federal justice employees in 2010 was $79,629, whereas for state justice employees, it was $53,619. Local personnel earned, on average, $58,665. Moreover, as we suggested, correctional workers are not among the highest paid employees in the criminal justice system. Evidence supporting this observation comes from a comparison of the law enforcement officers and corrections staff at state and local levels. On average, police officers at the state level earn $71,939 a year and local police officers earned $67,484, whereas state and local corrections workers had an average of $48,645 and $50,084 respectively (US Census Bureau 2010). At the federal level, correctional employees can expect to earn more than their state and local counterparts do, although less than their federal law enforcement peers. Clearly, justice system workers generally are not the highest-paid government employees.

INSTITUTIONAL CORRECTIONS: CORRECTIONAL OFFICERS AND COUNSELORS

Institutional work is one of the major employment areas in corrections. **Institutional corrections** involves employment in any facility in which state and local governments house accused or convicted offenders. According to the Bureau of Labor Statistics (2012), institutional corrections jobs are located in the following settings:

- prisons and penitentiaries;
- reformatories;
- jails;
- houses of correction;
- correctional farms;
- workhouses;
- industrial and training schools;
- institutions and facilities exclusively for the confinement of those who are criminally insane;

- institutions and facilities for the examination, evaluation, classification, and assignment of inmates; and

- certain facilities for the confinement, treatment, and rehabilitation of drug addicts and alcoholics

Correctional institutions employed roughly 60 percent of all state and local corrections workers in the United States (Hughes 2006; Stephan 2008; Kycklehahn 2012). They worked at all manner of jobs, from uniformed correctional officers to chief administrators (see Box 10.1). Bear in mind, however, that two-thirds of all institutional corrections employees work in custody or security positions (Stephan 2008, 4).

CORRECTIONAL OFFICERS

Most people who work in secure facilities start out as **correctional officers (COs)**, the staff members

---

WORKING IN INSTITUTIONAL CORRECTIONS: THE REST OF THE STORY   BOX 10.1

Correctional officer (CO) and correctional counselor are just two of the jobs available in secure facilities; there are many others. Actually, the easiest way to think about the institutional workplace is to think of a jail, detention center, prison or any institutional facility as a small city. A correctional facility must provide for its inmates every service that a city must provide its residents.

Consider, for example, medical services. Large facilities employ doctors, nurses, physicians' assistants, emergency medical technicians, dentists, dental hygienists, and pharmacists. In the medical services area—and we see this elsewhere as well—the corrections agency fills some of these positions; private contractors fill others.

Recreation is another area where correctional facilities need workers. Many prisons employ recreational specialists to help inmates organize team sports (softball, basketball) and individual activities (workouts, weightlifting). In addition, inmate arts and crafts programs constitute a recreational component. Prisons often provide instruction and materials (sometimes for a small fee) for inmates who want to paint, do sculpture or photography, or sew, for example.

Education is a major enterprise in most contemporary prisons and even in some local detention facilities. The educational programs found in most correctional settings include adult basic education to teach minimal literacy; General Educational Development (GED) classes to help inmates complete high school; vocational education and training give inmates job skills and then an industry-like setting in which to apply them; and personal improvement courses in financial management, or anger management, a subject that is especially important for inmates nearing release. There also may be academic courses for inmates working on college degrees. For example, the Prison University Project at San Quentin, a state-operated maximum security prison in California, enrolls 300 students in 20 classes per semester. A good source of information on teaching opportunities in jails and prisons is the Correctional Education Association (CEA).[1]

Another area for correctional employment is food services. Each year more facilities are contracting out the food services function. Private-sector food service providers operate all over the nation and many regularly advertise in magazines such as *Corrections Today* and *American Jails*, the official publications of the American Correctional Association and the American Jail Association, respectively. Indeed, such trade publications are another good source of job information.

SOURCES: PRISON UNIVERSITY PROJECT (2012); STEPHENS (1999); WILLIAMSON (1990).

directly responsible for monitoring the security of the facility, and for supervising, escorting, and ensuring the safety of inmates.[2] This is where most of the jobs are in corrections. College graduates may resist the suggestion that they begin their career as a CO, but in the twenty-first century, higher levels of education are common, and even expected, in institutional corrections (see, for example, Lee, Lee, and Beam 1998).

The Bureau of Labor Statistics (2012) notes that nationwide there were then 493,100 positions for bailiffs, COs, and jailers. About 60 percent of them were in state prisons, prison camps, and youth correctional facilities; slightly more than 3 percent were in federal facilities; and another 3 percent were in privately operated correctional institutions. The remainder worked in a variety of local institutions. In most of these institutional settings, COs wear a uniform like that of a police officer; in recent years, though, some jails and prison systems have made an effort to get away from traditional, military-style uniforms.

COs engage in a variety of tasks, but their principal job is institutional security. This means that they perform the most essential services in the institutions (Bureau of Labor Statistics 2012). In virtually every institution, COs are in direct contact with inmates. They are responsible for taking head counts, and they may be required to escort inmates as they move around the institution. COs also make rounds to check on inmate activities, and they have primary responsibility for issuing disciplinary reports (called *write-ups*) when inmates break a rule. COs may have special job assignments. In some facilities, for example, they are responsible for overseeing inmates' work assignments, which places them in food services, the laundry, or work programs. In other facilities, uniquely qualified COs may handle the facility's electrical and plumbing work.

THE WORK ENVIRONMENT To understand the CO's job more fully, it helps to examine the environment in which COs work. Many of the realities of that environment have both positive and negative aspects. For instance, one of the most positive, and challenging, is direct contact with inmates. However, for some COs, this can become a negative aspect of the job. Face-to-face contact with inmates can give COs a sense of accomplishment, the feeling that they are making a difference in the lives of their charges. It also can result in high levels of anxiety, a very cynical attitude toward life, and feelings of despair and hopelessness. More than other institutional corrections employees, COs have the greatest impact on inmates' lives. Therefore, their outlook and attitudes are very important.

A second crucial element of the CO's employment is shift work. Institutions must staff CO posts 24 hours a day, every day. Typically, fewer officers are on duty at night, but early career COs should prepare to work all different shifts, including weekends and holidays. Although working on holidays means overtime pay, it also means important time away from family and friends.

Most COs work a 40-hour week in five 8-hour days. Some institutions break up the workweek differently, into 10- or 12-hour shifts, and consequently COs work fewer days per week. Some like the extra days off, but the jury is still out on the effects longer shifts have on morale, energy, and general job performance.

The pay range for COs varies widely depending on the type of facility (detention center versus jail or prison) and the level of government (federal, state, or local). At the beginning of the chapter, we gave the average pay for all correctional employees by level of government. According to the Bureau of Labor Statistics (2012), a CO's median 2010 annual earnings (salary plus overtime pay) was $39,040. In the public sector, the median earnings for COs in federal facilities were $53,310; in state facilities, $38,690; and in local facilities, $38,980.[3] By comparison, private-sector COs had median annual earnings of $30,460.

The educational requirements for COs vary. In most state and local institutional settings, COs need just a high school diploma or a GED equivalent (Bureau of Labor Statistics 2012). Increasingly, however, state and even some local facilities are looking for candidates with an associate's or bachelor's degree, although some may accept military experience as an alternative to the degree requirement. We will return to this issue later in the chapter when we consider the movement toward greater professionalization.

The reasons for this new emphasis on education are simple. First, there is no position in a jail or prison that requires more in the way of human relations management skills than that of the CO. Therefore, the practice of hiring at the lowest possible level of qualifications is inconsistent with the expectations and complexities of the CO's job. In addition, in our litigious environment, corrections agencies are justifiably concerned about putting unqualified or underqualified workers into the cellblocks. Finally, many agencies have come to recognize that their supervisors, midlevel managers, and executives are likely to rise through the organization's ranks. This makes it important to hire, train, and retain well-educated people at even the entry levels.

That correctional agencies promote from within is good news for students thinking about a career in institutional corrections. So is the fact that general employment prospects in corrections are positive. Systems are adding new facilities and expanding existing ones all around the nation, and there is a steady demand to replace COs who transfer, are promoted, or retire. Job opportunities for new CO positions in the United States are projected to stay strong, but as a result of sentencing changes and diversion of offenders from secure confinement, the number of new CO positions is likely to increase by only about 5 percent from 2010 to 2020 (Bureau of Labor Statistics 2012). Some of the slowdown in growth is the result of decrease in prison expansion at both the state and federal levels.

It is simple to translate these numbers into prospects for promotion. Facilities in need of additional COs will have a concurrent need for additional supervisors and managers. Linked to the issue of promotions is the issue of transfers. In local systems, transfers are not likely: most counties have only one local detention facility, which limits job assignments and promotion potential. But large urban counties—like Dade County, Florida, and San Diego and Los Angeles counties—usually have several different detention facilities, including juvenile detention centers and separate men's and women's jails, which means opportunities to move on and up.

Opportunities to transfer within a state corrections system also vary. California has 100 state correctional facilities of varying security levels, including 32 state prisons. Likewise, the US Bureau of Prisons operates prison camps, federal correctional institutions, metropolitan correctional and detention centers, and penitentiaries from coast to coast—although most are located in the East and South.

The more facilities a particular level of government operates, the greater the potential to move up within that organization. However, the need to relocate may also increase with the number of facilities. This is not a problem in Texas, where the state operates many correctional institutions but historically has sited them in just a few localities. Relocation can be an issue in California, for example, where facilities are located throughout the state. Of course, the willingness to relocate has obvious career benefits, and many people enjoy living in and learning about different places. For others, though, a move, even within a state, is difficult.

Promotion through the ranks—upward mobility—in a correctional facility may well depend on one's willingness to make a number of moves between different institutions. Nationwide, there were more than 9,500 high-level administrative jobs in correctional institutions: 1,821 of them—1,719 in state facilities and 102 in federal facilities—were for the position of **warden**, the chief administrator of an adult correctional facility, and 473 jobs were for **superintendent**, the chief administrator in a juvenile correctional facility (Maguire and Pastore 1999, 80; Stephan 2008). Both positions are challenging, and the salaries are commensurate with the increased responsibilities.

HIRING REQUIREMENTS A college education is increasingly becoming a requirement of employment in secure facilities (Bureau of Labor Statistics 2012). Moreover, most institutions require one or more of the following as well: certain physical characteristics, written examinations, a background check, and a polygraph examination.

Like many law enforcement agencies, correctional agencies may require applicants to meet certain physical standards; however, the nature of those standards can be very different. Most police and sheriff's departments set height, weight, and eyesight requirements for their officers, and would-be recruits must pass strength or endurance tests (for example, run a mile in a certain time limit or do so many push-ups). These requirements are what the law calls *bona fide occupational qualifications*, also known colloquially as a BFOQ, meaning physical and other requirements essential to performing the job.

In general, COs do not have to meet the same physical requirements or to perform at the same level as police officers do. There are at least two very important exceptions.

- Local detention officers hired as sheriff's deputies must demonstrate the same physical agility required of all employees.

- State and federal corrections agencies require reasonable levels of physical fitness for their COs.

Indications of heart disease or hypertension (high blood pressure) are of particular concern. COs are subject to high levels of stress (Bureau of Labor Statistics 2012), a topic to which we return later in this chapter. In addition to applicant screening, some corrections departments dictate that employees maintain physical fitness, pass regular certification for strength and agility, and have an annual medical checkup.

Virtually all applicants for CO positions must take a battery of written tests. Usually, these are general aptitude tests, although they may require some broad knowledge of corrections philosophies and practices. Aptitude in two areas—reading and writing—is especially important. Throughout their careers, COs must review and respond to written directives (De Lucia and Doyle 1998; Bureau of Labor Statistics 2012).

Background checks and polygraph examinations are necessary to certify an applicant's suitability for work in a secure environment. The background check can be extensive, lengthy investigations into an applicant's family life, financial status, work record, academic experience, and criminal history. A felony conviction disqualifies applicants for most positions; even a misdemeanor conviction can cost an applicant a job. There are two issues at work here. A drunk-driving offense on an applicant's record may not be relevant to the job at hand—driving is seldom part of a CO's job description—but it could have an impact on the institution's public image. A driving while intoxicated (DWI) conviction may prevent an applicant from being hired, and it can be grounds for dismissal. Another concern is the institution's liability: a record of any kind could raise questions about a CO's qualifications and the facility's negligence in hiring that individual. Both of these issues apply to applicants with convictions for either theft or drug offenses as well. Items occasionally disappear in prisons, and having a convicted thief on the payroll simply does not make sense. More important, many inmates in jails and prisons have a history of abusing drugs; to bring a CO into their midst who has used or sold drugs is clearly negligent. We will address some of these concerns in the section on ethics at the end of the chapter.

WORK IN THE PRIVATE SECTOR The final issue we examine here is the likelihood of private-sector employment. The number of private correctional facilities in the United States has increased sharply. What 20 years ago would have seemed highly unlikely is now an essential component of corrections systems throughout the nation. For example, the Bureau of Justice Statistics reported 37 private jails and 415 secure and community-based private adult correctional facilities in the US (Stephan 2008; Stephan and Walsh 2011). In 2010 private prisons held 128,195 prisoners (33,830 federal and 94,365 state inmates). This was about 8 percent of the nation's prison inmate total (Guerino, Harrison, and Sabol 2011). Although we do not expect private corporations to take over corrections in the United States, we do expect they will continue to expand. That growth should be especially rapid among three types of facilities: local jails and detention centers, specialized facilities (for example, those housing illegal aliens, women, juveniles, drug-dependent inmates, or people who are mentally ill), and low-security prisons and boot camps. Recent surveys have shown that corrections workers in the private

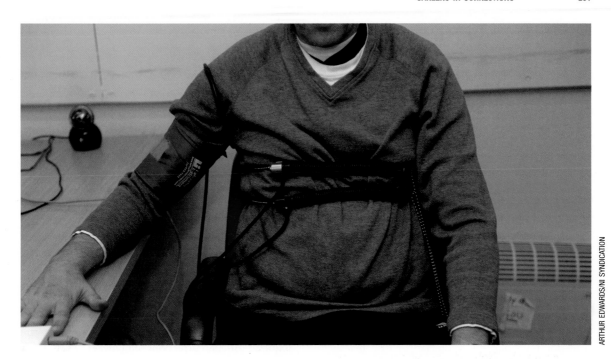

ARTHUR EDWARDS/NI SYNDICATION

sector earn about $8,500 a year less than state-level public sector employees (Bureau of Labor Statistics 2012). However, private-sector corrections provides an additional arena for correctional employment opportunities.

CORRECTIONAL COUNSELORS

Counselors who work in secure facilities typically operate in one of two capacities. Some **correctional counselors** carry out screening and psychological testing to determine the most appropriate security classification and treatment programs for new inmates (Bureau of Labor Statistics 2012). These **psychological technicians** or **psychological diagnosticians** also may be responsible for conducting group and individual counseling sessions on substance abuse or anger management. In some state corrections departments, psychological technicians or treatment specialists are called **classification officers**; in the US Bureau of Prisons (BOP) they are **case managers**. Whatever the label, essentially these people serve as first-line counselors.

At a higher level in most institutional settings is a **clinical psychologist**, the person who is responsible for supervising the psychological technicians and for approving all treatment plans (De Lucia and Doyle 1998, 78–79). The actual responsibilities and titles people in the clinical-psychologist position hold link directly to their education and experience. Requisite skills sets include such things as high functioning interpersonal skills, which are important for working with a culturally and racially diverse population with multiple problems; strong written and oral communications skills; critical analysis and decision-making skills, high-level organizational skills, and the ability to multi-task (see especially Onetonline.org 2012).

The workload of institutional counselors and psychologists varies depending on their assignments and the size of the unit or facility in which they work. Counselors who are treating inmates with serious needs—long-term substance abuse problems or with HIV/AIDS, for example—usually have smaller caseloads than those with "ordinary" inmates.

One of the important aspects of any job is the opportunity for advancement. For correctional counselors, the nonhierarchical organization of counseling services limits advancement within many facilities. Clinical psychologists may earn more money as they move up through pay grades; however, as a rule those grades are not associated with additional supervisory or managerial responsibilities. The lack of advancement at the higher level of counseling services translates into limited promotion potential for those at the lower level. If they wish to continue to interact directly with inmates, promotion may mean relocation to another facility. However, for psychological technicians and case managers who are willing to forgo regular direct contact with prisoners, there are jobs to move into within the facility—chief of classification or associate warden for programming, for example—positions that could eventually take them to the correction system's highest administrative level.

The educational requirements for correctional counselors are generally high. At a minimum, candidates for psychological technician or case manager positions should have a bachelor's degree in counseling, psychology, social work, or criminal justice, and some positions require a master's degree (Bureau of Labor Statistics 2012). Although generally considered entry-level jobs, some institutions may require at least a year's experience in either an internship or a similar full-position to secure these jobs. Psychologists working in prison settings often hold a doctorate in psychology, counseling, or education (Williamson 1990, 134). As a requirement of that degree or of state licensing practices, clinical psychologists also may have had to complete a clinical internship. However, specific licensing requirements vary from state to state and job to job. In many cases, all that is required is a drug screening, a valid state driver's license, and the absence of a felony conviction record.

One website lists correctional treatment specialist salaries that vary from $26,000 per year for overnight residential counselors to $88,000 per year for psychologist mental health counselors. Most salaries in this classification range from $40,000 to $60,000 per year (Indeed.com 2012). Clinical psychologists are among the highest-paid prison workers, although they tend to make less than equivalently trained individuals in the private sector. For both groups of correctional counselors, the necessary education and experience, and the demands of their jobs, explain their higher-than-average salaries.

If the facility or state correctional organization classifies correctional counselors as professional employees, they may be exempt from the civil service testing required of COs and probation and parole officers. In addition, correctional counselors generally are not required to demonstrate the same physical fitness levels as would-be COs. In addition, they seldom have to take written examinations. Correctional facilities treat clinical psychologists, like medical personnel, as professional employees. They usually are hired based on an evaluation of their credentials (degrees plus experience) and they may be required to hold a professional license or to complete requirements for state licensing within a specified time. But all correctional counselors, including clinical psychologists, are subject to background checks and even to polygraph tests if those tests are required of all corrections employees with direct inmate contact.

Private employment prospects for individuals interested in working in correctional psychology are promising on two counts. First, the private sector is expanding its operations in jails, detention centers, and prisons throughout the nation: those facilities are going to need increasing numbers of treatment personnel to keep up with their growing inmate populations. Second, it is becoming more common for public institutions to contract out certain functions, among them counseling and treatment services.

COMMUNITY-BASED CORRECTIONS: PROBATION AND PAROLE OFFICERS

This career field is difficult to describe for several reasons. First, titles are not uniform from state to state. Some states refer to probation and parole officers as probation or parole *agents* (California Department of Corrections and Rehabilitation 2012; see also Chapters 4 and 9); other states use very different titles. Second, the functions of probation and parole officers can vary markedly if they deal exclusively

with juveniles or with adults. Third, in different places in the country, we can find probation and parole officers working for local, state, or federal governments. Fourth, some local and state governments separate the supervision of probationers and parolees; others combine them. These variations make it difficult to describe the day-to-day job activities of probation and parole officers or gain a reasonably accurate perspective on the job market for these community-based employees of the criminal justice system. By necessity we are speaking here in generalities. If you are applying for a job as a probation/parole officer (PPO), you need to learn all you can about the particular responsibilities of that position.

Most PPOs assume one or more of four roles in their day-to-day work, each with unique demands (see either Chapter 4 or 9 for more on their duties):

- *Investigator*—their responsibility for preparing presentence investigation (PSI) reports and monitoring their clients means PPOs must function as an investigator, much like a detective in a police agency.

- *Therapist*—PPOs help released offenders live in the community. In this role, they function much like counselors. Although most PPOs would probably refer a client for psychological counseling if needed, certainly they can recognize psychological disorders in their clients.

- *Service broker*—PPOs assess their clients' needs (for a job, an apartment, a program), explore the available community services, and bring clients and services together. Usually this task involves a kind of brokering; but it also can require *advocacy*—that is, a PPO may be called on to lobby a community agency to develop or provide needed resources (Abadinsky 2009).

- ● *Law enforcer*—PPOs must enforce the conditions of release and all other applicable laws. In some jurisdictions, a PPO's responsibility in this area ends with the reporting of any violations of law to the local police or sheriff's department; in others, the PPOs are sworn peace officers with the authority to carry a weapon and make arrests. We address this issue, along with the arming of probation officers in particular, in Chapter 4.

Probationers and parolees place different demands on PPOs. Remember that probationers generally are first-time offenders, and that their offenses tend to be minor. By definition, PPOs are willing to take risks with this group of releasees, to give them a second chance. To that end, their meetings are likely to consist of drug and alcohol counseling, marriage counseling, or other therapies. However, as many probation and parole officers quickly come to realize, their caseload generally is too large to provide much attention to individual clients.

Parolees, having endured longer terms of incarceration and an inclination for higher levels of criminal involvement, tend to present more adjustment problems than probationers, and nationwide statistics generally show lower rates of success with paroled offenders. For example, of all persons who exited supervision in 2010, only 65 percent of probationers and 52 percent of parolees were successfully discharged (Glaze and Bonczar 2011, 6, 9). The biggest challenge facing PPOs who work with parolees is reintegration. In particular, this means locating housing for releasees, finding appropriate job training programs or job placements, and trying to smooth the transition back into their family lives.

The PPO's job has both positive and negative aspects. Many probation and parole officers are able to point to success stories. Unfortunately, the failures occasionally make headlines. Among the negative aspects of probation and parole work, three seem especially prominent. First, probation and parole work can be emotionally intense. When PPOs get involved in their clients' lives and problems, they find it difficult to leave their work at the office. Burnout can be a problem for PPOs who do not learn to cope with this particular aspect of the job. Second, PPOs seldom get feedback about how they are doing. The problem is largely because probation and parole agencies do not have particularly good record-keeping systems, which makes it difficult for officers to develop tangible measures of their performance. This can be a serious problem when politicians and the public are criticizing an office or a particular officer. Third, as probation and parole officers come to recognize, some clients seem doomed to fail despite an officer's best intentions to help. This realization may ultimately sap the optimism and enthusiasm with which most newly appointed PPOs start their careers.

PPOs' salaries generally are better than are those of front-line COs, and they are about the same or slightly less than are those of correctional counselors. The Bureau of Labor Statistics (2012) found that in 2010, PPOs (and correctional treatment personnel) had annual median earnings of $47,200, or over $8,000 a year more than a CO. One reason they earn more is because they have higher education and experience requirements. In addition, most state and local governments employ fewer PPOs than they do COs. For instance, in 2010, there were about 93,200 PPOs and correctional treatment specialists nationwide (Bureau of Labor Statistics 2012), equivalent to about 21 percent of the number of institutional employees overall.

As we discussed in Chapter 4, PPOs' caseloads vary from jurisdiction to jurisdiction. As we revealed in that chapter, the probationer population grew steadily during the last several decades of the twentieth century; the parolee population actually fell between the late 1970s and the end of the 1980s, as states eliminated discretionary parole. However, crowding in prisons soon led those states to adopt or implement mandatory parole statutes (Mays 1989). By the end of the 1990s, both probation and parole numbers were increasing (see Figure 4.1). In 2005, for example, the probationer population grew 0.5 percent, and the parole population grew 1.6 percent in a year's time (Glaze and Bonczar 2006). By 2010, however, the probation and parole populations were declining, the former faster than the latter (Glaze and Bonczar 2011, 1). The result of this growth is that PPOs who could not imagine caseloads of 100 clients 20 years ago today routinely carry caseloads in the hundreds (American Correctional Association (ACA) 2003, 75; Bureau of Labor Statistics 2012). The exception is those officers working in intensive probation or parole supervision programs who generally carry a maximum caseload of 25 clients (ACA 2003, 75).

The caseload picture means three things for PPOs. First, in recent years, because the probationer population is so large, PPOs are seeing many more probationers than they are parolees. Second, the increasing number of probationers means that more, and more serious, offenders are being placed on probation, which in turn diminishes the possibility that PPOs can intervene meaningfully in the lives of their clients (Champion 1990). Third, probation and parole officers can expect excellent job security. The demand for PPOs is not likely to decrease in the near future, and some projections indicate that these positions will grow about 18 percent from 2010 to 2020 (as fast as average for other occupations) (Bureau of Labor Statistics 2012).

Education and experience separate PPOs from COs (Williamson 1990, 91, 93). In most US jurisdictions, juvenile and adult probation officers are required to have a minimum of a bachelor's degree (Bureau of Labor Statistics 2012). This requirement may reduce the potential applicant pool, but probation and parole agencies typically accept a wide range of undergraduate majors—for example, counseling, criminal justice or criminology, psychology, social work, sociology, or even political science or business administration—for the positions they advertise. Furthermore, although many agencies require a bachelor's degree, some prefer or require a master's degree in an area related to probation and parole. For students interested in applying for these positions, the key factor may be the competitiveness of the application process. If there are hundreds of applicants for a handful of jobs, the chances are that the jobs will go to those with graduate degrees, related experience, or both.

As an alternative to the bachelor's degree requirement, some jurisdictions may substitute a certain number of years of experience for each year of education required. For example, an agency might treat an associate's degree and 5 years' experience as a CO as the equivalent of a bachelor's degree.

Actually, the small number of PPO positions makes the competition very stiff. Moreover, because the organization of probation and parole agencies tends to be less hierarchical than that of correctional institutions, there also may be fewer promotional opportunities. At the state level, we typically find different ranks or pay grades for PPOs. For instance, the entry-level job may be classified a PPO I. Promotion to PPO II and PPO III may depend on experience, additional education, specialized caseloads, or even a willingness to relocate. Very large probation and parole offices also may have supervisory positions of varying ranks. In most states, the top official in a local or regional probation and parole office frequently holds the title chief probation and parole officer.

Physical restrictions are not as common for probation and parole officers as they are for COs. People with physical disabilities may qualify for probation and parole positions, whereas their prospects might be much more limited in prisons and law enforcement.

Some states have written qualifying examinations for entry-level positions, but then base all promotions on performance evaluations and supervisors' recommendations. Others require written examinations for the initial hiring process and for all promotions as well. Finally, some states do not require initial testing, instead relying on an evaluation of the applicant's academic training and experience, perhaps combined with an oral interview. To prepare adequately for the application process, students should check with the nearest probation and parole office or state labor, employment, or civil service office to determine what the practices are for the particular agency in which they are most interested.

Applicants for probation and parole jobs undergo a background investigation, particularly if they apply for employment with an agency like Federal Probation and Pretrial Services. Unlike prison personnel,

ZUMA PRESS INC/ALAMY IMAGES

these applicants may not have to submit to a polygraph test and drug testing.

In line with the general trend toward privatization, we are beginning to see work in the private sector for PPOs. Indeed, the Salvation Army began to provide probation supervision for low-risk offenders in the mid-1970s; and since that time it has spread to at least ten states (Schloss and Alarid 2007). This is especially true in large metropolitan areas on the East Coast, where probation and parole agencies have backlogs for PSI reports. In some large cities, criminal defendants with the money to do so can hire an individual or a company to write a presentence investigation report for the sentencing judge. Most of the people preparing these reports at

one time worked as PPOs for state or federal governments.

COMMUNITY-BASED CORRECTIONS: COUNSELORS AND OTHER WORKERS

In addition to probation and parole officers, many other positions are available in community-based corrections (Bureau of Labor Statistics 2012; see also, De Lucia and Doyle 1998; Henry 1994). Here, we look at counselors and other corrections employees who work outside secure facilities, in group homes and halfway houses and in the agencies that operate other treatment programs and alternatives to incarceration. Although it is impossible to discuss every possible job in community-based corrections, we can draw their general parameters (Latessa and Smith 2011).

First, the people who staff community-based programs have chosen to work outside secure facilities. As we mentioned at the beginning of the chapter, many people who are interested in corrections are not necessarily interested in working in prisons. Some individuals are fearful of what they perceive to be a dangerous setting; others choose to work with offenders in the community because those offenders seem much more receptive to treatment than do many inmates. Some employees base their decisions on the structural differences between a secure facility and a local agency. Remember the high level of regimentation found in most jails and prisons, and the ever-present resistance to any change in routine. These people cannot see themselves working in an environment where one key difference between the keepers and the kept is that the former go home at night and the latter go to their cells. However, in community-based agencies, programming is flexible and staff members have the freedom to experiment.

Another important difference has to do with program success. Community-based programs typically demonstrate higher success levels than do institutional-based programs. At least two factors are at work here. For one thing, first-offender clients in community-based programs have far more intact support systems, particularly if they live at or near home. Those in diversionary programs such as those described in Chapter 4 have the added advantage of not having to be concerned about reintegrating into the community: they have never left it. Second, offenders ordered into community-based programs by definition pose a less serious threat to public safety, which may mean that the public is more amenable to funding job training and educational programs for them. Personnel working in successful community-based programs may have the sense that they are contributing to some positive social goal. The result is a higher degree of job satisfaction than is found among other correctional employees (Lambert, Hogan, and Barton 2002).

Of course, there are negative aspects to working in community corrections as well. We address two in particular. The first is job burnout, a particular issue for people who work in halfway houses or similar residential programs for any length of time. Close and often intense exposure to offenders and their problems can take an emotional toll. The second negative aspect is the lack of financial stability. Many community corrections programs receive their operating funds from year to year through a combination of private, local, state, and federal money. Promised funding can be late, and in some cases it never comes through. To keep the programs going, administrators are always on the verge of cutbacks—in program scope and in staff, which can create a sense of insecurity among agency employees.

Salaries in community corrections often reflect the lack of financial stability. Typically, jobs in community-based programs pay less than those in state or federal institutional settings, but are on par with those in probation and parole work (Bureau of Labor Statistics 2012). Furthermore, community-based programs often do not provide the range of benefits available to those who work in a state or federal prison.

Caseloads in community-based programs vary depending on the setting. Staffers in residential programs typically work with between eight and ten residents; seldom does a residential program house more than 15 offenders. In these situations, client numbers are limited, but the exposure to each client is more intense and prolonged than it is in a nonresidential program. Counselors in nonresidential community-based programs find their caseloads to be roughly equivalent to those of psychologists and counselors working in institutional settings. Again, probation and parole officers may not have the time, knowledge, or inclination to do a lot of counseling. Instead, they are likely to refer clients to community-based counselors hired specifically to diagnose and counsel probationers and parolees (see, especially, De Lucia and Doyle 1998, 78). These counselors see clients with different needs and often work with them in groups. Counselors and other treatment personnel may also occupy positions in community-based drug and alcohol treatment programs and in halfway houses.

When filling counseling positions, program administrators tend to look for the same educational levels and experience found in counselors and psychologists who work in prisons. In filling other positions, though, community programs may turn to **paraprofessionals**, people who lack the educational background of professionals (for example, most have only a high school diploma or an associate's degree), but who are trained to work alongside professionals. Cost is an obvious advantage here: paraprofessionals receive lower pay than professional staff. Another is the flexibility to bring into a program both community residents and ex-offenders, people who are able to interact with clients in different ways. Some community-based programs use ex-offenders as leaders or facilitators in their group treatment sessions.

Their willingness to hire paraprofessionals makes community programs a good place to accumulate the experience that positions in institutional corrections require. Our students often ask, "How can I get experience if no one will hire me to begin with?" This is how: Some small agencies look for availability and willingness to learn; the experience comes in time.

There are many positive aspects to working in community corrections: the close client contact, the flexibility, the opportunity to be creative, the ability to help others. But in many community corrections programs, opportunities for promotion are lacking. As most of these programs operate with a small number of staff members, there typically are few supervisors or managers. This means that caseworkers, as one example, have ready access to decision makers, but it also means that there is little likelihood of promotion. In addition, most community corrections programs in this country operate at the local level. They have no ties to a larger network of agencies, and this absence of a network can restrict the possibility of transferring from one location or agency to another.

Community corrections organizations tend to have the fewest hiring restrictions of any correctional agencies. They seldom set physical standards for candidates, and virtually none require a written entrance examination. There may be a cursory background check, but this usually consists of calling the candidate's references—the same kind of check any prospective employer might make. Moreover, community-based programs often are looking to hire ex-offenders for paraprofessional positions, people who would have a difficult time finding work in an institutional setting. A critical element in this hiring decision, however, is that the ex-offender is no longer on probation or parole. In fact, the best case scenario for employment is if the individual has received an executive pardon where the sentencing took place (state or federal government).

It is difficult to make the public–private distinction in talking about community corrections. Private organizations fund and operate many community-based programs; many others blend public and private financing. What we can say is that private and quasi-private agencies and organizations dominate this area of corrections. As long as there are community-based programs, private employment prospects in corrections will be good.

WORKPLACE CHALLENGES

Whenever people consider a criminal justice job, three issues arise: job-related stress, the potential for job-related injury or death, and the possibility of getting sued.

JOB-RELATED STRESS

Nearly all positions within corrections have some stress associated with them. However, all of life is full of stress, so what is unique about the stress of working with accused and convicted offenders? The questions turn, then, to what is workplace stress and how much is unacceptable. According to Hans Seyle (1974, 14), stress is "the nonspecific response of the body to any demand made upon it." Occupational stress, then, has its origins in the demands and conditions of the workplace, but may be related to other stress points in a person's life, such as family, social life, and the like, that simply manifest themselves in the individual's response to the workplace. Occupational stress has at least two origins: organizational factors and environmental factors (Schaufeli and

Peeters 2000; also see Lambert, Hogan, and Barton 2002). For example, organizational factors originate with how a prison hierarchy administers the facility and include management style, communication, and work schedules. Environmental factors are stressors caused by physical, social, and psychological elements within the location where the person works, and include the need for and exercise of personal security in the workplace, extent of personal contact with offenders, and even the age and condition of the physical workspace itself.

Response to job-place stress takes many forms (Carlson, Anson, and Thomas 2003; Lambert 2004; Owen 2006). For some, minor forms translate into tardiness or absenteeism. For others, stress may mean more sick leave or problems at home. At its extreme levels, workplace stress manifests itself in chronic depression, job burnout, and even suicide. The level of job satisfaction one feels has a lot to do with whether the job is valued or not. The nature and extent of job-related stress have a great deal to do with expressions of job satisfaction and continued employment and career development (Lambert, Hogan, and Barton 2002). As one review of job satisfaction literature observed (Lambert, Hogan, and Barton 2002, 137): "Worker stress should be lowered. This can be done by reducing role conflict and role ambiguity for staff. Staff responsibilities should be clearly defined and should not be in conflict with one another."

Stress is not equally distributed among all correctional workers. Given the significant role of environmental factors, those in direct daily physical contact with offenders experience the greatest environmental stress (Owen 2006). The farther one moves from clients in the correctional arena, the greater the role of organizational stressors becomes. Moreover, workplace stress is not limited to institutional corrections. Indeed, probation officers and other community-based service providers also experience similar levels, albeit with fewer originating in the institution's environment (Slate, Wells, and Johnson 2003). Stress also varies by one's position in the administrative hierarchy. Although those at the top do apparently experience lower stress levels than do those in direct contact with accused and convicted offenders, they nonetheless experience

workplace stress. Even though much stress among line-personnel comes from below—from those being watched—upper-level supervisors experience stress from above, from their bosses. Moreover, they have another set of demands: politics. One corrections administrator observed that a key stress point originated with "politicians who do not have a clue about an adult correctional facility making laws governing my job" (Owen 2006, 175).

JOB INJURIES AND DEATHS

Do corrections personnel get injured or killed on the job? The answer obviously is yes. Is this a major problem in corrections? The answer to this question is "it depends." All correctional personnel would say that if even one person gets injured or killed on the job, that is one too many. But, realistically, injuries and deaths can occur on any job. What we need to examine, then, are comparative figures. What do job safety statistics tell us about corrections versus other areas of employment?

First, based on aggregate numbers, correctional employees are more likely to be injured in the bathtub at home or in a car driving to and from work than they are to be killed on the job. In fact, in all of 2010 a total of 15 correctional staff members were killed in the United States compared with 145 law enforcement officers. Do correctional staff members die because of inmate actions? The answer to this question is affirmative, but the occurrence is quite rare, especially when compared with deaths in other high stress, dangerous workplaces (Bureau of Labor Statistics 2010).

Second, COs are more likely to incur work-related injuries from improper lifting and other routine activities than they are to be hurt by an inmate. COs occasionally are injured by accident when they try to intervene in inmate-on-inmate assaults, but they are seldom directly attacked by one or more inmates in a correctional facility.

Third, job-related injuries are much more common than job-related deaths. Indeed, the BLS notes that correctional officers have one of the highest rates of nonfatal on-the-job injuries.

Finally correctional employees sometimes say that they feel safer in prison than they do driving on the freeway or walking on city streets. This is true even of COs, who have the most direct and, occasionally, confrontational contact with inmates.

Once again, is corrections work safe? For the most part, the answer is yes.

LAWSUITS

Students concerned about litigation often ask, "Could I get sued if . . . ?" The answer is always yes. Anyone who works in the criminal justice system today *could* be sued for doing or not doing certain job-related tasks. As you will see in Chapter 12, corrections is a very fertile area for litigation. Inmates sue COs for mistreatment and wardens for a lack of programming; crime victims sue parole boards for releasing offenders who then reoffend, and the list goes on. But the real question is whether these lawsuits succeed.

Briefly, lawsuits or administrative disciplinary actions must be based on official misconduct, which legally refers to malfeasance, misfeasance, or nonfeasance (Champion 2005). **Malfeasance** is the commission of an act prohibited under any circumstance. An extreme example of malfeasance would be taking the life of a prisoner who failed to return to his or her cell in a timely manner. **Misfeasance** is the improper performance of an act that is within the scope of the worker's authority. An example of this would be a CO's disciplining an inmate by having the inmate wash the officer's uniforms and shine the officer's uniform shoes. Although COs are authorized to discipline inmates, they are not authorized to make inmates their personal servants. Finally, **nonfeasance** is the failure to act in a situation where one should act. The classic example of this is a CO who stands and watches one inmate beat another inmate into unconsciousness. The failure to act is nonfeasance.

The fear of litigation is very real for most corrections personnel, particularly those who work in secure facilities. Nevertheless, there are at least two good defenses. First, it can be wise to buy insurance for legal services from the agency or a professional group like the ACA, just in case. Second, corrections staffers should follow departmental policies and procedures to the letter. This is one of the best defenses in a lawsuit, another topic we come back to in Chapter 12.

THE TREND TOWARD PROFESSIONALIZATION

For many years in corrections, there has been a push toward professional recognition for the people who work in this field. Beginning in the 1970s (and perhaps before that) four factors started to emerge that have added increased emphasis and urgency on the notion of corrections as a profession. However, before we consider these four factors, it is important to acknowledge that many positions in corrections—particularly the position of CO—have not been highly regarded by the general public or even by university students who are considering criminal justice careers. Therefore, we will turn our attention to the impact that education, training, accreditation and certification, and technology have on correctional professionalization (Kohnke 2001).

Education is one of the key measures of the increased emphasis on professionalization in the corrections workplace. As we mentioned previously, most states and the federal government require the minimum of a bachelor's degree for positions of probation and parole officers and correctional treatment specialists (Bureau of Labor Statistics 2012). Furthermore, advertisements for some of these positions may express a preference for a master's degree, additional work experience, or both. By contrast, CO positions often only require a high school diploma or GED, but some states and the US Bureau of Prisons require beginning COs to have either a college degree or previous experience (Bureau of Labor Statistics 2012). Thus, the trend increasingly is for correctional agencies to require or prefer college degrees as educational requirements.

Training is another element related to the professionalization movement. Correctional agencies, like their law enforcement counterparts, traditionally trained new employees on the job. Decades ago, line-staff supervisors tended to assign rookie officers to work with one or more veterans until the rookies caught on to what was required of them. The veterans had to "sign-off" on the probationary employees; once this happened, the training process was complete. No ongoing or in-service training was required. Today, new corrections officers in the US Bureau of Prisons are required to complete 200 hours of basic training within their first year, and to complete another 120 hours of specialized training within 60 days of appointment (Bureau of Labor Statistics 2012). State agencies typically require anywhere from four weeks (160 hours) to 10 weeks (400 hours) of training for new employees. A quick online search shows that St. Petersburg College in Florida offers a basic corrections academy that consists of 15 weeks of training (576 hours), and New Mexico Junior College has a comparable academy of 8 weeks (320 hours). Rhode Island's state correctional academy is 9 weeks long (360 hours). The past three decades have seen a widespread recognition that many corrections positions—especially those in institutional settings—require employees well trained in a variety of specialized topics.

Accreditation and certification by professional organizations such as the American Correctional Association (**www.aca.org**) and the American Jail Association (**www.aja.org**) have further strengthened the professionalization movement. The ACA publishes a series of volumes on standards relating to the operations of various kinds of correctional agencies. These standards become the basis for site visits and operational reviews to determine whether the agencies meet the ACA standards for certification. Professional certification has several benefits. It can provide the basis for defense against inmate or client lawsuits. It also serves as a point of "bragging rights" for the agencies and organizations that meet the ACA standards. Additionally, the National Institute of Corrections (part of the US Department of Justice) and groups like the American Probation and Parole Association provide a great deal of training to corrections professionals every year, and the American Jail Associate has certification programs for individuals who meet certain qualifications and who pass certification examinations. The most prominent certification for the AJA is its Certified Jail Manager (CJM) program.

Finally, although we will address technology and the future of corrections in Chapter 15, it is sufficient to say at this point that technology is affecting every segment of corrections employment. As a result, employees who can understand and use technology are increasingly a part of corrections agencies. For example, technological applications include extensive use of laptop computers by community surveillance and supervision officers. Today, most states use some form of electronic monitoring of clients. In addition, states now use websites to provide information on certain released offenders (such as sex offenders), and corrections departments must maintain and update these sites frequently.

What these four elements demonstrate is that the field of corrections today is a complex and sophisticated employment arena. Therefore, agencies need to recruit well-educated employees, provide them with extensive preservice and inservice training, and give them the technological tools to do their jobs adequately. This means even greater emphasis on professionalization. We seem to have only scratched the surface at this point, something we share with our international colleagues (see Box 10.2).

FINDING A JOB

In some cases, corrections agencies with open positions send recruiters to college campuses looking for recent graduates or students about to graduate. However, active recruiting is the exception rather than the rule. In this section, we examine the places to look to find current, accurate, and complete information on jobs in corrections.

WHERE TO LOOK

One of the first places to look for general information on employment in the corrections system is with professional associations. Throughout this text, we mention organizations that have played a significant role in the professionalization of corrections over the past decades. Several—especially the ACA, the AJA, the APPA, the NIC, and the CEA—are also good sources of information on corrections careers. Those online resources maintained by organizations, however, may require that those using the site be members or, in some cases, student members, in

AMERICAN CORRECTIONAL ASSOCIATION

order to gain full access to the website. You can locate these organizations through the Corrections Connection Network website (**www.corrections.com**); moreover, they all maintain their own websites. Each of these associations has a different focus, and each has publications that reflect something of the current state of corrections professions. In addition to the national organizations, there are state or regional affiliates. Two mega-sites are the Government Jobs site (**www.governmentjobs.com**), a commercial site, and USAJobs, a government-sponsored site (**www.usajobs. gov**) tailored specifically to federal-level employment positions. Both allow the applicant to search according to their skills, experience, education, and regional interests.

You also can contact your state corrections department or the US Department of Justice. If there is a state or federal prison or probation and parole office located near you, you can obtain employment information and applications from the agency head or personnel office. Two major websites with job listings and links to job information are **www.criminaljusticejobs.com** and **www.usajobs.gov**, particularly for jobs with the federal government. Any of the major search engines can help you locate these and other sources of criminal justice job information on the web. In fact, as we were revising this edition, we did a quick online search using one of the common search engines available to college students. A query on the key words *corrections employment* resulted in more than 59 million hits.

Your career services office may receive regular notices of job openings in corrections even if the agencies do not come to campus to recruit. Additionally, some college career services offices sponsor (or are willing to sponsor) job fairs. Where they do not, a student organization—the criminal justice club, for example—may be able to organize its own job fair. This is a good way to make contacts with employing agencies, to get them to campus to meet

SPOTLIGHT ON INTERNATIONAL CORRECTIONS: WHY SHOULD A CORRECTIONAL EMPLOYEE BE CONCERNED ABOUT THE INTERNATIONALIZATION OF CORRECTIONS?   BOX 10.2

Crime is increasingly becoming a transnational phenomenon. Consider, for example, organized crime, terrorism, technological crime, illegal immigration, money laundering, and drug trafficking. No single nation can hope to respond holistically to crime in the twenty-first century without considering the policies and practices of the international community. Everything from children sold as slaves to nuclear materials can cross international borders with amazing ease.

According to Richard H. Ward, to attack these problems effectively, there has to be collaboration and a sharing of information among the world's corrections agencies. On one level, "tomorrow's criminal justice practitioner must have a broader understanding of the legal systems of other countries and respect for the customs and practices of immigrants, as well as an increasing number of international visitors" (267).

At another level, knowing how other nations respond to threats to the safety and security of their citizens has the potential to shape US responses as well. Whether we are talking about law, police, courts, or corrections, a worldview is becoming increasingly important in this century. Adopting an international perspective on all components of the criminal justice system is more than a worthy goal; it is rapidly becoming a practical necessity.

Think about international criminals, for example, and the challenges posed by their cultural, religious, dietary, and linguistic differences. Knowing how other nations deal with foreign inmates is one way to help those who administer corrections facilities in this country. Ignoring international practices is at best shortsighted; at worst, it is an invitation to greater problems.

SOURCE: WARD (2000).

with students who are looking for jobs or to make class presentations. The result is that students get the information they need to make career choices, and the agencies may begin coming to campus regularly to recruit.

Another good source of job information is job-listing services. Some are commercial, for-profit entities; professional law enforcement and corrections organizations at local, state, and federal levels compile others. To find out about these services, check with your college career services office or the nearest state employment commission or labor office listed in the government section of your telephone directory.

The final source of job information is books. Check the library and your college's placement services office and career center. These entities also regularly receive many publications that deal with job prospects.

We offer one last point. When you contact a correctional agency, a professional organization, or a job-listing service, ask questions. You want to know the following:

- when jobs normally become available;
- where the announcements are posted;
- where and to whom applications should be submitted; and
- how long the application process typically takes.

The last item is important because it gives you a sense of when to start applying for jobs.

WHEN TO APPLY

Just about every April, students graduating in May contact their professors and ask, "When is a good time to start applying for jobs?" The honest answer is always the same: "Six months ago." A good rule of thumb for most criminal justice positions is that the application, testing, interview process, and background check take six to nine months. Some agencies hire on a probationary basis: that is, they allow new employees who have passed aptitude and physical tests and who have done well in the interviews to start work pending the completion of the background check.

INTERNSHIPS AND COOPERATIVE EDUCATION

Before we turn to job prospects, we need to examine two often overlooked but effective ways of entering corrections careers: internships and cooperative education (Gordon and McBride 2011).

Many criminal justice academic programs offer **internship** courses either as an elective or as part of the required curriculum. The objective is to expose students to the actual demands and expectations of various careers. In most colleges and universities, students enroll in internships for a certain number of academic credits. They may be full-time (that is, 40 hours a week for the academic term) or part-time.

Occasionally undergraduate internships are paid, but most often they are learning, rather than earning, experiences. Some agencies offer internships as a favor to a faculty member at a nearby college or university; other agencies look at internships as a recruitment device, a way to find and develop potential employees; for understaffed agencies, internships are a way to fill urgent vacancies. What students should consider when deciding whether and where to do an internship is the possibility that the experience could turn into a job. Student interns are a known quantity, and that certainly gives them an advantage over applicants who mail a résumé or simply walk in off the street.

Some colleges and universities offer **cooperative (co-op) education**, and many criminal justice agencies prefer internships to co-ops. State and federal agencies do offer co-op placements, and those placements offer some unique advantages over internships. For instance, co-op students are in paid positions. Essentially, they are job placements. In a typical co-op experience, the student works for six months and goes to school for six months. Most agencies want students to go through at least one of these two work–education cycles. Internships, conversely, tend to be one-time propositions. For some students, the biggest drawback of co-op programs is that they can delay graduation by as much as a year. However, students who complete co-op placements— particularly with certain federal agencies—may be eligible for immediate employment when they graduate. Agencies are sometimes able to hire on a non-competitive basis (all the normal testing is bypassed) those students who have successfully completed a co-op experience.

The value of experiential learning cannot be overstressed. This kind of learning meets several needs. First, students get real-world experience. This makes classroom learning more meaningful, and it helps combat the burnout some juniors and seniors feel. Second, co-op placements and paid internships provide seasonal income for college students. Third, these programs give agencies a no-risk chance to recruit students and prepare them for employment. Finally, these programs give students the opportunity to try out a particular job for a limited time to see if this is where they want to spend the rest of their professional lives. Interestingly, there is a fairly high percentage of students who receive employment offers after such placements.

JOB PROSPECTS

Fortunately or unfortunately, depending on your perspective, corrections is a growth industry in the United States. Between 1982 and 2010, the number of state and federal inmates increased from 400,000 to 1.61 million, and the number of local inmates grew from 200,000 to over 748,000. As a result, 600 new state and 51 new federal correctional facilities were built. Additionally, many jurisdictions expanded existing jails or built new ones, and increased their PPO staffs. Both for the short term and for the long term, employment prospects in virtually every segment of the corrections systems—and in both public and private sectors—seem very good. Although the growth of correctional populations has slowed somewhat in the last few years, there will continue to be a demand for well-qualified employees, particularly those with 2-year and 4-year college degrees. Students with advanced degrees will find their career prospects even brighter as agencies begin looking for and preparing future supervisors and managers.

In the past, progression on the career ladder in state and federal correctional agencies was steady but slow. Today, there is limited expansion of institutional and noninstitutional programming; however, with baby boomer retirements escalating more entry-level and managerial positions will be opening. Where it might have taken an individual 15 to 18 years to move up to warden in the past, today wardens and superintendents may have only 8 to 12 years' experience. Therefore, the jobs are there; the salaries, though not spectacular, are reasonable; job security is very high; and promotions seem very likely for capable individuals. In sum, the career prospects in adult and juvenile corrections continue to look very strong.

CORRECTIONAL EMPLOYEE ETHICS

No discussion of correctional employment would be complete without touching on the topic of ethics. Like every aspect of the criminal justice system, correctional employees regularly face ethical dilemmas. In this section, we will briefly address a few of the key ethical issues in corrections.

Professional corrections organizations are especially aware of the role of ethics. Box 10.3 contains the ACA Code of Ethics. From this code, and from other sources, we can see that ethical issues seem to cluster around the following topics: (1) use of discretion, (2) use of force, (3) the code of silence and whistle-blowing, (4) improper relations with inmates or clients, (5) loyalty to conflicting standards, (6) a general concern with corruption, and (7) sexual harassment (see Albanese 2008; Braswell, McCarthy, and McCarthy 2012).

First, much like police officers, correctional employees enjoy a great deal of discretion in the performance of their duties. This means that institutional employees and those working in community-based programs have the authority to act or not act in a variety of situations. COs can decide to ignore misconduct by inmates or they can write reports on any number of disciplinary infractions. Likewise, probation and parole officers can keep their clients on a "short leash," or they can sanction them for only the most serious violations. Supervisors may review some of these actions, but some may be unknown to them. Although *discretion* is a value-neutral term, it can lead to discrimination and work to the detriment of some inmates or clients relative to others.

Second, although the misuse of authority is equally likely to occur throughout corrections, the misuse of force is much more likely to occur in institutional settings. COs are taught when and how to use force lawfully, and many prisons now routinely videotape forceful events such as cell extractions of uncooperative inmates. Nevertheless, prisons can cover large areas and not every spot is under closed-circuit camera surveillance. Therefore, it is still possible that a CO, or group of COs, could physically abuse an inmate identified as a troublemaker.

Third, in every segment of the criminal justice system, there is a strong sentiment toward institutional and coworker loyalty. In both institutional corrections and community-based programs, employees may be very reluctant to come forward and report misconduct by coworkers and supervisors. **Whistle-blowing** is sometimes overtly discouraged, but at other times, the organizational culture subtly conveys the message that being a "rat" or a "snitch" is disloyal (see Whitehead 2012). Therefore, for fear of being shunned or retaliated against, many correctional employees simply say nothing. They may rationalize this behavior with the qualifier: "At least *I'm* not doing anything illegal or unethical."

Fourth, both institutional correctional employees and community corrections personnel (such as probation and parole officers) can have improper relationships with inmates or clients. These relationships can involve exchanging favors (including sex), smuggling contraband into and out of jails and prisons, and accepting gratuities.

THE AMERICAN CORRECTIONAL ASSOCIATION'S CODE OF ETHICS

BOX 10.3

Preamble

The American Correctional Association expects of its members unfailing honesty, respect for the dignity and individuality of human beings, and a commitment to professional and compassionate service. To this end, we subscribe to the following principles.

1 Members shall respect and protect the civil and legal rights of all individuals.

2 Members shall treat every professional situation with concern for the welfare of the individuals involved and with no intent to personal gain.

3 Members shall maintain relationships with colleagues to promote mutual respect within the profession and improve the quality of service.

4 Members shall make public criticism of their colleagues or their agencies only when warranted, verifiable, and constructive.

5 Members shall respect the importance of all disciplines within the criminal justice system and work to improve cooperation with each segment.

6 Members shall honor the public's right to information and share information with the public to the extent permitted by law subject to individuals' right to privacy.

7 Members shall respect and protect the right of the public to be safeguarded from criminal activity.

8 Members shall refrain from using their positions to secure personal privileges or advantages.

9 Members shall refrain from allowing personal interest to impair objectivity in the performance of duty while acting in an official capacity.

10 Members shall refrain from entering into any formal or informal activity or agreement, which presents a conflict of interest or is inconsistent with the conscientious performance of duties.

11 Members shall refrain from accepting gifts, services, or favors that is or appears to be improper or implies an obligation inconsistent with the free and objective exercise of professional duties.

12 Members shall clearly differentiate between personal views/statements and views/statements/positions made on behalf of the agency or Association.

13 Members shall report to appropriate authorities any corrupt or unethical behaviors in which there is sufficient evidence to justify review.

14 Members shall refrain from discriminating against any individual because of race, gender, creed, national origin, religious affiliation, age, disability, or any other type of prohibited discrimination.

15 Members shall preserve the integrity of private information; they shall refrain from seeking information on individuals beyond that which is necessary to implement responsibilities and perform their duties; members shall refrain from revealing nonpublic information unless expressly authorized to do so.

16 Members shall make all appointments, promotions, and dismissals in accordance with established civil service rules, applicable contract agreements, and individual merit, rather than furtherance of personal interests.

17 Members shall respect, promote, and contribute to a work place that is safe, healthy, and free of harassment in any form.

SOURCE: AMERICAN CORRECTIONAL ASSOCIATION (2012). ADOPTED BY THE BOARD OF GOVERNORS AND DELEGATE ASSEMBLY IN AUGUST 1994. REPRINTED WITH PERMISSION OF THE AMERICAN CORRECTIONAL ASSOCIATION, ALEXANDRIA, VA.

Fifth, particularly among professional employees such as psychologists and counselors, there can be conflicting loyalties. For example, professional codes of conduct generally dictate that in a counseling setting, staff must treat certain information the client discloses with confidentiality. However, concerns for jail and prison security might necessitate the disclosure even if the client relayed information he or she believed had an expectation of confidentiality. In effect, employees in these kinds of positions may find themselves torn between competing sets of ethical mandates.

Sixth, there is a general concern with corruption. Bernard McCarthy (2012: 270–71) identifies four specific types of corruption in prisons (and a miscellaneous category), and some of these fall within the categories of ethical issues already mentioned. The types of corruption described by McCarthy include the following:

- *Theft of items from inmates* is normally committed by COs.
- *Trafficking in contraband* may involve prison staff members at various levels, and the contraband items can include drugs, alcohol, money, and weapons. Trafficking in contraband may be associated with the fourth item we discussed earlier: improper relations with inmates or clients.
- *Embezzlement* is where prison employees (perhaps with inmates' help) convert money or materials from government accounts and supplies to their own use.
- *Misuse of authority* is an area related to our discussion of discretion and accepting gratuities from inmates or clients or their families.

Seventh, correctional employees often find themselves dealing with situations where sexual harassment may be an issue. These situations may involve inmates or clients or they may involve their coworkers (Pollock 2007). We will return to this issue in the next chapter.

In concluding this section on employee ethics, we want to emphasize two points. First, as should be apparent from the ACA Code of Ethics, some issues are distinct and unique to certain employee or supervisory groups, and others cut across all ranks and types of agencies. Second, research with jail and prison employees indicates that most at least overtly express a fairly strong ethical orientation (see Stohr et al. 2000), and experience teaches us that many correctional employees act consistent with their opinions. However, a few act unethically or illegally and, unfortunately, their behavior reflects on others who work in the profession.

SUMMARY

In this chapter, we have examined the working environment of the world of corrections. The key points of interest are the following:

- Corrections is a large and growing field of employment.
- Institutional corrections typically has two employment entry points: correctional officers and counselors. However, secure facilities employ people to provide recreation services, education services, and a variety of other services.
- Community corrections offers several employment opportunities for college graduates. These include probation and parole, nonsecure residential treatment facilities, halfway houses, and reintegration centers.

- Among the greatest concerns expressed by prospective employees is an injury or death on the job and the likelihood of lawsuits, but job-related stress is a very real factor.
- Although job prospects are good, finding the jobs is not always easy. The numerous online sources can help, and college career services offices can be very useful as well. Additionally, students that have completed a co-op experience or internship have a much stronger chance in the application process.

THINKING ABOUT CORRECTIONAL POLICIES AND PRACTICES: WRITING ASSIGNMENTS

1   Prepare a one-page summary in the form of a briefing paper for a correctional administrator. Address the issue of whether a college degree should be required for a position as a corrections officer in a jail or prison. Does a degree really make a difference? What about the applicant's major in college? Carefully explain and be prepared to defend your position.

2   This exercise involves two parts. First, interview someone in your community who currently works in some capacity in corrections. Think about a series of five to six questions that you want to ask before you schedule the interview (do not ask "How do you like your job?"). After the interview, write a synopsis of the

information you gathered and share it with the other members of your class.

3   Prepare a one-page paper that describes two actions corrections employees can take to minimize the likelihood that a successful lawsuit will be brought against them. Can you think of other preventive actions? Explain.

4   Complete a one-page essay, with examples for corrections, on the following topic: "Career exploration should be part of a freshman-level course in all curriculums."

5   Of the seven general concerns mentioned by McCarthy, which one do you believe threatens job integrity the most and why?

KEY TERMS

case managers
classification officers
clinical psychologist
cooperative (co-op) education
correctional counselors
correctional officers (COs)

institutional corrections
internship
malfeasance
misfeasance
nonfeasance
paraprofessionals

psychological diagnosticians
psychological technicians
superintendent
warden
whistle-blowing

CRITICAL REVIEW QUESTIONS

1   Whose salary is typically higher, law enforcement officers or corrections officers? If there is a pay disparity, why does it exist?

2   What do you think are the most positive parts of the CO's position? What do you see as the most negative?

3   Why are correctional personnel in the private sector, especially at the entry level positions, paid less money? Is this a disincentive to seek

employment in the private sector? Explain your reasoning in coming to these conclusions.

4   What is the purpose of the background check for employment in corrections? Why is a polygraph test required? A drug test? What kinds of activities might disqualify a person from employment in a secure facility?

5   You are the warden of a 1,000-bed medium-security prison. At a staff meeting, someone

raises the issue of salaries. A representative from the state personnel office mentions that your director of corrections is considering a plan to pay your clinical psychologists as much or more than you make. What is your reaction?

6 What do we mean when we say that probation and parole officers function partly as service brokers? Can PPOs themselves deliver most of the services needed by their clients?

7 Should probation and parole authorities pay their officers more than correctional officers? Explain your answer.

8 Should we expand the use of private-sector probation? What about parole? Is there a difference between the two that could make this a higher risk to the community?

9 Suppose you have a strong rehabilitation orientation. Select one of the following job settings as a place to work: a secure facility, a halfway house, or a community-based agency. Why did you pick that one?

10 Which position in corrections holds the least appeal for you and why?

NOTES

1 Check **www.corrections.com** for links to the CEA and other professional groups.
2 Some jails and other local detention facilities refer to a CO as a *jail deputy*, *detention officer*, or *custody officer*. We use the title *correctional officer* throughout this section because it is the most common term in prisons.
3 Students typically assume that federal jobs pay better than state jobs, and that state employees make more than local-government employees do. The figures cited here and previously indicate that this may be true, but it is not always true. For the most complete information on pay, consult the personnel office of your local detention facility, the corrections departments in your state and neighboring states, the US Bureau of Prisons, or any of the websites noted in this chapter.

REFERENCES

Abadinsky, Howard. 2009. *Probation and parole*, 10th edn. Upper Saddle River, NJ: Pearson.

Albanese, Jay S. 2008. *Professional ethics in criminal justice*, 2nd edn. Boston: Allyn & Bacon.

American Correctional Association (ACA). 2003. *Directory: Adult and juvenile correctional departments, institutions, agencies, and probation and parole authorities*, 64th edn. Lanham, MD: American Correctional Association.

American Correctional Association (ACA). 2012. "ACA Code of Ethics." Retrieved July 16, 2013 from: **http://www.aca.org/pastpresentfuture/ethics.asp**

Braswell, Michael C., Belinda R. McCarthy, and Bernard J. McCarthy. 2012. *Justice, crime, and ethics*, 7th edn. Burlington, MA: Anderson/Elsevier.

Bureau of Labor Statistics. 2010. *Census of fatal occupational industries*. Washington, DC: US Department of Labor.

Bureau of Labor Statistics. 2012. *Occupational outlook handbook, 2012–13 edition*. Washington, DC: US Department of Labor.

California Department of Corrections and Rehabilitation. 2012. "Parole Agent Careers." Retrieved July 16, 2013 from: **http://www.cdcr.ca.gov/career_opportunities/HR/PA.html**

Carlson, Joseph R., Richard H. Anson, and George Thomas. 2003. Correctional officer burnout and stress: Does gender matter? *Prison Journal* 83: 277–88.

Champion, Dean. 1990. *Probation and parole in the United States*. Columbus, OH: Merrill.

Champion, Dean. 2005. *The American dictionary of criminal justice*, 3rd edn. Los Angeles, CA: Roxbury.

De Lucia, Robert C., and Thomas J. Doyle. 1998. *Career planning in criminal justice*, 3rd edn. Cincinnati, OH: Anderson.

Glaze, Lauren E., and Thomas P. Bonczar. 2006. *Probation and parole in the United States, 2005*. Washington, DC: US Department of Justice.

Glaze, Lauren E., and Thomas P. Bonczar. 2011. *Probation and parole in the United States, 2010*. Washington, DC: Bureau of Justice Statistics, U.S. Department of Justice.

Gordon, Gary R. and R. Bruce McBride. 2011. *Criminal justice internships: Theory into practice*, 7th edn. Burlington, MA: Anderson/ Elsevier.

Guerino, Paul, Paige M. Harrison, and William J. Sabol. 2011. *Prisoners in 2010*. Washington, DC: Bureau of Justice Statistics, US Department of Justice.

Henry, Stuart, ed. 1994. *Inside jobs*. Salem, WI: Sheffield.

Hughes, Kristen A. 2006. *Justice expenditure and employment in the United States, 2003*. Washington, DC: US Department of Justice.

Indeed.com. 2012. Retrieved July 16, from: http://www. indeed.com/salary/Correctional-Counselor.html

Kohnke, William R. 2001. Professionalism in corrections. *American Jails* 15(1): 75–6, 78.

Kycklehahn, Tracey. 2012. *Criminal justice expenditures and extracts 2008: Final*. Washington, DC: US Department of Justice. Retrieved on July 16, 2013 from: http://bjs.ojp.usdoj.gov/index.cfm?ty=pbdetail&iid =4333

Lambert, Eric G. 2004. The impact of job characteristics on correctional staff members. *Prison Journal* 84: 208–27.

Lambert, Eric G., Nancy Lynne Hogan, and Shannon M. Barton. 2002. Satisfied correctional staff: A review of the literature on the correlates of correctional staff job satisfaction. *Criminal Justice and Behavior* 29: 115–43.

Latessa, Edward and Paula Smith. 2011. *Corrections in the community*, 5th edn. Burlington, MA: Anderson/ Elsevier.

Lee, Mary Price, Richard S. Lee, and Carol Beam. 1998. *100 best careers in crime fighting*. New York: Macmillan.

Maguire, Kathleen, and Ann C. Pastore (eds.) 1999. *Bureau of Justice statistics sourcebook of criminal justice statistics 1998*. Washington, DC: US Department of Justice.

Mays, G. Larry. 1989. The impact of federal sentencing guidelines on jail and prison overcrowding and early release. In *The US sentencing guidelines: Implications for criminal justice*, edited by Dean J. Champion. New York: Praeger, 181–200.

McCarthy, Bernard J. 2012. Keeping an eye on the keeper: Prison corruption and its control. In *Justice, crime and ethics*, 7th edn., edited by Michael C. Braswell, Belinda R. McCarthy, and Bernard J. McCarthy. Burlington, MA: Anderson/Elsevier, 265–83.

Onetonline.org. 2012. US Department of Labor. Retrieved July 16 from: www.onetonline.org

Owen, Stephen S. 2006. Occupational stress among correctional officers. *Prison Journal* 86: 164–81.

Pollock, Joycelyn. 2007. *Ethical dilemmas and decisions in criminal justice*, 5th edn. Belmont, CA: Wadsworth.

Prison University Project. 2012. San Quentin college program. Retrieved November 5, 2012 from: http:// www.prisonuniversityproject.org/pages/programs/san-quentin- college-program.html

Schaufeli, W. B., and M. C. W. Peeters. 2000. Job stress and burnout among correctional officers: A literature review. *International Journal of Stress Management* 7: 19–48.

Schloss, Christine, and Leanne F. Alarid (2007). Standards in the privatization of probation services: a statutory analysis. *Criminal Justice Review* 32(3): 233–45.

Seyle, Hans. 1974. *Stress without distress*. New York: Signet.

Slate, Risdon N., Terry L. Wells, and W. Wesley Johnson. 2003. Opening the manager's door: State probation officer stress and perceptions of participation in workplace decision making. *Crime & Delinquency* 49: 519–41.

Stephan, James J. 2008. *Census of state and federal correctional facilities, 2005*. Washington, DC: Bureau of Justice Statistics, US Department of Justice.

Stephan, James J., and Georgette Walsh (2011). *Census of jail facilities, 2006*. Washington, DC: Bureau of Justice Statistics, US Department of Justice.

Stephens, W. Richard. 1999. *Careers in criminal justice*. Boston: Allyn & Bacon.

Stohr, Mary K., Craig Hemmens, Misty Kifer, and Mary Schoeler. 2000. We know it, we just have to do it: Perceptions of ethical work in prisons and jails. *Prison Journal* 80(2): 126–50.

US Census Bureau. 2010. *Annual survey of public employment and payroll*. Retrieved on November 19,

2012 from http://www.census.gov//govs.apes/historical_data_2010.html

Ward, Richard H. 2000. The internationalization of criminal justice. In *Boundary changes in criminal justice organization*, vol. 2, edited by Charles Friel. Washington, DC: US Department of Justice, 267–321.

Whitehead, John T. 2012. Ethical issues in probation, parole, and community corrections. In *Justice, crime, and ethics*, 7th edn., edited by Michael C. Braswell, Belinda R. McCarthy, and Bernard J. McCarthy. Burlington, MA: Anderson/Elsevier, 212–34.

Williamson, Harold E. 1990. *The corrections profession*. Newbury Park, CA: Sage.

11 THE ADMINISTRATION OF CORRECTIONS PROGRAMS

YAKONIVA/ALAMY IMAGES

Outline

Objectives

- To help you understand the concepts of administration and management

- To illustrate to you different leadership styles

- To examine the types of issues faced by correctional administrators

- To explain to you the complexities of managing inmates

- To introduce you to the role of ethics in correctional management

Essentials of Corrections, Fifth Edition. G. Larry Mays and L. Thomas Winfree, Jr.
© 2014 John Wiley & Sons, Inc. Published 2014 by John Wiley & Sons, Inc.

INTRODUCTION

The administration of correctional agencies is a largely under-researched area, and the administration of secure facilities is one of the most overlooked subjects in contemporary corrections. One reason may be that corrections is a difficult area for academics to study because by design, jails and prisons are closed societies. Another reason: corrections in general has never received the attention afforded the other components of the criminal justice system— for example, law enforcement. Except when there is a large-scale and bloody prison riot or the jail escape of an infamous prisoner or the failure on probation of a sex offender, corrections is perhaps best described as the stepchild of the criminal justice system, and that characterization extends to the administration of corrections as well.

Why are we concerned at all with the corrections administrator's world in a textbook on the essentials of corrections? We do not expect that you will step from the classroom into an administrative position; however, if you choose to work in corrections, you will be working in an administrative environment. And if you choose a related career—police officer, prosecutor or defense attorney, social worker— understanding the administrative environment in the corrections system can only help you do a better job.

ADMINISTRATION AND MANAGEMENT

Two terms that are central to all organizations are *administration* and *management*. Although we use them somewhat interchangeably, **administration** typically refers to the act of supervising or managing an office or an organization. In criminal justice practice, administrators are the people at the top of the authority hierarchy, the organization's policy makers and chief executives. In community corrections, they include chief probation and parole officers and community corrections managers. In institutional corrections, there are several facility managers, including wardens and assistant wardens, institutional superintendents, and directors or administrators. At the state level, the head of the department of corrections may be known as a director, commissioner, superintendent, or secretary (McShane and Williams 1993, 1996, 4). By virtue of their positions, these individuals are likely to be more responsive to pressure from outside the organization than from within.

Alan Coffey (1974, 23–24) divided the administrative process in a correctional organization into three levels: administrative, managerial, and supervisory. Those at the *administrative level* define and integrate goals. Those at the *managerial level* define and integrate objectives and staffing concerns. The *supervisory managers* are the closest to the organization's line employees: they are responsible for defining and directing program personnel.

By comparison, **management** is using organizational resources to achieve specific goals. However, this definition says nothing about offices or the people in them (Stojkovic, Kalinich, and Klofas 1998, 6). Management is a process, not a title or a person. All personnel, from the highest to the lowest, manage—but only a few administer. Corrections administrators' authority comes from their organizational positions. Corrections managers, irrespective of rank, receive their professional authority from the breadth and depth of their knowledge about the positions they occupy and the personnel they supervise in the organization.

WHY STUDY ADMINISTRATION AND MANAGEMENT?

We started this chapter with an acknowledgment that little attention has been paid to administration and management in corrections. More than 35 years ago, Harry More noted, "The literature on correctional management is limited" (1977, 232). Fourteen years later, Alvin Cohn added, "A review of several recent journals suggests that administration and management of correctional agencies are issues hardly examined—if studied at all" (1991, 12).

Today, this is less true, although studies of corrections administration and management continue to be underrepresented in the literature. If this is the case, why is it important to study the administration of correctional agencies and institutions? Cohn provides us with an answer. He says that most failures in corrections programs are not the product of inadequate programming or underdeveloped philosophy, but the result of "inadequate management and leadership" (Cohn 1977, 235). John DiIulio, in studying prison governance in three states, expands on this theme, adding, "The quality of prison life depends far more on management practices than on any other single variable" (DiIulio 1987, 6). He concludes, "If most prisons have failed, it is because they have been ill managed, under-managed, or not managed at all" (7). Thus, there is good reason to turn our attention to corrections administration and management.

MANAGING INMATES AND MANAGING STAFF

Corrections management really has two distinct aspects. There is *inmate management*, in the form of institutions, programming efforts, and discipline, and there is *organizational management*, which is concerned with keeping the various institutional and agency functions operating efficiently (Peak 2007). Cohn recognizes what he calls an "organizational contradiction": "Even the lowest status members of the hierarchy, such as probation, parole, and correctional officers, are also responsible for *managing* people as well as for the development of goals, albeit for clients" (Cohn 1991, 13). Our focus is on organizational management, although we return to a brief discussion of inmate management before the end of the chapter.

The most common tasks performed by corrections administrators fall into the categories of finance and personnel. Financial considerations include functions from purchasing office supplies to preparing annual budgets. However, staff should always be the primary focus of corrections administrators. Among the issues that revolve around staff are hiring, firing, initial and in-service training, job assignments, scheduling, and benefits.

Administration is much more than what administrators do. For our purposes, it is probably much more useful to assess *how* things get done rather than *what* gets done. In the sections that follow, then, we examine various administrative styles and related issues. Although we offer examples throughout the chapter, our emphasis is not on the administration of a specific agency or component. What we hope to give you is information applicable to different contexts.

OVERVIEW OF BUREAUCRACY

Nearly every contemporary correctional organization could be described as a **bureaucracy**, a structure that assigns individuals specific authority and responsibilities according to their position in a predetermined hierarchy. Historically, the most common way of managing complex organizations has been from the top down. Picture a pyramid. The chief administrator of the organization sits at the top, at the narrow point. He or she has general authority over, and responsibility for, everyone below. As you move down the organization, managers and their staff take on more specific authority and responsibility for different functions of the organization, and the pyramid widens. The more specialized the organization's functions, the wider and higher the pyramid.

The Roman Catholic Church is the world's oldest continually operating bureaucracy. Government agencies are all bureaucracies, and so are the branches of the military. Traditionally, prisons have operated much like the military: there is a chain of command, and custody staff members hold rank and wear uniforms (DiIulio 1987, 1994).

One of the organizational theorists most frequently associated with the bureaucratic management school is Max Weber (1864–1920), a German economist. Several of the principles he defined in describing the ideal bureaucracy are especially relevant to corrections. First, he believed that bureaucracies are based on controls established through an organization's rules. The emphasis is on rationality: the bureaucracy's members must assume the *rules are rational*, and correct, and must follow them. Second, in Weber's ideal bureaucracy, *rules and regulations limit discretion*. Some would say that the exercise of discretion is incompatible with the concept of bureaucracy (Mouzelis 1967, 41). Third, although it may not seem so today, Weber believed that *bureaucracy contributes to organizational efficiency*. Efficiency is a by-product of both task specialization and the strict application of policies and procedures. In other words, if you work in an area of competence and "go by the book," you *should* be working efficiently.

Standards of conduct are key to the operation of any bureaucracy. Such standards generally consist of policy statements that prescribe organizational behavior (More 1977, 227). Predictability and stability are both highly prized by and closely associated with bureaucratic organizations. Also important to the functioning of a bureaucracy is maintaining a record of processes and accomplishments. This record defines and controls the organizational culture (Mouzelis 1967, 47). A useful but unintended consequence is that bureaucratic record keeping has provided a wealth of information to students of organizational life in general and of correctional organizations in particular.

The standardization that underlies the bureaucratic organizational form gives the organization its stability, but it also limits the organization in important ways. Procedures are an effective means of dealing with routine tasks (Peak 2007); in corrections, however, few administrative tasks are routine. An organization's stability becomes a weakness when the organization cannot respond to rapid change or to periods of political, social, or financial uncertainty (More 1977, 228). Perhaps even worse, the inflexibility of bureaucratic rules and regulations can reduce employees' initiative (Mouzelis 1967, 47).

Bureaucratic standards of conduct often overlook the fact that employees are people, that there are times when the organization's rules are going to come into conflict with their personal beliefs or goals. The reality of organizational life is that during such conflicts, individuals may pursue goals that are fundamentally different from those of the organization. According to Nicos Mouzelis (1967, 59–60), when employees break the rules, the bureaucracy typically responds by enforcing existing rules more fully or by imposing stricter rules, both responses that can reduce employees' morale and stifle their individual initiative.

To understand the significance of bureaucratic ideals to corrections, we next turn to an examination of leadership styles. Some of these styles are consistent with bureaucratic organizations and some are not.

LEADERSHIP STYLES

To this point, we have been talking about administration and management in abstract terms. From the standpoint of corrections organizations, however, the most important consideration is how these concepts translate into leadership styles.

There are three basic types of leaders: authoritarian, laissez-faire, and democratic (see Blau and Scott 1962; Etzioni 1964; Weber 1947). The **authoritarian leader** gives orders and is concerned with productivity. This person is the boss, and he or she expects subordinates to do as they are instructed. Authoritarian leaders communicate primarily by telling or commanding. Communication is almost exclusively from top down. Marilyn McShane and Frank Williams (1993, 9) characterize the authoritarian leader as an autocrat. Consistent with authoritarianism, the autocrat is task oriented rather than people oriented, and dogmatic, and expects compliance with whatever orders are issued. This type of leader is found in many paramilitary organizations and may be particularly prevalent among prison administrators (1993, 1996).

The **laissez-faire leader** is an administrator who provides little or no direction to subordinates. Employees are encouraged to do more or less as they think best, to use their discretion. This approach may work fine in a small community-based program or with highly trained medical personnel, but it is not conducive generally to goal- or task-oriented activities.

The third basic leadership style stresses democratic ideals. The **democratic leader** communicates through explanation and elaboration rather than by orders. A democratic, or participatory, leader often is viewed as the first among equals; all of the people working under the leader's direction recognize their organizational roles and understand exactly what is expected of them. A difficulty associated with applying the democratic leadership style in corrections is confusion about who should be participating in decision making and to what degree (McShane and Williams 1993, 10). Should all employees have a say in important decisions? In prisons, should inmates play a role in decision making? Today, these questions remain largely unanswered.

Although the three basic leadership styles are useful for understanding how many administrators in the corrections system behave, they are by no means definitive. The National Advisory Commission on Criminal Justice Standards and Goals (1973, 449—50) identifies four other types of leaders.

The first is the **bureaucratic leader**. Much like the authoritarian or autocratic leader, this leader is rule oriented and tends to lead from the top down. The bureaucratic leader also demands loyalty from subordinates and expects subordinates to follow policies without asking questions. A strong orientation toward the status quo can make it difficult for the bureaucratic leader to respond quickly and appropriately in times of crisis.

The bureaucratic leader is common in corrections systems. In his study of three state prison systems, DiIulio (1987) characterized the Texas Department of Criminal Justice (formerly the Texas Department of Corrections) as a largely bureaucratic system, particularly before the federal court intervened in the system in the early 1980s. He suggested that the prison system in Texas operated under a "control model" for staff—inmate relations, in which "the chain of command was followed rigorously by employees" (5, 105). He concluded that the department experienced some of its most difficult problems when it tried to run a largely bureaucratic system during a highly volatile period, when it was facing both court mandates and changes in departmental and state leadership.

A second style listed by the National Advisory Commission is the **technocratic leader**. This is a manager who has achieved his or her position based on some area of expertise. For example, in corrections, technocratic leaders might be psychologists or social workers who find themselves in management roles. Technocratic leaders are not as likely as generalists to be at the very top of an organization—a warden of a prison, for example—but they may be responsible for a particular division (programming, treatment, mental health services, or the like). Unlike the bureaucratic leader, the technocrat typically is not concerned about *how* a job gets done as long as it gets done. So this leader may not strictly follow the organization's policies, procedures, and traditional chain of command.

The **idiosyncratic leader** is a little bit laissez-faire but mostly autocratic. He or she is likely to work over, under, around, and through the hierarchy by exerting direct contact and control over decision making. Sometimes idiosyncratic leaders play one employee off against another. And they may create fear and suspicion in the ranks, a practice that places them in the position of having the fullest knowledge and, therefore, the greatest power.

According to the commission, idiosyncratic leaders like to walk around their facilities, "not to make a grand inspection but to keep in close touch with operations" (National Advisory Commission 1973, 450). Walking around was a routine George Beto adopted in his years as the director of the Texas corrections system (see Box 11.1). The problem, according to the commission, is that this kind of hands-on leadership sacrifices the general for the specific. Idiosyncratic leaders may become so caught up in the details that they lose sight of their primary responsibility, the overall operations of a system, facility, or program.

Idiosyncratic leaders create two other serious problems in agencies and institutions. First, because they reserve most of the decision-making authority for themselves, decisions are made slowly or not at all. Second, idiosyncratic leaders suffer from blind spots that their employees are either afraid to warn them about or choose to take advantage of. These leaders may have a difficult time discerning good decisions from bad, and they are unlikely to ask for or get much help from their subordinates.

The **participative leader**, the final category in the commission's list, is much like the democratic leader. Participative leaders are more group oriented than autocratic or bureaucratic leaders are, and they frequently have informal contacts with employees under their direction. The chief weakness of many of these managers is that they dislike conflict almost to the point of trying to avoid it at all costs. The problem is that in healthy organizations, conflicts are bound to occur; in trying to reach a group consensus, some decisions may not be made or less-than-optimal solutions may be chosen. Box 11.2 presents a brief biographical sketch of Tom Murton, a classic example in corrections of a participative leader.

GEORGE BETO (1916–1991)   BOX 11.1

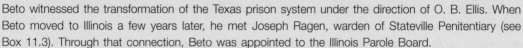

One of the best-known names in twentieth-century corrections is that of George Beto, director of the Texas Department of Corrections (TDC) during the 1960s and early 1970s. Beto carefully cultivated the reputation of the TDC as "the best prison system in the nation."

Beto did not set out to be a corrections administrator. He trained in theology at Concordia Theological Seminary in Illinois and became a Lutheran minister. After a short period in the ministry, he began teaching at and later became president of Concordia Lutheran College in Austin, Texas. Beto's link to corrections began in 1953, when the governor of Texas appointed him to the state prison board. As a member of that board, Beto witnessed the transformation of the Texas prison system under the direction of O. B. Ellis. When Beto moved to Illinois a few years later, he met Joseph Ragen, warden of Stateville Penitentiary (see Box 11.3). Through that connection, Beto was appointed to the Illinois Parole Board.

When Ellis died in 1961, Beto was contacted and offered the position of director of the TDC. He accepted. His leadership style was idiosyncratic: "Walking George," as he was sometimes called, would regularly tour the prisons in the system to see for himself how they were operating. Over time, Beto's style of managing the Texas prisons came to be known as the *control model*. According to Charles Jeffords and Jan Lindsey, "The control model involved the strict enforcement of discipline and the tight regulation of the inmate's daily routine, down to how he buttoned his prison uniform" (59). These were details to which Beto often personally responded.

Beto's control model has been praised by some and seriously questioned by others. But during his lifetime, it earned Beto a great deal of recognition and the Texas prisons "a national reputation based on an enviable record for order, efficiency, and inmate safety" (Dilulio).

SOURCES: DIIULIO (1987); T. GRAY AND MEYER (1996); JEFFORDS AND LINDSEY (1996).

TEXAS DEPARTMENT OF CRIMINAL JUSTICE

TOM MURTON (1928–1990)   BOX 11.2

Tom Murton was both academic and practitioner. He earned both the master of arts and doctoral degrees from the University of California at Berkeley; moreover, he served in a number of correctional positions, both military and civilian, before and after earning his advanced degrees. He also served as a faculty member at several universities, including Southern Illinois University and the University of Minnesota. In 1983, Murton received the Paul Tappan Award from the Western Society of Criminology for "outstanding contributions to the field of criminology."

Murton helped to establish the Alaska state prison system in the 1960s. However, he is perhaps best known for his 1967–1968 service in the Arkansas prison system, where, as superintendent at the 1,300-inmate Cummins State Prison Farm, he exposed widespread corruption and violence, including the alleged deaths of hundreds of inmates. A 1980 movie, *Brubaker*, was a highly fictionalized account of Murton's experience in Arkansas. After working less than a year in his position as a "professional penologist," he was fired by then governor Winthrop A. Rockefeller. Murton returned to Berkeley, where he completed his doctoral degree in criminology and was for nearly a decade a faculty member at the University of Minnesota. He formally left teaching in 1980, returning to his native Oklahoma to work the family farm, occasionally lecturing on corrections at his nearby alma mater, Oklahoma State University.

NOTE: TARA GRAY, ONE OF OUR COLLEAGUES AT NEW MEXICO STATE UNIVERSITY AND A STUDENT OF MURTON'S AT OKLAHOMA STATE UNIVERSITY, PROVIDED MATERIAL FOR THIS BIOGRAPHICAL SKETCH; FOWLER (1990).

JP LAFFONT/SYGMA/CORBIS

In its assessment of leadership styles, the National Advisory Commission (1973) drew three important conclusions. First, seldom do any of the management styles appear in their purest form (451). Many administrators combine two or more styles (see Box 11.3). Second, the most common forms in correctional organizations are the bureaucratic and idiosyncratic styles (450). Finally, although the bureaucratic and idiosyncratic styles are most common, "neither is ideally suited to the administration of large, complex systems under conditions of rapid change" (National Advisory Commission 1973, 450).

The correctness of the commission's assessment has been borne out many times over the intervening 30-plus years. The rapid change that characterizes contemporary corrections has made the deficiencies of traditional administrative approaches all too clear. Adding to the difficulty is that administrators tend to rely on what has worked in the past. Although some administrators can change their leadership styles to fit the situation (see Box 11.4), most rely on familiar ways of managing, even if those ways are not especially effective (McShane and Williams 1993, 8).

ISSUES FACING CORRECTIONS MANAGERS

Certainly corrections administrators face issues that are unique to the times, but a number of the problems facing contemporary corrections administrators have been with us for decades and are likely to be with us for decades to come.

MANAGING BUDGETS, MANAGING PERSONNEL: THE SCOPE OF MANAGERIAL DUTIES AND RESPONSIBILITIES

Corrections is big business. A report issued by the National Association of State Budget Officers (NASBO) (2010) found that in fiscal year 2010 states spent $51.1 billion for corrections (a 3.2 percent

decrease over fiscal 2009), and this figure represented 3.1 percent of total state spending.

However, it is important to note that this figure does not represent the true costs of correctional operations. For example, 23 states do not include counseling for juvenile offenders in their correctional budgets and 19 states do not include juvenile institutions (NASBO 2010, 53). Other states did not include funding for drug treatment centers, institutions for the criminally insane, or aid to local jails. Therefore, in order to estimate the true cost of institutional corrections, the Vera Institute issued a report including the ancillary or hidden costs associated with corrections (Henrichson and Delaney 2012).

In a survey to which 40 states responded, the Vera Institute found that true correctional costs annually were more than $5.4 billion (or 13.9 percent) more than the figures reported in states' correctional budgets.[1] Additional, but indirect, costs included employee benefits and taxes, pension contributions by the state, health care costs for retirees, capital construction costs, payments for legal judgments, and health care and educational costs for inmates. All of these items (and others like them) are included in state budgets somewhere, but they are not always reflected directly in corrections budgets. This means that for these 40 states (with 1.2 million prison inmates) the true annual cost per inmate was $31,286 (Henrichson and Delaney 2012, 9). This can be added to the roughly $1,250 per year that it costs to supervise nearly 5 million people on probation and parole (Glaze 2011; Pew Center on the States 2009).

In terms of employment figures, in 2011 the US Census Bureau reported that there were 462,549 full-time equivalent state employees working in corrections with an annual payroll of $1.92 billion. This translates into an average salary of about $42,000 each. Additionally, the US Bureau of Prisons employed 38,5000 people and there were another 234,000 working in local jails. The picture portrayed in this brief analysis of correctional budgets and personnel is rather daunting: more than $60 billion in expenditures and over 735,000 local, state, and federal employees indicate that corrections is a significant industry measured by any standards.

JOSEPH E. RAGEN (1896–1971)   BOX 11.3

Joseph E. Ragen symbolizes what most correctional scholars would characterize as the old school of prison administration. Ragen was a small-town sheriff when he was appointed warden of Stateville Penitentiary, the largest maximum-security facility in Illinois. He served in that capacity until 1961, when he became the state's public safety director.

In some ways, Ragen typified the autocratic leader; in others, he was a model of the idiosyncratic leader. James Jacobs, in his history of the Stateville prison, described the warden this way:

> The "old boss" devoted his life to perfecting the world's most orderly prison regime. He exercised personal control over every detail no matter how insignificant. He tolerated challenges neither by inmates nor by employees nor by outside interest groups. He cultivated an image which made him seem invincible to his subordinates as well as to the prisoners. (29)

Two features characterized Ragen's tenure as warden at Stateville and his personal management style. First, he was well respected in corrections circles in the United States and abroad. Second, Ragen kept partisan politics out of personnel decisions and prison operations. According to Jacobs, "Ragen established a patriarchal organization based upon his own charismatic authority," and an independence that is probably no longer possible in prisons in the United States (31).

SOURCE: JACOBS (1977).

FRANCIS MILLER/TIME & LIFE PICTURES/GETTY IMAGES

MARY BELLE HARRIS (1874–1957)   BOX 11.4

Mary Belle Harris was an early twentieth-century prison reformer and one of the first female prison administrators in the United States. Harris, who earned a PhD from the University of Chicago, became superintendent of the Women's Workhouse at Blackwell Island in New York City in 1913, at the age of 39. When she took over, the facility "was considered to be the worst among twelve institutions" under the direction of the New York Commissioner of Corrections (225).

Harris's approach to dealing with inmates clearly was rehabilitative. She tried to maximize and humanize staff contacts (particularly her own) with the inmates. Under her leadership, inmates took fresh-air walks and gardened. Drug-dependent inmates and those with venereal diseases were identified, classified, placed in separate units, and treated.

Harris worked at the state reformatory in Clinton, New Jersey, in several positions: as assistant director of the War Department's Section on Detention Houses and Reformatories for Women and as superintendent of the State Home for Girls in Trenton, New Jersey. In 1925, she was chosen as the first superintendent of the new women's federal prison at Alderson, West Virginia, a post she held until her retirement in 1941. During her tenure at Alderson, the prison "was considered a model institution with relatively few serious disciplinary actions and no escapes" (227).

SOURCE: ROGERS (1996).

REPRODUCED WITH PERMISSION FROM THE COLLECTIONS OF SPECIAL COLLECTIONS/UNIVERSITY ARCHIVES, BUCKNELL UNIVERSITY, LEWISBURG, PA. PHOTO HARRIS AND EWING

WHO MANAGES? THE CHARACTERISTICS OF CORRECTIONS MANAGERS

The managers of both institutions and community-based programs traditionally have not been especially well regarded for their qualifications, competence, or expertise. Several factors seem to have contributed to this situation.[2] First, for much of our history, corrections agencies have been *closed systems.* This means that these institutions and agencies have not been open to public scrutiny and that promotions have come from within. By the time employees rise to management or administration positions, they are thoroughly indoctrinated in the way functions should be performed in their organization. The problem with a closed system and promotion from within is that top administrators are unlikely to have a very broad understanding of how other facilities and programs approach common problems. We expand on this issue in the next section.

In addition, the status of corrections managers has reflected the traditionally low qualification levels required to work in corrections. In most institutional settings, entry-level employees need only have a high school diploma or General Educational Development (GED) certificate; when promotions come from within, the people with entry-level requirements move up to become supervisors, managers, and administrators. We will return to this issue in the discussion of professionalization at the end of the chapter.

By contrast, virtually all probation and parole administrators have a bachelor's degree at least and many hold a master's degree as well. The same can be said of technocrats who become facility or agency administrators. The employment requirements have become more stringent in the last decade or so, and the educational level of corrections administrators generally continues to increase.

The third, and possibly most influential, factor affecting corrections administrators' stature is **political patronage**. For most of the twentieth century, state corrections commissioners and wardens were political appointees. They did not earn their positions through their qualifications or experience. Instead, they were placed in office because they had worked for some politician. An unintended consequence of political patronage was frequent turnover; when the politicians left office, so did their appointees. This resulted in a lack of both long-term planning and organizational stability. Only in the past 20 years or so have the states moved away from the political appointment of wardens and most other corrections administrators. The one exception, of course, is the position of state corrections secretary or commissioner, a position that is typically part of a governor's cabinet and so, by definition, involves a political appointment.

CORRECTIONS ADMINISTRATORS' BACKGROUNDS

A lingering issue raised by the traditional promotion processes in corrections systems is the background corrections administrators should have. When administrators are promoted from within an organization, they have very specific experience within the organization and the local system. That means a relatively short learning curve to become familiar with their new responsibilities, which is a good thing in terms of how a facility or program operates. But it also can mean limited exposure to different ways of thinking and doing. One important question, then, is whether agencies should make a point of looking for administrative candidates outside the facility or possibly even outside the state. Another question along the same line is whether an individual with public administration experience in a field other than corrections is a suitable or even a better candidate for appointment to a high-ranking corrections position. These questions become increasingly important as states expand their corrections systems, especially as states build new prisons and face a growing need for experienced and competent administrators. The demand for seasoned correctional administrators, which began in earnest beginning in the 1980s and continued well into the twenty-first century, may have exhausted the existing candidate pool. Even though the demand for senior prison administrators due to prison growth may, as recent trends suggest, decline, the aging of the current leadership, including retirements of "baby-boomer" prison officials, will continue to stretch the leadership resources well into this century. These factors may leave the federal system, states and even local correctional authorities

UNIT MANAGEMENT IN THE US BUREAU OF PRISONS

BOX 11.5

One form of participatory, nonhierarchical management is found in the institutions operated by the US Bureau of Prisons (BOP) and the Michigan Department of Corrections. John Dilulio describes unit management as one of many strategies designed to demilitarize prison operations. Unit management began as the *functional-unit concept* developed by Robert Levinson and Roy Gerard. Each unit is organized around the function it is designed to perform, and treatment is provided for the inmates within their assigned units.

The BOP implemented the unit management system in the early 1970s. Each prison is divided into units housing between 50 and 250 inmates. The offices of staff members assigned to each unit are located within the unit. Each unit has a unit manager who is responsible for all the unit's programming and activities, and, depending on the unit's size, several case managers, correctional counselors, and correctional officers. In effect, each unit is a miniature prison.

Unit management is an example of one alternative to the traditional bureaucratic management of prisons. It is loosely based on a technocratic leadership style but involves all members of the unit staff in team-oriented decision making. A chief advantage of unit management, in addition to its more democratic leadership style, is that it minimizes many of the traditional divisions between treatment and custody staff.

SOURCES: DIIULIO (1987, 1994); FARMER (2012); LEVINSON AND GERARD (1973).

with few choices: they simply will not be able to wait for employees to work their way up through the ranks. Other hiring practices, including lateral hires of mid- and senior-level administrators from other criminal justice agencies and even from non-correctional private sector jobs may become increasingly common.

CENTRALIZATION VERSUS DECENTRALIZATION

One of the defining characteristics of bureaucracy is **centralization**, the concentration of power in one location. Historically, many states operated their corrections systems from a centralized corrections department. Although probation and parole offices by their function have had to be decentralized in locations and administration, prisons for the most part have continued to be controlled centrally. Today, however, several forces are moving corrections agencies in the direction of decentralization.

One is the movement away from megaprisons, the very large prisons housing thousands of inmates (McShane and Williams 1993, 1996). Several states have built 500- to 800-bed prisons in different locations throughout the jurisdiction. This makes it more challenging to create and administer policies from a central headquarters.

A second factor in the move toward decentralization is **unit management**. In effect, unit management creates prisons within prisons. It allows for more personal inmate contact and greater decentralization of decision making for most routine matters (Box 11.5).

A third factor in the movement toward decentralization is the competition among state agencies for scarce resources. At budget time, each prison in the state and the different probation and parole offices all are vying for funding from the same finite pool of tax dollars. This pits one agency against the others and makes each institution and office build its best case for why it should be listed as a higher priority. The result is an organization more fragmented than unified.

MODERN MANAGEMENT TASKS

One of the most difficult aspects of any corrections administrator's job is that the governor, the state legislature, or the courts often set the policy agenda.

As McShane and Williams (1996, 7) note in speaking about prison wardens, "Many of the aspects of the job are simply out of one's control." Nevertheless, certain basic tasks seem to cut across all jurisdictions, agencies, and institutions.

RECRUITING AND RETAINING STAFF

One of the key functions performed by corrections administrators is the recruitment of qualified staff members. As we have noted, many positions in corrections suffer from a poor public image, which can make it difficult to recruit the best-qualified individuals on a consistent basis. In addition, as some workforce projections indicate, in the coming decades there will be fewer people of any qualification from which to choose as the baby boom generation retires (Bureau of Labor Statistics 2012). Corrections administrators are going to have to be aggressive and proactive in locating qualified personnel. They are also going to have to make a conscious effort to diversify their staffs. The bottom line is that more women and members of minority groups have to be located and recruited for a work world that traditionally has been male and white.

Retention is clearly related to the recruitment issue. Contemporary corrections administrators must pay attention to employee turnover and morale, especially given the investment in recruitment and training (McShane and Williams 1993). High turnover and excessive use of sick leave are typical indicators of some type of organizational ailment. In the past, administrators might have been inclined simply to dismiss employees they believed were shirking, but this becomes less feasible as it becomes more difficult to find good workers. Instead, corrections managers must be adept at locating the sources of employees' problems and correcting those problems.

Morale is another issue related to retention, to job satisfaction and, ultimately, to job performance. The difficulty facing public-sector managers is that they may not have a broad range of employee incentives at their disposal. Therefore, corrections managers now and in the future will have to be creative in designing incentive plans to build and maintain employee morale. Such strategies might include periodic pay bonuses, if they are allowed by union contracts and state personnel regulations; days off with pay; or plaques designating the employee of the month, quarter, and year. Interestingly, one of the most effective morale builders—simple recognition of achievement—can cost little or no money.

DEALING WITH EMPLOYEE UNIONS

Now that we have mentioned employee unions, we should describe how these organizations fit into the administrative environment. During the past four decades, public-service employees have lobbied for legislation that would allow for unionization. Legislation was necessary in those states where laws prohibited public employees from forming or joining labor unions.[3]

One effect of unionization is that administrators cannot simply enact policy changes. For example, most union contracts specify the number of hours employees can work in a given pay period and typically restrict reassignments or disciplinary actions unless certain procedures are followed. Wardens may not be able to transfer employees within a prison or from one prison to another without carefully consulting the provisions of the union contract.

BUILDING AND REMODELING FACILITIES

All administrators at the level of corrections secretary or commissioner are faced with the prospect of building new facilities or remodeling older ones. This task primarily involves the construction of prisons and jails, but even probation and parole agencies must have office space, and that space must be reviewed for suitability on an ongoing basis. Therefore, top-level corrections administrators must be concerned with site selection, and building design and construction (Lawrence and Travis 2004).

MANAGING INMATE POPULATIONS

Institutional crowding is a chronic problem plaguing corrections managers (see Stephan 2008). A 2011 US

Supreme Court decision could have massive repercussions in California. In *Brown v. Plata*, a divided (5-4) Court ruled that the crowding situation in California violated the Eighth Amendment's provisions against cruel and unusual punishment.[4] The fate of 30,000 prison inmates was impacted by this decision, although a year after the decision California had made little progress and was heading toward a crisis involving the federal judiciary and state officials (St. John 2012). A 2012 Government Accountability Office report provided a scathing look at the problems associated with crowding in the Federal Bureau of Prisons and five selected state prison systems. Crowding negatively impacted inmates, staff, and even the infrastructure of the prisons themselves—causing facilities essentially to "wear out" before their time (GAO 2012).

At first glance, this problem would seem to be confined to jail and prison administrators, but even the managers of community-based programs are faced with the problem of controlling their caseloads. Corrections agencies of all sizes and types are being asked to do more with the same resources—or to do the same with fewer resources. And the problem does not look as if it will go away in the near future.

Historically, inmate populations were set by the courts—that is, facilities accepted whatever number of inmates the courts sent them. Increasingly, however, corrections administrators are taking a proactive stance, advocating long and hard for alternatives to incarceration. They are refusing to be simply victims of the broader political and legal environment, choosing instead to take an active role in policy creation and implementation. This can mean lobbying for changes in state laws to reduce prison populations, or for the use of private facilities inside or outside the state to handle overflow. Or corrections officials may meet with judges to inform them of institutional capacity issues and to encourage them to be cautious in sentencing convicted offenders to confinement.

The report by the Governmental Accountability Office (2012, 32) noted that states can take three types of actions to reduce institutional crowding and the increasing costs associated with corrections. These actions include:

- modifying criminal statutes and sentencing laws—much of what has driven correctional populations upward since the late 1970s has been the movement toward determinate sentencing along with mandatory minimum sentences for certain crimes; in effect, it is not just more sentenced offenders, but more offenders sentenced to longer periods of incarceration;

- relocating inmates, especially to lower security, less costly facilities; and

- providing inmates with good time credits or, in some cases, with more good time credits to hasten their release.

CONTAINING COSTS

An unspoken but real concern in all of the areas addressed is cost containment. Most corrections administrators today know that the public and its elected representatives are concerned about the spiraling costs of corrections, especially the costs of institutional placements. They recognize that the supply of tax dollars is finite. This recognition, as hard as it is to accept, means that top administrators in all corrections agencies, at all levels of government, have to be concerned about cost containment. Particularly important are the medical costs incurred in jails and prisons today. The rate of serious illness in secure facilities is rising, as is the age of the population because inmates must serve a higher percentage of longer prison sentences. Both disease and illness are likely to send medical costs in jails and prisons soaring, topics we return to in Chapter 15.

DEALING WITH THE COURTS

Administrators spend a great deal of time with legal issues. Virtually every corrections commissioner who comes into office immediately becomes a party to one or more lawsuits. That means time learning about all of the ongoing lawsuits that are facing the department. Given the litigation potential in all parts of the corrections system, this also means setting aside time to deal with issues before they become lawsuits.

INMATE MANAGEMENT

Most of what we have examined to this point has had to do with the internal processes of corrections organizations: managers dealing with their employees. However, all corrections employees, including top administrators, have at least some responsibility for managing inmates or clients as well (Peak 2007). Greg Newbold reminds us of a popular saying among prison employees: "There are two ways of running a prison: with the inmates or without them" (Newbold 1992, 53). The second way assumes that inmates are obstinate, uncooperative, and resistant to change. This is somewhat akin to Douglas McGregor's (1960) notion of Theory X management, the traditional approach to inmate and client management. By this approach, "a rigidly authoritarian relationship between inmates and keepers [is] maintained" (Newbold 1992, 53). Although this orientation can

work for a time, it has the tendency to alienate and isolate the inmates from the staff (or from probation and parole officers in community settings). In the end, authoritarian management deepens inmates' commitment to the inmate subculture (see Chapter 7), and this can mean serious problems for the administration (56).

The other approach to dealing with inmates takes the view that inmates are adults and that they will respond to the level of responsibility expected of them. This is much like McGregor's (1960) Theory Y management style. The immediate response of most people to this idea is something like "You can't trust inmates, and you can't give them power over their own lives or the lives of others." Some prison administrators, notably Tom Murton when he was an Arkansas prison warden, believe that inmates will act in accord with our expectations of them (see T. Gray and Meyer 1996). Box 11.6 contains a

---

A COMPARISON OF MCGREGOR'S THEORY X AND THEORY Y   BOX 11.6

Assumptions Theory X makes about workers and the workplace:

1 People dislike work and avoid it if they can.

2 As people dislike work, most of them must be "coerced, controlled, directed, [or] threatened with punishment" to get them to make an effort (33).

3 The average person is not ambitious.

4 Most people avoid responsibility.

5 The average person wants to be directed and is security oriented.

6 In work environments, most people do not use their intellectual capacity.

Assumptions Theory Y makes about workers and the workplace:

1 The physical and mental aspects of work are as natural as rest or play.

2 People do not need external control if they are committed to the organization's goals.

3 People's commitment to organizational goals is related to the rewards attached to achieving those goals.

4 Most people learn to accept and even search out responsibility.

5 Imagination, ingenuity, and creativity are widely distributed throughout an organization's personnel.

6 The work environment can release the intellectual capacity of most people.

SOURCE: MCGREGOR (1960).

description of the assumptions that underlie McGregor's X and Y theories.

As we end this brief discussion of inmate management, we need to turn to two conclusions from Newbold, a criminologist who has served time in prison himself. First, Newbold maintains that as the level of threat from administration to inmates decreases, the tension in the inmate population also decreases. Second, he says that the "peaceful interface between management and inmates makes a prison a simpler place to operate and live in" (1992, 56). Implementing such an approach to institutional corrections in the United States may prove difficult. An anecdote may be instructive. In 2006, Winfree took a group of students to a medium security prison situated outside London, England. One of the students was a former correctional officer from the Correctional Institution Division of the Texas Department of Criminal Justice, having worked for several years at the infamous "Walls Unit" (i.e., the Texas State Penitentiary at Huntsville). This student immediately expressed a high level of personal distress when he saw the level of nearly collegial familiarity between correctional staff and inmates. There was no "line" down the center of the hallways for the inmates to walk, and there were no set uniforms, allowing for clear demarcation of who was an inmate and who was a staff person. The head of security for the facility was a pregnant woman, who walked the halls of the unit without regard for her personal safety. Talking with staff, he found that inmates and staff regularly exchanged ideas on how to minimize problems in the facility, both sides listening to the other. "I might not have quit my job as a CO," he noted, "if we did things like this in the States." But he continued, "I doubt that this approach would fly in Texas."

TRENDS IN CORRECTIONAL MANAGEMENT

Some of you taking this course will be corrections managers in the coming years. What does the future hold for you? Although we cannot say with absolute certainty, several issues undoubtedly will carry over into the next decade. Cohn (1995), who

often comments on corrections management, suggests three.

THE DEVELOPMENT OF TECHNOLOGY

Technology encompasses many different devices and applications. For corrections, perhaps no technology has surpassed that of the computer. Historically, administrators had to consult with subordinates to gather information on agency operations. As Cohn notes, now "managers have the ability to find out what is happening in institutions and in caseloads, as examples, without having to confer directly with staff" (1995, 12). Technology will clearly shift power relationships in corrections organizations: the most powerful will be those who know and can use the technology the best. The result may be that "the traditional role of the correctional supervisor and, in fact, the need for such are about to be changed and, perhaps, even eliminated!" (12).

THE ADVENT OF TOTAL QUALITY MANAGEMENT

Total quality management (TQM) is a concept that has been widely applied in US businesses. From a correctional standpoint, TQM demands that "clients" be considered "consumers," and that agencies or organizations develop a strong consumer orientation. Cohn again gives us insights into how this will affect corrections staff: "Workers are being asked to reconsider their routines, to bring qualitative improvements to their services to consumers, and to ensure that the defined goals and objectives of the organization are met—and in ways that can be quantified" (1995, 13).

Two dilemmas face corrections agencies in relation to the adoption of total quality management. First, corrections systems exhibit a tendency to do things the way they have always been done. Second, and perhaps even more problematic, is the definition of who the consumers are. Does the corrections system serve the general public? The governor? The state legislature? Inmates, probationers, and parolees? Until this question can be answered with some degree of certainty, TQM can only be a possibility, not a reality, in corrections management.

RESTRUCTURING GOVERNMENT

Governments of all sizes, at all levels, and from all parts of the United States are faced with the prospect of being restructured or reinvented. In simplest terms, most agencies are being asked to do more with less. This tactic can result in downsizing or right-sizing. Whatever we call it, agencies are faced with the likelihood that budgets may not increase and that some positions may be lost or may have to be altered. Resources may be redirected toward those functions that are considered essential, and nonessential functions may be eliminated or placed in a much lower position of priority than they have traditionally held (see Cohn 1995). Of course, determining what is or is not essential is a hotly debated issue in the process of organizational downsizing.

Before we end this consideration of trends in corrections administration, let's look at some solutions to these problems. McShane and Williams (1993, 59–64) make ten "recommendations for correctional managers" that should be given very serious consideration. We present them here in somewhat abbreviated form.

1   Corrections agencies should not be promoting from within. They should select top administrators from different professional backgrounds who have experience in human-services management.

2   Effective managers should develop a "management style that is consistent with their personality and beliefs . . . Managers need to be both adaptable and adaptive" (60).

3   Although a central office may hire for the agency, administrators should let that office know what qualifications they are seeking in their employees. Managers should also monitor employee morale and track the reasons that employees resign from their positions. This gives some measure of the nature and quality of the work environment.

4   When the facility uses shift work, especially in jail and prison settings, managers should make every effort to equalize the duties and responsibilities of each shift. That is, no one shift should be more or less desirable than any other. Although this is a difficult task, it is not impossible.

5   Management concepts such as unit management and direct supervision (discussed in Chapter 5) should receive serious consideration. The literature on these topics, particularly direct supervision and new-generation facilities, is growing, and future corrections managers would be well served by reviewing this research carefully.

6   Whenever changes in management style or organizational structure are anticipated, managers must plan well in advance and solicit substantive input from all parts of the agency. Top-down management is less effective in most organizations.

7   Administrators should be actively looking for ways to enrich and enlarge the jobs of all corrections employees. Very few individuals working in corrections today are so tied to their jobs that they would not consider leaving for more rewarding opportunities. Unfortunately, certain positions, both inside and outside institutions, are mind-numbingly routine. If we want to attract high-quality personnel and retain them for some length of time, we must think seriously about career development strategies.

8   Corrections managers must recognize that they are part of a larger community and should become involved in community activities. It is virtually impossible for corrections administrators to ignore the larger legal, political, and social environments in which they operate. Corrections agencies are fast becoming more open systems.

9   Managers should become active consumers of management research. Very few agencies or managers can afford to learn by trial and error. The learning curve is simply too steep. One way to find out quickly what does and does not work is to review current management research in both public and private sectors.

10   Corrections agencies, particularly those that operate jails and prisons, should move beyond the nine-to-five mentality. A number of assignments can be accomplished throughout the day, and accommodations should be made for equalizing work assignments and duties.

TEN IDEAS FOR EFFECTIVE MANAGERS

BOX 11.7

Robert Wiggins, a criminal justice practitioner turned college professor, suggested ten ideas for effective managers.

1 Cultivate positive personal relationships. Organizations do not forget negative behaviors. Treat people as if they will have authority over you someday—some may very well be your boss.

2 Remember that great leaders can be poor managers. Managers, in addition to leading, are also skilled at planning, organizing, and controlling.

3 Use personal power. Person~~al pow~~er is more effective than positional power
~~~~r's personality, ability to inspire, or charisma.

~~~~ganizational structure is to coordinate and communicate. There is
~~~~cept of chain of command is no longer sacred. Decentralization
~~~~making.

~~~~ure can be more effective than policy statements.

~~~~oductivity and organizational intelligence. In brain storming
~~~~gh-level cohesive groups can do incredibly dumb things.

~~~~ning and program evaluation. Take time for strategic planning.
~~~~uation.

~~~~eakening restraining forces—rules and regulations that keep
~~~~ Weakening restraining forces works better than strengthening
~~~~spects the dignity of workers and makes use of the personal-

~~~~ss. We need to recognize the importance of getting the job
~~~~But if standard rules and procedures don't get it done, they

~~~~ right kind of behavior.~~ Rewards, morale, ingenuity, and productivity go together in the workplace.

SOURCE: WIGGINS (1996).

Recommendations like these and the ones in Box 11.7 should substantially improve corrections administration and, in turn, the effectiveness of corrections systems into the future. Good luck to those of you who will take us there.

ADMINISTRATIVE PROFESSIONALIZATION

In addition to the three factors noted by Cohn, there has been an ongoing movement toward professionalization within the field of corrections. As we mentioned in Chapter 10, this has been true for front-line positions such as correctional officers, but it has been even more so for those individuals occupying administrative positions. In Europe and other nations around the globe, the paths to senior correctional administrators appear rather different from those found in the United States (see Box 11.8). Four factors seem to have played a role in increasing professionalization in the United States.

SPOTLIGHT ON INTERNATIONAL CORRECTIONS: DEVELOPING CORRECTIONS PROFESSIONALS

BOX 11.8

Directors, superintendents, governors, wardens, or "the boss" at prisons in other nations may not resemble their counterparts in the United States. As previously noted, most senior-level administrators in US prisons and jails worked their way up through the ranks; few have college degrees beyond a baccalaureate. Movement between major component parts of the criminal justice system in the United States, from prison work to law enforcement or the judiciary, let alone the reverse path, is rare. In European civil law systems, however, it is not uncommon to find that a facility's warden possesses a PhD, although in all likelihood it is a doctorate in law because academic criminology tends to reside largely, if not exclusively, in law schools. Wardens may also have extensive experience in another part of the criminal justice system, as all are civil servants in the national government. They could have been a judge, a police agency head, or a prison facility warden.

Another feature of the correctional systems of many nations is the correctional college, a national or regional facility that offers advanced education and training for corrections professionals. Much of this training is the equivalent of graduate-level coursework in the United States. It is also common to see prison personnel from one nation training at the facility of another country. Correctional agencies in the United States, because of four main jurisdictional levels—municipal, county, state, and federal—have a difficult time achieving the same level of professionalism in standards and training for the career development of upper-level administrators that we find in many other nations. Professional organizations, including the American Correctional Association and the American Probation and Parole Association, are making inroads. Other professionalism initiatives, such as those offered by the National Institute of Corrections through its facility in Boulder, Colorado, regional training activities, video and online training, and self-study resources, have expanded corrections professionalism in the United States.

SOURCES: PERSONAL OBSERVATIONS OF L. THOMAS WINFREE, JR; REICHEL (2013); TERRILL (2007).

Although some corrections agencies allow experience to substitute for formal education, corrections administrators are, today, more likely to have college degrees. This is true of prison and jail administrators, and it is especially true in probation and parole where college degrees (and even advanced degrees) have been the norm for decades. Some of the movement toward more formal education comes from state and local human resources agencies, and some of it has come about as a result of informal pressures among corrections employees to further their education for increased pay and mobility. As a result, the Bureau of Labor Statistics (2012) reports that in 2010 corrections supervisors/managers were earning an average of $58,290 and the top 10 percent were

earning more than $90,050. Slightly higher salaries were reported for probation and parole supervisors and those working in managerial capacities with correctional treatment specialists.

Management training also has been increasing. Many state corrections academies provide regular advanced training for their managers, and several colleges and universities around the country offer areas of emphasis in their bachelor's and master's degree programs or they offer highly focused certificate programs for corrections managers who want to obtain additional training although they may not necessarily be interested in obtaining another degree. Nongovernmental organizations like the American Correctional Association and the American Jail

Association also offer training and certification programs, as does the Department of Justice's National Institute of Corrections.

Additionally, as we mentioned in Chapter 10, the movement toward accreditation and certification has influenced correctional professionalization. These two processes often mandate that individuals demonstrate that they possess certain types of knowledge or certain skill sets that are related to the performance of their jobs.

Finally, as a result of responding to litigation (which we will address more fully in the next chapter), corrections agencies must carefully consider their policies on recruiting, hiring, training, and promoting individuals. In effect, the courts have placed additional pressures on corrections agencies to employ highly trained and highly qualified professional personnel.

ADMINISTRATIVE ETHICS

A quick glance at the American Correctional Association Code of Ethics (2012) included in Chapter 10 reveals that many of the ethical issues facing corrections employees cut across all types and all levels of the organizations that they serve. However, from this list at least two major areas—conflicts of interest and fairness and equity—that are composed of seven items seem to be particularly relevant to administrators. In this section, we will briefly discuss these two areas.

The first area of concern involves conflicts of interest. Four items from the ACA Code of Ethics (numbers 8, 9, 10, and 11 in Box 10.3) deal with this issue. Administrators need to be especially careful not to use their professional positions to obtain personal privileges or advantages. They should not let their personal feelings or values negatively affect their objectivity as they perform their duties. They also must scrupulously avoid any arrangements that would result in a conflict of interest, or that would appear to be a situation involving a conflict of interest. Finally, they should not accept gifts from inmates or clients, their families, or others who do business with their agency. A few brief scenarios will illustrate the kinds of ethical dilemmas that may confront corrections administrators.

- A new warden takes over at a prison located in a small community. In the process of getting settled in, the warden visits a local automobile dealership to buy a car for his teenage son. During the negotiations, the warden reminds the salesperson and the manager of the importance of the prison to the local economy and strongly suggests that he is deserving of a substantial discount off of the purchase price of the car. Is the warden acting ethically or unethically? Is it inappropriate for criminal justice officials to ask for discounts on goods and services?

- The director of purchasing for the state corrections department has negotiated contracts for the purchase of supplies from a major national vendor for several years. At some point the president and CEO of the supplier contacts the purchasing director and offers her a job with his company at a substantial increase in salary. Although it is not part of the employment offer, there may be an implicit understanding that hiring this individual will help the contractor's future business with the state because the purchasing director already knows the ins-and-outs of the state purchasing process. Should the purchasing director take this position? Is there a problem with her doing business with the state in the future?

- Mega-Corrections Corporation is a private company supplying services to federal, state, and local governments around the country. One of the agents for Mega-Corrections contacts the secretary of the state corrections department to offer him a free week of golf at a luxury resort on the South Carolina coast. Is there a problem presented by accepting such a gift?

The second area of ethical concern deals with fairness and equity (items 14, 16, and 17 in Box 10.3). Corrections administrators must be fair when it comes to promotions, transfers, disciplinary actions, and so forth regarding race, gender, age, religious affiliation, or any other legally protected category. Both federal and state laws—as well as union contracts—protect employees from discriminatory treatment, but sometimes discrimination is difficult to prove. For example, if promotions are based to a large degree on seniority, then women and minorities (who typically have less seniority than white males) may be particularly disadvantaged. Also, given the rural locations of many prisons in the United States, it is possible that family connections may be taken into the decision of who gets employed and who gets promoted; this is known as **nepotism**. Finally, one of the most problematic issues for corrections has been that of sexual harassment. The number of female correctional officers and supervisors has steadily increased during the past 30 years. Unfortunately, these jobs often place women in positions where they can be sexually harassed by inmates. However, most of the legal claims of sexual harassment have been directed at supervisors and administrators more than at the inmates. For most of its history, corrections has been a male-dominated field of employment. With increasing numbers of women entering the corrections workforce, administrators must be very diligent about not allowing sexual harassment to occur.

SUMMARY

After reading this chapter, even the casual student of administration should recognize that corrections positions—especially those in prisons and jails—are much more interdependent than many law enforcement jobs are. The following are among the key points presented in this chapter:

- In some ways, in their operations, probation and parole officers working in the field resemble the police.
- By contrast, prisons and jails are institutions where functions are more integrated, which means they need a more coordinated or team approach to accomplishing their goals.
- There is much closer supervision of jail and prison employees than there is of their law enforcement counterparts. Therefore, correctional officers typically enjoy less discretion than police officers.
- Although we have talked about ideal management types, we should not assume that any type occurs in its purest form or that one management type is necessarily preferable to another.
- Bureaucratic management and the bureaucratic leadership style are still prevalent in corrections. Although this approach may diminish, it is not likely to disappear.
- Various factors are causing changes in corrections management. We should see more democratic and participatory management styles as the bureaucratic approach becomes less popular.
- Two factors that have influenced corrections management during the past 30 years are increasing concerns regarding ethical issues and an expanded emphasis on professionalization.

THINKING ABOUT CORRECTIONAL POLICIES AND PRACTICES: WRITING ASSIGNMENTS

1   When you think of a bureaucratic organization, which term comes to mind: *efficiency* or *inefficiency*? Provide a short (2–3 paragraphs) essay to explain your answer.

2   Look back over the various leadership styles that we have discussed. Pick one of these styles and explain in one to two pages why you would prefer to work with an administrator who uses this particular style.

3   To what extent should a college degree (or even a master's degree) be a requirement for prison and jail administrators, as well as

probation and parole supervisors? Develop a chart with side-by-side comparisons indicating the positive and negative aspects of requiring additional education for those who administer corrections programs and agencies.

4   Crowding has been and continues to be a problem for institutional corrections of all kinds in the twenty-first century. What would you identify as the greatest single problem associated with crowding? What if your state was, like California, ordered to free 10 or even 20 percent of its prison population? What would be the public response? Provide as much documented support for your answer as possible.

5   Ethical practices are central to any profession. Correctional administrators face additional layers of ethical concerns. Given what you have learned about managing and administering correctional agencies, rank these concerns from the most difficult to attain to the least difficult to attain and provide your assessments for these rankings.

KEY TERMS

administration	idiosyncratic leader	technocratic leader
authoritarian leader	laissez-faire leader	total quality management
bureaucracy	management	(TQM)
bureaucratic leader	nepotism	unit management
centralization	participative leader	
democratic leader	political patronage	

CRITICAL REVIEW QUESTIONS

1   What are the advantages associated with an authoritarian or autocratic leader? What are the disadvantages? Consider the advantages and disadvantages of laissez-faire and democratic leaders as well.

2   Which of the four leadership styles identified by the National Advisory Commission are you most likely to find in a prison? Would your answer be different if you considered probation and parole agencies? Why or why not?

3   How do you feel about the trends in correctional expenditures? What does your state spend on corrections? Is it possible that the corrections budget doesn't really reflect true correctional costs? (*Note:* This information is available online. For example, see the website maintained by the Bureau of Justice Statistics.)

4   Respond to this proposition: Correctional employees with a college degree should begin at a higher ranking position than that of correctional officer. What factors enter into your answer?

5   Should corrections administrators reflect a cross-section of society in the United States? In other words, should more women and minority group members be administrators? Does it make any difference to operations? Why or why not?

6   Can corrections administrators really motivate their employees? How? What motivates you to work harder or more effectively?

7   What approach makes the most sense in managing inmates, a firm hand or substantial inmate participation? Can all inmates (or prisons) be managed the same way?

8   Look at the "Ten Ideas for Effective Managers." Are these simply common-sense notions? Is this something that can be learned in management

training, or does this come with experience on the job?

9 What are Theory X and Theory Y? What factors shape the worldviews of those who employ the Theory X approach? The Theory Y approach? Are these attitudes something learned?

10 Total quality management has been embraced by businesses, particularly in Japan and now in the United States. Do you think this business orientation can be applied to corrections? Why or why not?

CASE CITED

Brown v. Plata, 131 S.Ct. 1910 (2011).

NOTES

1 The ten states that did not respond to the survey or that could not certify data were Alaska, Hawaii, Massachusetts, Mississippi, New Mexico, Oregon, South Carolina, South Dakota, Tennessee, and Wyoming.

2 Much of the information used in this section is taken from McShane and Williams (1993, 1996).

3 For a thorough treatment of the history and development of public-sector employee unions, see Ayres and Wheelen (1977), Stanley (1972), and Zagoria (1972).

4 The Court denied the state's appeal for relief from a three-judge federal court panel that mandated California reduce its prison population to 137.5 percent of capacity; translated: The prisons in California will still be 37.5 percent over-capacity on the day that all 30,000 inmates are reassigned.

REFERENCES

American Correctional Association (ACA). 2012. ACA Code of Ethics. Retrieved July 16, 2013 from: **http://www.aca.org/pastpresentfuture/ethics.asp**

Ayres, Richard M., and Thomas L. Wheelen. 1977. *Collective bargaining in the public sector*. Gaithersburg, MD: International Association of Chiefs of Police.

Blau, Peter M., and W. Richard Scott. 1962. *Formal organizations*. San Francisco: Chandler.

Bureau of Labor Statistics. 2012. *Occupational outlook handbook 2012–13*. Washington, DC: US Department of Labor.

Coffey, Alan R. 1974. *Correctional administration*. Englewood Cliffs, NJ: Prentice Hall.

Cohn, Alvin W. 1977. *Criminal justice planning and development*. Beverly Hills, CA: Sage.

Cohn, Alvin W. 1991. The failure of correctional management-reviewed: Present and future dimensions. *Federal Probation*, June, 12–16.

Cohn, Alvin W. 1995. The failure of correctional management: Recycling the middle manager. *Federal Probation* 59(2): 10–16.

DiIulio, John J., Jr. 1987. *Governing prisons: A comparative study of correctional management*. New York: Free Press.

DiIulio, John J., Jr. 1994. The evolution of executive management in the Federal Bureau of Prisons. In *Escaping prison myths*, edited by John W. Roberts. Washington, DC: American University Press, 195–74.

Etzioni, Amitai. 1964. *Modern organizations*. Englewood Cliffs, NJ: Prentice Hall.

Farmer, J. Forbes. 2012. Testing the conceptual path to correctional staff safety: A Study of the implementation of unit management in two medium security state institutions in the USA. *International Journal of Criminal Justice Sciences* 7(1): 431–49.

Fowler, Glenn. 1990. Thomas Murton, 62, a penologist who advocated reforms, is dead. New York Times. Retrieved on July 17, 2013 from: http://www.nytimes.com/1990/10/19/obituaries/thomas-murton-62-a-penologist-who-advocated-reforms-is-dead.html

Glaze, Lauren. 2011. *Correctional populations in the United States, 2010.* Washington, DC: US Department of Justice.

Government Accountability Office. 2012. *Bureau of prisons: Growing inmate crowding negatively affects inmates, staff and infrastructure.* Washington, DC: GAO.

Gray, Tara, and Jon'a F. Meyer. 1996. Expanding prison industries through privatization. In *Privatization and the provision of correctional services: Context and consequences,* edited by G. Larry Mays and Tara Gray. Cincinnati, OH: Anderson, Academy of Criminal Justice Sciences, 125–31.

Henrichson, Christian, and Ruth Delaney. 2012. *The price of prisons: What incarceration costs taxpayers.* New York: Vera Institute of Justice.

Jacobs, James B. 1977. *Stateville: The penitentiary in mass society.* Chicago: University of Chicago Press.

Jeffords, Charles, and Jan Lindsey. 1996. George Beto (1916–1991). In *Encyclopedia of American prisons,* edited by Marilyn D. McShane and Frank P. Williams III. New York: Garland, 58–61.

Lawrence, Sarah, and Jeremy Travis. 2004. *The new landscape of imprisonment: mapping America's prison expansion.* Washington, DC: The Urban Institute.

Levinson, Robert B., and Roy E. Gerard. 1973. Functional units: A different correctional approach. *Federal Probation* 37: 8–16.

McGregor, Douglas. 1960. *The human side of enterprise.* New York: McGraw-Hill.

McShane, Marilyn D., and Frank P. Williams III. 1993. *The management of correctional institutions.* New York: Garland.

McShane, Marilyn D., and Frank P. Williams III. 1996. Administration. In *Encyclopedia of American prisons,* edited by Marilyn D. McShane and Frank P. Williams III. New York: Garland, 4–8.

More, Harry W., Jr. 1977. *Criminal justice management: Text and readings.* St. Paul, MN: West.

Mouzelis, Nicos P. 1967. *Organization and bureaucracy: An analysis of modern theories.* Chicago: Aldine.

National Advisory Commission on Criminal Justice Standards and Goals. 1973. *Corrections.* Washington, DC: US Department of Justice.

National Association of State Budget Officers (NASBO). 2010. *State expenditure report: Examining fiscal 2009–2011 state spending.* Washington, DC: National Association of State Budget Officers.

Newbold, Greg. 1992. What works in prison management: Effects of administrative change in New Zealand. *Federal Probation* 56(4): 53–7.

Peak, Kenneth J. 2007. *Justice administration: Police, courts, and corrections management,* 5th edn. Upper Saddle River, NJ: Prentice Hall.

Pew Center on the States. 2009. *One in 31: The long reach of American corrections.* Washington, DC: Pew Center.

Reichel, Philip. 2013. *Comparative criminal justice systems: A topical approach,* 7th edn. Upper Saddle Creek, NJ: Prentice Hall.

Rogers, Joseph W. 1996. Mary Belle Harris (1874–1957). In *Encyclopedia of American prisons,* edited by Marilyn D. McShane and Frank P. Williams III. New York: Garland, 364–8.

St. John, Paige. 2012. California unlikely to meet prison crowding reduction requirement. *Los Angeles Times,* 12 August. Retrieved on July 17, 2013 from: http://articles.latimes.com/2012/aug/12/local/la-me-prisons-20120811

Stanley, David T. 1972. *Managing local government under union pressure.* Washington, DC: Brookings Institution.

Stephan, James J. 2008. *Census of state and federal correctional facilities, 2005.* Washington, DC: Bureau of Justice Statistics, US Department of Justice.

Stojkovic, Stan, David Kalinich, and John Klofas. 1998. *Criminal justice organizations,* 2nd edn. Belmont, CA: West/Wadsworth.

Terrill, Richard J. 2007. *World criminal justice systems: A survey,* 6th edn. Cincinnati, OH: Anderson.

US Census Bureau. 2011. 2011 Public employment and payroll data. Retrieved on July 17, 2013 from: http://www2.census.gov/govs/apes/11stus.txt

Weber, Max. 1947. *The theory of social and economic organization.* Trans. A. M. Henderson and Talcott Parsons. New York: Oxford University Press.

Wiggins, Robert R. 1996. Ten ideas for effective managers. *Federal Probation* 60: 43–9.

Zagoria, Sam, ed. 1972. *Public workers and public unions.* Englewood Cliffs, NJ: Prentice Hall.

12 CORRECTIONS LAW AND INMATE LITIGATION

BRETT COOMER/AP/PRESS ASSOCIATION IMAGES

Outline

The History of Inmate Litigation

Inmate Litigation and Postconviction Relief

Laws and Litigation Dealing with Probation and Parole

Issues Raised by Corrections Lawsuits

Recent Trends in Inmate Litigation

Capital Punishment and Prisoner Litigation

The Future of Litigation

Objectives

- To provide you with a brief history of inmate litigation

- To illustrate for you some of the case law dealing with probation and parole

- To help you understand the range of issues presented in inmate lawsuits

- To show you the legal dimensions of the death penalty

- To help you anticipate some future issues that may arise in correctional law

Essentials of Corrections, Fifth Edition. G. Larry Mays and L. Thomas Winfree, Jr.
© 2014 John Wiley & Sons, Inc. Published 2014 by John Wiley & Sons, Inc.

INTRODUCTION

"Prisons have traditionally been closed organizations, and it has been difficult for citizens in the outside world to learn about conditions inside them" (Rhodes 1992, 215). This organizational isolation was often reinforced by geographic isolation. Most prisons are sited well away from population centers. Moreover, the truth was that the pubic did not really want to know what was going on behind prison walls.

That changed in 1971, when New York's Attica Correctional Facility erupted. By the time rioting broke out at the Penitentiary of New Mexico in 1980, many policy makers and private citizens understood that something was very wrong in the nation's prisons (see, especially, Mahan 1982). In addition, policy makers and citizens wanted to know what it was and what could be done about it. According to Susan Rhodes (1992, 205–06), what was wrong was endemic to all secure facilities in the country: rising inmate populations, aging prison facilities, and restrictive state budgets. As to what could be done about it, there were a number of alternatives. Since the 1970s, one of the most effective has been litigation. Beginning with cases like *Holt v. Sarver* (1970) and *Pugh v. Locke* (1976), appellate courts in Arkansas, Alabama, and many other states challenged a broad range of prison conditions.

In 2000, 357 state (324) and private (33) facilities were under court order or consent decree to improve the general conditions of confinement or to limit their populations—by 2005 the numbers had declined to 239. Interestingly, while the number of public facilities decreased by 125, the private facilities increased by seven (Stephan 2008, 149). The number of state facilities under court order to limit their populations decreased from 119 in 2000 to 21 in 2005, and those under court orders for specific conditions decreased from 303 to 190 in the same period (Stephan 2008, 14). No federal prisons were under court orders for these reasons.

In this chapter, we trace the history of corrections litigation in the United States, especially the large body of cases relating to prisons and jails. Of particular interest is the concept of inmates' access to the courts and the issues addressed in inmate lawsuits. Finally, we examine what may be the most important issue in contemporary corrections, the impact of 50 years of prisoner lawsuits.

THE HISTORY OF INMATE LITIGATION

Legislation, particularly at the federal level, has been an important instrument of social change for women and minority groups in the United States as each has sought access to such things as voting and equal pay for equal work. However, that method has not been effective for jail and prison inmates. Instead, they have turned to the appellate courts during the past five decades to remedy the circumstances of their convictions or of their confinement.

Corrections law has gone through three distinct periods of development. Jack Call (1995, 36) identified them as the *hands-off period*, before 1964; the *rights period*, from 1964 to 1978; and the *deference period*, from 1979 to the present (36).

THE HANDS-OFF PERIOD: 1871–1963

Any discussion of corrections law must begin with *Ruffin v. Commonwealth* (1871). In this Virginia case, the court held that prisoners are slaves of the state and so have no more rights than slaves do (see Palmer 2010). According to this ruling, offenders suffer a **civil death** in the wake of their conviction and imprisonment (Alexander 1994; Palmer 2010). In practical terms, this status means that they forfeit many of their citizenship rights (Harris and Spiller 1977).

By considering prisoners slaves of the state, the decision in *Ruffin* assigned them **nonperson status**. This meant the courts were largely free to ignore pleas based on alleged deprivations of their rights: inmates had few, if any, constitutional rights. For almost a century following *Ruffin*, the courts took a hands-off approach toward prison policies and practices (Bronstein 1985; Chilton 1991; DiIulio 1990; Nagel 1985; Robertson 1985–1986).

The courts justified their inaction on three grounds (Coles 1987; Schuster and Widmer 1978; Thomas 1988). First, federal courts expressed some reluctance to intervene in corrections departments' affairs because those departments are state executive agencies (Alpert, Crouch, and Huff 1984; also see Collins 2010). The US Constitution established a federal system of government that gave the national and state governments distinct powers and authority. The judiciary cited the "division of responsibility between federal and state courts" (Mays 1983, 29) to explain its failure to act. Others brought the separation of powers into the argument. They reasoned that the Constitution had divided authority among the three branches of government (executive, legislative, and judicial). It was improper, then, for a court—particularly a federal court—to tell a state corrections system how it should run its prisons (see,

especially, Frug 1978). These interpretations may have been convenient, but they were not necessarily correct. Even in a federal system of government, jurisdictions overlap. In addition, the separation of powers served as a system of checks and balances on the conduct of each branch of government, restricting each branch's ability to operate without constraint.

Second, many judges were hesitant to get involved in prison litigation cases because they lacked corrections expertise. This gave prison administrators broad discretion, effectively shielding them from public scrutiny and judicial review. The third defense had to do with prison security. Corrections administrators maintained that court intervention would interfere with their authority and would reduce the ability of institutional personnel to operate safe prisons, and the judiciary believed them.

JACQUELYN MARTIN/AP/PRESS ASSOCIATION IMAGES

THE RIGHTS PERIOD: 1964–1978

By the early 1960s, attitudes were changing. Increasingly, racial minority groups, resident aliens, people with handicaps, and women were laying claim to civil rights protections. In a sense, state prison inmates became another minority group wanting to expand its civil rights. In addition, by the 1960s, the effectiveness of **public interest law** was clear: in a number of landmark cases, activist groups, among them the National Association for the Advancement of Colored People (NAACP) and the American Civil Liberties Union (ACLU), had successfully used litigation to change social conditions. Finally, both publicity and a heightened sensitivity to civil rights claims made federal district and appellate courts more receptive to lawsuits from state prison inmates (Call 1995, 36–37).

The US Supreme Court seemed particularly attentive to state prisoners' due process claims (see, for example, Smith 1986; Thomas 1988). Call (1995, 38) takes issue with the assertion by some that during this period the Court was engaged in a "prisoners' rights revolution." He says, instead, that the Court recognized that prisoners had constitutional rights and that those rights were equal to the rights of prisons.

Two Supreme Court cases in the early 1960s opened the door to prisoner litigation. The first, *Monroe v. Pape* (1961), simplified the procedures for suing state officials in federal court for alleged violations of constitutional rights (see Prigmore and Crow 1976). The other—*Cooper v. Pate* (1964)—raised the issue of the free exercise of religion by black Muslim prisoners. In both of these cases, the Court held that the Civil Rights Act of 1871 (known in the statutes as 42 USC 1983) provided an appropriate mechanism by which to challenge state actions (C. E. Smith 1986).

With its decisions in *Monroe* and *Cooper*, the Supreme Court signaled its willingness to take a hands-on approach to state prison litigation (Nagel 1985). Now state prisoners had two options for filing federal lawsuits. They could follow the traditional path, petitioning for a **writ of habeas corpus**, or they could travel a new path, filing a **civil rights claim**, or what lawyers and others call a **Section 1983 suit**.

Inmates can also file *tort claims*, in which they allege negligence on the part of corrections personnel, but these claims typically are filed in state courts (Collins 2010).

THE DEFERENCE PERIOD: 1979–PRESENT

The final period, the period that continues today, began with the Supreme Court's decision in *Bell v. Wolfish* (1979). In *Bell*, the Court decided just one issue—cell size—in favor of the inmates; on four other issues, the justices ruled for the corrections department. According to Call,

> In ruling against the inmates, the Court set the tone for the Deference Period. During this period, inmates would lose on most prisoners' rights issues before the Court, which would stress the need to give deference to the expertise of corrections officials. (1995, 39)

In the three decades since *Bell*, inmates have had a few victories in court, and those have come only in cases of the most blatant violations of prisoners' rights. In most cases, corrections agencies have been given wide latitude to exercise their authority (Pollock 2002; Robertson 2006).

INMATE LITIGATION AND POSTCONVICTION RELIEF

We should note that inmates could choose the legal mechanism for bringing suit, the forum (type of court) for the suit, and the targets of litigation. For instance, a prisoner can challenge the actions of individual correctional officers or officials—a superintendent, a warden, or the commissioner of corrections (Collins 2010). Alternatively, a lawsuit can be broader, challenging the totality of institutional conditions under which the inmate is confined (Pollock 2002; Stephan 2008).

ACCESS TO THE COURTS

In habeas corpus appeals, inmates allege that their confinement is unjust and that the state should demonstrate why their incarceration should continue (Mays 1984). Writs of habeas corpus challenge the legality of incarceration; and if a court substantiates a prisoner's allegations, he or she may be released (Cheesman et al. 1998; Collins 2010). In its 1962–1963 term, the US Supreme Court decided three cases—*Townsend v. Sain*, *Fay v. Noia*, and *Sanders v. United States*—that expanded habeas corpus relief for state prisoners. As a result, writs of habeas corpus became the primary legal mechanism for most prisoners' appeals.

As Table 12.1 illustrates, state prisoner habeas corpus petitions nearly tripled between 1980 and 2000, the peak year for filings. However, since 2000 the number of habeas corpus petitions has decreased to the point that in 2010 there were 4,502 fewer habeas petitions than there were in 2000. This represents a 21.1 percent decline in filings.

Victor Flango reports that habeas corpus petitions "are not used by the typical state prisoner" (1994, 160). Inmates charged with serious offenses bring most of these appeals, and most allege deficiencies in one of eight areas: ineffective assistance of counsel, due process concerns, trial court error, Fifth Amendment protections, detention and punishment concerns, prosecutor misconduct, police misconduct, and charges to the jury. Flango (1994, 168) also notes that those who do file habeas corpus claims generally file multiple petitions in federal and state courts.

Beginning in 1966, the Department of Justice began tracking civil rights actions as a separate category of prisoner claims. Between 1980 and 2000, civil rights claims by state inmates increased more than 97 percent, from 12,395 to 24,463 (Scalia 2002). Civil rights petitions by state prison inmates peaked in 1995 with 40,569 claims. However, changes in federal laws (see later) had a significant effect on the number of Section 1983 claims filed: by 2010, in a period of 15 years, that number had dropped by over 40 percent.

A Section 1983 action must satisfy several requirements (Collins 2010):

● *The defendant must be a person*—the courts have held that states and state agencies, including corrections departments, are not persons and so are immune from civil rights claims.

TABLE 12.1 Petitions filed in Federal District Courts by State Inmates, 1980–2010.

Year	Writs of habeas corpus	Civil rights claims
1980	7,029	12,395
1981	7,786	15,639
1982	8,036	16,739
1983	8,523	17,686
1984	8,335	18,034
1985	8,520	18,490
1986	9,040	20,071
1987	9,524	22,972
1988	9,867	23,558
1989	10,545	25,039
1990	10,817	24,843
1991	10,325	25,043
1992	11,296	29,645
1993	11,574	33,018
1994	11,908	37,925
1995	13,627	40,569
1996	14,726	39,996
1997	19,956	27,658
1998	18,838	25,478
1999	20,493	24,732
2000	21,345	24,463
2001	20,446	12,703
2002	19,616	13,268
2003	18,872	13,708
2004	8,646	14,396
2005	19,190	14,993
2006	18,959	23,123
2007	18,907	22,779
2008	18,268	24,375
2009	17,454	23,573
2010	16,843	23,774

SOURCES: ADMINISTRATIVE OFFICE OF US COURTS (2010); SCALIA (2002, 2).

However, cities and counties, if they are incorporated, are persons.

- *The defendant must be acting under color of state law*—the alleged violation must have occurred in the course of the defendant's employment with the government agency.

- *The injury to the inmate-plaintiff must involve a violation of a protected right*—the US Constitution or a federal statute may protect the right. Often, allegations of injury or abuse are based on broad constitutional language—for example, the Eighth Amendment's prohibition against cruel and unusual punishment.

- *The defendant (or defendants) must have been personally involved in the alleged injury.* The exception to this item is **vicarious liability** (or *supervisory liability*).

Supervisors are not automatically liable for the actions of their subordinates (Collins 2010). Under two sets of circumstances—failure to train and failure to supervise—supervisors can become parties to Section 1983 suits. In these suits, the inmate-plaintiff must make a direct connection between the supervisor's action or failure to act and the resulting injury.

As is readily apparent from Table 12.1, prisoner litigation increased dramatically from 1980 to 2000. At least two factors were at work here. First, beginning in the 1970s, US prison populations began expanding rapidly. One reason for the increase in prisoners' lawsuits, then, was simply an increased number of prisoners. Second, prisoners began to file many more lawsuits—that is, there was an increase in inmate *litigiousness*—and the opportunities for litigation increased as well. The fact that for most of the period between 1980 and 2000, the growth of inmate lawsuits outpaced the growth in prison population supports these conclusions.

To understand fully the data in Table 12.1, however, we must consider three pieces of federal legislation enacted over the last two decades of the twentieth century. All had as their objective the restriction of inmate appeals.

In 1980, Congress passed the Civil Rights of Institutionalized Persons Act (CRIPA) (42 U.S.C. 1997). The intent of this law (in Section e) was to reduce the number of Section 1983 claims filed by state inmates by requiring prisoners to exhaust all state administrative remedies before filing a federal suit. However, as Table 12.1 demonstrates, the number of civil rights petitions did not decrease after 1980. In fact, before the decade was over, the number of petitions had more than doubled. Some suggest that much of that increase reflected the growth in inmate populations (see Scalia 2002). The rate of petitions filed per 1,000 inmates supports this argument: it fell from 75 in 1980 to 60 in 1990 and to 40 in 2000.

Jim Thomas (1988, 63) says that the growth of civil rights petitions—versus writs of habeas corpus—came about because state inmates were not interested in using the federal courts to secure their release—as would be the case with habeas corpus petitions; they were much more interested in challenging their conditions of confinement. An equally plausible explanation is that the federal courts were demonstrating a lack of receptivity toward state prisoners' habeas corpus writs (Burger 1985; Powers 1987; Remington 1986).

Second, in 1996 Congress passed the Prison Reform Litigation Act (PRLA) together with the Antiterrorism and Effective Death Penalty Act (AEDPA) (Public Laws 104–134 and 104–132 respectively). Again, both were designed to reduce appeals in federal courts by prison inmates. The PRLA affirmed that state inmates must exhaust all of their state administrative remedies before filing a claim in a federal court; it also required inmates to pay appropriate appellate fees. The law did not take away inmates' right to file *in forma pauperis* (that is, as indigents), but they could no longer claim indigence if two previous petitions had been dismissed as frivolous or malicious (Belbot 2004). It also required that there must be a showing of physical injury if the petitioner was claiming mental or emotional injury (American Civil Liberties Union 2011). The AEDPA set strict time limits for filing habeas corpus writs in federal courts and required that a federal appeals court panel approve habeas corpus petitions for filing in federal district courts (see Scalia 2002).

Both of these acts became law in 1997, and the results have been somewhat unexpected. By the end of that year, the number of civil rights claims filed by state inmates dropped almost 31 percent, even as the nation's prison population continued to grow. In that same year, the volume of habeas corpus writs went up almost 36 percent. In 1993, there were roughly three times the number of civil rights petitions as habeas corpus petitions; by 2000, the difference was much smaller, but by 2010 the gap had once again widened somewhat.

LEGAL ASSISTANCE AND LEGAL ACCESS

Does the state have to provide inmates with legal aid? If the state is so obligated, when and how must it provide this aid? The Supreme Court rulings in two cases addressed the issue of legal assistance for inmates. *Johnson v. Avery* (1969) centered on a prison regulation that prohibited inmates from giving one another legal help:

> No inmate will advise, assist, or otherwise contract to aid another, either with or without a fee, to prepare Writs or other legal matters. It is not intended that an innocent man be punished. When a man believes he is unlawfully held or illegally convicted, he should prepare a brief or state his complaint in letter form and address it to his lawyer or a judge. A formal Writ is not necessary to receive a hearing. False charges or untrue complaints may be punished. Inmates are forbidden to set themselves up as practitioners for promoting a business of writing Writs.

The case involved a prison in Tennessee, but at that time, a number of prisons banned **jailhouse lawyers**, or **writ writers**. The concern was not the quality of the legal help. Rather, the power such knowledge and skills gave the writ writers over other inmates concerned prison administrators. In its decision, the Court ruled that states could only prohibit inmates from helping others file appeals if the states provide legal assistance to inmates who need it.

Eight years later, in *Bounds v. Smith*, the Court extended the states' responsibility to provide legal aid to inmates. In its ruling, the Court noted that inmates must have *meaningful* legal access. This meant an adequately stocked law library within the institution for the use of inmates and jailhouse lawyers, or the legal assistance of paralegals or attorneys.

The standards developed in *Johnson* and *Bounds* strengthened the foundation of contemporary prison litigation. In a long line of right-to-counsel cases—among the most famous of those cases are *Powell v. Alabama* (1932), *Gideon v. Wainwright* (1963), *Miranda v. Arizona* (1966), and *Argersinger v. Hamlin* (1972)—the Supreme Court has made clear that the effective assistance of counsel could well be one of the Constitution's most fundamental due process rights. Most states have fulfilled the Court's mandates by establishing law libraries and allowing jailhouse lawyers to work in them. Although some states discourage jailhouse lawyers from "practicing," to our knowledge none actually prohibit inmates from helping other inmates prepare appeals. Moreover, some jurisdictions do hire attorneys for inmates or allow public defenders to handle appeals. In addition, groups like the ACLU's National Prison Project may take inmates' suits, typically with no charge.

There are no data on the relative costs of having inmates versus lawyers prepare appeals. There is a sense that hiring attorneys to represent inmate-plaintiffs could well save the state money in the end. The use of licensed attorneys should reduce the number of frivolous *pro se* **actions**, suits in which inmates represent themselves, and the costs of those suits. Attorneys are in a better position to understand the merits of cases and are more objective in trying to reach negotiated settlements with corrections officials (*Correctional Law Reporter* 1995, 67, 79). Fewer frivolous suits also translate into real monetary savings for the facility in the costs of security and transportation, not to mention time savings as well.

INMATE ADVOCATES AND ADVOCACY GROUPS

Inmates are a relatively powerless social group (see Hanson 1987; Thomas, Wheeler, and Harris 1986). Moreover, their families are typically not wealthy or influential. What mechanisms, then, do they have to make their concerns heard by the public, politicians, and corrections administrators? Two answers come to mind: riots and lawsuits.

Prison riots during the 1970s and 1980s brought national attention to the plight of inmates (Braswell,

Dillingham, and Montgomery 1985; Useem and Kimball 1989). However, it has been through litigation that some of the most far-reaching and long-lasting changes have come about in prison policies and practices. Litigation has given prisoners a forum in which they can air their grievances against state authorities. Thomas and his colleagues assert that litigation is one of the final "nonviolent and legitimate" mechanisms at prison inmates' disposal (Thomas, Wheeler, and Harris 1986, 794).

Inmates seldom have the economic resources to undertake a wide-ranging and protracted **class action lawsuit**—a suit brought on behalf of prisoners as a group. Instead, prisoners' rights groups—such as the National Prison Project—have acted as their advocates (Bronstein 1985; Mays and Taggart 1985, 1988; Rhodes 1992). Changes in federal legislation concerning the bases for civil rights actions and expanded grants of lawyers' fees undoubtedly have contributed to an increase in inmate litigation and to the interest of prisoners' rights advocacy groups.

LAWS AND LITIGATION DEALING WITH PROBATION AND PAROLE

Until the late 1960s, probation officers enjoyed a great deal of freedom in discharging their duties. For some, that meant cooperating with the police to revoke a term of probation based on information that would not stand up to legal scrutiny. The probation officer would simply take the probationer into custody, claiming some violation, and would request resentencing, which normally resulted in a quick trip to prison for the probationer. Rarely were either the formalities of due process or a hearing on the alleged charges part of the process.

That practice ended in 1967, when the Supreme Court ruled in *Mempa v. Rhay* that the right of an accused to be represented by an attorney is not confined to trials alone, that counsel is required at every stage where substantial rights of the accused may be affected. Sentencing, particularly on revocation of probation, qualifies as a critical stage.

The Court's ruling in *Morrissey v. Brewer* (1972) expanded legal protections to parolees. At the heart of *Morrissey* was the contention of Iowa authorities that parolees do not enjoy a basic right to conditional release from prison, that parole is a privilege extended by the executive branch of government. The Court rejected the state's position. In its ruling, the Court observed that parole had emerged as an integral part of correctional practices, and that it occurred too regularly to be considered a privilege. The Court also noted that by whatever means freedom is obtained, "it must be seen within the protection of the Fourteenth Amendment. Its termination calls for some orderly process, however informal." Finally, citing the fact that parole revocations occur as often as 35 percent to 40 percent of the time, the Court maintained that the protection of parolees' rights is essential.

In *Morrissey*, the Court addressed the nature of due process for parolees. The parole revocation hearing should be a two-stage process: (1) the arrest and preliminary hearing and (2) the revocation hearing. For these hearings, the Court extended to parolees the following due process rights:

- written notice of the alleged parole violation;
- disclosure of the evidence against the parolee;
- the opportunity to be heard in person and to present witnesses and documentary evidence;
- the right to confront and cross-examine adverse witnesses (unless the hearing officer finds good cause for not allowing a confrontation);
- a "neutral and detached" hearing body—like a traditional parole board, for example—whose members need not be judicial officers or lawyers; and
- a written statement by the fact finders concerning the evidence relied on and the reasons for revoking parole.

As it did with probation, the Court left unanswered the question of the right to counsel. In practice, parolees may have attorneys present, but the government need not provide them.

The Court emphasized that the hearings should be informal. The justices noted, "It is a narrow inquiry; the process should be flexible enough to consider evidence, including letters, affidavits, and other material that would not be admissible in an adversary criminal trial." In short, like a discretionary-parole hearing, the standards of evidence and of proof required are lower than those required in a trial court for conviction.

In *Gagnon v. Scarpelli* (1973), the Supreme Court formally defined the due process rights of probationers. At a minimum, a probationer is entitled to the following:

1 Notice of alleged violations concerning the probation violation.

2 A preliminary hearing to decide if probable cause exists.

3 A revocation hearing, which in the words of the Court is "a somewhat more comprehensive hearing prior to the making of the final revocation decision." The revocation hearing should allow the accused the opportunity to appear, to present witnesses and evidence.

4 An opportunity to confront any accusatory witnesses or evidence.

Again, the Court failed to clarify the right to counsel at these hearings. The justices suggested that the need for counsel should be determined on a case-by-case basis. In practice, most jurisdictions provide the accused with counsel or allow private counsel at the preliminary hearings.

A final set of legal questions centers on the use of the presentence investigation report in the punishment phase of a criminal trial. As we learned in Chapter 4, a probation officer often prepares this document, which has the potential to determine an offender's sentence.

ISSUES RAISED BY CORRECTIONS LAWSUITS

According to a study of 239 state prisons under court order or consent decree in 2005, the most common causes of inmate litigation are related to specific conditions such as visitation/mail/telephone policies, medical treatment, and recreation (218

prisons) and crowding (44 prisons) (Stephan 2008). While crowding is not the most significant issue in prison litigation, it affects many aspects of prison operations and has long been one of the most common factors cited in court orders. Some prisons are filled beyond operational capacity, and some states, among them Texas, have had their entire prison system under court order because of persistent crowding (Alpert, Crouch, and Huff 1984; Crouch and Marquart 1989; DiIulio 1990). Therefore, it should come as no surprise to find that 44 of the 239 state prisons under court order in 2005 had orders to limit their populations.

Crowding certainly is a factor in facilities' reliance on *double-bunking* (sometimes called *double-celling*), when two inmates are housed in a cell that was designed to hold one. In *Bell v. Wolfish* (1979), the Supreme Court ruled definitively on the constitutionality of double-bunking. The majority opinion—it was a seven to two vote—stated that double-bunking does not necessarily constitute cruel and unusual punishment and, so, is not unconstitutional (*Correctional Law Reporter* 1994; Mays and Bernat 1988). At least one observer has characterized this case as one of the most important cases the Supreme Court has decided (Collins 2010). That assessment rested not on the issue of crowding but on a ruling that signaled the end of the rights period in corrections law.

Another source of inmate litigation is health and safety issues. Medical care standards, including dental care and mental health therapies, often have been points of legal contention (Alpert, Crouch, and Huff 1984; Hopper 1985; Prigmore and Crow 1976; Selke 1985; Yarbrough 1984). Health care was an area in which corrections officials felt they could save money by cutting services. As a result, in some prisons, physician's assistants served as primary care providers (see *Corrections Digest* 1994, 7), and in others, inmates were given the title "medical technician" and were allowed to provide health care and even to dispense drugs (see Alpert et al. 1984). The courts have not ordered that a doctor be available 24 hours a day at all facilities, but today a physician regularly visits most facilities or they have a physician on call. The medical staff includes registered nurses, certified nurse practitioners, certified nursing assistants, and medical technical assistants (correctional officers with some medical training). In many cases, the federal courts have ordered prisons to implement or upgrade medical care to the levels proposed by the American Correctional Association and the American Medical Association.

The standard articulated in _Estelle v. Gamble_ (1976), and typically employed by the courts in assessing blame, is **deliberate indifference**—that corrections officials knew but did nothing about the inmate's physical or medical condition, and that the failure to act had long-term effects on the inmate's condition. Moreover, at least one federal judge has ruled that county commissioners and a sheriff can be held personally liable for refusing to provide treatment to a jail inmate who is suffering from cancer (_Corrections Digest_ 1993a, 10).

Food and fire hazards are inmate health and safety concerns too. A number of cases have mandated nutrition and fire-safety standards for prisons (Mays and Taggart 1985). Food service is a perennial point of inmate dissatisfaction, and the courts have ruled that inmates must be provided nutritious, well-balanced meals. Also, some inmates may have special dietary needs. This is particularly true for inmates of certain religions. For example, Muslim inmates do not eat pork, one of the most common meat items in prison diets. In _Cooper v. Pate_ (1964), the Supreme Court ruled that the states must consider inmates' special dietary needs, religious or medical.

Fire-safety standards range from access to fire extinguishers to the use of flame retardant materials in inmates' clothing and bedding (American Correctional Association (ACA) 1991). Given necessary security restrictions on inmate movements in jails and prisons, fire safety is crucial.

Staffing is another issue that can fall into the health and safety category. Several inmates have petitioned for additional custodial and treatment staff to increase prisoners' safety and service levels. Moreover, some have sought particular deployment patterns for personnel (Bingaman 1980; Mays and Taggart 1985). Although the courts have generally been reluctant to tell corrections departments how many people to employ and where to use them, some inmate lawsuits have resulted in facilities' hiring more COs and health care personnel.

Education, recreation, and general library services fall into the area of inmate programs and services. Much prison and jail time is unproductive. Therefore, educational and recreation programs can benefit the inmates and assist in the facility's smooth operation. Library services provide inmates with recreational reading opportunities.

The final issue of concern is a broad area called _institutional governance_. This encompasses visitation and correspondence policies, administrative segregation, classification policies, and disciplinary and grievance procedures. Concerns about institutional governance, especially discipline and inmate grievances, seem to be a constant source of inmate litigation. It is important to remember that prisons have the authority to discipline inmates for infractions of institutional rules; however, there must be an orderly process of reviewing complaints, especially those that might result in administrative segregation, loss of privileges, or the loss of good-time credits (Cohen 1988, 338–42).

RECENT TRENDS IN INMATE LITIGATION

In the previous sections, we have examined the history of corrections litigation. Recent litigation also is significantly affecting the operations of contemporary corrections agencies and institutions.

EXPANDING LITIGATION TO JAILS

Many of the corrections lawsuits brought in the 1960s and 1970s dealt with prisons. Although prison litigation led the way, suits involving jails and other local detention facilities have not been far behind. For example, many of the same issues raised initially in prison lawsuits have since found their way into lawsuits filed by jail inmates (Mays and Bernat 1988; Pollock 2002). Among those issues are crowding, recreation, medical care, staffing levels and staff training, food service, disciplinary practices, and treatment programs (see Guynes 1988; Kerle and Ford 1982). If jail administrators want to know the potential source of litigation, all they have to do is read the major prison cases from the 1960s and 1970s.

NEW AREAS OF LITIGATION

We have been describing several persistent sources of inmate litigation. Today's lawsuits, however, raise new issues. Here we examine four of these emerging issues—inmates' right to privacy in terms of being supervised by members of the opposite sex, receipt of sexually explicit materials and access to the Internet, smoke-free environments, and the use of excessive physical force by prison officials—and the impact each may have on corrections policy and practice.

GENDER AND STAFF One of the earliest cases addressing the issue of opposite-gender staff guarding inmates was *Lee v. Downs* (1981). This case dealt with the issue of whether a female inmate, while being examined by a doctor, could be forced to remove her underclothing in the presence of male COs. The court held that because the inmate was willing to remove her clothing if the male officers would withdraw, forcing her to undress in their presence constituted an improper invasion of her privacy.

In a related case, *Timm v. Gunter* (1990), a group of male inmates at the Nebraska State Penitentiary filed suit to prevent female COs from performing pat down searches and from seeing them in the nude. With an increasing number of female COs working in all-male institutions, it is not surprising that the issue is being raised. In *Timm*, the inmates alleged that their privacy rights were violated when the female officers saw them showering, using toilet facilities, dressing and undressing, and sleeping. There, contrary to the ruling in *Lee v. Downs*, the appellate court held that "opposite-sex surveillance of male inmates, performed on the same basis as same-sex surveillance, is not 'unreasonable,'" and that the practice "neither impermissibly violate[s] the inmates' privacy rights nor impermissibly violate[s] the guards' equal employment rights."

SEXUALLY EXPLICIT MATERIALS AND ACCESS TO THE INTERNET Although the Supreme Court has not addressed these particular concerns yet, a number of appellate courts have. Much like the question of supervision by members of the opposite sex, these two issues typically are couched in "right to privacy"

or freedom of expression terms (see Robertson 2006).

For many years, some states and the US Bureau of Prisons (BOP) have prohibited inmates from possessing or displaying nude "pin-up" photos in their cells and from receiving magazines of a sexually explicit nature. In *Ramirez v. Pugh* (2004), a federal prison inmate challenged the BOP's restriction against receiving sexually explicit magazines. The federal district court in this case found in favor of the BOP policy. In addition, though not completely supporting the inmate's claim, the US Third Circuit Court of Appeals remanded the case to the district court with instructions that such rulings must examine the impact of the policy on inmate rehabilitation.

Use of the Internet by jail and prison inmates represents a completely new legal domain. Some facilities have experimented, often only briefly, with allowing inmates to have access to the Internet through library or law library computers (Mandak 2007). However, some of these experiments have resulted in abuses—including attempts to solicit money or legal help, or attempts to commit additional crimes—and currently no state allows inmates to have direct access to the Internet (Johnson 2007; Locke 2007). As a result, inmates use personal visits, letters, and phone calls to intermediaries who then can access the Internet for them or post items on various social media sites.

To date, jail and prison inmates have won a few victories (*Clement v. California Department of Corrections*, 2004), but the courts have been deferential to corrections authorities who maintain that unrestricted access to the Internet would threaten the stability and safety of corrections facilities.

In perhaps the most unusual legal challenge involving the Internet, Maricopa County, Arizona, Sheriff Joe Arpaio (the self-described "meanest sheriff in the country") has been sued over his practice of installing webcams throughout his jail showing the inmates and their daily routines. From his perspective, this practice is not cruel and unusual punishment, and it is not an invasion of privacy. Although potentially humiliating to the inmates, Arpaio maintains that it allows the public to see what really goes on in jail.

A SMOKE-FREE ENVIRONMENT During the past few years, prison and jail inmates have filed suit asserting their right to live in a smoke-free environment. Lawsuits have charged that environmental tobacco smoke is a potential health risk. This issue is especially problematic for inmates because they cannot choose their cellmates. A federal district judge in Indiana ruled against an inmate who claimed to have a constitutional right to a smoke-free environment. In his decision, Judge Allen Sharp stated that if the corrections department wants to create smoke-free areas in its institutions, it certainly could do so; however, nothing in the Constitution compels the state to provide inmates with smoke-free surroundings (*Substance Abuse Report* 1992, 7–8).

By contrast, when Nevada inmate William McKinney appealed to the US Supreme Court, he argued successfully that "involuntary exposure to cigarette smoke could be regarded as 'cruel and unusual' punishment and a violation" of his rights (*Corrections Digest* 1993b, 4; *Criminal Law Reporter* 1993, 2229). In *Helling v. McKinney* (1993), the Court ruled that potential harm might result from exposure to environmental tobacco smoke and noted that actions should be taken to reduce or eliminate that harm. As a result of this case and other administrative changes, 96 percent of the prisons in the United States have established smoke-free living areas, and 60 percent have banned tobacco use altogether (Eldridge and Cropsey 2009).

EXCESSIVE FORCE The use of physical force certainly is not new in prisons, and inmates have long complained about the use of force to maintain order and discipline. According to Rolando del Carmen (1992, 44), "The question . . . is not whether force can be used, but when and how."

The Supreme Court provided a partial answer in *Hudson v. McMillian* (1992), a Louisiana case. Inmate Hudson was restrained after arguing with CO McMillian. Hudson was taken from his cell in handcuffs and shackles and placed in lockdown. On the way to lockdown, McMillian and another correctional officer continued to punch Hudson while a supervisor watched but did not intervene.

Hudson brought a Section 1983 suit against the state prison officials, and the case eventually reached the US Supreme Court. The Court was asked to decide whether the use of excessive force constituted cruel and unusual punishment even though Hudson did not suffer serious physical injury. The Court decided that the COs' actions were malicious and sadistic and constituted a violation of Hudson's Eighth Amendment protections against cruel and unusual punishment. Del Carmen concludes, "The good news is that the *Hudson* decision has articulated a test for all excessive use of force cases in a prison setting; the bad news is that it fails to lay the issue to rest" (1992, 46).

THE IMPACT OF INMATE LITIGATION

Litigation has been one of the major influences in changing correctional practices since 1970 (Collins 2010). The number of writs of habeas corpus and civil rights actions filed by state prisoners alone between 1980 and 2010—over 930,000 petitions—indicates that prisoner litigation is a major enterprise. However, is all that legal action working? Is there any evidence that lawsuits lead to real change? Richard Schuster and Sherry Widmer say that the essential question is "Has court intervention made an appreciable difference in prisoners' daily lives?" (1978, 11).

In an early assessment of the impact of prison litigation, M. Kay Harris and Dudley Spiller (1977, 21) concluded that broad-based prison lawsuits have generally had four outcomes. First, they believe that there have been qualitative improvements in the particular prisons cited in the suits and generally in the state corrections departments. Second, contrary to the fears of hands-off proponents, the suits have not undermined state authority. Third, the suits also have not created "country club" prisons. Fourth, federal judges have not taken over the day-to-day administration of the prisons that have faced litigation.

The experience of Texas in the wake of the decisions in *Estelle v. Gamble* (1976) and *Ruiz v. Estelle* (1980) may be more indicative of the effect inmate litigation is having on corrections systems today. Geoffrey Alpert and his colleagues acknowledge that the decisions produced system-wide improvements in "personal living space, medical care, access to the courts, and working conditions" (1984, 298). However, they add that an unintended consequence of *Ruiz* has been rising expectations by prisoners that have "set in motion a chain of events that has undermined the traditional stability, safety, and regularity" of the state's corrections department.

Mississippi has also been the target of a significant amount of inmate litigation. The positive effects of that litigation include an end to racial segregation and improvements in prison conditions relating to mail censorship, disciplinary procedures, access to legal materials, religious freedom, medical care, and cell space. However, as Columbus Hopper (1985, 61) notes, the improvements changed the state prison at Parchman from a "feudal system to a fortress"; that is, the prison went from a plantation-style farm prison to a high-security, walled institution.

Litigation that originated in Indiana resulted in "hiring more personnel, upgrading prison programs, and repairing the physical facilities" (Selke 1985, 34). Much to the disappointment of some prison reform advocates, however, instead of ending up with more treatment programs and more-humane conditions, the state ended up with both new and expanded high-security facilities.

In the end, most assessments of the outcome of inmate litigation are optimistic or, at worst, reserved. Jim Thomas (1988, 250, 252), an optimist, insists that litigation has had a profound impact on corrections systems by expanding the base of prison reformers, creating inmate grievance mechanisms, granting additional mail privileges, eliminating at least some of the outrageous administrative practices, reducing arbitrariness in the staff, and widening prisoners' legal access. In a more-cautious appraisal, G. Larry Mays and William Taggart say that court-ordered prison reform "will be a labored process even under the best of circumstances." They add, "The formulation and implementation of court-ordered reforms is most likely to be measured in decades instead of years" (1988, 194).

However, William Collins (2010) gives the best summary of corrections litigation. He notes that in as many as 98 of every 100 suits filed, the defendants—that is, the state corrections officials—win; inmate-plaintiffs succeed in just 2 percent of the suits filed. In spite of this win-loss record, he

concludes, these lawsuits have made an impact on corrections administration in this country.

Whatever the substantive changes produced by inmate litigation, one fact is clear: as a result of state inmates' civil rights actions, more than 10 percent of civil suits filed in the federal district courts involve a prisoner's claim (Dilworth 1995, 98; Hanson and Daley 1995, 38). Of course, most of these cases do not go through trial or settlement. The federal courts dismiss about 75 percent of them, and another 20 percent are terminated on motions to dismiss from the states. As inmates are not guaranteed the right to counsel in Section 1983 suits, many of these cases are dismissed outright for lack of merit or on procedural grounds (Dilworth 1995, 98, 100).

CAPITAL PUNISHMENT AND PRISONER LITIGATION

Some people question whether capital punishment is a corrections issue. After all, its use as a punishment arises out of legislative actions or judicial decisions (see Chapter 3). Here, capital punishment is an area we address because death row inmates file their appeals from their cells, and because corrections authorities are ultimately responsible for carrying out death sentences.

For the more than 3,100 prisoners on death row at the end of 2010, capital punishment is a very real concern and the source of a good deal of litigation (Snell 2011). Perhaps the place to start in an examination of litigation and the death penalty is *Furman v. Georgia* (1972). In *Furman*, a divided Supreme Court struck down as unconstitutional the death penalties of Georgia and most other states. In simplest terms, the Court held that the death penalty was unconstitutional because of overly broad jury discretion. The Court did not say that the death penalty is unconstitutional in and of itself—only that it is unconstitutional when its application is arbitrary and capricious. This interpretation allowed the states and the federal government to redraw death penalty statutes that responded to the Court's criticisms. In 1976, the Court heard *Gregg v. Georgia*. There, in a seven to two decision, the Court upheld the revised

Georgia statute. Only Justices William Brennan and Thurgood Marshall, both ardent opponents of the death penalty, dissented.

Under the revised law, Georgia and a number of other states adopted a bifurcated system of adjudication for death penalty cases. In the first phase, the jury decides the question of guilt. If in the trial phase, the jury finds the defendant guilty, they must then begin the sentencing phase. In the sentencing hearing, several factors come into play:

- Juries now must consider **mitigating** and **aggravating circumstances**—any factors that diminish (mitigate) or enhance (aggravate) the seriousness of the crime. In most states, only murder is punishable by death. Although the actual statutory definitions vary from state to state—for instance, the definitions of *first-degree murder*, *aggravated murder*, and *felony murder* may vary—the death penalty is generally reserved for the most serious type of murder (US Department of Justice 1994).

- A sentencing jury must return a unanimous verdict for the death penalty. In the absence of a unanimous verdict, life or a similar prison term becomes the default sentence. This means that the 12 members of the jury must support the decisions relating both to guilt or innocence and to the sentence.

- In 37 of the 38 states that allow capital punishment, death sentences are automatically reviewed, whether the defendant wants a review or not, South Carolina being the exception (Snell 2006). Most of these appeals go directly to the state supreme court. This practice ensures that the trial judge made no errors of law or in the judge's instructions to the jury before either of its deliberations.

Box 12.1 describes several recent cases regarding the imposition and the parameters of the death penalty.

Each year the number of people sentenced to death is roughly the same as the number that leave death row for any reason. However, there have been some year-to-year fluctuations. For instance, the United States' death row population increased by an average of 228 inmates per year between 1995 and 2005, but the annual increases declined from 325 to 128 during this period. In the same period, various jurisdictions executed an average of 68 inmates per

RECENT SUPREME COURT DEATH PENALTY CASES

BOX 12.1

Recent cases before the Supreme Court have seldom raised the issue of the death penalty's constitutionality. Instead, the Court has been asked to deal with technical issues: When is the death penalty appropriate? Are there individuals for whom capital punishment is not appropriate? Are the procedures employed by state and federal trial courts in imposing death sentences adequate? The following list briefly outlines some of the cases and issues that have come before the Court.

- *Penry v. Johnson* (2001): The essential question in this case, although it was never fully addressed, is whether the death penalty is appropriate for people who are mentally retarded. This case went to the Supreme Court twice, and both times was decided on a procedural issue. The point the Court addressed was whether jurors should be informed of the criminal defendant's "mental impairments and childhood abuse" and whether these facts should be considered mitigating circumstances that outweigh any and all aggravating circumstances. The Court held that the jury instructions in the second *Penry* trial had not complied with its ruling in the first appeal. In a unanimous decision (with three justices concurring in part and

(Continued)

(Continued)

dissenting in part), the Supreme Court ruled that the court's instructions "made the jury charge as a whole internally contradictory, and placed law-abiding jurors in an impossible situation."

● *Atkins v. Virginia* (2002): The *Atkins* case resolved the issue that had been left dangling in *Penry*, namely: whether it is constitutional to execute a person who is mentally retarded. The Supreme Court's majority opinion (by a six-to-three vote) noted that a number of states now prohibit the execution of mentally retarded persons, and that even those states that allow such executions rarely carry them out. Therefore, based on the concept of evolving standards of decency, the Court held that "executions of mentally retarded criminals are 'cruel and unusual punishments' prohibited by the Eighth Amendment."

● *Ring v. Arizona* (2002): The jury in Ring's trial was deadlocked on the charge of premeditated murder but found him guilty of felony murder, the result of an armed robbery. To sentence a defendant to death under these circumstances, Arizona law requires the trial judge to conduct a separate hearing to decide whether there were aggravating or mitigating circumstances. Ring's appeal was based on the constitutionality of entrusting the judge with fact-finding concerning the capital sentence. In a seven-to-two vote, the Court held that judicial fact finding in relation to capital sentences is no insurance against arbitrariness, and that most states entrust those kinds of decisions to juries. In simplest terms, judges cannot be the decision makers in cases where the death penalty can be imposed.

● *Roper v. Simmons* (2005): This is perhaps one of the most significant death penalty cases to be decided by the Supreme Court since *Gregg v. Georgia* (1976). A series of appeals that came before the Court beginning in the 1980s had questioned the constitutionality of the death penalty for individuals whose crimes had been committed before they turned 18, and the Court had allowed capital sentences for 16- and 17-year-old offenders (see, for example, *Stanford v. Kentucky*, 1989). At the time *Roper* was decided, 14 states allowed capital sentences for youngsters between the ages of 14 and 17. However, in this case the Supreme Court—in a five-to-four decision—held that because of "evolving standards of decency," the death penalty should no longer be imposed on persons under 18.

● *Panetti v. Quarterman* (2007): The Supreme Court recently ruled on the issue of execution of mentally ill inmates (as opposed to those who are mentally retarded). The question in this case was, "Does the Eighth Amendment permit the execution of an inmate who has a factual awareness of the State's stated reason for his execution, but who lacks, due to mental illness, a rational understanding of the State's justification?" (*Oyez* 2007): In a five-to-four decision, the Supreme Court ordered a stay of execution and returned Panetti's case to the courts of Texas to allow them to decide more fully the claims of incompetence. However, the "High Court declined to establish a new standard for mental competence before an individual may be subject to capital punishment" (Richey 2007).

● *Baze v. Rees* (2008): This was another of the technical issue cases decided by the Supreme Court. The case challenged the use of lethal injection by Kentucky in carrying out death sentences. The Supreme Court ruled that nothing in the Constitution prohibits states from employing lethal injection as a means of capital punishment.

SOURCE: SOME OF THE MATERIAL HERE WAS ADAPTED FROM THE CORNELL UNIVERSITY LAW SCHOOL WEBSITE (WWW.LAW.CORNELL.EDU).

year—with a contemporary high of 98 in 1999. Since 1999 there has been a fairly consistent decline in the number of executions annually, and in 2010 there were only 46 (Snell 2011).

Additionally, every Supreme Court term some death-row inmates appeal their convictions. As a result, the Court sees a variety of death penalty issues. Given the Court's current composition, it seems unlikely that the death penalty will be abolished in the near future. Therefore, prisons will have to accommodate substantial death row populations, and this means expensive housing in what amounts to segregation units. In California (with 699 inmates on death row), Florida (with 395), and Texas (with 315), this is a substantial corrections expenditure.

Public opinion polls show strong, but declining, support for the death penalty. The topic is also a source of political capital among politicians. Capital punishment will continue to be on the statute books in most states, a few states every year will execute inmates, and, as a result, the death penalty will continue to be a source of litigation.

BETTMANN ARCHIVE/CORBIS

THE FUTURE OF LITIGATION

With the number of jail and prison inmates in the United States increasing every year, the future would seem to hold more inmate litigation. However, since the late 1970s, Congress and the federal courts, particularly the US Supreme Court, have become less receptive to inmate lawsuits. (Box 12.2 describes the ways other countries deal with inmate grievances.) Confirmation that the rights period was well over came in 1987, in *Turner v. Safley* (see Robertson 2006). The case dealt with Missouri's prohibition against inmate romances and inmates' corresponding with one another. To determine the constitutionality of prison officials' actions, the Supreme Court established the *reasonableness test*, which is a measure of inmates' rights against the prison's need for security. Rudolph Alexander says that this test, in contrast to the strict-scrutiny test, is "highly deferential to prison officials and has the potential for a significant erosion in prisoners' rights" (1994, 104). That deference gives this period in the history of inmate litigation its name.

At the start of this chapter, we identified three periods in the history of inmate lawsuits. The hands-off period lasted from 1871 through 1963. The appellate courts were very much hands-on during the rights period, from 1964 to 1978. In the deference period, notes Collins (2010), one hand is on, and one hand is off. In the prisoner lawsuits decided by the Supreme Court since 1979, inmates have seldom won. Moreover, the decisions in many of these cases make it unlikely they will succeed in the future (Call 1995, 41).

A low probability of winning will not stop inmates from trying, though. The crowding in jails and prisons is likely to continue, as the growth in inmate population outpaces available prison and jail space. Faced with limited resources, corrections systems across the country have begun to curtail or eliminate programs, diverting funds to inmates' basic needs: food, shelter, and security. More inmates, with more idle time, will use some of that time to bring suits against their keepers.

Collins (2010) tells us that the Court's message in *Bell v. Wolfish* (1979) was that prisoners have constitutional rights but that those rights are restricted. He

SPOTLIGHT ON INTERNATIONAL CORRECTIONS: INMATE LITIGATION AND LEGAL SYSTEMS   BOX 12.2

Different legal systems have different ways of dealing with question of prisoners' rights. In Saudi Arabia, an Islamic kingdom, appeals go the Saudi royal family through the Interior Ministry. Russia has struggled with its prison system since the fall of Communism and, like Saudi Arabia, has been a frequent target of Amnesty International for its treatment of prisoners. Inmates under the control of the Russian Ministry of Internal Affairs have few mechanisms for asserting their human rights. Similarly, Japanese inmates have few rights and little access to treatment programs like those in Western countries.

Even in Western Europe, where the nations have well-developed procedures for dealing with questions of prisoners' rights, there is considerable variability in the ways of addressing these concerns. The United Kingdom has long employed a Board of Visitors, which operates under the authority of the Home Office.* Its members are laypeople who come into prisons to mediate problems of discipline between prison administrators and inmates. In the 1990s, the United Kingdom also began using prison ombudspersons, accountable only to the Home Secretary, the person ultimately responsible for the operation of prisons. The ombudspersons are the final domestic arbiters of appeal for issues involving internal discipline. Since shortly after the founding of the European Union in 1992, the United Kingdom has taken prisoner grievances to the European Court of Human Rights, but this court hears cases only after all domestic remedies are exhausted.

France employs the Office of Corrections Judges to resolve prisoners' concerns. These courts normally oversee the administration of criminal sanctions to convicted offenders, hence the formal name of its judges, *juges de l'application des peines* [judges for the application of punishments]. These judges also oversee prison conditions and discipline. The judges in these courts must visit all the prisons in their jurisdictions at least once a month to hear the formal complaints of individual inmates about prison resources and general conditions. In essence, these judges perform the same function as the Board of Visitors in the United Kingdom, but in France, they are part of the judiciary, rather than the executive.

Germany's approach to a prisoner's rights is very formal. Prisons are administered at the *Länder* (state) level. The Prison Act of 1976 guarantees inmates access to courts for any violations of their rights. Special court panels must hear inmate grievances, and they carry appeals to the state high courts as needed. Despite the formality of the process the system has led to an increase in prisoners' claims.

Erika Fairchild observes that the mechanisms for handling inmate complaints in these three European countries reveal a lot about each nation's character. The United Kingdom, a common law nation, relies on laypeople to hear inmates' complaints. France, a nation known for its formidable bureaucratic structure, uses bureaucratic judges to perform that duty. Germany, a nation that embodies the idea of *Rechtsstaat* (a law-based state), resolves inmates' complaints through legal channels. However, since the creation of the European Union, inmates have increasingly accessed the European Court of Human Rights in Strasbourg, France.

NOTE: *THE EUROPEAN CONVENTION OF HUMAN RIGHTS (1950) EXTENDED CERTAIN RIGHTS TO PRISON INMATES. THE UNITED KINGDOM WAS A SIGNATORY AND HAS USED THE CONVENTION AS ITS FINAL AUTHORITY FOR THE TREATMENT OF PRISONERS SINCE 1950. THE ONLY EXCEPTION: PRISONERS CONVICTED OF TERRORISM BECAUSE OF ACTIONS TAKEN IN NORTHERN IRELAND AND ENGLAND.
SOURCES: FAIRCHILD (1993); GLENDON, GORDON, AND CAROZZA (1999); REICHEL (2013); TERRILL (1999).

speculates that corrections litigation in the future will focus on four areas. First, conditions of confinement—particularly crowding—will continue to be the basis of much litigation. Therefore, state and federal governments will have to devote increasingly larger segments of their budgets to building and operating facilities. Second, inmates will continue to litigate in areas involving previously articulated rights—medical care, for example. Medical care may be a critically important issue as we put more people in prison and keep them there for longer periods. The next decade may see the practice of geriatric medicine become common in the nation's correctional facilities. Third, inmates will not be the only group asserting their rights. Staff members will enter the fray, raising concerns over pay, safety, and other workplace conditions. Finally, newly created statutory rights, like those mandated by the Americans with Disabilities Act (1990) will provide fertile ground for inmate and staff litigation (see, especially, Collins 2010).

In the United States there are many alternative mechanisms for dealing with the volume of inmate lawsuits, particularly civil rights actions. In fact, through CRIPA, the procedures are already in place for internal dispute resolution. The 1980 legislation authorizes the US attorney general and the federal courts to certify administrative grievance mechanisms that would allow the states to hear and act on routine inmate complaints. For those states with certified plans, inmates must exhaust all administrative mechanisms before they can file suit in federal court (Belbot 2004; Collins 2010). The procedure is designed to handle most problems as close to the source as possible, and to keep a large number of cases off federal court dockets. Unfortunately, most states have not sought certification of their grievance procedures, and there has been little prompting from the federal courts to so do. The result is that CRIPA remains an underused, though potentially very significant, vehicle for settling inmate complaints (*Criminal Justice Newsletter* 1995, 6–7; Hanson and Daley 1995, 40).

In the absence of viable alternatives to litigation, and with inmate populations continuing to rise, inmates will continue to file lawsuits alleging that their conditions of confinement constitute cruel and unusual punishment. Probation and parole, too, will be a fertile area for litigation. With more offenders—and more serious offenders—being placed in community supervision programs, lawsuits will escalate here too. Offenders will sue because they are not receiving adequate treatment. Citizens will sue because they are not being protected adequately. Moreover, corrections employees will sue because they work long hours—sometimes more than 40 per week—in a dangerous and stressful environment. The end is not in sight.

SUMMARY

The areas of prisoners' rights and inmate litigation are complex. However, from this chapter you should especially note the following:

- For a long period in our nation's early history, the courts took a "hands-off" approach to prisoners and prisoners' rights.

- During the 1960s, prison inmates, along with other groups in society, frequently turned to the courts seeking redress for their grievances.

- Although the courts still hear appeals from prison inmates, courts have largely been deferential to prison authorities and prison policies for the past 30 years.

- Inmates have a variety of legal mechanisms for their appeals, and two of the most common have been writs of habeas corpus and civil rights actions (Section 1983 suits).

- Prison inmates have challenged a wide range of conditions of confinement—such as crowding and medical care—and litigation has extended to jails and probation and parole clients.

● One of the most visible areas of inmate litigation has been in challenges to the death penalty.

● Some states have seen significant changes in their corrections systems because of inmate lawsuits and oversight by the federal courts.

THINKING ABOUT CORRECTIONAL POLICIES AND PRACTICES: WRITING ASSIGNMENTS

1 Develop a one-page summary of some of the reasons inmate lawsuits increased so dramatically in the 1970s. Which of these reasons do you think had the greatest impact? Why?

2 Prepare an op-ed (opinion-editorial) for the local newspaper on the issue of whether and to what extent inmates have a right to privacy. What would this mean in terms of COs of one gender monitoring prisoners of the other?

3 Provide a written answer to the following question: What impact does a death row population have on prison operations? Is current information available on the Internet? In your

answer, pay particular attention to operating costs and security concerns.

4 In what area of litigation have inmates been most effective in getting basic rights? In what area have they been least effective in getting these same rights? Support your answer with reference to the cases involved.

5 "The European Union model of an appellate court for inmate litigation outside of the national court provides a superior method of guaranteeing inmate rights to that used in the United States." Support or attack this statement.

KEY TERMS

aggravating circumstances
civil death
civil rights claim
class action lawsuit
deliberate indifference

jailhouse lawyers
mitigating circumstances
nonperson status
pro se actions
public interest law

Section 1983 suit
vicarious liability
writ of habeas corpus
writ writers

CRITICAL REVIEW QUESTIONS

1 What is your reaction to a federal judge telling a state prison how many prisoners it should house? Would you feel differently if you were a prison warden?

2 Jailhouse lawyers increase the number of lawsuits filed by prisoners. Give at least two other reasons why prison administrators would want to limit or prohibit the practice of inmates helping other inmates file appeals.

3 After examining some of the statistics in the chapter, list some of the ways the Prison

Litigation Reform Act and the Antiterrorism and Effective Death Penalty Act have changed the nature of prison inmate litigation.

4 Compare and contrast inmate habeas corpus petitions with civil rights actions. Are the goals of each the same or different? Explain.

5 Should inmates' rights groups, such as the ACLU's National Prison Project or the Southern Poverty Law Center, be filing lawsuits on behalf of inmates? Why do inmates need advocacy groups?

6 How do the legal status and constitutional protections of probationers and parolees differ?

7 Should attorneys represent offenders during parole revocation proceedings? If offenders cannot afford an attorney, should the state appoint counsel?

8 How would you characterize the present period in terms of inmate litigation and the courts? Are we in a hands-off, hands-on, or some other type of environment? Provide evidence to support your contention.

9 Do you think prisons and jails should be smoke-free environments for inmates and staff members? Are there other issues at work here beyond health? What would you do to change an institution from a smoking facility to a smoke-free facility?

10 What evidence do we have that litigation is improving the lives of jail and prison inmates? Describe the two areas where you see the greatest improvement.

CASES CITED

Argersinger v. Hamlin, 407 U.S. 25 (1972)
Atkins v. Virginia, 536 U.S. 304 (2002)
Batson v. Kentucky, 476 U.S. 79 (1986)
Baze v. Rees, 553 U.S. 35 (2008)
Bell v. Wolfish, 441 U.S. 520 (1979)
Bounds v. Smith, 430 U.S. 817 (1977)
Clement v. California Department of Corrections, 364 F. 3d 1148 (9th Cir., 2004)
Cooper v. Pate, 378 U.S. 546 (1964)
Estelle v. Gamble, 429 U.S. 97 (1976)
Fay v. Noia, 372 U.S. 391 (1963)
Furman v. Georgia, 408 U.S. 238 (1972)
Gagnon v. Scarpelli, 411 U.S. 778 (1973)
Gideon v. Wainwright, 372 U.S. 335 (1963)
Gregg v. Georgia, 428 U.S. 153 (1976)
Helling v. McKinney, 509 U.S. 25 (1993)
Holt v. Sarver, 309 F.Supp. 362 (ED Ark., 1970)
Hudson v. McMillian, 501 U.S. 1279 (1992)
Johnson v. Avery, 393 U.S. 483 (1969)
Lee v. Downs, 641 F.2d 1117 (4th Cir., 1981)

Mempa v. Rhay, 389 U.S. 128 (1967)
Miranda v. Arizona, 384 U.S. 436 (1966)
Monroe v. Pape, 365 U.S. 167 (1961)
Morrissey v. Brewer, 408 U.S. 471 (1972)
Panetti v. Quarterman, 551 U.S. 930 (2007)
Penry v. Johnson, 532 U.S. 782 (2001)
Powell v. Alabama, 287 U.S. 45 (1932)
Pugh v. Locke, 406 F.Supp. 318 (MD Ala., 1976)
Ramirez v. Pugh, 379 F.3d 122 (3rd Cir. 8-12-04, 2004)
Rhodes v. Chapman, 452 U.S. 337 (1981)
Ring v. Arizona, 536 U.S. 584 (2002)
Roper v. Simmons, 543 U.S. 551 (2005)
Ruffin v. Commonwealth, 62 Va. 790 (1871)
Ruiz v. Estelle, 503 F.Supp. 1265 (S.D. Tex., 1980)
Sanders v. United States, 373 U.S. 1 (1963)
Stanford v. Kentucky, 492 U.S. 361 (1989)
Timm v. Gunter, 917 F.2d 1093 (8th Cir., 1990)
Townsend v. Sain, 372 U.S. 293 (1963)
Turner v. Safley, 482 U.S. 78 (1987)

REFERENCES

Administrative Office of US Courts. 2010. *Annual report to the director*. Retrieved on July 17, 2013 from: http://www.uscourts.gov/uscourts/Statistics/JudicialFactsAndFigures/2010/Table406.pdf

Alexander, Rudolph, Jr. 1994. Hands-off, hands-on, hands semi-off: A discussion of the current legal test used by the United States Supreme Court to decide inmates' rights. *Journal of Crime and Justice* 17(1): 103–28.

Alpert, Geoffrey P., Ben M. Crouch, and C. Ronald Huff. 1984. Prison reform by judicial decree: The unintended consequences of *Ruiz v. Estelle*. *Justice System Journal* 9(3): 291–305.

American Civil Liberties Union. 2011. Know your rights: The Prison Litigation Reform Act (PLRA). Retrieved on July 17, 2013 from: http://www.aclu.org/prisoners-rights/know-your-rights-prison-litigation-reform-act

American Correctional Association (ACA). 1991. *Standards for adult local detention facilities*, 3rd edn. Laurel, MD: American Correctional Association.

Belbot, Barbara. 2004. Report on the prison litigation reform act: What have the courts decided so far? *The Prison Journal* 84(3): 290–316.

Bingaman, Jeff. 1980. *Report of the attorney general on the February 2 and 3, 1980, riot of the Penitentiary of New Mexico*. 2 vols. Santa Fe, NM: Office of the Attorney General.

Braswell, Michael C., Steven Dillingham, and Reid Montgomery, eds. 1985. *Prison violence in America*. Cincinnati, OH: Anderson.

Bronstein, Alvin J. 1985. Prisoners and their endangered rights. *Prison Journal* 65(1): 3–17.

Burger, Warren E. 1985. The need for change in prisons and the correctional system. *Arkansas Law Review* 38(4): 711–26.

Call, Jack E. 1995. The Supreme Court and prisoners' rights. *Federal Probation* 59(1): 36–46.

Cheesman, Fred, Roger Hanson, Brian Ostrom, and Neal Kauder. 1998. Prisoner Litigation in Relation to Prisoner Population. *Caseload Highlights* 4(September). Williamsburg, VA: National Center for State Courts.

Chilton, Bradley. 1991. *Prisons under the gavel: The federal court takeover of Georgia prisons*. Columbus: Ohio State University Press.

Cohen, Fred. 1988. The law of prisoners' rights: An overview. *Criminal Law Bulletin* 24(4): 321–49.

Coles, Frances S. 1987. The impact of *Bell v. Wolfish* upon prisoners' rights. *Journal of Crime and Justice* 10(1): 47–69.

Collins, William C. 2010. *Correctional law for the correctional officer*, 5th edn. Laurel, MD: American Correctional Association.

Correctional Law Reporter. 1994. Corrections court cases with greatest impact identified by CLR Poll. June, 1–15.

Correctional Law Reporter. 1995. Access to a law library and inmates assisting inmates may not be the best ways of guaranteeing prisoners' right to court access. February, 67–9.

Corrections Digest. 1993a. Federal court ruling holds official personally liable for inmate's medical help. August 25, 10.

Corrections Digest. 1993b. Nevada not obligated to provide nonsmoking facilities, state argues. January 27, 4–5.

Corrections Digest. 1994. ACLU joins inmates in federal suit over prison conditions. January 12, 7–8.

Criminal Justice Newsletter. 1995. Inmate suits a growing burden on federal courts, study finds. February 15, 6–7.

Criminal Law Reporter. 1993. Opinion of the U.S. Supreme Court. June 16, 2229.

Crouch, Ben M., and James W. Marquart. 1989. *An appeal to justice: Litigated reform of Texas prisons*. Austin: University of Texas Press.

del Carmen, Rolando. 1992. The Supreme Court and prison excessive use of force cases: Does one test fit all? *Federal Probation* 56(2): 44–7.

DiIulio, John J., Jr. ed. 1990. *Courts, corrections, and the Constitution: The impact of judicial intervention on prisons and jails*. New York: Oxford University Press.

Dilworth, Donald. 1995. Prisoners' lawsuits burden federal civil courts. *Trial* 31(5): 98, 100.

Eldridge, Gloria D., and Karen L. Cropsey. 2009. Smoking bans and restrictions in U.S. prisons and jails: Consequences for incarcerated women. *American Journal of Preventive Medicine* 37(2): 179–80.

Fairchild, Erika. 1993. *Comparative criminal justice systems*. Belmont, CA: Wadsworth.

Flango, Victor E. 1994. Federal court review of state court convictions in noncapital cases. *Justice System Journal* 17(2): 153–70.

Frug, Gerald E. 1978. The judicial power of the purse. *University of Pennsylvania Law Review* 126(4): 715–94.

Glendon, Mary Ann, Michael W. Gordon, and Paolo G. Carozza. 1999. *Comparative legal traditions*. St. Paul, MN: West Group.

Guynes, Randall. 1988. *Nation's jail managers assess their problems*. Washington, DC: US Department of Justice.

Hanson, Roger A. 1987. What should be done when prisoners want to take the state to court? *Judicature* 70(4): 223–27.

Hanson, Roger A., and Henry W. K. Daley. 1995. *Challenging the conditions of prisons and jails: A report on Section 1983 litigation*. Washington, DC: US Department of Justice.

Harris, M. Kay, and Dudley P. Spiller, Jr. 1977. *After decision: Implementations of judicial decrees in correctional settings*. Washington, DC: National Institute of Law Enforcement and Criminal Justice.

Hopper, Columbus B. 1985. The impact of litigation on Mississippi's prison system. *Prison Journal* 65(1): 54–63.

Johnson, Kevin. 2007. Inmates go to court to seek right to use the Internet. *USATODAY.com*. Retrieved July 17, 2013 from: **http://www. usatody.com/ tech/news/2006-11-23-prison-net_x.htm**

Kerle, Kenneth E., and Francis R. Ford. 1982. *The state of our nation's jails*. Washington, DC: National Sheriffs' Association.

Locke, Michelle. 2007. Dot-cons: Inmates take to the Web. *Prison Legal News*. Retrieved June 19, 2007 from: **www.prisonlegalnews.org/Visitors/ (S(uej45yi1lei3qz45uhn0jg55))/95_displayNews.aspx**

Mahan, Sue. 1982. An "orgy of brutality" at Attica and the "killing ground" at Santa Fe: A comparison of prison riots. In *Coping with imprisonment*, edited by N. Parisi. Beverly Hills, CA: Sage, 65–78.

Mandak, Joe. 2007. Inmates use intermediaries to escape to the Internet. *USATODAY.com*. Retrieved July 17, 2013, from **http://usatoday30.usatoday.com/tech/ news/2005-05-01-inmates-internet_x.htm?csp=34**

Mays, G. Larry. 1983. *Stone v. Powell:* The impact on state supreme court judges' perceptions. *Journal of Criminal Justice* 11(1): 27–34.

Mays, G. Larry. 1984. The Supreme Court and development of federal habeas corpus doctrine. In *Legal issues in criminal justice: The courts*, edited by Sloan Letman, Dan Edwards, and Daniel Bell. Cincinnati, OH: Anderson, 55–69.

Mays, G. Larry, and Frances P. Bernat. 1988. Jail reform litigation: The issue of rights and remedies. *American Journal of Criminal Justice* 12(2): 254–73.

Mays, G. Larry, and William A. Taggart. 1985. The impact of litigation on changing New Mexico's prison conditions. *Prison Journal* 65(1): 38–53.

Mays, G. Larry, and William A. Taggart. 1988. The implementation of court-ordered prison reform. In *Research in law and policy studies*, vol. 2, edited by Stuart S. Nagel. Greenwich, CT: JAI Press, 179–98.

Oyez. 2007. Panetti v. Quarterman (Docket no. 06–6407) 555 U.S. 930 (2007). Retrieved June 30, 2007, from **http://www.oyez.org/cases/2000–2009/2006/ 2006_06_6407/**

Palmer, John W. 2010. *Constitutional rights of prisoners*, 9th edn. Newark, NJ: Anderson/Matthew Binder and Co.

Pollock, Joycelyn. 2002. Prisoner rights. In *Encyclopedia of crime and punishment*, edited by David Levinson. Thousand Oaks, CA: Sage, 1246–50.

Powers, Richard A., III. 1987. Comment: Restrictions on state prisoner habeas corpus review by federal courts. *Criminal Law Bulletin* 23(1): 30–5.

Prigmore, Charles S., and Richard T. Crow. 1976. Is the Court remaking the American prison system? *Federal Probation* 40: 3–10.

Reichel, Philip L. 2013. *Comparative criminal justice systems: A topical approach*. Boston, MA: Pearson.

Remington, Frank J. 1986. Change in the availability of federal habeas corpus: Its significance for state prisoners and state correctional programs. *Michigan Law Review* 85(3): 570–91.

Rhodes, Susan L. 1992. Prison reform and prison life: Four books on the process of court-ordered change. *Law & Society Review* 26(1): 189–218.

Richey, Warren. 2007. Court strikes down death sentence for mentally ill man. *The Christian Science Monitor*. Retrieved June 30, 2007 from: **http:// www.csmonitor/com/2007/0629/p10s01-usju.htm**

Robertson, James E. 1985–1986. Surviving incarceration: Constitutional protection from inmate violence. *Drake Law Review* 35(1): 101–60.

Robertson, James E. 2006. Correctional case law: 2004–2005. *Criminal Justice Review* 31(2): 185–204.

Scalia, John. 2002. *Prisoner petitions filed in U.S. district courts, 2000*. Washington, DC: US Department of Justice.

Schuster, Richard L., and Sherry Widmer. 1978. Judicial intervention in corrections: A case study. *Federal Probation* 42(3): 10–17.

Selke, William L. 1985. Judicial management of prisons? Responses to prison litigation. *Prison Journal* 65(1): 26–37.

Smith, Christopher E. 1986. Federal judges' role in prison litigation: What's necessary? What's proper? *Judicature* 70(3): 144–50.

Snell, Tracy L. 2006. *Capital punishment, 2005*. Washington, DC: US Department of Justice.

Snell, Tracy L. 2011. *Capital punishment, 2010—statistical tables*. Washington, DC: Bureau of Justice Statistics, US Department of Justice.

Stephan, James J. 2008. *Census of state and federal correctional facilities, 2005*. Washington, DC: Bureau of Justice Statistics, US Department of Justice.

Substance abuse report. 1992. Federal court says inmate has no right to smoke-free prison. December 15, 7–8.

Terrill, Richard J. 1999. *World criminal justice systems: A survey*. Cincinnati, OH: Anderson.

Thomas, Jim. 1988. *Prison litigation: The paradox of the jailhouse lawyer*. Totowa, NJ: Rowman and Littlefield.

Thomas, Jim., Devin Wheeler, and Kathy Harris. 1986. Issues and misconceptions in prisoner litigation: A critical view. *Criminology* 24(4): 775–97.

US Department of Justice. 1994. *Capital punishment 1993*. Washington, DC: US Government Printing Office.

Useem, Bert, and Peter Kimball. 1989. *States of siege: U.S. prison riots, 1971–1986*. New York: Oxford University Press.

Yarbrough, Tinsley E. 1984. The Alabama prison litigation. *Justice System Journal* 9(3): 276–90.

GENDER ISSUES IN CORRECTIONS

Outline

Objectives

● To explain to you how gender shapes the corrections world, from inmates to employees

● To acquaint you with the range of correctional experiences, from institutional corrections to alternatives to incarceration, that are affected by gender

● To give you a sense of the special needs of female offenders in the corrections system

● To help you develop an appreciation for the extent to which gender plays a role in how and to what extent women gain access to key services outside prison and jail

● To give you a sense of the special issues confronting the nation's correctional system as it struggles to accommodate increasing numbers of female offenders

Essentials of Corrections, Fifth Edition. G. Larry Mays and L. Thomas Winfree, Jr.
© 2014 John Wiley & Sons, Inc. Published 2014 by John Wiley & Sons, Inc.

INTRODUCTION

Despite changes in the gender makeup of the various correctional client populations, females do not receive certain services, programs, and other resources routinely offered to males (Green et al. 2005; Islam-Zwart and Vik 2004; Maeve 2001; Mosher and Phillips 2006). As correctional clients, women have many of the same short- and long-term problems and daily concerns as men. They also have special psychological, medical, and physical needs that often go unrecognized or unmet. For example, those who are mothers may feel the loss of their children in ways that differ from those of incarcerated fathers. Moreover, those who are pregnant or have gynecological problems often cannot get needed medical services. In many cases, corrections administrators even fail to acknowledge those needs.

The result is a form of **benign neglect**: there is no specific intent to create these disparities in treatment, services, and programming; rather they happen largely by default, as the incarcerated females compared to their male counterparts simply get far less attention—and resources—from state and federal legislators and policy makers. Why? Consider the number of female inmates, the lack of jails and prisons exclusively for women, the relatively small number of bed spaces allocated to women in other facilities; moreover, criminal courts tend to convict women of less serious crimes than men. Then there is the endemic sexist perspective attributed to many policy makers within the criminal justice system: female offenders somehow deserve what they get because they have betrayed society and other women by their misdeeds (Belknap 1996; Chesney-Lind 1998; Covington 2001; Harris 1998; Pollock 2002; Wesley 2006). Other experts claim that women adjust to prison somewhat better than men; in particular, they do not call attention to themselves through riots and other inmate uprisings (Bartollas and Conrad 1992, 467; Covington 2001). As a consequence, female offenders present unique challenges to the nation's corrections systems, challenges that are largely unmet.

This chapter is about more than female offenders. Recall that the organizing focus is gender issues.

Hence, we include an overview of female correctional employees. If gender-related information about correctional clients is sparse, for female employees of the nation's corrections systems it is even more so. Before addressing either the female correctional employee or client, we turn to an examination of the nature and extent of female criminality, which even before we begin this review is acknowledged to be less than that of males. Exactly how and to what extent remains important, since many of these offenders eventually become the female clients of the nation's correctional system.

NATURE AND EXTENT OF FEMALE CRIMINALITY

Women are arrested less often than men and generally for less serious crimes, although the range of offenses is identical to that for men. For example, look at Table 13.1. Notice that overall in 2010, women made up 25.5 percent of the 8,221,468 arrestees. The message is clear: Given that women make up roughly 50 percent of the nation's adult population, they are disproportionately lower among arrestees than the proportion of females in the general population. However, if we find women's percentage of a given arrest category higher than 25.5 percent, then this is a crime where the number of female arrestees is disproportionately higher *given their contribution to the entire arrestee population*. If it is below 25.5 percent, then the reverse is true: the arrest rate for women is disproportionately lower than we would expect.[1] Certain economic crimes present several examples of the former, as women's arrest rates are higher than we might expect for overall property crime, larceny-theft, fraud, and forgery and counterfeiting. For embezzlement, women achieve parity with men. In the arrest category of prostitution and commercialized sex, women dominate.

Women's involvement in violent crime presents an entirely different picture. Overall, women are underrepresented, but far more so in some categories such as forcible rape, murder and nonnegligent manslaughter, and robbery. Women's arrest rates are

TABLE 13.1 Ten-Year Trends for Male and Female Arrestees.

Offense charged	Male Total 2001	2010	Percent change	Female Total 2001	2010	Percent change	Percent Female 2001	2010
TOTAL[a]	6,568,579	6,122,413	−6.8	1,899,440	2,099,055	+10.5	22.5	25.5
Murder and nonnegligent manslaughter	7,011	6,276	−10.5	1,060	751	−29.2	12.5	10.9
Forcible rape	16,552	12,475	−24.6	193	113	−41.5	1.2	1.1
Robbery	61,315	62,383	+1.7	6,978	9,010	+29.1	10.1	12.2
Aggravated assault	243,381	208,367	−14.4	61,311	60,145	−1.9	20.1	22.6
Burglary	158,422	159,813	+0.9	25,654	30,627	+19.4	13.6	15.3
Larceny-theft	468,276	454,079	−3.0	272,887	359,414	+31.7	36.5	43.9
Motor vehicle theft	71,385	36,238	−49.2	13,918	7,887	−43.3	16.4	17.5
Arson	9,369	6,237	−33.4	1,690	1,277	−24.4	15.9	17.4
Violent crime[b]	328,259	289,501	−11.8	69,542	70,019	+0.7	17.3	19.5
Property crime[b]	707,452	656,367	−7.2	314,149	399,205	+27.1	30.4	37.6
Other assaults	624,982	603,501	−3.4	194,814	226,024	+16.0	23.4	26.9
Forgery and counterfeiting	43,623	29,878	−31.5	29,625	17,967	−39.4	40.2	37.6
Fraud	116,414	69,079	−40.7	100,089	51,685	−48.4	45.4	41.5
Embezzlement	6,940	5,538	−20.2	6,750	5,763	−14.6	49.6	50.5
Stolen property; buying, receiving, possessing	62,888	50,045	−20.4	12,664	12,229	−3.4	17.9	19.7
Vandalism	144,703	131,349	−9.2	27,876	30,319	+8.8	16.2	18.9
Weapons; carrying, possessing, etc.	91,440	89,693	−1.9	8,283	8,374	+1.1	8.2	8.4
Prostitution and commercialized vice	16,245	10,844	−33.2	31,011	25,961	−16.3	66.6	68.7
Sex offenses (except forcible rape and prostitution)	52,815	42,833	−18.9	4,448	3,256	−26.8	8.0	7.7
Drug abuse violations	786,831	816,307	+3.7	174,225	198,076	+13.7	17.8	19.1
Gambling	4,365	2,614	−40.1	548	432	−21.2	9.5	9.3
Offenses against the family and children	68,431	52,116	−23.8	20,097	17,455	−13.1	23.1	25.2
Driving under the influence	715,610	639,291	−10.7	144,788	196,727	+35.9	16.6	23.7
Liquor laws	307,444	230,230	−25.1	95,624	91,025	−4.8	23.6	28.5
Drunkenness	344,649	308,784	−10.4	55,186	65,102	+18.0	13.7	17.3
Disorderly conduct	287,509	251,193	−12.6	93,137	99,580	+6.9	23.9	27.8
Vagrancy	13,512	16,981	+25.7	3,276	4,271	+30.4	19.1	19.9
All other offenses (except traffic)	1,777,951	1,782,491	+0.3	483,874	557,410	+15.2	21.3	24.1
Suspicion	1,772	427	−75.9	528	110	−79.2	24.3	23.3
Curfew and loitering law violations	66,516	43,778	−34.2	29,434	18,175	−38.3	31.0	29.6

[a]DOES NOT INCLUDE SUSPICION.
[b]VIOLENT CRIMES ARE MURDER AND NONNEGLIGENT MANSLAUGHTER, FORCIBLE RAPE, ROBBERY, AND AGGRAVATED ASSAULT. PROPERTY CRIMES ARE BURGLARY, LARCENY-THEFT, MOTOR VEHICLE THEFT, AND ARSON.
SOURCES: FEDERAL BUREAU OF INVESTIGATION (2002, TABLE 42; 2011, TABLES 33, 42).

also disproportionately low for burglary, motor-vehicle theft, and arson. In fact, for the UCR Index Crimes, only in the cases of aggravated assaults and larceny thefts are the percentages of women at or above where we would expect given the overall arrest rate. In all remaining non-Index Crime arrest categories, women are at or below what we would expect.

Table 13.1 also illustrates that arrest rates for women between 2001 and 2010 increased more than 10 percent; the rates for men dropped by nearly 7 percent for the same period, creating a difference of more than 17 percent. Much of the increase for women can be attributed to changes in larceny-theft arrests, as this is the largest Index Crime category. However, several other non-Index Crime categories also saw large increases over the time period represented, including other assaults, drug abuse violations, driving under the influence, and all other offenses (except traffic), crime categories in which women were either at or below their overall arrest percentages in both 2001 and 2010. But the differences between the genders were shrinking, owing to the larger gains by women. Also, going back to Table 6.2, note the rather dramatic increases in the prison per capita[2] (per 100,000) incarceration rate for women over the past 30 years.

Collectively, these figures suggest that women commit fewer crimes than men, or the police arrest women less frequently than they arrest men. Second, male and female offenders are predisposed to commit different offenses, with men more prone to commit the more serious Index Crimes (especially violent crime) and women are disproportionately more likely to be arrested for crimes of financial gain. The question then becomes, how much attention do female offenders get from the criminal justice system in general and corrections systems in particular? Moreover, what might account for the differences between men's and women's outcomes after arrest? The evidence suggests that female offenders and female corrections workers are second-class citizens in a system that places a great premium on status. To gain a more complete perspective on this phenomenon, we briefly return to criminological theory, especially theories specifically developed to explain female criminality.

EXPLAINING FEMALE OFFENDERS

We explored general theories of crime and criminality in Chapter 1. Most of those explanations, largely developed by men to explain the propensities of other men for crime, are generally gender-neutral or gender-negative. That is, either they do not make a distinction between boys and girls, men and women, or they simply do not address gender. Not everyone, however, would agree that crime theories are or should be gender neutral. For example, some biogenic theorists—those who look to human biology for answers—might look to female biochemistry for answers about the presence or absence of crime propensities. Other theorists suggest we look at the power-sharing arrangements or lack of them in contemporary society as yielding insights into past and present crime statistics for women. Most students of human nature would agree that women are different from men, in this case in the kinds and volume of crimes they commit. Few can tell us why these differences exist.

More than 100 years ago, criminologists noticed these differences in offending rates and found female offenders to be a mystery. Italian prison doctor Lombroso (1876), writing in the last quarter of the nineteenth century, believed women criminals were an aberration, basically masculinized women. Early in the twentieth century, psychoanalyst Freud (1933) considered female criminals to be women who lacked proper maternal instincts. These views, sexist in orientation and impact, lasted well into the twentieth century.

By mid-century, cracks began appearing in the sexist body of theorizing about female criminality. For example, Pollack (1950) observed that the crimes with the highest prevalence among women—including shoplifting, domestic theft, and theft by prostitution—had low detection rates; that even when detected, the victims were generally unwilling to report the incidents; and, last, that even when detected and reported, female offenders were unlikely to suffer the full brunt of the criminal justice system. This last point led to the idea that the police responded chivalrously to female offenders, while the courts may act in a paternalistic fashion, viewing their crimes as evidence of a wayward or willful "child," the result being a form of "gendered justice" (Simpson 1989; Visher 1983).

In the mid-1970s, two criminologists, Adler (1975) and Simon (1975), expounded on the **liberation hypothesis**. Adler posited that women's liberation had opened up criminal activities to a new generation of women, and she predicted an end to the traditional male-female distinctions in crime. Simon, looking at the same data, came to a slightly different conclusion. She argued that women's liberation alone did not cause the changes in the incidence of women's involvement in crime; rather, its role in creating the rising tide of female criminality was indirect by increasing opportunities in the labor market.

Researchers have found the idea of a new type of female offender to be largely unsupportable (Steffensmeier 1980; Steffensmeier and Cobb 1981; Weis 1981; but also see R. L. Austin 1982). Nevertheless, the work of Adler and Simon recast the debate on women's criminality. After Adler and Simon, society could no longer view women as less criminally involved simply because of their biology; other forces were at work, perhaps women's liberation and changes in the workplace. In their intellectual wake, three forms of feminist criminology emerged in the 1970s and 1980s. First, **radical feminism** argued that male power and privilege both define all social relations and are the primary cause of all social inequities—two factors related to women's criminality. In the behaviors of many young female offenders, Chesney-Lind (1973) saw attempts to flee abusive and controlling fathers; their crimes—running away from home, incorrigibility, even prostitution—were simply survival strategies. Petty criminality, insisted Chesney-Lind, is a way out, a means of empowerment, for many young women. Moreover, the police and the courts are extensions of the patriarchal system: they assume the paternal role in the public sphere.

The intersection of social class and gender is the nexus of crime for the third form of feminist criminology, **socialist feminism**, which tells us that we must consider both variables to appreciate fully the role of either on female criminality. Blending neo-Marxism and socialist feminism, Hagan (1989) believed that family structure creates differential

power dynamics between husbands and wives, and between their male and female children. From this perspective, **patriarchal families** produce daughters whose futures are limited to domestic labor and consumption; moreover, the families, but especially the fathers, exercise great control over the lives of these girls and young women. The future and career opportunities of the male children of patriarchal families are far more open, as are their opportunities and their family's expectations of youthful misbehavior. In **egalitarian families**, by contrast, husbands and wives share power, and their positions in society are equal. The families transfer this equanimity to their children: both boy and girl offspring enjoy equal access to normalcy and criminality. **Power-control theory**, then, suggests that the presence of power and the absence of control in egalitarian families create conditions conducive to common forms of delinquency for both boys and girls (Hagan, Simpson, and Gillis 1985).

The third variant of feminist criminology derives from Marxism. According to **Marxist feminism**, male dominance reflects a social ideology that is willing to subjugate women, first to capital and second to men (Beirne and Messerschmidt 2000). Women's often-trivialized labor is essential to capitalism's success, and women's crimes—including shoplifting, prostitution, and domestic violence against their children or spouses—are a reflection of their enforced domesticity (Balkan, Berger, and Schmidt 1980, 211).

What does the empirical evidence say about the ability of these perspectives to explain crimes by women? Both radical feminism and Marxist feminism offer explanations that are more ideology than theory (Winfree and Abadinsky 2010). Given the relatively unchanging nature of male dominance and other aspects of patriarchal society, adequate tests of these theories are nearly impossible (Akers 1994). However, tests of power-control theory have yielded generally positive results for delinquency (Winfree and Abadinsky 2010, 325). Perhaps the most important contribution of feminist criminologists has been to focus research on gender differences. After all, the best single predictor of crime and delinquency is a person's gender. In corrections research, the introduction of gender into program studies holds great potential to increase our understanding of crime and the criminality of both men and women, not to mention the functioning of corrections agencies.

INSTITUTIONAL CORRECTIONS FOR FEMALE OFFENDERS

Historically, female offenders—as was the case with their male counterparts—were rarely imprisoned for long periods of time, unless they were members of the nobility and they threatened the current ruler. Specialized facilities for female offenders were uncommon in medieval England. In the eighteenth century, Becarria railed against keeping male and female prisoners in the same cells, as was a common practice for another 100 years. One of the first specialized prisons for women was Amsterdam's *Spinhuis*, a former Ursulan convent that opened its doors in 1597; women labored in this workhouse prison under what even at the time were appalling conditions that approached slavery. In Colonial America, when women were punished for wrongdoings, they generally went to the stocks or the pillory for petty crimes or in more serious cases, including accusations of witchcraft, they were burned or hung, although the imposition of the death penalty was a rarity (Newman 2008).

New York's Auburn Prison first admitted women in 1825, 4 years after the prison was first occupied (Harris 1998). Pennsylvania's Eastern State Penitentiary admitted women almost from the day the facility opened in 1829. At Auburn, officials housed female inmates above the penitentiary kitchen, subject to not-so-benign neglect, abuse, and outright indifference. In the Pennsylvania facility, where extreme isolation and repentance were the order of the day, the women languished in their cells, suffering the same physical and psychological distress as the men. After several scandals at Auburn, including an inmate pregnancy, New York opened a separate women's facility, the Mount Pleasant Female Prison, in 1835. This prison, which remained open for 33 years, was the first separate women's facility in the United States.

In 1873, nearly a century after Beccaria first called for separating inmates by age and gender, and several years after Mount Pleasant closed its doors because of crowding, Indianapolis, Indiana opened the first US prison for women run by women. Similar facilities in Massachusetts (1877) and New York (1887) soon followed. However, in some states, like Maryland, prisons housed men and women in the same facilities from their nineteenth century openings until well into the twentieth century (Young 2001).

The first women-only prisons were cottage-like in appearance. They more closely resembled Brockway-style reformatories than Auburn-style prisons, which is not surprising because Brockway operated the Detroit House of Shelter for Women as a reformatory in the 1870s. In the cottage-style **women's reformatory**, female staff supervised inmates and taught them appropriate domestic skills.

In the women's reformatories, prison officials tended to treat the inmates at best as wayward children and at worst as contemptible and beyond redemption (L. M. Dodge 1999; Freedman 1981; Rafter 1985). In fact, that was the standard treatment of women in prison throughout the nineteenth century and much of the twentieth century. The general thinking was that these women, by breaking the law, also had betrayed their gender (L. M. Dodge; Harris 1998; also see Butler 1997). The idea of betrayal was particularly strong in the nineteenth century in the American West, where women often lived in men's penitentiaries:

> The woman prisoner may have appeared divorced from the gender dynamics that affected womanhood, but that perception rested on a shallow foundation. The incarcerated female of the nineteenth century bore a double identity—woman and criminal. Conversely, noncriminal women, although they often denied it, shared commonality with the incarcerated woman; if the slender thread of social acceptability—a sometimes frayed and tangled line—snapped, a woman's existence changed in an instant. (Butler 1997, 21)

Women of color in the Old West often faced even more desperate conditions when they conflicted with the law than their white sisters. This was the same for black women in the East (Young 2001).

An emergent philosophy about women guided late-nineteenth-century women's prisons. That is, the ideal woman was "pure, honest, and innocent on the one hand, and . . . deceitful, designing, and susceptible to corruption on the other" (Harris 1998, 76). This violation of the social construct of ideal womanhood most offended Victorian moralists (cf., Abrams and Curran 2000; Zedner 1995). In the 1860s, the English social critic Henry Mayhew emphasized this **duality of women**—Madonna and whore—in his description of criminal women: "In them one sees the most hideous picture of all human weakness and depravity—a picture the more striking because exhibiting the coarsest and rudest moral features in connection with a being whom we are apt to regard as the most graceful and gentle form of humanity" (Mayhew quoted in Zedner 1995, 332). As Mara Dodge so succinctly notes, "The woman who violated the law transgressed not only legal norms, but the boundaries of femininity itself" (1999, 908).

As a result of prevailing social values, the task of the women-only prisons was to instill in inmates an appreciation for the proper role of women in society. Prison staff taught women domestic skills. Inmates were encouraged to create make-believe families in their cottage-style prisons.

By 1940, 23 states had separate women's prison facilities; by 1975, that number had increased to 34. The remaining states contracted with other states or the private sector to house female prisoners. The first federal women's prison was in rural Alderson, West Virginia, now FCI-Alderson and opened in 1927 as a cottage-style reformatory. States abandoned the reformatory model in the mid-1930s, to be replaced by a campus model taken from the vocational training programs in men's correctional facilities. In women's prisons, the programs emphasized marketable and gender-specific skills, consistent with the philosophical underpinnings of women's prisons (Rafter 1985).

WOMEN IN JAILS TODAY

The proportion of women in the nation's jail population nearly doubled between 1983 and 2010, from 6 percent to almost 13 percent.[3] Of a total jail population of 748,728 in 2010, 92,368 were women, over six times the number of women incarcerated in 1983. In this same period, the number of male jail inmates increased from 205,000 to 656,360. By any measure, then, the increases for females were remarkable. However, to keep things in perspective, in the most recent jail inmate survey (2005), the per capita rate for females was one-seventh the rate of males.

Most jails—roughly 85 percent—hold both males and females, although by law and practice all jails must maintain sight and sound segregation.[4] Another 13 percent held men only. Only 32 jails in the United States held women only, half of them in the South and another 20 percent in California. Finally, the nation's Bureau of Prisons (BOP) operated 12 federal jails (mainly metropolitan detention centers), ten of which held both genders, while the remaining two confined only men.

JAIL INMATES The most recent gender-specific analyses of US jail populations found more female jail inmates were black (44 percent) than any other racial or ethnic group, followed by whites (36 percent), Hispanics (15 percent), and others (5 percent).[5] Their median age was 31, with about half between 25 and 34 years of age. More had been married at some time in their lives than not, but only 15 percent were currently married. Jailed women were less likely than were those in the general population to have been married; but nearly 80 percent of them were mothers—the average was two children apiece—and many had minor children. Between 5 and 10 percent of them were pregnant on admission. Fifty-five percent had finished high school, about the same rate as jailed men. The percentage of convicted female inmates (46 percent) was about the same as for males.

GENDER-BASED DIFFERENCES IN JAIL INMATE POPULATIONS During the past decade, researchers have identified four distinct differences in the sociolegal characteristics of female and male jail inmates, distinctions that may play important roles in women inmates' adjustment to life in and out of jail. First, as a rule, women do not have the breadth and depth of contacts with the jail system that we find among men. The net result is that a larger proportion of women than men have special problems adjusting to both the jail experience and the stigma of jail (Lindquist and Lindquist 1997; Singer et al. 1995).

Second, offense-specific programming in jails generally targets the needs of the largest resident group—male inmates. Hence, there are far fewer jail-based interventions that address women's gender-specific needs (Green et al. 2005).

Third, drugs play a proportionately larger role in the illegal activities of women than they do for men, and this fact adds more to the legal and social stigma

of women than it does for men, apart from the fact that their treatment needs may also be different from those of male inmates (Peters et al. 1997). More than just an intra-jail programming issue, drug use by jailed women has implications beyond jail (or prison), as documented in Box 13.1.

Fourth, there are significant gender-specific differences in the area of physical and sexual abuse. In a 1996 survey, nearly half of all female jail inmates indicated that they were abused either physically or

---

WELFARE BAN IMPACTS FEMALE DRUG OFFENDERS AND THEIR CHILDREN   BOX 13.1

In 1996, Congress passed the Welfare Reform Act. Section 115 of the act placed a lifetime ban on temporary aid to needy families (TANF) and food stamps for people convicted of using or selling drugs.[6] This ban affects only those convicted of drug-related crimes; no other offenders suffered a similar loss of entitlement. Section 115 received bipartisan support in Congress after two minutes of debate.[7]

Critics charge that Section 115 is discriminatory. That is, 48 percent of the women affected by it were black or Hispanic. In Alabama, Delaware, Illinois, Mississippi, and Virginia the majority of women affected by the ban were black; in Pennsylvania and Texas, black women and Latinas represented more than 50 percent of those affected. The law's opponents claim women of color are particularly susceptible to this law for several reasons. First, drug-law enforcement policies are racially biased, which accounts for the rapid growth of both African American women and Latinas in the offender population. Second, socioeconomic inequalities based on race and gender place black and Hispanic mothers at a unique risk of poverty and an equally unique dependence on the welfare system.

Dalley observes that most mothers when released from jails and prisons will be reunited with their children, but many will not be able to live crime-free or drug-free lives or maintain stable relationships with their children. Drug-involved female offenders, including those sent to jail and prison, are not by definition bad parents, lacking in parenting skills, or abusive mothers. However, they may need monetary and other support when they leave correctional facilities. Given the number of states that have opted out of Section 115, it would appear that many in government believe the lifetime ban is a poorly conceived policy. Nonetheless, tens of thousands of women and their children remain under its grip.

During the past decade, many interest groups have petitioned Congress and the Department of Health and Social Services, asking for the elimination or severe curtailment of this law. However, it remains unchanged. Connecticut, Michigan, New Hampshire, New York, Ohio, Oklahoma, Oregon, Vermont, and the District of Columbia opted out of the support program since the law's inception. Increasingly, other states have taken advantage of ways to limit these restrictions. For example, by 2005, 32 states had exempted all or some convicted felons from restrictions on TANF and 35 states had modified the ban on food stamps. In a study of 23 states with the ban, Allard estimated it impacted the lives of 92,000 women and 135,000 children.

SOURCES: ALLARD (2002); DALLEY (2002); GAO (2005); KING (2002); SURRATT (2003).

sexually before incarceration, and a quarter of them reported being raped (Harlow 1998, 1999). The abuse rate for women inmates was almost four times that reported for men inmates; the rape rate was almost ten times greater. By 2002, even more female inmates reported being physically or sexually abused (55 percent). Although men reported abuse primarily as children, women reported similar rates as children and as adults (Harlow 1998, 1999; James and Glaze 2006). While in jail, 3.1 percent of the females—compared to 1.3 percent of the males—reported an inmate-on-inmate sexual victimization; females were less likely to report a staff-initiated sexual assault than were males (1.5 percent versus 2.1 percent) (Beck et al. 2010).

These four factors, combined with the general lack of treatment programs for women in jails (Ross and Lawrence 1998), make the incarceration experience even more threatening for and more potentially damaging to female inmates than for their male counterparts (Maeve 2001). Bill (1998) suggests that women's correctional facilities re-victimize many women, largely through security procedures that perpetuate feelings of powerlessness. According to Heney and Kristiansen (1998), many women relive their experiences of abuse through the security procedures—the pat-downs and body searches—that are a common part of correctional operations. Moreover, the potential for sexual assault is a constant when male correctional officers (COs) supervise female inmates (Stein 1996; Zupan 1992).

The failure to provide adequate or even marginal health care services in jail often translates into long-term problems for women. Maeve (2001, 166) summarizes the issue: "Dumping women in the middle of the night, without money, with no way to let friends or family know that they are out, back into neighborhoods already disorganized, leaves already vulnerable women with the worst possible 'new beginnings.'" Women who enter jail with problems rarely find themselves in better physical or mental shape when they leave. As Lynch and associates (2012) make clear, significant numbers of women inmates enter jail with serious mental illness, post-traumatic stress induced by a lifetime of victimization, and substance use disorder—the latter often associated with the previous two issues; collectively, these issues and the absence of meaningful gender-specific programs to address them in jail create a recipe for reentry disaster.

WOMEN IN PRISONS

In Chapter 6, we noted that the per capita prison rate for women is rising faster than for men. The proportion of state and federal prisoners who are female is also increasing. In 1995, less than 6 percent of all prisoners were female; in 2010, the nation's state and federal prisons held nearly 113,000 females, or 7 percent of the prison population. In 2000, the per capita rate for females was 59; in 2010 their rate was 67. For males, the per capita rate increased from 904 to 943. In absolute numbers, proportions, and per capita rates, women prison inmates are a growing problem, but prison populations, like those of jails, are clearly dominated by men.

PRISON INMATES The average federal female prisoner is 36 years old, about the same age as the average federal male prisoner.[8] She is black or Hispanic, she has a high school diploma or its equivalent, and she has never been married. The average woman in a state prison is a bit different: she is 33 years old (a year older than the average male inmate in a state prison), she is far more likely to be black, she is less educated (40 percent do not have a high school diploma or its equivalent), and she has never married.

GENDER-BASED DIFFERENCES IN PRISON INMATE POPULATIONS In 2010, the most serious crime committed by 41 percent of the women entering federal prison was a drug offense, compared to 33 percent of the males.[9] For men, the percentages for the remaining types of federal crimes, in descending order, were immigration offenses (30) weapons offenses (13), property offenses (9), public order offenses (8) and violent offenses (5). For women, the percentages were as follows: property offenses (29), immigration offenses (14), public order offenses (9), weapons offenses (3), and violent offenses (3).

In terms of new commitments to state prisons in 2010, drug offenses accounted for 34 percent of newly committed female prisoners' most serious crimes, compared to 26 percent for males.[10] For men, the percentages for the remaining types of state crimes, in descending order, were violent offenses (31), property offenses (26), and public order offenses (17). For women the percentages are: property offenses (38), violent offenses (18), and public order offenses (10).

The nation's antidrug policies have had a gender-specific impact, as disproportionately more women find their way into state and federal prisons for drug-related crimes than do men. Owen finds fault with both the policies and incarceration as punishment:

> Women in prison represent a very specific failure of conventional society—and public policy—to recognize the damage done to women through the oppression of patriarchy, economic marginalization, and the wider-reaching effects of such short-sighted and detrimental policies as the war on drugs and the overreliance on incarceration as social control. (Owen 1998, 192)

In general, women receive substantially lighter sentences than men. As Starr (2012) has reported for federal sentences, women are significantly more likely to avoid charges and convictions than men. However, once convicted they are twice as likely to avoid incarceration as men. Overall, men's sentences are over 60 percent longer than women for the same federal offenses. Doerner (2009, 2010) finds the gender gap at the federal level is smaller for fraud cases than drug-related and firearms cases. She further speculates on these differences, by suggesting:

> [G]ender continues to influence the sentencing process in U.S. federal courts despite guidelines designed to avoid differential sentencing. For instance, judges and prosecutors circumvent the guidelines through the use of sentencing departures and ultimately treat female defendants more leniently than male defendants. Although many explanations may exist for this behavior, one possibility may be that judges treat women more leniently for practical reasons, such as their greater caretaking responsibility. (2009, v)

At the state level, the sentences for 40 percent of all female prisoners were less than 5 years, compared with about 25 percent of male prisoners. About 25 percent of the women had sentences of 15 years or more, including life in prison and the death penalty; the equivalent for men was 33 percent. These disparities are at least in part a product of differences in offense patterns: "Women [are] more likely than men to be in prison for drug and property offenses, which [have] shorter average sentences than violent offenses" (Snell 1994, 4; also see Ditton and Wilson 1999, 6).

More than receiving shorter sentences, female offenders serve less time in prison (Ditton and Wilson 1999). In the mid-1990s, women served an average of 18 months for all offenses, compared with 26 months for men. Drug and public-order offenders experienced the smallest disparities, averaging four and two months respectively, with women serving less time on average. For violent offenses, women served an average of nine months less than men did. Similarly, women whose commitment offense was a property offense served eight months less than males convicted of the same offenses. In no category of offenses did women serve longer sentences than men. This is also true of federal sentences, where sentencing guidelines wield an especially heavy guiding hand.

Of course it could also be that women are less inclined to "act out" in the prison environment, and, thereby, are able to take advantage of the few benefits of good time accorded under current sentencing regimes. At this point, we simply do not know how to explain the observed differences in time served or any of the other disparities between the fate of men and women in the correctional system, just as similar insights into the sentencing practices of federal judges elude us.

OPERATING WOMEN'S CORRECTIONAL FACILITIES

The operation of correctional facilities for women shares all of the characteristics and concerns found in men's prisons, plus a few additional ones. This is true whether local, state, or federal governments operate the facility, or it is a privately operated jail or prison. This is also true whether the facility is for women only or is a **co-correctional unit**, the latter a facility housing both men and women, although they use sound and sight separation to the greatest extent possible.

CLASSIFICATION SCHEMES

Classification systems are central to the daily operation of any institutional correctional facility, a fact underscored in Chapter 6. What should the classification system for a women's prison look like? How should it differ from the one employed in a men's prison? For the federal government, the US Bureau of Prisons (2000) uses standardized gender-specific classification schemes. This system is based on a combination of threat assessment (past criminal and antisocial behavior and affiliations) and possible mitigating factors, including family or community ties and precommitment status, such as release on recognizance and voluntary surrender. There are subtle differences between the forms employed for the classification of women and men. By way of example, belonging to what essentially is a gang does not have an effect on the classification of women, while it can have a profound impact on where male inmates are housed. In addition, women's **custody variance score**, which represents the sum of risk factors and can determine an increase or decrease in their security levels, is different from that of men.

The states present a different and quite diverse picture of classification schemes, as revealed by two important studies, conducted a decade apart. In Burke and Adams's (1991, 6) survey of 48 departments of corrections (DOCs), four states reported significant differences in classification; and four others adapted their classification systems or used them differently for women, but used identical institutional policies and procedures. The remaining 40 states used the same classification system for women and men. As a rule, states generally classify women's prisons as lower-risk facilities than men's prisons. Such facilities typically place less emphasis on security and more emphasis on **habilation**, or the process of acquiring the basic life skills needed to function

in society. Nevertheless, acquiring such skills can only happen when those prisons use a distinct classification system and operate with distinct policies and procedures.

Ten years later, Van Voorhis and Presser (2001) explored state *and* federal classification schemes. Their findings were very similar to those in Burke and Adams's report. Again, four states (Idaho, Massachusetts, New York, and Ohio) indicated that they used separate classification systems for women, and another four used different cutoff scores for women. Fourteen state DOCs responded that they assess women and men differently. When asked whether women have unique needs that required addressing in correctional settings, most of the survey respondents, respondents replied yes. Among the issues they identified were trauma and abuse, self-esteem and assertiveness, vocational and job skills, medical care, mental health, parenting and childcare, and relationships. Most agreed that classification should address issues of security and public safety. However, many classification personnel suggested that it also should address goals that are more central to women offenders, including habilation *and* rehabilitation, transitional programming related to parenting and family issues, and moving women who have committed minor offenses to lower custody levels or out of prisons and jails and into community facilities (Van Voorhis and Presser 2001, 13).

Given the fact that most states in the two studies of classification systems used the same system for both genders, whatever the type of institution, the logical conclusion is that the systems in place in many states are failing to meet women's needs.

Based on a careful examination of the DOCs that employed gender-specific classification systems, Burke and Adams (1991) make several recommendations for change:

- Classification systems for women's facilities must be system-specific and perhaps even institution-specific. Simply importing classification models from other states or institutions may not provide a workable solution.
- The development of a risk-based classification tool for women offenders must incorporate gender-specific elements. That is, it must

address the real and objective risks posed by the inmate population at a given institution. As we have seen, women and men do not commit the same kinds of crimes in the same proportions. Women tend to be less violent and so pose different security risks for one another in prison. All risk-based classification tools should include these factors.

● Emergent classification schemes should consider the greater emphasis on habilitation—especially the interactive living arrangements—found in most women's prisons when compared with men's prisons.

● Those responsible for the classification system must guard against creating a *completely* gender-specific classification system, as opposed to one that is informed by and sensitive to the unique needs of female inmates. The statewide system should be gender neutral, just as it should be racially neutral. Legal and constitutional principles guide this gender-neutrality position.

In sum, inmate classification is one area that appears to need more attention from prison managers, who can minimize legal challenges and constitutional concerns by careful assessment of current and prospective classification schemes. The key to a workable system, claimed Burke and Adams, was to ground inmate classification in the institution's mission and the needs of the institution's inmate population. Judging by Van Voorhis and Presser's reexamination of state classification systems 10 years later, it appears that few DOCs have taken that recommendation to heart.

Some penologists suggest that states may employ identical systems for men and women as a legal shield.[11] That is, classification systems traditionally have fallen into the same legal category as equal access to housing, legal services, programming, employee wages, and the like. Critics view the adoption of a system of classification that uses gender to assign people to different programs and to different security levels as a form of gender discrimination (Brennan 1998). According to Van Voorhis and Presser (2001, 9), that thinking is faulty on three counts:

1 a system that is valid for men may not be valid for women;

2 a system that recognizes men's needs more so than women's is already biased; and

3 more maximum-security male inmates commit predatory acts than do maximum-security female inmates, which suggests that the system already lacks parity.

The Michigan Supreme Court agreed with this analysis. Its decision in *Cain v. Michigan Department of Corrections* (1996) led the state's DOC to adopt different cutoff scores for women.[12] Given the disparate nature of existing classification systems, corrections agencies may well come to the opinion that they are more likely to be targeted with litigation for failing to provide separate classification systems for women and men than for doing so (J. F. Austin, Chan, and Elms 1993). Is this the right decision? We offer a partial answer in Box 13.2.

The debate over the need for gender-specific or gender-sensitive classification schemes, and their links to post-prison survival, is unlikely to disappear (Hannah-Moffat 2009; Heilbrun et al. 2008). A meta-analysis by Smith, Cullen, and Latessa (2009) of 27 studies that used the scores of 14,737 women has found that the Level of Service Inventory-Revised (LSI-R) predicts recidivism equally well for male and female offenders. Holtfreter and Cupp (2007; see too Holtfreter, Reisig, and Morash 2004) find that the LSI-R does work reasonably well for predicting outcomes for females whose criminality resembles that of males; however, the LSI-R may not work well with women who follow a "gendered pathway" to crime, which often includes intense victimization experiences, abuse, and poverty as children. Central to this problem, maintains Hannah-Moffat (2009, 216), is the absence of interdisciplinary research on the complex relationships between risk prediction, which such instruments have as their reason for being, and gender, race, and penal policy.

INMATE CULTURE IN WOMEN'S PRISONS AND JAILS

In Chapter 7, we looked at the general inmate subculture. We now examine how the inmate communities differ by gender. Actually, many similarities exist in all inmate communities. We find prisonization

PREDICTING PRISON VIOLENCE: A COMPARISON OF MALE AND FEMALE PRISON INMATES   BOX 13.2

Since the late 1980s, women's adjustment to prison life, particularly their avoidance of involvement in prison-based violence, has taken center stage in prison-classification schemes. The environmental stressors associated with prison life clearly affect men differently from women. Women tend to report more anxiety, depression, and psychotic episodes than men. In short, women and men may have different risk factors. Harer and Langan explored this premise by using data collected from nearly 25,000 women and 178,000 men newly admitted to the federal prisons between 1991 and 1998. Harer and Langan wanted to assess the predictive validity of an eight-item risk classification scheme: Would it accurately predict who is at greater risk for violence-related misconduct in the year following prison admission? The eight items were: (1) *type of detainer* in place for the offender, that is, did another jurisdiction want to prosecute the inmate; (2) *severity of current offense*; (3) *history of escapes*; (4) *history of violence* in and out of prison; (5) *precommitment status* while being tried; (6) *age*; (7) *criminal history*, as a measure of prior criminal record; and (8) *education* at admission.

What did they find? First, the instrument equally predicted male and female violence-related misconduct. Second, just as is the case in the free society outside prison, women in prison commit far less serious rule violations than men. Third, education is an equally powerful predictor for men's and women's success on parole. With respect to having separate male and female classification systems, the researchers were unclear. The instrument worked well for both; however, given the variances in types of violence reported for men versus women, and the tendency to use rank-ordering systems (i.e., minimum, low, medium and high levels of risk), the system should consider the gender differences in types and seriousness of inmate behavior. (Remember: The federal government uses a slightly different system for men and women.) Harer and Langan propose that the BOP use the same instrument, but cut the interval scores, which range from 0 to 27, differently for men and women. If the BOP had adopted their recommendations, they suggest 97 percent of the women would be classified as minimum security, with 2 percent as low and 1 percent as medium or high. Such a system would more accurately reflect the actual threat posed by female inmates to the institution and their peers than does the current system.

SOURCES: HARER AND LANGAN (2001); LINDQUIST AND LINDQUIST (1997); WARREN ET AL. (2004).

in both women's and men's facilities with women feeling the deprivations of incarceration just as intensely as men. Women also suffer deprivations not reported by men, including the loss of their children (Baunach 1985; Pollock 2002; Smart 1976). Indeed, women's pains of imprisonment may be greater than that experienced by men, especially if we factor in fear (Pogrebin and Dodge 2001).

The reality of life in women's facilities—that is generally less violent than in men's facilities—may be less important than inmate perceptions. Women also may be affected more than men by the shame of their confinement (M. Dodge and Pogrebin 2001).

By way of example, consider one woman's memory of her first hours in prison:

> I try to forget what it was like in prison most of the time. When I just got there they stripped me down and this guard did a full body search. I was shocked. I never had anyone touch me like that, especially with other guards just standing there watching me. Then they threw me these clothes and took me to a cell. While we were walking, some girls were yelling names at me. It was the most scary thing I had ever seen. (Pogrebin and Dodge 2001, 538)

Women also display acute needs for emotional support in prison, particularly the need to establish emotional relationships with other women (Giallambardo 1966; Ward and Kassebaum 1965). Female inmates are far less criminalized than their male counterparts; that is, they generally have committed less-serious crimes and were far less involved in criminal subcultures outside prison (Bowker 1981, 410). Cut off from their children and families and friends, women in prisons appear to experience feelings of helplessness, powerlessness, dependency, and despair far more than their male peers do (Mahan 1984, 381; also see Gibson 1976, 99; Harman, Smith, and Egan 2007). Conversely, where women maintain better social support networks with those living outside prison, but especially their children, they experience fewer conflicts with the prison administration (Jiang and Winfree 2006).[13]

Women in prisons also live by an inmate code and adopt various roles to cope with incarceration (Giallambardo 1966; Mahan 1984). Those roles, like those male inmates adopt, center on the exercise of power, the delivery of goods and services, and sexual relationships (Giallambardo 1966; Simmons 1975). Heffernan (1972) employed Sykes's (1958) hypothesis about these pains of imprisonment in her study of the District of Columbia Women's Reformatory at Occoquan, Virginia. Heffernan identified roughly half of the participants in the study as *squares*: primarily women who were situational offenders, "good Christian women" who wanted to rectify their mistake through good deeds and clean living. Some female inmates, however, were *in the life*—that is, they were leading the same antisocial lives in prison that they had led on the streets. Prison life was not going to change them. Their hardcore stance and lengthy experience with the criminal justice system demanded that they adopt an antiauthoritarian and, in particular, anti-institutional perspective. Still others were **cools**, inmates who manipulated other inmates to make their own time pass more quickly and easily. These roles, argued Heffernan, were largely extensions of the women's preprison identities.

Owen's (1998) study of the Central California Women's Facility, the largest women's prison in the world, provides unique insights. The term she used to describe the defiance exhibited by certain inmates was **the mix**. According to Owen, the mix "is characterized by a continuation of the behavior that led to imprisonment, a life revolving around drugs, intense, volatile, and often destructive relationships, and non-rule abiding behavior" (3). Like Heffernan, Owen also believes that women's lives in prison are closely tied to their lives before and predictive of their lives after. Women in prisons, especially the economically or racially marginalized, have much in common with male inmates. However, women also face the unique challenges generated by pervasive sexual and personal oppression. Surviving the mix, or making it in prison and on the outside, is a constant struggle for some women. For others, whom Owen described as a small minority of women inmates, the lure and excitement of the life—drugs, fighting, volatile intimate relationships—is too hard to resist.

The functions of the inmate subculture in prisons for men and women are generally viewed as different. The subculture in men's prisons exists largely to protect inmates from one another; it also helps to neutralize the rejection associated with incarceration and provides a buffer between inmates and staff. In women's prisons, the subculture exists for these reasons plus one more: emotional support (B. Owen 1998; Pollock-Byrne 1990, 59–63; Welch 1996, 360).

Evidence that women in prison need more emotional support than men comes from their tendency to create **play families** or **pseudo-families**, to assume the role of spouse, parent, child, sibling, or grandparent for one another (Heffernan 1972; MacKenzie, Robinson, and Campbell 1995, but also see Girshick 1999; Ward and Kassebaum 1965). In some instances, the role-play is so serious that inmates prepare "official" papers documenting an adoption, a wedding, even a divorce. Owen explains it this way:

> These relationships with other prisoners mediate how women learn to do their time and may also provide some protection from the self-destruction of the mix. Thus, surviving the mix is grounded in a woman's ability to develop a satisfying and productive routine within the prison and the nature of her relationships with other prisoners. (1998, 8)

Pseudo-families exist in twenty-first century women's prisons, although it would appear that their intent is less sexual or emotive and more for the creation of an extended social support network (Huggins, Capeheart, and Newman 2006). Their prevalence may also be declining. Pollock (2002) argues that play families are much less important now than they were in the past (see also, Greer 2000; Severance 2005). Female inmates, Pollock says, are "less inclined to introspection and continue to involve themselves in relationships, drugs, and other distractions to divert their attention away from looking at their own behavior" (Pollock 2002: 39). The contradictory nature of these findings appears to signal that the culture of women's prisons is changing (see Box 13.3).

WOMEN AND ALTERNATIVES TO INCARCERATION

In this section, we examine whether there is a gender bias in the use of alternatives to incarceration. We focus on a central question: to what extent are women being disproportionately placed in community corrections programs rather than institutional programs?

FEMALE PROBATIONERS AND PAROLEES

Looking at the percentage of arrestees who are female (24 percent), we would assume, all things being equal (and random), that the percentages of females on probation and in prison or jail would match this figure. One alternative interpretation is that for some reason the police are disproportionately arresting innocent women. We already know from earlier discussions in this chapter that in jails and in both state and federal prisons, convicted women account for less than 24 percent of the inmates. Women accused of crimes are even less likely than men to spend time in jail before trial or, once convicted, to serve their sentences in jail (Stephan 2001). Women convicted of felonies, it also appears, are less likely to end up in prison.

In absolute numbers, the probation sector has grown like no other part of the nation's corrections system (see Figure 4.1). This statement is true of the entire sector, but it is especially true for female probationers. From 1990 to 2010, the number of women on probation increased from 481,000 to 712,084; the proportion of female probationers increased from 18 percent to 24 percent (Glaze and Bonczar 2006; 2011). In this regard, the percentage of females placed on probation is very close to the percentage of female arrestees.

The parole sector experienced similar growth trends. The number of female parolees increased from 42,500 in 1982 to 103,374 in 2010 and from 8 percent to 12 percent of all parolees in each year, respectively (Glaze and Bonczar 2006, 2011). Although the number of female parolees has increased over the past nearly 30 years, and is even higher than their proportion of the prisoner population, it is far below the female proportion of either arrestees or probationers.

These trends suggest that community corrections alternatives, but especially intermediate sanctions, for women will continue to grow in the next decade. This generalization is especially true of reentry programs, as the number of females in prison increases at unprecedented rates. The question now becomes a different one: What is a successful gender-specific community corrections program?

GENDER AND COMMUNITY CORRECTIONS

McCarthy and McCarthy (1991, 286–91) suggest that to be successful, community-based programs for female offenders should focus on three areas. The first is the development of economic independence, which relies heavily on job-readiness training, including vocational testing, using public transportation, job-seeking skills, interviewing skills, and self-esteem training; vocational training, which emphasizes in-house training and pretraining readiness for those who will receive on-the-job training with new employers; job development and placement with special emphasis on how to deal with the workplace, including dealing with harassment; and follow-up services. Follow-up is especially important because women experience more problems than men, for example, with child-care, self-esteem, and sexual harassment.

Second, McCarthy and McCarthy (1991) believe that community-based programs should incorporate

THE CHANGING NATURE OF THE FEMALE INMATE SUBCULTURE   BOX 13.3

Recent research on life in women's prisons reveals findings so contradictory that we could question whether the researchers were studying the same phenomenon. Greer interviewed 35 female inmates in a Midwestern state correctional institution. She made the following observations about the women she studied:

● *Friendships among female offenders*: few of the friendships she observed or heard described seemed to be more than superficial, tied largely to the immediate experience. Most of the female inmates—and the study's author—expressed high levels of skepticism about the durability and depth of friendships forged in prison.

● *Sexual relationships among inmates*: the inmates expressed either very positive or very negative attitudes about sexual relationships between women in prison. Although most believed that many women were engaging in homosexual activities, less than a third admitted to it. Where inmates in earlier studies had formed homosexual relationships to lessen the pains of imprisonment, the women in Greer's study expressed the opinion that homosexual relationships, though an important part of the prison culture, are all about manipulation and power, not the attraction or compatibility between partners. Economics played a central role; a primary reason given for engaging in sexual relations with another woman was economic. Wanting to fit into the prison culture and wanting affection were also mentioned as reasons, but less frequently. By contrast, female inmates who participated in sexual relationships for money or merchandise were called canteen or commissary whores.

● *Lack of play families*: the play families that were reported in previous research on the inmate culture in women's prisons are nearly absent from Greer's study. Where they existed, the families were not highly structured, nor did they seem to be an important response to the pains of imprisonment as earlier researchers had described them. The subjects did not see clearly defined family relationships as part of the prison's interpersonal environment or their own. In the nineteenth century, prison officials encouraged female inmates to engage in play families as a way of practicing and extending family values.

Greer suggests that the changes in the female inmate culture may reflect the power of the cultural-importation model (see Chapter 7). Prisons, like city streets, are far more complex today than they were in the 1950s, 1960s, or 1970s when much of the previous research on prison culture was carried out. Greer also observes, as have others, that contemporary prisons are far more open than the total institutions of earlier generations. Inmates are no longer closed off from outside influences, good or bad. What is important, she maintains, is to use the physical and emotional circumstances of female inmates as a guide for the design of "institutional programs and environments that address the unique gender and cultural needs of the women confined therein" (465).

SOURCES: GIRSHICK (1999); GREER (2000); KOSCHESKI AND HENSLEY (2001); MCCORKLE, MIETHE, AND DRASS (1995); B. OWEN (1998); POLLOCK (2002).

a parenting element—a topic we have addressed previously. Program participants who are mothers have special problems in this area that do not disappear when they leave a correctional facility (nearly everyone who receives intermediate sanctions is incarcerated for some period of time) or have completed a nonresidential program. For mothers who are confined, furloughs and other temporary-release programs can help improve their parenting skills and renew ties with their children (1991, 290).

Finally, women released back into the community often need more survival training than men in order to live independently. For much of their lives, women who come in contact with the criminal justice system may have been dependent on others, often abusive and uncaring family members, to meet their short-term and long-term needs. Ex-offenders may need something as complex as problem-solving skills or something as straightforward as how to open, use, and balance a checking account. As McCarthy and McCarthy observe, "Knowing that she can work out solutions to her own problems may encourage the offender to take greater responsibility for her life and to be less vulnerable to victimization" (1991, 290).

WOMEN AND REENTRY

To their detriment, state correctional programs often use policies and procedures with female parolees that have been created for men, while the evidence supports the view that gender-specific or gender-sensitive programs for women yield positive results (Wells and Bright 2005; Wright, Salisbury, and Van Voorhis 2007). One of this chapter's lessons is that women face additional burdens when incarcerated, and, upon release, these problems are amplified by either nonexistent or male-focused reentry programs. For example, a study of the factors affecting female reentry in one program found higher risks of failure if the woman has:

- a psychiatric history (formal diagnosis and/or emotional/psychological difficulties);
- contemplated suicide;
- attempted suicide; or
- difficulty controlling her temper or demonstrate hostile/violent behavior.

Changing any of these factors in a positive fashion becomes central to successful reentry.

The National Institute of Justice (2005) reviewed program evaluations for four reentry projects with unique gender components. Two programs—Delaware's CREST and KEY programs—were therapeutic communities for women. Originally designed for men, such prison-based communities can also work for women because both exhibited relatively high success rates. The researchers observed that female counselors created a less confrontational atmosphere. Moreover, it may be the case that the programs should be single-gender because the researchers noted that women tend to fall silent when confronted by men, a situation that is likely to hinder the overall therapeutic process (KEY was single gender; CREST had both men and women).

Forever Free was a California residential treatment program available during parole and entered only after the women completed an institutional-based component. Participation in both elements was voluntary. This two-pronged program, which viewed addiction as a disease, emphasized relapse prevention. Several sessions related specifically to women's issues, including self-esteem, anger management, assertiveness training, physical and psychological abuse, posttraumatic stress disorder, codependency, parenting, gender, and health. Again, participants in this program fared well upon release, perhaps because of the bridging of services between the closed and free communities (see Travis's elements of successful reentry in Chapter 9). Indeed, a significant finding from the evaluation of the Forever Free program was the importance of treatment after release from custody.

The fourth reentry program was Seeking Safety, which attempts to address the fact that some female inmates have a **dual diagnosis** upon entering prison: they use illegal substances or abuse legal ones and they suffer from posttraumatic stress disorder. This program uses group and individual therapy settings, in outpatient or residential treatment facilities. The program's intent is to help clients gain a level of self-control to avoid dangerous behavior, including self-inflicted injuries; risky behavior in relationships, such as HIV infection; and distorted thinking, such as that which occurs while intoxicated.

Helping women reenter the community means knowing what works with women. We have much information in this regard, but translating that knowledge into policies and practices is the difficult task. As Bloom, Owen, and Covington (2003, 1) state, such programs demonstrate "that investing in gender-responsive policy and procedures will likely produce long-term dividends for the criminal justice system and the community as well as the women offenders and their families."

WOMEN'S CORRECTIONAL ISSUES

Gender issues in prisons and jails tend to cluster around two topics: policy concerns and gender-specific programs for women offenders. In their general operations, most facilities have different policies for female and male inmates in just two areas. First, women are typically given a greater range of options with respect to the health and beauty items they can purchase at the commissary. Second, the allowed list of personal property is different for women and men. Most DOCs—four in five—report implementing the same policies for women and men regarding diet, transportation, visits by children, and even pat-down searches. Only about one in three agencies report gender differences in parenting programs and personal-grooming policies.

Two areas are particularly important to the study of female inmates. We refer here to parenting issues and the unique health and medical problems faced by female inmates.

PARENTING AND INCARCERATED MOTHERS

More than 2,000 years ago, an emperor of India appointed welfare workers to expedite the release of prisoners who had children (Ling 1973, 199). Forty years ago, Baunach and Murton (1973) began a discussion about allowing inmates to keep their babies while in prison. More than 30 years ago, two important studies—McGowan and Blumenthal's *Why Punish the Children?* (1978) and Henriques's *Imprisoned Mothers and Their Children* (1982)—chronicled how little had changed for incarcerated mothers and

their children. Since then, an emerging body of research has extended this theme: the loss of children negatively influences both the incarcerated women and the children they leave behind (Dalley 2002; George et al. 2011; Kauffman 2001; Surratt 2003).

This discussion has taken on a world-wide significance, as other nations express the same concerns, reservations and dilemmas, such as in New Zealand, where it has been observed that the female offender population is both disproportionately Maori (the indigenous peoples of New Zealand) and maternal, as nearly nine in ten are parents. Kingi (2000, 9) notes that the policies and practices of the government ignore the needs of these women and their children. This lack of a compassionate governmental response is not limited to New Zealand. Importantly, as shall become clear in this chapter, some actions of government have made a bad situation even worse.

INMATE PARENTS: GENDER DIFFERENCES Key to understanding the scope of this problem is a single fact: seven in ten female inmates have offspring younger than age 18. Jails and prisons present slightly different insights into this problem. In the late 1990s, researchers at the Bureau of Justice Statistics estimated that women in jail had 105,300 minor children, or roughly two children per woman. Jailed fathers accounted for roughly 11 times the number of minor children attributed to female inmates. However, there are important differences between mothers and fathers who are jail inmates. Forced separation from children seems particularly hard on women (Baunach 1985): more than six in ten of the mothers women lived with their children before imprisonment, versus four in ten of the fathers. Moreover, when a father goes to jail, minor children usually live with their mother or another relative. When mothers enter jail, the children are often placed in foster care or approved for adoption (Baunach).

State and federal prisons hold an estimated 809,800 parents of minor children.[14] The number of minor children with a mother in prison has doubled since 1991. About six in ten women in state prisons and over one-half of women in federal prisons have offspring younger than 18. Nearly two in three

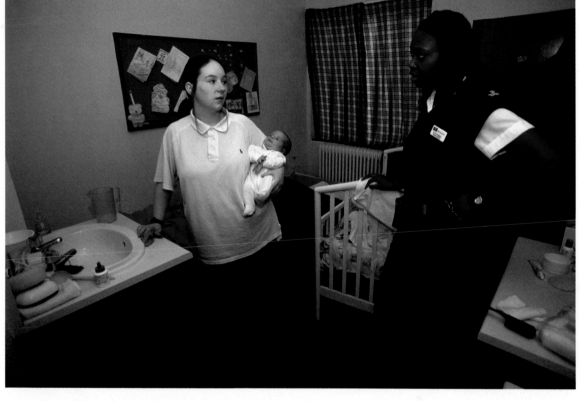

women in state prisons with young children had lived with those children before entering prison, and so had more than four in five of the mothers in federal prisons. The net result is that an estimated 1.7 million children in the United States had a parent in prison in 2008, an increase of nearly 80 percent since 1991. More than one-third of all these children will reach their eighteenth birthday before their parents return home from prison.

Among the males, four in ten of the fathers were black and three in ten were white. For females, three in ten were black and nearly five in ten were white. Slightly less than two in ten of either male or female parents were Hispanic. Most fathers in prison (90 percent) reported that their minor children lived with their mother. However, less than 40 percent of the mothers in prison report that their minor children currently lived with their father. In fact, the children of female inmates were more likely to live with grandparents (45 percent) than their father. Foster care, adoption, or, at best, another relative was often the only viable option for the rest of these children.

A comparison of inmates' contact with their children tells us that more than 60 percent of the mothers in state prisons reported weekly contact versus 40 percent of the fathers. We should not construe these rates to mean that inmate fathers are less attached to their children than inmate mothers are. What they may reflect are differences in programming as much as differences in personal priorities. Moreover, these contacts may prove crucial for women as they attempt to adjust to prison life (Jiang and Winfree 2006).

One area where the genders were very similar was financial support prior to incarceration: Slightly more than one-half of the male and female inmates reported that they provided the primary financial support for their children prior to incarceration; more than three-fourths were employed in the month prior to incarceration, mainly from legitimate wages or salaries.

PROGRAMMATIC RESPONSES Many jails and prisons have instituted programs intended to bridge the institutional gap between mothers and their children. In the United States, programs that address the needs of incarcerated mothers range from simply helping mothers and their children keep in touch through letters and journals, phone calls, emails, and even instant messaging, to allowing mothers to keep their children in prison, to arranging furloughs and home visits and, finally, to coordinating appropriate foster-care placements (Bartlett 2000;

Kauffman 2001; Temin 2001). Parenting courses are also viewed as essential elements of successful prerelease and community-based programming (Surratt 2003). Reunification with family members—especially minor children—is inevitable. Prisons and jails need to sponsor programs intended to enhance parenting skills and ease reunification where appropriate (Dalley 2002, 261).

There is some debate as to where to locate such programs. For example, in the 1990s Australia began to allow children up to the age of three to be housed in prison with their mothers; however, a decade into that program it was recommended that the inmate mothers and their children should reside in a secure facility away from the main prison for women (Clay and Burfitt 2000). Box 13.4 provides some details on

---

SPOTLIGHT ON INTERNATIONAL CORRECTIONS: A GERMAN MODEL FOR FAMILIES IN PRISON   BOX 13.4

In Preungesheim Prison, a maximum-security prison for women (and a limited number of men) near Frankfurt, Germany, mothers and their children live together in a somewhat isolated segment of the prison known as the *closed mother–child house*. The building and contiguous yard are set in an area near the center of the enclosed century-old prison. Windows tend to look out into the neighboring free world rather than the prison itself. Standing in the grass-filled play area, one must know where to look to see prison walls.

The facility's administrators accept motherhood as a legitimate work assignment, although many of the women perform other jobs in the facility while staff and other inmates monitor their children. Infants live with their mothers in the facility; toddlers to the age of three are allowed to attend a neighborhood preschool program. The children often join the children of staff members and parents in the adjoining area at the preschool. During this time, the mothers return to their assigned duties in the facility; but except for mothers who are security risks, they live with their children in the closed mother–child house during off hours. When they are inside this special residential center, mothers must assume total responsibility as caregivers for their children.

Children must leave Preungesheim Prison once they are school age. Moreover, the special housing unit has limited bed spaces. Many mothers of older children at the facility are eligible for a special form of work release: They may leave the prison to prepare their children for school and to take care of various domestic aspects of the child's home in the free world.

This program, of course, assumes that the residences of the older children are accessible by public transportation. The mothers must return to prison at the end of the day, when their child (or children) returns to the care of another adult family member or caregiver.

SOURCES: KAUFFMAN (2001); PERSONAL OBSERVATIONS OF L. THOMAS WINFREE, JR.

another international example of one such program that creates a family setting within the heart of a prison.

WOMEN'S HEALTH CARE AND RELATED MEDICAL ISSUES

A critical cluster of inmates are those suffering from medical and mental health issues, and these inmates are disproportionately female. As you read about the nature and scope of the various health and medical issues facing women and men, bear in mind that few correctional facilities offer the breadth and scope of treatment programs required to adequately address problems of this range and complexity (Heney and Kristiansen 1998; Ross and Lawrence 1998).

Given that prisons house persons for longer than the average jail sentence, they are as a rule better equipped to deal with many of these problems (Ross and Lawrence 1998). One difficulty is that the range of problems and issues that women's prisons must address often is related to the inmates' sexual and drug practices before entering prison (Levin, Bick, and Stubblefield 2002). Those practices when combined can have deadly results.

AIDS/HIV Jail surveys reveal that HIV is several times higher within the inmate population than the general population (Maruschak 2006, 8). Moreover, the percentage of female inmates testing positive for HIV is twice that for males (2.3 percent versus 1.2 percent). The rate is even higher (3 percent) among black women, the largest single group of female inmates in jails, followed closely by Hispanic males and females (2.9 percent).

In 2002, the rate of AIDS in prison was three times the rate in the general population (Maruschak 2006, 5), which is down from nearly five times the national rate in 1998. By 2007, the ratio of AIDS cases in prisons to cases in the general population was half that reported for 1998. Among women in state prisons in 2002, who were tested and whose results were reported, the percentage of women who were HIV-positive was higher than it was for men (2.4 percent versus 1.7 percent). By 2010, the percentage of women who were HIV-positive was still roughly 30 percent higher than were men (1.9 percent versus 1.4 percent), but both percentages were lower than previously reported (Maruschak 2012, 6).

What is interesting, and not well understood, is that federal prisons have among the lowest HIV-positive rates—about 1 percent overall and no differences by gender—and that federal drug offenders have the absolutely lowest HIV rate among offender groups. The differences here may reflect the fact that federal prisons tend to house people who primarily sold drugs, whereas state prisons tend to house people who used them. This interpretation is supported by the observation that inmates being held on drug offenses in state prisons report the highest HIV-positive rate (Maruschak 2006).

OTHER INFECTIOUS DISEASES Sexually transmitted diseases (STDs), tuberculosis, and hepatitis are major health threats faced by all inmates. Although information about STDs and both hepatitis B and C is incomplete, prison inmates are clearly at higher risk than the general population. The 2000 Census of State and Federal Adult Correctional Facilities provides some information (Beck and Maruschak 2004). Health experts view hepatitis C (HCV) as the more deadly strain of the disease, although any variant can cause problems for inmates and administrators. HCV causes lifelong infection, cirrhosis (scaring) of the liver, cancer, liver failure, and death. Being a blood-borne disease, the most common transmission mechanism is either sexual contact or shared needles. Most prisons (79 percent) test inmates for HCV. Random tests find that more than one-quarter of the inmates have HCV (Beck and Maruschak 2004, 1). Although gender breakdowns are unavailable, other studies lead us to speculate that women have higher rates of hepatitis C than men (Ross and Lawrence 1998).

Tuberculosis (TB), including the multidrug resistant (MDR) strain, is a growing problem for the nation's prisons. Every untreated case of TB has the potential to infect 10 to 15 more individuals. Mycobacterium tuberculosis, which has infected one-third of the world's population, kills more adults worldwide than any other infectious agent. More than 40 percent of all TB victims in the United States passed through a correctional facility (Hammett, Harm, and

Rhodes 2002). In the federal prison system, about 12 percent of both men and women test positive for TB, whereas for states, the figure is about 4 percent for both (Maruschak 2006; Hammett, Harm, and Rhodes 2002).[15] Although men are slightly more likely to test positive than are women, both groups are at high risk if not treated, and the risk to women, given the tendency toward benign neglect, may be even greater than for men.

MENTAL ILLNESS In the adult population nationwide, we find more women than men (12.5 percent versus 8.7 percent) present symptoms of mental illness.[16] In jails, the differences are even more pronounced: three-quarters of women and nearly two-thirds of men report a mental health problem. Moreover, two in ten men in jail have a *diagnosed* mental illness versus four in ten women. Jail is a stressful environment, so we would expect existing problems to percolate to the surface. However, these numbers suggest that jails have become *de facto* mental health repositories, a use for which they are ill suited.

This characterization is also true of the nation's prison system. In state prisons, more women inmates than men inmates reported a mental health problem (73 percent versus 55 percent); federal prisoners reported similar percentage differences (61 percent versus 44 percent). The percentage of women and men diagnosed with a mental illness in state prisons is nearly identical to that found in the jail population. State prison officials reported that 40 percent of female inmates received medication for a mental problem. Roughly 16 percent of male inmates likewise received mental-health medications. The rates in federal prisons are about half those observed in state facilities.

PHYSICAL AND SEXUAL ABUSE The proportion of mentally ill female inmates who have been physically abused is nearly double that of other female inmates (Ditton 1999, 7). Sexual abuse presents similar patterns for both sets of inmates. However, the percentage of males and females reporting sexual abuse at the hands of other inmates is higher in prison than

was previously reported for jail inmates. Beck, Harrison et al. (2010, 5) observed that female prison inmates (4.7 percent) were more than twice as likely as male prison inmates (1.9 percent) to report experiencing inmate-on-inmate sexual victimization; imprisoned females were also more likely to report sexual activity with staff than male inmates. As previously described, female prisoners who are mentally ill are extremely vulnerable. The problem is that although most prison inmates, female and male, receive some form of mental health treatment during incarceration, the mixture of problems—physical and sexual abuse, drug involvement, mental illness—compounds many of the existing physical and mental problems.

GENERAL HEALTH ISSUES Women in jail have more general health problems than their male counterparts (Maruschak 2006). More than 50 percent of the jailed women in 2005 reported one or more medical problem, compared with about 30 percent of the men. Women with three or more medical problems outnumber men two to one in jail. For 11 of 14 medical problems surveyed, women reported more than men, including arthritis, asthma, cancer, diabetes, heart problems, hypertension, kidney problems, liver problems, hepatitis, and sexually transmitted diseases. In short, women, but especially pregnant women, are by definition *special-needs inmates* because they have medical requirements beyond the ability of most physicians working in jails (see Chapter 8).

Between 5 and 10 percent of all female jail inmates are pregnant upon arrival. Pregnant inmates present unique problems for facilities that house them. For example, major questions surround the restraint and transportation of pregnant inmates. Minimal-restraint policies are the rule. Also, most DOCs require that a medical staff member sign off before a pregnant inmate is transported or restrained. Where any differences in diet between facilities for men and women are observed, they typically involve pregnant inmates.

Among the specific programs intended to address these needs are parenting skills and domestic violence awareness. Nursery programs allow incarcerated mothers to keep their babies near them in prison or jail. Eight DOCs report specific mentoring programs for female inmates, and another three target improvements in female inmates' self-esteem. In addition, survivors' groups address issues of domestic violence and sexual abuse. In many cases, these programs are merged into, or offered with, programs on substance abuse, life skills, and mental health. The goal here is to alter what is arguably a contributing factor to women's criminality.

Jail and prison responses to women's health care issues differ. Nine in ten female prison inmates reported having a gynecological examination after their admission; by contrast, only two in ten female jail inmates reported the same service (Greenfield and Snell 1999, 8). About 50 percent of pregnant jail inmates reported that they had received prenatal care since their admission, compared with 80 percent of pregnant prison inmates.

Overall, women in both state and federal custody were more likely than men to report a medical problem, excluding an injury, in both state and federal custody (Maruschak and Beck 2001, 8). However, one medical problem stands out for imprisoned women, even though it is not "gender-specific," as is the case for gynecological or obstetrical issues. Specifically, drugs are more than an offense for some inmates; they are a way of life. For example, women in state prisons and federal facilities were far more likely than men to have used methamphetamine in the month before the current commitment offense (Mumola and Karberg 2006). For any drug, the percentage of women using is also slightly higher than men in state prisons, whereas in federal prisons half of all men and women reported drug use in the month before offending. Drug dependence and abuse reveals a similar pattern: more female state prisoners than male state prisoners reported being drug dependent or drug abusers. In the federal system, women and men reported roughly the same level of involvement with drugs. Drug abuse also demonstrates an important if poorly understood tie to mental illness. Persons who use alcohol or drugs prior to incarceration in either prison or jail are, on average, 50 percent more likely to report a mental problem.

Illicit drug use is a problem for all prisoners, but more so for women in the state system and men in the federal system. While the differences are small, we must remember the caveat given earlier in this chapter: even when the problems are similar, women suffer more, given their smaller numbers and lower level of attention paid to their needs.

RESPONDING TO GENDER-SPECIFIC HEALTH ISSUES

Developing and maintaining adequate health care delivery in women's prisons and jails should be a high priority for the nation's corrections system. The issues identified in this section go beyond simply providing for women's health needs while they are incarcerated. Ross and Lawrence challenge both female inmates and facilities' health-care providers:

> Women offenders need to develop living skills that raise self-esteem and build confidence necessary to avoid high risk behaviors; to negotiate the complexities of the health care system as consumers; and to adopt wellness as a primary personal value . . . Many medical professionals would do well to learn and adopt a less judgmental approach to their patients and trouble themselves less over whether offenders deserve their skill and effort. (Ross and Lawrence 1998, 129)

Ideally, the adequate provision and proper utilization of health care in prison should help female inmates break the cycle of crime and victimization. The problem is that "jail and prison health care systems have largely been defined and operated by men for a nearly exclusive male clientele" (Ross and Lawrence 1998, 122).

WOMEN IN THE CORRECTIONAL WORKPLACE

Until well into the twentieth century, the traditional roles played by women in the corrections workplace were limited to matron and juvenile correctional officer. Also, until the 1970s, the number of women employed in corrections was relatively low. In the last three decades of the century, those conditions

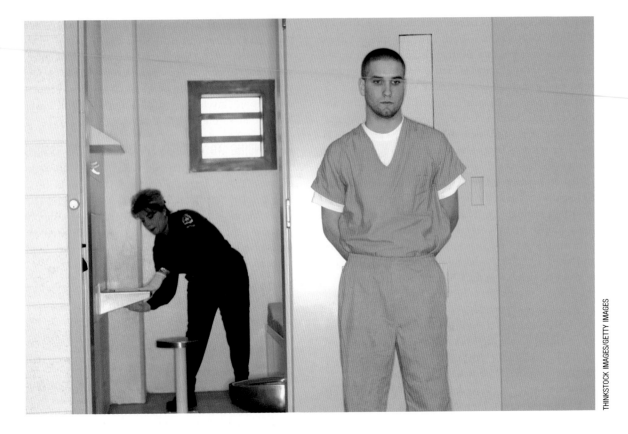

changed, but women who work in corrections continue to face problems, and many of those problems they share with women inmates. As we move into the second decade of the twenty-first century a key question remains: How much has the correctional workplace changed for female employees?

FEMALE EMPLOYEES: WHO IS DOING WHAT?

The Bureau of Labor Statistics (BLS) (2012) reports that women accounted for 24 percent of all correctional first-line supervisors or managers, although it is impossible to separate out jails from prisons in these numbers. The BLS also reports for that same time period women accounted for 27 percent of all bailiffs, correctional officers, and jailers, the most relevant category included in their annual reports. There is a certain irony here: The percentage of

female employees of the correctional system closely mirrors the percentage of women arrested and on probation.

We do have other information about jail and prison female staff, but it is fragmentary and limited. For example, Kerle (2002, 54) notes that staffing is one of the chief concerns of jail administrators in the nation: most of the nation's jails are understaffed. Estimates place the total number of jail employees at about 210,000; roughly 33 percent of those employees are women. Among COs, the employees who most often come into direct contact with inmates, the rate drops to 28 percent—which suggests that women are more likely to work in support areas than on the front line in jails. These proportions are roughly the same for female employees in federal metropolitan correctional centers and in local jails. In privately operated jails, the gender ratios are different: female staffers account for 46 percent of the work force and nearly 41 percent of the COs.

Most women who worked in jails historically supervised and managed female offenders or juveniles, especially female juveniles. Kerle (2002, 55) suggests that the implementation of direct supervision changed the job description of many female COs. He reports that in many cases, the tasks assigned to female jail employees now include strip-searching female prisoners after they are booked, observing them while they shower, issuing them clothing, and supervising them. For liability reasons, Kerle also recommends that at least one woman be on all shifts, and he suggests that male officers who are asked to supervise female inmates without a female colleague should resign.

As suggested by the previously reviewed BLS report, women also have assumed leadership roles in the nation's jail systems. The 1991 edition of *Who's Who in Jail Administration*, published by the American Jail Association (AJA), listed 150 female jail administrators. By the end of the decade, the AJA (1999) reported 480 female jail administrators (also see Kerle 2002).

Female staff members are the norm in women's prisons; they occupy more than half of all custodial, programmatic, and administrative positions in the state systems. In the BOP, women account for slightly fewer than three in ten staff members. Overall, in all state correctional facilities, women make up nearly one in three of all corrections staff members (Stephan 2008, 20). In the average women-only prison, female staff members serve in half of the custodial positions; and they dominate administrative and program-related positions, filling nearly 70 percent of positions in both categories. Where private-public comparisons are possible, women occupy positions in all three areas at a slightly higher rate in the private sector than they do in the public sector. These higher-than-expected rates may reflect a preference in some agencies to assigning women staff members to women's prisons.

BURNOUT AND JOB SATISFACTION

Burnout is said to exist when people deplete their physical or mental resources. In the corrections

environment, staff burnout typically follows three stages: (1) an employee becomes frustrated with the job itself and subsequently neglects clients; (2) the employee feels less personal achievement and accomplishment in the job; and (3) the employee is emotionally exhausted and is less productive. Corrections work is generally acknowledged to be highly stressful (Anson and Bloom 1988; Lindquist and Whitehead 1986). This is especially true of COs: as many as one-third of COs report work-related stress or burnout.

Does gender play a part in job stress? Do female corrections employees experience more or less burnout than their male counterparts? In the 1980s, studies found that female COs experienced more occupational stress than men (Cullen et al. 1985; Zupan 1986); however, more-recent research found few or no differences (Gross et al. 1994; Morgan, Van Haveren, and Pearson 2002; S. Owen 2006; Triplett, Mullings, and Scarborough 1996). Morgan and his colleagues (2002) observed that female correctional officers were more likely than their male counterparts, to respond impersonally to inmates. The women also experienced lower levels of burnout—suggesting that "correctional work for females remains a relatively new phenomenon in comparison to male employment standards, and it is possible that women have learned to adjust to the demands and stressors of the correctional environment" (2002, 152). Women COs also may access support mechanisms that male officers are reluctant to call on because they feel asking for help is a sign of weakness.

Burnout is one concern for corrections workers; another is job satisfaction. Satisfied workers are better workers: they have higher job performance ratings, higher job retention rates, and lower rates of absenteeism. In general, research has failed to find a gender bias in this area: men and women are equally satisfied or dissatisfied. Although many factors can influence how one perceives his or her work world, gender does not appear to be one of them (Lambert, Hogan, and Barton 2002). Researchers find that female and male COs are relatively homogeneous groups, particularly in emotional exhaustion and depersonalization (Carlson, Anson, and Thomas 2003).

SUMMARY

Women in the corrections system—as both clients and employees—must confront issues, setbacks, challenges, and general neglect unlike those faced by men. The following are among the key points presented in this chapter:

- The absolute number of women under sanctions has increased dramatically since the mid-1980s.

- The relative proportion of women also has reached record levels, straining the system as it has never been before.

- The institutional world of female inmates appears to be changing, as women are subject to pains of imprisonment that equal or exceed those of men.

- The culture of women's prisons may also be in a state of flux, as increasing demands are made on a system whose resources do not appear to be keeping pace with its population.

- Correctional experts have pointed to health care issues, drug treatment programs, parenting programs, family contact initiatives, and post-release and extra-institutional support services as areas that need to be expanded or, in some jurisdictions, initiated.

- A particularly important lesson of this chapter is the lack of gender-specific information available to the correctional practitioner.

- For far too long, both practitioners and researchers have neglected the gender variable in corrections.

THINKING ABOUT CORRECTIONAL POLICIES AND PRACTICES: WRITING ASSIGNMENTS

1   Look again at Table 13.1. Did any of the increases or decreases in the by-offense arrest rates for women between 1996 and 2005 seem particularly intriguing? Choose two, and suggest why the change occurred in each instance. (*Hint:* The Internet is a good source for this kind of research.)

2   Much is made of the drug-involved female offender. What do you find to be the most troubling aspect of this discussion? Explain your answer.

3   Select a nation other than your own. (You should not worry about making a selection because there are about 200 nations worldwide from which to select.) Now use your favorite search engine to find out the fate of incarcerated women in that nation. How many women are incarcerated in that nation? What percentage do they contribute to the entire prison population? Can you find anything about the quality of their lives as prison inmates? Include

in your single-page response a brief comparison of what you have learned about female inmates in that country with those in your own nation. A good starting point might be the International Centre for Prison Studies, a partner of the University of Essex: **http://www.prisonstudies. org/info/worldbrief/**

4   Review the two gender-based problems that are confronting the nation's jail administrators today. Prepare a single-page paper in which you identify which one you think administrators can remedy the fastest, and how they can accomplish this feat.

5   You are a correctional officer in a women's prison. What do you see as the greatest source of job stress? What can the facility do to rectify this problem? It is not appropriate to answer either question (or both) with nothing. Summarize your thinking about these issues in a single page.

KEY TERMS

benign neglect
co-correctional unit
cools
custody variance score
dual diagnosis
duality of women

egalitarian families
habilitation
liberation hypothesis
Marxist feminism
patriarchal families
play families

power-control theory
pseudo-families
radical feminism
socialist feminism
the mix
women's reformatory

CRITICAL REVIEW QUESTIONS

1 Define *benign neglect*. Is it benign or malign? (*Hint:* You may want to consider theoretical explanations of female criminality before answering this question.)

2 Which single explanation of female criminality do you find most insightful? How has this theory increased your understanding of female offenders?

3 What aspects of the evolution and history of female correctional facilities in the United States do you think tells us the most about our contemporary problems?

4 "Women are different from men; they have different needs in and out of prison." Defend or attack this assertion, providing supporting documentation.

5 Describe what you see to be the important links between inmate classification systems and the inmate social system.

6 Greer suggests that play families have largely disappeared from women's prison experience. What role do you think the women's liberation movement had in this? Describe two other areas where that movement seems to have affected women's lives in jails and prisons.

7 What gender-specific aspect of intermediate sanctions is missing from the literature that you would like to know about?

8 How much has the correctional workplace changed for female employees in the twenty-first century?

9 Did you expect male and female employees of the correctional system to feel much the same about their work world? What do you think explains this level of consistency?

10 "All this discussion of gender and corrections is misplaced because . . ." Finish this sentence, and explain what you mean.

CASE CITED

Cain v. Michigan Department of Corrections, 451 Mich. 470; 548 N.W.2d 210 (1996)

NOTES

1 In the interest of somewhat more parsimonious comparisons, the following discussion is limited to those differences greater than plus or minus 5.5 percent or, in this case, below 20 percent or above

31 percent. These breakpoints are arbitrary. Given that we have the entire population of data for arrestees, there is no such thing as a statistically significant difference, a difference greater than we would expect by chance alone. Rather, what we are looking at are differences that are substantively significant, and for these comparisons we are using differences greater or less than 5.5 percent.

2   Per capita here and throughout this chapter refers to per 100,000 of population.

3   Following discussion based on Harrison and Beck (2006) and Minton (2011).

4   Following discussion based on Stephan and Walsh (2011).

5   Following discussion based on Greenfield and Snell (1999).

6   Congress codified this rule as 42 U.S.C. Section 862a; however, supporters and critics alike tend to refer to it as Section 115. For more on the racial bias in US drug enforcement policies and practices, see Chapter 14.

7   Other bans accorded to persons convicted of drug-related offenses exist as well, including ones restricting access to post-secondary education, federally assisted housing, and some federal contracts and licenses; however, these bans are generally for relatively short periods of time and not for the lifetime of the convicted person (GAO 2005).

8   The insights on women in prison come largely from Greenfield (1991) and Snell (1994); the Bureau of Justice Statistics only sporadically provides this information for men or women.

9   Following discussion is based on Bureau of Justice Statistics (2013).

10 Following discussion is based on Bureau of Justice Statistics (Federal Bureau of Investigation 2011). The states include weapons offenses as public order offenses, whereas the federal system disaggregates them.

11 We purposefully limit our discussion of inmate classification systems to state and federal prisons. Few jails classify women inmates at all, and that is a mistake says jail expert Ken Kerle (2002, 46).

12 That decision held. The US Supreme Court refused to hear the case on a writ of certiorari in 1999.

13 For male inmates, the primary source of extra-institutional social support was their wives.

14 Following discussion based on Glaze and Maruschak (2008).

15 One reason offered for the higher rate in the federal prison system is the fact that it holds a disproportionately high number of foreign-born inmates; TB is higher among this group than among native-born prisoners (Hammett, Harms, and Rhodes 2002).

16 Unless otherwise indicated, the following discussion based on James and Glaze (2006).

REFERENCES

Abrams, Laura S., and Laura Curran. 2000. Wayward girls and virtuous women: Social workers and female juvenile delinquency in the Progressive Era. *Affilia* 15: 49–64.

Adler, Freda. 1975. *Sisters in crime: The rise of the new female criminal.* New York: McGraw-Hill.

Akers, Ronald. 1994. *Criminological theories: Introduction and evaluation.* Los Angeles: Roxbury.

Allard, Patricia. 2002. *Life sentences: Denying welfare benefits to women convicted of drug offenses.* Washington, DC: Sentencing Project.

American Jail Association (AJA). 1991. *Who's who in jail management.* Hagerstown, MD: American Jail Association.

American Jail Association (AJA). 1999. *Who's who in jail management,* 3rd edn. Hagerstown, MD: American Jail Association.

Anson, Richard H., and Mary Ellen Bloom. 1988. Police stress in an occupational context. *Journal of Police Science and Administration* 16: 229–35.

Austin, Roy L. 1982. Women's liberation and increases in minor, major and occupational offenses. *Criminology* 20: 407–30.

Austin, James F., L. Chan, and W. Elms. 1993. *Indiana Department of Corrections: Women classification study.* San Francisco: National Council on Crime and Delinquency.

Balkan, Sheila, Ronald J. Berger, and Janet Schmidt. 1980. *Crime and deviance in America: A critical approach.* Belmont, CA: Wadsworth.

Bartlett, Rini. 2000. Helping inmate moms keep in touch—Prison programs encourage ties with children. *Corrections Today* 62: 102–4.

Bartollas, Clemens, and John P. Conrad. 1992. *Introduction to corrections*, 2nd edn. New York: HarperCollins.

Baunach, Phyllis. 1985. *Mothers in prison*. New Brunswick, NJ: Transaction Books.

Baunach, Phyllis, and T. O. Murton. 1973. Women in prison—An awakening minority. *Crime and Corrections* 1(2): 4–12.

Beck, Allen, Paige Harrison, Marcus Berzofsky, Rachel Caspar, and Christoper Kreps. 2010. *Sexual victimization in prisons and jails reported by inmates, 2008–2009*. Washington, DC: US Department of Justice.

Beck, Allen, and Laura M. Maruschak. 2004. *Hepatitis testing and treatment in state prisons*. Washington, DC: US Department of Justice.

Beirne, Piers, and James Messerschmidt. 2000. *Criminology*, 3rd edn. Boulder, CO: Westview Press.

Belknap, Joan. 1996. *The invisible woman: Gender, crime and justice*. Belmont, CA: Wadsworth.

Bill, Louise. 1998. The victimization . . . and revictimization of female offenders. *Corrections Today*, December, 106–12.

Bloom, Barbara, Barbara Owen, and Stephanie Covington. 2003. *Gender-responsiveness strategies: Research, practice, and guiding principles for women offenders*. Washington, DC: US Department of Justice.

Bowker, Lee M. 1981. Gender differences in prisoner subcultures. In *Women and crime in America*, edited by Lee M. Bowker. New York: Macmillan, 409–19.

Brennan, Tim. 1998. Institutional classification of females: Problems and some proposals for reform. In *Female offenders: Effective critical prospects and interventions*, edited by Ruth T. Zaplin. Gaithersburg, MD: Aspen, 179–204.

Bureau of Justice Statistics. 2013. *Federal criminal case processing statistics, 2010*. Retrieved July 24, 2013 from: http://www.bjs.gov/fjsrc/

Bureau of Labor Statistics. 2012. *Women in the labor force: A databook*. Washington, DC: US Bureau of Labor Statistics.

Burke, Peggy, and Linda Adams. 1991. *Classification of women offenders in state correctional facilities: A handbook for practitioners*. Washington, DC: US Government Printing Office.

Butler, Anne M. 1997. *Gendered justice in the American West: Women prisoners in men's penitentiaries*. Urbana: University of Illinois Press.

Carlson, Joseph R., Richard H. Anson, and George Thomas. 2003. Correctional officer burnout and stress: Does gender matter? *Prison Journal* 83: 277–88.

Chesney-Lind, Meda. 1998. Women in prison: From partial justice to vengeful equity. *Corrections Today* 60(7): 66–73.

Chesney-Lind, Meda. 1973. Judicial enforcement of the female sex role. *Criminology* 8: 51–69.

Clay, C., and Ann Burfitt. 2000. Do children and prison go together? Paper presented at the Women in Corrections: Staff and Clients Conference. Adelaide, Australia, 31 October–1 November.

Covington, Stephanie S. 2001. Creating gender-responsive programs: The next step for women's services. *Corrections Today* 63(2): 85–7.

Cullen, Francis T., Bruce G. Link, Nancy T. Wolf, and James Frank. 1985. The social dimensions of correctional officer stress. *Justice Quarterly* 2: 505–33.

Dalley, Lanette P. 2002. Policy implications relating to inmate mothers and their children: Will the past be prologue? *Prison Journal* 82: 234–68.

Ditton, Paula M. 1999. *Mental health and treatment of inmates and probationers*. Washington, DC: US Government Printing Office.

Ditton, Paula M., and Doris James Wilson. 1999. *Truth in sentencing in state prisons*. Washington, DC: US Government Printing Office.

Dodge, L. Mara. 1999. One female prisoner is more trouble than twenty males: Women convicts in Illinois prisons, 1835–1896. *Journal of Social History* 32(4): 907–30.

Dodge, Mary, and Mark R. Pogrebin. 2001. Collateral costs of imprisonment for women: Complications of reintegration. *Prison Journal* 81: 42–54.

Doerner, J. K. 2009. Explaining the gender gap in sentencing outcomes: an investigation of differential treatment in U.S. federal courts. Unpublished dissertation. Bowling Green, OH: Bowling Green State University.

Doerner, J. K. 2010. Independent and joint effects of race/ethnicity, gender and age on sentencing outcomes in U.S. federal court. *Justice Quarterly* 27(1): 1–27.

Federal Bureau of Investigation. 2002. *Crime in the United States, 2001*. Washington, DC: US Department of Justice.

Federal Bureau of Investigation. 2011. *Crime in the United States, 2010*. Washington, DC: US Department of Justice.

Freedman, Estelle B. 1981. *Their sisters' keepers: Women's prison reform in America, 1830–1930*. Ann Arbor: University of Michigan Press.

Freud, Sigmund. 1933. *New introductory lectures on psychoanalysis*. New York: Norton.

George, S., R. Holst, H. Jung, R. LaLonde, and R. Varghese. 2011. *Incarcerated women, their children and the nexus with foster care*. Washington, DC: National Institute of Justice.

Giallambardo, Rose. 1966. *Society of women: A study of women's prison*. New York: Wiley.

Gibson, Helen C. 1976. Women's prisons: Laboratories for penal reform. In *The female offender*, edited by Laura Crites. Lexington, MA: Heath, 93–119.

Girshick, Lori B. 1999. *No safe haven: Stories of women in prison*. Boston: Northeastern University Press.

Glaze, Lauren E., and Thomas P. Bonczar. 2006. *Probation and parole in the United States, 2005*. Washington, DC: US Department of Justice.

Glaze, Lauren E., and Thomas P. Bonczar. 2011. *Probation and parole in the United States, 2010*. Washington, DC: US Department of Justice.

Glaze, Lauren E., and L. M. Maruschak. 2008. *Parents in prison and their minor children*. Washington, DC: US Department of Justice.

Government Accounting Office (GAO). 2005. *Drug offenders: Various factors may limit the impacts of federal law that provide for denial of selected benefits*. Washington, DC: Government Accounting Office.

Green, B., J. Miranda, A. Daroowalla, and J. Siddique. 2005. Trauma exposure, mental health functioning, and program needs of women in jail. *Crime & Delinquency*, 51: 133–51.

Greenfield, Lawrence A. 1991. *Women in prison*. Washington, DC: US Department of Justice.

Greenfield, Lawrence A., and Tracy L. Snell. 1999. *Women offenders*. Washington, DC: US Department of Justice.

Greer, K.R. 2000. The changing nature of interpersonal relationships in a women's prison. *Prison Journal* 80: 442–69.

Gross, George R., Susan J. Larsen, Gloria Urban, and Linda Zupan. 1994. Gender differences in occupational stress among correctional officers. *American Journal of Criminal Justice* 18: 219–34.

Hagan, John. 1989. *Structural criminology*. New Brunswick, NJ: Rutgers University Press.

Hagan, John., John H. Simpson, and A.R. Gillis. 1985. The class structure of gender and delinquency: Toward a power-control theory of common delinquency behavior. *American Journal of Sociology* 90: 1151–78.

Hammett, Theodore M., Mary Patricia Harm, and William Rhodes. 2002. The burden of infectious diseases among inmates and releasees of US correctional facilities, 1999. *American Journal of Public Health* 92: 1789–94.

Hannah-Moffat, K. 2009. Gridlock and mutability: Reconsidering "gender" and risk assessment. *Criminology & Public Policy* 8: 209–19.

Harer, Miles D., and Neal P. Langan. 2001. Gender differences in predictors of prison violence: Assessing the predictive validity of a risk classification system. *Crime & Delinquency* 47: 513–36.

Harlow, Caroline Wolf. 1998. *Profile of jail inmates 1996*. Washington, DC: US Department of Justice.

Harlow, Caroline Wolf. 1999. *Prior abuse reported by inmates and probationers*. Washington, DC: US Department of Justice.

Harman, Jennifer J., Vernon E. Smith, and Louisa C. Egan. 2007. The impact of incarceration on intimate relationships. *Criminal Justice and Behavior* 34: 794–815.

Harris, M. Kay. 1998. Women's imprisonment in the United States: A historical analysis of female offenders through the early 20th century. *Corrections Today*, December, 74–8, 80.

Harrison, Paige M., and Allen J. Beck. 2006. *Prison and jail inmates at midyear, 2005*. Washington, DC: US Department of Justice.

Heffernan, Esther. 1972. *Making it in prison: The square, the cool and the life*. New York: Wiley.

Heilbrun, K., D. DeMatteo, R. Fretz, J. Erickson, K. Yasuhara, and N. Anumba. 2008. How "specific" are gender-specific rehabilitation needs? An empirical analysis. *Criminal Justice and Behavior* 35: 1382–97.

Heney, Jan, and Connie M. Kristiansen. 1998. An analysis of the impact of prison on women survivors of childhood sexual abuse. *Women & Therapy* 20(4): 29–44.

Henriques, Zelma Weston. 1982. *Imprisoned mothers and their children*. Washington, DC: University Press of America.

Holtfreter, K., and R. Cupp. 2007. Gender and risk assessment: The empirical status of the LSI-R for women. *Journal of Contemporary Criminal Justice* 23: 363–82.

Holtfreter, K., M. D. Reisig, and M. Morash. 2004. Poverty, state, capital, and recidivism among women offenders. *Criminology & Public Policy* 3: 185–208.

Huggins, Denise, Loretta Capeheart, and Elizabeth Newman. 2006. Deviants or scapegoats. *The Prison Journal* 86(1): 114–39.

Islam-Zwart, Kayleen, and Peter W. Vik. 2004. Female adjustment to incarceration as influenced by sexual assault history. *Criminal Justice and Behavior* 31: 521–41.

James, Doris J., and Lauren E. Glaze. 2006. *Mental health problems of prison and jail inmates, 2006.* Washington, DC: US Department of Justice.

Jiang, Shanhe, and L. Thomas Winfree, Jr. 2006. Social support, gender, and inmate adjustment to prison life: Insights from a national sample. *Prison Journal* 86: 32–55.

Kauffman, Kelsey. 2001. Mothers prison. *Corrections Today* 63(1): 62–5.

Kerle, Kenneth E. 2002. Women in the American world of jails: Inmates and staff. *Margins* 2(Spring): 41–61.

King, Elizabeth. 2002. Benefits ban impacts women and children. *Corrections Today* 64(4): 1–4.

Kingi, V. 2000. The children of women in prison: A New Zealand study. Paper presented at the Women in Corrections: Staff and Clients Conference. Adelaide, Australia, 31 October–1 November.

Koscheski, Mary, and Christopher Hensley. 2001. Inmate homosexual behavior in a southern female correctional facility. *American Journal of Criminal Justice* 25: 269–77.

Lambert, Eric G., Nancy Lynne Hogan, and Shannon M. Barton. 2002. Satisfied correctional staff: A review of the literature on the correlates of correctional staff job satisfaction. *Criminal Justice and Behavior* 29: 115–43.

Levin, Jules, Joseph Bick, and Elizabeth Stubblefield. 2002. Recommendations for those on the frontline against hepatitis C. *HIV & Hepatitis Education Prison Project* (HEPP) 5(8 & 9, Aug./Sept.).

Lindquist, Charles A., and C. A. Lindquist. 1997. Gender differences in distress: Mental health consequences of environmental stress among jail inmates. *Behavioral Sciences and the Law* 15: 503–23.

Lindquist, Charles A., and John T. Whitehead. 1986. Correctional officers as parole officers: An examination of a community supervision function. *Criminal Justice and Behavior* 13: 197–222.

Ling, Trevor. 1973. *The Buddha.* Harmondsworth, UK: Penguin Books.

Lombroso, Cesare. 1876. *L'uomo delinquente* [*The criminal man*]. Milan: Hoepli.

Lynch, S. M., D. D. Dehart, J. Belknap, and B. L. Green. 2012. *Women's pathways to jail: The roles & intersections of serious mental illness and trauma.* Washington, DC: US Department of Justice.

MacKenzie, Doris L., James Robinson, and Carol S. Campbell. 1995. Long-term incarceration of female offenders: Prison adjustment and coping. In *Long-term imprisonment,* edited by Timothy Flanagan. Thousand Oaks, CA: Sage, 128–37.

Maeve, M. Katherine. 2001. Waiting to be caught: The devolution of health for women newly released from jail. *Criminal Justice Review* 26: 143–69.

Mahan, Sue. 1984. Imposition of despair: An ethnography of women in prison. *Justice Quarterly* 1: 357–83.

Maruschak, Laura M. 2006. *Medical problems of jail inmates.* Washington, DC: US Department of Justice.

Maruschak, Laura M. 2012. *HIV in Prisons, 2001–2010.* Washington, DC: U.S. Department of Justice.

Maruschak, Laura M., and Allen J. Beck. 2001. *Medical problems of inmates, 1997.* Washington, DC: National Institute of Justice.

McCarthy, Belinda Rogers, and Bernard J. McCarthy, Jr. 1991. *Community-based corrections,* 2nd edn. Monterey, CA: Brooks/Cole.

McCorkle, R. C., T. D. Miethe, and K. A. Drass. 1995. Roots of prison violence: A test of the deprivation, management, and "not-so-total" institution models. *Crime & Delinquency* 41: 317–31.

McGowan, Brenda G., and Karen L. Blumenthal. 1978. *Why punish the children? A study of children of women prisoners.* Hackensack, NJ: National Council on Crime and Delinquency.

Minton, Todd D. 2011. *Jail inmates at midyear 2010— statistical tables.* Washington, DC: US Department of Justice.

Morgan, Robert D., Richard A. Van Haveren, and Christy A. Pearson. 2002. Correctional officer burnout: A further analysis. *Criminal Justice and Behavior* 29: 144–60.

Mosher, Clayton, and Dretha Phillips. 2006. The dynamics of a prison-based therapeutic community for women: Retention, completion, and outcomes. *Prison Journal* 86: 6–31.

Mumola, Christopher, and Jennifer C. Karberg. 2006. *Drug use and dependence, state and federal prisoners, 2004.* Washington, DC: US Department of Justice.

National Institute of Justice. 2005. Reentry programs for women. *NIJ Journal.* 252.

Newman, Graeme. 2008. *The punishment response,* 2nd edn. Piscataway, NJ: Transaction Publishers.

Owen, Barbara. 1998. *"In the mix": Struggle and survival in a women's prison.* Albany: State University of New York Press.

Owen, Stephen S. 2006. Occupational stress among correctional officers. *Prison Journal* 86: 164–81.

Peters, R. H., A. L. Strozier, M. R. Murrin, and W. D. Kearns. 1997. Treatment of substance abusing jail inmates: Examination of gender differences. *Journal of Substance Abuse Treatment* 14: 339–49.

Pogrebin, Mark R., and Mary Dodge. 2001. Women's accounts of their prison experiences: A retrospective view of their subjective realities. *Journal of Criminal Justice* 29: 531–41.

Pollack, Otto. 1950. *The criminality of women.* Philadelphia: University of Pennsylvania Press.

Pollock, Joycelyn. 2002. *Women, prison and crime,* 2nd edn. Belmont, CA: Wadsworth.

Pollock-Byrne, Joycelyn M. 1990. *Women, prison and crime.* Pacific Grove, CA: Brooks/Cole.

Rafter, Nicole Hahn. 1985. *Partial justice: Women in state prison, 1800–1935.* Boston: Northeastern University Press.

Ross, Phyllis Harrison, and James E. Lawrence. 1998. Health care for women offenders. *Corrections Today,* December, 122–29.

Severance, T. A. 2005. "You know who you can go to": Cooperation and exchange between incarcerated women. *Prison Journal* 85: 343–67.

Simmons, I. 1975. Interaction and leadership among female prisoners. PhD dissertation, University of Missouri, Columbia.

Simon, Rita James. 1975. *Women and crime.* Lexington, MA: Heath.

Simpson, S. 1989. Feminist theory, crime and justice. *Criminology* 27: 605–37.

Singer, M. I., J. Bussey, J., L.Y. Song, and L. Lunghofer. 1995. The psychosocial issues of women serving time in jail. *Social Work* 40: 103–13.

Smart, Carol. 1976. *Women, crime and criminology.* Boston: Routledge and Kegan Paul.

Smith, P., F. T. Cullen, and E. J. Latessa. 2009. Can 14,737 women be wrong? A meta-analysis of the LSI-R and recidivism for female offenders. *Criminology & Public Policy* 8: 138–208.

Snell, Tracy L. 1994. *Women in prison: Survey of state prison inmates, 1991.* Washington, DC: US Department of Justice.

Starr, S. B. 2012. Estimating gender disparities in federal criminal cases. August 29. University of Michigan Law and Economics Research Paper, No. 12-018. Retrieved on July 18, 2013 from: http://dx.doi.org/10.2139/ssrn.2144002

Steffensmeier, Darrell. 1980. Sex differences in patterns of adult crime, 1965–1977. *Social Forces* 58: 1080–90.

Steffensmeier, Darrell, and M. J. Cobb. 1981. Sex differences in urban arrest patterns, 1934–1979. *Social Problems* 29: 37–50.

Stein, Robbie. 1996. Sexual abuse: Guards let rapists into women's cells. *Progressive,* July, 23–4.

Stephan, James J. 2001. *Census of jails, 1999.* Washington, DC: US Department of Justice.

Stephan, James J. 2008. *Census of state and federal correctional facilities, 2005.* Washington, DC: US Department of Justice.

Stephan, James J., and G. Walsh. 2011. *Census of jail facilities, 2006.* Washington, DC: US Department of Justice.

Surratt, Hilary L. 2003. Parenting attitudes of drug-involved women inmates. *Prison Journal* 83: 206–20.

Sykes, Gresham M. 1958. *The society of captives: A study of a maximum security prison.* Princeton, NJ: Princeton University Press.

Temin, Carolyn Engel. 2001. Let us consider the children. *Corrections Today* 63: 66–8.

Triplett, Ruth, Janet L. Mullings, and Kathryn E. Scarborough. 1996. Work-related stress and coping among correctional officers: Implications from organizational literature. *Journal of Criminal Justice* 24: 291–308.

US Bureau of Prisons (BOP). 2000. *Change notice. Security designation and custody classification.* Washington, DC: US Government Printing Office.

Van Voorhis, Patricia, and Lois Presser. 2001. *Classification of women offenders: A national assessment of current practices.* Washington, DC: National Institute of Corrections.

Visher, K. 1983. Gender, police arrest decisions, and notions of chivalry. *Criminology* 21: 5–28.

Ward, David, and Gene Kassebaum. 1965. *Women's prison: Sex and social structure.* Chicago: Aldine-Atherton.

Warren, Janet I., Susan Hurt, Ann Booker Loper, and Preeti Chauhan. 2004. Exploring prison adjustment among female inmates: Issues of measurement and prediction. *Criminal Justice and Behavior* 31: 624–45.

Weis, Joseph. 1981. Liberation and crime: The invention of the new female criminal. *Social Justice* 1: 17–27.

Welch, Michael. 1996. Prisonization. In *Encyclopedia of American prisons,* edited by Marilyn D. McShane and Frank P. Williams III. New York: Garland, 357–63.

Wells, Doris, and Laurie Bright. 2005. Drug treatment and reentry for incarcerated women. *Corrections Today.* December: 98–9.

Wesley, Jennifer K. 2006. Considering the context of women's violence: Gender, lived experiences, and cumulative victimization. *Feminist Criminology* 4: 303–28.

Winfree, Jr., L. Thomas, and Howard Abadinsky (2010). *Understanding crime: Essentials of criminology*, 3rd edn. Belmont, CA: Wadsworth.

Wright, E. M., E. J. Salisbury, and P. Van Voorhis. 2007. Predicting prison misconducts of women offenders: The importance of gender-responsive needs. *Journal of Contemporary Criminal Justice* 232(4): 310–40.

Young, Vernetta D. 2001. All the women in the Maryland state penitentiary: 1812–1869. *Prison Journal* 81: 113–32.

Zedner, Lucia. 1995. Wayward sisters: The prison for women. In *The Oxford history of the prison: The practice of punishment in western society*, edited by Norval Morris and David J. Rothman. New York: Oxford, 329–61.

Zupan, Linda L. 1986. Gender-related differences in correctional officers' perceptions and attitudes. *Journal of Criminal Justice* 14: 344–61.

Zupan, Linda L. 1992. Men guarding women: An analysis of the employment of male correctional officers in prisons for women. *Journal of Criminal Justice* 20: 297–309.

14 RACE, ETHNICITY, AND CORRECTIONS

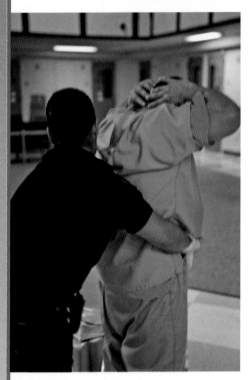

MARMADUKE ST JOHN/ALAMY IMAGES

Outline

Arrest Disparities

Sentencing Disparities

Confinement Disparities

Race, Ethnicity, and Prison Life

Probation and Parole Disparities

Race and the Death Penalty

Race and Corrections: Final Comments

Objectives

- To reveal to you the significance of race and ethnicity in contemporary correctional practice

- To acquaint you with the ideas of sentencing disparity and disproportionate minority contact and their impact on corrections

- To show you how race and ethnicity shape prisoners' lives

- To explain how discretion and discrimination influence such diverse penal practices as probation, parole, and the death penalty

Essentials of Corrections, Fifth Edition. G. Larry Mays and L. Thomas Winfree, Jr.
© 2014 John Wiley & Sons, Inc. Published 2014 by John Wiley & Sons, Inc.

INTRODUCTION

Throughout this text, we have referred to the place of gender, race, and ethnicity in the study of corrections. In Chapter 13, we explored the implications of gender for contemporary corrections. In this chapter, we turn to a similar treatment of race and ethnicity.

The special emphasis given to gender, on the one hand, and race and ethnicity, on the other, is ironic. An emphasis on gender points to one group—females—that is *underrepresented* in jails, prisons, and other parts of the corrections system. An emphasis on race and ethnicity focuses our attention on another category of people, those who are *overrepresented* in the corrections system. Moreover, females and members of racial and ethnic minority groups receive sanctions, services, and treatments that differ qualitatively and quantitatively from those described for white men.

To gain a better appreciation for the depth and breadth of these differences, it is important to distinguish between race and ethnicity and to emphasize that both of these characteristics play an important role in corrections.

The terms *race* and *ethnicity* are often used interchangeably; however, they represent two distinct, though related, ideas. First, **race** divides human beings into distinct groups based on hereditary characteristics. Indeed, the first systematic and scientific applications of this term were used by anthropologists who wanted to categorize the species *Homo sapiens*. Early racial identifications turned on physical characteristics such as skin color, hair texture, facial features, and stature.[1] Differing combinations of these characteristics provided the basis for the major racial groups and subgroups. Using these types of characteristics, four major racial groups emerged: Caucasoid, Mongoloid, Negroid, and Australoid.

Racial distinctiveness depends on the physical, geographical, national, and cultural isolation of the various groupings. In the twentieth century, these distinctions took on less biological and anthropological significance. Nowhere is that more clearly demonstrated than in the United States, where racial distinctions have blurred even further in the children of mixed-race parents.

Ethnicity, by contrast, refers to a group's common social or cultural traits. Ethnic groups may have their own language, religion, and customs. Perhaps the most important element of ethnicity is the in-group identification shared by members, the sense that as a group they are traditionally distinct from the larger society.

Based on these two definitions, African Americans are identified as a racial group, whereas Hispanics are an ethnic group. However, Hispanics present an interesting case for two reasons. First, they are the fastest-growing minority group in the United States. Second, several different racial groups claim the cultural modifier of Hispanic or Latin. This makes their classification—in a study, for example—complicated. For instance, there are Hispanics of European descent (from Spain, for example); there are Hispanics of Afro-Caribbean descent (from the Dominican Republic or Puerto Rico, for example), who are also descended from people whose origins are African and Spanish; and there are Hispanics descended from both Spanish colonialists and various indigenous peoples in North, Central, and South America.

In the early 1990s, the American Anthropological Association (AAA) entered the debate. The AAA criticized the race and ethnic distinctions developed by the Office of Management and Budget (OMB) for use by the federal government and, by default, nearly all state and local governments as well. The OMB definition recognized five races: American Indian or Alaskan Native, Asian, Native Hawaiian or Pacific Islander, black or African American, and white. It recognized two ethnic designations: Hispanic and non-Hispanic. However, the OMB acknowledged that it had no scientific basis for this particular classification system. What the AAA suggested was that the concept of race is more useful in social and cultural contexts than in a purely biological one. The association acknowledged the difficulty many people have in making distinctions between race and ethnicity; in particular, it acknowledged that some Hispanics consider being Hispanic a racial designation (also see Gerber and de la Puente 1996; Rodriguez and Cordero-Guzman 1992). Finally, the AAA suggested that multiethnic and multiracial identifications were becoming increasingly common in the United States and that to ignore these new distinctions was to ignore the realities of contemporary US life.

In 1998, the AAA published a formal statement on race, acknowledging that it did not even reflect the consensus of its own membership. The statement noted that there is more human variability found within racial groups than there is among them, and that interracial distinctions are even less pronounced when the people of the races in question live in close physical proximity to one another. In the final analysis, the AAA concluded that race as a means of distinguishing among different groups of peoples may have outlived its scientific usefulness—if it ever had any:

> Given what we know about the capacity of normal humans to achieve and function within any culture, we conclude that present-day inequalities between so-called "racial" groups are not consequences of their biological inheritance but products of historical and contemporary social, economic, educational, and political circumstances. (AAA 1998, 4)

To date, the OMB allows people to identify with more than one race, but the ethnicity choice is still either Hispanic or non–Hispanic.

Governmental entities and social scientific communities are sensitive to definitions of race and ethnicity. The idea that race and ethnicity play a significant role in the distribution of criminal justice is a source of discomfort for many and a wellspring of resentment for others. **Racism** and **ethnocentrism**—the beliefs that, respectively, either certain races or certain ethnic groups are by definition better or worse than others—have long and unhappy histories in the United States, and most US citizens are not proud of that. However, racial and ethnic distinctions serve a purpose if they can help us identify and eliminate discrimination in the way people of color move through the criminal justice system (see, for example, Mann 1987; Wilbanks 1987).

Disproportionate minority contact (DMC) refers to the overrepresentation of minority group members at all stages of the criminal justice process, including arrest, trial, and punishment. DMC has long been the subject of scrutiny by policy analysts and other social scientists. In fact, the term, as first used, referred to disproportionate minority confinement, reflecting the overrepresentation of people of color in the nation's jails and prisons. In 1992, the Office of Juvenile Justice and Delinquency Prevention made disproportionate minority confinement one of its major national initiatives, and it funded research and technical assistance for states to address this problem. As the study of the phenomenon evolved, it became clear that this term was somewhat limited, and that the strained relationship between minority communities and the justice system was far broader than just the question of confinement (Pope, Lovell, and Hsia 2003). In 2002, the mandate changed, as "contact" replaced "confinement" in DMC.

Disproportionate minority contact may start with juveniles, but it is also devastating to adult people of color. Hence, the term is commonly used today to examine the disproportionate number of minority adults *and* juveniles that come into contact with elements of the nation's criminal justice system. That contact typically begins with arrest.

ARREST DISPARITIES

African Americans are arrested less often than whites but for generally more serious crimes, although the range of offenses is identical to that for whites. For example, look at Table 14.1. Notice that overall in 2010, blacks made up 29.1 percent of the 6,216,983 adult arrestees of either race. The message is clear: Given that blacks make up roughly 13 percent of the nation's adult population, they are disproportionately higher among arrestees, over twice the percentage of blacks in the general population. However, if we find the percentage blacks in a given arrest category higher than 29.1 percent, then this is a crime where the number of black arrestees is substantively higher *given their contribution to the entire arrestee population.*[2] (That is, blacks are already disproportionately higher overall in the arrest statistics.) If the percentage of blacks in an arrest category is below 29.1 percent, then the reverse is true: that arrest rate for blacks is substantively lower than we would expect.

In certain Index Crimes, blacks have higher than expected arrest figures, particularly murder and nonnegligent manslaughter and robbery; moreover, in

TABLE 14.1 Ten-Year Trends for White and Black Adult Arrestees.

Offense charged	White			Black			Percent Black	
	Total			Total				
	2001	2010	Percent change	2001	2010	Percent change	2001	2010
TOTAL[a]	5,363,012	6,216,983	+15.9	2,207,001	2,447,613	+10.9	29.2	29.1
Murder and nonnegligent manslaughter	4,138	3,929	−5.1	4,130	3,770	−8.7	50.0	46.8
Forcible rape	9,723	8,809	−9.4	5,285	4,138	−21.7	35.2	29.4
Robbery	26,905	31,236	+16.1	30,711	34,108	+11.1	53.3	55.1
Aggravated assault	183,290	182,663	−0.3	94,639	91,900	−2.9	34.1	33.1
Burglary	93,380	120,671	+29.2	41,032	50,884	+24.0	30.5	31.5
Larceny-theft	367,568	543,818	+48.0	184,795	211,413	+14.4	33.5	29.0
Motor vehicle theft	40,018	28,288	−29.3	27,113	13,631	−49.7	40.4	24.6
Arson	4,666	3,915	−16.1	1,602	1,194	−25.5	25.6	21.6
Violent crime[b]	224,056	226,637	+1.2	134,765	133,916	−0.6	37.6	37.1
Property crime[b]	505,632	696,692	+37.8	254,542	277,122	+8.9	33.5	29.1
Other assaults	484,830	562,177	+16.0	232,197	256,270	+10.4	32.4	32.3
Forgery and counterfeiting	49,514	39,294	−20.6	22,474	18,946	−15.7	31.2	30.7
Fraud	138,651	92,426	−33.3	63,430	44,740	−29.5	31.4	28.7
Embezzlement	8,213	8,356	+1.7	4,060	3,918	−3.5	33.1	31.6
Stolen property; buying, receiving, possessing	39,182	41,817	+6.7	25,174	19,629	−22.0	39.1	29.3
Vandalism	80,175	98,292	+22.6	29,959	34,448	+15.0	27.2	26.9
Weapons; carrying, possessing, etc.	52,617	56,660	+7.7	34,295	40,672	+18.6	39.5	44.7
Prostitution and commercialized vice	32,937	25,850	−21.5	23,093	19,929	−13.7	41.2	40.7

(Continued)

TABLE 14.1 (*Continued*)

Offense charged	White Total			Black Total			Percent Black	
	2001	2010	Percent change	2001	2010	Percent change	2001	2010
Sex offenses (except forcible rape and prostitution)	37,547	34,178	−9.0	11,696	10,542	−9.9	23.8	23.0
Drug abuse violations	600,938	748,697	+24.6	338,318	373,034	+10.3	36.0	34.3
Gambling	2,018	2,074	+2.8	4,424	4,129	−6.7	68.7	63.5
Offenses against the family and children	58,395	54,119	−7.3	26,325	25,724	−2.3	31.1	32.0
Driving under the influence	813,242	919,048	+13.0	98,894	123,935	+25.3	10.8	12.2
Liquor laws	266,558	263,175	−1.3	36,506	42,241	+15.7	12.0	14.1
Drunkenness	342,235	353,568	+3.3	55,243	65,987	+19.4	13.9	16.1
Disorderly conduct	201,113	235,684	+17.2	98,953	113,713	+14.9	33.0	34.0
Vagrancy	10,753	12,810	+19.1	6,550	9,544	+45.7	37.9	49.3
All other offenses (except traffic)	1,414,348	1,744,872	+23.4	708,417	828,898	+17.0	33.4	33.8
Suspicion	1,058	511	−51.7	686	276	−59.8	39.3	23.1

NOTES: [a]DOES NOT INCLUDE RUNAWAYS; [b]VIOLENT CRIMES ARE OFFENSES OF MURDER AND NON-NEGLIGENT MANSLAUGHTER, FORCIBLE RAPE, ROBBERY, AND AGGRAVATED ASSAULT. PROPERTY CRIMES ARE OFFENSES OF BURGLARY, LARCENY-THEFT, MOTOR VEHICLE THEFT, AND ARSON.

SOURCES: FEDERAL BUREAU OF INVESTIGATION (2002, 254; 2011, TABLES 43C).

four non-Index Crime categories, including weapons offenses, prostitution, gambling, and vagrancy, the percentage of blacks is, in 2010, well above the 29.1 percent figure. Blacks' involvement in certain arrest categories presents an entirely different picture. Overall, blacks are underrepresented in only a few crime categories, but they are instructive. For example, their arrest rates are substantively lower than whites for the following non-Index Crimes: sex offenses (except forcible rape and prostitution), DUI, liquor law violations, drunkenness, and suspicion. Blacks' arrest rates are also substantively lower than whites for burglary, motor-vehicle theft, and arson, all of which are Index Crimes.

Table 14.1 also illustrates that arrest rates for blacks between 2001 and 2010 increased by almost 11 percent; the rates for whites increased by nearly 16 percent for the same period, creating a difference of 5 percent between the two racial groupings. Much of the increase for whites can be attributed to changes in larceny-theft arrests, as this is the largest Index Crime category. However, several other non-Index Crime categories also saw large increases (more than 20 percent) over this same time period, including vandalism, drug abuse violations, and all other offenses (except traffic), all offenses with large base figures. White arrest rates for the following crimes decreased by more than 20 percent: motor vehicle theft, forgery and counterfeiting, fraud, prostitution and commercialized vice, and suspicion.

For their part, blacks saw increases in a different set of crime categories, including large increases (more than 20 percent) for burglary, DUI, and vagrancy. Large decreases (more than 20 percent) were reported for blacks in the following crime categories: forcible rape, motor vehicle theft, and arson, all three being Index Crimes. Among the non-Index Crimes, blacks saw large decreases for fraud, stolen property, and suspicion.

Collectively, these figures suggest that blacks commit a disproportionately higher number of violent crimes, including murder and nonnegligent manslaughter and robbery. Second, blacks also commit a similarly disproportionate number of crimes associated with contemporary street life, including weapons offenses, gambling, prostitution and commercialized vice, and vagrancy. Taken together, these observations about crime and violence correspond with other studies of contemporary life in many of the nation's black communities (Massey 1994; Massey and Denton 1993; Sánchez-Jankowski 1991; Shihadeh and Flynn 1996; Wilson 1987; Zimring and Hawkins 1997), as well as its Hispanic communities (Ramirez 2002). As Massey and Denton conclude, much of the violent crime and associated social ills found in minority communities can be attributed to the extreme level of **hypersegregation**, the social and legal separation of racial minorities but especially blacks into discrete geographic areas, that characterizes the nation's inner cities.

SENTENCING DISPARITIES

In Chapter 3, we discussed the long tradition of indeterminate sentencing in the United States. Legislatures set the outside limits of indeterminate sentences, but within those limits, judges have wide discretion in imposing sentences, and parole boards enjoy equally wide discretion in deciding when an individual will be released and under what conditions. The result of this broad discretion often is sentencing disparity. **Sentencing disparity** can take a variety of forms. For instance, when a judge sentences two similar defendants to distinctly different types of punishments—say prison sentences of different durations—that is a sentencing disparity. Another is when different judges sentence offenders charged with similar offenses to different punishments—one to probation, for example, and the other to prison. Often an unintended consequence of judicial discretion and sentencing disparity is that members of minority groups are punished more frequently and more harshly than others are.

THE ROLE OF SENTENCING GUIDELINES IN REDUCING DISPARITIES

To minimize sentencing disparities, especially as they affect minority groups, states have moved in the direction of creating *sentencing guidelines* (see Chapter 3). In 1980, Minnesota became the first state to implement sentencing guidelines (Knapp 1982, 1984). The guidelines are expressed in the form of a grid with two legally relevant dimensions: the offense with which the person is charged and the offender's criminal history.[3] Factors such as race, income, employment history, and drug use are not legally relevant for determining a sentence and should not be used.

The Minnesota Sentencing Guidelines Commission (2003) lists five goals of the guidelines.

1 To ensure public safety by incarcerating the most dangerous offenders for the longest time.

2 To promote uniformity in sentencing by imposing similar sentences on similar offenders.

3 To promote proportionality in sentencing by supporting a just-deserts philosophy of punishment.

4 To provide truth and certainty in sentencing by requiring prisoners to serve at least two-thirds of the sentence imposed.

5 To coordinate sentencing practices with available prison space.

Of these goals, the second and third, which promote uniformity and proportionality, are most closely related to questions of race and ethnicity.

After 30 years, the Minnesota sentencing guidelines have become a component of the criminal justice system in many jurisdictions: 20 states, the District of Columbia, and the federal government have guided sentencing in place.[4] Proponents insist that the sentencing process in these jurisdictions is more objective, and so sentences are more uniform. Whether guidelines have totally eliminated discretion from the sentencing process is not clear. Some states have yet to consider sentencing guidelines, and other state legislatures debated and then rejected the use of guidelines.

Not all states have approached guided sentencing in the same way. For instance, Minnesota's guidelines are mandated by statute: judges are bound to adhere to the guidelines unless they can point to a **manifest injustice**, a sentence that is simply not appropriate given the facts in the case. Manifest injustice can be invoked any time a judge thinks the prescribed sentence is too severe for the crime given the offender's individual circumstances. When judges depart from

prescribed sentences, they must provide written justification for that departure, and this kind of deviation becomes grounds for appeal ("Sentencing reform act" 2003). Minnesota's judges seldom depart from the guidelines. By contrast, sentencing guidelines in Maryland are less mandatory and more advisory: judges are not legally bound to follow them, and most do not. A review of sentencing practices in Maryland found that judges depart from the guidelines in nearly 80 percent of their sentencing decisions (Maryland Commission on Criminal Sentencing Policy 1998).

Kauder and Ostrom (2008) examined the extent to which sentencing guidelines in the 21 jurisdictions employing them are either voluntary or mandatory. At the voluntary end of the continuum, from most to least voluntary, are Ohio, Wisconsin, Missouri, Alabama, District of Columbia, Tennessee, Arkansas, Louisiana, Delaware, Utah, and Virginia. On the more mandatory side of the continuum, from most to least mandatory, are North Carolina, Minnesota, Oregon, Kansas, Washington, Pennsylvania, Michigan, Alaska, Massachusetts, and Maryland. Simply having such guidelines is no guarantee that they will remove the possibility of judicial discretion entering the actual sentencing process.

FELONY SENTENCING

Figure 14.1 shows the distribution of felony convictions for black and white defendants in state courts in 2006 (Rosenmerkel, Durose, and Farole 2009). The bar labeled *All offenses* in each figure defines the racial group's average contribution. For example, among all persons convicted in state court, 38 percent were black defendants and 60 percent were white defendants, the remainder being other racial groups. The bars that show a greater percentage than the *all offences* bar indicate conviction rates that are higher than average for that group—black or white defendants are overrepresented among those convicted for these crimes.[5] For example, Figure 14.1b shows that 74 percent of all those convicted of sexual assault in state courts in 2006 were white; the dark bar shows that 60 percent of all persons convicted of felonies in state courts that year were white.

FIGURE 14.1 Black and White Defendants Convicted in State Courts, by Most-Serious Felony Conviction, 2006. *Source:* Rosenmerkel, Durose, and Farole (2009).

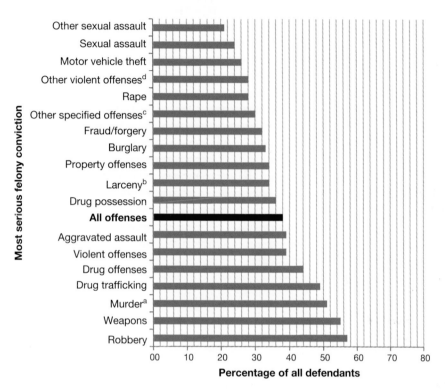

a. Black defendants

Notes: [a]Murder includes nonnegligent manslaughter.
[b]Larceny includes forgery and embezzlement.
[c]Other offenses include nonviolent offenses like receiving stolen property and vandalism.
[d]Other violent offenses include offenses like negligent manslaughter and kidnapping.

Whites, then, were overrepresented in sexual assault convictions.

Does one racial group or the other dominate certain types of crimes? Yes. Figure 14.1a shows blacks were markedly overrepresented, where their share of the defendants is more than 5 percent above their "average" (all offenses), in five offense categories: robbery, weapons offenses, murder, drug trafficking, and all drug offenses.[6] As importantly, blacks are markedly underrepresented, where their share of the defendants is more than 5 percent below their "average" (all offenses), in the following eight offense categories: burglary, fraud/forgery, other specified offenses, rape, other violent offenses, motor vehicle theft, sexual assault, and other sexual assault. It is drug offenses in particular that can have very serious consequences for defendants of color. A study of sentencing behavior in Maryland (see previous discussion about that state's sentencing guidelines) revealed that judges' sentences of black and Hispanic drug defendants are longer than for white defendants (Souryal and Wellford 1997). We return to drug crimes later in this chapter.

White defendants were markedly overrepresented—that is, more than 5 percent above their average proportion of the defendants (all offenses)—in eight

FIGURE 14.1 (*Continued*)

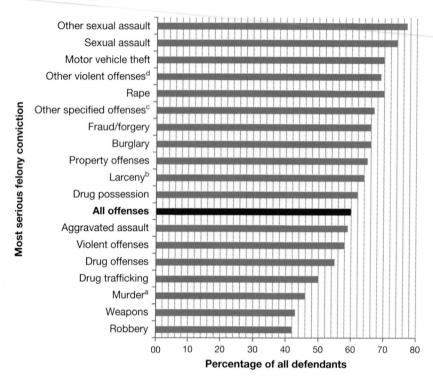

b. White defendants

Notes: [a]Murder includes nonnegligent manslaughter.
[b]Larceny includes forgery and embezzlement.
[c]Other offenses include nonviolent offenses like receiving stolen property and vandalism.
[d]Other violent offenses include offenses like negligent manslaughter and kidnapping.

offense categories: other sexual assault, sexual assault, rape, motor vehicle theft, other violent offenses, other specified offenses, fraud/forgery, and burglary. Notice that whites "dominated" all of the sex-related offenses and two of the three Index Property Crimes included in the analysis. White defendants were markedly underrepresented in four offenses: drug trafficking, murder, weapons offenses, and robbery.

That black defendants were overrepresented in the robbery and murder categories seems inextricably linked to blacks' high rates of violent victimization: that is, blacks are more likely to commit certain violent crimes, and they also are more likely to be the victims of those violent crimes. When a black

person kills another person, the victim is most likely to be a black stranger or a black friend; a black person is far less likely to kill a white stranger and would almost never kill a white friend (Rennison 2001, 2). Also, blacks are far more likely to present a weapon—which in half the cases is a gun—during the commission of a violent crime.

We do not have exactly comparable federal sentencing data. In 2005, fewer than 69,000 people were convicted in federal courts, about one-tenth the number convicted of felonies in state courts (Durose and Langan 2004; US Sentencing Commission 2007). Moreover, far fewer violent crimes find their way into federal court. A few comparisons are nonetheless instructive. In 2005, whites accounted for 29 percent of all sentenced defendants, blacks another 24 percent, and Hispanics 43 percent. Five crimes constituted more than 80 percent of all federal convictions. For example, drug trafficking accounts for 36 percent of all convictions; however, none of the groups were represented disproportionately from their overall conviction percentages. In the case of immigration convictions, 90 percent involved Hispanics, the consequences of which we addressed in Chapter 8. Blacks dominated firearms charges (47 percent), whereas whites were overrepresented in fraud and larceny (48 percent each). What is important to remember is that 75 percent of all persons convicted in federal court are either Hispanic or black.

DRUG OFFENSES: A SPECIAL CASE?

During the 1980s, critics of the federal government's "War on Drugs" pointed out that people convicted of drug law violations involving crack cocaine receive far longer sentences than those whose offenses involved the chemically identical powder version of the drug (Inciardi 1992; Walker 2011). According to federal law, 1 gram of crack cocaine is equal to 100 grams of powder cocaine (Free 1997, 276). Hence, a suspect with even a small amount of crack cocaine would not be charged with simple possession (21 USC 844). Instead, he or she could be charged with a general drug trafficking offense—for example, the intent to distribute illicit drugs (21 USC 841) or the importation of illicit drugs (21 USC 960)—either of which is a far more serious crime. Also, in some states, a person convicted of possessing less than 10 grams of *powder cocaine* might face up to 5 years in prison, while someone with as little as 3 grams of crack would face 20 years in prison (Alexander and Gyamerah 1997, 111).

Many critics of current sentencing guidelines—in particular, drug sentencing policies—remain convinced that there are two different systems of punishment in the United States for the possession of drugs, one for blacks and one for whites. According to Alexander and Gyamerah (1997), current drug laws continue discriminatory practices begun during slavery (see, for example, Sellin 1976). Alexander and Gyamerah point to changes in the 1960s in the laws governing the possession of marijuana to lessen the potential for those possessing small amounts of the drug to serve significant prison sentences. They compare that change with the harsher penalties imposed in the 1980s for the possession of crack cocaine, the form of cocaine most widely used among blacks. And they argue that this discrimination must stop, that the government should ease the laws governing the possession of crack as it did those governing marijuana.

A particular target of critics is the *Anti-Drug Abuse Act of 1986*. This law affected sentencing in two ways. First, it established mandatory minimum penalties for drug trafficking based on the quantity of the drug involved (US Sentencing Commission 1991); second, it differentiated crack cocaine from powder cocaine for sentencing purposes (McDonald and Carlson 1993). Another is the *Omnibus Anti-Drug Abuse Act of 1988*, which mandates a sentence of at least 5 years in federal prison for the possession of 5 grams of crack cocaine—the weight of two pennies and about the amount of crack a serious user might smoke in a weekend (Free 1997, 276).

Free (1997) believes that the national campaign against drugs has disproportionately affected blacks through sentencing guidelines (also see Inciardi 1992). Black defendants, who are more likely to possess and use crack cocaine, more often receive sentences at or above the mandatory minimum than either whites or Hispanics (US Sentencing Commission 1991, 80). Racial discrimination may not have been the intent of the War on Drugs, but drug use patterns and unreasonably harsh sentencing practices have certainly made it a result of that campaign. For example, among those sentenced in 2005 in federal courts for "powder" cocaine crime (accounting for roughly 20 percent of all federal drug sentences) 15 percent were white, 27 percent black, and 57 percent Hispanic (US Sentencing Commission 2007). Crack presented a far different picture: 80 percent were black, 9 percent Hispanic, and 9 percent white.

After two failed Supreme Court challenges asserting facial bias in the crack cocaine sentencing laws, *United States v. Armstrong* (1996) and *Edwards v. United States* (1998), Congress passed the Fair Sentencing

Act (FSA) in 2010, which changed the 100 to 1 sentencing disparity between minimum sentences for crack and powder cocaine to 18 to 1. That is, prior to the FSA, 1 ounce of crack was the equivalent at sentencing of 100 ounces of the powder form of cocaine; under the provision of the FSA, this ratio was lowered to one ounce of crack equal to 18 ounces of powder cocaine at sentencing. A year later the US Sentencing Commission made the reduced crack cocaine penalties retroactive, making some 12,000 current federal inmates eligible to request reduced sentences. There was some resistance to the retroactive provision; however, the Supreme Court examined this issue in *Dorsey v. U.S.* (2012). Defendant Dorsey was convicted of the possession of 5.5 grams of crack in 2008; he was sentenced to 10 years after full implementation of the FSA. The Court, in a five to four decision, ruled that the retroactive application provision of the FSA should apply to persons who committed a crack cocaine crime before the act was signed into law, but were sentenced after its effective date.

CONFINEMENT DISPARITIES

The nation's state and federal prison systems, along with its jail system, experienced unprecedented growth during the 1980s and 1990s (see Chapter 6). Before we look at how that growth affected the racial and ethnic makeup of the inmate population, another cautionary note is necessary. That is, from the earliest time that prisons began to report data on inmates, race was noted as either black or white. Other races, which could cover a great deal of racial and ethnic territory, were grouped in the black category. Beginning in the 1980s, the Bureau of Justice Statistics (BJS) sporadically published estimates of the number of Hispanic inmates per 100,000 Hispanics nationally, but these figures were notoriously unreliable because many states still did not collect accurate racial and ethnic information (Brown et al. 1996, 9). An OMB directive in 1997 (discussed earlier in this chapter) established guidelines for collecting data on race and ethnicity. Beginning in 1999, the BJS used three racial and ethnic categories for persons incarcerated by state and federal jurisdictions: white non-Hispanics (or those we call *whites*), nonblack Hispanics (those we call *Hispanics*), and non-Hispanic blacks (those we call *blacks*).[7] These changes mean that it can be very difficult to find comparable information.

JAIL INMATES

Jails house significantly fewer inmates at any one time than do prisons. However, as we noted in Chapter 5, in a given year millions of individuals pass through the 3,000-plus jails in the United States. Hence, jail population disparities mean that a significant number of people of color pass through the nation's jails yearly. Both the race- and ethnicity-adjusted jail population figures and rates by group per 100,000 residents help us understand the scope of this problem over the entire 26 years represented in Figure 14.2.

Although none of the group-specific changes in the racial and ethnic breakdown of the jail population were very large, the increase in absolute numbers was substantial. More importantly, when we combine the figures for blacks and Hispanics, we find that by 2010, 55 percent of the inmates in the nation's jails are people of color, a fact that has not changed substantially since 1988 when it was 56 percent.

The per 100,000 incarceration rates listed in Table 14.2 suggest that the disparities observed in prison rates also appear in jails. The rates for whites and blacks more than doubled between 1985 and 2005.[8] As whites went from 73 to 166 inmates per 100,000 white residents, blacks increased from 368 to 800 per 100,000 black residents. Among Hispanics, the rate changed little between 1996—the first time the rate was systematically reported—and 2006. In 2006, the Hispanic rate was more than 50 percent greater than that for whites, whereas the rate for blacks was close to five times greater than whites.

PRISON INMATES

Our information about prisons and race covers a longer period of time than is available for jails. For example, Figure 14.3 offers a historical perspective

FIGURE 14.2 **Local Jail Inmates by Race and Hispanic Origin, 1985–2010.** *Sources:* Gillard and Beck (1997b); Harrison and Karberg (2003, 2004); Harrison and Beck (2005); Minton (2010, 2011); Minton and Sabol (2009).

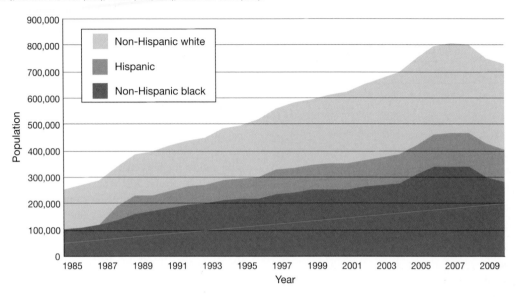

FIGURE 14.3 **Prisoners Admitted to State and Federal Institutions, by Race, 1930–1985.** *Source:* Adapted from Langan (1991).

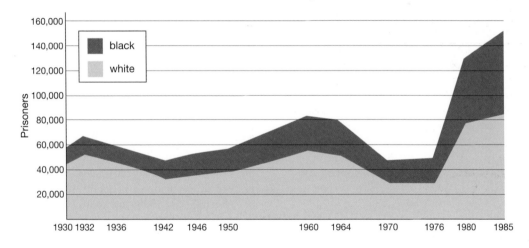

on the racial makeup of prisoners *admitted* to state and federal institutions from 1930 to 1985. Throughout the period, blacks were overrepresented among prisoners admitted to state and federal facilities—that is, their percentage in this population was larger than their percentage in the general population. Through

the mid-1970s, their proportion among prisoners admitted grew very gradually, and their numbers largely increased or decreased in tandem with the numbers of white prisoners admitted to state and federal facilities. There was significant change in that pattern in the late 1970s and early 1980s, just as the

TABLE 14.2 **Inmates in local jails, per capita rates (per 100,000) by gender, race, and Hispanic origin, 1985–2006.**

Year	Number of inmates per 100,000 residents		
	White	Black	Hispanic
1985	73	368	—
1986	79	375	—
1987	86	392	—
1988	96	478	—
1989	106	568	—
1990	106	569	—
1991	109	604	—
1992	109	619	—
1993	111	665	—
1994	117	688	—
1995	122	700	—
1996	111	666	290
1997	118	737	304
1998	125	747	302
1999	127	730	288
2000	132	736	280
2001	138	703	263
2002	147	740	256
2003	151	748	269
2004	160	765	262
2005	166	800	268
2006	170	815	283

—NOT CALCULATED.
SOURCES: HARRISON AND BECK (2001, 2005, 2006); HARRISON AND KARBERG (2004); SABOL AND MINTON (2008).

nation's overall prison population began to experience a steep climb: The ratio of white-to-black inmates changed markedly from 1976 to 1980 (see Figure 14.3). This meant that, at the beginning of the penal harm movement (see too Chapter 1), there was even greater disproportionality of black-to-white inmates entering the nation's prison systems. This was a time when leaving prison before the end of one's sentence—which was often very long—

became an increasingly difficult proposition. The net result of this movement was that sentences—but mainly incarceration—became intentionally more harsh and retributive with the ultimate goal that the unpleasantness associated with such criminal sanctions would stop future criminality; however, as this figure suggests, people of color in particular were negatively impacted by the implementation of these practices (Cullen 1995).

Figure 14.4 reflects not the admissions to the nation's prisons, as was the case in Figure 14.3, but the *actual number* of federal and state prison inmates. This figure suggests that the number incarcerated in each group—black and white inmates—grew exponentially, as the overall prison population more than doubled from 1985 to 1997. The slope or angle of the line for blacks is steeper than for whites, suggesting that the rate of growth was slightly higher for the former. In 1997, blacks accounted for about 47 percent of the prison population, roughly where they were in 1985. However, from 1985 to 1994, the percentage of black inmates increased every year, peaking at 52 percent in 1994.

Figure 14.5 reflects the number of federal and state prison inmates from 1999 to 2010 in the three major racial/ethnic groupings available after the definitional changes imposed in 1997–1998. The percentage of blacks declined over this period of time from 46 percent in 1999 to 38 percent by 2010. The percent of white inmates fluctuated only slightly over this time frame, from a high of 36 percent in 2001 to a low of 32 percent by 2010. The percentage of Hispanics increased over the 12 years, rising from a low of 16 percent in 2001 to a high of 22 percent by 2010. Put another way, 64 percent of the nation's prisoners were either black or Hispanic in 1999; by 2010, this figure had dropped to 60 percent. Before drawing the conclusion that disproportionate minority confinement was on the decline, it is important to realize that between 2003 and 2010, the percentage of inmates identifying as being something other than white, black, or Hispanic and those indicating that they were multiracial increased from less than 3 percent to nearly 8 percent, which translates into a non-white prison population of 68 percent in 2010, whereas it had been 67 percent in 1999.

FIGURE 14.4 **Inmates in State and Federal Prisons by Race, 1985–1997.** *Sources:* Beck and Mumola (1999); Gillard and Beck (1994); and Mumola and Beck (1997).

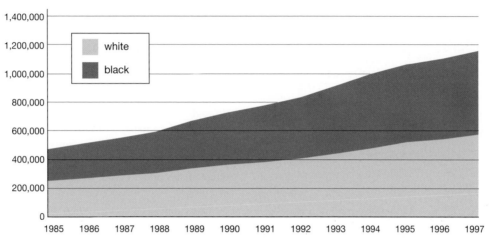

NOTE: Hispanics are included in both white and black totals, depending on the racial identification of the individual inmate.

FIGURE 14.5 **Inmates in State and Federal Prisons by Race, 1999–2010.** *Sources:* Beck (2000, 10); Guerino, Harrison, and Sabol (2011).

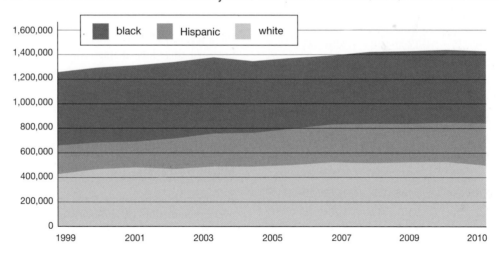

Table 14.3 provides a different view of the over-representation issue (and the question of changing ethnic/racial definitions), this time focusing on per 100,000 rates, rather than the raw number of inmates. This figure also shows the rates of prisoners by gender and race. Between 1985 and 1997, the rates for men and women, and blacks and whites increased,

and in some cases the starting rates were already high. For example, in 1985 there were 1,559 black men in prison for every 100,000 black residents in the United States. By 1997, that rate had more than doubled, increasing to 3,253. The rate for white male inmates rose from 246 for every 100,000 white residents in the country in 1985 to 491 in 1997. The

TABLE 14.3 Inmates in state and federal prisons (per 100,000) rates by gender, race, and Hispanic origin, 1985–2010.

| | Number of inmates per 100,000 residents | | | | | |
| | White | | Black | | Hispanic | |
Year	Male	Female	Male	Female	Male	Female
1985	246	10	1,559	68	—	—
1986	261	12	1,695	77	—	—
1987	277	13	1,800	82	—	—
1988	290	15	1,951	91	—	—
1989	317	17	2,200	115	—	—
1990	339	19	2,376	125	—	—
1991	352	19	2,523	135	—	—
1992	372	20	2,678	143	—	—
1993	398	23	2,920	165	—	—
1994	427	26	3,158	179	—	—
1995	449	27	3,095	176	—	—
1996	468	30	3,164	185	—	—
1997	491	32	3,253	192	—	—
1998	—	—	—	—	—	—
1999	417	27	3,408	212	1,335	87
2000	449	34	3,457	205	1,220	60
2001	462	36	3,535	199	1,177	61
2002	450	35	3,437	191	1,176	80
2003	465	38	3,405	185	1,231	84
2004	463	42	3,218	170	1,220	75
2005	471	45	3,145	156	1,244	76
2006	487	48	3,042	148	1,261	81
2007	481	50	3,138	150	1,259	79
2008	487	50	3,161	149	1,200	75
2009	487	50	3,119	142	1,193	74
2010	459	47	3,074	133	1,258	77

SOURCES: BECK (2000); BECK AND HARRISON (2001); BECK AND MUMOLA (1999); GILLIARD AND BECK (1994); HARRISON AND BECK (2002, 2003, 2004, 8, 2005, 8, 2006, 8); GUERINO, HARRISON, AND SABOL (2011, 27).

rate for black women in prison almost tripled over the period; the rate for white women more than tripled between 1985 and 1997.

The BJS's change in definitions also had the effect of lowering the rate for white inmates in 1999, while the rates for black inmates increased. This statistical quirk is explained by the fact that traditionally between 80 percent and 90 percent of Hispanic inmates self-identify as white (Gilliard and Beck 1997a, 9). The rate for Hispanic inmates of both genders fell between 1999 and 2010, as did the rate for black male and female inmates. Interestingly, but given the analyses in Chapter 13 not surprisingly, the rates for white females showed an overall increase throughout the period shown in Table 14.3. The rates for white males and females—like the absolute numbers of inmates shown in Figure 14.5—rose between 1999 and 2010: the per capita rates for white males and females were higher in 2010 than in 1999.

These rates, especially when one considers that multiracial inmates have been excluded from the totals, suggest that the disproportionate minority confinement was an established and intractable pattern by the mid-1990s. The grossly disparate rates per 100,000 residents reported for black and Hispanic males are all the more important because together blacks and Hispanics make up more than 30 percent of the nation's population. Driving down the rates for these two categories of inmates has the potential to reduce dramatically the nation's prison population. If nothing is done, as shown in Box 14.1, the results could be catastrophic for minority communities.

EXPLAINING DISPROPORTIONATE MINORITY CONTACT

A number of explanations have been offered for the overrepresentation of minority group members in both the adult and juvenile components of the criminal justice system. One reason typically offered is that people of color commit more crimes because they happen to grow up and live in urban areas, usually in parts of inner cities where crime is common. Criminologists observed at the beginning of the twentieth century, and others have confirmed since, that indeed certain places are more prone to crime than others, no matter who lives there. For example, in the early 1900s, immigrants from Europe lived in the crime-prone inner cities of the United

WHAT WILL HAPPEN IF NOTHING CHANGES?   BOX 14.1

What will happen if the population trends reflected in the reported figures and the rate trends are not curbed or reversed? Bonczar has a chilling answer. He calculated that in 2001, nearly 2.2 million blacks in the United States and a similar number of whites had served time in prison, and that about 1 million Hispanics were ex-convicts. The proportion of black males who had been in prison at some time in their lives (17 percent) was more than twice that of Hispanic males (8 percent) and almost six times that of whites (3 percent). For black males aged 35 to 44 in 2001, the picture was even bleaker: 22 percent of these individuals had been in prison at some time.

According to Bonczar, as bad as things are today, the future may be even worse. Using a sophisticated demographic technique and nearly 20 years of prison data, he predicts that 7 percent of all children born in 2001 eventually will go to prison. For some males, the picture is worse: 32 percent of black males, 17 percent of Hispanic males, while 6 percent of white males can expect to spend some time in prison during their lifetime, *but only if current incarceration rates remain unchanged*. If they increase, and given the downward trend driven largely by changes in California's incarceration practices, that remains a difficult question. Black women, says Bonczar, will have the highest incarceration rates for females—6 percent will probably go to prison—almost the same rate as white males. White females have a substantially lower likelihood of being sent to prison: only about 1 percent of those born in 2001. The rate for Hispanic females will be twice that: 2 percent.

SOURCE: BONCZAR (2003).

States. This is where all new immigrants lived, despite the crime and other social problems. It was where they could afford to live or where they were allowed to live by a society that was well aware of their immigrant status. Criminologists studying crime and migration noted that the inner cities were deviant places, and they incorporated that idea in *social disorganization theory* (see Chapter 1). Among the factors that contributed to that deviance was a lack of adequate infrastructure, including police and fire services, trash removal, and parks. Also, residents had no real sense of community: this was not where they hoped to live out their days; it was simply the first rung on the ladder of success.

At the start of the twenty-first century, blacks, Hispanics, and other nonwhite immigrants from around the world populate those same streets, and the criminality of these places has changed little in the intervening century. Proponents of modern variants of social disorganization theory would argue, as their predecessors did in the 1930s and 1940s, that traditions of deviance are passed along to successive generations of newcomers, even if the next group of residents is of a different race or ethnicity (Sampson and Grove 1989). Proponents would insist that crime statistics do not reflect high-crime groups but, rather, reflect high-crime areas. As William Julius Wilson (1987) has observed, many urban black and Hispanic youths grow up in poverty-ridden, crime-infested neighborhoods, where lawbreaking is viewed as a way of life.

A second explanation is **justice by geography**, the idea that urban jurisdictions tend to deliver harsher sentences than nonurban jurisdictions do (see, for example, Feld 1981; Pope and Freyerherm 1991). Justice by geography could explain the treatment of members of minority groups and their overrepresentation in secure facilities and juvenile residential placements. James F. Austin and John Irwin (2001, 94–95) also observe that a major factor in the continual increase in racial skewing of the adult prison population is that most convicts come from inner-city, lower-class groups. This unique segment of the national population is increasingly made up of

African Americans and Hispanics. Justice by geography begins with delinquents and continues to influence which individuals are sentenced to what kinds of sanctions through adulthood.

A third explanation for minority overrepresentation involves overt **discrimination** based on the policies and practices of criminal justice system actors and agencies. This argument posits that these prejudicial policies and practices, combined with the socioeconomic levels of many minority communities, place minority-group members at distinct disadvantages when they face criminal prosecution. However, recent studies of differential arrest rates for adults and juveniles have failed to find a link between police conduct and DMC (Pope and Snyder 2003; Sorensen, Hope, and Stemen 2003). Given the presence of **institutional racism**, a form of prejudicial treatment whereby practices at many points in the justice system disproportionately affect people of color, it is doubly important to ensure that sentencing disparities do not disadvantage minority defendants or, worse, add to the disparities that already exist in the system.

Howard Snyder and Melissa Sickmund (1999) note that the same conditions—disparity and overrepresentation—could have their roots in the differential behaviors of minority youths *and* be related to legal factors. However, to date, we do not have the data necessary to test their hypothesis adequately. Race and ethnicity do appear to affect decisions in the processing of adult and juvenile cases. In approximately two-thirds of the studies examined by Pope and Freyerherm (1990a, 1990b, 1991), the offender's race or ethnicity appeared to influence the outcome of the case. As Snyder and Sickmund conclude, "Existing research suggests that race/ethnicity does make a difference in juvenile justice decisions in some jurisdictions at least some of the time" (1999, 193).

RACE, ETHNICITY, AND PRISON LIFE

In 2010, 40 percent of state and federal prison inmates were African American, and another 20 percent were Hispanic—or 60 percent of prison inmates were people of color. In that same year, 39 percent of jail inmates were black, and 15 percent

were Hispanic. Addressing racial and ethnic concerns is a fact of life for today's prison and jail administrators. In this section, we look at four areas where race and ethnicity play an especially important role in the daily operation of secure facilities: inmate–inmate relations, inmate–staff relations, prison riots and other inmate disturbances, and prison gangs.

INMATE–INMATE RELATIONS

The racial composition of a prison or prison system affects the relationships among groups of inmates. Not all states and not all prisons have the same racial mix of inmates. Prisons that primarily incarcerate convicts from urban areas—such as New York State's Attica prison in the 1970s and contemporary prisons in California—generally have large minority populations. Within prisons, there is often conflict over power and control, and this can manifest in inmate cliques. Racial tension is often a by-product of prison cliques and gangs.

Prison inmates are relatively powerless. One of the few ways they can exert power is by forming groups, and a natural basis for forming groups is race or ethnicity. It is not unusual for prison inmate groups to promote racial or ethnic pride or identity. Group members may ask to wear certain types of clothing or hairstyles, or to engage in certain religious practices. Prison officials have honored some of these requests; others have been denied for fear that they might be a disruptive influence. The US Supreme Court has decided at least two cases that centered on the First Amendment guarantee of religious freedom, one involving black Muslim inmates and the other Native American inmates. The Court's decisions have guaranteed some religious freedom to particular racial or ethnic groups, but they also recognize that the ultimate standard by which any inmate request must be measured is the safety and orderliness with which the prison operates.

INMATE–STAFF RELATIONS

Very seldom does the racial or ethnic composition of a prison's inmate population reflect the racial or ethnic composition of the staff. In fact, in a few well-publicized cases, numerous white staffers were in charge of an inmate population that was substantially black and Hispanic. For example, in the Attica facility, the staff was primarily white and from rural areas of New York; the inmates, by contrast, were primarily black and Hispanic, and from neighborhoods in New York City. Although the racial differences between workers and inmates were not the primary reason for the riot in Attica, some believe that those differences contributed to the difficulty in bringing the institution back under control (Wicker 1975).

It would be easy to say that discrimination underlies the problems of inmates and staffers from different racial and ethnic backgrounds but other factors may also be at work here. Differences in race and ethnicity can mean differences in language or speech patterns, social class, and politics or religion. It is very difficult for people to relate to one another in meaningful ways when they cannot communicate easily or hold totally different worldviews.

PRISON RIOTS AND INMATE DISTURBANCES

Earlier we noted the confounding effect that race and ethnicity had in the prison riot at Attica. This was not an isolated incident. Racial tensions between inmate groups and between inmates and staff have led to riots in other state and federal prisons. At the root of many of those disturbances were inmates of color who believed that they were being treated unfairly or that white inmates were somehow receiving preferential treatment. Moreover, prisons are often located in rural United States and the correctional officers drawn from the local population. Potentially the correctional officers have little contextual understanding of the inner-city minority group inmates.

PRISON GANGS

One of the most visible ways that racial and ethnic issues shape prison society is through prison gangs. Most prison gangs are formed along strict racial and ethnic lines. In some very large prisons, it is not uncommon to find two or more gangs representing one racial or ethnic group. In California and Texas facilities, for example, where the Hispanic inmate populations are high, there may be several Hispanic gangs in a facility, each representing a different

geographic region or local neighborhood in their respective states. The American Correctional Association classifies prison gangs as security-threat groups. All prison gangs are security-threat groups, but not all security-threat groups are gangs.

Gangs—as *security-threat groups*—exist in prisons for any number of reasons, but two are particularly important (see Chapter 7). The first is protection: when a group threatens an individual or another group one response is to band together in a gang (Fong and Vogel 1997). Typically, when a gang forms in a prison, other gangs form in response. It becomes something of an arms race to see which gang can establish the most power and thus provide the most protection. Ironically, in most prisons—as on most city streets—being a member of a gang not only provides protection, but also increases the likelihood of a member needing protection.

The second reason behind the formation of inmate gangs is to establish control within the prison. This control may take the form of claiming a certain part of the facility—an area in the recreation yard, for example—as the gang's territory. More important, however, prison gangs exercise economic control over drugs, gambling, work assignments, and sexual favors. Being part of a gang can make "doing time" easier.

PROBATION AND PAROLE DISPARITIES

All things being equal, the various punishments handed out to people convicted of crimes should be proportionate regardless of race or ethnicity. That is, whites, blacks, and Hispanics should receive jail and prison sentences, and probation and discretionary parole at the same rate. However, members of minority groups—especially African Americans—are sentenced to jails and prisons at disproportionate rates and for longer terms. What about probation and parole? Are minority-group members at the same disadvantage when the sanction for crime suspends or shortens a term of confinement?

As we indicated in Chapter 4, probation is the most common correctional disposition in the United States for adults. At the end of 2010, some 7 million people were under some form of correctional supervision in the United States at all levels of government. Of this number, more than 4 million people (almost 60 percent of the total) were on probation. Probation is the mainstay of the nation's correctional system.

Is probation administered fairly? When we compare the percentage of minority probationers to their proportion in the nation's population, the answer would appear to be no. Remember that minority groups make up less than 40 percent of the nation's population. If decisions were made without consideration of other factors—randomly, that is—we would expect them to make up a similar proportion of the probationer population. However, in 2010, minority-group members (nonwhites) constituted about 45 percent of probationers (see Figure 14.6a). Blacks, in particular, who accounted for only about 13 percent of the nation's population that year, made up 30 percent of the probationer population. Between 1990 and 2010, these figures changed little, except for Hispanics: their share of probationers dropped from 18 percent 1990 to 14 percent in 1995, where it has remained within 1 percent ever since. The percentage of black probationers changed little, whereas whites increased from 52 percent to 55 percent. Other minorities (American Indians/Alaska Natives and Asians/Pacific Islanders) accounted for more modest increases (from less than 1 percent to about 2 percent).

Several factors may explain these distributions. It is possible, for instance, that actors in the criminal justice system are basing their decisions on the race or ethnicity of the individuals who come before them for disposition. If this is true then racism is overt in the criminal justice system. A greater likelihood is that extralegal factors enter into the decision-making process. Remember that the decision to sentence an offender rests on a number of factors—all examined in the presentencing investigation—among them family stability, employment history, financial status, education, and criminal history. Although these factors are not explicitly tied to race, in most instances they act as surrogates for race. In social science research, we would say that these factors are *highly correlated* with race.

The second part of Figure 14.6 provides a look at race and ethnicity among the nation's parolees. The data here mirror those of prison populations.

This correlation is logical: the people placed on supervised release have served time in prison. Looking at the rates from 1990 to 2010, we can see that the proportion of white parolees increased from 36 percent in 1990 to 42 percent in 2010; the proportion of black parolees dropped from 46 percent to 39 percent during this same period; and the proportion of Hispanic parolees fluctuated between 18 and 21 percent. Given the increase in the black prison population during the 1990s, that the rate of black parolees has dropped would indicate an increasing disadvantage for them.

As we close this section on probation and parole decision making, we must emphasize several points. First, although blacks account for fewer probationers than jail or prison inmates, they still are present at a rate that is more than twice their proportion in the general population. Hispanics are only slightly overrepresented among probationers. Other members of minority groups are only about 2 percent of the overall probation population.

Second, legislatures still allow judges a great deal of discretion in deciding who should be placed on probation. Overt racism is difficult to prove in a discretionary decision-making environment. Race may play a factor, but it may be masked by a variety of other conditions that are highly correlated but that do not constitute racism per se.

Finally, when jail and prison populations are compared with probation and parole caseloads, it becomes apparent that all racial and ethnic groups do not fare equally well at all stages of the criminal justice process.

RACE AND THE DEATH PENALTY

Perhaps no aspect of criminal justice in the United States has been more controversial in the past 30 years than the death penalty. Certainly no other criminal justice practice has raised such important questions about discrimination. Here, three types of information are instructive: inmates on death row, inmates executed, and inmates leaving death row other than by execution.

In 2010, 13 states executed 46 prisoners; 17 of those executions were in Texas. At year's end, there

FIGURE 14.6 **Probationers and Parolees by Race and Ethnicity, 1990, 1995, 2000, 2005, and 2010.** *Sources:* Glaze (2002, 5, 8; 2003); Glaze and Bonczar (2006, 5, 8; 2011, 33, 43).

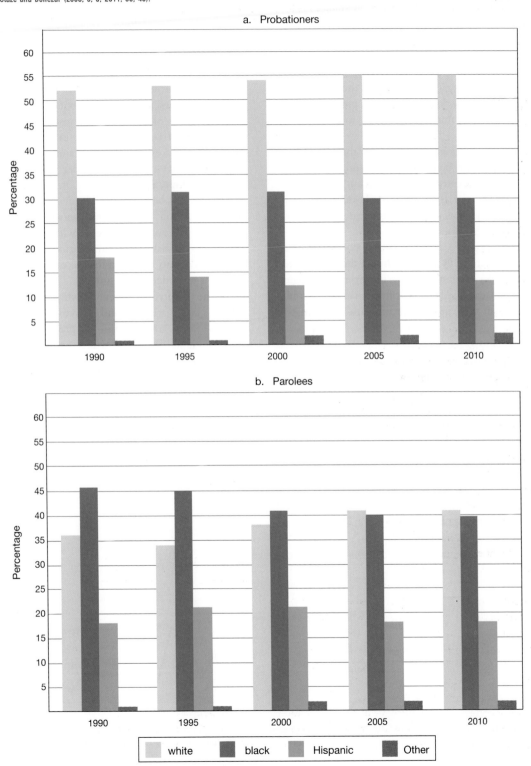

were 3,158 inmates under death sentences. Three states—California, Texas, and Florida—housed 40 percent of the nation's death row population (Snell 2011). Of the 46 people executed, 33 were white and 19 were black. Although whites constituted a numerical majority (72 percent) of those executed, the number of blacks executed was proportionately greater than the number of blacks in the general population.

As shown in Figure 14.7, between the reintroduction of the death penalty in 1977 and 2010, 1,235 people were executed: 700 (57 percent) were white and 424 (34 percent) were black. However, the majority of persons sentenced to death during this same time were black.

In closing, once again people of color are overrepresented on death row and among those executed. It remains an interesting irony, however, that whites have been executed more often than we would expect given their proportion of death row inmates.

RACE AND CORRECTIONS: FINAL COMMENTS

No discussion of contemporary corrections is complete without addressing race and ethnicity. In every stage of the corrections process, members of racial and ethnic minority groups are overrepresented.

Overrepresentation means that a particular group is present in a higher proportion than we would expect given its proportion of the nation's population. The disparities we describe in this chapter do not provide direct evidence of racism in the justice system, and explorations of race as a factor in arrests do not support the idea of racist police actions whether they involve juveniles (Pope and Snyder 2003) or adults (Sorensen, Hope, and Stemen 2003). However, there does seem to be considerable regional variation across the nation and variation between urban and rural areas, patterns that coincide with the residential patterns of the nation's minority groups. Geography, it seems, accounts for at least some of the differential treatment accorded racial groups.

In the future, prisoners serving time in the nation's jails, prisons, and juvenile correctional facilities—and the nation's probationers and parolees—in all likelihood will resemble the prisoners, probationers, and parolees of today. That is, they will be drawn disproportionately from the most disadvantaged groups in society, what Wilson (1987) calls the **underclass**. (Box 14.2 provides an international example.) For this group, crime is as institutionalized as poverty.

FIGURE 14.7 Inmates Executed, by Race, 1977–2010. *Source:* Snell (2011, 13).

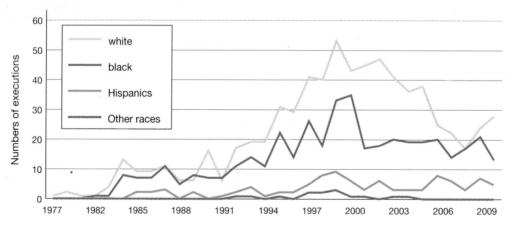

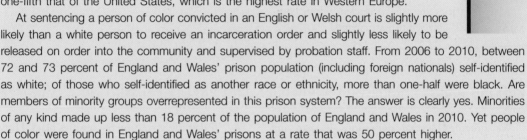

SPOTLIGHT ON INTERNATIONAL CORRECTIONS: CORRECTIONAL POPULATIONS IN ENGLAND AND WALES

BOX 14.2

Accurate data on the racial and ethnic composition of inmates in jail and prison systems around the world are hard to find. Not all nations are as open with this information as the United States. An exception to this generalization is the legally and politically distinct part of the United Kingdom known as England and Wales.* First, England and Wales have an incarceration rate of 148 per 100,000 residents, or about one-fifth that of the United States, which is the highest rate in Western Europe.

At sentencing a person of color convicted in an English or Welsh court is slightly more likely than a white person to receive an incarceration order and slightly less likely to be released on order into the community and supervised by probation staff. From 2006 to 2010, between 72 and 73 percent of England and Wales' prison population (including foreign nationals) self-identified as white; of those who self-identified as another race or ethnicity, more than one-half were black. Are members of minority groups overrepresented in this prison system? The answer is clearly yes. Minorities of any kind made up less than 18 percent of the population of England and Wales in 2010. Yet people of color were found in England and Wales' prisons at a rate that was 50 percent higher.

Probation services are over a century old in England and Wales, having been created in 1907 by the Probation of Offenders Act. Major changes occurred early in this century, with the creation of the National Probation Service in England and Wales in 2001 and a restructuring of probation services in 2004 that led to the establishment of the National Offender Management System (NOMS), which provided for an "end-to-end management of offenders, regardless of whether they were given a custodial or community sentence" (Home Office 2004, 14). NOMS became part of the new Ministry of Justice in 2007. According to annual reports on the activities of NOMS, roughly 73 percent of all pre-post-release supervision order commencements between 2006 and 2010 were white, which corresponds roughly to the percentages found in England and Wales' prisons; however, the percentage of supervisees who were black ranged from only 8 to 9 percent, far lower than the case for prison inmates.

The overrepresentation of minority-group members is a problem that the United States shares with many nations, not just England and Wales. However, given the absolute number of people in the United States under some form of supervision, few countries around the world can challenge its supremacy as the most racially and ethnically diverse corrections system in the world.

NOTE: *THE UNITED KINGDOM INCLUDES FOUR REGIONS: ENGLAND, SCOTLAND, WALES, AND NORTHERN IRELAND. SEPARATE STATISTICS ARE AVAILABLE FOR ALL FOUR. HOWEVER, THE MINISTRY OF JUSTICE REPORTS GROUP THE STATISTICS FOR ENGLAND AND WALES, AS REPORTED HERE.

SOURCES: ANNISON (2013); CENTRAL INTELLIGENCE AGENCY (2013); INTERNATIONAL CENTRE FOR PRISON STUDIES (2013); HOME OFFICE (2004); MINISTRY OF JUSTICE (2011).

SUMMARY

Race and ethnicity are two ideas that underscore much of our nation's response to crime and justice. Images of racism in its many forms haunt the nation's policy makers and practitioners as they review the statistics summarized in this chapter. The following are key points presented:

- Race and ethnicity, although closely related, refer to two quite different aspects of human social and physical conditions.

- Disparities based on race and ethnicity may begin at arrest, but they continue into the sentencing process in both state and federal courts.

● In the area of federal drug law enforcement, especially for certain kinds of drug offenses (for example, differences in sentences accorded crack versus powder cocaine possession), and immigration-law enforcement, questions about the racial and ethnic biases of policy makers come easily.

● Clear racial and ethnic disparities exist at each juncture in the criminal justice process, but the racial disparities are especially clear when comparing black and white participants.

● Hispanics, nonetheless, frequently account for a far disproportionate number of persons—male and female—in probation, parole, jail, and prison statistics.

● The death penalty is the prime example of institutional racism in the US criminal justice system. Minorities, but especially blacks, find themselves sentenced to death in disproportionate numbers.

THINKING ABOUT CORRECTIONAL POLICIES AND PRACTICES: WRITING ASSIGNMENTS

1 We provided several definitions of *race* and *ethnicity*, definitions used by the US Census Bureau, the Bureau of Justice Statistics, and others. What do you think about the process of defining race and ethnicity? Why is it important? Why is it divisive? Prepare a one- to two-page answer to these questions.

2 We limit our discussions of Table 14.1 to current areas where blacks are over- or under-represented in the arrest population, given their "share" of arrestees. First, what is wrong with this argument? Second, what happened to areas where blacks were either over- or under-represented in 2001 compared to 2010?

3 Prepare a one-page argument for abandoning the sentencing differences for crack cocaine and powder cocaine. Next, prepare a single-page rationale for keeping the law the way it is. Which argument wins, in your opinion?

4 Today, the government classifies black Hispanics for many purposes as Hispanics, rather than blacks. Is there a problem with this approach? Which is more important in the life of an offender: race or cultural identity? Is one or the other piece of information potentially more useful to policy makers and program designers? Prepare a two-page response to these questions.

5 Government agencies are being forced to cut costs. Suppose one measure Congress is considering would severely curtail the activities of the Bureau of Justice Statistics, the government entity that collects and publishes data on crime and justice. Prepare a one- to two-page response on the effects this would have on those studying corrections and developing correctional programs and public policy.

KEY TERMS

discrimination
disproportionate minority
    contact (DMC)
ethnicity
ethnocentrism

hyper-segregation
institutional racism
justice by geography
manifest injustice
race

racism
sentencing disparity
underclass

CRITICAL REVIEW QUESTIONS

1   What one aspect of the racial and ethnic disproportion in the history of US corrections disturbs you most? Why?

2   What fact, historical or contemporary, surprised you about the racial makeup of *arrestees* in the United States?

3   How do you respond to the claim that sentencing practices in the United States are basically unfair?

4   What fact, historical or contemporary, surprised you about the racial and ethnic makeup of *prisoners* in the United States?

5   What fact, historical or contemporary, surprised you about the racial and ethnic makeup of *probationers* in the United States?

6   What fact, historical or contemporary, surprised you about the racial and ethnic makeup of *parolees* in the United States?

7   If you had to characterize the conditions for blacks in the nation's corrections system, what would you say? Are conditions getting better or worse for blacks? Explain your answer.

8   If you had to characterize the conditions for Hispanics in the nation's corrections system, what would you say? Are conditions getting better or worse for Hispanics? Explain your answer.

9   Read Box 14.2. Now go on the Internet and try to find similar information for some other nation's corrections system. Why is this exercise useful?

10 What would be the fastest legal means to resolve the DMC problem?

CASES CITED

Edwards v. United States, 523 U.S. 511 (1998)
Dorsey v. United States, 567 U.S. 132 S.Ct. 2321 (2012)

United States v. Armstrong, 517 U.S. 456 (1996)

NOTES

1   The indiscriminate use of *race* and *ethnicity* to refer to biologically different groups can be traced to early beliefs that even social and cultural differences were biologically transmitted (Theodorson and Theodorson 1969, 328).

2   In the interest of somewhat simpler comparisons, the following discussion is limited to those differences greater than plus or minus 5 percent or, in this case, below 24.2 percent or above 34.2 percent. These breakpoints are arbitrary. Given that we have the entire population of data for arrestees, there is no such thing as a statistically significant difference, a difference greater than we would expect by chance alone. Rather, what we are looking at are differences that are substantively significant, and for these comparisons we are using differences greater or less than 5 percent.

3   The goals of the guidelines and other information about their implementation are available at the commission's website (**www.msgc.state.mn.us**).

4   The US Sentencing Commission website (**www.ussc. gov**) lists 20 state sentencing commissions and one for the District of Columbia.

5   As we move through the corrections process in this chapter, it is important to bear in mind the essential disparity that underlies the distribution of whites and

blacks in the corrections system. According to the US Census Bureau (2011), in 2010, white-only individuals constituted 72.4 percent of the US population, and black-only composed 12.6 percent.

6   As with the gender comparisons, to simplify the discussion we arbitrarily use plus or minus 5 percentage points from the all-offenses (average) rate as an indicator of substantive significance.

7   The Bureau of Justice Statistics has not completed a fully explicated report on the state of jails and jail inmates since 2006, providing only "statistical tables" that do not provide the per capita (per 100,000) breakdowns by gender or race.

8   According to the US Census Bureau (2011), in 2010, there were an estimated 37.7 million black non-Hispanics, 26.7 million non-black Hispanics, and 1.2 million black Hispanics/Hispanic blacks. However, the total number of blacks, whatever their ethnicity, was 38.9 million; and the total number of Hispanics, black or not, was 50.5 million. Confusing the picture of race and ethnicity even more is the fact that 9 million Americans report that they are two or more races.

REFERENCES

American Anthropological Association (AAA). 1998. *American Anthropological Association statement on "race."* Arlington, VA: AAA.

Alexander, Rudolph, Jr., and Jacquelyn Gyamerah. 1997. Differential punishing of African Americans and whites who possess drugs: A just policy or a continuation of the past? *Journal of Black Studies* 28: 97–111.

Austin, James F., and John Irwin. 2001. *It's about time: America's imprisonment binge*, 3rd edn. Belmont, CA: Wadsworth.

Beck, Allen J. 2000. *Prisoners in 1999.* Washington, DC: US Government Printing Office.

Beck, Allen J., and Paige M. Harrison. 2001. *Prisoners in 2000.* Washington, DC: US Government Printing Office.

Beck, Allen J., and Christopher J. Mumola. 1999. *Prisoners in 1998.* Washington, DC: US Department of Justice.

Bonczar, Thomas P. 2003. *Prevalence of imprisonment in the US population, 1974–2001.* Washington, DC: US Department of Justice.

Brown, Jodi M., Darrell K. Gilliard, Tracy L. Snell, James J. Stephan, and Doris James Wilson. 1996. *Correctional populations in the United States, 1994.* Washington, DC: US Department of Justice.

Durose, Matthew R., and Patrick A. Langan. 2004. *Felony sentences in state courts, 2002.* Washington, DC: US Department of Justice.

Federal Bureau of Investigation. 2002. *Crime in the United States, 2001.* Washington, DC: US Department of Justice.

Federal Bureau of Investigation. 2011. *Crime in the United States, 2010.* Washington, DC: US Department of Justice.

Feld, Barry. 1981. Legislative policies toward the serious juvenile offender. *Crime & Delinquency* 27(4): 497–521.

Fong, Robert S., and Ronald E. Vogel. 1997. A comparative analysis of prison gang members, security threat groups, and general population prisoners in the Texas Department of Corrections. In *Gangs and gang behavior*, edited by G. Larry Mays. Chicago: Nelson-Hall, 382–95.

Free, Marvin D. 1997. The impact of sentencing reforms on African Americans. *Journal of Black Studies* 28: 268–86.

Gerber, Eleanor, and Manuel de la Puente. 1996. *The development and cognitive testing of race and ethnic origin questions for the year 2000 decennial census.* US Census Bureau Annual Research Conference. Rosslynn, VA: US Bureau of the Census.

Gilliard, Darrell K., and Allen J. Beck. 1994. *Prisoners in 1993.* Washington, DC: US Department of Justice.

Gilliard, Darrell K., and Allen J. Beck. 1997a. *Prison and jail inmates, 1995.* Washington, DC: US Department of Justice.

Gilliard, Darrell K., and Allen J. Beck. 1997b. *Prison and jail inmates at midyear, 1996.* Washington, DC: US Department of Justice.

Glaze, Lauren E. 2002. *Probation and parole in the United States, 2001.* Washington, DC: US Department of Justice.

Glaze, Lauren E. 2003. *Probation and parole in the United States, 2002.* Washington, DC: US Department of Justice.

Glaze, Lauren E., and Thomas P. Bonczar. 2006. *Probation and parole in the United States, 2005.* Washington, DC: US Department of Justice.

Glaze, Lauren E., and Thomas P. Bonczar. 2011. *Probation and parole in the United States 2010.* Washington, DC: US Department of Justice.

Guerino, Paul, Paige M. Harrison, and William J. Sabol. 2011. *Prisoners in 2010.* Washington, DC: Bureau of Justice Statistics, US Department of Justice.

Harrison, Paige M., and Allen J. Beck. 2001. *Prisoners in 2000.* Washington, DC: US Department of Justice.

Harrison, Paige M., and Allen J. Beck. 2002. *Prisoners in 2001.* Washington, DC: US Department of Justice.

Harrison, Paige M., and Allen J. Beck. 2003. *Prisoners in 2002.* Washington, DC: US Department of Justice.

Harrison, Paige M., and Allen J. Beck. 2004. *Prisoners in 2003.* Washington, DC: US Department of Justice.

Harrison, Paige M., and Allen J. Beck. 2005. *Prisoners in 2004.* Washington, DC: US Department of Justice.

Harrison, Paige M., and Allen J. Beck. 2006. *Prison and jail inmates at midyear, 2005.* Washington, DC: US Department of Justice.

Harrison, Paige M., and Jennifer C. Karberg. 2003. *Prison and jail inmates at midyear 2002.* Washington, DC: US Department of Justice.

Harrison, Paige M., and Jennifer C. Karberg. 2004. *Prison and jail inmates at midyear 2003.* Washington, DC: US Department of Justice.

Home Office. 2004. *Reducing crime, changing lives.* London: Home Office.

Inciardi, James. 1992. *The war on drugs II.* Mountain View, CA: Mayfield.

Kauder, Neal B, and Brian J. Ostrom. 2008. *State sentencing guidelines: Profiles and continuum.* Williamsburg, VA: National Center for State Courts.

Langan, Patrick A. 1991. *Race of prisoners admitted to state and federal institutions, 1926–1986.* Washington, DC: US Department of Justice.

Knapp, Kay. 1982. The impact of the Minnesota sentencing guidelines on sentencing practices. *Hamline Law Review* 5: 237–56.

Knapp, Kay. 1984. What sentencing reform in Minnesota has and has not accomplished. *Judicature* 68: 181–9.

Mann, Caramae Richey. 1987. Racism in the criminal justice system: Two sides of a controversy. *Criminal Justice Research Bulletin* 3(5): 1–6.

Maryland Commission on Criminal Sentencing Policy. 1998. *Final report.* Annapolis.

Massey, D. 1994. Getting away with murder: Segregation and violent crime in the United States. *University of Pennsylvania Law Review* 143: 1203–32.

Massey, D., and N. A. Denton. 1993. *American apartheid.* Cambridge: Harvard University Press.

McDonald, D., and K. Carlson. 1993. *Sentencing in the federal courts: Does race matter? The transition to sentencing guidelines, 1986–1990 (summary).* Washington, DC: US Department of Justice.

Minnesota Sentencing Guidelines Commission. 2003. Retrieved on August 6, 2013 from: **www.msgc. state.mn.us**

Minton, Todd D. 2010. *Jail inmates at midyear 2009—statistical tables.* Washington, DC: US Department of Justice.

Minton, Todd D. 2011. *Jail inmates at midyear 2010—statistical tables.* Washington, DC: Bureau of Justice Statistics, US Department of Justice.

Minton, Todd D., and William J Sabol. 2009. *Jail inmates at midyear 2008—statistical tables.* Washington, DC: US Department of Justice.

Mumola, Christopher, and Allen J. Beck. 1997. *Prisoners in 1996.* Washington, DC: US Department of Justice.

Pope, Carl, and W. Freyerherm. 1990a. Minority status and juvenile justice processing. Part I. *Criminal Justice Abstracts* 22(2): 327–36.

Pope, Carl, and W. Freyerherm. 1990b. Minority status and juvenile justice processing. Part II. *Criminal Justice Abstracts* 22(3): 527–42.

Pope, Carl, and W. Freyerherm. 1991. *Minorities and the juvenile justice system. Final report.* Washington, DC: US Department of Justice.

Pope, Carl, and Howard N. Snyder. 2003. *Race as a factor in juvenile arrests.* Washington, DC: US Department of Justice.

Pope, Carl, Rick Lovell, and Heidi M. Hsia. 2003. *Disproportionate minority confinement: A review of the literature from 1989 through 1991.* Washington, DC: US Department of Justice.

Ramirez, Roberto R. 2002. *We the people: Hispanics in the United States.* Washington, DC: US Census Bureau.

Rennison, Callie. 2001. *Violent victimization and race, 1993–1998.* Washington, DC: US Department of Justice.

Rodriguez, C. E., and J. M. Cordero-Guzman. 1992. Place race in context. *Ethnic Racial Studies* 15: 523–43.

Rosenmerkel, Sean, Matthew Durose, and Donald Farole, Jr. 2009. *Felony sentences in state courts, 2006—statistical tables*. Washington, DC: Bureau of Justice Statistics, US Department of Justice.

Sabol, W. J., and T. Minton. 2008. *Jail inmates at midyear, 2007*. Washington, DC: US Department of Justice.

Sampson, Robert J., and W. Byron Groves. 1989. Community structure and crime: Testing social disorganization theory. *American Journal of Sociology* 94: 774–802.

Sánchez-Jankowski, M. 1991. *Islands in the street: Gang and American urban society*. Berkeley: University of California Press.

Sellin, Thorsten J. 1976. *Slavery and the penal system*. New York: Elsevier.

Sentencing reform act: Historical background. 2003. Retrieved on July 20, 2013 from: http://www.sgc.wa.gov/Informational/historical.htm

Shihedah, E. S., and N. Flynn. 1996. Segregation and crime: The effects of black social isolation on rates of black urban violence. *Social Forces* 74(4): 1325–52.

Snell, Tracy L. 2011. *Capital punishment, 2010—statistical tables*. Washington, DC: Bureau of Justice Statistics, US Department of Justice.

Snyder, Howard, and Melissa Sickmund. 1999. *Juvenile offenders and victims: 1999 national report*. Washington, DC: US Department of Justice.

Sorensen, Jon, Robert Hope, and Don Stemen. 2003. Racial disproportionality in state prison admissions: Can regional variation be explained by differential arrest rates? *Journal of Criminal Justice* 31: 73–84.

Souryal, Claire, and Charles Wellford. 1997. *An examination of unwarranted sentencing disparity under Maryland's voluntary sentencing guidelines*. College Park: Department of Criminal Justice and Criminology, University of Maryland.

Theodorson, George A., and Achilles G. Theodorson. 1969. *Modern dictionary of sociology*. New York: Apollo Edition.

US Census Bureau. 2011. *Overview of race and Hispanic origin: 2010*. US Department of Commerce: Washington, DC.

US Sentencing Commission. 1991. *Mandatory minimum penalties in the federal criminal justice system*. Washington, DC.

US Sentencing Commission. 2007. Table 4: Race of offenders in each primary offense category 1, Fiscal year 2006. 2006 Datafile, USSCFY0. Washington, DC: US Sentencing Commission. Retrieved November 30, 2007, from http://www.ussc.gov/Research_and_Statistics/Annual_Reports_and_Sourcebooks/2006/table4.pdf

Walker, Samuel. 2011. *Sense and nonsense about crime and drugs*, 7th edn. Belmont, CA: Wadsworth.

Wicker, Tom. 1975. *A time to die*. New York: Quadrangle.

Wilbanks, William. 1987. *The myth of a racist criminal justice system*. Pacific Grove, CA: Brooks/ Cole.

Wilson, William Julius. 1987. *The truly disadvantaged: The inner city, the underclass and public policy*. Chicago: University of Chicago Press.

Zimring, F.E., and G. Hawkins. 1997. *Crime is not the problem: Lethal violence in America*. New York: Oxford Press.

THE FUTURE OF CORRECTIONS

Outline

Future Correctional Philosophies

Future Correctional Practices

Future Correctional Problems

Future Correctional Research

The Challenges Ahead for Corrections

Objectives

● To help you understand the struggles over competing correctional philosophies

● To acquaint you with correctional practices that present unresolved issues

● To introduce to you the opportunities to carry out research in the field of corrections

● To provide you with ten changes that could significantly alter the world of corrections

INTRODUCTION

One of the exciting things about studying or being a practitioner in corrections is that there always seem to be more questions than there are answers. This condition is a challenge to those trying to discover the answers to society's long-term crime and punishment dilemmas.

In this chapter, we examine several issues that have troubled students of corrections for some time. There are no easy answers, no clear-cut solutions. These issues are both persistent and critical. They remain ones our nation and those who work in its criminal justice system seem destined to continue to deal with well into the future. Our list is by no means exhaustive: your instructor might add others, and you may feel there are problems that we do not address here.

As you read this final chapter, you will no doubt recognize material we have discussed elsewhere. We also present new content, statistics, observations, and speculations. Our goal is to suggest that the future answers to corrections problems are firmly rooted in the past and in the present. We begin this review where we began this book, with the philosophical bases of corrections.

Essentials of Corrections, Fifth Edition. G. Larry Mays and L. Thomas Winfree, Jr.
© 2014 John Wiley & Sons, Inc. Published 2014 by John Wiley & Sons, Inc.

FUTURE CORRECTIONAL PHILOSOPHIES

An ongoing issue in contemporary corrections is the correctional philosophy we choose to follow. We could call this the choice of a **corrections paradigm**. Simply put: What underlying social values will guide our approach to correcting criminal behavior through the twenty-first century? For most people in the United States today, the guiding principle is punishment. The interrelated philosophies of retribution, deterrence, and incapacitation appear to influence our corrections policies. The actions we take in the name of justice often have far-reaching implications, some of which are not anticipated by legislators. Three-strikes legislation is a clear example of this problem (see Box 15.1). The public seems to have a thirst for more severe criminal sanctions, and policy makers seem eager to quench it. But when we examine what people are saying about getting tough on crime and criminals, do we find that the public truly wants these specific policies? Or, are these strategies a quick fix, a way for politicians to allay public fears without addressing the real problem or its underlying causes?

Listwan et al. (2008) in examining the penal harm or "get-tough" movement in the United States say that there are "four important fissures" or "cracks" that indicate that the public's view toward punishment may not be monolithic. First, they note that the view of a "punitive public" is largely a myth and that there is not a singular world view on this topic. Second, the use of "smarter" forms of punishment (for example, boot camps, three-strikes laws, and mandatory minimum sentences) has not been effective and has added to correctional costs. Third, there are a number of recent pieces of federal and state legislation that have demonstrated support for inmate treatment and rehabilitation programs. Finally, programs that employ "effective treatment" methods and that are carefully evaluated have demonstrated that corrections truly can correct law-violating behavior.

In the short term, the dominant model driving the nation's penal philosophy is retribution. One word captures the effect retribution is likely to have on jail and prison populations: *more*. After Congress adopted sentencing guidelines in 1987, social scientists predicted massive growth in federal prison populations (Block and Rhodes 1987; Mays 1989). They were right. In Chapter 6 we learned that the nation's inmate population grew by more than five times between 1980 and 2010. As a result of the Violent Offender Incarceration and Truth in Sentencing Initiative (VOITIS) Congress encouraged the states to adopt truth-in-sentencing laws requiring the most serious offenders to serve 85 percent of their sentences before being released. The National Institute of Justice found that 41 states and the District of Columbia had adopted some form of truth-in-sentencing and 28 states and the District of Columbia had met federal guidelines for qualifying for grants. In analyzing the impact of truth-in-sentencing (TIS) laws on prison populations in seven states studied, the conclusion was that "State TIS reforms did not uniformly account for changes in prison populations" (Rosich and Kane 2005). Nevertheless, the nation's prison population increased nearly threefold between 1987 and 2010.

The policies of three-strikes statutes, truth in sentencing, mandatory sentences, sentencing guidelines, determinate sentences, more criminal sanctions, and fewer mechanisms for early release have all contributed to the enormous growth in inmate populations. All of these add to the retributive punitive approach to dealing with offenders. Box 15.2 provides a list of principles for state legislators to consider when they adopt or modify sentencing laws.

Whatever the merits of retribution as a corrections philosophy, at some point the imprisonment binge must stop. We simply cannot afford to keep increasing the number of people in secure facilities. Eventually, taxpayers are going to realize that every dollar spent on incarceration is a dollar not available for the schools, roads, health care, and parks that benefit all citizens, or for the entitlement programs that meet the needs of the elderly and the poor. At some point, taxpayers will say, "Enough." Voters, angry and frustrated by the endless incarceration, may vote down capital bonds for jail and prison renovation and construction. Additionally, they may begin to elect legislators who promise to bring a halt to our increasingly punitive policies.

THREE STRIKES AND YOU'RE OUT—BUT AT WHAT COSTS?   BOX 15.1

"Three Strikes—We Are All Out" is how Samuel Walker (2011) describes three-strikes laws in his book, *Sense and Nonsense about Crime, Drugs, and Communities*. Forty states have lengthened sentences for repeat offenders, and 26 of them include a three-strikes provision. By the late 1990s, two-thirds of the states with a three-strikes provision had used it no more than a dozen times. Only in California and, to a lesser extent, Georgia is the law used with any regularity. California's 1994 law is severe: a person convicted for the second time of a "strikeable" offense (a felony or certain misdemeanors labeled "wobblers") earns a doubled sentence, and a third strike means life with no parole for at least 25 years. In the first 5 years of implementation, the law was invoked more than 40,000 times (R. S. King and Mauer). Georgia's 1995 statute is even harsher: life in prison without parole for the second conviction on a "serious violent felony." By the late 1990s, Georgia had invoked the law some 1,000 times (R. S. King and Mauer).

Criminologists doubt that even these tough penalties will reduce crime. Three-strike provisions, like other mandatory sentences, fail to consider the human factors. Walker believes three-strikes laws are the worst of the get-tough measures. He gives five reasons:

● such laws demonstrate overreactions to cases that are exceptional rather than routine (celebrated cases);

● they prove to be overreaching policies that punish nonserious as well as serious offenders;

● they are applied inconsistently;

● they alter the so-called going rate and add further costs to local justice systems; and

● there is no evidence that they reduce the crime rate. (2011)

The RAND Corporation, a leading research organization, foresaw disastrous consequences for California in the wake of its three-strikes legislation. A report predicted that new prisons would have to be built to hold those convicted for their third felony and sentenced to life. However, two studies of the impact of three-strikes laws on the nation's courts and corrections systems suggest that those fears were unfounded. James Austin and his colleagues observed that except for California, "there has been virtually no impact on the courts, local jails or state prisons. Neither does there appear to be an impact on the crime rates. Even in California where the law was expected to have a major impact, it appears that all the projections were in error" (i). Elsa Chen examined data from all 50 states for the period 1986 to 1997. She, too, found little evidence that three-strikes laws affected prison populations. Austin and his associates' appraisal of three-strikes laws remains the bluntest: "[Our] report proffers that this form of legislation was carefully crafted to be largely symbolic" (i).

In 2003, in *Lockyer v. Andrade* and *Ewing v. California*, the US Supreme Court ruled that California's three-strikes law does not violate the Constitution's ban on cruel and unusual punishment. Justice Sandra Day O'Connor noted that the majority opinion was that defendants still enjoy the possibility of a parole, no matter how distant. Symbolic or otherwise, three strikes and you're out is the law in the majority of the nation's jurisdictions.

SOURCES: AUERHAHN (2002); AUSTIN ET AL. (1999); CHEN (2001); KING AND MAUER (2001); MAUER (2002); MOODY (2002); WALKER (2006, 2011).

PRINCIPLES FOR EFFECTIVE SENTENCING

BOX 15.2

The following set of principles was developed by the National Conference of State Legislatures to provide guidance in developing or altering criminal sentencing laws. Of particular concern to this group was the impact of sentencing changes on correctional populations.

- The overriding principles guiding sentencing and correctional policies should be fairness, consistency, proportionality, and the impact convictions may have on future housing and employment opportunities.

- State sentencing and correctional policies should set forth clear and purposeful rationales. They should be "logical, understandable, and transparent to stakeholders and the public."

- There should be a range of correctional options from prison for "the most serious offenders" to community-based programs for others.

- All sentencing and correctional policies should be sensitive to the resources that the state can provide to incarcerate and treat offenders.

- Sentencing and correctional policies should be "data-driven."

- Sentencing and correctional policies should "reflect current needs, standards, and values."

- Crime control policies "should involve prevention, treatment, health, labor, and other state policies," and they should be developed using a broad range of expertise.

Relying on these principles should help state legislatures develop sentencing and corrections policies that are rational instead of emotional and such policies should be both efficient and cost effective.

SOURCE: LAWRENCE AND LYONS (2011, 1–3).

History reveals that society's response to crime and punishment is cyclical. Bernard and Kurlychek (2010) point to the experience of the juvenile justice system in the United States during the past century. When the public perceives that leniency is not working, that it is promoting delinquency, there is a cry for much harsher penalties for juvenile offenders, as if more severe punishment will solve the delinquency problem. When those punishments fail, reformers advocate new, more lenient responses. Ultimately, Bernard and Kurlychek note, those responses will fail too, and the cycle will repeat. Society expects juvenile justice policy to solve the problem of delinquency but the reality is that juveniles are a high-crime group: no policy, no matter how well intended or conceived, can change this basic fact. On this point, Bernard and Kurlychek

observe that the only hope we have for lowering juvenile crime is if we discover a previously undiscovered policy that will somehow convert juveniles into a low-crime group. This, they argue, is the best rationale for making the juvenile justice system as lenient as possible.

The cycle Bernard and Kurlychek identify in the juvenile justice system also exists in the criminal justice system. At some point it becomes apparent— at least to many criminal justice practitioners—that getting tougher does not seem to be working. What happens next? Often they adapt the harsher penalties to make them less severe. Samuel Walker (2011) calls this response the **law of criminal justice thermodynamics.** By this he means that the more severe criminal penalties become, the less likely practitioners are to apply them with full force. In essence, the crime is made to fit the punishment, and the result is a much more lenient approach to dealing with offenders than policy makers had envisioned.

You might be wondering how, with mandatory sentences, practitioners are able to modify the intent of the laws. Consider the laws about firearms used in the commission of a crime. Several states have passed laws requiring mandatory minimum sentences or extra time served for individuals convicted of crimes committed with a firearm. Researchers have found that in some cases prosecutors ignore the presence of the firearm as part of a plea bargain; moreover, the police may ignore a concealed weapon found on a local storeowner, dentist, or other "good citizen" (Pierce and Bowers 1981). In effect, the criminal justice system's actors are negating the harsh response mandated by the statute. That behavior weakens the law, but it also means that the law is applied arbitrarily. According to Walker (2011), the less often practitioners apply the law as it is written, the more arbitrary its application, and that leads to bias and discrimination (see Chapter 14).

Corrections officials also make adaptive responses. One of the most obvious cases involves the use of determinate sentencing. Beginning with Maine in 1976, a total of 14 states moved to sentencing systems that were exclusively or primarily determinate in nature (Steen 2002). This change came about for many reasons. Liberals believed that indeterminate sentences granted too much discretion to parole boards. By contrast, conservatives believed that indeterminate sentences were dishonest, that the sentences imposed were not the sentences actually served. Under indeterminate sentences, a 1- to 10-year sentence might result in less than a year in prison. By the mid-1980s, several state legislatures, followed by Congress, had changed sentencing laws to provide for flat-time sentences.

After a few years of determinate sentences, corrections officials recognized their impact on prisons. To cope with the surge in prison populations, those officials began developing adaptive responses. One of the most obvious has been the use of good-time credits. In some states, the **discount rate** for good-time credit is as much as half the original sentence (see especially Lawrence and Lyons 2011). For instance, some prison inmates in New Mexico can earn one day of good-time credit for every day served, a 50 percent discount rate. This practice represents an example of Walker's law of criminal justice thermodynamics. What is yet to be determined is how, or even if, the conflict will be resolved between adaptive responses and truth-in-sentencing laws.

It is possible that between them, taxpayers and practitioners will change the direction of correctional policy and that a less-punitive philosophy will come to dominate the twenty-first century. Will we see a new age of rehabilitation? What we may see is a growing emphasis on treatment programs that have as their objectives behavioral change and greater accountability on the part of offenders. Only time will tell.

FUTURE CORRECTIONAL PRACTICES

In this section, we address a number of programmatic or institutional practices that present unresolved issues for the near future.

INTERMEDIATE SANCTIONS

Intermediate sanctions include correctional approaches that fall between traditional probation and incarceration (see Chapter 4). These sanctions have become widespread since the 1980s. Several factors explain why.

The first reason was institutional crowding. With little or no room available in many jails and prisons for more inmates, corrections administrators looked for alternatives to incarceration or alternative forms of incarceration. A second reason for the growth of intermediate sanctions was dissatisfaction with traditional probation. Many people believed that probation was not working, and that more punishment was necessary. In reality, the conditions surrounding probation's administration have changed so much in the past four decades that probation was almost destined to fail. More offenders and more serious offenders are being placed on probation, and probation resources have been stretched to the limit. Probation officers have so many clients that they could go weeks without ever seeing clients in the field. Not surprisingly, then, probation has become almost meaningless for many probationers. A third factor promoting intermediate sanctions was operational costs. The presumption behind all of these programs was that anything short of jail or prison time was cheaper and thus better.

Although programs proliferated, research efforts during the 1990s showed that most of them failed to deliver on their promises (Austin and Irwin 2001; Clear 1988; MacKenzie 1997; Sechrest 1989b). For instance, house arrest with electronic monitoring fails on at least two counts: (1) it monitors location, but it does not monitor behavior, and (2) instead of being an alternative to incarceration, it often is used with individuals who would not be incarcerated anyway (Clear). If that is the case, house arrest—with or without electronic monitoring—becomes a probation add-on (MacKenzie 1997; Walker 2011).

Intensive supervision programs (ISPs) for both probationers and parolees also have been criticized on two counts. First, some observers suggest that offenders who need intensive supervision belong in a secure facility (McShane and Krause 1993; Smykla and Selke 1995). Second, offenders on ISPs have high failure rates—largely because increased surveillance is more likely to detect technical violations (McShane and Krause 1993).

PAROLE SUPERVISION

Related to the issue of intermediate sanctions is the question of parole supervision (see Chapter 9). Following the imposition of structured-sentencing practices and truth-in-sentencing laws, critics worried that where parole supervision existed it would increasingly focus on accountability versus treatment (Ringel et al. 1994). Parole officers would worry less about providing their clients with services and concentrate instead on preventing them from reoffending. Since the late 1990s, this concern has become fact (Petersilia 2000, 3). The number of officers has not kept pace with client demand; fewer officers and more clients mean less time for each client and an emphasis on supervision over services. The balance between the two is only possible if the parole function is adequately funded and staffed. Inmate accountability, reinforced by treatment programs intended to aid inmates' reentry, should go a long way toward improving the success rate for returning offenders.

One way to improve the treatment component of parolees' reentry is to use **specialized caseloads**, to assign parole officers groups of clients with very specific problems—for example, drug offenders and sex offenders (see Box 15.3). Over time, the officers will develop an expertise in working with these clients (Clear 1994; English, Pullen, and Jones 1996). One drawback to specialized caseloads is economics. First, the officers handling these cases need specialized training: many drug users and sex offenders are high-risk clients (English, Pullen, and Jones 1996; Zevitz and Farkas 2000). Thus, funds have to be allocated at least at the start of the programs for that training. Second, supervising moderate- to high-risk clients is labor-intensive, which means officers cannot carry a normal caseload (Zevitz and Farkas 2000). Most agencies, already strained with handling their existing caseloads, will have to hire additional staff. Considering budget constraints, there is legitimate concern about finding the resources to support specialized caseloads. And even if funding can be found, some question the wisdom of concentrating limited supervisory resources on sexual offenders in particular. Despite the widespread belief to the contrary, research tells us that this population is less likely to reoffend than, for example, burglars are (compare Dethlefsen and Hansen 2011; Pallone 2003; Sample and Bray 2003; Wright 2003).

Some observers argue that another important factor is the reconfiguration of parole boards, staffing them with trained civil servants (Petersilia 2000). To appreciate this approach fully, we must consider the two functions that parole boards have historically served. First, they decide parolees' release dates, a task that has largely been eliminated by sentencing practices. Second, parole boards decide when prisoners are ready for release and supervise the release plan. As Jeremy Travis characterizes it,

> This baby may have been thrown out with the bathwater of discretionary release. Although imperfect, the system integrated the prerelease and postrelease functions of the relevant government agencies and provided a rationale for the offender's reentry. (2000, 2)

THE IMPACT OF SEX OFFENDERS ON CORRECTIONS   BOX 15.3

In the early 1990s, the image of convicted pedophiles at large in the community caused many states to pass **sex-offender notification laws**, requiring sex offenders to notify the police when they move to a new neighborhood. In some jurisdictions, the laws required that police officials notify local residents. In others, the sex offender registry is open for public viewing. Pictures of convicted sex offenders are available on the Internet in many states; their home addresses easily found, pinpointed on maps linked from police department homepages.

An extension of these preventive measures is the **civil detention of sex offenders**. This practice, ruled constitutional by the Supreme Court in 1997, allows states to transfer convicted sex offenders to hospitals for the criminally insane after they have served their prison sentences if they are judged likely to commit another sexual offense. Civil libertarians argue that the practice amounts to punishment for crimes not yet committed. In the High Court's majority opinion, sex offenders are clearly different from other citizens and, because they pose a threat to society, that they can be confined to institutions with periodic review of their status. Moreover, in an eight-to-one decision in *Seling v. Young* (2001), the Court reaffirmed its stand on civil detention but added that the state has a duty to treat those held involuntarily.

Managing sex offenders under community supervision poses unique problems that sometimes require novel solutions. For example, Kim English and her associates suggest a **total containment model** for managing sex offenders in the community that is heavily dependent on agency coordination, multidisciplinary partnerships, and specialized personnel. This model holds sex offenders accountable through external and internal control measures. The former include traditional monitoring and surveillance while the latter require periodic polygraph testing. A "bad" polygraph may not be considered a violation, but it does lead to stricter supervision, increased surveillance, and a reassessment of the treatment program.

A study by the Colorado Division of Criminal Justice examined 689 adult sex offenders who had been successfully discharged from probation (356 offenders) or parole (333 offenders) between July 1, 2005 and June 30, 2007. The authors of the study found that after 1 year there was 13.1 percent recidivism, and after 3 years 28 percent had recidivated. Interestingly, only five offenders had a new sex offense after 1 year, and 18 had a new sex offense after 3 years. About half of the recidivists committed nonviolent, nonsexual crimes, and 90 of the recidivists from year 1 and 193 of the recidivists from year 3 had no offense other than failing to register as a sex offender.

Another supervision method relies on GPS to supervise high-risk sex offenders. A study funded by the US Office of Justice Programs found that California sex offenders placed on global positioning satellite (GPS) monitoring did significantly better in terms of "compliance and recidivism" than a similar group of offenders who received traditional parole supervision. While the daily cost for GPS monitoring is slightly higher than traditional parole, the difference in effectiveness seems to justify the cost.

SOURCE: DETHLEFSEN AND HANSEN (2011); ENGLISH, PULLEN, AND JONES (1996); GIES ET AL. (2012); "SEXUAL PREDATOR LAW UPHELD" (2001).

Professional parole boards, with less discretionary power and more focus on integrated release plans, could be in the future of US corrections.

THE RELEASE PLAN

US citizens fear crime, and that fear drives the movement to harsher and longer sentences. However, the reality is that all offenders cannot be kept off the streets forever: "Longer prison sentences cannot obviate the reentry phenomenon: They all come back" (Travis 2005; also see Chapter 9). The goal must be to help offenders reenter the community with the support they need to live crime-free lives. Central to meeting that goal is a release plan. Certainly parole supervision is an important part of many release plans, but other programs can also be

critical to successful reentry. As we learned in Chapter 9, such programs exist, have been implemented and evaluated, and show much promise for success. However, policy makers must show the will to implement them widely. By using reentry plans that bridge what the inmates achieve in the prison and what happens in the community, practitioners may be able to harness the enthusiasm that characterizes most ex-convicts' reentries as a positive force for change, rather than another part of the failed promises of new beginnings.

JAIL AND PRISON INDUSTRIES

Jail and prison industries will increasingly be a focus of attention and resources (Dwyer and McNally 1994; Lammay 1996). There are many reasons. One in particular is inmate idleness, an important concern for corrections administrators nationwide. Work programs are a productive way for inmates to spend their time. Although prisons have pioneered this effort, jails will increasingly begin to implement these programs, especially for inmates who are serving misdemeanor sentences of three months or more.

Industries programs also help inmates develop job skills and a work ethic. We have relatively good evidence that one of the best ways to ensure reintegration in the community and to forestall recidivism is to help inmates develop the skills and motivation they need to find work when they are released (Chapter 6; see also McShane and Krause 1993).

Finally, for corrections agencies with increasingly tight funding, industries programs may offset at least some operational costs. Today, the general public and politicians alike want to hear that inmates are helping pay their own way, and that they are not simply another weight on overburdened taxpayers.

BANISHMENT

In corrections, everything old is new again. For example, consider the move to reinstitute chain gangs in Alabama and Arizona in the 1990s or the 20-year boot camp experiment that had its roots in Zebulon Brockway's Elmira Reformatory. Periodically, legislative or administrative bodies put a new face on an abandoned practice. A likely candidate is banishment, a practice that ended when the French stopped sending prisoners to Devil's Island in the 1940s. The time may be rapidly approaching when banishment could be practiced again. Two questions need answering. First, where would we send the offenders? Second, how much would it cost?

The location question raises a number of interesting prospects. For instance, the United States has many remote regions that could serve as penal colonies. There are large tracts of land owned by the federal government in some of the less populated Western states, and they might provide sites for banishment that are still within the continental United States. Imagine, for example, Federal Penal Colony–Nevada or Federal Penal Colony–Utah. Before you reject this idea as pure speculation, remember that

the US Bureau of Prisons (BOP) has a huge correctional complex in a mountainous region near Florence, Colorado. Is this Federal Penal Colony–Colorado?

We could be more creative. What about placing penal colonies in outer space? One story line in several science fiction television shows and movies involved prison satellites and planets. Is it possible? Is it practical? Currently, it is probably neither. Nor is it likely in the near future that we can locate penal colonies under our planet's oceans. What is speculation today at some point may become a serious discussion of places never before considered for housing convicted criminals.

The problem with remote locations is infrastructure, the support systems needed to operate a secure facility. By definition, areas that are remote and unpopulated are not going to have roads, utilities, or places for staff members to live (other than in the prison compound itself). The cost of preparing a site in a remote location would be enormous. Then there is the staff to consider. When keepers are forced to live and work in a prison setting, they eventually have more in common with the kept than with the rest of society. If these barriers could be overcome, banishment might be a realistic option in the future. Then there are those who argue that we already are practicing banishment. They point to the three-strikes and habitual-offender laws that are sending offenders to prison for life without the possibility of parole. After all, the idea behind banishment is that convicted criminals are not allowed to rejoin the community. Where these people live from sentencing to death is what will be negotiated in the future.

TECHNOLOGICAL APPLICATIONS

Electronic monitoring gives us a glimpse of what technology might hold for the future of corrections (see Fabelo 2000), and although we are clearly doing a bit of fantasizing here, most of the technology we mention already exists. Consider **telemedicine**, health care provision over a distance using telecommunications technology. It is already in use in the public health sector and has been shown to be both possible and practical for use in jails and prisons (Nacci et al. 2002).

Most current forms of electronic monitoring are passive: monitoring is done in one place (usually the offender's home) on a periodic basis by a computer-based dial-up system. *Active monitoring devices* track individuals such as sex offenders continuously, meaning **global positioning satellite (GPS) surveillance** 24 hours a day (Gies et al. 2012; National Institute of Justice 2011). It is also a way of knowing where to send surveillance officers to check on an offender if a location is suspect. The technologies to monitor and control community-based inmates exist now, and we are close to having even more sophisticated devices.

An extension of house arrest could use an invisible **electronic fence**, like the fences used to keep dogs in their yards. An electric wire would be buried along the perimeter of the yard, and the offender could wear an electronic collar or bracelet. If the offender tries to cross the boundary, the collar or bracelet would first vibrate and then send out a shock. Of course, we would have to be sure that the wiring is tamper-proof, but the rest of the technology is available. Some might argue that administering a shock is cruel (to people and animals), but it may well be less cruel than incarceration in a secure facility.

An **acoustic fence** would serve the same purpose as an invisible one, but the inmate would not wear a receiving device (Pasternak 1997, 41). Arrays of high-frequency sound would surround the containment area. As the inmate nears the sonic barrier, the discomfort level increases, internal organs resonate, and the inner ear vibrates, causing nausea and even death. Such acoustic devices are not as far-fetched as you might think: The US military has tested them as less-than-lethal ways to control crowds and unlawful assemblies.

Electronic brain implants combine mechanical and biological technologies. These implants could control certain types of thoughts or behaviors. Does this sound far-fetched? It shouldn't. What's needed is an understanding of which centers in the brain correspond to which forms of thought or behavior—and that is already a goal of the ongoing Human Brain Project (Koslow and Hyman 2000). To date, abnormal brain structure has been related to mental diseases and even to drug dependency

(Megalooikonomou et al. 2004). What this strategy ignores, though, is free will—the individual's ability to respond or not to respond to an impulse.[1]

Biological methods, at a minimum, include pharmacology and genetics. Drugs have been used for years to treat mentally ill offenders. New drugs to control emotions and behaviors, a generation or two removed from the primitive drugs used in the 1960s and early 1970s, are nearing implementation. Their use with offenders who are not mentally ill will be a matter of policy—and possible litigation. Research is under way into the correctional application of certain biochemicals, including serotonin and monoamine oxidase, both of which have demonstrated links to violent and criminal behavior (Fabelo 2000, 2).

Eugenics, or genetic engineering, is an expanding field of research and practice (Fishbein 1990). If scientists find that certain criminogenic factors are biological, they might be able to genetically reengineer people so that these factors are controlled or eliminated. The specter of scientists doing genetic experiments on people causes much concern for very legitimate reasons. Both the Germans and the Japanese conducted biological experiments on human subjects during World War II.

Even if we could effect the changes openly sought by the Nazis and whispered about by some academics today, should we? More than 80 years ago, the author Aldous Huxley described a society where each individual's fate was determined chemically and genetically at conception. Of course, we do not yet have the technology to control behavior and attitudes genetically. Although scientists have mapped human DNA, our ability to effect behavior changes in individuals may be a long way off (Nelkin and Lindee 1995; Winfree and Abadinsky 2010). Nonetheless, if scientists can identify genes that put offenders into high-risk categories, **genetic mapping**— examining the arrangement of genes on the chromosome—could become a form of inmate screening.

Finally, technology is allowing both jails and prisons to expand their inmate visitation programs while controlling costs and maintaining institutional security (Campbell 2012). For instance, the Washoe County, Nevada jail implemented a web-based inmate visitation program in 2010. Inmates are charged $9.00 per half-hour visit, and the jail found that the use of such technology has the following benefits: (1) it reduces the amount of time people spend waiting for a visit, (2) it enhances the safety of inmates and staff by reducing the likelihood of contraband entering the jail, (3) visits can be scheduled at different times and from any location with a computer and a web cam, (4) it prevents children from having to accompany parents on jail visits, and (5) it extends the number of hours in which visits can be scheduled. For law enforcement purposes all visits are recorded and can be reviewed for potential illegal activities that might be discussed. Not only do inmates benefit from expanded visitation opportunities but also some of the funds generated are returned to the jail to support inmate programs.

THE FUTURE OF THE DEATH PENALTY

For most of the public, and for many of the criminal justice system's personnel, the death penalty issue is settled. In *Gregg v. Georgia* (1976), the US Supreme Court upheld the death penalty's constitutionality, and some states carry out executions on a regular basis. Recent Supreme Court death penalty cases could be characterized as fine-tuning, but there seems little chance that the death penalty will be overturned in the near future. At least five issues face the corrections subsystem as its employees carry out executions, and Box 15.4 presents a sixth issue: gender.

THE RATE OF EXECUTIONS: SPEEDING UP OR SLOWING DOWN? Will the death penalty continue to be employed at the current rate? Or can we expect the pace of executions to quicken? Since the death penalty was affirmed in 1976, legal authorities in the United States have averaged 39 executions a year; between 2000 and 2010, the number of inmates executed ranged from a low of 37 (2008) to a high of 85 (2000), an average of 58 a year (Snell 2011, 13).

It is interesting to note that the pace at which executions occurred in the late twentieth century has consistently declined since 1999, when it peaked at 98. It is also significant to note that the number

of people sentenced to death has declined from a peak of 315 in 1996. By 2010, more than 3,100 people in the nation's prisons faced the possibility of execution and 46 were actually executed (Snell 2011, 8).

ACCESS TO THE COURTS: FEWER OR MORE LIMITATIONS? There has been much talk about eliminating what some characterize as "excessive" appeals by death row inmates. In 2010 the average death row inmate waited nearly 15 years before the sentence was finally carried out; in some cases, that interval extends beyond 20 years. If access to the courts by death row inmates is restricted to a set number of appeals, we may be faced with much shorter time frames from conviction to execution. This could mean that the size of our death row populations would continue to decrease as the pace of executions nears the number of newly convicted death row inmates.

Discontent over lengthy delays has resulted in federal legislation to limit the appeals by death row inmates. The *Antiterrorism and Effective Death Penalty Act (1996)* is one such piece of legislation. The act was passed in the wake of the 1995 bombing of the Alfred P. Murrah Federal Building in Oklahoma City. Specifically, the act imposes limits on habeas corpus appeals in federal courts for capital cases and reduces the time allowed for appeals. Essentially, convicted murderers have one "bite at the apple" in the appeals process. All subsequent appeals are refused unless a three-judge panel of a US Circuit Court of Appeals rules that a case involves very specific new factual evidence or legal developments. To date, the law has withstood legal challenge (*Mumia Abu-Jamal v. Pennsylvania* 1999).

METHOD OF EXECUTION: DOES IT MATTER? The third issue facing us is the method of execution. As we discussed in Chapter 3, states employ various methods for executing inmates, including electrocution, firing squads, hanging, and the gas chamber. However, lethal injection seems to have gained the acceptance of the public, corrections officials, and the courts. For example, between 1977 and 2010, 1,234 people were executed in the United States, and of this number 1,060 died by lethal injection (Snell 2011, 14). Until

CAPITAL PUNISHMENT: DON'T FORGET THE WOMEN

BOX 15.4

Women kill far fewer people than men do.* At the end of the 1990s, the estimated homicide rate for women was 1.3 per 100,000 female residents; the rate for men—11.5 per 100,000 male residents—was almost nine times that of women. The good news for both women and men is that the rates have been going down: at the end of the 1990s, they were the lowest since such statistics were first collected in 1976. Women's rates have been falling since 1980; men's rates peaked in 1991 and have dropped steadily each year since.

As of December 31, 2010, 58 women—about 2 percent of the 3,158 death row inmates—were under death sentences in the United States. That figure included 40 whites, 14 blacks, and four of other races. Since restoration of the death penalty, 12 women have been executed, of which ten were white.**

Objectively, the likelihood of a woman's ending up on death row is very small. Although men kill at a rate that is nine times greater than women, men are 71 times more likely to be sentenced to death. Moreover, once corrections authorities take custody of a female murderer, her likelihood of execution seems equally remote.

Could chance alone account for these differences? Is it the workings of a patriarchal criminal justice system? Perhaps patriarchal values are at work, but they are more likely to work against, rather than for, women. Whitney George observed the following about Aileen Wuornos: "The only thing more threatening to patriarchy than a woman who does not want men in her life is a 'lesbian killer'" (16). The more likely explanation is that legal factors also enter the equation, and that the kinds of homicides committed by women (i.e., unplanned, lacking a felony-murder component, not involving a law enforcement victim) simply do not fit the statutory requirement for capital murder. This observation, however accurate, does not explain why lesbians are overrepresented on death row, and why women of color are underrepresented. Nor does it explain why these disparities have received little attention. Perhaps the more interesting question is what will happen to public support for the death penalty when women are executed routinely.

NOTE: *WOMEN WHO KILL ARE THREE TIMES MORE LIKELY THAN MEN ARE TO MURDER AN INTIMATE FRIEND OR FAMILY MEMBER; **GIVEN THEIR NUMBERS ON DEATH ROW, BLACK WOMEN WERE UNDERREPRESENTED IN THE DEATH CHAMBER.
SOURCES: GEORGE (1998); SNELL (2011).

a more humane way of carrying out the death penalty is devised, lethal injection will likely be the preferred method, despite well-publicized botched executions.

PRIVATE-SECTOR EXECUTIONS: WHO DOES THE EXECUTING?

A fourth issue involves the private sector's participation in corrections. Will private corporations be asked to carry out executions? Legally, is it possible for a private corporation to serve as a state's executioner? The answer in all likelihood is yes (Chaires and Lentz 1996; Mays 1996). In the past, the US Supreme Court and other appellate courts have looked at the function being performed, not the actor's public or private status, to determine legality. More than likely, private corporations will not rush to execute prisoners, but unless specifically prohibited by state law (or by some provision of their contracts), they could do so if the need arose.

EXECUTING MURDERERS: DOES IT MAKE A DIFFERENCE?

The final question related to capital punishment is straightforward: Does the death penalty have an impact on the crime rate? Unfortunately, the answer is not simple. Crime rates generally? No. Relatively few crimes committed in this country are eligible for the death penalty. In most states, only first-degree murder (and several variations on that offense) qualifies as a capital crime. By definition, then, the death penalty cannot have much of an effect on the overall US crime rate.

What about the effect of the death penalty on the murder rate? Does the death penalty deter killers? The answer to these questions is that we do not know (Walker 2011). The death penalty *might* be a deterrent, but we have no way of knowing the number of murders that did not occur. However, if executions did lower the murder rate, we would expect Texas—with the most executions of any state—to have the nation's lowest per 100,000 murder rate. It does not: to date there is little evidence that the number of executions carried out by Texas has had an appreciable effect on the number of murders there.

Finally, it is important to remember that not all convictions for first-degree murder result in capital sentences, even in the death penalty states. Each year, between 125 and 325 inmates enter death row nationwide, and on average between 50 and 60 inmates are executed each year. Therefore, it may be that to most murderers, execution seems a remote possibility. Although this may not eliminate the deterrent effect of the death penalty, it may certainly diminish it.

FUTURE CORRECTIONAL PROBLEMS

The problems we could discuss here are virtually limitless. We have chosen the following issues because they are among the most difficult concerns facing us. They also are likely to remain troublesome for years to come.

WOMEN IN THE CORRECTIONAL WORKPLACE

Women have entered the correctional workforce in increasing numbers during the past 30 years, but not without difficulties. Most female correctional employees end up working in female facilities, although the trend since the 1970s has been to hire women as frontline COs and in other staff positions in all-male institutions. Their entrance into an exclusively male world has raised two concerns.

First, corrections administrators at least initially questioned women's ability to handle the danger and stress of working in male prisons. The concern seemed to be primarily for the women's safety. Second, administrators also recognized the potential for workplace disruption caused by incidents of **sexual harassment** (Stohr et al. 1997).

The reality of women in the correctional workplace has been somewhat surprising to everyone involved. In terms of safety, women staff members do not seem to be in any greater danger than male staff. In fact, female COs seem to get into fewer confrontations and physical altercations with inmates. Apparently, because they tend to be smaller and weaker than inmates, they have learned to diffuse situations that male officers might allow to escalate into security threats. Safety, then, has proved to be a nonissue. By contrast, early findings indicate that sexual harassment does occur: female staff members were harassed by just about everyone—their male supervisors, coworkers, and inmates. However, the rates reported, given the unique environment in which female corrections staffers work, are probably not substantially higher than the rates in other male-dominated workplaces.

In the future, female employees will play a critical role in the corrections workplace. The reason is simple: workforce demographics in the United States are changing dramatically (Gido 1996). For corrections agencies to meet their quotas of educated, qualified employees, they are going to have to employ women much more frequently.

LEGISLATIVE TRENDS

Legislative bodies often set the corrections agenda in this country. Understanding legislative trends, then, is critical to understanding the issues the corrections system will be facing in the future. Four trends are especially important:

- Legislatures nationwide are continuing to expand the definition of *criminality*. We can expect more and more behaviors to be defined as crimes.

- Legislatures will continue to exhibit punitiveness toward juvenile and adult offenders. The corrections system will continue to incarcerate more people and to confine them, on average, for longer periods.

- Much has been made of the privatization movement. In some states, leadership in this area has come from the governor, but in virtually every state, lawmakers also have been important players. So we can expect the privatization trend to continue. However, based on more than three decades of experience, we also can expect growth here to be slow.

- In recent years, legislatures have been busy reinventing government. They are asking agencies to do more with less, to scale back on essential services to save money. This means that corrections agencies are likely to face tight budgets and possibly budget and hiring freezes. Inevitably funding constraints will complicate the task of supervising larger inmate populations in secure facilities and offenders in community-based programs.

REFORM MOVEMENTS

The next few decades are likely to see more calls for correctional reform in the United States. Some of the reform initiatives will come—must legally come—from legislatures and executives. However, there are at least three additional sources of reform, including the courts. We do not see sweeping reforms ordered, like the reforms that were carried out in Alabama, Arkansas, and Texas in the 1970s. Conversely, we are nowhere near a return to a complete hands-off period. Judges seem somewhat more restrained in their dealings with corrections agencies, but the notion of prisoners' rights is well established.

A second group that may influence the shape and texture of corrections in the twenty-first century is researchers. Their work will involve analyzing the problems and suggesting solutions for those problems. Consider James Austin and John Irwin (2001),

who, in several editions of their book *It's about Time: America's Imprisonment Binge,* have repeatedly warned about a coming crisis in US prisons. More recently, Michael Tonry has urged policy makers to reconsider indeterminate sentencing. He warns that sentencing and corrections policies are "fractured or fracturing" (1999b, 1). Indeed, the entire discussion of parole reassessment owes much to corrections researchers and other experts (compare Petersilia 2000; Smith and Dickey 1999; Tonry 1999a, 1999b; and Travis 2000).

The final major influence on correctional reform will be internal. Professional organizations such as the American Correctional Association, the American Probation and Parole Association, and the American Jail Association have developed training materials and seminars as well as standards for jails, prisons, and juvenile detention centers. The movement toward management certification and **accreditation** seems to be gaining momentum, and there is increasing professional pressure from peers and professional organizations to operate accredited facilities.

Reform of any bureaucratic structure is difficult, time consuming, and often frustrating. Even when changes appear to happen—a new policy or procedure, for example—the net result may be something less than that intended by those promoting change. However, if the various constituencies and interest groups—and the public—could be shown that a reasonable and safe alternative exists, many of these barriers could be overcome.

CONTROLLING COSTS

Corrections philosophies, practices, and populations all determine the system's costs. One of the most difficult challenges facing corrections agencies is controlling costs without changing the essential character of the system, losing important programming, or neglecting inmates' general and individual needs.

We cannot address this issue extensively here, but we can examine several of the most important numbers. Construction costs are an example. The costs of building, expanding, or renovating facilities are, on average, $50,000 per bed space. The more secure the facility, the higher the costs, largely because of the special-grade materials used. New construction methods can save money and time, but building correctional facilities still entails very large capital outlays. Despite high construction costs, during the life of most correctional facilities, 90 percent of expenditures are for *operating costs*: salaries and fringe benefits, utility and maintenance expenses, programming costs, and a host of other day-to-day obligations—spending that averages anywhere from $25,000 to $50,000 per inmate a year, depending on the jurisdiction and facility.

Acknowledging that corrections agencies need facilities and need to operate them, what, if anything, can be done to contain costs? First, the most effective cost-saving measure is to keep people out of correctional facilities. Alternatives to incarceration can substantially contain corrections costs if the following two conditions are met:

- if the alternatives do not shift costs to the public by increasing the amount of crime committed by those diverted into the programs; and

- if the alternatives truly are alternatives, not add-ons to bring more offenders under some form of social control.

Second, as noted earlier, the use of standardized or prefabricated materials can reduce construction costs. Where possible, the use of lower-cost commercial-grade materials also can save money, a fact already demonstrated in many of the podular-design jails (Nelson 1988).

Third, some degree of privatization may result in cost savings (Mays and Gray 1996). This could include financing, construction, programming, or total operations. For most states, a public-private partnership is the most cost-effective solution (Cox and Osterhoff 1991). However, recent examinations of direct and indirect costs attributed to private prison suggest that the early claims about private prisons being cost-effective may have been incorrect (Levine 2010). In particular, private prisons often take the less expensive low-security inmates, leaving states with the costlier high-security prisoners (Oppel 2011). The evidence simply does not support the long-term claims of lower operating costs attributed to private prisons (Maahs and Pratt 1999).

Finally, even in those prisons operated exclusively by government agencies, operations can be improved. Most public bureaucracies have never been held to account to achieve high standards of efficiency, and will have to change. All state agencies, rather than just corrections departments, must identify and then eliminate the regulations that make them inherently inefficient.

INSTITUTIONAL VIOLENCE AND INMATE UPRISINGS

Violence is very much a part of life in US prisons and jails (see Chapter 7). Prison and jail experts speculate that the nature of institutional life today creates conditions ripe for violence (Austin and Irwin 2001). This violence can take several different forms. Three are most common.

Perhaps the most prevalent form of institutional violence involves *inmate-on-inmate* assaults. Several factors can precipitate this kind of violence (see Sechrest 1989a; Welch 1996). For instance, some states—particularly California and Texas—have to deal with gangs in their prison systems (see, for example, Fong 1990; Fong and Vogel 1997). Where prison gangs are common, assault rates go up. Many violent outbursts are spontaneous, but it is not unusual for members of one gang to target one or more members of a rival gang. More often, though, inmate-on-inmate assaults are the result of interpersonal conflicts. Disputes arise over lost or stolen property, personal insults or challenges, the refusal of sexual advances, and various other factors. Often, crowding compounds individual conflicts.

Inmate-on-staff violence is rare, but incidents of assault and even murder are reported each year. Often, the injuries to staff members are accidental, incurred when they try to break up inmate fights or other disturbances. More troubling are direct attacks on COs or other staff. Here, the cause is often retaliation for discipline. Some attacks happen because a staff member has manipulated or lied to an inmate. Not "playing straight" is considered a personal insult, and it is common for inmates to harbor resentment until they see an opportunity to retaliate.

The most extreme form of institutional violence is *collective violence*, or a *riot* (see Chapter 7). During the past several decades, the United States has experienced a number of notorious riots in both state and federal institutions (Braswell, Montgomery, and Lombardo 1994; Saenz 1986; Useem et al. 1995; Wicker 1975).

Randy Martin and Sherwood Zimmerman (1990, 715–16) offer a typology of prison riots:

1   *Environmental conditions* include institutional food, staff brutality, lack of treatment programs, and the nature of the inmates themselves—the so-called preconditions of a prison riot.

2   *Spontaneity* combines preexisting environmental conditions with some event that sets off the collective violence. This element is the proximate cause of the disturbance.

3   *Conflict* suggests that inmates respond to a repressive environment with collective violence. An essential element here is that inmates tend to disregard any positive contributions associated with official power and control.

4   *Social control/collective behavior* addresses the delicate balance between staff control and inmate cooperation. Any failure of formal or informal control mechanisms can precipitate collective violence.

5   *Power vacuum* recognizes that either the inmates or the staff "run the joint." If there is instability resulting from a lack of decisiveness or from staff turnover, collective violence may result as inmates try to assert their power.

6   *Rising expectations* recognize that as jails and prisons have gone through periods of reform, inmates have come to expect improved conditions of confinement. When improvements are not made—in the wake of an inmate's successful lawsuit, for example—prisoners may express their frustration through collective violence.

The best way to deal with violence is to prevent it in the first place. This may not be possible with some types of interpersonal violence, but well-trained, vigilant staff members may be able to prevent or to intercede quickly in many cases. Box 15.5 presents some strategies for coping with the threat of a prison riot.

If recent history is any indicator, as long as we have prisons, and as long as some of those prisons are crowded, we are likely to have inmate disturbances and riots. The challenge for all correctional personnel will be to prevent, contain, and respond effectively to each incident.

CROWDING

The final problem was, is, and will be institutional crowding. In medicine, practitioners talk about two kinds of conditions: *acute* (severe, immediate, and potentially life threatening) and *chronic* (long-term or persistent). Institutional crowding has moved from being an acute problem to being a chronic problem.[2]

At the end of 2010, 19 states and the federal government reported inmate populations over their **highest rated capacity** (essentially the number of inmates that the facility can hold at a maximum); 25 states and the federal government exceed their **lowest rated capacity** (essentially the number of inmates that the facility should hold for maximum operational efficiency and effectiveness) (Guerino, Harrison, and Sabol 2011, 34). Overall, state prisons were operating at 1 percent under their highest rated capacity and 9 percent above their lowest rated capacity in 2010; the federal prison system was at 36 percent above their capacity (Guerino, Harrison, and Sabol 2011, 34). However, these figures tell only part of the story. Variations by state were striking. Using only highest rated capacity (the most generous view of how many inmates a facility can hold), we find seven states above 125 percent of capacity, including: Alabama (196 percent); Illinois (144 percent); Indiana (131 percent); Iowa (131 percent); Massachusetts (139 percent); North Dakota (136 percent); and Ohio (127 percent). At the other extreme, the following four states are below 75 percent of their highest rated capacities: Mississippi (46 percent); New Mexico (53 percent); Rhode Island (44 percent); and Tennessee (71 percent).

A temporary solution has been to "back up" inmates into local jails (Allinson 1982; Taft 1979). In

STRATEGIES FOR RESPONDING TO THE THREAT OF PRISON DISTURBANCES   BOX 15.5

Burt Useem and his associates say that several factors related to staff vigilance and physical control can prevent prisoner uprisings and disturbances. Among them are:

- *Experienced staff and supervision*—high-security units that house violent or potentially violent inmates must have experienced COs and supervisors.

- *Post orders*—the orders for posts in restricted units should "anticipate the possibility" of riots or other inmate disturbances.

- *Physical plant and equipment*—prisons need to pay particular attention to reinforced glass, blind spots both inside and outside the facility, and other structural or security weaknesses.

- *Escalation of conflict*—many full-scale riots are preceded by an escalation of inmate-on-inmate or inmate-on-staff conflicts. Line staff and corrections administrators need to pay particular attention to an increase in the number and seriousness of these incidents.

- *Riots with warning*—staff members may be advised formally or informally, through the institution's grapevine, that an inmate disturbance is pending. Although not every rumor proves to be true, staff members must weigh and assess the likelihood of a disturbance. They should never discount a rumor without attempting to verify the information.

SOURCE: USEEM ET AL. (1995, 6–7).

---

fact, in 2005, more than 83,400 inmates—slightly more than 5 percent of all state and federal prisoners—were being held in local jails, largely because the courts had ordered that something be done about prison crowding (Guerino, Harrison, and Sabol 2011; Harrison and Beck 2006).

Again, crowding in the nation's jails and prisons is a long-term problem. However, in recent years, secure facilities have faced the **crisis of overcriminalization**. As we have increased the number of punishable offenses, we have increased the number of offenders who need punishing. More-punitive laws, mandatory sentences, determinate sentences, sentencing guidelines, and truth-in-sentencing are also a factor here because they increase the time each inmate serves.

The result is that much of the crowding in prisons today is legislatively mandated. Moreover, lawmakers have increased the pool of inmates and the time they spend behind bars, while underfunding

correctional budgets. This "perfect storm" has left prison and jail administrators, many of whom start out with inadequate facilities, scrambling to house burgeoning inmate populations. The consequences have been predictable. Some state and federal facilities have experienced inmate uprisings, even full-scale riots (Braswell, Montgomery, and Lombardo 1994). In nearly all states, inmate lawsuits have increased significantly. Although inmates are not winning a significant number of cases, the number of suits indicates their resistance to their conditions of confinement (Mays and Olszta 1989; Thomas 1988).

Since the 1980s, state and local governments have tried to deal with institutional crowding by building new facilities and renovating old ones. We find ourselves in the midst of a corrections building boom (Stephan 2008), and a quarter century of building has left us only slightly better off regarding crowding in some jurisdictions.

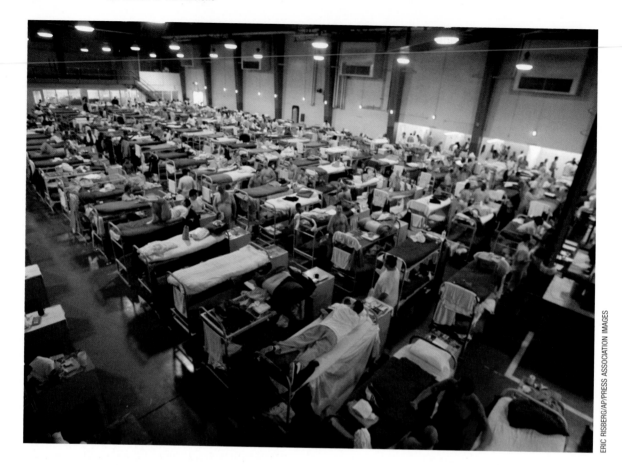

FUTURE CORRECTIONAL RESEARCH

We do not want to end this chapter on a note of despair. Many components of the corrections system in the United States are among the world's best. What prevents us from doing even better, however, is a lack of information. Research cannot rescue us from many of the dilemmas in which we find ourselves. (See Box 15.6 for a look at the international scope of this problem.) Researchers can tell us what we are doing right and what we are doing wrong . . . and possibly how to fix it.

According to Tonry and Petersilia, corrections research is important because "apparent relations between crime and punishment may be . . . misleading" (1999, 1). They ask whether crime rates affect rates of incarceration, or whether incarceration rates affect crime rates. Actually, it is possible that the two are only marginally related if at all. However, in a study that linked court mandated changes in prison populations and crime rates, Levitt (1996) found that "Incarcerating one additional prisoner reduces the number of crimes by approximately fifteen per year." Nevertheless, "prevention or rehabilitation would likely be preferable to long-term incarceration from both a cost-benefit and humanitarian perspective" (348). By contrast, a definitive study by King, Mauer, and Young concluded that "[w]hile incarceration is one factor affecting crime rates, its impact is more modest than many proponents suggest, and is increasingly subject to diminishing returns." Therefore, "[in]creasing incarceration while ignoring more effective approaches will impose a heavy burden upon courts, corrections, and communities, while providing a marginal impact on crime" (King, Mauer, and Young 2005, 8).

SPOTLIGHT ON INTERNATIONAL CORRECTIONS: WHO HAS THE LARGEST PRISON SYSTEM IN THE WORLD?

BOX 15.6

Following is a list of 20 nations selected from among the top 100 largest prison systems in the world, with their most recent rankings and per 100,000 prison populations.

Rank	Nation	Inmates per 100,000 population
1	United States	716
7	Russian Federation	486
10	Belarus	438
13	Azerbaijan	413
24	Dominica	356
28	Ukraine	320
29	Kazakhstan	316
31	Lithuania	314
37	Latvia	297
39	South Africa	286
50	Estonia	246
58	Georgia	232
62	Turkmenistan	224
63	Poland	223
77	Moldova (Republic of)	185
78	Kyrgyzstan	181
89	Saudi Arabia	162
96	Uzbekistan	152 (estimated)
99	United Kingdom: England and Wales	149
99	Spain	149

For decades, the Soviet Union, South Africa, and the United States have been first, second, and third on the list. The Soviet Union's breakup into independent nations and affiliated republics added several new nations; many of them are in the top 100, including the Russian Federation in the seventh position. South Africa has moved down into the 39th position. Take a close look at the list. Notice how quickly the rates drop from the high and mid-three digits. The 24th nation on the list (Dominica) has a rate one-half that of the United States. The rate for Poland, the first Eastern European nation to appear on the list in the 63rd position, is less than one-third that of the United States. As a rule, Western European nations report per 100,000 rates in the low 100s or high double digits. With the exception of the one former superpower and one fading superpower, most of the top 100 nations with the largest prison systems are developing nations. For the most recent listing, visit the International Centre for Prison Studies' website (www.prisonstudies.org).

Although the question posed in the title of this box is easily answered (the United States), more research is needed to provide insights into why the United States and the Russian Federation are in league with so many developing and impoverished nations when it comes to the number of inmates they incarcerate per 100,000 population.

SOURCE: *INTERNATIONAL CENTRE FOR PRISON STUDIES* (2013).

What corrections needs is what Larry Sherman (1998) calls "evidence-based" policies and practices. Although Sherman was talking about policing, his suggestions apply to corrections. Researchers, he said, should do more than finish their work and hand in their reports. Instead, they should be proactive, pushing "accumulated research evidence into practice through national and community guidelines" (1).

Evidence-based corrections would use the best available research on the outcomes of correctional programs and practices "to implement guidelines and evaluate agencies, units, and others" (Sherman 1998, 1). As Francis Cullen and Jody Sundt observed, "[t]he current movement toward 'evidence-based' corrections is an attempt to free us—as well as offenders and their future victims—from the costs of using programs that have no hope of ever working" (Cullen and Sundt 2003, 355). We have already provided examples of evidence-based corrections in this text. Consider the work of Kim English, Suzanne Pullen, and Linda Jones (1996), which consists of both evidence for the containment approach to sex offenders *and* policy and practice guidelines (see Box 15.3). Their work embodies the best of evidence-based corrections.

By contrast, three-strikes laws and other knee-jerk policies represent the other end of the spectrum—laws created in response to celebrated cases with little thought about their impact on the corrections process (see Walker 2011). Some evidence even suggests that three-strikes laws promote homicide: witness the increase in short- and long-term homicide rates in cities in states with those laws (Kovandzic, Sloan, and Vieraitis 2002; also see Marvell and Moody 2001). It would appear that some felons, to avoid the possibility of a third strike and life in prison, are turning ordinary felonies into homicides. That is, rather than leaving any witnesses at the scene of an ordinary felony, say a robbery or burglary, they are killing anyone who could later testify in a trial on a "third strike" (Kovandzic, Sloan, and Vieraitis 2002). However, there is some reason to question this alleged association, especially in the case of police officer homicides (Guffey, Larson, and Kelso 2009).

In this regard, corrections research should also examine the impact of social changes—poverty and unemployment, chaotic families—on criminal behavior. Furthermore, research should examine the impact of legislative changes on incarceration rates across all racial and ethnic groups and ages, and by gender. We have to determine the environmental impact of legal changes on social groups, not just individuals.

Three other areas are critically important to the future of corrections:

- *Sentence length:* What are the long-term effects of lengthy prison sentences? What happens to inmates who are serving sentences of more than 10 years, both within the institution and in the society once they are released?

- *Workplace performance:* What can we do to help corrections workers do a better job? What are the appropriate qualifications for COs and other employees? What are the essential motivators (or sources of discouragement) in the work environment? What are the stressors, and how should staff handle them? What are the best ways to recruit, train, retain, and promote employees?

- *Improving inmate programming:* How can we use institutional design to improve both the custody and the treatment of inmates? How can we design and build affordable facilities that are safe for staff, the public, and inmates? What designs promote employee safety and efficiency, as well as inmate rehabilitation?

Only research can answer these kinds of questions. Some of you reading this book will use or even conduct this type of research—the job market for corrections researchers is expanding. Practitioners and theorists alike are desperate for valid and useful research, for definitive answers to the questions that continue to cast doubt on correctional philosophies, programs, and practices.

THE CHALLENGES AHEAD FOR CORRECTIONS

As we come to the end of this text, it is important to make a point that we have not dealt with explicitly. Although the corrections system in the United States is something of a loose confederation of agencies, organizations, and institutions, all of these entities are interconnected. This association means that changes in the number and size of prisons, and the number of inmates sentenced to prison, have an impact on jail populations as well. As corrections professionals painfully learned during the 1990s, when prisons become crowded, inmates back up in local jails that are not equipped to deal with long-term populations or with serious offenders. Similarly, incarceration rates and the policies that affect those rates have an impact on probation, parole, and community-based programming. If we have learned anything about corrections in the past 40 years, it is that we cannot tinker with one part of the system without affecting the others.

Here, we list ten changes in policies or practices or both that could have a positive impact on the nation's corrections system, particularly the number of people under its control. Some are not likely to be implemented, whereas others already have support in state and federal legislatures and among corrections professionals. All have been addressed to some extent in this text. As you consider each in turn, assess the likelihood of its full implementation.

1 *Change the current correctional philosophy:* Currently, the state and federal governments are operating their corrections systems under what can best be described as a retributionist philosophy. Many corrections experts believe that this philosophy has led to huge increases in jail, prison, and probation populations, and they describe it as "the penal harm movement." Why not consider a change to restorative justice, or a return to rehabilitation—a model that can help offenders reenter society?

2 *Legalize, or at least decriminalize, most drugs:* The nation's prisons are full of people whose offense is drug related. Legalization may be a difficult path for the nation to take now, but decriminalization, where possession is treated as a civil rather than as a criminal matter, could result in far fewer people being incarcerated (perhaps cutting our prison population by as much as one-half). Money currently spent on prisons and probation services for drug-using offenders could be diverted to community drug treatment programs and early-intervention and prevention programs. Moreover, sentencing disparities associated with different forms of drugs and their use by respective racial groups would disappear.

3 *Depoliticize the corrections system:* Bad politics can interfere with good correctional practices. Without politicians, however, corrections programs would have a hard time getting funded or, in the case of new programs, seeing the light of day. The question is one of balance: How do we juggle the needs of politicians to appear tough on crime and the programmatic needs of the corrections system? Perhaps if politicians understood that good programs have the potential to make them look good, they could be persuaded to support alternatives to penal harm.

4 *Abandon three-strikes and truth-in-sentencing laws:* The pundits predicted huge increases in the nation's prison populations following the widespread adoption of truth-in-sentencing laws. In large measure, those predictions have come to pass. Three-strikes provisions have not yielded the same dire consequences, but they remain largely symbolic and so should be abandoned as well. Existing habitual-offender laws will continue to protect the public even in the absence of three-strikes provisions.

5 *Develop and use an index of dangerous or convicted offenders:* Most practitioners agree that perhaps 80 percent to 90 percent of all inmates could be released from prison today with no ill effects on society. The key is to determine the identity of the 10 to 20 percent who should stay behind bars. What we need are more-effective models that would allow us to predict who needs to be incarcerated and who would benefit more from community-based correctional programming.

6 *Increase meaningful educational and vocational programs in prisons:* Money spent on helping prisoners is an investment in crime prevention. Increased educational and vocational training programs for convicted offenders—in and out of prison—are necessary if releasees are to assume more meaningful roles in society.

7 *Return to the full use of parole:* The conditional release of offenders from prison means that the corrections system has some measure of control over them. Parole is useful for prison operations (that is, the use of good time as an inmate control mechanism is viewed by some as essential) and within the community (inmates returned without supervision are a greater threat to themselves and to the community than are those under supervision). Concurrent with this approach, however, is the creation of prerelease programs intended to ease the return to the free society.

8 *Treat most violations of immigration laws as civil, rather than criminal, matters:* In 2010, nearly 21,377 undocumented aliens were being housed in federally operated facilities, state prisons, and local jails (Guerino, Harrison, and Sabol 2011, 30). Changing federal policies on immigration law violations could result in a significant decrease in the nation's jail and prison populations.

9 *Expand the use of unified prison-jail systems that are operated by state governments rather than local authorities:* The creation of state-run facilities would help standardize treatment and programs. Jails would continue to operate with far more limited functions—for example, for the temporary detention of people being tried or for inmates awaiting transfer to a state prison or a federal facility. The costs of operating this system could be spread throughout the state.

10 *Fully implement evidence-based corrections:* Rather than creating feel-good programs and laws, or programs and laws that are politically popular but pragmatically difficult to implement, politicians should turn to the research generated by partnerships between social scientists and practitioners for guidance in developing programs and laws that work.

There are two final factors that will drive all such discussions. First, in any society, people are going to violate laws or other rules. Second, when violations occur, some attempt is going to be made to punish or correct those who ignore the society's laws or sense of decency or order. Society will always need some mechanism to deal with criminal offenders, a mechanism that we call *corrections*.

SUMMARY

Much remains to be accomplished in corrections, and much is attainable. The agenda is full; all that is required is a cohort of policy makers and practitioners at all levels who are willing to engage the challenges ahead. The following are among the key findings contained in this chapter:

- We know a great deal about the issues that confront the nation's corrections system. The key is to bring public opinion into line with a corrections philosophy that achieves better results and imprisons fewer people.

- The policies and practices that have their roots in the current retributive justice philosophy do not work.

- The future of prisoner reentry may lie with an invigorated parole system that includes reentry philosophies and programs that do more than just dump inmates back into the community.

- Work programs for inmates that build marketable skills and have applications outside prison will also aid in prisoner reentry.

- Prisons, jails, probation and community corrections, parole, and prisoner reentry systems must all come to recognize the changing nature of the offender population.

- The nation must find some way to remove the institutional racism that plagues its corrections system, particularly as the United States moves toward becoming a country where people of color are in the majority.

● Researchers should fill the voids in what we know about the corrections process, many of them created by changes in funding from the federal government. Increasing this body of knowledge will help state and federal legislatures make informed decisions about current or projected corrections practices.

● Many challenges remain unaddressed; most will call for rethinking how we view criminals and what we do to and for them.

THINKING ABOUT CORRECTIONAL POLICIES AND PRACTICES: WRITING ASSIGNMENTS

1 Prepare a brief essay explaining your feelings about the idea of banishment. Do you think it really is a punishment? Looking at a map of the United States, identify three or four potential areas for a penal colony. Would you be likely to run up against the "not-in-my-backyard" syndrome in those locations?

2 Is support for the death penalty decreasing? In one page explain why we seem to be seeing a decrease in the number of inmates sentenced to death rows in the United States and why the number of executions has been declining.

3 Go to your state corrections department's website and see if you can find the trends in

prison inmates incarcerated by year for the last 10 years. What is the trend? Prepare a brief analysis of why inmate populations are increasing, decreasing, or remaining the same.

4 This chapter explores five sets of problems facing contemporary corrections. Which one must be addressed first and why?

5 Which one of the ten policy/practice changes would have the greatest impact on corrections in the United States today? Justify your selection. Which one has the highest chance of success in today's political climate? Which one has the lowest chance of success? Do any of the three questions have the same answer?

KEY TERMS

accreditation
acoustic fence
civil detention of sex
   offenders
corrections paradigm
crisis of overcriminalization
discount rate
electronic brain implants

electronic fence
eugenics
genetic mapping
global positioning satellite
   (GPS) surveillance
highest rated capacity
law of criminal justice
   thermodynamics

lowest rated capacity
sex-offender notification laws
sexual harassment
specialized caseloads
telemedicine
total containment model

CRITICAL REVIEW QUESTIONS

1 Much has been made concerning the implementation of three-strikes laws in several states. Initially these laws seemed to be aimed at

violent, personal offenders. Has this really been the target based on the people incarcerated for receiving their third strike? Explain.

2   What do we mean by truth-in-sentencing? Is this a shorthand way of saying we are going to get tough on certain offenders? What have been the consequences, intended or unintended, of truth-in-sentencing laws?

3   Consider the nature of intermediate sanctions. What two factors do you believe have most influenced their growth? What two factors do you think are most likely to limit their growth?

4   Is parole on its last legs in the United States, or do you think it is likely to be revitalized?

5   Have we prematurely given up on treating sex offenders in this country? What does the recent research say about the likelihood of reoffending when these offenders are released from prison?

6   Where does your state stand on the death penalty? Visit your state department of correction's website and research the issue. Do you believe your legislators made a good decision?

7   Are electronic monitoring and the use of GPS technology a solution to some of our crime control problems, or are they solutions in search of a problem? Explain your answer.

8   Do you think genetic engineering is a real solution? What about using genetics as a crime control or treatment method? What ethical issues would this raise?

9   What are some of the problems facing women in the corrections workplace? Are these the same kinds of problems found throughout the criminal justice system, or are they unique? Explain your answer.

10 What is the relationship between incarceration rates in this country and crime rates? Which seems to be driving the other? Does the research show that the relationship is intuitive or counterintuitive?

CASES CITED

Ewing v. California, 538 U.S. 11 (2003)
Gregg v. Georgia, 428 U.S. 153 (1976)
Lockyer v. Andrade, 538 U.S. 63 (2003)

Mumia Abu-Jamal v. Pennsylvania, 501 U.S. 1214 (1991)
Seling v. Young, 531 U.S. 250 (2001)

NOTES

1   The antihero in Anthony Burgess's *A Clockwork Orange* (1962) refrains from violent sexual acts— not because he understands that they are bad, but because his body has been conditioned to respond negatively to the mere thought of such behavior.

2   Some authors use the term "overcrowding." We believe that a prison or jail is either crowded or not crowded; overcrowding is not a very useful word to describe what is happening and somehow diminishes a rather bleak picture of prison and jail crowding. Hence we talk about chronic and acute crowding.

REFERENCES

Allinson, Richard. 1982. Crisis in the jails: Overcrowding is now a national epidemic. *Corrections*, April, 18–24.

Auerhahn, Kathleen. 2002. Selective incapacitation, three strikes, and the problem of aging prison populations: Using simulation modeling to see the future. *Criminology & Public Policy* 1: 353–87.

Austin, James F., John Clark, Patricia Hardyman, and D. Alan Henry. 1999. *Three strikes and you're out: The implementation and impact of strike laws.* Washington, DC: US Department of Justice.

Austin, James F., and John Irwin. 2001. *It's about time: America's imprisonment binge*, 3rd edn. Belmont, CA: Wadsworth.

Bernard, Thomas J., and Megan C. Kurlychek. 2010. *The cycle of juvenile justice*, 2nd edn. New York: Oxford University Press.

Block, Michael, and William K. Rhodes. 1987. *The impact of the federal sentencing guidelines.* Washington, DC: US Department of Justice.

Braswell, Michael C., Reid H. Montgomery, and Lucien X. Lombardo, eds. 1994. *Prison violence in America*, 2nd edn. Cincinnati, OH: Anderson.

Campbell, Debi. 2012. Web-based inmate visitation improves security and access in Washoe County, Nevada. National Jail Exchange. Retrieved on July 21, 2013 from: **http://community.nicic.gov/blogs/national_ jail_exchange/archive/2012/11/01/web-based-inmate- visitation-improves-security-and-access-in-washoe-county- nevada.aspx**

Chaires, Robert, and Susan Lentz. 1996. Some legal considerations in prison privatization. In *Privatization and the provision of correctional services: Context and consequences*, edited by G. Larry Mays and Tara Gray. Cincinnati, OH: Anderson, Academy of Criminal Justice Sciences, 31–60.

Chen, Elsa. 2001. *Impact of three strikes and truth in sentencing on the volume and composition of correctional populations.* Washington, DC: US Department of Justice.

Clear, Todd R. 1988. A critical assessment of electronic monitoring in corrections. *Policy Studies Review* 7(3): 671–81.

Clear, Todd R. 1994. *Harm in American penology: Offenders, victims, and their communities.* Albany: State University of New York Press.

Cox, Norman R., Jr., and William E. Osterhoff. 1991. Managing the crisis in local corrections: A public– private partnership approach. In *American jails: Public policy issues*, edited by Joel A. Thompson and G. Larry Mays. Chicago: Nelson-Hall, 227–39.

Cullen, Francis T., and Jody L. Sundt. 2003. Reaffirming evidence-based corrections. *Criminology & Public Policy* 2: 353–8.

Dethlefsen, Amy, and Jesse Hansen. 2011. *Outcome evaluation of the Colorado sex offender management*

board standards and guidelines. Denver, CO: Colorado Division of Criminal Justice.

Dwyer, Diane C., and Roger B. McNally. 1994. Public policy and prison industries for the 1990s. In *Critical issues in crime and justice*, edited by Albert R. Roberts. Thousand Oaks, CA: Sage, 277–95.

English, Kim, Suzanne Pullen, and Linda Jones. 1996. *Managing adult sex offenders: A containment approach.* Lexington, KY: American Probation and Parole Association.

Fabelo, Tony. 2000. *"Technocorrections": The promises, the uncertain threats.* Washington, DC: US Government Printing Office.

Fishbein, Diana. 1990. Biological perspectives in criminology. *Criminology* 28: 27–42.

Fong, Robert S. 1990. The organizational structure of prison gangs. *Federal Probation* 54(4): 36–43.

Fong, Robert S., and Ronald E. Vogel. 1997. A comparative analysis of prison gang members, security threat groups, and general population prisoners in the Texas Department of Corrections. In *Gangs and gang behavior*, edited by G. Larry Mays. Chicago: Nelson-Hall, 382–95.

George, Whitney. 1998. Women on death row. *Off Our Backs*, January, 16–17.

Gido, Rosemary. 1996. Organizational change and workforce planning: Dilemmas for criminal justice in the year 2000. In *Visions for change: Crime and justice in the twenty-first century*, edited by Roslyn Muraskin and Albert R. Roberts. Upper Saddle River, NJ: Prentice Hall, 272–82.

Gies, Stephen V., Randy Gainey, Marcia I. Cohen, Eoin Healy, Dan Duplantier, Martha Yeide et al. 2012. *Monitoring high-risk sex offenders with GPS technology: An evaluation of the California supervision program.* Bethesda, MD: Development Services Group, Inc.

Guffey, J. E., J. G. Larson, and C. Kelso. 2009. Three- strikes laws and police officer murders: Do the data indicate a correlation? *Professional Issues in Criminal Justice* 4(2): 9–26.

Guerino, Paul, Paige M. Harrison, and William J. Sabol. 2011. *Prisoners in 2010.* Washington, DC: Bureau of Justice Statistics, US Department of Justice.

Harrison, Paige M., and Allen J. Beck. 2006. *Prisoners in 2005.* Washington, DC: US Department of Justice.

International Centre for Prison Studies. 2013. World prison brief online. Compiled by Roy Walmsley, Director of the World Prison Brief. International Centre for Prison Studies: University of Essex, UK.

Retrieved on July 21, 2013 from: **www. prisonstudies.org/**

King, Ryan S., and Marc Mauer. 2001. *Aging behind bars: Three strikes seven years later.* Washington, DC: Sentencing Project.

King, Ryan S., Marc Mauer, and Malcolm Young. 2005. *Incarceration and crime: A complex relationship.* Washington, DC: The Sentencing Project.

Koslow, S., and S. Hyman. 2000. Human brain project: A program for the new millennium. *Einstein Quarterly Journal of Biological Medicine* 17: 7–15.

Kovandzic, Tomislav V., John J. Sloan III, and Lynne M. Vieraitis. 2002. Unintended consequences of politically popular sentencing policy: The homicide promotion effects of "three strikes" in US cities. 1980–1999). *Criminology & Public Policy* 1(3): 399–434.

Lammay, Rich. 1996. The role of corporate America in prison industries: A practitioner's view. In *Privatization and the provision of correctional services: Context and consequences*, edited by G. Larry Mays and Tara Gray. Cincinnati, OH: Anderson, Academy of Criminal Justice Sciences, 119–23.

Lawrence, Alison, and Donna Lyons. 2011. *Principles of effective state sentencing and corrections policy.* Washington, DC: National Conference of State Legislatures.

Levine, M. A. 2010. What's costlier than a government run prison? A private one. *Fortune*. August 12. Retrieved on July 21, from: **http://money.cnn.com/ 2010/08/17/news/economy/private_prisons_economic_ impact.fortune/**

Levitt, Steven D. 1996. The effect of prison population size on crime rates: Evidence from prison overcrowding litigation. *Quarterly Journal of Economics* 111(2): 319–51.

Listwan, Shelley Johnson, Cheryl Lero Jonson, Francis T. Cullen, and Edward J. Latessa. 2008. Cracks in the penal harm movement: Evidence from the field. *Criminology & Public Policy* 7(3): 423–65.

Maahs, J., and Pratt, T. 1999. Are private prisons more cost-effective than public prisons? A meta-analysis of evaluation research studies. *Crime & Delinquency*, 45(3): 358–71.

MacKenzie, Doris L. 1997. Criminal justice and crime prevention. In *Preventing crime: What works, what doesn't, what's promising?*, edited by Lawrence W. Sherman. Washington, DC: US Department of Justice, 661–91.

Martin, Randy, and Sherwood Zimmerman. 1990. A typology of the causes of prison riots and an analytical extension to the 1986 West Virginia riot. *Justice Quarterly* 7: 711–37.

Marvell, Thomas B., and Carlisle E. Moody. 2001. The lethal effects of three-strikes laws. *Journal of Legal Studies* 30: 89–106.

Mauer, Marc. 2002. Analyzing and responding to the driving forces of prison population growth. *Criminology & Public Policy* 1: 389–92.

Mays, G. Larry. 1989. The impact of federal sentencing guidelines on jail and prison overcrowding and early release. In *The US sentencing guidelines: Implications for criminal justice*, edited by Dean J. Champion. New York: Praeger, 181–200.

Mays, G. Larry. 1996. Correctional privatization: Defining the issues and searching for answers. In *Privatization and the provision of correctional services: Context and consequences*, edited by G. Larry Mays and Tara Gray. Cincinnati, OH: Anderson, Academy of Criminal Justice Sciences, 3–10.

Mays, G. Larry, and Tara Gray, eds. 1996. *Privatization and the provision of correctional services.* Cincinnati, OH: Anderson, Academy of Criminal Justice Sciences.

Mays, G. Larry, and Michelle Olszta. 1989. Prison litigation: From the 1960s to the 1990s. *Criminal Justice Policy Review* 3(3): 279–98.

McShane, Marilyn D., and Wesley Krause. 1993. *Community corrections.* New York: Macmillan.

Megalooikonomou, V., Z. Obradovic, J. Gee, O. B. Boyko, and D. S. Woodruf-Pak. 2004. Mining brain image data. Paper presented at the annual meeting of Neuroinfomatics. Bethesda, MD: National Institutes of Health.

Moody, Carlisle E. 2002. Simulation modeling and policy analysis. *Criminology & Public Policy* 1: 393–8.

Nacci, Peter L., C. Allan Turner, Ronald J. Waldron, and Eddie Broyles. 2002. *Implementing telemedicine in correctional facilities.* Washington, DC: US Department of Justice.

National Institute of Justice. 2011. *Electronic monitoring reduces recidivism.* Washington, DC: US Department of Justice.

Nelkin, Dorothy, and M. Susan Lindee. 1995. *The DNA mystique: The gene as a cultural icon.* New York: Freeman.

Nelson, W. Raymond. 1988. *Cost savings in new generation jails: The direct supervision approach.* Washington, DC: US Department of Justice.

Oppel, Richard A. 2011. Private prisons found to offer little in savings. *New York Times*. May 18. Retrieved on July 21, 2013 from: **http://www.nytimes.com/2011/ 05/19/us/19prisons.html?_r=3&ref=us&**

Pallone, Nathaniel J. 2003. Without plea bargaining, Megan Kanka would be alive today. *Criminology & Public Policy* 3: 83–96.

Pasternak, Douglas. 1997. Special report: Wonder weapons. *US News & World Report* 123(1): 38–41, 45–46.

Petersilia, Joan. 2000. *When prisoners return to the community: Political, economic, and social consequences.* Washington, DC: US Department of Justice.

Pierce, Glenn L., and William J. Bowers. 1981. The Bartley-Fox gun law's short-term impact on crime. *Annals of the American Academy of Political and Social Science* 455(May): 120–37.

Ringel, Cheryl L., Ernest L. Cowles, and Thomas C. Castellano. 1994. Changing patterns and trends in parole supervision. In *Critical issues in crime and justice*, edited by Albert R. Roberts. Thousand Oaks, CA: Sage, 296–320.

Rosich, Katherine, and Kamala Mallik Kane. 2005. Truth in sentencing and state sentencing practices. *NIJ Journal* 252(July), retrieved on July 21, 2013 from: **http://www.nij.gov/journals/252/sentencing.html**

Saenz, Adolph. 1986. *Politics of a riot.* Washington, DC: American Correctional Association.

Sample, Lisa L., and Timothy M. Bray. 2003. Are sex offenders dangerous? *Criminology & Public Policy* 3: 59–82.

Sechrest, Dale K. 1989a. Population density and assaults in jails for men and women. *American Journal of Criminal Justice* 14(1): 87–103.

Sechrest, Dale K. 1989b. Prison "boot camps" do not measure up. *Federal Probation* 53(3): 19–24.

Sexual predator law upheld. 2001. *Las Cruces (NM) Sun–News*, January 23, A8.

Sherman, Lawrence W. 1998. Evidence-based policing. *Ideas in American policing.* Washington, DC: Police Foundation.

Smith, Michael E., and Walter J. Dickey. 1999. *Reforming sentencing and corrections for just punishment and public safety.* Washington, DC: US Department of Justice.

Smykla, John Ortiz, and Selke, William L. 1995. *Intermediate sanctions: Sentencing in the 1990s.* Cincinnati, OH: Anderson.

Snell, Tracy L. (2011). *Capital punishment, 2010—statistical tables.* Washington, DC: Bureau of Justice Statistics, US Department of Justice.

Steen, Sara. 2002. Determinate sentences. In *Encyclopedia of crime and punishment*, edited by David Levinson. Thousand Oaks, CA: Sage, 509–12.

Stephan, James J. 2008. *Census of state and federal correctional facilities, 2005.* Washington, DC: Bureau of Justice Statistics, US Department of Justice.

Stohr, Mary K., G. Larry Mays, Ann C. Beck, and Tammy Kelley. 1997. Sexual harassment in women's jails. *Journal of Contemporary Criminal Justice* 14(2): 135–55.

Taft, Philip B., Jr. 1979. Backed up in jail. *Corrections*, June, 26–33.

Thomas, Jim. 1988. *Prison litigation: The paradox of the jailhouse lawyer.* Totowa, NJ: Rowman and Littlefield.

Tonry, Michael. 1999a. *The fragmentation of sentencing and corrections in America.* Washington, DC: US Department of Justice.

Tonry, Michael. 1999b. *Reconsidering indeterminate and structured sentencing.* Washington, DC: US Department of Justice.

Tonry, Michael, and Joan Petersilia. 1999. *Prisons research at the beginning of the 21st century.* Washington, DC: US Department of Justice.

Travis, Jeremy. 2000. *But they all come back: Rethinking prisoner reentry.* Washington, DC: US Department of Justice.

Travis, Jeremy. 2005. *But they all come back: Facing the challenges of prisoner reentry.* Washington, DC: Urban Institute.

Useem, Bert, Camille Graham Camp, George M. Camp, and Renie Dugan. 1995. *Resolution of prison riots.* Washington, DC: US Department of Justice.

Walker, Samuel. 2006. *Sense and nonsense about crime and drugs: A policy guide*, 6th edn. Belmont, CA: Wadsworth.

Walker, Samuel. 2011. *Sense and nonsense about crime, drugs, and communities: A policy guide*, 7th edn. Belmont, CA: Wadsworth/Cengage.

Welch, Michael. 1996. *Corrections: A critical approach.* New York: McGraw-Hill.

Wicker, Tom. 1975. *A time to die.* New York: Quadrangle.

Winfree, L. Thomas, Jr., and Howard Abadinsky. 2010. *Understanding crime*, 3rd edn. Belmont, CA: Wadsworth/Cengage.

Wright, Richard. 2003. Sex offender registration and notification: Public attention, political emphasis, and fear. *Criminology & Public Policy* 3: 97–104.

Zevitz, Richard G., and Mary Ann Farkas. 2000. Sex offender community notification: Assessing the impact in Wisconsin. *National Institute of Justice Research in Brief.* Washington, DC: US Department of Justice.

GLOSSARY

Numbers in parentheses indicate the chapter(s) in which the term is primarily discussed.

accessory (3): An individual who contributes in some way to a crime's commission either before (*accessory before the fact*) or after (*accessory after the fact*) the crime is committed.

accreditation (15): The process of reviewing operating procedures and policies against a set of standards published by a professional organization such as the American Correctional Association (ACA).

accusatorial system (3): See *inquisitorial system*.

acoustic fence (15): Much like an electronic fence, an acoustic fence uses sound waves to keep people contained within a certain area.

***actus reus* (3):** (Latin: "guilty act") The legal requirement that an act is criminal only if it was committed overtly and resulted in harm.

administration (11): The act of administering or managing an office, employment, or organization.

administrative facilities (6): Special use prisons that provide a range of security classifications for different groups of inmates.

Administrative Maximum United States Penitentiary (ADMAX) (6): The only BOP supermax prison, a 400-person facility for men, located at the BOP Florence (Colorado) Federal Correctional Complex.

administrative segregation unit (6): A supermax area (a cell, hallway, or wing) within a maximum-security jail or prison where inmates who break the facility's rules or are violent are isolated, usually for short periods.

adversarial system (3): The Anglo-American legal system, in which legal disputes are resolved by two parties confronting each other in a court of law. The initiating party is called the *plaintiff* (in civil cases) or *prosecutor* (in criminal matters); the responding party is called the *defendant*. In criminal cases, the prosecution bears the burden of proof. Compare *inquisitorial system*.

affirmative defense (3): An argument made by a defendant who admits to the facts of the crime but claims some mitigating circumstance: for example, a defendant on trial for murder might admit to killing the victim but would argue it was done in self-defense. See also *entrapment*, *infancy defense*, and *insanity defense*.

Age of Enlightenment (2): The eighteenth-century movement in Europe and the United States to apply reason to all aspects of life. See also *natural law*.

aggravating circumstance (12): Circumstance relating to the commission of a crime that causes its gravity to be greater than that of the average instance of the given type of offense. Compare *mitigating circumstance*.

AIDS (8): Acquired immunodeficiency syndrome; disease resulting from individuals exposed to the human immunodeficiency virus (HIV).

alibi (3): An affirmative defense; the defendant does not dispute the facts of the case but argues that he or she was somewhere else when the crime was committed.

anomic trap (1): The realization that one can either accept what fate dictates—that is, work hard and achieve little—or become a criminal, a rebel, or a hermit; a component of Merton's anomie theory.

anomie (1): (French: "normlessness") Durkheim's term to describe the rejection of laws and other norms by a society that has undergone critical social or economic change. Merton uses the term to describe the gulf between the culture's goals and the individual's capacity to achieve them.

arousal theory (1): Theory that because of their brain functioning, psychopaths quickly become habituated to incoming stimuli; they may seek sensory stimulation through risk taking or criminal activity.

Essentials of Corrections, Fifth Edition. G. Larry Mays and L. Thomas Winfree, Jr.
© 2014 John Wiley & Sons, Inc. Published 2014 by John Wiley & Sons, Inc.

Ashurst-Sumners Act (6): Legislation passed by Congress in 1935 that restricted the movement across state borders of prison-manufactured goods. See also *Hawes-Cooper Act*.

asset forfeiture (4): The governmental seizure of personal assets obtained from or used in a criminal enterprise.

Auburn system (2): Method of imprisonment developed at the Auburn (New York) Prison in the nineteenth century, where serious offenders worked and ate with one another during the day but were confined to small solitary cells at night, and where silence was strictly enforced at all times. Compare *Pennsylvania system*; see also *silent system*.

authoritarian leader (11): An individual who approaches administration from the top down; he or she believes in a system in which orders will be carried out without question or hesitation.

bail (4): A security (money or property) pledged to or held by the court to ensure that an individual who has been arrested and booked will appear in court for hearings and trial.

behavior modification (1): A psychological approach to altering human conduct, based on a form of conditioning, whereby subjects are rewarded for appropriate conduct and punished for inappropriate conduct.

benign neglect (13): Ignoring or refusing to address a problem, but without bad intentions, often in the hope that others will address the problem or it will solve itself; this concept was introduced by Daniel Patrick Moynihan (1965) in his description of the government's policy toward violence precipitated by the Civil Rights movement.

bifurcated hearing (3): Two-part trial proceeding in which the question of guilt is determined in the first part and, if a conviction results, the sentence is determined in the second. The two steps of a bifurcated trial generally take place in separate hearings but use the same jury.

biological determinism (1): As applied to crime and justice, the theory that social or psychological phenomena are determined by biological factors, including genetics.

body cavity search (6): A search of mouth, anus, or vagina for contraband.

BOP (6): See *US Bureau of Prisons*.

***bote* (2):** The monetary compensation, described in the *lex salica*, that offenders (or their family) had to pay victims (or their family).

building tenders (7): A system of inmate-guards used extensively in Texas and Arkansas, among other states. This system became the basis of litigation against the operation of cruel and unusual penal systems.

bureaucracy (11): An organizational structure that assigns individuals specific authority and responsibilities according to their positions in a predetermined hierarchy.

bureaucratic leader (11): Similar to Weber's autocratic leader, this leader is rule oriented and tends to lead from the top down; such a leader frequently demands loyalty from his or her subordinates and expects obedience to policies without questions.

camper (6): A low-risk inmate in the federal security level classification scheme; an inmate in a federal prison camp.

campus-design prison (6): A facility in which the living units are laid out like dormitories and other buildings on the grounds of a small college.

canon law (2): The body of laws that governs a church, especially the Roman Catholic Church; evolved from the *Corpus Juris Civilis*.

case law (2): An outgrowth of the Roman *jus honorarium*, whereby judges, as they decide cases and render decisions, create new law.

caseload (4): The number of clients assigned to a particular probation (or parole) officer for supervision. Compare *workload*.

case manager (10): A prison official who works with inmates on such matters as classification, prison-work assignments, and staff-inmate and inmate-inmate complaints. The case manager approach to unit management has been employed by the BOP since the 1970s.

centralization (11): Concentration of power in one location within a bureaucracy.

citation (9): A legal document ordering the parolee to appear in court; generally issued by a court, when, in the estimation of the parole officer, a supervisee poses a threat to the community or is a flight risk.

Citizenship and Immigration Services (8): Federal law enforcement agency that is part of the Department of Homeland Security; it is responsible for processing visas and naturalization petitions, as well as granting refugee status.

civil death (12): The legal idea that offenders lose most if not all of their citizenship rights once they have been convicted and incarcerated.

civil detention of sex offenders (15): The continued incarceration of sex offenders after they have served their prison sentence until it is determined that their presence in the community does not pose a threat; civil detainees are, however, entitled to treatment, unlike prison inmates.

civil rights claim (12): A suit filed under Section 1983 of the US Code that permits prison and jail inmates, as well as probationers and parolees, to sue those responsible for their care and custody under the due process and equal protection clauses of the Fourteenth Amendment; also called *Section 1983 suit*.

class action lawsuit (12): Litigation involving a group of similarly situated petitioners, such as jail or prison inmates.

classification officer (6, 10): Prison official who uses testing, inmates' histories, and interviews to determine inmates' security level.

clinical psychologist (10): A person who treats individuals with mental and behavioral problems; in corrections, this person is responsible for supervising counselors and approving treatment plans.

close-custody unit (7): A form of administrative detention used in some prison systems to maintain control over dangerous inmates, including members of prison gangs.

co-correctional unit (13): A prison that houses both male and female inmates, although in separate living areas.

Code of Hammurabi (2): Babylonian legal code compiled during the reign of Hammurabi, in the eighteenth century BCE perhaps the oldest codified system of crime and punishment.

common law (3): Unwritten law based on custom and precedent that developed in England primarily from judicial decisions; the basis of the English legal system and the legal system in the United States (with the exception of Louisiana).

community service (4): A form of community corrections, usually recommended in cases of vandalism and minor property offenses. The intent is to secure some benefits for the public from the offender, increase offender accountability, and reduce the need for incarceration.

commutation of sentence (9): An extraordinary action by the executive branch of government. In law, *commutation* literally means exchanging one punishment for another, less severe one.

concurrent sentence (3): Two or more terms of imprisonment imposed and then served at the same time. Compare *consecutive sentence*.

conjugal visits (8): Visits allowed between inmates and spouses or intimate partners in which privacy and sexual relations are permitted.

con-politician (7): One of Schrag's prison role types: the inmate who attempts to manipulate guards and other inmates with money and influence; tends to be pseudosocial, that is, pretends to be prosocial but in reality is antisocial. Compare *outlaw*, *right guy*, and *Square John*.

consecutive sentence (3): Two or more terms of imprisonment imposed at the same time but served in sequence, or a new sentence imposed on a person already under sentence for a previous offense. Compare *concurrent sentence*.

consensus-based classification system (6): An inmate classification scheme in which the factors that determine risk are identified by prison personnel, based on their experiences with problem inmates. Compare *equity-based classification system* and *prediction-based classification system*.

consolidated parole board (9): Consists of an autonomous (independent) panel within a state-level corrections department or division; makes all decisions about conditional release from prison, but delegates supervision to another part of the system. Also called the *institutional model*. Compare *independent parole board*.

contract system (6): The practice of wardens' selling inmate labor to private vendors, who provided raw materials, machinery, and even supervisory staff; the work was done in factories near the prison or at the prison, in space rented to the vendors by the wardens. Compare *lease system* and *state-use system*.

cools (13): Heffernan's term to describe female inmates who manipulate other inmates to try to pass their own prison time as pleasantly as possible.

cooperative (co-op) education (10): Paid experiential learning placement in which students alternate between work and a period of class enrollment; many "co-ops" result in job offers.

***corpus delicti* (3):** (Latin: "body of the crime") The facts that prove a crime.

***Corpus Juris Civilis* (2):** The recodification of Roman laws completed by 12 scholars in 535 at the order of Justinian I of Constantinople; the criminal and civil code of most of the Byzantine Empire until the end of the Middle Ages, and the basis for Germanic law and canon law. Also known as the *Justinian Code*.

Correctional Classification Profile (6): An inmate classification system created by the Correctional Services Group that assesses inmates' needs based on the risk posed to the institution and the public at large.

correctional counselor (10): A professional staff member who provides individual or group treatment to correctional clients. This could take place in institutional (prison or jail) settings or extrainstitutional (community corrections, probation and parole) settings.

correctional officer (CO) (10): A custody officer in a jail or prison.

corrections (1): All government actions intended to manage adults who have been accused or convicted of a criminal offense and juveniles who have been charged with or found guilty of an act of delinquency or a status offense.

corrections paradigm (15): The operational model or philosophy under which correctional programs are designed and administered.

courtyard-design prison (6): A facility in which the cells and functional areas are built around an open plaza.

criminal intent (3): The intent to commit an act that violates the law; can be specific (the offender intended to harm victim this way) or general (the offender understood that harm was possible).

criminology (1): The scientific study of crime and criminals.

crisis of overcriminalization (15): A recent spike in the number of people serving time, brought about by a legislative increase in the number of punishable offenses and the amount of time each offender must serve. This crisis has made crowding in jails and prisons a greater concern than ever before.

cultural importation hypothesis (7): Clemmer's idea that convicted offenders bring key elements of the inmate code, along with most inmate role adaptations, into the prison community. Compare *deprivation hypothesis*.

cultural transmission thesis (1): A key explanatory element of the Chicago school of sociology's social disorganization theory. It states that there are no criminal groups, only criminal areas of neighborhoods that pass the criminality from one generation to the next as part of the area's culture.

custody (6): The legal or physical responsibility for detaining a person.

Custody Determination Model (6): A classification scheme, developed by the National Institute of Corrections, that bases an inmate's assignment on factors such as the offender's expression of violence before and since incarceration, his or her history of alcohol and drug abuse, and the severity of the current offense.

custody variance score (13): A score created from the sum of risk factors that is used by the BOP classification scheme to determine a person's security level while in custody.

day fine (3): A monetary sanction that converts punishment units (a nonmonetary measure) into a dollar amount based on the offender's average daily income; also called *structured fine*. See also *means-based penalties*.

dehumanization (6): The process described by Goffman of stripping inmates of their personhood in total institutions. See also *rites of passage*.

deinstitutionalization (1): Removing certain groups or individuals from secure confinement and placing them in alternative correctional settings; especially used with groups such as juvenile status offenders.

deliberate indifference (12): The legal test used by courts to determine whether correctional officials ignored the physical (medical) conditions of an inmate to that inmate's long-term detriment.

democratic leader (11): Person in a position of trust, power, and authority over others who relies on explanation and elaboration as means of communicating.

deportable person (8): Any person illegally in the United States whether that person entered illegally or entered legally but whose legal status has lapsed.

deprivation hypothesis (7): The view, derived from the work of Clemmer, that prison culture, including its code and inmate role types, results directly from the act of incarceration and the pains of imprisonment. Compare *cultural importation hypothesis*.

detention facilities (5): Any place of short-term confinement; may include jails as well as facilities designed to hold juveniles or persons on immigration holds.

determinate sentence (3): A sentence to confinement, specified by statute, for a fixed period. Compare *indeterminate sentence*.

deterrence (1): One of eight philosophical responses to crime; asserts that certain and severe punishment discourages the criminal from committing additional offenses (*specific deterrence*) and keeps others from committing crimes as well (*general deterrence*). See also *incapacitation, isolation, rehabilitation, reintegration, restitution, restoration,* and *retribution*.

diagnostician (10): Corrections employee charged with administering (and in some cases assessing) classification instruments and psychometric examinations to determine inmates' institutional classification or treatment needs.

differential association theory (1): Sutherland's explanation for why people commit crimes: that criminals learn motives, ideas, and rationalizations from others, and that those definitions vary by duration, frequency, intensity, and priority.

differential reinforcement (1): According to Akers's social learning theory, a mechanism for learning in which people retain and repeat rewarded behavior and extinguish behavior that is punished. See also *discriminative stimuli* and *imitation*.

direct supervision (5): A pattern of inmate management that eliminates many of the traditional barriers between inmates and staff, and that affords staff members greater interaction with and control over inmates 24 hours a day. Compare *intermittent supervision* and *remote supervision*.

discount rate (15): The amount of time removed from an inmate's sentence as a result of good behavior and participation in programming efforts.

discretionary release (9): Release of inmates from incarceration at the discretion of parole boards within limits set by the sentence and penal law.

discrimination (14): The unequal treatment of individuals or groups based on some trait, characteristic or attribute, including, for example, race, skin color, gender, or sexual orientation.

discriminative stimuli (1): According to Akers, positive or neutralizing definitions that motivate people to violate the law. See also *differential reinforcement*.

disproportionate minority contact (DMC) (1, 14): The disproportionate rates at which members of minority groups are convicted of crimes and sentenced to prison in the United States.

diversion (4): The process of removing individuals from the formal system of prosecution and adjudication, and placing them in a less-formal treatment setting.

doing time (7): Irwin's term to describe the outlook expressed by some inmates in which prison is viewed as a temporary break in their criminal career. Compare *gleaning* and *jailing*.

drug education (6): An information-oriented program available to almost all inmates in federal and state facilities.

drug offense (7): Crime involving a psychoactive substance; includes the actual or attempted unlawful sale, purchase, distribution, manufacture, cultivation, transport, possession, or use of a controlled or prohibited substance.

dual diagnosis (13): Two disease conditions or syndromes existing at the same time in the same individual; for example, a person diagnosed as a substance abuser and as suffering from a mental health issue, such as depression.

duality of women (13): A nineteenth century idea that women were either good or bad, Madonna or whore; this notion shaped how social and legal institutions of the day, including the courts and prisons, viewed and treated female offenders, who were often viewed as the latter, having fallen from grace.

economic exploitation (7): The idea that inmates are taken advantage of within prisons and jails because of the monopolistic prices they must pay for goods and services in the inmate *sub rosa* economy; also called *economic victimization*.

egalitarian families (13): Family units where no gender assumes primacy and where decisions for all or nearly all aspects of social life are shared equally by parents or parent substitutes; moreover, there are few if any distinctions in the treatment of male and female children within the family.

ego (1): According to Freud the part of the mind that is influenced by parental training and the like.

electronic brain implants (15): An experimental technology that is proposed to control the behaviors and, ultimately, the thought patterns of convicted offenders.

electronic fence (15): A device that can be buried in the ground that provides an electric perimeter around a certain area keeping people (or animals) contained.

entrapment (3): An affirmative defense claiming that a legal authority induced the criminal behavior, that the defendant would not have committed the crime in the absence of the authority's intervention.

equity (3): In criminal justice, that similar offenders and similar offenses should be treated the same.

equity-based classification system (6): An inmate classification scheme that attempts to treat all inmates the same and that bases classification only on factors related to the current offense. Compare *consensus-based classification system* and *prediction-based classification system*.

ethnicity (14): The shared social or cultural traits by which a group is identified, such as language, religion, and customs. Compare *race*.

ethnocentrism (14): The belief that certain races or ethnic groups are by definition better or worse than others.

eugenics (15): A form of genetic engineering that selects for positive traits and attempts to eliminate negative traits.

expiration release (9): The unconditional release from custody or supervision when an offender has served his or her sentence (minus any good-time credits).

extrainstitutional punishment (4): The idea that offenders may be adequately punished for their crimes by means other than prison or jail.

false negatives (9): A term taken from statistics and used to refer to prison inmates who are assessed to be poor risks for parole and are, therefore, denied conditional release from prison, but who, in reality, are actually unlikely to return to prison; nearly always unknown because they are not released.

false positives (9): A term taken from statistics and used to refer to prisoners who are assessed to be good risks for parole, but who actually are high risks for return to prison by either violating the terms of their conditional release or otherwise engaging in violating behavior; these prisoners nearly always come to the attention of the parole authority by their actions.

Federal Correctional Complex (FCC) (6): Clusters of federal prisons serving a variety of purposes that are located in closed proximity to one another.

Federal Correctional Institution (FCI) (6): A federal low- or medium-security facility.

Federal Detention Center (FDC) (6): A BOP holding facility not intended for long-term confinement.

Federal Medical Center (FMC) (6): A BOP medical facility.

Federal Prison Camp (FPC) (6): A federal minimum-security facility.

Federal Prison Industries, Inc. (6): See *UNICOR*.

Federal Transfer Center (6): Located in Oklahoma City, this facility is responsible for moving federal inmates from one facility to another.

felony (3): A criminal offense punishable by death or incarceration in a state or federal prison facility generally for more than 1 year. Compare *misdemeanor*.

fish (7): An inmate term for new inmates; signifies their low status in the prison social system.

frustration riot (7): A type of riot prevalent during the 1950s and 1960s, representing open conflict between a unified inmate subculture and prison authorities.

gender identity (8): A person's self-concept of gender status apart from biological designation as male or female.

Gender Identity Disorder (GID) (8): Presence and persistence of a cross-gender identification.

gender orientation (8): See *gender identity*.

genetic mapping (15): Analysis of individuals' unique DNA patterns to determine identity and risk factors associated with certain behaviors.

general deterrence (1): See *deterrence*.

GLBT inmates (8): Abbreviation for jail and prison inmates identified as gay, lesbian, bi-sexual, or transgender.

gleaning (7): Irwin's term to describe the practice of some inmates to gain as much personal improvement from their incarceration as they can. Compare *doing time* and *jailing*.

global positioning satellite (GPS) surveillance (15): The use of satellites positioned over the Earth to monitor activities (such as the location of probationers and parolees) on the Earth's surface.

good-time credits (3): Time, usually measured in days, deducted from a prison sentence for good behavior; a part of determinate sentencing.

good-time laws (9): Laws originating in New York in 1817 that allow a reduction of a prisoner's term for "good behavior" while in prison.

Guardians (9): A term used in the nineteenth century to describe citizen volunteers in New York, to whom released prisoners reported while on parole.

guilt beyond a reasonable doubt (3): The standard of proof in criminal cases. Compare *preponderance of the evidence*.

Habeas Corpus Act of 1679 (4): An early English Parliamentary act that established the presumption for release on recognizance in cases where the accused were not required to post bail.

habeas corpus, writ of (3, 12): (Latin: "[that] you have the body") An order requiring that the named prisoner be brought before a court at a stated time and place to decide the legality of his or her incarceration.

habilitation (13): The process of acquiring the basic life skills needed to function in society.

habitual-offender statutes (2): Laws that increase the penalty for those designated as repeat offenders; for example, a law that mandates a sentence of life without parole for the commission of a third felony. Also called *three-strikes-and-you're-out laws*.

halfway house (4): Originally a residential center for paroled offenders who were halfway out of prison; now includes any residential program on the spectrum between incarceration and total freedom.

Hawes-Cooper Act (6): A law enacted by Congress and approved by President Hoover in January 1929 that made all inmate-manufactured goods transported through a state subject to that state's laws, in effect ending manufacturers' reliance on prisoners as a source of cheap labor. See also *Ashurst-Sumners Act*.

hearing officer (9): An officer who presides over preliminary parole hearings, typically a supervisory-level or senior member of the parole agency staff.

hepatitis C virus (8): The more deadly strain of this highly communicable viral disease that can cause inflammation of the liver; typically spread through blood or blood product; also known as *HCV*.

high-use jail (5): Klofas's term for a jail that both books and holds high numbers of inmates. Compare *holding jail*, *low-use jail*, and *processing jail*.

highest rated capacity (15): The maximum number of inmates that a given correctional facility can hold.

HIV-positive (8): Persons who have tested positive for the human immunodeficiency virus, the precursor to acquired immunodeficiency syndrome (AIDS).

holding jail (5): Klofas's term for a jail that books inmates at a low rate but holds them for some time. Compare *high-use jail*, *low-use jail*, and *processing jail*.

horizontal overcharging (3): A prosecutorial practice whereby the state charges a defendant with every possible criminal charge related to the offense for tactical advantage in the plea-bargaining process; also called *bedsheeting*. Compare *vertical overcharging*.

hyper-segregation (14): Extreme separation between social classes and races within a city.

ICE detainees (8): Individuals held by the Immigration and Customs Enforcement agency on suspicion of immigration violations.

id (1): According to Freud, the part of the mind that is the source of primitive, hedonistic urges.

idiosyncratic leader (10): A leader that works over, under, around, and through the hierarchy by exerting direct contact and control over decision making.

imitation (1): According to Akers's social learning theory, a mechanism for learning; the idea that behavior is modeled after that observed in others. See also *differential reinforcement*.

Immigration and Customs Enforcement (ICE) (8): The federal law enforcement agency located within the Department of Homeland Security that is responsible for enforcing the nation's immigration laws.

imprisonment binge (7): Irwin and Austin's term to describe the trend in the mid- to late-1990s of using incarceration as the primary—if not sole—method for combating crime; results in an ever-increasing reliance on prisons and more prison construction, consuming ever-increasing proportions of the state and federal budgets.

incapacitation (1): One of eight philosophical responses to crime; the belief that separating offenders from society reduces the likelihood of their committing new crimes. See also *deterrence*, *isolation*, *rehabilitation*, *reintegration*, *restitution*, *restoration*, and *retribution*.

inchoate offense (3): In criminal law, a solicitation, an attempt, or conspiracy to commit a crime.

independent parole board (9): An entity, not under the power of any other state agency, that controls the release of inmates from prison and makes revocation decisions. Compare *consolidated parole board*.

indeterminate sentence (3): A term of imprisonment defined by statute as a range of time (for example, a minimum of 2 years and a maximum of 5 years) rather than a specific amount of time (3 years). Compare *determinate sentence*.

infancy defense (3): An affirmative defense that the defendant was too young at the time the crime was committed to distinguish between right and wrong. The age, usually between eight and ten, is defined by statute.

inmate code (7): Informal set of rules reflecting the values of the prison society.

inmate count (6): A security practice in which COs must physically account for each inmate in their areas of responsibility; conducted regularly at certain places or times (at meals, at work, in the evening) and randomly at others.

inquisitorial system (3): (From the Latin *inquisitor*, "to search or inquire") The legal system in civil law countries, which places the burden of proof on the defendant; also called *accusatorial system*. Compare *adversarial system*.

insanity defense (3): An affirmative defense in which the defendant denies accountability for the criminal act because he or she was incapable of knowing right from wrong at the time the act was committed, or was incapable of acting on that difference because of a defect of reason. See also *irresistible-impulse test* and *M'Naughton* rule.

inspector of released prisoners (9): A nineteenth-century civilian governmental employee who aided the police in the supervision of ex-convicts released from prison under the Irish ticket-of-leave system; essentially the first parole officers.

institutional corrections (10): Refers to employment in any facility in which accused or convicted offenders are housed, such as prisons and jails but also including halfway houses and other integrative institutions that provide some level of secure offender management.

institutional model (9): See *consolidated parole board*.

institutionalized racism (14): An endemic or society-wide problem in which stereotypes, discrimination, and prejudices shape how most people view members of racial and ethnic minority groups.

intake (2): The information gathering and personal interviews conducted when an inmate is first brought to a corrections facility.

intensive supervision program (ISP) (4): A supervisory system in which probation officers have lighter caseloads, perhaps as few as ten clients per month, institute regular drug tests, and carry out other intensive measures, such as work and home visits.

intermediate sanction (3, 4): A punishment that is more severe than standard probation but less severe than imprisonment; can include fines and other forms of extra-institutional diversion.

intermittent supervision (5): A pattern of inmate management that requires COs to actually look into inmates' cells to observe prisoners' activities; by its nature, this form of supervision tends to be less regular than others. Compare *direct supervision* and *remote supervision*.

internship (10): College course (for pay, credit, or both) in which students observe and participate in some agency activities; also called *field experience* or *practicum*.

Irish ticket-of-leave system (2, 9): A four-stage program instituted in the Irish prison system in the mid-1800s; inmates who advanced through the first three stages, each allowing them greater independence, were rewarded in the fourth stage with a ticket of leave (parole).

iron law of imprisonment (9): Travis's term to express the idea that nearly all prison inmates leave prison under some legal authority and return to the community.

iron law of prison populations (9): The notion that prison populations are a function of both the number of people we send to prison, and the amount of time those individuals must spend in prison.

irresistible-impulse test (3): A test of the insanity defense that concedes the defendant's ability to distinguish between right and wrong but suggests that a mental defect prevented the defendant from using that knowledge at the time the offense was committed to control his or her actions; the assumption: the inability to control criminal behavior means the defendant could not have been acting with criminal intent. See also *M'Naughton* rule.

isolation (1): One of eight philosophical responses to crime; the belief that offenders should be separated from the rest of the community. See also *deterrence*,

incapacitation, *rehabilitation*, *reintegration*, *restitution*, *restoration*, and *retribution*.

jail (5): A facility, usually under the control of a city or county government, that houses a diverse population of pretrial detainees, convicted misdemeanants serving short sentences, and convicted felons awaiting transportation to prison.

jail annex (5): A facility that houses the overflow from a main jail; also called *satellite jail*.

jailhouse lawyer (12): An inmate in a prison or jail who becomes skilled in the law and assists other prisoners in filing suits largely against prison or jail administration; sometimes called *writ writer*.

jailing (7): Irwin's term to refer to the inmate practice of seeking positions of power and authority within the facility; prison or jail is, for these inmates, home.

joint-venture program (6): An association of people or business organizations that undertakes a commercial enterprise.

judicial reprieve (4): In the Middle Ages, an action by a judge that suspended imposition of a sentence until a convicted offender could appeal to the monarch for a pardon.

***jus civile* (2):** (Latin: "civil law") The law created by Roman jurists for resolving issues between Roman citizens.

***jus gentium* (2):** (Latin: "the law of nations") The law developed by Roman jurists for trying aliens (non-Roman citizens).

***jus honorarium* (2):** (Latin: "supplemental law") Magisterial law meant to supplement and correct existing law; the basis of case law.

justice by geography (14): Feld's term to describe the variability in juvenile justice outcomes that can be associated with where the court is found; urban jurisdictions tend, he claimed, to render harsher justice than do nonurban ones.

justice model (2): A punishment model that assumes individuals choose to violate laws and so deserve punishment, not treatment. Often attributed to Fogel and Von Hirsch, among others; the goals of the justice model are to confine as punishment, to provide a safe and humane system of offender control, to offer treatment programs (but not require them), and to provide public safety.

Justinian Code (2): Roman law codified by the 12 scholars under the direction of Emperor Justinian I. See also *Corpus Juris Civilis*.

juvenile detention center (8): A facility much like an adult jail that has responsibility for short-term detention of accused (and sometimes adjudicated) juvenile offenders.

King's Peace (2): crimes committed in the king's presence or against one of his officers.

labeling (4): A theoretical approach to deviant behavior attributed to Lemert; asserts that the formal designation of an individual as a criminal (as in a convicted offender) can result in a negative self-concept that will push the person deeper into crime.

laissez-faire leader (11): An administrator who provides little or no direction for subordinates.

law of criminal justice thermodynamics (15): As originated by Walker, the idea that as punishments become increasingly harsh, they are concomitantly and decreasingly likely to be enforced.

Law of Moses (2): The Judaic laws set forth in the first five books of the Old Testament (Genesis, Exodus, Leviticus, Numbers, and Deuteronomy) and summarized in the Ten Commandments; also called *Mosaic Code*, *Pentateuch*, and *Torah*.

lease system (6): A modification of the contract system in which vendors paid a fixed fee for prison labor and the work was done outside the prison, typically on farms or in mines. Compare *contract system* and *state-use system*.

legitimate inmate economy (7): The commerce conducted through the facility's commissary or store that "sells" inmates food and other products; to make purchases at these "stores," inmates must have money in their accounts, often described as an inmate "trust fund," into which relatives, friends and others may make contributions.

lex salica **(2):** (Latin: "law of the Salian Franks, or Germans") Germanic tribal law.

lex talionis **(1):** (Latin: "law of the claw") Law of retaliation (for example, "an eye for an eye, a tooth for a tooth").

liberation hypothesis (13): The 1970s view, voiced by Adler and Simon, that the increased opportunities of women's liberation opened up criminal activities to a new generation of women.

linear design (5, 6): A jail or prison layout in which individual or two-person cells are located off a central hallway that is entered through a sally port. Compare *modified linear design* and *podular design*.

lowest rated capacity (15): The minimum number of inmates that a facility can hold and still operate efficiently.

low-use jail (5): Klofas's term for a jail that both books and holds inmates at very low rates. Compare *holding jail*, *high-use jail*, and *processing jail*.

malfeasance (10): Commission of a prohibited act by a justice employee.

management (11): In corrections: inmate management and organizational management; both are concerned with keeping the functions of institutions and agencies operating relatively efficiently.

mandatory minimum (3): By statute, the least-severe penalties that can be imposed on offenders convicted of committing certain crimes.

mandatory release (9): A conditional release from prison required by statute when an inmate has been confined for a period equal to his or her full sentence minus statutory good time, if any.

mandatory sentence (3): Penalty required by law for those convicted of certain offenses.

manifest injustice (14): An outcome, generally in a legal case, that is clearly and indisputably unfair, for example, a sentence that appears far too severe, given the circumstances in the criminal case.

marks of commendation (2): A set of rewards given to inmates for good behavior developed by Alexander Maconochie.

Marxist feminism (13): A variant of feminist criminology derived from Marxism; the belief that male dominance reflects a social ideology that is willing to subjugate women, first to capital and second to men.

maximum security (6): The highest level of security found in most jails and prison systems, reserved for inmates who pose the greatest threat to society, the institution, and other inmates.

means-based penalty (3): A monetary sanction that takes into account individual offenders' ability to pay. See also *day fine*.

medical model (2): A treatment plan that equates crime with illness, and rehabilitation with cure, and that relies for both the definition and treatment of criminals on scientific study.

medium security (6): A level of security in jails and prisons that is less restrictive than maximum security in terms of recreational activities for inmates and visitation, but in which some direct supervision of inmates is maintained.

mens rea **(3):** (Latin: "guilty mind") The intention to carry out a criminal act. See *criminal intent*.

mental health problem (8): A broad designation for a variety of mental functioning issues including those that are genetic as well as those resulting from drug and alcohol induced psychoses.

mental illness (8): Medical conditions such as schizophrenia, bipolar disorder, delusions, and hallucinations.

Metropolitan Correctional Center/Metropolitan Detention Center (MCC/MDC) (6): A special-mission facility operated by the BOP and used primarily to house pretrial detainees and convicted offenders awaiting transfer to other federal facilities; all are located in or near large metropolitan centers.

minimum security (6): The least-restrictive level of custody in most correctional systems; allows inmates the most freedom of movement throughout the institution.

misdemeanor (3): The least serious type of crime; punishable in most states by a fine or a combination of a fine and incarceration for less than 1 year, typically in a county jail or similar facility. Compare *felony*.

misfeasance (10): Improper performance of an otherwise permitted act by a justice employee.

mitigating circumstance (12): A factor or situation surrounding the commission of a crime that would cause a jury to consider a lesser penalty once a person has been found guilty of a law violation. Compare *aggravating circumstance*.

mix, the (13): Owen's term to describe how the drug use and other self-destructive behaviors of certain female inmates continue after they are incarcerated.

mixed caseload (4): A situation in which a probation officer may have a both misdemeanants and felons among the probationers being supervised.

***M'Naughton* rule (3):** A test of the insanity defense that focuses on the defendant's ability to distinguish between right and wrong at the time an offense was committed; the assumption: if the offender did not understand the illegal nature of the act, he or she could not have been acting with criminal intent. See also *irresistible-impulse test*.

modified linear design (6): A jail or prison layout in which cells usually are arranged in clusters, inmates in each cluster share a common living area, and entry to each cluster is controlled by means of a sally port. Compare *linear design* and *podular design*.

Multiple drug-resistant tuberculosis (MDR-TB) (8): A form of tuberculosis that has developed resistance to most of the currently available drug treatment therapies.

natural law (2): A system of rules and principles growing out of and conforming to human nature that can be discovered through reason. See also *Age of Enlightenment*.

needs principle (4): Use of assessment instruments to learn the needs of offenders that are related to their criminal tendencies.

nepotism (11): Hiring individuals who may be related to another person by birth or by marriage. Many civil service systems prohibit this and may not allow one person to supervise another who is related.

net widening (4): The idea that the more options a correctional program—or any criminal justice agency—has, the more people will be brought under some form of social control.

new-generation jail (5): A facility in which the podular design allows for the direct supervision of inmates.

nonfeasance (10): Failure to act when an employee is authorized and expected to act.

nonperson status (12): Having no legal status; a basis for denying any constitutional rights.

nonresidential drug abuse treatment (6): A community-based, outpatient program consisting of individual and group counseling, self-help groups, and seminars.

operant conditioning (1): The psychological process of using rewards to encourage certain actions, and punishment to discourage others; often an element of behavior modification programs.

outlaw (7): Schrag's role type of inmate that relies on force and physical violence to get what he or she wants from other, more easily exploited inmates. Compare *con-politician, right guy, Square John*.

pains of imprisonment (7): According to Sykes, the deprivations associated with imprisonment, including loss of freedom, autonomy, goods and services, security, and heterosexual relationships.

paraprofessional (10): An individual who may not possess requisite educational qualifications (for example, college degrees, training, experience) but nonetheless assists in correctional treatment; sometimes such an individual is a community volunteer or an ex-offender.

pardon (9): A form of executive clemency or mercy; a unique and rare event, whereby the governor or president, depending on the legal authority by which the sentencing occurred, has the power to pardon or forgive the offender for his or her criminal misdeeds and, in some cases, restore some or all rights lost by the conviction.

parole (2, 9): An administrative function; the conditional and supervised release of convicted offenders before their sentences are completed.

parole agents (9): State-level civil service employees, working for the executive branch of government, who monitor, supervise, and otherwise provide oversight for ex-prisoners upon their release.

parole agreement (9): A document, signed by the paroling authority and the parolee, that specifies the general and special conditions under which the prisoner is released into the community.

parole eligibility date (9): The earliest possible point at which an inmate can leave prison.

parole officers (9): See *parole agents.*

participative leader (11): A group-oriented leader who frequently has informal contacts with employees under his or her direction.

patriarchal families (13): Family units where progenitor and or dominant male assumes the role of the primary decision-maker in nearly all or all aspects of family life; literally refers to "rule by the father"; moreover, male and female offspring are treated quite differently, with far more control exercised over female children.

PC units (8): prison units designed to hold inmates who need additional protection. See *protective custody.*

penal colony (2): An isolated place used for the confinement of convicted offenders; in most penal colonies, the geography or topography provided the means of confinement and control.

penal harm (1): The idea that punishment, in particular incarceration, should be uncomfortable.

Penal Servitude Act of 1853 (2): An act of Parliament allowing prisoners to be paroled.

Penitentiary Act of 1779 (2): Parliamentary act promoted by John Howard in order to provide more humane treatment for English prisoners.

Pennsylvania system (2): A nineteenth-century method of imprisonment developed in Pennsylvania; the method was reflected in a layout designed to isolate inmates from one another to give them an opportunity for reflection and self-reform. Compare *Auburn system.*

penologists (1): People who engage in the systematic study of punishment.

personal offense (3): A crime that threatens the physical well-being of the victim; includes aggravated assault, rape, murder, and robbery.

petty misdemeanor (3): The most minor criminal offense, usually punishable by a fine or a very brief period of incarceration; also called *infraction.*

pillory (2): Wooden timbers set on a post, with restraining holes for head and hands cut into the timbers; a means of public punishment and humiliation.

play family (13): See *pseudo family.*

plea bargaining (3): Negotiations over sentences, counts, and charges that go on between the defense and the prosecution; the exchange of a guilty plea for some form of leniency.

podular design (5, 6): A jail or prison layout in which cells line the perimeter of pods (often triangular), and inmates share a central common area. Compare *linear design* and *modified linear design.*

police lockup (5): An incarceration facility, generally located in a police station, for the temporary detention of suspects until they can be interrogated or fully processed by the police before being transferred to a county jail.

political patronage (11): The appointment of an individual to an office based on whom he or she knows, not what he or she knows.

political riot (7): A type of prison uprising common in the late 1960s and 1970s; an expression of inmates' concerns politically about the oppressed nature of the prison inmate population.

positivists (1): Social scientists who believed that human behavior was determined by factors beyond the individual's control and that science must be used to understand criminal behavior. *Positivism* was a major trend in criminological theory from the mid-nineteenth century through the early twentieth century.

post (5): Any position in a correctional facility that must be staffed 24 hours a day.

power-control theory (13): The view that the presence of power and the absence of control in egalitarian families create conditions conducive to common forms of delinquency for both boys and girls.

prediction-based classification system (6): A prisoner classification scheme based on a range of legal, psychological, social, and medical information about offenders; the goal is both to predict the likelihood of the inmate's being the perpetrator or victim of violence and to control that behavior. Compare *consensus classification system* and *equity-based classification system.*

preponderance of the evidence (3): The standard of proof in civil cases; establishes that one party to a suit is more liable than the other; a less rigorous standard than the guilty-beyond-a-reasonable-doubt standard applied in criminal cases.

presentence investigation (PSI) (4): The detailed examination, by a probation officer, case worker, or other court officer, of the criminal defendant's life; culminates in a report that suggests the appropriate method for disposing of the case.

pressing (2): A method used to convince people to confess of their crimes; boards were placed on the individual and heavy stones of increasing weights were placed on the boards.

presumption of innocence (3): The common law idea that in criminal matters, a person is assumed to be innocent until proved guilty beyond a reasonable doubt.

presumptive sentence (3): A sentence determined through the application of a statutory method that does not consider mitigating or aggravating circumstances.

principal (3): The individual accused of actually committing a crime; the person most directly involved in the criminal act.

prisoner reentry (9): A term used to refer to the general reentry of convicted, sentenced, and incarcerated offenders back into the community, whether through parole or some other legal means, including expiration of sentence; often used to indicate programmatic and procedural actions taken against and on behalf of those being released.

prison gang (7): A clique or informal group found in US prisons today, examples are the "Aryan Brotherhood," the "Black Guerrilla Family," "Mexican Mafia," "La Nuestra Familia," and the "Texas Syndicate." See also *security threat group*.

prisonization (7): According to Clemmer, the taking on to a greater or lesser extent of the folkways, mores, customs, and general culture of the penitentiary; a form of institutionalization in which the prison is home and other inmates are fellow citizens of the prison community.

prison riot (7): According to Hawkins and Alpert, a "collective attempt by inmates to take over part or all" of a prison.

prison subculture (7): According to Clemmer and others, the inmate social community, governed by the inmate code; traditionally aligned against staff and legitimate society.

Private Sector/Prison Industries Enhancement Certification (PS/PIEC) (6): A law passed by Congress in 1979 that removed most of the restrictions created by the Hawes-Cooper and Ashurst-Sumners acts on prisoner-made goods.

privatization (5): The movement toward having corrections facilities or specific functions within those facilities constructed or operated by private contractors.

probation (3, 4): The conditional freedom granted an alleged or adjudged adult or juvenile offender in lieu of incarceration.

probation/parole officers (PPOs) (9): State- or local-level civil servants, working for local or state units of government or state-level courts, depending on state law and local traditions, provide the same services for prison releasees as parole officers/parole agents, but also supervise probations; see also Chapter 4.

procedural law (3): The legal procedures under which criminal laws must be enforced and applied to those accused and convicted of crimes.

processing jail (5): Klofas's term for a jail that books inmates at a high rate but holds them for a relatively short time. Compare *holding jail, high-use jail,* and *low-use jail*.

property offense (3): A crime that involves the destruction or theft of something of value but that does not threaten the physical well-being of the victim; includes arson, larceny and theft, burglary, auto theft, and fraud and embezzlement.

proportionality (3): In criminal justice, the belief that the severity of the punishment should increase with the seriousness of the crime.

***pro se* action (12):** (Latin: "one's self") Acting as one's own defense attorney in criminal proceedings.

protective custody (8): Special housing units in correctional facilities designed to provide extra security and protection for inmates who are particularly susceptible to victimization by other inmates.

pseudo family (12): Often used to describe nuclear and extended family units found in women's prisons as a response to a unique set of imprisonment pains suffered by female inmates, specifically, being cut off physically and emotionally from their own families; also called *play family*.

psyche (1): The totality of the human mind, both conscious and unconscious.

psychological determinism (1): A form of positivism in which psychological or mental factors are believed to cause most human behavior, including criminal behavior.

psychological diagnostician (10): See *psychological technician*.

psychological technician (10): An entry-level psychologist at a corrections facility; not certified as a counselor or clinician, but can conduct certain types of screening tests and other preliminary psychometric testing.

psychological victimization (7): The threat of physical harm.

psychopath (1): Person who commits crimes with no thought of conventional morality or the consequences of the actions; individual may be immune to traditional behavior modification therapies. Also called *sociopath*.

public interest law (12): An approach to law in which activist groups effect social change through litigation.

public–private partnership (5): An arrangement in which a government makes a legal agreement to purchase specific services from a private-sector supplier.

public whipping (2): A public method of punishment in which the person was beaten of flogged.

punk (7): An inmate personality or type according to Sykes and Messinger; an otherwise heterosexual inmate coerced into a submissive homosexual role. Compare *wolf.*

race (14): A group defined by shared hereditary characteristics. Compare *ethnicity.*

race riot (7): A type of prison disturbance common during 1960s: largely apolitical uprisings based on racial conflict within the institution.

racism (14): The belief that certain races are by definition better or worse than others.

Racketeer Influenced and Corrupt Organizations (RICO) Statute (3): Title IX of the Organized Crime Control Act of 1970; allows the use of large fines to recover funds accumulated through illegal activities. The statute was crafted to stem the influence of organized crime on legitimate commerce, but since the early 1980s, it has been applied more broadly.

radial-design prison (6): A facility in which the cell blocks and functional areas of the prison are laid out like the spokes of a wheel.

radical feminism (13): The theory that male power and privilege both define all social relations and are the primary cause of all social inequities.

radical noninterventionism (1): Notion developed by Edwin Schur that most minor indiscretions committed by juveniles should be overlooked in order that they not be labeled as delinquents and subsequently treated as such.

rage riot (7): A spontaneous prison uprising; often an expression by inmates of their frustration with mistreatment, but also a means to pay back disloyal inmates or to destroy the facility.

reality therapy (RT) (1): A therapy with roots in behaviorism that holds offenders accountable for their actions; uses praise and concern to reinforce appropriate behavior and the withdrawal of praise to punish inappropriate behavior.

release on recognizance (ROR) (4): Discharge on one's personal word, unsecured by money or property, to return to court at a scheduled time.

rehabilitation (1, 2): One of eight philosophical responses to crime; asserts that "providing psychological or educational assistance or job training to offenders"

makes "them less likely to engage in future criminality"; the process of returning offenders to orderly or acceptable behaviors. See also *deterrence, incapacitation, isolation, reintegration, restitution, restoration,* and *retribution.*

rehabilitative services (5): A variety of treatment programs designed to provide jail (and prison) inmates with help to meet their physical, emotional, recreational, and spiritual needs.

reintegration (1, 2): One of eight philosophical responses to crime; asserts that the most positive method of corrections is the phased-in, controlled reentry of the offender into the community, based on the observation that more than 90 percent of prison inmates leave confinement and reenter society; also the process of learning life skills to prepare inmates to reenter the community. See also *deterrence, incapacitation, isolation, prison reentry, rehabilitation, restitution, restoration,* and *retribution.*

remote supervision (5): A pattern of inmate management that augments the physical surveillance of prisoners in their cells with supervision of inmates and staff in common areas by means of monitoring devices. Compare *direct supervision* and *intermittent supervision.*

residential drug abuse treatment program (6): Institutional-based, which requires inmates to live together in special wings or buildings, and halfway-house-based programs; most such programs are voluntary, and participating inmates must engage in a fixed period of drug education and intensive individual and group counseling.

responsivity principle (4): Matching offenders' learning styles and cognitive abilities with the appropriate treatment programs.

restitution (1, 4, 8): One of eight philosophical responses to crime; asserts that offenders must repay their victim or community "in money or services." See also *deterrence, incapacitation, isolation, rehabilitation, reintegration, restoration,* and *retribution.*

restoration (1): One of eight philosophical responses to crime; stresses the importance of balance between three key elements: accountability, community protection, and competency development. See also *deterrence, incapacitation, isolation, rehabilitation, reintegration, restitution,* and *retribution.*

retribution (1): One of eight philosophical responses to crime; asserts that punishment must avenge or retaliate for a harm or wrong done to another. Its essence was codified in the biblical injunction "an eye for an eye, a tooth for a tooth." See also *deterrence, incapacitation, isolation, lex talionis, rehabilitation, reintegration, restitution,* and *restoration.*

right guy (7): According to Schrag, an inmate who follows all the precepts of the inmate code. Compare *con-politician, outlaw,* and *Square John.*

risk principle (4): An assessment of an offender's likelihood of recidivism.

rites of passage (6): The formal and informal rituals through which inmates in total institutions come to understand that they are the property of the institution.

sally port (6): In a prison, an entryway with two steel or barred doors that must be opened in turn to allow movement in and out of a secure area.

satellite jail (5): See *jail annex.*

Satellite Prison Camps (SPC) (6): Low security federal prison camps operated by the Bureau of Prisons and located adjacent to more secure facilities.

Section 1983 suit (12): See *civil rights claim.*

Secure Female Facility (SFF) (6): Secure federal women's prison located at USP Hazelton, West Virginia.

security threat group (7): The ACA's term for *prison gang.*

selective incapacitation (1): The long-term incarceration of offenders who have been identified by various criteria as likely to keep repeating serious crimes.

sentencing disparity (14): The practice of assigning different punishments to similar defendants, or offenders charged with similar crimes; an unintended consequence is that members of minority groups are punished more frequently and more harshly than others are.

sentencing guidelines (3): The sentences judges must impose for certain offenders (based on the individual's criminal history) and for certain crimes (based on the seriousness of the particular crime).

sex-offender notification laws (15): Statutes that require convicted sex offenders to register with local law enforcement when they move into a neighborhood.

sexual harassment (15): Unsolicited and unwanted sexually based acts, ranging from lewd remarks to groping and touching.

sexual orientation (8): Status based on the gender of the partner chosen by a person.

sexual reassignment surgery (8): The process of surgically changing from one biological gender to another.

shakedown (6): A search of a jail or prison cell or an inmate, by force if necessary, to discover contraband or evidence of crimes or infractions.

sight-and-sound separation (8): The operating principle for correctional facilities that some inmates (especially females and juveniles) must be housed in such a way that they cannot see or hear (or be seen or heard by) male inmates.

silent system (2): The enforced silence of inmates at all times, even when they are working or eating with other prisoners. See also *Auburn system.*

social bond (1): The sum of the forces in a person's social and physical environment that connect that person to society and its moral constituents.

social control theory (1): A theory of crime that emphasizes the social mechanisms, strategies, and practices that ultimately lead to conformity, or at least obedience, to society's rules.

social debt (3): In criminal justice, the idea that a sentence should incorporate some recognition of the offender's criminal history.

social disorganization (1): A sociological explanation for crime; the physical deterioration and lack of cohesive community in inner-city neighborhoods that find expression in high crime rates.

socialist feminism (13): A form of feminist criminology based on the belief that the intersection of social class and gender is the nexus of crime and that to fully appreciate either social class or gender, the other variable must be considered.

social learning theory (1): Akers's theory, which stresses the importance of acquiring definitions, motivations, and methods supportive of criminal conduct (and, conversely, noncriminal conduct). See also *differential association theory, discriminative stimuli,* and *imitation.*

solidary opposition (7): The hostility or resistance of a group of inmates, banded together by common rules, norms, expectations, and deprivations.

specialized caseloads (15): Probation and parole caseloads in which the supervisor has the training and skills required to deal with problematic and high-risk ex-offenders, including drug users and sex offenders.

special needs (5, 8): Physical, psychological, or medical problems that require individual treatment and access to services beyond those available generally.

specific deterrence (1): See *deterrence.*

Square John (7): Schrag's role type played by inmates who are noncriminal types and considered situational offenders. This type of inmate does not adjust well to prison life and does not conform to the inmate code. Compare *con-politician, outlaw,* and *right guy.*

state-use system (6): The use of prison labor to produce products for consumption by the prison or the state government; a response to charges of unfair competition. Compare *contract system* and *lease system*.

stocks (2): A public method of punishment and humiliation in which a person was placed in timbers into which holes had been cut for the hands, feet, and head. The individual was required to stand or sit in this position; often used for crimes like public drunkenness.

subcultural hypothesis (1): A sociological theory that crime emerges from groups of delinquent youths or deviant persons who share symbols, beliefs, and values.

***sub rosa* inmate economy (7):** The illegal means by which inmates acquire and distribute valued goods and services in prisons and jails; the "black market."

substantive law (3): The statutes enacted by legislative bodies that define the elements of crimes.

summary arrest (9): The act of taking a person, in this case a parolee, immediately into secure custody, without a warrant or other legal instrument, based on the legal principle that the parolee's freedom is conditioned upon his or her good behavior and the parole officer has reason to suspect that this freedom has been abused.

superego (1): According to Freud, that part of the mind that is concerned with moral values.

superintendent (10): The chief administrative officer in most juvenile correctional institutions. See *warden*.

supermax prison (6): A state or federal prison facility in which high-risk inmates are locked up for 23 hours a day under extremely secure conditions.

supervised release (9): A term that has become popular because of state and federal efforts to move away from parole as a form of release from prison; largely indistinguishable from parole; irrespective of how they are released from the BOP, such ex-inmates are supervised by US probation officers.

***sursis* (4):** (French: "deferment") In European civil law, the unsupervised release of a convicted offender conditioned solely on good behavior.

surveillance officers (4): Employees of the court or probation authority who provide physical oversight of probationers in the community; may be either sworn peace officers with full arrest powers or other court employees who have powers of detainment to hold a probationers until someone with arresting powers arrives on the scene.

technical violation (4): In both probation and parole, an infraction of the rules or conditions of release that is not related to the commission of a new offense.

technocratic leader (11): A manager who has achieved his or her position based on an area of expertise.

telemedicine (15): Use of technology to deliver medical advice to patients located some distance from a doctor or hospital.

telephone-pole design prison (6): A facility in which the cells and functional areas of the prison are at right angles to both sides of a central hallway.

therapeutic community (1): A residential program in which all members work together to change the attitudes and behaviors of every member of the group.

ticket of leave (2): Maconochie's term for early release from a prison or penal colony.

total containment model (15): As developed by English and her associates, this approach to managing sex offenders in the community brings to bear on the offender a broad range of agency coordination, multidisciplinary partnerships, and specialized staff.

total institution (6): Goffman's term for a facility in which others control nearly every aspect of residents' daily lives.

total quality management (TQM) (11): The approach to operations that defines success in terms of customer orientation, maximum worker input, and concern for the quality of the product.

transportation (2): The deportation of convicted criminals to work in penal colonies or to settle a nation's colonies.

treatment (6): A particular method of therapy based on a particular diagnosis; an essential element in the medical model of corrections.

tuberculosis (8): An infectious disease of the lungs caused by the organism *Mycobacterium tuberculosis;* transmitted by airborne droplets containing the tubercle bacillus.

Twelve Tables (2): Rome's first major civil and criminal code.

underclass (14): According to William Julius Wilson, the most disadvantaged groups in society; a disproportionate number of offenders come from this segment of society.

UNICOR (6): The trade name of Federal Prison Industries, Inc., a work program operated by the US Bureau of Prisons.

US Bureau of Prisons (BOP) (6): The federal agency created in 1930 to ensure consistent administration of the federal prison system, a professional prison service, and more humane care for federal prisoners.

US Penitentiary (USP) (6): A high-security facility in the federal prison system.

unit management (7, 11): Supervision by the same team of correctional specialists of the inmates in a given unit, all of whom have similar classifications and release dates; pioneered by the US Bureau of Prisons, it creates prisons within prisons.

vertical overcharging (3): The practice of charging a suspect with more serious charges than can be proved in court for tactical advantage in the plea-bargaining process. Compare *horizontal overcharging.*

vicarious liability (12): Liability for the actions of another in the absence of fault, when the person did not know of, did not encourage, and did not assist in the act(s); usually imposed because of the person's supervisory position over the offender; also called *supervisory liability.*

warden (10): Chief administrative officer in most adult (and many juvenile) correctional facilities. See *superintendent.*

wergild (2): Under Germanic law the value placed on a murder victim that had to be paid by the offender.

whistle-blowing (10): Actions by employees who make public any illegal, unethical, or improper activities that have been committed by their supervisors or other employees in the organization.

wites (2): Legal device created by a king or local ruler that allowed him or her to keep the botes or monetary fines in the case of serious crimes.

wolf (7): One of three role types based on sex roles; a predatory inmate who provides protection for weak inmates in return for sexual favors. Compare *punk.*

women's reformatory (13): A correctional facility intended for the reform or rehabilitation of its female inmates, often patterned on existing institutional models for juveniles, which had been brought to the United States from England and Europe; such facilities provided females with instruction in household skills, morality, and social responsibility.

workload (4): The amount of effort necessary to supervise the number of clients assigned to a probation (or parole) officer. Compare *caseload.*

writ of habeas corpus (3, 12): See *habeas corpus, writ of.*

writ writer (12): See *jailhouse lawyer.*

INDEX

Essentials of Corrections, Fifth Edition. G. Larry Mays and L. Thomas Winfree, Jr.
© 2014 John Wiley & Sons, Inc. Published 2014 by John Wiley & Sons, Inc.